TAKING SIDES

Clashing Views in

Abnormal Psychology

FIFTH EDITION

Selected, Edited, and with Introductions by

Richard P. Halgin
University of Massachusetts–Amherst

McGraw-Hill
Higher Education

Boston   Burr Ridge, IL   Dubuque, IA   New York   San Francisco   St. Louis
Bangkok   Bogotá   Caracas   Kuala Lumpur   Lisbon   London   Madrid   Mexico City
Milan   Montreal   New Delhi   Santiago   Seoul   Singapore   Sydney   Taipei   Toronto

McGraw-Hill
Higher Education

TAKING SIDES: ABNORMAL PSYCHOLOGY,
FIFTH EDITION

Published by McGraw-Hill, a business unit of The McGraw-Hill Companies, Inc., 1221 Avenue of the Americas, New York, NY 10020. Copyright © 2009 by The McGraw-Hill Companies, Inc. All rights reserved. Previous edition(s) 2000–2007. No part of this publication may be reproduced or distributed in any form or by any means, or stored in a database or retrieval system, without the prior written consent of The McGraw-Hill Companies, Inc., including, but not limited to, in any network or other electronic storage or transmission, or broadcast for distance learning.

Some ancillaries, including electronic and print components, may not be available to customers outside the United States.

Taking Sides® is a registered trademark of the McGraw-Hill Companies, Inc.
Taking Sides is published by the **Contemporary Learning Series** group within the McGraw-Hill Higher Education division.

1 2 3 4 5 6 7 8 9 0 DOC/DOC 0 9 8

MHID: 0-07-351526-4
ISBN: 978-0-07-351526-7
ISSN: 1527-604X

Managing Editor: *Larry Loeppke*
Production Manager: *Faye Schilling*
Senior Developmental Editor: *Jill Peter*
Editorial Assistant: *Nancy Meissner*
Production Service Assistant: *Rita Hingtgen*
Permissions Coordinator: *Lori Church*
Senior Marketing Manager: *Julie Keck*
Marketing Communications Specialist: *Mary Klein*
Marketing Coordinator: *Alice Link*
Project Manager: *Jane Mohr*
Design Specialist: *Tara McDermott*
Senior Administrative Assistant: *DeAnna Dausener*
Cover Graphics: *Kristine Jubeck*

Compositor: ICC Macmillan Inc.

Cover Image: PhotoAlto/Picture Quest

Library of Congress Cataloging-in-Publication Data

Main entry under title:
Taking sides: clashing views in abnormal psychology/selected, edited, and with introductions by Richard P. Halgin. —5th ed.

Includes bibliographical references.
1. Psychology, Pathological. I. Halgin, Richard P. *comp.*
616.89

www.mhhe.com

Preface

T he field of abnormal psychology is inherently controversial because we lack a clear delineation between normal and abnormal behavior. Most phenomena in the realm of abnormal psychology fall along continua; the point on a continuum at which behavior moves from being considered "normal" to being considered "abnormal" varies considerably and is influenced by a number of factors. Consider the example of an active boy's behavior. His running around impulsively and shouting out aimless comments would be viewed as normal behavior on a playground but abnormal behavior in a quiet classroom. In a classroom setting, his behavior might be referred to as impulsive and hyperactive, possibly prompting his teacher to refer him to a mental health professional for therapy and medication to help him settle down and pay attention. Although such referrals are commonplace in American schools, some people contend that we pathologize the normal behavior of children when we view their high levels of energy as mental disorders. This is but one of the debates about which you will read in this book, and it is a good example of the kind of controversy found in the field of mental health.

There are many complex issues that arise in the field of abnormal psychology; in this book you will read about 19 controversial matters with which mental health experts struggle. Unit 1 looks at psychological conditions and treatments about which there has been vehement disagreement in recent years, with some experts expressing intense skepticism about the validity of specific clinical problems and interventions that have been in the spotlight. Unit 2 looks at the trend toward biological interventions for an array of psychological problems and mental disorders. Unit 3 explores pertinent social issues that interface with the field of abnormal psychology, particularly debates about ethical and legal issues that pertain to the field of mental health.

Most students who enroll in a course in abnormal psychology begin the semester with the belief that they will be learning about problems that affect "other people," rather than themselves. In a short period of time, however, they come to realize that they are reading about conditions that have much more personal salience than they had anticipated. Sooner or later, they recognize conditions that they or someone close to them have experienced, and their interest in the topic intensifies. In all likelihood, you will have a similar reaction as you read this book. To capture the essence of each debate, you will find it helpful to connect yourself in a personal way to the issue under consideration; you might imagine yourself dealing with the issue personally, or as the relative of a client with the particular problem, or even as a professional trying to provide mental health assistance.

Plan of the book   To assist you in understanding the significance of each issue, every issue begins with an *introduction* that provides important background about the issue and summarizes the perspective in each of the pieces. Points and counterpoints are enumerated to help you appreciate the specific areas of disagreement between the two pieces. Each issue concludes with a set of *challenge questions* that can serve as the basis for further thought or discussion on the topic as well as a list of suggested additional readings. In addition, Internet site addresses (URLs) have been provided on the *Internet References* page at the beginning of each unit, which should prove useful as starting points for further research on the issues. At the back of the book is a listing of all the *contributors to this volume* with a brief biographical sketch of each of the prominent figures whose views are debated here.

Changes to this edition This fifth edition of *Taking Sides: Clashing Views in Abnormal Psychology* includes some important changes from the fourth edition. This edition includes eleven new articles, ten of which comprise the content of five new chapters, and the eleventh serving as a replacement for an article in the previous edition. The five new topics address provocative debates which have emerged in recent years. "Is Forced Treatment of Seriously Mentally Ill Individuals Justifiable?" (Issue 1) discusses the ethical quandary about the decision to administer treatment to seriously disturbed individuals against their will. "Should Memory-Dampening Drugs Be Used to Alleviate the Symptoms of Trauma?" (Issue 8) tackles a thorny bioethical debate about the value and wisdom of minimizing memories of trauma. "Is It Ethical to Support the Wish for Healthy Limb Amputation in People with Body Integrity Identity Disorder (BIID)?" (Issue 13) focuses on an unusual variant of body dysmorphic disorder in which individuals feel compelled to rid themselves of a healthy limb, and the ethical dilemma faced by health professionals to whom they turn for help. "Would Legalization of Virtual Child Pornography Reduce Sexual Exploitation of Children?" (Issue 16) addresses a socio-legal debate regarding First Amendment protection of speech on the one hand, and the proliferation of media that might increase the victimization of children on the other hand. "Must Mentally Ill Murderers Have a Rational Understanding of Why They Are Being Sentenced to Death?" (Issue 19) addresses a legal matter that has arisen to the level of the United States Supreme Court. "Is ADHD a Real Disorder?" (Issue 5) has been updated in order to include an official document of the National Institute of Mental Health specifying the characteristics of what NIMH regards as a valid diagnostic condition.

A word to the instructor An *Instructor's Resource Guide with Test Questions* (multiple-choice and essay) is available through the publisher for the instructor using *Taking Sides* in the classroom. A general guidebook, *Using Taking Sides in the Classroom,* which discusses methods and techniques for integrating the procon approach into any classroom setting, is also available. An online version of *Using Taking Sides in the Classroom* and a correspondence service for *Taking Sides* adopters can be found at http://www.mhcls.com/usingts/.

Taking Sides: Clashing Views in Abnormal Psychology is only one title in the Taking Sides series. If you are interested in seeing the table of contents for any of the other titles, please visit the Taking Sides Web site at http://www.mhcls.com/takingsides/.

Acknowledgments   Very special gratitude goes to Ilana Klarman, Senior Editorial Assistant for the fifth edition. Ilana did an absolutely remarkable job conducting exhaustive bibliographic research, analyzing and editing each new chapter, and contributing to the Instructor's Manual. Ilana's sophisticated grasp of the issues, her outstanding efficiency, and her diligent attention to detail proved to be invaluable at every step of the way. The chapters developed by Ilana include: "Is Forced Treatment of Seriously Mentally Ill Individuals Justifiable?" (Issue 1); "Should Memory-Dampening Drugs Be Used to Alleviate the Symptoms of Trauma?" (Issue 8); "Is It Ethical to Support the Wish for Healthy Limb Amputation in People with Body Integrity Identity Disorder (BIID)?" (Issue 13); "Would Legalization of Virtual Child Pornography Reduce Sexual Exploitation of Children?" (Issue 16); and "Must Mentally Ill Murderers Have a Rational Understanding of Why They Are Being Sentenced to Death?" (Issue 19). She also updated "Is ADHD a Real Disorder?" (Issue 5). Special gratitude also goes to the research assistants whose contributions to previous editions continue to be evident in the fifth edition: Molly Burnett, Rebecca Gray, Joseph Greer, Kerry Halgin, Eric Nguyen, Diana Rancourt, Barbara Sieck, and Justin Smith.

Thanks also to Jill Peter and the staff at McGraw-Hill. Jill's conscientious oversight and thoughtful direction played a pivotal role in the current and previous editions, and I feel especially fortunate to have benefited from her editorial guidance.

Richard P. Halgin
University of Massachusetts–Amherst

*To my wonderful wife, Lucille, whose love
and support provide me with immeasurable
amounts of energy, and to our children,
Daniel and Kerry, whose values
and achievements have been
inspiring.*

Contents In Brief

Contents

Psychologists Grant J. Devilly and Peter Cotton assert that critical incident stress debriefing (CISD) is poorly defined and has been shown to do more harm than good. They propose alternative approaches for responding to trauma survivors, which they consider more effective. Jeffrey T. Mitchell of the International Critical Incident Stress Foundation (ICISF) argues that Devilly and Cotton have misrepresented important information about psychological debriefing and have confused several aspects of this system of responding to trauma survivors.

Psychologist David Gleaves and his colleagues assert that for some people, memories of traumatic events are blocked but may subsequently be recovered. Psychologist John Kihlstrom disputes the validity of blocked and recovered memories. He views the phenomenon of "false memories" as a serious problem in contemporary society.

NIMH views ADHD as a valid disorder affecting between 3 and 5 percent of American children, many of whom will continue to deal with symptoms of this condition into adulthood. According to NIMH, ADHD warrants careful diagnosis and treatment by skilled professionals. Psychologist Rogers H. Wright argues that ADHD has vague diagnostic criteria that lead to over-diagnosis and over-medication of an excessive number of people.

Science writers Robert Mathias and Patrick Zickler argue that MDMA has skyrocketed in popularity and that insufficient attention has been paid to the physical and psychological risks associated with its use. June Riedlinger, an assistant professor of clinical pharmacy, and Michael Montagne, a professor of pharmacy, contend that the risks associated with MDMA use have been exaggerated and that there are legitimate therapeutic uses for this substance.

Psychologist Patricia Owen asserts that abstinence is the safest and most honest treatment goal for most people who are dependent on alcohol. Health and medical writer Anne Fletcher contends that many people with alcohol problems can be successful in their efforts to control their drinking, particularly if they are given professional guidance and support.

Professor Adam Kolber asserts that victims of trauma who experience terrifying residual symptoms can benefit from drugs that make the trauma feel less horrible. Such drugs can help trauma survivors make life transformations that they would otherwise be incapable of making. The President's Council on Bioethics, chaired by Dr. Leon Kass, objects to the use of biotechnical interventions to ease the psychic pain of bad memories, because identities are formed in part by what people undergo and suffer.

Psychiatrist E. Fuller Torrey, an outspoken advocate for the needs of the mentally ill and their families, contends that antipsychotic medications play a centrally important role in alleviating psychotic symptoms and reducing the likelihood of rehospitalization. Journalist and social critic Robert Whitaker asserts that antipsychotic medications make people chronically ill, cause serious side effects, and increase the likelihood of rehospitalization; furthermore, reliance on these medical treatments for the mentally ill neglect important questions such as what it means to be human.

Physician Peter R. Breggin asserts that Ritalin and similar stimulants are dangerous addictive medications that should not be prescribed to children because they suppress growth and lead to a number of worrisome physical and psychological symptoms. Psychologist and prominent ADHD researcher Russell A. Barkley objects to criticisms of Ritalin and similar stimulants, asserting that these medications serve as important parts of interventions and aim at helping children increase their attention and concentration.

Psychologist Robert Resnick endorses the recommendation that psychologists be given prescription privileges in order to expand psychopharmacological availability to people needing medication. Psychologist William Robiner and his colleagues object to the notion of granting prescription privileges to psychologists, and express several concerns pertaining to training and competence.

Physician Max Fink asserts that electroconvulsive therapy (ECT) is an effective intervention whose use has been limited as a result of social stigma and philosophical bias, which have been reinforced by intimidation from the pharmaceutical and managed care industries. Leonard R. Frank, editor and cofounder of the Network Against Psychiatric Assault, criticizes the use of ECT because of its disturbing side effects, some of which he personally has suffered, and asserts that its resurgence in popularity is economically based.

Attorney Arnold Loewy views the issue of virtual child pornography from a legal perspective, asserting that such material is a form of free speech that ought to be constitutionally protected. He also contends that legalizing virtual child pornography would reduce the extent to which real children would be exploited. Writers Diana Russell and Natalie Purcell express vehement objections to any forms of pornography involving images of children, asserting that Internet users with no previous sexual interest in children may find themselves drawn into a world in which the societal prohibition against adult-child sex is undermined.

Evolutionary biologist Randy Thornhill and evolutionary anthropologist Craig T. Palmer assert that the reasons why men rape are misunderstood. They contend that, rather than an act of gratuitous violence, rape can be understood as a biologically determined behavior in which socially disenfranchised men resort to this extreme act in order to gain access to women. Journalist Susan Brownmiller argues that rape is an exemplification of the male-female struggle in which men humiliate and degrade women in a blunt and ugly expression of physical power.

Rhea K. Farberman, director of public communications for the American Psychological Association, makes the case that mental health professionals should be called upon to assess terminally ill people who request hastened death in order to ensure that decision making is rational and free of coercion. Psychiatrists Mark D. Sullivan, Linda Ganzini, and Stuart J. Youngner argue that the reliance on mental health professionals to be suicide gatekeepers involves an inappropriate use of clinical procedures to disguise society's ambivalence about suicide itself.

The American Psychological Association, American Psychiatric Association, and the National Alliance on Mental Illness collaborated in the preparation of an *amici curiae* brief pertaining to the case of Scott Panetti who was sentenced to death for murder. In this brief the argument is made that mentally ill convicts should not be executed if their disability significantly impairs their capacity to understand the nature and purpose of their punishment, or to appreciate why the punishment is being imposed on them. An opposing argument is made by Nathaniel Quarterman who asserts that punishment for murder does not depend on the rational understanding of the convicted individual, but rather on the convict's moral culpability at the time the crime was committed.

Correlation Guide

The *Taking Sides* series presents current issues in a debate-style format designed to stimulate student interest and develop critical thinking skills. Each issue is thoughtfully framed with an issue summary, an issue introduction with points and counterpoints, and challenge questions. The pro and con essays—selected for their liveliness and substance—represent the arguments of leading scholars and commentators in their fields.

Taking Sides: Clashing Views in Abnormal Psychology, 5/e is an easy-to-use reader that presents issues on important topics such as *anorexia, sexual orientation,* and *ADHD.* For more information on *Taking Sides* and other *McGraw-Hill Contemporary Learning Series* titles, visit www.mhcls.com.

This convenient guide matches the issues in **Taking Sides: Abnormal Psychology, 5/e** with the corresponding chapters in two of our best-selling McGraw-Hill Abnormal Psychology textbooks by Nolen-Hoeksema and Halgin/Whitbourne.

Taking Sides: Abnormal Psychology, 5/e by Halgin	Abnormal Psychology: Media & Research Update, 4/e by Nolen-Hoeksema	Abnormal Psychology: Clinical Perspectives on Psychological Disorders, 5/e by Halgin/Whitbourne
Issue 1: Is Forced Treatment of Seriously Mentally Ill Individuals Justifiable?	**Chapter 18:** Mental Health and the Law	**Chapter 15:** Ethical and Legal Issues
Issue 2: Should Individuals with Anorexia Nervosa Have the Right to Refuse Life-Sustaining Treatment?	**Chapter 15:** Eating Disorders **Chapter 18:** Mental Health and the Law	**Chapter 14:** Eating Disorders and Impulse-Control Disorders **Chapter 15:** Ethical and Legal Issues
Issue 3: Is Psychological Debriefing a Harmful Intervention for Survivors of Trauma?	**Chapter 3:** The Research Endeavor **Chapter 6:** Stress Disorders and Health Psychology	**Chapter 5:** Anxiety Disorders
Issue 4: Are Blocked and Recovered Memories Valid Phenomena?		
Issue 5: Is Attention-Deficit/ Hyperactivity Disorder (ADHD) a Real Disorder?	**Chapter 13:** Childhood Disorders	**Chapter 11:** Development-Related Disorders
Issue 6: Should MDMA (Ecstasy) Be Prohibited, Even for Therapeutic Use?	**Chapter 17:** Substance-Related Disorders	
Issue 7: Should Abstinence Be the Goal for Treating People with Alcohol Problems?	**Chapter 17:** Substance-Related Disorders	**Chapter 13:** Substance-Related Disorders

continued

Taking Sides: Abnormal Psychology, 5/e by Halgin	Abnormal Psychology: Media & Research Update, 4/e by Nolen-Hoeksema	Abnormal Psychology: Clinical Perspectives on Psychological Disorders, 5/e by Halgin/Whitbourne
Issue 8: Should Memory-Dampening Drugs Be Used to Alleviate the Symptoms of Trauma?	**Chapter 6:** Stress Disorders and Health Psychology	
Issue 9: Are Antipsychotic Medications the Treatment of Choice for People with Psychosis?	**Chapter 5:** Treatments for Abnormality	**Chapter 5:** Anxiety Disorders
Issue 10: Is Ritalin Overprescribed?	**Chapter 13:** Childhood Disorders	**Chapter 11:** Development-Related Disorders
Issue 11: Should Psychologists Prescribe Medication?	**Chapter 1:** Looking at Abnormality	**Chapter 2:** Classification and Treatment Plans
Issue 12: Is Electroconvulsive Therapy Ethical?	**Chapter 5:** Treatments for Abnormality **Chapter 9:** Mood Disorders **Chapter 11:** Schizophrenia **Chapter 14:** Cognitive Disorders and Life-Span Issues	**Chapter 4:** Theoretical Perspectives **Chapter 8:** Mood Disorders
Issue 13: Is it Ethical to Support the Wish for Healthy Limb Amputation in People with Body Integrity Identity Disorder?		
Issue 14: Is Sexual Orientation Conversion Therapy Ethical?	**Chapter 16:** Sexual Disorders	**Chapter 7:** Sexual Disorders
Issue 15: Does Exposure to Media Violence Promote Aggressive Behavior?	**Chapter 12:** Personality Disorders	**Chapter 10:** Personality Disorders
Issue 16: Would Legalization of Virtual Child Pornography Reduce Sexual Exploitation of Children?		
Issue 17: Does Evolution Explain Why Men Rape?	**Chapter 9:** Mood Disorders **Chapter 16:** Sexual Disorders	
Issue 18: Should Mental Health Professionals Serve as Gatekeepers for Physician-Assisted Suicide?	**Chapter 10:** Suicide	
Issue 19: Must Mentally Ill Murderers Have a Rational Understanding of Why They Are Being Sentenced to Death?		

Introduction

What's "Abnormal" about Abnormal Psychology?

Richard P. Halgin

The field of abnormal psychology lends itself well to a discussion of controversial issues because of the inherent difficulty involved in defining the concept of "abnormal." The definition of abnormality is contingent on a myriad of influences that include cultural, historical, geographical, societal, interpersonal, and intrapersonal factors. What is considered everyday behavior in one culture might be regarded as bizarre in another. What was acceptable at one point in time might seem absurd in contemporary society. What seems customary in one region, even in one section of a large city, might be viewed as outrageous elsewhere. Even on a very personal level, one person's typical style of emotional expression might be experienced by another person as odd and disruptive. This introductory essay looks at some of the complex issues involved in defining and understanding abnormality and, in doing so, will set the stage for the controversial issues that follow. With this theoretical foundation, you will be better equipped to tackle the thorny issues in this volume and to develop an approach for reaching your own conclusions about these controversies.

Defining Abnormality

One of the best ways to begin a discussion of the complexity of defining abnormality is by considering our own behavior. Think about an outlandish costume that you wore to a Halloween party and the fun you had engaging in this completely normal behavior. Now imagine wearing the same costume to class the following day, and think about the reactions you would have received. What seemed so normal on the evening of October 31 would have been considered bizarre on the morning of November 1. Only a day later, in a different context, you would have been regarded as abnormal, and your behavior would have been viewed as both disturbed and disturbing. Consider another example: Recall a time in which you were intensely emotional, perhaps weeping profusely at a funeral. If you were to display similar emotionality a few days later in a class discussion, your behavior would cause considerable stir, and your classmates would be taken aback by the intensity of your emotions. Now consider a common behavior that is completely acceptable and expected in American culture, such as shaking a person's hand upon meeting. Did you know that in some cultures such behavior is regarded as rude and unacceptable? These simple examples highlight the ways in which the concept of "normal" is contingent on many factors. Because of the wide variability in definitions of what is abnormal, psychologists have spelled out criteria that can be used in determining abnormal human behavior. These criteria fall into four categories: distress, impairment, risk to self or other people, and socially and culturally unacceptable behavior.

Distress

I begin with the most personal criterion of abnormality because the experience of inner emotional distress is a universal phenomenon and a powerful way in which every person at some point in life feels different from everyone around them. Distress, the experience of emotional pain, is experienced in many ways, such as depression, anxiety, and cognitive confusion. When people feel any of these responses to an extreme degree, they feel abnormal, and they typically look for ways to alleviate their feelings of inner pain. Some of the issues in this book illustrate the various ways in which different people respond to similar life events. For example, following the devastating events of September 11th, the Asian tsunami, and Hurricane Katrina, many mental health professionals were called upon to intervene with the survivors of these life-threatening traumas. Although providing a therapeutic response in the form of psychological debriefing might seem beneficial, some critics argue that such efforts might make a dificult emotional situation even worse (Issue 3). In recent years efforts have been made to find medications that alleviate the memories associated with the experience of a trauma; Issue 8 addresses the possible benefits as well as the disadvantages of dampening memories of a traumatic experience.

Impairment

People who are intensely distressed are likely to find it difficult to fulfill the everyday responsibilities of life. When people are very depressed or anxious, they typically have a difficult time concentrating on their studies, attending to their work responsibilities, or even interacting with other people. Impairment involves a reduction in a person's ability to function at an optimal or even an average level. Although distress and impairment often go hand in hand, they do not always; a person can be seriously impaired but feel no particular distress. This is often the case with substance abuse, in which people are incapable of the basic tasks of physical coordination and cognitive clarity but feel euphoric. Some of the debates in this book address the issue of impairment and the difficulty in assessing the extent to which people are impaired. For example, Issue 18 focuses on physician-assisted suicide, with particular attention to the role of mental health professionals in determining a person's competency to choose suicide. One aspect of the controversy pertains to the issue of whether or not a terminally ill person is too impaired to make a rational life-ending decision.

Risk to Self or Others

Sometimes people act in ways that cause risk to themselves or others. In this context, risk refers to danger or threat to the well-being of a person. In the case of suicide or self-mutilating behavior, the personal risk is evident. In the case of outwardly directed violence, rape, or even emotional exploitation, the risk is to other people. Although the issue of risk to self or others might not seem controversial on the surface, there are many facets of risk that provoke debate. For example, does an individual have the right to engage in self-injurious, perhaps even life-ending, behavior, or does society have a right, even a responsibility, to intervene? As addressed in Issues 1 and 2, do individuals who are at risk of harming other people (i.e., by means of violence) or themselves (i.e., self-starvation) have the right to refuse intervention, or do health professionals have a responsibility to protect such individuals from engaging in such potentially dangerous behavior? The choice of suicide, even by terminally ill people, has prompted heated debate in our society, but so have less-extreme issues, such as the choice to view pornography. The debate about pornography becomes especially heated when the sexual images involve children (discussed in Issue 16). Although no reasonable person would defend real child pornography, some argue that virtual images generated by computers are not only legally permissible, but could reduce the victimization of real children by the pornography industry. Critics of that stance argue that pornography involving children, whether virtual or not, increases the likelihood of real-life victimization.

Socially and Culturally Unacceptable Behavior

Another criterion for defining abnormality pertains to the social or cultural context in which behavior occurs. In some instances, behavior that is regarded as odd within a given culture, society, or subgroup is common elsewhere. For example, some people from Mediterranean cultures believe in a phenomenon called *mal de ojo,* or "evil eye," in which the ill will of one person can negatively affect another. According to this belief, receiving the evil eye from a person can cause a range of disturbing physical and emotional symptoms; consequently, individuals in these cultures often take steps to ward off the power of another person's evil eye. Such beliefs might be regarded as strangely superstitious, almost delusional, in American culture, but they are considered common elsewhere. Even more subtle contexts can influence the extent to which a behavior is defined as abnormal, as illustrated by the example of the Halloween costume mentioned previously. This book features issues related to social and cultural variables, such as whether media violence promotes violent behavior in young people (Issue 15).

What Causes Abnormality?

In trying to understand why people act and feel in ways that are regarded as abnormal, social scientists consider three dimensions: biological, psychological, and sociocultural. Rather than viewing these dimensions as independent, however, experts discuss the relative contribution of each dimension in influencing human behavior, and they use the term *biopsychosocial* to capture these intertwining forces. In the context of abnormality, the biopsychosocial conceptualization of human behavior conveys the sense that abnormal behavior arises from a complex set of determinants in the body, the mind, and the social context.

Biological Causes

During the past several decades scientists have made tremendous progress in discovering ways in which human behavior is influenced by a range of biological variables. In the realm of abnormal psychology, the contributions of the biological sciences have been especially impressive, as researchers have developed increasing understanding of the ways in which abnormal behavior is determined by bodily physiology and genetic makeup. As is the case with many medical disorders, various mental disorders, such as depression, run in families. Mental health researchers have made great efforts to understand why certain mental illnesses are passed from one generation to another and also to understand why certain disorders are not inherited even in identical twin pairs when one of the twins has the condition and the other does not.

In addition to understanding the role of genetics, mental health experts also consider the ways in which physical functioning can cause or aggravate the experience of psychological symptoms. Experts know that many medical conditions can cause a person to feel or act in ways that are abnormal. For example, a medical abnormality in the thyroid gland can cause wide variations in mood and emotionality. Brain damage resulting from a head trauma, even a slight one, can result in bizarre behavior and intense emotionality. Similarly, the use of drugs or alcohol can cause people to act in extreme ways that neither they nor those who know them well would have ever imagined. Even exposure to environmental stimuli, such as toxic substances or allergens, can cause people to experience disturbing emotional changes and to act in odd or bizarre ways. Several issues in this book explore conditions in which biology plays a prominent causative role. For example, attention deficit disorder (ADHD) is regarded as a disorder of the brain that interferes with a person's ability to pay attention or to control behavior (see Issue 5).

Psychological Causes

Biology does not tell the entire story about the causes of mental disorders; many forms of emotional disturbance arise as a result of troubling life experiences. The experiences of life, even seemingly insignificant ones, can leave lasting marks on a person. In cases in which an experience involves trauma, such as rape or abuse, the impact can be emotionally disruptive throughout life, affecting a person's thoughts, behaviors, and even dreams.

In trying to understand the psychological causes of abnormality, social scientists and mental health clinicians consider a person's experiences. Not only do they focus on interpersonal interactions with other people that may have left a mark, but they also consider the inner life of the individual—thoughts and feelings that may cause distress or impairment. Some conditions arise from distorted perceptions and faulty ways of thinking. For example, highly sensitive people may misconstrue innocent comments by acquaintances that cause obsessional worry about being disliked or demeaned. As a result, these people may respond to their acquaintances in hostile ways that perpetuate interpersonal difficulties and inner distress.

For several of the issues in this book, psychological forces play a significant causative role. For example, Issue 4 considers the disturbances of people who have suffered traumatic life experiences and the controversies surrounding the possibility that trauma might be repressed or might cause the development of multiple personalities.

Sociocultural Causes

The term *sociocultural* refers to the various circles of social influence in the lives of people. The most immediate circle is composed of people with whom we interact in our immediate environment; for college students, this includes roommates, classmates, and coworkers. Moving beyond the immediate circle are people who inhabit the extended circle of relationships, such as family members back home or friends from high school. A third circle is composed of the people in our environments with whom we interact minimally and rarely by name, such as residents of our community or campus, whose standards, expectations, and behaviors influence our lives. A fourth circle is the much wider culture in which people live, such as American society.

Abnormal behavior can emerge from experiences in any of these social contexts. Troubled relationships with a roommate or family member can cause intense emotional distress. Involvement in an abusive relationship may initiate an interpersonal style in which the abused person becomes repeatedly caught up with people who are hurtful or damaging. Political turmoil, even on a relatively local level, can evoke emotions ranging from intense anxiety to incapacitating fear.

This book discusses several conditions in which sociocultural factors are significant. For example, Issue 15 discusses the ways in which exposure to media violence may promote aggressive behavior, and Issue 17 addresses the ways in which pornography, even in virtual form, may contribute to the victimization of children.

The Biopsychosocial Perspective

From the discussion so far, it should be evident that most aspects of human behavior are determined by a complex of causes involving an interaction of biological, psychological, and sociocultural factors. As you read about the clinical conditions and mental disorders discussed in this book, it will be useful for you to keep the biopsychosocial perspective in mind, even in those discussions in which the authors seem narrowly focused. For example, a condition may be put forth as being biologically caused, leading the reader to believe that other influences play little or no role. Another condition may be presented as being so psychologically based that it is difficult to fathom the role that biology might play in causing or aggravating the condition. Other issues may be discussed almost exclusively in sociocultural terms, with minimal attention to the roles of biological and psychological factors. An intelligent discussion in the field of abnormal psychology is one that explores the relative importance of biological, psychological, and sociocultural influences. An intelligent discussion should avoid reductionistic thinking and simplistic explanations for complex human problems.

Why We View Behavior as "Abnormal"

In addition to understanding how to define abnormality and what causes abnormal behavior, it is important to understand how members of society view people who are abnormal and how this view affects people with emotional problems and mental disorders. Many people in our society discriminate against and reject mentally disturbed people. In so doing, they aggravate one of the most profound aspects of dealing with mental disorder—the experience of stigma. A stigma is a label that causes certain people to be regarded as different and defective and to be set apart from mainstream members of society. Today, several decades after sociologist Erving Goffman brought the phenomenon of stigma to public attention, there is ample evidence in American society that people with mental disorders are regarded as different and are often deprived of the basic human right to respectful treatment.

It is common for people with serious psychological disorders, especially those who have been hospitalized, to experience profound and long-lasting emotional and social effects. People who suffer from serious psychological problems tend to think less of themselves because of these experiences, and they often come to believe many of the myths about themselves that are perpetuated in a society that lacks understanding about the nature of mental illness and psychological problems.

Although tremendous efforts have been undertaken to humanize the experiences of people with psychological problems and mental disorders, deeply rooted societal reactions still present obstacles for many emotionally distressed people. Controversies continue to rage about the systems of diagnosis and assessment used by mental health professionals, about the validity of certain clinical conditions, and about the efficacy of various psychotherapeutic and medical interventions. As you read both sides of the debates in this book, it is important that you keep in mind the strong personal beliefs that influence, and possibly bias, the statements of each writer and to consider the ways in which various societal forces are intertwined with the comments of the author.

The most powerful force within the field of mental health during the twentieth century was the medical model, upon which many forms of intervention are based. This book frequently mentions a system of diagnosis developed by the American Psychiatric Association that has been revised several times during the past 50 years. This system is published in a book called the *Diagnostic and Statistical Manual of Mental Disorders*. The most recent version is the fourth edition, which is commonly abbreviated *DSM-IV-TR*. In this medical model diagnostic system, mental disorders are construed as diseases that require treatment. There are both advantages and disadvantages to this approach.

Not only does *DSM-IV-TR* rely on the medical model, but it also uses a categorical approach. A categorical approach assumes that diseases fit into distinct categories. For example, the medical disease pneumonia is a condition that fits into the category of diseases involving the respiratory system. In corresponding fashion, conditions involving mood fit into the category of mood disorders, conditions involving anxiety fit into the category of anxiety disorders, and so on. However, as the authors of *DSM-IV-TR* admit, there are limitations to the categorical approach. For one thing, psychological disorders are not neatly separable from each other or from normal functioning. For example, where is the dividing line between normal sadness and clinical depression? Furthermore, many disorders seem linked to each other in fundamental ways. In a state of agitated depression, for example, an individual suffers from both anxiety and saddened mood.

Several of the conditions and interventions discussed in this book have been debated for years. As you read about these issues, it will be helpful for you to keep in mind the context in which these debates have arisen. Some debates arise because of turf battles between professions. For example, psychiatrists may be more inclined to endorse the diagnostic system of the American Psychiatric Association (*DSM-IV-TR*) and to support biological explanations and somatic interventions for mental disorders. Psychologists, on the other hand, may urge mental health professionals to take a broader point of view and to proceed more cautiously in turning to biological explanations and causes.

The Influence of Theoretical Perspective on the Choice of Intervention

Although impressive advances have been achieved in determining why people develop various mental disorders, understanding how best to treat their conditions remains limited and also powerfully influenced by the ideological biases of many clinicians and researchers. For much of the twentieth century, various interventions emerged from markedly different schools of thought, each approach being tied to one of the three major realms—biological, psychological, or sociocultural. But how are biological, psychological, and sociocultural frameworks used in determining choice of intervention?

Within the biological perspective, disturbances in emotions, behavior, and cognitive processes are viewed as being caused by abnormalities in the functioning of the body, such as the brain and nervous system or the endocrine system. Treatments involve a range of somatic therapies, the most common of which is medication, the most extreme of which involves psychosurgery. Several issues in this book focus on debates about reliance on biological explanations and interventions, such as the issues on ADHD (Issue 5), rape (Issue 17), and electroconvulsive therapy (Issue 12).

The realm of psychological theories contains numerous approaches, although three schools of thought emerged as most prominent during the second half of the twentieth century: psychodynamic, humanistic, and behavioral. Proponents of the psychodynamic perspective emphasize unconscious determinants of behavior and recommend the use of techniques involving exploration of the developmental causes of behavior and the interpretation of unconscious influences on thoughts, feelings, and behavior. This is pertinent to the debate over repressed memories (Issue 4), which involves clinicians who believe that people are inclined to "forget" traumatic experiences in order to defend themselves from the disruptive anxiety they would otherwise experience.

At the core of the humanistic perspective is the belief that human motivation is based on an inherent tendency to strive for self-fulfillment and meaning in life. Humanistic therapists use a client-centered approach in which they strive to treat clients with unconditional positive regard and empathy. Mental health professionals are called upon to act in ways that are more client-centered as they deal with issues ranging from distress about sexual orientation (Issue 14) to matters involving a client's choice to end life due to a debilitating illness (Issue 18).

According to the behavioral perspective, abnormality is caused by faulty learning experiences, with a subset of behavioral theory focusing on cognitive functions, such as maladaptive thought processes. Because behaviorists and cognitive theorists believe that disturbance results from faulty learning or distorted thinking, intervention focuses on teaching clients more adaptive ways of thinking and behaving. Some of the discussions in this book focus on the ways in which behavioral and cognitive approaches might be preferable to medical approaches to conditions such as ADHD (Issue 5) and distress related to sexual orientation (Issue 14).

Clinicians working within sociocultural models emphasize the ways that individuals are influenced by people, social institutions, and social forces. According to this viewpoint, psychological problems can emerge from social contexts ranging from the family to society. In a corresponding vein, treatments are determined by the nature of the group. Thus, problems rooted within family systems would be treated with family therapy; societal problems caused by discrimination or inadequate care of the mentally ill would be dealt with through enactment of social policy initiatives. Several issues in this volume touch upon sociocultural influences, such as the effects of pornography (Issue 16), the most appropriate intervention for treating alcoholism (Issue 7), and how best to respond to survivors of life-threatening trauma (Issues 3 and 8).

Keeping the Issues in Perspective

In evaluating the content of the writings in this book, it is important to keep in mind who the writers are and what their agendas might be. Most of the contributors are distinguished figures in the fields of mental health, ethics, and law. They are regarded as clear and influential thinkers who have important messages to convey. However, it would be naive to think that any writer, particularly when addressing a controversial topic, is free of bias.

It is best to read each issue with an understanding of the forces that might influence the development of a particular bias. For example, as physicians, psychiatrists have been trained in the medical model, with its focus on biological causes for problems and somatic interventions. Nonphysician mental health professionals may be more inclined to focus on interpersonal and intrapersonal causes and interventions. Lawyers and ethicists are more likely to be further removed from questions of etiology, focusing instead on what they believe is justified according to the law or right according to ethical standards.

As you read about the issues facing mental health clinicians and researchers, you are certain to be struck by the challenges that these professionals face. You may also be struck by the powerful emotion expressed by the authors who discuss their views on topics in this field. Because psychological stresses and problems are an inherent part of human existence, many discussions about abnormal psychology are emotionally charged. At some point in life, most people have a brush with serious emotional problems, either directly or indirectly. This is a frightening prospect for many people, one that engenders worried expectations and intense reactions. By acknowledging our vulnerability to disruptive emotional experiences, however, we can think about the ways in which we would want clinicians to treat us. As you read the issues in this book, place yourself in the position of an individual in the process of being assessed, diagnosed, and treated for an emotional difficulty or mental disorder.

Before you take a side in each debate, consider how the issue might be personally relevant to you at some point in life. You may be surprised to discover that you respond in different ways to issues that might have special salience to yourself, as opposed to random people somewhere else. By imagining yourself being personally affected by a professional's controversial opinion regarding one or more of the debates in this book, you will find yourself immersed in the discussions about issues for which there is no clear right or wrong.

Internet References . . .

The Treatment Advocacy Center

A national nonprofit organization committed to removing barriers faced by mentally ill people who are seeking effective and timely treatment.

http://psychlaws.blogspot.com/

Schizophrenia Treatment

The Web site offers information, advice, and first-hand accounts of schizophrenic individuals and their relatives.

http://www.schizophrenia.com/sztreat.html

Children and Adults with Attention-Deficit/Hyperactivity Disorder (CHADD)

CHADD is a nonprofit organization that supports people with ADHD through advocacy and education.

http://www.chadd.org

The National Institute on Drug Abuse (NIDA)

This organization supports and conducts research on drug abuse and uses this information to help improve addiction prevention efforts, treatment, and policy.

http://www.nida.nih.gov

Healthy Place

This Web site provides information about the role of psychotherapy in the treatment of eating disorders.

**http://www.healthyplace.com/Communities/
Eating_Disorders/treatment_therapy_5.asp**

National Center for Post-Traumatic Stress Disorder

This site provides information and recommendations about psychological debriefing.

**http://www.ncptsd.va.gov/facts/disasters/
fs_debriefing_disaster.html**

Recovered Memories

This site brings together a body of evidence in favor of recovered memories, including background, response to critics, and case studies.

**http://www.brown.edu/Departments/
Taubman_Center/Recovmem/**

Additude: Living Well with ADD and Learning Disabilities

This Web site is sponsored by *Additude* magazine, a national monthly publication about child and adult ADD and ADHD, family support options, and doctors' treatment recommendations.

http://www.additudemag.com/

Psychological Conditions and Treatments

*A*t the heart of abnormal psychology are the psychological conditions and mental disorders for which people need professional treatment. The determination of need for professional intervention is especially problematic in cases in which an obviously disturbed person refuses treatment. For example, questions have arisen about the ethics and legality of forcing a possibly violent individual to take medications involuntarily. Similarly, there is debate about whether a person who engages in personally detrimental behavior, such as self-starvation in severe anorexia, has the right to refuse life-sustaining treatment. Particular controversy has emerged about the validity of phenomena of blocked and recovered memories. Questions have also arisen about the use of drugs such as MDMA (Ecstasy) and whether or not cognitive deficits may result from their use. Also, many questions have been raised about the most appropriate means of responding to individuals with psychological problems and disorders. For example, some eating-disordered individuals are at such medical peril that health professionals find it necessary to take forceful action to protect the health of these clients, a stance that some critics find objectionable. Other topics garnering media attention since the devastating events of September 11th, the Asian tsunami, and Hurricane Katrina focuses on the effectiveness of psychological debriefing with survivors of traumatizing events or the advisability of using drugs to dampen traumatic memories. Finally, the most appropriate intervention for treating people with alcoholism has been debated for decades; some argue that complete abstinence is the only option, while others believe that controlled drinking is possible.

- Is Forced Treatment of Seriously Mentally Ill Individuals Justifiable?
- Should Individuals with Anorexia Nervosa Have the Right to Refuse Life-Sustaining Treatment?
- Is Psychological Debriefing a Harmful Intervention for Survivors of Trauma?
- Are Blocked and Recovered Memories Valid Phenomena?
- Is Attention-Deficit/Hyperactivity Disorder (ADHD) a Real Disorder?
- Should MDMA (Ecstasy) Be Prohibited, Even for Therapeutic Use?
- Should Abstinence Be the Goal for Treating People with Alcohol Problems?

1

ISSUE 1

Is Forced Treatment of Seriously Mentally Ill Individuals Justifiable?

YES: **Samuel Jan Brakel**, from *Overriding Mental Health Treatment Refusals: How Much Process Is "Due"?* (The Berkeley Electronic Press, 2007)

NO: **James B. Gottstein**, from "How the Legal System Can Help Create a Recovery Culture in Mental Health Systems," *Leading the Transformation to Recovery* (2005)

ISSUE SUMMARY

YES: Attorney Samuel J. Brakel asserts that society has a responsibility to care for mentally ill individuals who are incapable of understanding their sickness or their need for treatment, even if treatment must be forced upon these individuals against their will.

NO: Attorney James B. Gottstein objects to the commonly held notion that mentally ill individuals are incapable of making rational decisions about their treatment. He views involuntary interventions as representing a curtailment of liberty.

T he deinstitutionalization movement which began in the final quarter of the 20th century was regarded as an important positive trend in the treatment of seriously mentally ill people. Although some patients who were transferred to community programs and halfway houses thrived in a less restrictive environment, other patients became lost in the maze, with many becoming homeless and destitute. In response to the social crisis following deinstitutionalization, some social critics have called for more aggressive efforts to reach out to seriously mentally ill people so that they can be provided with badly needed care, even if these individuals resist such solicitous efforts. A controversy has raged about whether therapeutic treatment should be forced upon seriously mentally ill people.

In the first reading, Attorney Samuel Brakel argues that many citizens with profound mental illness are incapable of caring for themselves, and will resist treatment because they do not view themselves as mentally ill. Without treatment many individuals will not only be at risk, but will be deprived of experiencing a better quality of life. Attorney Brakel believes that mental health professionals should be allowed to initiate treatment over a patient's objection in instances involving seriously ill individuals who cannot be convinced to accept treatment voluntarily.

In the second reading, Attorney James Gottstein argues vehemently against the idea of forcing treatment upon unwilling citizens. He argues that myths about mental illness need to be debunked, while efforts are made to provide more humane, effective, recovery-oriented, and non-coercive interventions. Gottstein contends that it is easier for the system to lock people up and drug them into submission than it is to engage them in a much more humane process of recovery.

POINT (Brakel)

- Without drugs as the base treatment for schizophrenia and other psychotic disorders, there is no hope for improvement. Talk and behavior therapy, by themselves, are useless treatment methods for schizophrenia.

- Many people suffering from psychosis have a neurological inability to appreciate that they are sick and need treatment (a condition called anosagnosia). These people will resist treatment because they do not view themselves as mentally ill.

- Antipsychotic drugs used in treatment are highly efficacious and without the purported negative side-effects portrayed by anti-psychiatry alarmists.

- If a patient cannot be convinced to accept prescribed treatment, the physician should be allowed to initiate treatment over the patient's objection with minimal legal interference.

- Patients who adhere to *continued* drug treatment benefit on virtually all important personal and social measures. They have lower rates of rehospitalization, criminal recidivism, and violent behavior.

COUNTERPOINT (Gottstein)

- It is far easier for the system to lock people up and drug them into submission than it is to spend the time with them to develop a therapeutic relationship, and thus be able to engage troubled individuals with voluntary humane alternatives leading to recovery.

- Mental patients are not by definition incapable of making rational decisions; nor are they necessarily less competent than non-mentally ill medical patients.

- Forced drugging simply cannot be scientifically proven to be in a person's best interest; information is lacking about the long-term effectiveness or the possible harm associated with these drugs.

- As posited by the United States Supreme Court, involuntary commitment does nothing to enhance autonomy, but rather represents a "massive curtailment of liberty."

- Rather than providing remarkable opportunities for growth and autonomy, the system of forced psychiatry leads a tremendous number of people down a road to permanent disability and poverty.

YES ⤺

Samuel Jan Brakel

Overriding Mental Health Treatment Refusals: How Much Process Is "Due"?

Abstract

Getting mental health treatment to patients who need it is today a much bele-galed enterprise. This is in part because law makers have a skewed view of the enterprise, in particular the treatment of patients with antipsychotic medica-tions. The properties and uses of these medications are misunderstood by many in the legal community, while the drugs' undesirable side-effects are typically overstated and the remedial effects undersold when not outright ignored. One specific legal effect has been to accord to mental patients a sub-stantively outsized right to refuse treatment that comes with a correspondingly action-stifling dose of procedural safeguards, this despite the patients' fre-quent lack of capacity to exercise the right wisely and the bad personal and systemic consequences that flow from that. The purpose of this article is to provide better balanced and accurate evidence of the properties of antipsy-chotic drugs so as to convince law makers and advocates for the mentally dis-abled that it is safe to roll back some of the more counterproductive legal strictures on the effort to provide mental health treatment. . . .

I. Introduction

"In 1991 the above listed authors published an article in the *Indiana Law Review* titled "Taking Harms Seriously: Involuntary Mental Patients and the Right to Refuse Treatment."[1] In it we argued that the extension to involuntarily committed mental health patients of a legal right to refuse mental health treatment (at least in the sense of its being protected by potentially multiple judicial hearings), was a legal/logical anomaly and one that had bad conse-quences for those patients who exercised the right, not to mention their fellow patients, the hospital doctors and the institutions in which the patients were (ware)housed. We felt, somewhat naively perhaps, that the reason the law was askew stemmed from the lack of good medical information on the part of law-yers, judges and legislators and that rectifying the situation required the pre-sentation in an appropriate legal forum of such information. Everyone's eyes would be opened and the law would change in the direction warranted by our confidence in the medical facts—*i.e.*, that the antipsychotic drugs predominantly used in treatment were highly efficacious and without anywhere near the negative side-effects profiles portrayed by antipsychiatric alarmists. There has been some success in the realization of this hope, though pinning much or any of it on the publication/dissemination of a legal academic article would be presumptuous.[2] There has been progress in the law in the sense that the cases and statutes today are somewhat more likely than a decade or so ago to reflect an appropriate appreciation of what the medications can do (and what they won't do), in multiple contexts. Whether the issue is civil commitment and treatment (inpatient or outpatient), or treatment in the criminal justice-mandated context of competency commitments (whether pre-trial or pre-sentence) or post-conviction treatment in the prison setting, medical authority to medicate unwilling patients has in the overall expanded while judicial review has been relegated to a lesser and later ("post-deprivation") role—a realignment of power that one would surmise has much to do with better knowledge of the (large) benefits vs. (relatively small) costs in potential negative consequences of the medications.

At the same time, however, there has been some jurisprudential backsliding as well, including at the U.S. Supreme Court level," (p. 5) . . . "where a small number of decisions has been handed down and some language articulated that seems to give new life to what one had hoped was the moribund view of psychotropic drugs as predominantly harmful and the accompanying disbelief in the competence and integrity of doctors to appropriately prescribe them.

Given the thus still uneven, not to say precarious, lay of the legal landscape on treatment refusals, we feel it is timely to do a reprise of sorts of our 1991 article and to present once again what we believe is a true picture of the risks and benefits of antipsychotic medications. It is a picture that in many respects is and can be more optimistic than before, consistent with another set of major advances over the last 10-15 years in psychiatric medicine (in particular, the development of the so-called atypicals, a new line of antipsychotic drugs with higher benefit potential and fewer risks than the "old" medications, and continuing improvement in their usage). . . .

"We will begin by presenting the new medical data because (1) it is the most significant (new) element in the debate on the matter of treatment rights, including the right to refuse it and (2) it immediately makes more intelligible what that debate is about as well as what our preferences/biases as authors are and from where these derive. We will present the research and anecdotal results documenting the heightened efficacy and the reduced possibility of untoward effects of the new antipsychotic drugs. This section of the paper will include information, new information to the extent it has been developed, on the harms, both personal and institutional, that result from withholding for legal reasons treatment that is medically indicated—in short we will present some indication at least of the costs of an inefficient legal treatment refusal regime, one that makes any conscientious and medically justified attempt to override the patient's resistance to treatment cumbersome to the point of impractical, if not impossible." . . .

II. Of Typicals and Atypicals: The Old and New Medical Data

"We begin this section on the new medical data by summarizing what we said in the old article. Under the heading "Separating Myth from Reality" we first reported on a review we conducted of the legal literature on the use of psychotropic drugs—law journals as well as judicial opinions—concluding that the vast bulk of it was woefully, even willfully, misinformed about the both the drugs' risks and benefits.[3] The prevalence and severity of negative (side-) effects were almost uniformly overstated, alleged misuse of "drugging" by state physicians was played up as rampant if not the norm (embellishments/inventions ranging from the charge that drugs were administered mostly for administrative convenience or punishment to the suggestion by analogy that it might be or at least risked being done to suppress political dissent), while the huge health benefits of proper drug usage for people with serious mental illness got no play at all (the whole helping rationale behind psychiatric treatment being simply ignored).[4] We wrote of the characteristic internal referencing aspect of this legal literature where reliance for authority was not on original medical publications but almost exclusively on a few biased analyses written by non-physicians or one or two radical anti-psychiatry doctors, leading to an inevitable repetition of false information and myth or even, as in the legal cases ruled by common law precedent, the outright transformation of medical myth into legal fact."[5] . . .

"One area where the law needs to adjust is the treatment of patients with antipsychotic drugs. When these drugs were first discovered in the early 1950's they were referred to as tranquilizers. The first antipsychotic drug, chlorpromazine, did have considerable sedative properties. Thence came the charge that the drugs "dulled the senses" or that they were a convenient chemical straightjacket. But even the early drugs did not act by sedation. Like the newer drugs their action is to counteract psychosis by blocking excessive dopamine in the brain, a hormone-like substance whose release in abnormal quantities is associated with "positive" psychiatric symptoms such as hallucinations and delusions.[6] While the drugs may quiet a highly agitated and excited patient, they also help restore apathetic, affect-less patients.[7] The restoration is in the nature of a regaining of cognitive skills, ideally as close as possible to normal pre-morbid thinking and functioning." . . .

"Treatment with antipsychotic drugs is the hallmark of psychiatric treatment of patients suffering from schizophrenia and other major mental disorders. In no institution today, whether the remaining state facilities, private general hospitals or specialized facilities, the medical schools, or for that matter in the doctor's office, is psychological or psychosocial treatment alone provided. Treatment is always given with drugs. It is not true that wealthy patients get verbal psychotherapy while poor patients are drugged. The wealthy get drugs *plus* psychotherapy. Medication dispensation and management have become primary aspects of psychiatric treatment for mentally ill patients of all classes and cultures. What is seen by unknowing critics as an orgy of pill pushing is no more than a reflection of the reality that without drugs as the base treatment for schizophrenia and other psychotic disorders there is no hope for improvement. Talk and behavior therapy are still provided, but such therapy builds on the substantial degree of cognitive and emotional restoration that can be achieved with medication. Often its focus is on developing the patient's and even the family's coping skills, to sharpen recognition of the onset of an episode, of the conditions, stresses that signal vulnerability, and what to do in the face of them. . . . By themselves however these treatment methods are useless for schizophrenia, potentially harmful even, particularly if used to the exclusion of needed pharmacology."[8]

Prior to the early 1950's most schizophrenic patients spent much of their life in state insane asylums. Since schizophrenia's onset is typically in adolescence, the illness took away most of the patients' normal lives. In the early 1950's 50% of the hospital beds in the country were in massive state mental facilities located in rural areas.[9] Up to half a million mental patients filled these beds.[10] When chlorpromazine was discovered in 1953 its use spread quickly throughout the world in two or three years. Violence in state hospitals in the United States dropped by 90% almost overnight.[11] The number of patients in hospitals began to drop year by year with comparable alacrity. Today the total of patients in state mental hospitals throughout the United States is less than 10% of what it was in the mid-1950's and the facilities themselves have almost completely disappeared, restructured for new use or torn down.[12]

When good care is available and patients take their medication the majority of them can return to work or school and be productive members of society. Unfortunately, many schizophrenic patients do not have access to high quality care. The emptying of the state hospitals was accompanied by the realization that much of the treatment burden would now fall on community, mostly outpatient, programs. But the will or wherewithal to create a community treatment system equal to the task never materialized. The result is that the hope of full social rehabilitation, a theoretical possibility for many schizophrenic patients, is realized in all too few cases. For other patients it is worse than that. They may get brief treatment in a hospital or, more likely today, in a jail but they will stop taking their medication once released. Their lives will spiral downward to where episodes of active schizophrenia grow more frequent and worse and recovery is less complete with each episode. Eventually the disease process may flatten out but by then too often alcoholism, drug abuse and homelessness will have become dominant if not permanent features of the patient's existence.[13] What used to be the back wards of hospitals for these patients have today become the back streets and jails. As presently structured, the law and the courts provide little in the way of relief from this pattern.

Schizophrenia is not normally thought of as a fatal illness. The average life expectancy of schizophrenic patients is lower than that of the normal population, but many live into old age. Much of the shorter life span is attributable to a high suicide rate among people suffering from schizophrenia, as well as accidental death and the negative life-style effects of those who are not well cared for. In that respect, it is relevant to note that schizophrenic patients not receiving drugs die at a rate ten times higher than patients on medication.[14] . . .

"[T]here is today a great deal more documented evidence of the concept of anosognosia.[15] More than just an assertion that mentally ill people sometimes lack full awareness of or adequate insight into their illness and distinct from denial as a psychologically-based defense tactic, the term is meant to describe a "biologically-based" or even "neurological" inability on the part of the sick person to appreciate that he/she is sick and needs treatment, which is a characteristic of the illness itself. It is said to afflict some 47%–57% of schizophrenic patients[16] with implications not just for health and behavior (as mentioned, untreated mental illness is strongly related to psychiatric deterioration and violence) but of course also the law's assessment of a treatment refuser's "competence" and the desirability/wisdom of honoring his or her wishes." . . .

"We also wrote of the costs of treatment delayed or denied because of the law's overprotections: individual clinical costs such as mental deterioration and the inability to recapture such psychiatric loss; institutional costs and harms on the order of increased violence in hospitals on the part of untreated patients and its effect on compliant patients and care givers; and the direct financial costs of warehousing patients before they can be treated, as well as legal process expenditures in judicially or administratively resolving treatment refusal disputes."[17]

Finally, we wrote of the "true risks of side effects" of the antipsychotic drugs (the first-generation drugs of that time), noting that on the one hand all drugs have side effects, and on the other, that as measured by both their efficacy (high but underappreciated) and their asserted bad effects (grossly overstated as to seriousness, general prevalence and particular risk to the patient or patient class) the antipsychotics predominantly used were relatively benign."[18] (p. 13) . . . "[T]he risk of death from untreated psychosis, drawn from hospital studies documenting large numbers of deaths from lethal catatonia, suicide, accidents, infection and other harms that used to befall chronically psychotic patients in pre-drug days, was infinitely larger than from the antipsychotic drugs, a situation we analogized to the benefits of penicillin which exponentially increased medical survival rates in homes, hospitals and on the battle fields despite the fact that an allergic reaction to the drug can on occasion be fatal."[19] (p. 13) . . . "To anticipate arguments about autonomy or (even) free speech, we emphasized, as we do today, the restorative properties of the drugs; that the evidence of cognitive/perceptual restoration to premorbid "normal" mental processing was substantial for many patients treated with the drugs; and the bearing this in turn should have on which of the patient's choices in what mental state to honor.[20]

This was the state of the medication treatment art in regard to what have since been called the "typicals" (*i.a.*, haloperidol, chlorpromazine, thioridazine, fluphenazine, perphenazine), the "old", "conventional" antipsychotic drugs that in the early 1990's began to be replaced by a newer line of pharmaceuticals called (of course) the "atypicals" (the forerunner clozapine and later olanzapine, quetiapine, risperidone, ziprasidone, and aripiprazole). Trials and other research on the atypicals tended to show substantial efficacy gains as well as a marked reduction in the prevalence and seriousness of undesirable side effects. . . .

"The evidence also continues to accumulate and solidify that all drugs, old or new, produce major gains and help safeguard against psychiatric loss which occurs in the absence of treatment and cannot be recouped even after treatment is initiated. Recent studies document disturbingly high percentages of untreated mental illness or treatment that is interrupted against medical advice (this, in a context where the law's preoccupation continues, anachronistically, to be with alleged unneeded and unwanted treatment). A 2001 report of a National Comorbidity Survey conducted between 1990 and 1992 found that fewer than 40% of a cohort of seriously mentally ill patients received stable treatment, with the primary reason for failure to seek treatment or failing to continue being the subjects' unwillingness or inability to see the need.[21] The prognosis for these patients is a diminishing chance of amelioration or recovery as relapses mount and symptoms increase in acuity, severity (negative symptoms in particular) and resistance to remediation.[22] At the same time, studies on adherence to drug treatment, many conducted in the context of attempts to evaluate the merits of so-called outpatient commitment (OPC),[23] show the benefits of treatment and especially *continued* treatment (even for the minimally symptomatic) on virtually all important personal and social measures: *i.a.*, reduced hospital recidivism and reduced criminal recidivism/violent behavior,[24] as well as reduced victimization;[25] quality of life improvements such as measured by reduced psychiatric symptomatology and better functioning;[26] and systemic gains in terms of less discordant and more appropriate use of the mental health and correctional systems, respectively, for mentally ill people who come into contact with the law as well as appreciable gains in housing situations (reductions in homelessness)."[27]

Finally, as mentioned, new findings and confirmation of older study results on anognosia, which document the relationship between schizophrenia and lack of insight as one of the latter being a neurological function/symptom of the former,[28] provide strengthening support for a best-medical-interests decision making model in mental health matters. The implications of the concept of anognosia for treatment adherence/compliance are self-evident. A person who believes he is not sick will resist treatment at all stages and levels. To the extent the implications for the person's mental health (negative, as they would be for most any untreated somatic illness) are not equally self-evident, they have been described and documented in studies such as those cited in the preceding paragraph. Last, while the details may ultimately bedevil some or many, we believe no spelling out is required of anognosia's implication *in principle* regarding the need for and propriety of the option of (legal) coercion in mental health treatment. Much as we might want, desirable as it may seem, we cannot afford to limit mental health treatment to its entirely voluntary provision and acceptance.

These then are the contemporary medical facts against whose backdrop we proceed with the analysis in the remainder of the paper.

III. Once Again: What Is the Legal Debate About?

. . . "All patients have a legally, even constitutionally, protected right to refuse treatment. There is no disagreement on this and need not be. Nor, despite its constitutionally protected status, is there any doubt that this right of a patient"

(p. 17) . . . "in some situations must yield to superior interests, in particular the interests of treating doctors and/or those they represent. The "issue" is how much/what kind of process must be observed to override the patient's refusal, should that be considered medically necessary. This is where opinions, both legal and lay, diverge. And the legal/medical context in which the refusal is asserted will have everything to do with what the answer is or, better, as there is no consensus here, what we think the answer ought to be. This is the crux of the matter[.]" . . .

VI. Legislative Process and Progress

"Reports by groups favoring psychiatric intervention when needed such as the Treatment Advocacy Center (TAC)[29] suggest that in regard to inpatient commitment observable strides have been made nationally—*i.e.,* jurisdiction by jurisdiction—to impart a more medically-oriented/*parens patriae* perspective and, if not replace, to at least supplement the danger-to-others/police power focus of the earlier statutes. This has been accomplished via a revival of the need for treatment standard to suffice for commitment and an accompanying refocus of the legal lens on indicators such as psychiatric treatment history, recent decompensation, deterioration or destabilization, or even mere risk of such—all of which avoid, conceptually, the implicit emergency/police power strictures that dominate the dangerousness formulation, and should help us move away in practice from the consequent futile pattern of repetitive one-at-a-time, typically post-crisis, interventions."

As for outpatient commitment statutes, the concept underlying them is not new, but they have over the past few years swept the country in terms of increased visibility and use.[30] The objective of these laws, at least partly met according to early studies,[31] is to ensure treatment for those who otherwise resist, avoid, stop, slip-through-the-cracks-of, and "recycle" through the mental health and criminal justice systems, to their own as well as their fellow citizens' detriment. More, and especially earlier, treatment for more people who need it is the aspiration here, as is the continuation of treatment already begun given the proven benefits of adherence/compliance and the well-documented negatives associated with the interruption or cessation of the treatment regimen. The concept's ancillary virtue" (pp. 42–43) . . . "is that it is and has been correctly perceived by many as a lesser infringement on patients' liberty than having the treatment need met by inpatient hospitalization (or the "police need" for segregation met by incarceration). In other words, it is a concept on which people of differing political/philosophical persuasion and orientation—*i.e.,* those on opposite sides of the traditional advocacy divide—should be able to agree.[32] . . .

A. Increased Treatment Focus in Commitment Statutes

1. Persistence of Dangerousness as the Sole Commitment Criterion (and Four Deviations)
"It is the view, correct in our opinion, that for determining the need for psychiatric intervention it is both apposite and sufficient to use psychiatric standards

and terms, and not those of law enforcement. The law is not asking a secondary question here such as it does in the context of, say, the insanity defense, where the psychiatric input is meant to address cognitive or volitional capacity so as to help resolve the ultimate legal issue of accountability/culpability, or any of a number of issues where the law seeks psychiatric consultation as it were via testimony on so-called penultimate issues.[33] This is direct and ultimate: it is about treatment and treatability. The question can both be posed and answered directly, in medical terms.[34] . . .

B. Outpatient "Commitment" Laws

VII. The ADA, *Olmstead* and the "Conversion" of Justice Kennedy

"It must be remembered that for the person with severe mental illness who has no treatment, the most dreaded of confinements can be the imprisonment inflicted by his own mind, which shuts reality out and subjects him to the torment of voices and images beyond our powers to describe. . . . It is a common phenomenon that a patient functions well with medication, yet, because of the mental illness itself, lacks discipline or capacity to follow the regime the medication requires."[35] . . .

Conclusions

"We believe that for civil commitment . . . and commitment for restoration to trial competence both the substantive standards and procedures can and should be medical. As we said at the outset, every patient or proposed patient has a right to refuse treatment if he/she does not want it. That is to say, patients as other citizens should be able to articulate their objection to prescribed treatment and that objection, if made, should be heard. Moreover, the physician who is responsible for treating the patient should try to convince the patient that the course prescribed is best for him/her or propose another course or courses that the patient finds more palatable but that, despite perhaps being suboptimal, still work(s). In short, we support the kind of therapist/patient dialogue about therapy that we will presume takes place in any hospital, community treatment center or doctor's office to the extent the patient's mental condition permits."[36]

However, if the patient cannot be convinced to accept the prescribed treatment, rejecting it and any plausible alternative courses (including trial and error), the physician should be allowed to initiate treatment over the patient's objection with minimal legal interference. That is, the only substantive criterion that need or should inform the physician's decision to proceed to treat is medical need/propriety. Inquiries into the patient's dangerousness, the government's (compelling) interest in prosecuting or any similarly diversionary issues should not be required. Procedurally, in-house medical review of the initial treatment decision should suffice to allow the primary physician to go ahead. The purpose after all of each of these commitments, simply stated even if not always simple to achieve, is to restore mental health and functioning as much and as quickly as possible[.] . . .

"Judges cannot be and should not be the baseline decision makers in any of these institutional (or non-institutional), post-legal judgment phases of the treatment process. Forced treatment can begin once the medical reviewer has approved the treating physician's recommendation. Post-deprivation judicial review, after treatment has been initiated and limited by the professional judgment rule, is all the law should call for at this juncture."[37]

Notes

1. Samuel J. Brakel & John M. Davis, *Taking Harms Seriously: Involuntary Mental Patients and the Right to Refuse Treatment*, 25 IND. L. REV. 429 (1991).

2. Indeed, it would be demonstrably wrong. (1) What success there is has been slow in coming and uneven. (2) The article has not been cited with great frequency, its appeal apparently being limited mostly to the already converted. And (3) the achievement of significant legal change tends to require a combination of many factors and forces, among which academic writings may play a role but not usually a prominent one. . . .

3. Brakel & Davis, *supra*, note 1, at 437–438 and notes.

4. *Ibid.*

5. *Id.* at 438–440, especially note 33, citing *In re* the Mental Commitment of M.P., 510 N.E. 2d 645 (IN 1987) and *In re* Orr, 531 N.E. 2d 64 (IL 1988) as textbook examples. The earlier Indiana case had made reference to a "virtually undisputed allegation that a person medicated with antipsychotic drugs has a 50% risk of contracting tardive dyskinesia." This in fact highly disputable, if not plain erroneous (the much less alarming facts were not widely known at the time), allegation was then cited by the Illinois court in a subsequent decision as a "fact" "found" by the Indiana Supreme Court. . . .

6. There are imaging data today from living schizophrenic patients that show excessive dopamine release in the brain when the patient is having hallucinations and delusions, as well as of the blocking effect on dopamine receptors when antipsychotics are administered. *See* A. Abi-Dargam, R.Gil, J. Krystal *et al., Increased Striatal Dopamine Transmission in Schizophrenia: Confirmation in a Second Cohort*, 155 AM. J. PSYCHIATRY 761 (1998); A. Bartolomeis, D.R. Weinberger, N. Weisenfeld *et al., Schizophrenia Is Associated with Elevated Amphetamine-Induced Synaptic Dopamine Concentrations: Evidence from a Novel Positron Emission Tomography Method*, 94 PROC. NAT'L ACAD. SCI. U.S.A. 2569 (1997).

7. The amotivational, apathetic, poor social skills aspects of schizophrenia are its so-called negative symptoms. Combined with cognitive/executive defects, these deficits contribute greatly to poor social and vocational functioning among people with the illness. But today's drugs can go a long way toward remedying these deficits and we have an understanding, albeit imperfect, of how they work. S. R. Marder, J.M. Davis & G. Chouinard, *The Effects of Risperidone on the Five Dimensions of Schizophrenia Derived by Factor Analysis: Combined Results of the North American Trial*, 58 J. CLIN. PSYCHIATRY 538 (1997); J.M. Davis & N. Chen, *Clinical Profile of an Atypical Antipsychotic: Risperidone*, 28 SCHIZOPHRENIA BULLETIN 43 (2002). . . .

8. It is less a matter of psycho-social treatments having no place or a lesser place in the treatment of severe mental illness today than that the treatments are entirely different. They *capitalize* today on the gains in thinking and functioning that

can be achieved by the medications, as distinct from trying the impossible, which is to achieve these gains directly through verbal or behavioral therapy. *See* Osherhoff v. Chestnut Lodge, Inc. 62 Md. App. 519, 490 A.2d 720 (1985) for an early case—the reported court case merely affirms an arbitration award for allegedly negligent treatment that took place in 1979—involving the recognition that verbal therapy as such is ineffective in treating mental illness with substantial biological components, in this instance a psychotic depressive reaction, and that the failure on the part of the defendant to initiate psychopharmacologic treatments may constitute negligence. The defendant institution, Chestnut Lodge, was a facility famous for furthering psychoanalytic theory and practice, having trained a number of prominent American psychiatrists of this school, a fact which seems to have influenced the diagnosis its staff made of the plaintiff's mental health problems as much as the treatment course that was pursued in the face of unmistakable evidence that the patient was getting worse rather than better.

9.   E. FULLER TORREY, OUT OF THE SHADOWS (1997).

10. *Ibid. See* also, H. Brill & R.E. Patton, *Population Fall in New York State Mental Hospitals in First Year of a Large-Scale Use of Tranquilizing Drugs*, 114 AM. J. OF PSYCHIATRY 509 (1957).

11. See Brill & Patton, *supra,* note 28.

12. *See* OUT OF THE SHADOWS, *supra*, note 27. The lawyer author of this paper conducted social/legal research in the early 1970's at Kankakee State Hospital 30 miles south of Chicago at a time when it housed some 4,000 patients. Within a few years the hospital was a relic, empty of mentally ill patients and in the process of being converted, to the extent possible, to other uses.

13. The neuropsychological deficits and the loss of grey matter seem to get worse after the patient's first psychotic episode and there is strong evidence that failure to treat the first episode with antipsychotic drugs leads to substantially worse outcome, in terms of repeat episodes and recovery therefrom, in the following five years. There is beginning evidence that at least some of the second-generation drugs in particular are effective in blocking the progression of these deficits and losses. K. Kasai, M.E. Shenton *et al.*, *Progressive Decrease of Left Superior Temporal Gyrus Grey Matter Volume in Patients with First-Episode Schizophrenia*, 160 AM. J. OF PSYCHIATRY 156 (2003); W. Cahn, H.E. Hulshoff Poll *et al.*, *Brain Volume Changes in First_Episode Schizophrenia: A One-Year Follow-Up Study*, 59 ARCH. OF GENERAL PSYCHIATRY 1002 (2002). Moreover, a large study carried out in Finland, based on that country's central register, found that the risk of untreated schizophrenic patients dying was 10 times higher than that of patients on medication. J. Tiihonen, K. Wahlbeck *et al., Effectiveness of Antipsychotic Treatments in a Nationwide Cohort of Patients in Community Care after First Hospitalization Due to Schizophrenia and Schizoaffective Disorder: Observational Follow-Up Study*, 333 BRITISH MED. J. 224 (2006).

14. *Ibid. . . .*

15. Researchers most prominently identified with the concept of anosognosia, through studies conducted in the early 1990's, are psychologist Xavier Amador at Columbia University in New York and psychiatrist Anthony David at the Institute of Psychiatry in London (UK). Psychiatrist Joseph McEvoy of the University of Pittsburgh however first explicitly linked the characteristic to the illness in the 1980's. Joseph P. McEvoy *et al., Why Must Some Schizophrenic Patients Be Involuntarily Committed? The Role of Insight*, 30 COMPR. PSYCHIATRY 13 (1989); Joseph P. McEvoy *et al., Measuring Chronic Schizophrenic Patients' Attitudes Toward Their Illness and Treatment*, 32 HOSP. COMMUNITY PSYCHIATRY 856 (1981).

16. Xavier Amador *et al., Awareness of Illness in Schizophrenia and Schizoaffective and Mood Disorders*, 51 ARCHIVES GEN. PSYCHIATRY 826 (1994); Xavier Amador

et al., Awareness Deficits in Neurological Disorders and Schizophrenia (abstract), 24 SCHIZOPHRENIA RES. 96 (1997). . . .

17. *Id.* at 453–461, under "Research Findings on the Harms Resulting from Delayed Treatment."

18. *Id.* at 461–467. . . .

19. *Ibid.* . . .

20. *Id.* at 465. . . .

21. Ronald C. Kessler, Patricia A. Berglund, Martha L. Bruce *et al., The Prevalence and Correlates of Untreated Serious Mental Illness*, 36 HEALTH SERVICES RESEARCH 978 (2001).

22. *E.g.,* Diana O. Perkins, Hongbin Gu, Kalina Boteva & Jeffrey A. Lieberman, *Relationships Between Duration of Untreated Psychosis and Outcome in First-Episode Schizophrenia: A Critical Review and Meta Analysis*, 162 AM. J. OF PSYCHIATRY 1785 (2005); D.A.W. Johnson, G. Pasterski, L. Ludlow *et al., The Discontinuance of Maintenance Neuroleptic Therapy in Chronic Schizophrenic Patients: Drug and Social Consequences*, 67 ACTA PSYCHIATR. SCAND. 339 (1983); Charles M. Beasley, Jr., Virginia K. Sutton, Cindy C. Taylor *et al., Is Quality of Life Among Minimally Symptomatic Patients with Schizophrenia Better Following Withdrawal or Continuation of Antipsychotic Treatment?* 26 J. OF CLINICAL PSYCHOPHARMACOLOGY 40 (2006).

23. See section on this topic *infra* at pp.—of this paper.

24. Jeffrey W. Swanson, Randy Borum, Marvin S. Swartz, Virginia A. Hiday *et al., Can Involuntary Outpatient Commitment Reduce Arrests Among Persons with Severe Mental Illness?* 28 CRIM. JUSTICE AND BEHAVIOR 156 (2001); Jeffrey W. Swanson, Marvin S. Swartz, Randy Borum, Virginia A. Hiday *et al., Involuntary Outpatient Commitment and Reduction of Violent Behaviour in Persons with Severe Mental Illness*, 176 BRITISH J. OF PSYCHIATRY 324 (2000); Marvin S. Swartz, Jeffrey W. Swanson, H. Ryan Wagner, Barbara J. Burns *et al., Can Involuntary Outpatient Commitment Reduce Hospital Recidivism?: Findings from a Randomized Trial with Severely Mentally Ill Individuals*, 156 AM. J. OF PSYCHIATRY 1968 (1999).

25. Virginia A. Hiday, Marvin S. Swartz, Jeffrey W. Swanson, Randy Borum & H. Ryan Wagner, *Impact of Outpatient Commitment on Victimization of People with Severe Mental Illness*, 159 AM. J. OF PSYCHIATRY 1403 (2002).

26. Jeffrey W. Swanson, Marvin S. Swartz, Eric B. Elbogen *et al., Effects of Involuntary Outpatient Commitment on Subjective Quality of Life in Persons with Severe Mental Illness*, 21 BEHAV. SCIENCES AND THE LAW 473 (2003).

27. Haya Ascher-Svanum, Douglas E. Faries, Baojin Zhu *et al., Medication Adherence and Long-Term Functional Outcomes in the Treatment of Schizophrenia in Usual Care*, 67 J. OF CLINICAL PSYCHIATRY 453 (2006).

28. See Amador and McEvoy articles, *supra,* notes 37 and 38. Also, Joseph P. McEvoy, Paul S. Appelbaum, L. Joy Apperson *et al., Why Must Some Schizophrenic Patients Be Involuntarily Committed? The Role of Insight*, 30 COMPR. PSYCHIATRY 13 (1989); Anthony S. David, *Insight and Psychosis*, 156 BRITISH J. OF PSYCHIATRY 798 (1990); Xavier F. Amador, David H. Strauss, Scott A. Yale & Jack M. Gorman, *Awareness of Illness in Schizophrenia*, 17 SCHIZOPHRENIA BULLETIN 113 (1991); Faith B. Dickerson, John J. Boronow, Norman Ringel & Frederick Parente, *Lack of Insight Among Outpatients with Schizophrenia*, 48 PSYCHIATRIC SERVICES 195 (1997); Xavier F. Amador & Regina A. Seckinger, *The Assessment of Insight: A Methodological Review,* 27 PSYCHIATRIC ANNALS 798 (1997); Graig Goodman, Gabriella Knoll, Victoria Isakov & Henry Silver, *Insight into Illness in Schizophrenia*, 46 COMPR. PSYCHIATRY 284 (2005).

29. See the CATALYST (Newsletter of the Treatment Advocacy Center) Spring/ Summer 2004. TAC also maintains a website, www.psychlaws.org, on which it provides, *i.a.*, updates on the latest legislative reforms. TAC advocates refer to the process as "assisted outpatient treatment" (AOT) which apart from deemphasizing the nonconsensual aspects of "outpatient commitment" also has the advantage of avoiding its oxymoronic quality, the term commitment being associated with confinement in an institution, *i.e.,* being an *in*patient.

30. *Ibid.*

31. CATALYST, Spring/Summer 2005 at 7 and 15. The latter page presents "realworld results" on New York's Kendra's law under the title "Kendra's Law families and participants laud program: Report shows sharp reductions in hospitalizations, incarcerations, homelessness." The TAC group points to a number of other studies supporting the notion that the outpatient commitment laws have achieved their intended effects: Guido Zanni & Leslie deVeau, *Inpatient Stays Before and After Outpatient Commitment,* 37 HOSP. & CMTY PSYCHIATRY 941 (1986); M.R. Munetz *et al., The Effectiveness of Outpatient Civil Commitment,* 47 Psychiatric Services 1251 (1996); B.M. Rohland, *The Role of Outpatient Commitment in the Management of Persons with Schizophrenia,* IOWA CONSORTIUM FOR MENTAL HEALTH SERVICES, TRAINING, AND RESEARCH (1998); and Gustavo A. Fernandez & Sylvia Nygard, *Impact of Involuntary Outpatient Commitment on the Revolving-Door Syndrome in North Carolina,* 41 HOSP. & CMTY PSYCHIATRY 1001 (1990). Later studies in North Carolina have been especially persuasive in documenting positive effects of mandated outpatient treatment in various respects. *See* (the titles are indicative) Marvin S. Swartz, Jeffrey W. Swanson, H. Ryan Wagner *et al., Can Involuntary Outpatient Commitment Reduce Hospital Recidivism?* 156 AM. J. PSYCHIAT. 1986 (1999); Jeffrey W. Swanson, Marvin S. Swartz, R. Borum *et al., Involuntary Outpatient Commitment and Reduction in Violent Behaviour in Persons with Severe Mental Illness,* 176 BRIT. J. PSYCHIAT. 224 (2000); Jeffrey W. Swanson, R. Borum, Marvin S. Swartz *et al., Can Involuntary Outpatient Commitment Reduce Arrests among Persons with Severe Mental Illness?* 28 CRIM. JUSTICE & BEHAVIOR 156 (2001); Virginia A. Hiday, Marvin S. Swartz, Jeffrey W. Swanson *et al., Impact of Outpatient Commitment on Victimization of People with Severe Mental Illness,* 159 AM. J. PSYCHIAT. 1403 (2002). . . .

32. In theory at least. A recent article by Richard J. Bonnie and John Monahan, *From Coercion to Contract: Reframing the Debate on Mandated Community Treatment for People with Mental Disorders,* 29 LAW AND HUMAN BEHAVIOR 485 (2005), confirms (by the title alone) that there is much less agreement on the value of the concept than its proponents once optimistically believed. See also note 277, *supra.* . . .

33. The law has gone back and forth on whether it is appropriate for mental health experts to offer testimony on ultimate legal issues, with the postHinckley reforms following the acquittal by reason of insanity of President Reagan's would-be assassin, enacted in 1984 for the federal courts, leading the way toward the currently dominant position of disallowing it.

34. It has been pointed out innumerable times by both judges and legal commentators that commitment is a social/legal decision rather than a medical one, but this does not alter the fact that medical criteria and medical facts are what that social/legal decision should be heavily based on. . . .

35. *Id.* at 609–610.

36. The law is allowed to, should in fact, assume basic medical/institutional realities including such that there ordinarily is communication about treatment prospects and plans between therapist and patient. As distinct from case law drawn from litigation where worst-case evidence is introduced, the statutory

or regulatory law ordinarily need not and should not be written based on worst-case scenarios. *Cf.* the discussion of *Rennie v. Klein* in the text, *supra*, at pp.—where we reproduce the administrative regulation—presumptively a codification of practices—guiding doctors in New Jersey on how to approach patients who resist prescribed treatment. Substantively, the regulation in fact incorporates the least intrusive/least restrictive principle and its procedural mandates suggest abundant deference to the patient's preferences via the physician's stated obligation to discuss alternatives with the patient, to try make the patient understand and to encourage voluntary acceptance (with the help of relatives and friends if so indicated) before seeking approval from the hospital medical director to proceed over the patient's objections. . . .

37. Post-deprivation judicial review should suffice because (1) judges have no expertise in medical matters and therefore should not be baseline (first-instance) decision makers and (2) the costs in time and treatment foregone, deflection of resources, and institutional bad effects of the judiciary's failing to show proper deference to medical professionals are large.

James B. Gottstein

NO

How the Legal System Can Help Create a Recovery Culture in Mental Health Systems

Summary

The purpose of this paper is to show how strategic litigation can and should be a part of efforts to transform mental health systems to culture of recovery. Currently, involuntary commitment and forced drugging are by far the "path of least resistance" when society is faced with someone who is disturbing and their thinking does not conform to society's norms.[1] In other words, it is far easier for the system to lock people up and drug them into submission, then it is to spend the time with them to develop a therapeutic relationship and thus able to engage the person with voluntary humane alternatives leading to recovery.[2] I estimate that 10% of involuntary commitments in the United States and none of the forced drugging under the *parens patriae* doctrine[3] are legally justified. This presents a tremendous opportunity to use litigation to "encourage" the creation of voluntary, recovery oriented services."[4]

In my view, though, in order to be successful various myths of mental illness need to be debunked among the general public and humane, effective recovery oriented, non-coercive alternatives must be made available. . . . The thesis of this paper is that strategic litigation (and public education) are likely essential to transforming the mental health system to one of a recovery culture. . . .

For example, debunking the myth among the general public that people do not recover from a diagnosis of serious mental health illness can encourage the willingness to invest in recovery oriented alternatives. Similarly, having successful, recovery oriented alternatives will help in debunking the myth that people don't recover from serious mental illness. In like fashion, judges and even counsel appointed to represent psychiatric defendants, believe the myth "if this person wasn't crazy, she would know these drugs are good for her" and therefore don't let her pesky rights get in the way of doing the "right thing," i.e., forced drugging. The myth of dangerousness results in people being locked up. In other words, the judges and lawyers reflect society's views and to the extent that society's views change, the judges and lawyers' responses will change to suit. That leads to taking people's rights more seriously. The converse is true as well. Legal cases can have a big impact on public views. *Brown v. Board of Education,*[5] which resulted in outlawing segregation is a classic example of this. Finally, the involuntary mental illness system[6] operates largely illegally, including through its failure to offer less restrictive alternatives.[7] Thus, litigation can force the creation of such alternatives. At the same time, as a practical matter, the availability of acceptable (to the person), recovery oriented, alternatives is necessary for anyone to actually be able to get such services when faced with involuntary commitment and forced drugging.

III. The Involuntary Mental Illness System Operates Largely Illegally

Involuntary "treatment"[8] in the United States largely operates illegally in that court orders for forced treatment are obtained without actual compliance with statutory and constitutional requirements. One of the fundamental constitutional rights that is ignored in practice is that of a "less restrictive alternative."[9] Thus, enforcement of this right through the courts can be instrumental in bringing about change. First, I will discuss the key constitutional principles. . . .

(2) Constitutional Limits on Involuntary Commitment

The Supreme Court went on to say in this and other cases that involuntary commitment was permissible only when the following factors were present:

> (1) "the confinement takes place pursuant to proper procedures and evidentiary standards," (2) there is a finding of "dangerousness either to one's self or to others," and (3) proof of dangerousness is "coupled . . . with the proof of some additional factor, such as a 'mental illness' or 'mental abnormality.'" [11a]

(3) Constitutional Limits on Forced Drugging

The United States Supreme Court has also held a number of times that being free of unwanted psychiatric medication is a fundamental constitutional right.[12] In the most recent case, *Sell,* the United States Supreme Court reiterated:

> [A]n individual has a "significant" constitutionally protected "liberty interest" in "avoiding the unwanted administration of antipsychotic drugs."[13] . . .

The Massachusetts Supreme Judicial Court has held people have the absolute right to decline medication unless they are incompetent to make such a decision and if they are incompetent they can not be medicated against their will except by a court made Substituted Judgment Decision that includes the following factors:

1. The patient's expressed preferences regarding treatment.
2. The strength of the incompetent patient's religious convictions, to the extent that they may contribute to his refusal of treatment.

3. The impact of the decision on the ward's family—this factor being primarily relevant when the patient is part of a closely knit family.
4. The probability of adverse side effects.
5. The prognosis without treatment.
6. The prognosis with treatment.
7. Any other factors which appear relevant." . . .

[I]n *Rivers v. Katz*[14], decided strictly on common law and constitutional due process grounds, New York's highest court held a person's right to be free from unwanted antipsychotic medication is a constitutionally protected liberty interest:

"[i]f the law recognizes the right of an individual to make decisions about . . . life out of respect for the dignity and autonomy of the individual, that interest is no less significant when the individual is mentally or physically ill."

✦

We reject any argument that the mere fact that appellants are mentally ill reduces in any manner their fundamental liberty interest to reject antipsychotic medication. We likewise reject any argument that involuntarily committed patients lose their liberty interest in avoiding the unwanted administration of antipsychotic medication.

✦

If . . . the court determines that the patient has the capability to make his own treatment decisions, the State shall be precluded from administering antipsychotic drugs. If, however, the court concludes that the patient lacks the capacity to determine the course of his own treatment, the court must determine whether the proposed treatment is narrowly tailored to give substantive effect to the patient's liberty interest, taking into consideration all relevant circumstances, including the patient's best interests, the benefits to be gained from the treatment, the adverse side effects associated with the treatment and any less intrusive alternative treatments. The State would bear the burden to establish by clear and convincing evidence that the proposed treatment meets these criteria." . . .

[I]n practice, people's rights are not being honored.[15] There are other states which have just as good legal rights and some that don't under state law, but the common denominator in all of them is whatever rights people have, they are uniformly ignored." . . .

In *Sell*, decided in 2003, the United States Supreme Court held someone could not be force drugged to make them competent to stand trial unless:

1. The court finds that *important* governmental interests are at stake.
2. The court must conclude that involuntary medication will *significantly further* those concomitant state interests.

3. The court must conclude that involuntary medication is *necessary* to further those interests. The court must find that any alternative, less intrusive treatments are unlikely to achieve substantially the same results.
4. The court must conclude that administration of the drugs is *medically appropriate*, i.e., in the patient's best medical interest in light of his medical condition. The specific kinds of drugs at issue may matter here as elsewhere. Different kinds of antipsychotic drugs may produce different side effects and enjoy different levels of success.

(italics in original) These are general constitutional principles and should apply in the civil context. Thus, for example, while in *Sell*, the "*important* governmental interest*" is in bringing a criminal defendant to trial, the governmental interest in the civil context is (supposedly) the person's best interest, i.e., the *parens patriae* doctrine.[16]

With respect to the second requirement that the forced drugging "will *significantly further*" those interests, the question in the competence to stand trial context is whether the forced drugging is likely to make the person competent to stand trial, while in the civil context, the question is whether it is in the person's best interest or is the decision the person would make if he or she were competent.

The third requirement that the forced drugging must be *necessary* and there is no less restrictive alternative is hugely important in the civil context because it is a potential lever to require less restrictive (i.e., non-drug, recovery oriented alternatives). It is important to note here that failure to find these alternatives does not give the government the right to force drug someone. If a less restrictive alternative could be made available, the forced drugging is unconstitutional."[17] . . .

"The fourth requirement is also very important because it essentially requires the state to prove the drugging is in the person's best interest and not merely recite "professional judgment."

The take away message is, in my view, people are constitutionally entitled to noncoercive, non-drugging, recovery oriented alternatives before involuntary commitment and forced drugging can occur and even then forced drugging can only constitutionally occur if it is in the person's best interest. There are a couple of ways to look at this since the reality is so far from what the law requires. One is to see it as a tremendous opportunity to improve the situation. The other is that there are forces operating to totally defeat people's rights. Both are true and this paper suggests there are actions that can be taken to have people's rights honored that can play a crucial part in transforming the mental health system to one of a recovery culture.

B. Proper Procedures and Evidentiary Standards

Mentioned above is the United States Supreme Court rulings that involuntary commitment can occur only pursuant to proper procedures and evidentiary standards. In contrast to this legal requirement, involuntary commitment and forced drugging proceedings can quite fairly be characterized as a sham, a farce, Kangaroo Courts, etc., in the vast majority of cases."[18] . . .

(1) Proper Procedures . . .

(a) **Proper evidentiary standards.** . . . "[I]involuntary commitment is constitutionally permissible only if the person is a harm to self or others as a result of a "mental illness." In *Addington v. Texas*[19] the United States held that this has to be proven by "clear and convincing evidence," which is less than "beyond a reasonable doubt," but more than the normal "preponderance of the evidence"[20] standard in most civil cases." . . .

"The truth is psychiatric testimony as to a person's dangerousness is highly unreliable with a high likelihood of over-estimating dangerousness.

> The voluminous literature as to the ability of psychiatrists (or other mental health professionals) to testify reliably as to an individual's dangerousness in the indeterminate future had been virtually unanimous: "psychiatrists have absolutely no expertise in predicting dangerous behavior—indeed, they may be less accurate predictors than laymen—and that they usually err by overpredicting violence."[21]

This is the primary reason why I estimate only 10% of involuntary commitments are legally justified. If people were only involuntarily committed when it can be shown, by clear and convincing evidence, under scientifically reliable methods of predicting the requisite harm to self or others, my view is 90% of current commitments would not be granted.

With respect to forced drugging, one of the pre-requisites is the person must be found to be incompetent to decline the drug(s). Here, too, psychiatrists, to be kind, overestimate incompetence.

> [M]ental patients are not always incompetent to make rational decisions and are not inherently more incompetent than nonmentally ill medical patients.[22] . . .

"The reason why I believe no forced drugging in the civil context is legally justified is it simply can not be scientifically proven it is in a person's best interest.[23] It would make this paper even more too long than it already is to fully support this assertion, but some will be presented. First, there is really no doubt the current overreliance on the drugs is at least doubling the number of people becoming defined by the system as chronically mentally ill with it recently being estimated it has increased the rate of disability due to "mental Illness" six-fold.[24] In the case where we litigated the issue in Alaska, the trial court found

> The relevant conclusion that I draw from [the evidence presented by the Respondent's experts] is that there is a real and viable debate among qualified

experts in the psychiatric community regarding whether the standard of care for treating schizophrenic patients should be the administration of anti-psychotic medication.

◦◦◦

[T]here is a viable debate in the psychiatric community regarding whether administration of this type of medication might actually cause damage to her or ultimately worsen her condition.[25]

A recent study in Ireland concluded the already elevated risk for death in schizophrenia due to the older neuroleptics was doubled with the newer, so-called "atypical" neuroleptics, such as Zyprexa and Risperdal.[26] More information on these drugs can be found on PsychRights' website at. . . .

In sum, my view is the state can never (or virtually never) actually meet its burden of proving forced drugging is in a person's best interest (assuming that is required) because of the lack of long-term effectiveness and great harm they cause. Again, this raises the question of why forced drugging is so pervasive and what might be done about it. In other words, it is an opportunity for strategic litigation playing a key role in a transformation to a recovery oriented system.

(1) Corrupt Involuntary Mental "Treatment" System

As set forth above, people are locked up under judicial findings of dangerous-ness and force drugged based on it being in their best interests without any legitimate scientific evidence of either dangerousness or the drugs being in a person's best interests. As Professor Michael Perlin has noted:

[C]ourts accept . . . testimonial dishonesty, . . . specifically where witnesses, especially expert witnesses, show a "high propensity to purposely distort their testimony in order to achieve desired ends." . . .

Experts frequently . . . and openly subvert statutory and case law criteria that impose rigorous behavioral standards as predicates for commitment. . . .

This combination . . . helps define a system in which (1) dishonest testimony is often regularly (and unthinkingly) accepted; (2) statutory and case law standards are frequently subverted; and (3) insurmountable barriers are raised to insure that the allegedly "therapeutically correct" social end is met. . . . In short, the mental disability law system often deprives indi-viduals of liberty disingenuously and upon bases that have no relationship to case law or to statutes.[27]

In other words, testifying psychiatrists lie,[28] the trial (but generally not appellate) courts don't care, and lawyers assigned to represent defendants in these cases, are "woefully inadequate—disinterested, uninformed, roleless, and often hostile. A model of "paternalism/best interests" is substituted for a tradi-tional legal advocacy position, and this substitution is rarely questioned."[29] Counsel appointed to represent psychiatric defendants are, more often than not, actually working for the other side, or barely put up even a token defense, which amounts to the same thing.[30]

No one in the legal system is taking psychiatric defendants' rights seriously, including the lawyer appointed to represent the person. There are two reasons for this: The first is the belief that "if this person wasn't crazy, she'd know this is good for her." The second is the system is driven by irrational fear. All the evidence shows people who end up with psychiatric labels are no more likely to be dangerous than the general population and that medications increase the overall relapse rate, yet society's response has been to lock people up, and whether locked up or not, force them to take these drugs.[31] . . .

IV. The Requirement and Necessity of Alternatives

Hopefully it is apparent from the foregoing that people should be allowed (less restrictive) alternatives when they are faced with forced drugging. The same is basically true of involuntary commitment.[32] These alternatives, I suggest, should primarily include non-coercive, for sure, and non-drug alternatives that are known to lead to recovery for many people.[33] The reality is likely a "which came first, the chicken or the egg?" situation, because judges will be reluctant to deny petitions for forced drugging on the basis that a less restrictive alternative could be made available, but in fact is not available. Thus, the actual availability of alternatives is important. However, where sufficient legal pressure is applied, the courts will simply not be able to order forced drugging. I know these are contradictory statements, but that is why they reinforce each other as set forth above (and below).

This can be illustrated by the way in which Advance Directives. As set forth above, everyone has the absolute constitutional right to decline psychiatric drugs, with one exception, which is if they are incompetent to do so. Currently, the competency determinations are not legitimate and Advance Directives are ignored. One reason I would posit, is that the system simply does not know what else to do with people so the system deals with it by finding people incompetent when they are not. . . .

V. The Importance of Public Opinion

It is perhaps easier to see how Public Education and the Availability of Alternatives reinforce each other. Alternatives to the hopelessness driven, medication only, stabilization oriented, system are not available because our society believes it is the only possibility, in spite of all kinds of evidence to the contrary. Thus, to the extent effective alternatives become known to society in general, these alternatives will become desired by society because they produce much more desired outcomes. Not only do people get better, but huge amounts of money will be saved by more than halving the number of people who become a permanent ward of government. At the same time, having successful Alternatives will show society that they are viable. Thus, as with the

Availability of Alternatives and Honoring Legal Rights, they reinforce each other." . . .

VI. Interplay Between Public Education and Honoring Legal Rights

"As set forth above, the judges and even the lawyers representing people facing forced psychiatry accept the current societal view that people need to be locked up and forcibly drugged for society's and the person's own safety and best interests. To the extent society becomes aware this is not true, the judicial system will reflect that and be much more willing to honor people's rights." . . .

VIII. Requirements for Successful Litigation— Attorneys & Expert Witnesses

The building blocks for mounting successful strategic litigation are recruiting attorneys who will put forth a serious effort to discharge their ethical duties to their clients and expert witnesses who can prove the junk science behind current "treatment" and the effectiveness of recovery oriented alternatives."

IX. Types of Legal Actions . . .

A. Establishing the Right to Effective Assistance of Counsel

If people's rights were being honored, the problem of forced psychiatry would be mostly solved and this would absolutely force society to come up with alternatives—hopefully recovery oriented. Thus, challenges to the effectiveness of counsel should be made. In light of the current state of affairs, there seems little downside to trying to get the United States Supreme Court to hold it is a right under the United States Constitution. I also believe that ethics complaints should be brought against the attorneys who do not discharge their duty to zealously represent their clients. If every involuntary commitment and forced drugging hearing were zealously represented, each case should take at least half a day. In my view it takes that long to fully challenge the state's case and present the patient's. This, in itself, would encourage the system to look for alternatives (the "path of least resistance" principle).

B. Challenges to State Proceedings

States that proceed under the "professional judgment" rule should be challenged. The right to state paid expert witnesses should be pursued. The right to less restrictive alternatives should be pursued. Challenges to "expert witness" opinion testimony regarding dangerousness and competence should be made. Challenges to *ex parté* proceedings should be made. There are a myriad of challenges that can be made in the various states, depending on the statutes and procedures utilized in them.[34] . . .

XI. Public Attitudes

Even though this paper is about the court's potential role in transforming mental health systems to a recovery culture, it seems worthwhile to also make a few comments about changing public attitudes. There is an historic opportunity right now to make substantial inroads against the Psychopharmacology/Psychiatric hegemony because of the revelations in the media regarding dangerous, ineffective drugs, but this must be seized or it will be lost. **A serious public education program must be mounted**.

A. An Effective Public Relations Campaign

In the main, perhaps unduplicated for any other issue, the power of the Psychopharmacology/Psychiatric Hegemony has so controlled the message that the media tends not to even acknowledge there is another side. For most issues, the media will present at least one spokesperson from each side. However, when the latest questionable breakthrough in mental illness research or "treatment" is announced, the other side is not even presented. One might want to pass this off as Big Pharma advertising money infecting the news departments, but I think that is way too simplistic and perhaps even largely untrue. . . .

XII. Alternatives

It also seems worthwhile to spend a little bit of space here on creating alternatives. Ultimately, in order to be successful, alternatives need to be funded by the public system.[35] One argument in its favor that should be attractive to government (but has not heretofore been) in the current system is breaking the bank. As Whitaker has shown, the disability rate for mental illness has increased six-fold since the introduction of Thorazine.[36] Making so many people permanently disabled and financially supported by the government, rather than working and supporting the government, is not only a huge human tragedy, but is also a massive, unnecessary governmental expense.

One of the simplest, but very important things that should be done is to compile a readily accessible, accurate, list of existing alternatives and efforts to get them going. I have seen lists of alternatives, but then I hear that this program or that is really not a true non-drugging and/or non-coercive alternative. It would be extremely helpful for there to be a description of each such program with enough investigation to know what is really happening. . . .

XIII. Conclusion

A final word about the importance of the potential role of the courts and the forced psychiatry issue. While it is true that many, even maybe most, people in the system are not under court orders at any given time, it is my view that the forced psychiatry system is what starts a tremendous number of people on the road to permanent disability (and poverty) and drives the whole public system. Of course, coercion to take the drugs is pervasive outside of court orders too, but again I see the legal coercion as a key element. If people who are now being dragged into forced psychiatry were given, non-coercive, recovery oriented options, they would also become available for the people who are not subject to forced psychiatry. I hope this paper has conveyed the role that strategic litigation can play in transforming mental health systems to a culture of recovery.

Notes

1. By phrasing it this way, I am not disputing that people become psychotic. I have been there. . . . However, there are lots of degrees—a continuum, if you will—and there are different ways of looking at these unaccepted ways of thinking, or altered states of consciousness. So, what I mean by this terminology is that people are faced with involuntary commitment and forced drugging when two conditions exist: One, they are bothering another person(s), including concern about the risk of suicide or other self-harm, and Two, they are expressing thoughts that do not conform to those accepted "normal" by society. Of course, this ignores the reality that a lot of both are often trumped up, especially against people who have previously been subjected to the system.

2. The system believes it is also less expensive, but the opposite is actually true. The overreliance on neuroleptics and, increasingly, polypharmacy, has at least doubled the number of people who become permanently reliant on government transfer payments. In *Anatomy of an Epidemic: Psychiatric Drugs and the Astonishing Rise of Mental Illness in America,* which is available at . . . Robert Whitaker demonstrates the rate of disability has increased six fold since the introduction of Thorazine in the mid '50s. The Michigan State Psychotherapy Project demonstrated extremely more favorable long-term outcomes for those receiving psychotherapy alone from psychotherapists with *relevant* training and experience. The short term costs were comparable to the standard treatment and the long term savings were tremendous. This study can be found at. . . .

3. "Parens Patriae" is legal Latin, literally meaning "parent of his or her country". Black's Law Dictionary, Seventh Edition defines it as "the state in its capacity as provider of protection to those unable to care for themselves." It is invoked with respect to minors and adults who are deemed incompetent to make their own decisions. In the context of forced drugging under the *parens patriae* doctrine, it basically is based on the notion, "If you weren't crazy, you'd know this was good for you."

4. At the same time there are impediments to doing so, primarily the lack of legal resources.

5. U.S. 294, 75 S.Ct. 753, 99 L.Ed. 1083 (1955).

6. In light of the system basically creating massive numbers of people who become categorized as chronically mentally ill, I call it the mental illness system, rather than the mental health system.

7. By saying the mental illness system operates largely illegally I mean that to the extent people are locked up and forcibly drugged when the statutory and constitutional requirements are not being met, that is illegal. Of course, this is done by filing paperwork and getting court orders, which looked at another way, makes it legal.

8. "Treatment" is in quotes because it is both (1) pretty clear the current, virtually exclusive reliance on psychiatric drugs by the public mental illness system hinders recovery for the vast majority of people, and (2) if it isn't voluntary, it isn't treatment.

9.   *See*, e.g., *Sell v. United States*, 539 U.S. 166 (2003). However, not everyone agrees with my legal analysis of the right to the least restrictive alternative.

10. *Humphrey v. Cady*, 405 U.S. 504 (1972).

11. *Addington v. Texas*, 441 U.S. 418 (1979).

11a. *Kansas v. Crane*, 534 U.S. 407 (2002).

12. *Mills v. Rogers*, 457 U.S. 291 (1982); *Washington v. Harper*, 494 U.S. 210 (1990; *Riggins v. Nevada*, 504 U.S. 127 (1992); and *Sell v. United States*, 539 U.S. 166 (2003).

13. *Sell v. United States*, 539 U.S. 166, 177-8 (2003), citing to the Due Process Clause, U.S. Const., amend. 5, and *Washington v. Harper*, 494 U.S. 210, 110 S.Ct. 1028 (1990). . . .

14. *Rivers v. Katz*, 495 N.E.2d 337, 341-3 (NY 1986).

15. *See*, Mental Hygiene Law Court Monitoring Project: Part 1 of Report: Do Psychiatric Inmates in New York Have the Right to Refuse Drugs? An Examination of Rivers Hearings in the Brooklyn Court, which can be accessed on the Internet at. . . .

16. I say, "supposedly," because in truth, controlling the person's behavior is a primary interest. "Police power" justification, which actually is based on controlling dangerous behavior, has also been used to justify forced drugging. *See*, *Rivers v. Katz*, 495 N.E.2d 337, 343 (NY 1986). However, the behavior presumably has to be very extreme to invoke "police power" and is not normally the stated basis for seeking forced drugging orders. It has been suggested there is an important government interest in ending indeterminate commitment and returning the individual to society, which can be done most effectively if the person is required to take the prescribed drugs. However, this is not the basis normally asserted and I would argue it is not a sufficient interest to override a person's rights to decline the drugs, particularly in light of the physical harms they cause.

17. There are likely limits on this, such as there being no requirement for Herculean efforts or where the cost is prohibitive. *See*, e.g., *Mathews v. Eldridge*, 424 U.S. 319, 334-35 (1976). . . .

18. An example is described in the recent Alaska Supreme Court brief we filed in *Wetherhorn v. Alaska Psychiatric Institute*, which can be found on the Internet at. . . .

19. 441 U.S. 418 (1979)

20. "Preponderance of the evidence," means more likely than not or, put another way, it only requires the balance to be slightly more on one side than the other. Yet another way to look at it is it just has to be more than 50% likely. . . .

21. Michael L. Perlin, *Mental Disability Law: Civil and Criminal*, §2A-4.3c, p. 109 (2d. Ed. 1998), footnotes omitted. *See*, also, Morris, Pursuing Justice for the Mentally Disabled, 42 San Diego L. Rev 757, 764 (2005) ("recent studies confirm that psychotic symptoms, such as delusions or hallucinations, currently being experienced by a person, do not elevate his or her risk of violence."

22. Perlin, "And My Best Friend, My Doctor/Won't Even Say What It Is I've Got: The Role And Significance Of Counsel In Right To Refuse Treatment Cases," 42 San Diego Law Review 735, 746-7 (2005), citing to Thomas Grisso & Paul S. Appelbaum, *The MacArthur Treatment Competence Study. III: Abilities of Patients to Consent to Psychiatric and Medical Treatments*, 19 Law & Hum. Behav. 149 (1995). . . .

23. While I believe this is true in the forced drugging context in terms of meeting the legal burden of justifying overriding a person's right to decline the medications, and I know this paper comes off as a polemic against psychiatric drugs, I absolutely believe people also have the right to choose to take them. I

do think people should be fully informed about them, of course, which is normally not done, but that is a different issue. Not surprisingly, in a study of people who have recovered after being diagnosed with serious mental illness, those who felt the drugs helped them, used them in their recovery and those that didn't find them helpful, didn't use the drugs in their recovery. "How do We Recover? An Analysis of Psychiatric Survivor Oral Histories," by Oryx Cohen, in *Journal of Humanistic Psychology*, Vol . 45 No. 3, Summer 2005 333-35, which is available on the Internet at. . . .

24. Anatomy of an Epidemic: Psychiatric Drugs and the Astonishing Rise of Mental Illness in America, by Robert Whitaker, *Ethical Human Psychology and Psychiatry*, Volume 7, Number I: 23-35 Spring 2005, which can be accessed on the Internet at. . . .

25. Order, in *In the Matter of the Hospitalization of Faith Myers,* Anchorage Superior Court, Third Judicial District, State of Alaska, Case No. 3AN-03-277 PR, March 14, 2003, pp. 8, 13, which can be accessed on the Internet at. . . .

26. Prospective analysis of premature mortality in schizophrenia in relation to health service engagement: a 7.5-year study within an epidemiologically complete, homogeneous population in rural Ireland, by Maria G. Morgan, Paul J. Scully, Hanafy A. Youssef, Anthony Kinsellac, John M. Owensa, and John L. Waddingtona, *Psychiatry Research* 117 (2003) 127–135, which can be found on the Internet at. . . .

27. *The ADA and Persons with Mental Disabilities: Can Sanist Attitudes Be Undone?* Journal of Law and Health, 1993/1994, 8 JLHEALTH 15, 33–34.

28. "It would probably be difficult to find any American Psychiatrist working with the mentally ill who has not, at a minimum, exaggerated the dangerousness of a mentally ill person's behavior to obtain a judicial order for commitment." Torrey, E. Fuller. 1997. *Out of the Shadows: Confronting America's Mental Illness Crisis*, New York: John Wiley and Sons, page 152. Dr. Torrey goes on to say this lying to the courts is a good thing. Of course, lying in court is perjury. Dr. Torrey also quotes Psychiatrist Paul Applebaum as saying when "confronted with psychotic persons who might well benefit from treatment, and who would certainly suffer without it, mental health professionals and judges alike were reluctant to comply with the law," noting that in "'the dominance of the commonsense model,' the laws are sometimes simply disregarded."

29. Perlin, *"And My Best Friend, My Doctor/Won't Even Say What It Is I've Got": The Role And Significance Of Counsel In Right To Refuse Treatment Cases*, 42 San Diego Law Review 735, 738 (2005).

30. This is a violation of professional ethics. For example, the Comment to the Model Rules of Professional Conduct for attorneys, Rule 1.3, includes, "A lawyer should pursue a matter on behalf of a client despite opposition, obstruction or personal inconvenience to the lawyer, and take whatever lawful and ethical measures are required to vindicate a client's cause or endeavor. A lawyer must also act with commitment and dedication to the interests of the client and with zeal in advocacy upon the client's behalf."

31. "Kendra's Law" in New York is a classic example of this. There a person who had been denied numerous attempts to obtain mental health services pushed Kendra in front of a moving subway and when he was grabbed, said something like "now maybe I will get some help." The response was to pass an outpatient commitment law requiring people to take psychiatric drugs or be locked up in the hospital. This is a characterization, but when this was challenged, New York's high court ruled Kendra's Law didn't require people to take the drugs;

that all it did was subject people to "heightened scrutiny" for involuntary commitment if they didn't. *See, In the Matter of K.L.*, 806 N.E.2d 480(NY 2004). . . .

32. Many state statutes certainly require it, and I would suggest it is constitutionally required as well.

33. *See*, Effective Non-Drug Treatments, which can be found on the Internet at. . . .

34. For example, I have identified a lot of things under Alaska law where I think valid challenges to what is going on can and should be made. . . .

35. However, I am also in favor of non-system alternatives.

36. *See*, Anatomy of an Epidemic: Psychiatric Drugs and the Astonishing Rise of Mental Illness in America, which is available at. . . .

CHALLENGE QUESTIONS

Is Forced Treatment of Seriously Mentally Ill Individuals Justifiable?

1. What legal protections can be put in place, and what specific procedures followed, to protect the right of individuals to make choices affecting their psychological and physical well-being?
2. What arguments can be made to support the idea that mental health professionals should be accorded the legal right to administer treatments against the will of a mentally ill person?
3. To what extent should family members of a seriously mentally ill individual be given the right to approve treatment for a loved one who is resisting such intervention?
4. In cases in which an involuntarily treated patient begins to recover from symptoms, how should decisions be made by mental health professionals to respect the prerogative of the patient to stop the treatment?
5. How would you go about designing a study to evaluate the psychological impact on individuals for whom treatment has been involuntarily administered?

Suggested Readings

Bassman, R. (2005). Mental illness and the freedom to refuse treatment: Privilege or right. *Professional Psychology: Research and Practice, 36* (5), 488–497.

Fritz, M. (2006, February 1). A Doctor's fight: More forced care for the mentally ill. *The Wall Street Journal*, p. A1.

Torrey, E. F. (2007, April 27). Commitment phobia. *The Wall Street Journal*, p. A17.

Treatment Advocacy Center, (Spring, 2006). *Catalyst*. Arlington, VA: Treatment Advocacy Center.

ISSUE 2

Should Individuals with Anorexia Nervosa Have the Right to Refuse Life-Sustaining Treatment?

YES: Heather Draper, from "Anorexia Nervosa and Respecting a Refusal of Life-Prolonging Therapy: A Limited Justification," *Bioethics* (April 1, 2000)

NO: James L. Werth, Jr., et al., from "When Does the 'Duty to Protect' Apply with a Client Who Has Anorexia Nervosa?" *The Counseling Psychologist* (July 2003)

ISSUE SUMMARY

YES: Heather Draper argues that clinicians need to accept the fact that individuals with anorexia nervosa may be competent, and may have legitimate reasons for refusing therapy. In such cases, therapists should respect the individual's wishes and should refrain from administering life-sustaining treatment.

NO: James Werth, Jr. and his colleagues contend that, due to the very nature of anorexia nervosa, individuals with anorexia cannot make rational decisions about nutrition and feeding. Because the behaviors of anorexics have such potential for health damage or even death, clinicians have a duty to protect the lives of their patients, even if it calls for compulsory treatment.

Health practitioners have long debated the ethics of treating individuals against their will. When an individual engages in behavior that may lead to self-harm, and possible death, it is assumed that professionals have an obligation to intervene. In the case of suicide, most would support hospitalization, with or without that person's consent. However, consider instances in which the individual may lack the competence to evaluate the extent to which a behavior is self-damaging, or instances in which the individual may reject medical assistance, regardless of medical recommendations. People with anorexia nervosa fall into this latter category. It is unclear whether a person in the throes of starvation and gross weight loss can make a competent decision about feeding and nutrition, even though this individual seems to demonstrate competence in other areas of life. Professionals trying to treat such individuals face the ethical dilemma about a 'duty to protect.' In other words, they confront decisions about whether to take actions to protect a patient, regardless of the patient's preference to be left to his or her own choices.

Heather Draper argues that mental health professionals need to consider the possibility that individuals with anorexia nervosa can make competent decisions about their treatment. Draper makes the case that professionals should respect the individual's refusal of therapy, especially when the refusal is grounded in arguments about the quality of life and the burden of therapy. Furthermore, Draper questions the effectiveness of forced feeding; it may save the life of the individual but does nothing to alleviate the underlying condition. Ultimately, it is the individual who is responsible for the consequences of his or her decisions, even if death is possible.

James Werth, Jr. and his colleagues assert that individuals with anorexia nervosa may experience significant harm and possible death as a result of behaviors related to the disorder. Due to this risk, Werth argues that there exists an obligation to take action when anorexia-related behavior progresses to the point at which it poses serious danger to the individual. Werth and his colleagues conclude that, while maintaining the individual's autonomy is indeed important to the success of the therapeutic process, health professionals have a duty to protect an anorexic client, even when this client refuses therapy.

POINT

- Some sufferers of anorexia nervosa may be competent to refuse therapy. In such cases, it would be wrong and unlawful to force them to undergo therapy that they choose to refuse.

- Mental health professionals should respect an individual's autonomy. This includes respecting the individual's refusal of therapy and accepting that the patient is responsible for the consequences of decisions, even if it may result in death.

- While forced feeding may save the life of the individual, it does nothing for the underlying condition, and may actually worsen the situation.

- Patients may be better off when the clinician agrees to work within their frame of reference. Agreeing with them that they may be better off anorexic is often a new experience for them and may allow them to proceed with much more confidence.

COUNTERPOINT

- The pattern of thinking demonstrated by an individual with anorexia nervosa can be considered to be a thought disturbance. Since the individual secretly thrives on the results of starvation, a reinforcing loop exists that prevents competent decisions about food intake.

- Experts in the treatment of anorexia state that clients are not competent to make decisions regarding treatment, and that they are often grateful for medical intervention once they are no longer in the downward spiral of the disorder.

- Once a person's weight is stabilized, the benefits of psychological and pharmacological treatment are more likely to accrue and be appreciated by the patient.

- Allowing patients to make their own decisions about treatment may facilitate the therapeutic relationship, but it also increases the risk of serious health deterioration. Clients are more likely to be grateful for the intervention once they are medically and psychologically stable.

YES ↵

Heather Draper

Anorexia Nervosa and Respecting a Refusal of Life-Prolonging Therapy: A Limited Justification

Introduction

The eating disorder anorexia nervosa results in the death of between 20–30 patients per year in the UK[1] and death rates internationally are reported to be between 4–20%.[2] This death rate would undoubtedly be higher if anorexics were not force-fed once their weight became dangerously low. Force-feeding (feeding without consent) has been recognised in the UK by the Mental Health Commission as a legitimate therapy to give under section 63 of the UK Mental Health Act 1983,[3] and the legitimacy of force-feeding in conjunction with other therapies is also supported in case law.[4] Force-feeding may take the form of literally forcing a patient to eat; coercing her to eat by putting her under pressure to feed herself; or, by tube feeding. Feeding alone is thought to be ineffective—unless it is done simply to restore the patient sufficiently to enable her to participate in other psychiatric therapies. Sectioning for feeding should, therefore, only be considered as an adjunct to other therapies if it is to be justified by appeals to best interest. It is also thought likely that repeated episodes of force-feeding—particularly of the literally forcing food into the mouths of sufferers kind—decrease the chances of long-term recovery and it is doubtful that it is actually in the best interests of a patient to be subjected to a regime of force-feeding on more than a few occasions.[5] Nevertheless, medical practitioners are understandably reluctant not to force-feed by one method or another when a patient is dying for want of nutrition. A recent article[6] suggesting that there might be a role for a palliative approach for patients who are both long term sufferers and refusing therapy, attracted more criticism than support from practitioners, and the possibility of respecting a sufferer from anorexia's decision not to proceed with therapy—whatever the circumstances—has been described as collusion.[7] It is asserted that sufferers from anorexia are not competent to make any decisions that relate in any way to food, and withdrawing therapy or treating palliatively effectively entails withdrawing feeding. On one level this assertion may be pointing out the obvious—someone who is on the point of starving to death, has uncontrollable (non) eating behaviour

From *Bioethics*, vol. 14, issue 2, April 2002, pp. 261–278. Copyright © 2000 by Blackwell Publishing, Ltd. Reprinted by permission.

and a completely distorted body image is not likely to be competent. Such an assertion, however, assumes that incompetence is a description of an individual (broad or global incompetence) rather than an assessment of the capacity of the individual to make a specific decision (narrow incompetence). Some anorexics may indeed be incompetent as individuals (be broadly incompetent): for example, those on the point of starving to death. Others are certainly not broadly incompetent; they are studying for school leaving exams, or degrees, or are running their own financial affairs, others are professionals working in demanding jobs. It is because incompetence is also task specific (narrow) that it is accepted that a patient who is sectioned for compulsory treatment for a specific mental disorder cannot be treated on an involuntary basis for any other health problem, however life-threatening it is thought to be.[8] Thus, sufferers from anorexia cannot be involuntarily subjected to any therapies unrelated to their eating disorder. But could an anorexic competently decide to withdraw from therapy not on the grounds that she didn't want to eat, nor that she was 'fat' but because the quality of her life was so poor that the therapy was no longer of benefit to her, or that it was on balance more of a burden than a benefit?

In this paper, it is argued that whilst it is generally legitimate to detain and treat sufferers from anorexia against their will, under some circumstances there is a failure to respect their competent refusal of therapy; namely where those who are refusing have been afflicted beyond the natural cycle of the disorder (which is between one and eight years); have already been force-fed on previous occasions; are competent to make decisions concerning their quality of life; have insight into the influence which their anorexia has over some aspects of their lives, and are not at death's door (they may, for instance, have just been released from a section for compulsory treatment). It will be argued that in these cases, the decision to refuse therapy is on a par with other decisions to refuse life-prolonging therapy made by sufferers of debilitating chronic, or acute onset terminal illness and that in such cases palliation might justifiably replace aggressive therapy. In order to do this the paper will first revisit the distinction between competent refusal of therapy and passive euthanasia and the distinction between incompetent and irrational decisions. Both distinctions will then be applied to decision to refuse food. Finally, the extent to which sufferers from anorexia nervosa can be categorised as either incompetent or irrational will be examined. It is against this background that it will be argued that at least some of those who suffer from anorexia should have their refusals of therapy respected, even if they may die as a result.

The Distinction Between Passive Euthanasia and Competent Refusal of Life-Prolonging Therapy

A distinction is drawn in many jurisdictions between passive euthanasia—which may be viewed as murder or a similar crime and respecting a competent patient's decision to refuse lifesaving or life-prolonging therapy—which is part of respecting the right to consent. This distinction can also be important in ethics where passive euthanasia is considered wrong, but respecting a patient's decision to withdraw or withhold therapy is not only permissible but may be required.[9] Clearly, the distinction is irrelevant for those who think that euthanasia can be permissible, but for those who disagree, it is perceived to form the boundary between acceptable and unacceptable withdrawal of therapy. The distinction will be used in this paper to argue that whilst it might be wrong for clinicians to give up on anorexics, and therefore for them to decide to withdraw therapy, it is acceptable for the anorexic herself to make a decision to withdraw from therapy, under certain circumstances and for reasons which will be addressed in the second half of this paper. So, can the distinction between passive euthanasia and competent withdrawal from therapy be defended?

In passive euthanasia therapy is withdrawn or omitted with the intention that the patient will die as a result. To be euthanasia, the omission or withdrawal must be thought to be in the patient's best interests, whether or not the patient is party to this decision.[10] The final judgement about whether or not to omit therapy rests with the clinician and not the patient, even when the patient is party to the decision, or even when the patient goes to considerable lengths to persuade the clinician of her point of view. . . . However, if the patient simply said that she withdrew her consent for the therapy to continue, the clinician would have to comply but would comply without compromising his view that her life was worth living. When a competent patient refuses therapy—whether or not she has a terminal illness or a poor quality of life or will die as a result—professional carers are ethically and legally bound to accept this refusal.

The moral difference between passive euthanasia and competent refusal of therapy lies in who makes the final decision. Euthanasia is something which one person gives to another—whether or not it is voluntary. Withdrawing from therapy is something which one does to, or for, oneself. Respecting autonomy means that we bound to take our own moral decisions and others are bound not to interfere; but it also means that we are responsible for the decisions which we make. There is, then, a strong sense in which clinicians are responsible for decisions to give euthanasia, and patients are responsible for decisions which they make to withdraw from therapy.[11,12]

Distinction Between Irrational Decisions and Incompetent Decisions

Patients can refuse therapy for a variety of reasons. They may have religious objections to some procedures which are life saving (like Jehovah's Witnesses do to blood transfusions); they may have moral objections (perhaps a strongly held view that it is wrong to terminate the life of the unborn even to save one's own life); they may be objecting on economic moral grounds (believing that the money which is to be spent on them would be put to better use saving someone else); they may hold the personal belief (whether or not well founded) that they have become too much of a burden upon their family; or, they may consider that the burden of the therapy has become too great so that even though they would rather live, they would rather risk dying than continue with this therapy. None of these reasons requires us to be convinced that it is in the patient's best interests to be dead—as would be necessary in passive euthanasia—but any of these reasons given by a competent patient would be sufficient to suppose that her decision should be respected.

Of course, we might want to argue that it is irrational to put religious beliefs before life itself—particularly when the religious belief is based on a literal interpretation of the bible. We might argue that it is irrational to prefer to save the life of an unborn child to one's own, particularly if the unborn child may die anyway as a result of one's own death. We might argue that it is irrational to give up one's own chance of life when one has no control over where the resources will be spent instead. We might argue that it is irrational to perceive oneself as a burden to relatives because burdensomeness is in the eye of the beholder. But we should be wary of confusing irrational reasons with reasons with which we simply do not agree. Furthermore, we should be wary of confusing either irrationality or strong disagreement with incompetence. . . .

To summarise, a competent decision to refuse therapy can be made on rational or irrational grounds, or even no grounds at all. A request for voluntary, passive euthanasia, however, must, in addition to being competent, be rational to the extent that the doctor concerned can be persuaded to become party to the decision. But the doctor can also refuse to be party to the decision not because it is an incompetent one, nor because it is an irrational one, but because he disagrees that euthanasia is the appropriate clinical or moral option under the circumstances. At least two things follow from this distinction. The first is that patients who might otherwise request passive euthanasia could instead refuse all therapy necessary to sustain or save life. If food is considered to be a therapy,[13] then no competent patient is without the means to end her life since she simply has to refuse to eat and decline her consent to tube feeding. The advantage of so doing is that it is not necessary for the patient to make the clinician an accomplice to her decision. This does not mean that she has to conceal her desire for death from her clinician—indeed, this desire is likely to be discussed when any patient makes such a request. Rather it means that the patient remains in control, since it is her decision, rather than that of her clinician, which is the decisive one. The second is that since it is already legal for competent patients to refuse therapy, there is no need, in addition, to legalise voluntary, passive euthanasia in order to give patients autonomy over their own bodies. Both these arguments may meet some of the ethical problems with euthanasia previously outlined.[14]

Refusal of Feeding

But can these distinctions between voluntary passive euthanasia and competent refusal of consent be applied to feeding? It certainly seems so, for a decision to withhold/withdraw tubefeeding from an incompetent patient on the grounds that their interests were best served by being dead would certainly be euthanasia,[15] whilst competent decisions to refuse food (whether by tube or other means) are not.

Once more, the distinction seems to turn upon who makes the final decision, the doctor (in euthanasia) or the patient (in refusal of food). Moreover, a decision to commence (tube) feeding once a patient is so weak that they become incompetent is at odds with the judgement that Jehovah's witnesses carrying cards saying they do not want to receive blood products cannot be given transfusions—even if they are unconscious upon arrival at hospital.[16] . . .

Anorexia Nervosa and the Decision to Refuse Food

The condition which challenges these distinctions is anorexia nervosa where food is refused because the patient is completely obsessed with the idea of weight loss, or maintaining weight at a level incompatible with active life or even any life at all. Here the lack of distinction between providing food and therapy is even more marked because nutrition is very definitely part of the therapy required to restore the anorexic to 'health'.

Inverted commas around health are necessary here because anorexia nervosa is commonly, but often uncomfortably, described as an illness—a mental illness. The ambivalence with which this categorisation is viewed by treating clinicians is very evident in Crisp's textbook *Anorexia Nervosa: Let me be.*[17] Crisp—widely recognised as an international expert on eating disorders—claims in the first chapter that in his opinion the condition is an illness. His theory is that anorexia is a psychological adaptive stance operating through biological mechanisms, as the sufferer tries either to avoid puberty or return to a pre-pubescent state.[18] Nevertheless, he almost invariably puts 'illness' in inverted commas when referring to anorexia and frequently compares it to alcoholism, another state that is only uncomfortably described as an illness.

The anorexic's determination to starve in the face of abundance is essentially seen as irrational—what ever psychological theory is used to explain this behaviour. As has already been indicated, whether it is a sufficiently irrational obsession to be categorised as a mental illness cannot be taken for granted, but even if it is, it is far from obvious that simply being classed as suffering from a mental illness is necessarily an indication that one is an incompetent individual. Nor is it obvious that anorexics refusing therapy are sufficiently irrational to be classed as incompetent to make decisions regarding their food intake.

There are two justifications for associating irrationality with incompetence in the case of anorexia. One is that the desire not to eat undermines an even stronger desire not to die. Another is that the desire not to eat might itself be an involuntary one, grounded in some other deeply held, but false, belief about their body image—usually that they are 'fat'.

It is interesting that although the irrational nature of their beliefs is often cited (alongside the desire to prevent them from dying) as a reason to overrule their refusal of food, working with this irrational belief is also perceived to be a valuable clinical option. For instance, Crisp writes:

> '. . . a statement that he (the therapist) agrees that the patient is probably better off, all things considered, remaining anorexic, can be the most

helpful and often totally new experience for the anorexic. She can approach the task of limited weight gain with much more confidence under such circumstances.'[19]

This suggests that therapists are prepared to work within the anorexic's frame of reference, provided that the anorexic is making decisions, which are life-promoting rather than decisions that are likely to result in her death. Of course, it is rational for the therapist to do this because it achieves his aim of preventing his patient's death. This does not, however, make the anorexic's beliefs any more rational. Accordingly, either the relationship is still one of the clinician's proxy determination of the best therapy for his patient (her wishes just happen to coincide with the therapy he has chosen for her); or, if the patient is considered to be competent to decide for herself, she is only as competent as she was when she decided to refuse food[20]—which makes any previous decision to over-ride her wishes and force-feed her highly paternalistic and even a battery, however well motivated. There is always a danger in clinical relationships that competence is more likely to be questioned when the patient disagrees with the judgement of the clinician. This questioning itself highlights the ease with which assessments about a patient's competence can be muddied by disagreements over the relative value of deep-seated beliefs.[21]

It is at this point that the clinical management of eating disorders begins to challenge the established view that competent refusals of consent must be respected. Let us return to one example and introduce yet another. Earlier, the point was made that it would be deemed unacceptable for clinicians to forcibly prevent from eating those whose over-eating was life-threatening. One reason for this is that over-eating is not considered to be a mental disorder. Yet, neither is the vast majority of under-eating—namely that which is done for the sake of current fashion and in conformity with current trends about body image and healthy living. Anorexia nervosa differs from this kind of under-eating in two important respects. First, the diagnosis is usually only made once the under-eating threatens life and health. Second, it is believed that the compulsion not to eat is somehow involuntary or beyond the control of the sufferer. If this is the case, then there are good grounds for supposing that in regard to eating, sufferers from anorexia are not competent. There is no one, universal explanation for this disorder but it is often associated with other psychological problems such as low self-esteem, a sense of having no control over one's lives, or a history of sexual abuse. . . .

The second example concerns those women who refuse to undergo radical breast surgery when they are diagnosed with breast cancer, because they consider that their breasts are so integral to their identity and/or quality of life that they would rather die with their breasts intact, than live without them. This is a view that attracts a great deal of sympathy, despite the fact that it seems irrational to give greater weight to one's body image than to one's life expectancy. But provided that she is competent and understands the dangers of refusing to consent, such a patient would never be compelled to undergo surgery. In this case, competence and irrationality are clearly differentiated.

But what of the sufferer from anorexia who refuses therapy, not because she thinks that her condition is not life-threatening, nor because she refuses to accept that she has a problem at all, but because for her too the burden of therapy and the side-effects of successful therapy—in terms of the body with which she will be left—are such that she prefers to take her chances with death? Such a sufferer would not be a typical case (any more than a woman who refuses surgery for breast cancer would). However, what we need to be mindful of at this point is that some sufferers from anorexia nervosa are never cured, not even to the extent that they are able to live with their disorder by maintaining an abnormally low but constant, life-sustaining body weight.[22] Granted that the received wisdom is that of an illness with a natural cycle of anywhere between one and eight years, under discussion here is someone who has endured a decade or more of repeated painful weight loss and traumatic weight gain. The stress of living with anorexia nervosa prompted Crisp to write:

> (m)any anorexics feel constantly like alcoholics, that they are just one step away from disaster. When suicide occurs it is often within this context. The individual is seeking relief from the endless terror and the exhaustion of a battle to maintain her position.[23]

Crisp acknowledges that the tension between the desire to eat and fear of the consequences of eating is a constant battle; one that can leave the sufferer from anorexia feeling so battle-weary that death becomes a viable and preferred option. If this is true for those sufferers from anorexia who decide to take their own lives, why can it not also be true for some of those sufferers from anorexia who refuse the therapy which will save their lives?

[S]ome refusals of consent by sufferers from anorexia may actually be voluntary. It was noted earlier that many sufferers are not broadly incompetent. Granted that broad competence is intact,[24] we should be open to the possibility that sufferers are actually as competent as anyone else to make decisions about the quality of their lives, and to assess the relative value of their lives in the light of its quality. For this reason, it is proposed that it may be wrong, as well as unlawful, to force patients to comply with therapy simply because they are anorexic.

It is undoubtedly awful to watch someone—possibly a young someone—die when they can so easily be saved. However, if justice is to be given to those sufferers who can neither live with their anorexia nor live without it, we must listen carefully to their refusals of therapy. The first step on this road is to accept that at least some sufferers from anorexia may be competent to refuse therapy—even if this is only a tiny minority. To do this we will have to listen to the reasons that they give for their refusal, not to determine whether or not these reasons are rational per se, but to hear whether these reasons reflect the burden that life with anorexia and therapy has become. We need to bear in mind that there is a difference between saving the life of a sufferer and curing them of their anorexia. Whilst feeding may be life-saving, it does nothing for the underlying condition—indeed it may even worsen it. Accordingly, we may also have to be open to the possibility that some sufferers from anorexia will never be cured, and that offering palliative care in such cases should not be dismissed as collusion with a mental illness. Rather it should be see as offering the same services to incurable anorexics as are available to others who cannot be cured.

There is a wider danger in rejecting the possibility that some refusals of therapy by sufferers from anorexia are actually about quality of life and not involuntary refusals of food. This danger is that of weakening of the distinction between passive euthanasia and competent refusal of life saving therapy. If we exclude the possibility of a competent refusal being made for reasons which we cannot endorse—which I am suggesting may be happening in a minority of anorexia cases—there is a danger that a refusal of life-prolonging therapy will need to become as convincing to a physician as a request for passive euthanasia needs to be. Respecting a patient's autonomy is not simply about letting her make some decisions, or even all decisions. It is also about accepting that it is the patient who is responsible for the consequences of her decisions, and not the person who records this refusal of consent in the patient's medical notes.

References

1. Crisp, Anorexia Nervosa: Let Me Be (Baillere Tindell, London, 1990), p. 31.

2. The death rate varies according to study and length of follow up. For instance, see Phillip W. Lang. The Harvard Mental Health Letter, Oct./Nov. 1997 who also cites a prevalence for anorexia nervosa of 0.1-0.6% in the general population in the USA (a figure which he claims is several times higher amongst adolescent girls).

3. Mental Health Act Commission Guidance Note 3: Guidance on the Treatment of Anorexia Nervosa Under the Mental Health Act 1983 (Issued August 1997).

4. See Riverside Health NHS Trust v. Fox [1994] 1 FLR and B v. Croydon H.A. [1995] 1 AUER 683.

5. This argument was made very forcefully by Penny Lewis 'Feeding anorexic patients who refuse food,' Medical Law Review, 7, 1, (1999), pp. 21–37.

6. J. O'Neill, American Journal of Hospice and Palliative Care Nov./Dec. 1994 pp. 36-8. In 1998, the British Medical Journal 18 July 1998 pp. 195–197 also addressed the issue of palliation in its 'Education and Debate' section. In this discussion, C. J. Williams, L. Pieri, & A. Sims, argued that patients should always be treated actively, whilst L. Russon, & D. Alison, argued that there was a case for extending palliative care to anorexics.

7. Janet Treasure speaking at 'Food, Glorious Food?', Kings College, London 4th July 1997.

8. In one dramatic example a patient, who was sectioned for treatment for paranoid schizophrenia, refused to have his leg amputated even though medical advice was that the gangrene would otherwise kill him. A court upheld his fight to refuse treatment on the grounds that he was competent to do so. Re C (refusal of medical treatment) [1994] 1 All ER 819 (FD).

9. For instance, it might be argued that whilst it is acceptable to take one's own life, it is wrong to enlist the help of others in so doing, or that it is wrong for doctors to take life, or that permitting any form of euthanasia is the first step on a dangerous slippery slope.

10. For more on the definition of euthanasia and distinctions between euthanasia and other forms of killing—including self-killing—see Heather Draper 'Euthanasia' in Encyclopaedia of Applied Ethics, ed. R. Chadwick, (Academic Press, San Diego, 1997). pp. 175–187.

11. Though, as one of the referees for this paper helpfully pointed out, there is a sense in which a patient who goes to great lengths to persuade a clinician to perform euthanasia upon her, shares some of the responsibility for her own death. More generally this point is well taken because otherwise we would be able to avoid responsibility for any action by persuading an accomplice to undertake it for us.

12. Obviously, some people would want to argue that voluntary euthanasia also respects the autonomous decision of the patient.

13. In the UK, it was established that tube-feeding was a medical intervention in Airedale NHS Trust v. Bland [1993] 3 WLR 316.

14. See the points made in footnote 9.

15. This point is well made by James Rachels 'Active and Passive Euthanasia' in Applied Ethics ed. Peter Singer, (Oxford University Press, Oxford, 1986) pp. 29–35.

16. See for instance the Canadian case Malette v. Shulman NW Ont CA (1009) 67 DLR (4th) 321.

17. Crisp, Anorexia Nervosa: Let me be.

18. This is, of course, only one view about the origins of the disorder. For an excellent critique of Crisp and outlines and critiques of other theories, see Morag MacSween Anorexic Bodies, (Routledge, London and New York, 1996), Chapters Two and Three.

19. Crisp, Anorexia Nervosa: Let me be, p. 146.

20. Competent in a general sense. I do not, of course, mean an incompetent refusal of food on the point of near death. A patient who has been force-fed under a section, who is released from the section and then requests that this cycle is not repeated would qualify for the kind of consideration I am suggesting here.

21. There are many examples of this in practice, particularly where patients refuse life-saving therapy. The issue is discussed in Heather Draper, 'Consent and Midwifery' in ed. Frith, L. Ethics and Midwifery (Butterworth Heinemann, Oxford, 1994). pp. 17–33 and Heather Draper, 'Women, reproductive responsibilities and forced caesareans', Journal of Medical Ethics, 22, 6 (1996), pp. 327–333.

22. Statistics for recovery vary. Lang, The Harvard Medical Letter cites a recovery rate of between 50–70% over ten years. E. D. Eckert, et al 'Ten year follow-up of anorexia nervosa: clinical course and outcome', Psychological Medicine, 25 (1995), pp. 143–156 suggest a 24% full recovery rate and just under 50% benign outcome. Obviously, taken together these sources suggest a failure rate of between 25–50% over ten years.

23. Crisp, Anorexia Nervosa: Let me be, p. 81.

24. Which, again, would exclude those on the point of starving to death.

James L. Werth, Jr., et al.

 **NO**

When Does the "Duty to Protect" Apply with a Client Who Has Anorexia Nervosa?

. . . While the literature abounds with protocols that will assist the counselor in case conceptualization and treatment (see Stein et al., 2001), a minimally addressed issue is the ethical and legal quagmire that ensues as the health of clients with eating disorders, particularly those with anorexia nervosa, declines. For the therapist, the task is to balance the therapeutic needs of these clients, particularly autonomy, with concerns about the person's health. Allowing clients to make their own decisions about treatment and recovery may facilitate the therapeutic relationship but may increase the risk of medical deterioration. Maintaining the balance between respecting the client's autonomy and protecting the client's health is especially challenging. It is within this context that practitioners, trainers, and supervisors could benefit from a discussion of their ethical, legal, and clinical obligations when a client with anorexia is in medical jeopardy (i.e., her or his life is in danger).

The purposes of this article are to (a) discuss the intersection between the duty to protect (i.e., an obligation to take some action when a person is engaging or considering engaging in a behavior that may lead to self-harm) and the treatment of people with eating disorders, specifically anorexia nervosa; and (b) provide some general guidelines for intervention. To determine whether there may be an essentially heretofore neglected duty to protect in the case of counseling with people who have certain eating disorders, this article first provides a brief overview of anorexia nervosa and then reviews the incidence of mortality in people with this condition. The next section outlines the duty to protect in instances of self-harm and discusses legal options when a person is considered to be at risk. Then, based on the information about anorexia and the ethical and legal issues associated with the duty to protect, the question of when this duty applies with clients who have anorexia is examined. The article concludes with implications of this analysis.

Anorexia Nervosa

Cognitive Functioning

Unfortunately, the *DSM-IV-TR* is silent about how anorexia can affect cognitive functioning beyond mentioning comorbid mental disorders. Experts on anorexia (e.g., Goldner, 1989; Goldner, Birmingham, & Smye, 1997; Kluge, 1991) and forensics (e.g., Appelbaum & Rumpf, 1998; Dresser, 1984a, 1984b; Dresser & Boisaubin, 1986) have noted that self-starvation can interfere with conceptualization, perceptions, and decision making. These cognitive deficits can impact the person's ability to realistically assess her situation and then impair judgment to the point that she is legally incompetent, specifically in areas related to eating and receiving treatments designed to increase weight and/or become medically stable. "The question of competence for individuals with anorexia nervosa centers on their specific ability to make rational decisions about nutrition, refeeding, and other medical treatments" (Goldner et al., 1997, p. 454). In other words, the disorder itself impairs judgment. Because they are often high functioning in other areas, the lack of severe delusions or other psychotic features in these clients can deceive some clinicians, attorneys, and judges (see Gutheil & Bursztajn, 1986). Depending on the course of the condition, these deficits may be apparent in standardized psychological and neuropsychological testing (Bowers, 1994; Hamsher, Halmi, & Benton, 1981; Watson, Bowers, & Andersen, 2000). In more severe cases, the inability to care for self as well as the person's medical jeopardy will be evident to observers (Appelbaum & Rumpf, 1998; Dresser, 1984a, 1984b).

Although not a cognitive deficit in and of itself, the pattern of thinking by the person with anorexia can be considered to be a thought disturbance. Importantly, it is the ego-syntonic dimension of this thought disturbance that negatively affects help seeking, treatment compliance, and retention in therapy (Stein et al., 2001). Despite their obvious physiological decline, these clients refuse to acknowledge the extent of their disorder and are secretly pleased with their emaciation. Unlike those with other conditions, clients with anorexia value and seek the symptoms of their disorder (i.e., thinness and starvation). Because clients with anorexia rely on and value their symptoms to organize and manage their lives, there is little or no incentive for change, especially given their almost delusional capacity to ignore their emaciation. There is, then, a synergy between the ego-syntonic dimension of the disorder and the physiological-cognitive response to starvation. These cognitive factors create a reinforcing loop that fuels and maintains the need for personal control, to control food intake, and to resist change (and therefore treatment).

Mortality

The *DSM-IV-TR* indicates that the long-term mortality for individuals with anorexia admitted to university hospitals is 10%; death usually results from the effects of starvation, an electrolyte imbalance, or suicide. These conclusions were likely based on several studies and reviews that have been conducted in the past 20 years on the causes and rate of mortality of those who exhibit the condition (e.g., Crow, Praus, & Thuras, 1999; Deter & Herzog, 1994; Eckert, Halmi, Marchi, Grove, & Crosby, 1995; Herzog et al., 2000; Neumarker, 1997, 2000; Nielsen et al., 1998; Ratnasuriya, Eisler, Szmukler, & Russell, 1991; Schwartz & Thompson, 1981; Theander, 1985). After reviewing this research, Sullivan (1995) recounted this list of comparisons:

> The aggregate annual mortality rate associated with anorexia nervosa is more than 12 times higher than the annual death rate due to all causes of death for females 15-24 years old in the general population . . . and more than 200 times greater than the suicide rate in the general population. . . . The annual mortality rate associated with anorexia nervosa is more than twice that of a national study group of female psychiatric patients. (p. 1074)

This led Sullivan to conclude, "These data highlight the status of anorexia as a serious psychiatric disorder with a substantial risk of mortality" (p. 1074). More succinctly, Neumarker (2000, p. 181) stated that "it is clear that anorexia nervosa has the highest mortality rate of all the psychiatric illnesses" (see also Griffiths & Russell, 1998; Harris & Barraclough, 1998; Herzog et al., 2000; Nielsen et al., 1998; Vitiello & Lederhendler, 2000). . . .

Ethical and Legal Issues When a Client May Be at Risk of Self-Harm

Ethical Considerations

An integral part of the psychotherapeutic process is the client's understanding and belief that what is discussed with the therapist will remain confidential. Although what a client says in the therapy room is considered confidential and is also protected by law (i.e., it is privileged communication) in most situations, there are situations where the counselor is legally and ethically able (or obligated, in some cases) to divulge what the client said (Kitchener, 2000).

One of the limitations to confidentiality occurs when a person is perceived to be at risk of self-harm. Although harm-to-self is often discussed in the context of suicide, a close examination reveals that it is not the *intent* to die or to cause harm to one's being that is the key; it is that the behavior itself, or the inability to manage one's behavior, has the potential of causing significant damage or death (Appelbaum & Rumpf, 1998). Therefore, whether a client has suicidal ideation, expressed intent to kill herself or himself, or taken actions that could be interpreted as suicidal is not the issue; the outcome is the key point (Werth & Rogers, 2003). In such situations, a therapist must exercise reasonable care to prevent foreseeable harm or danger that may result from a client's mental or physical incapacity (Bongar, 2002). This is an example of the "duty to protect" applied to self-harm as opposed to harm to others (see *Bellah v. Greenson*, 1978). Thus, although the duty to protect grew from case law related to harming others (i.e., *Tarasoff v. Regents of the University of California*, 1976), it has since been expanded to become an ethical and clinical standard of care and to encompass other client actions (Bongar, 2002; Vande-Creek & Knapp, 2001). . . .

Ethical Meta-Principles

The ethical meta-principles such as autonomy, beneficence, nonmaleficence, justice, and fidelity have been discussed as important aspects of ethical decision making in counseling psychology for nearly two decades (Kitchener, 1984; Kitchener & Anderson, 2000). Although the interpretations of these principles are culture-bound and potentially problematic (see, e.g., Blackhall, Murphy, Frank, Michel, & Azen, 1995; Carrese & Rhodes, 1995), the principles are relevant in this context, and the interplay between them contributes to the dilemma faced by the clinician (Goldner et al., 1997). For example, many authors have emphasized that autonomy (i.e., control) is such an important issue for individuals with anorexia (e.g., Russell, 2001; Stein et al., 2001) that a desire may exist to maximize this principle; however, beneficence and non-maleficence may conflict with autonomy, given that death may result, and therefore may temporarily override autonomy (Griffiths & Russell, 1998). Thus, the question for the counselor may revolve around when, if ever, the client's autonomy should give way to the therapist's interpretation of what constitutes beneficence and nonmaleficence.

Legal Considerations

For the purposes of this analysis, three important legal issues are germane: (a) whether state law mandates intervention when a counselor believes a person may harm himself or herself, (b) when involuntary hospitalization (i.e., civil commitment) is possible in situations involving self-harm, and (c) when treatment can and cannot be refused. These matters are discussed in turn.

Just as some psychologists may erroneously believe the APA ethics code (2002) mandates breaking confidentiality (or some other intervention) when a person is believed to be at risk of self-harm, some may think that state laws require intervention in such situations. However, with only a few exceptions, this is mistaken. Most state laws related to potential harm-to-self are similar to the APA ethics code in that they allow, but do not mandate, action (Werth, 2001; see also Barret et al., 2001). The intervention discussed in state laws related to self-harm is involuntary hospitalization.

In terms of civil commitment related to self-harm, a person can be judged to be a danger to herself or himself to a degree that legally allows for intervention in two ways: The self-harm must be the result of (a) a mental illness or (b) grave disability (Appelbaum & Rumpf, 1998; Werth, 2001). Although the mental illness criterion is typically vaguely defined in laws, a *DSM* Axis I disorder would likely suffice. Grave disability, in essence, means that judgment is so impaired that the individual cannot take care of herself or himself: One example of this may be intentional malnutrition (Appelbaum & Rumpf, 1998).

However, even if involuntarily hospitalized, a person has a right to refuse treatment unless (a) declared legally incompetent or (b) competency is in question and a life-threatening emergency arises. In the latter case, after stabilization, competence must be reassessed, and treatment refusal may take place unless a court declares the person incompetent (Appelbaum & Rumpf, 1998; Dresser 1984a, 1984b; Dresser & Boisaubin, 1986). If deemed incompetent, a person with anorexia can be force-fed; this situation is referred to as *compulsory treatment.*

Summary

Psychologists who have a client in danger of self-harm must practice up to the standards of care, which means that they have a duty to protect the client. Many interventions may satisfy the duty, and both the APA ethics code (2002) and most state laws allow for (but do not mandate) the breaking of confidentiality and attempts at involuntary hospitalization in certain situations. However, except in rare circumstances, the client has the right to refuse treatment.

Is There a Duty to Protect with Clients Who Have Anorexia?

The preceding discussion on anorexia and on the duty to protect leads to the following key points:

- Anorexia is a diagnosable mental condition in both the *DSM-IV-TR* and the *ICD-10* (World Health Organization, 1992).
- People with anorexia have a high mortality rate because of medical complications associated with the disorder and because of suicide.
- An ethical duty to protect exists when a client is a potential harm-to-self (although the actual intervention is dependent on the standard of care for that clinical situation).
- The APA (2002) ethics code permits the breaking of confidentiality to protect a person from self-harm.
- Possibilities exist for involuntary hospitalization of a person whose self-harm is not necessarily intentional but is the result of a mental disorder or grave disability.
- Involuntarily hospitalized persons can refuse treatment unless declared incompetent.

It is in this context that the counselor may be faced with the clinical, ethical, and legal dilemma of how to protect a client with anorexia from the life-threatening impact of the disorder while maintaining the client's autonomy (which is especially significant given that control typically is such an important issue for individuals with eating disorders).

If a client with anorexia is explicitly suicidal, then a duty to protect likely exists (for studies specifically on suicidality among people with eating disorders, see Bulik, Sullivan, & Joyce, 1999; Favaro & Santonastaso, 1996, 1997; and Viesselman & Roig, 1985). However, the issue to be examined next is the broader one of whether the eating-related behaviors associated with anorexia nervosa *in and of themselves* activate the duty to protect. In other words, in the discussion that follows, we are *not* saying that client behaviors associated with severe anorexia amount to suicidality but rather that the client's disorder-related actions may at some point put her health at significant risk and this is what engenders the duty to protect.

Given that low-burden standard interventions (e.g., increasing session frequency, adding a therapeutic modality) are not likely to be controversial, the focus here is on the most forceful actions: involuntary hospitalization and compulsory treatment. These must be discussed, even if these interventions are used relatively rarely, because (given the arguments made above) a duty to protect exists with clients who have anorexia, and the counselor must be willing to implement any ethically and legally acceptable intervention to meet that duty and protect the client.

Because the possibility that the behaviors of clients with anorexia nervosa may engender a duty to protect requiring extreme intervention has been discussed more frequently outside the United States (Appelbaum & Rumpf, 1998), we review this literature first. Analysis specific to the United States follows, along with responses to concerns about these interventions.

International Perspectives

In the international literature, the issue of what to do when faced with a client whose anorexia is quite severe is usually examined in terms of compulsory treatment. Distinguishing between involuntary hospitalization and compulsory treatment is important. In the treatment of eating disorders, *involuntary hospitalization* refers to the client's being placed into a restrictive environment where she is able to partake of the same treatment program as voluntary clients. *Compulsory treatment* is more specific and may include forced or nasogastric feeding. This distinction is not always made clear in the literature, but it is significant in the United States because of the assumption that a person is competent, and therefore able to refuse treatment, unless proven otherwise in court.

Therapists and physicians in the United Kingdom and Australia have been the most attentive to the issue of compulsory treatment. Tiller, Schmidt, and Treasure (1993; see also Lanceley & Travers, 1993) considered whether compulsory treatment for anorexia nervosa was compassion or coercion. They mentioned the case of a 16-year-old female who had appealed to an English court to refuse treatment for her anorexia (see also Brahams, 1997; Dolan, 1998). Tiller and colleagues said that given the mortality rate for anorexia, they found it hard to understand why compulsory treatment was so controversial. They concluded that compulsory treatment should be considered when the person is at a BMI below 13.5 (e.g., 5'5" and 81 pounds) and has considerable physical complications and concomitant psychiatric diagnoses. Serfaty and McCluskey (1998) reviewed instances of people receiving compulsory treatment in their specialty unit, and they, too, used the criteria of a BMI below 13.5 and serious physical complications.

English researchers Ramsay, Ward, Treasure, and Russell (1999) examined the conditions associated with compulsory inpatient treatment. They compared 81 compulsory patients (16% of all admissions), virtually all of whom had anorexia nervosa, with 81 voluntary patients. The investigators gave four reasons for compulsory treatment:

(i) Detention was necessary in the interest of the patient's health, for example by virtue of extreme weight loss and persistent avoidance of food;
(ii) Detention was in the interest of the patient's safety, for example he or she was making suicidal plans or had already attempted self-harm;
(iii) The detention was in the interest of both health and safety;
(iv) Other reasons (e.g., aggression or violence). (p. 148)

Note that both anorexic behaviors in and of themselves as well as specific plans for self-harm were considered acceptable reasons for compulsory treatment. Ramsay's team found that those individuals who received compulsory treatment did not significantly differ from the voluntary patients in admission weight or BMI, but the members of the compulsory group were significantly more likely to have a history of childhood physical/sexual abuse, prior admissions, longer hospitalizations, and explicit self-harm. . . .

United States

The literature in the United States has also attended to the dangers associated with anorexia, but the focus has been on mandatory withdrawal from a university (e.g., Glenn, Pollard, Denovchek, & Smith, 1986; Pavela, 1985) and involuntary hospitalization (Appelbaum & Rumpf, 1998; Dresser, 1984a, 1984b; see also Goldner et al., 1997). Of special relevance to counseling psychologists who work on college campuses, Pavela (1985) asserted that students with eating disorders made up one of three groups that may warrant involuntary withdrawal from a university because of the effects of the condition on the person, the impact on the university community, or the fact that the student could not receive adequate treatment on campus (the other groups were suicidal students and students with mental disorders who commit offenses without awareness of the nature of their actions). He stated that after other measures have been tried, "Unresponsive patients with potentially life threatening complications should be committed to a medical facility for prompt intervention, if necessary" (p. 60); but he did not indicate when such action would be "necessary." Glenn and colleagues (1986) provided four levels of interventions for students with eating disorders. The highest-level intervention is warranted when a student is "behaving in ways that are a threat to the life or health of self or others" (p. 164). They reported that there were two instances at their university where intervention began at the highest level because of the severity of the students' behavior.

Recently, Appelbaum and Rumpf (1998; see also Dresser, 1984a; Dresser & Boisaubin, 1986; Fost, 1984) discussed the prospect of involuntary hospitalization for people with anorexia. These authors explicitly stated that civil commitment in the case of anorexia is analogous to "other areas of mental health practice, involving the treatment of overtly suicidal patients or those so gravely disabled as to be unable to meet their basic needs" (p. 225). Yet the authors noted that it appears rare for people with anorexia to be involuntarily hospitalized (see also Fost, 1984), perhaps because many therapists do not consider a client with anorexia, who is not explicitly suicidal, to be a harm-to-self and, therefore, do not consider attempting involuntary hospitalization if other interventions fail. However, as previously reviewed, neither overt suicidality nor intent to harm oneself is necessary for the duty to protect to apply. Furthermore, given the mortality data previously cited, it should be clear that

> the effect of anorexic behavior can be fully as lethal as the more direct suicidal actions of a severely depressed patient. Thus, the focus on expressed intent is misleading and potentially harmful to the patient. . . . Even without the intent to end their lives, anorexics often act in ways that make that outcome likely. (p. 227)

As a result, Appelbaum and Rumpf concluded, therapists should consider involuntary hospitalization if a client's anorexia-related behaviors are severe enough to suggest that the individual's life is in jeopardy.

Objections to Involuntary Hospitalization

Although a few authors have made the case that some individuals with anorexia may be acting in ways, or have progressed far enough in their disease process, to warrant strong interventions, others object to the consideration of involuntary treatment for these clients. Reasons most often cited include potential violation of client rights, questionable efficacy of enforced treatment, and the likely deterioration of the therapeutic relationship.

One of the primary concerns regarding the use of involuntary hospitalization or compulsory treatment is that this imposition violates the client's right to decide for herself—her autonomy is taken away. This violation of client rights is seen as running counter to good therapeutic practice and believed to be counterproductive in both the short and long run (Dresser, 1984a, 1984b; Rathner, 1998). Although this may be true in principle, experts in anorexia indicate that clients are often grateful for such intervention once they are not in the downward spiral of the disorder (Fost, 1984; Goldner et al., 1997; Griffiths & Russell, 1998).

Experts have also suggested that involuntary hospitalization serves the temporary purpose of medical stabilization but does not actually treat the eating disorder because this requires the cooperation of the client (Rathner, 1998). Although short-term results are positive, the long-term success rates of involuntary treatment have been less clear. Only three studies to date have assessed the outcome of involuntary treatment (Griffiths et al., 1997; Ramsay et al., 1999; Watson et al., 2000). Although the investigations were not directly comparable, Russell (2001) summarized the results of research from these three outcome studies (one each in Australia, London, and Iowa). All three indicated that the involuntary patients experienced successful refeeding, although the results took longer than with the voluntary patients (mean 113 days compared to mean 88 days, respectively). Long-term follow-up was not done, but mortality comparisons were made with the London data. At an average of 5.7 years postadmission, the involuntary patients had a higher mortality rate (10 of 70 involuntary patients had died compared with 2 of the 70 voluntary patients). This was believed to be the result of the more severe pathology of the involuntary patients (Russell, 2001). How many deaths were prevented by the hospitalization, however, is unknown. More research is required to determine the long-term therapeutic impact of involuntary hospitalization.

Another concern about involuntary treatments is that such efforts could irreparably damage the therapeutic relationship and make it less likely that the client would seek treatment in the future (Richmond, 2001). There are no data to suggest that this is true, however, and some authors offer anecdotal evidence that clients are more likely to be grateful for the intervention once they are medically and psychologically stable (Andersen, Bowers, & Evans, 1997; Fost, 1984). Furthermore, it is argued, mere admission does not mean the person will necessarily improve (Dresser, 1984a), and if all that is achieved through hospitalization is medical stabilization without treatment for the actual disorder(s), positive treatment outcome is less likely. Once a person's weight is stabilized, however, the benefits of psychological and pharmacological treatment are more likely to accrue. A recent study (Watson et al., 2000) comparing voluntary and involuntary in-patients with eating disorders demonstrated that treatment outcomes were not significantly different and that the involuntary patients were just as likely to benefit from the treatment as were the voluntary patients. Long-term follow-up is still needed to determine whether these positive outcomes are sustained.

Objections to Applying the Duty to Protect with Clients Who Have Anorexia

Although we have attempted to make the case that counselors have a duty to protect with clients who have anorexia and that discharging this duty may even lead to attempts at involuntary hospitalization and compulsory treatment, readers may object to this line of reasoning. Some may argue that because the incidence of anorexia is lower than that of other mental disorders, even a mortality rate of 10% represents a relatively small number of deaths compared to those associated with other conditions. However, the number of deaths associated with anorexia is not the issue; the *probability* of death is the key. Because anorexia will lead to death if the course is not interrupted, the clinician has a duty to intervene if the course has progressed far enough (i.e., to the point of medical jeopardy). . . .

Implications for Practice

Based on the foregoing, we contend that there is a duty to protect with clients who have anorexia and, therefore, the counselor must be prepared to attempt involuntary hospitalization with clients whose conditions warrant extreme intervention. Regardless of whether a therapist considers the behaviors associated with anorexia nervosa to be overtly suicidal or to be the result of a condition that has compromised the ability to think clearly and care for oneself, it would appear obvious that such behaviors are dangerous and the counselor needs to intervene in some way. How to intervene is shaped, in part, by whether a duty to protect exists. Because the diagnosis of anorexia nervosa alone is not sufficient, the duty to protect applies when the client's behaviors have become extreme or are associated with significant health risks. The uninterrupted course of anorexia will inevitably lead to medical jeopardy and death. The goal of treatment is to slow the progression of symptoms until the client is able to develop healthy coping mechanisms. Depending on the client's response, decisions will need to be made about whether to maintain the current course of treatment or to develop a more aggressive plan, which would include more protective measures.

An example of how the physical and psychological decompensation of a client with anorexia can lead to (a) significant health concerns, (b) consideration as to whether the duty to protect applies and, if so, (c) decisions about what interventions are necessary illustrates the dilemma for the counselor.

> Jan was an 18-year-old first-year student at a large university. She had been treated for eating disorder behaviors in an outpatient clinic during high school and, although not fully recovered, she was attending college 1,500 miles from home. She lived in the residence hall on campus. Despite her best intentions to maintain her progress, she started restricting her food intake shortly after classes began in the fall. Initially friendly, she began to withdraw from her new friends and roommates, particularly avoiding activities that involved meals. By late fall, her roommates expressed their concern about Jan's avoidance and declining weight to the resident assistant. The residence hall staff referred her to the campus counseling center. She began counseling and medical monitoring through student health services as part of a multidisciplinary treatment team and remained stable through winter break. After returning to campus in the spring semester, her weight continued to drop. Although she agreed to have her parents notified that she was in counseling, she denied the extent of her decline both medically and psychologically. She had developed a strong therapeutic relationship with her counselor but was terrified of making any changes in her eating behavior. In an attempt to maintain her autonomy and avoid a power struggle, treatment options were discussed with her, but she refused inpatient treatment and refused to leave school voluntarily. Despite her weakened condition, she was seen by acquaintances exercising excessively. She had alienated her friends and had reduced her contact with her family.
>
> The treatment team worked carefully to maintain Jan's engagement and cooperation in the treatment process. Although she maintained her counseling and medical appointments, her disorder continued to progress. Her mood became more dysphoric, she had little energy, and her memory showed impairment. Furthermore, her weight had fallen to 95 pounds (given her height of 5'5", this equated to a BMI of 15.8), so her therapist and physician constructed a behavioral contract that included more frequent counseling sessions, nutritionist appointments, weight expectations and monitoring, and activity restrictions. She signed the contract to avoid

being involuntarily withdrawn from school, although she continued to claim that she was medically stable and functioning well. Jan felt some pressure to sign the contract, but by allowing the team physician to monitor the medical consequences, the counselor was able to maintain an empathic connection and address Jan's fears. As a result, the therapeutic relationship did not seem to suffer by implementing the contract.

By spring break, Jan had been taken to a local emergency room twice: once for rehydration after fainting and once because of cardiac dysrhythmia. Her treatment team had already escalated interventions in response to her physical and psychological condition and, again, determined that more aggressive treatment was necessary to preserve her life. As outpatient treatment on campus proved insufficient in reversing the course of her disorder, and her BMI dropped to 15 (90 pounds), they decided to call her parents to make arrangements for more intensive treatment, with or without Jan's consent.

Although counselors routinely intensify treatment with clients who are decompensating, it is unclear in the literature when counselors engage in an assessment of the need to protect the client from the probable death associated with continued anorexic behavior. Although no one has specifically identified a set of criteria that would implicate the duty to protect when a client, such as Jan, has anorexia nervosa, a tentative list of conditions may be generated based on the research and analysis associated with compulsory treatment in the United Kingdom and Australia (Griffiths et al., 1997; Griffiths & Russell, 1998; Ramsay et al., 1999; Serfaty & McCluskey, 1998), the reviews of civil commitment in the United States (Appelbaum & Rumpf, 1998; Dresser, 1984a, 1984b; Goldner et al., 1997), and discussions of the physical complications associated with and treatments for anorexia nervosa (American Psychiatric Association, 2000a; Andersen et al., 1997; Becker, Grinspoon, Klibanski, & Herzog, 1999; Brotman & Stern, 1983; Casper & Davis, 1977; Garner & Needleman, 1997; J. E. Mitchell, Pomeroy, & Adson, 1997; see also Stein et al., 2001). Unfortunately, the rate of progression toward medical danger in anorexia is difficult to predict. Death in these cases is often the result of a cardiac event for which there was no warning (Birmingham, 1989; Brotman & Stern, 1983).

Given the medical risk associated with this disorder, the therapist must work closely with medical personnel or as part of a multidisciplinary treatment team in evaluating the health risk of the individual patient (Kalodner, 1998). In fact, the American Psychiatric Association (2000b) guidelines prescribe that eating disorder treatment decisions be made by a multidisciplinary team. The American Psychiatric Association guidelines also highlight certain characteristics that would warrant immediate hospitalization: increase in pulse of greater than 20 beats per minute (bpm) or a drop in blood pressure of greater than 20 mm Hg/minute standing, bradycardia less than 40 bpm, tachycardia greater than 110 bpm, or inability to sustain body core temperature above 97.0 degrees. Having no motivation for recovery is also cited as an indicator for inpatient hospitalization. Short of these emergent physical signs, the risk factors listed below indicate more protective/aggressive treatment strategies are necessary, which may include behavioral contracts, intensive outpatient treatment, and, ultimately, voluntary or involuntary hospitalization.

High-risk indicators include

1. BMI below 15 (e.g., 5′2″ and 82 pounds; 5′5″ and 90 pounds; 5′8″ and 98 pounds)
2. Any of the following medical conditions: cardiac arrhythmia, seizures, syncopol episodes, organic brain syndrome, bradycardia (less than 40 bpm), exercise-induced chest pain, reduced exercise tolerance, dysrhythmias, renal dysfunction, tetany, blood volume depletion
3. Abnormalities in electrolyte levels
4. Rapid weight loss into dangerous weight range for height
5. Comorbid psychiatric conditions (e.g., major depression, obsessive-compulsive disorder, bipolar disorder, post-traumatic stress disorder, substance abuse)
6. History of self-harm or prior hospitalizations
7. Cognitive impairment that interferes with judgment to the point that the person is incompetent or gravely disabled

The clinician who has a client meeting one or more of the above criteria (in particular, 1, 2, or 7) should consider herself or himself to have an affirmative duty to take explicit action to protect the health of the client (if the client is a minor, special duties apply; see Dresser, 1984a, 1984b, for a discussion of these). Any combination of the above risk factors should alert the clinician that more aggressive treatment is warranted. Because the progression of symptoms is typically gradual, it will be the cumulative clinical judgment of the treatment team that determines whether a duty exists to intensify the interventions. In general, the counselor might proceed from establishing a behavioral contract, to using intensive outpatient treatment, to instituting partial hospitalization or day treatment. When these efforts have failed to bring about sufficient change, voluntary or involuntary hospitalization should be considered.

Appelbaum and Rumpf (1998; see also Gutheil & Bursztajn, 1986) made a compelling case that the most aggressive form of intervention—civil commitment—is a possible course of action for therapists working with clients whose health is in jeopardy because of the behaviors associated with anorexia nervosa. Although framed within the auspices of the duty to protect, Appelbaum and Rumpf did not discuss other, less extreme, interventions that may be both appropriate and necessary under this duty. Ideally, the therapist should proceed from the least restrictive (e.g., verbal contract) to more restrictive treatment options (e.g., breaking confidentiality) and only consider involuntary hospitalization when other treatment attempts have failed or medical risks necessitate (Andersen et al., 1997). . . .

Conclusion

To practice up to the standard of care when working with clients who are at risk of self-harm, psychologists must take some action to protect the person (Bongar, 2002). We have asserted that when a counselor is seeing a client with anorexia, the therapist may eventually have a duty to take action to protect the client's health even if the client is not explicitly suicidal and is not engaging in anorexic behaviors with the explicit intent of self-harm. The specific diagnosis is not the key; the behaviors associated with the diagnosis are what trigger the duty. For example, just as a diagnosis of major depression does not automatically require intervention to protect the well-being of the client unless the behaviors or potential behaviors associated with the depression (e.g., suicidal ideation with a plan or attempt) signaled that significant harm was believed likely, the diagnosis of anorexia in and of itself is not sufficient. However, if the behaviors associated with the condition are such that the therapist, after medical consultation, perceives the client's life to be in danger, then the duty would apply.

The goal of this article is to make explicit what may have been implicit: At times, there is a duty to protect with clients who have anorexia nervosa. The medical danger associated with this condition invokes the ethical and legal responsibility to protect clients in an acute state of the disorder. Counseling psychologists and trainees would benefit from an increased understanding of the overlap of clinical and ethical dimensions of decision making and treatment planning with clients with anorexia. We hope that this article will prompt others to examine this issue and that researchers will work to further define the conditions under which the duty to protect applies. Until then, counselors are reminded that even if their clients with anorexia nervosa are not explicitly suicidal, the behaviors associated with this condition do put these clients at risk of significant self-harm and death, and the therapist therefore may have an affirmative duty to protect clients with anorexia.

References

American Psychiatric Association. (2000a). *Diagnostic and statistical manual of mental disorders* (4th ed., text revision). Washington, DC: American Psychiatric Press.

American Psychiatric Association. (2000b). *Practice guideline for the treatment of patients with eating disorders* (2nd ed.). Washington, DC: Author.

American Psychological Association. (2002). Ethical principles of psychologists and code of conduct. *American Psychologist, 57,* 1060–1073.

Andersen, A. E., Bowers, W., & Evans, K. (1997). Inpatient treatment of anorexia nervosa. In D. M. Garner & P. E. Garfinkel (Eds.), *Handbook of treatment for eating disorders* (2nd ed., pp. 327–353). New York: Guilford.

Appelbaum, P. S., & Rumpf, T. (1998). Civil commitment of the anorexic patient. *General Hospital Psychiatry, 20,* 225–230.

Barret, B., Kitchener, K. S., & Burris, S. (2001). Suicide and confidentiality with the client with advanced AIDS: The case of Phil. In J. R. Anderson & B. Barret (Eds.), *Ethics in HIV-related psychotherapy: Clinical decision making in complex cases* (pp. 299–314). Washington, DC: American Psychological Association.

Becker, A. E., Grinspoon, S. K., Klibanski, A., & Herzog, D. B. (1999). Eating disorders. *New England Journal of Medicine, 340,* 1092–1098.

Bellah v. Greenson, 146 Cal.Rptr. 535, 81 Cal.App.3d 614 (1978).

Birmingham, C. L. (1989). Anorexia nervosa and bulimia: Medical complications and management. *British Columbia Medical Journal, 31,* 155–158.

Blackhall, L. J., Murphy, S. T., Frank, G., Michel, V., & Azen, S. (1995). Ethnicity and attitudes toward patient autonomy. *Journal of the American Medical Association, 274*, 820–825.

Bongar, B. (2002). *The suicidal patient: Clinical and legal standards of care* (2nd ed.). Washington, DC: American Psychological Association.

Bongar, B., Berman, A. L., Maris, R. W., Silverman, M. M., Harris, E. A., & Packman, W. L. (Eds.). (1998). *Risk management with suicidal patients.* New York: Guilford.

Bowers, W. A. (1994). Neuropsychological impairment among anorexia nervosa and bulimia patients. *Eating Disorders: Journal of Treatment and Prevention, 2*, 42–46.

Brahams, D. (1997). UK compulsory detention for anorexia makes legal history. *Lancet, 349*, 860.

Brotman, A. W., & Stern, T. A. (1983). Case report of cardiovascular abnormalities in anorexia nervosa. *American Journal of Psychiatry, 140*, 1227–1228.

Bulik, C. M., Sullivan, P. F., & Joyce, P. R. (1999). Temperament, character, and suicide attempts in anorexia nervosa, bulimia nervosa and major depression. *Acta Psychiatrica Scandinavica, 100*, 27–32.

Carrese, J. A., & Rhodes, L. A. (1995). Western bioethics on the Navajo reservation. *Journal of the American Medical Association, 274*, 826–829.

Casper, R. C., & Davis, J. M. (1977). On the course of anorexia nervosa. *American Journal of Psychiatry, 134*, 974–978.

Crow, S., Praus, B., & Thuras, P. (1999). Mortality from eating disorders—A 5- to 10-year record linkage study. *International Journal of Eating Disorders, 26*, 97–101.

Deter, H.-C., & Herzog, W. (1994). Anorexia nervosa in a long-term perspective: Results of the Heidelberg-Mannheim study. *Psychosomatic Medicine, 56*, 20–27.

Dolan, B. (1998). Food refusal, forced feeding and the law of England and Wales. In W. Vandereycken & P. J. V. Beumont (Eds.), *Treating eating disorders: Ethical, legal and personal issues* (pp. 151–178). New York: New York University Press.

Dresser, R. (1984a). Feeding the hunger artists: Legal issues in treating anorexia nervosa. *Wisconsin Law Review*, pp. 297–374.

Dresser, R. (1984b). Legal and policy considerations in treatment of anorexia nervosa patients. *International Journal of Eating Disorders, 3*, 43–51.

Dresser, R. S., & Boisaubin, E. V. (1986). Psychiatric patients who refuse nourishment. *General Hospital Psychiatry, 8*, 101–106.

Eckert, E. D., Halmi, K. A., Marchi, P., Grove, W., & Crosby, R. (1995). Ten-year follow-up of anorexia nervosa: Clinical course and outcome. *Psychological Medicine, 25*, 143–156.

Favaro, A., & Santonastaso, P. (1996). Purging behaviors, suicide attempts, and psychiatric symptoms in 398 eating disordered subjects. *International Journal of Eating Disorders, 20*, 99–103.

Favaro, A., & Santonastaso, P. (1997). Suicidality in eating disorders: Clinical and psychological correlates. *Acta Psychiatrica Scandinavica, 95*, 508–514.

Fost, N. (1984). Food for thought: Dresser on anorexia. *Wisconsin Law Review*, pp. 375–384.

Garner, D. M., & Needleman, L. D. (1997). Sequencing and integration of treatments. In D. M. Garner & P. E. Garfinkel (Eds.), *Handbook of treatment for eating disorders* (2nd ed., pp. 50–63). New York: Guilford.

Glenn, A. A., Pollard, J. W., Denovchek, J. A., & Smith, A. F. (1986). Eating disorders on campus: A procedure for community intervention. *Journal of Counseling and Development, 65*, 163–165.

Goldner, E. (1989). Treatment refusal in anorexia nervosa. *International Journal of Eating Disorders, 8*, 297–306.

Goldner, E. M., Birmingham, C. L., & Smye, V. (1997). Addressing treatment refusal in anorexia nervosa: Clinical, ethical, and legal considerations. In D. M. Garner & P. E. Garfinkel (Eds.), *Handbook of treatment for eating disorders, second edition* (pp. 450–461). New York: Guilford.

Griffiths, R. A., Beumont, P. J. V., Russell, J., Touyz, S. W., & Moore, G. (1997). The use of guardianship legislation for anorexia nervosa: A report of 15 cases. *Australian and New Zealand Journal of Psychiatry, 31*, 525–531.

Griffiths, R., & Russell, J. (1998). Compulsory treatment of anorexia nervosa patients. In W. Vandereycken & P. J. V. Beumont (Eds.), *Treating eating disorders: Ethical, legal and personal issues* (pp. 127–150). New York: New York University Press.

Gutheil, T. G., & Bursztajn, H. (1986). Clinicians' guidelines for assessing and presenting subtle forms of patient incompetence in legal settings. *American Journal of Psychiatry, 143*, 1020–1023.

Hamsher, K. S., Halmi, K. A., & Benton, A. L. (1981). Prediction of outcome in anorexia nervosa from neuropsychological status. *Psychiatry Research, 4*, 79–88.

Harris, E. C., & Barraclough, B. (1998). Excess mortality of mental disorder. *British Journal of Psychiatry, 173*, 11–53.

Herzog, D. B., Greenwood, D. N., Dorer, D. J., Flores, A. T., Ekeblad, E. R., Richards, A., et al. (2000). Mortality in eating disorders: A descriptive study. *International Journal of Eating Disorders, 28*, 20–26.

Kalodner, C. (1998). Eating disorders. In S. Roth-Roemer, S. E. Robinson Kurpius, & C. Carmin (Eds.), *The emerging role of counseling psychology in health care* (pp. 253–278). New York: Norton.

Kitchener, K. S. (1984). Intuition, critical evaluation and ethnical principles: The foundations for ethical decisions in counseling psychology. *The Counseling Psychologist, 12*(3), 43–55.

Kitchener, K. S. (2000). *Foundations of ethical practice, research, and teaching in psychology*. Mahwah, NJ: Lawrence Erlbaum.

Kitchener, K. S., & Anderson, S. K. (2000). Ethical issues in counseling psychology: Old themes—New problems. In S. D. Brown & R. W. Lent (Eds.), *Handbook of counseling psychology* (3rd ed., pp. 50–82). New York: John Wiley.

Kluge, E.-H. (1991). The ethics of forced feeding in anorexia nervosa: A response to Hebert and Weingarten. *Canadian Medical Association Journal, 144*, 1121–1124.

Lanceley, C., & Travers, R. (1993). Anorexia nervosa: Forced feeding and the law [letter]. *British Journal of Psychiatry, 163*, 835.

Mitchell, J. E., Pomeroy, C., & Adson, D. E. (1997). Managing medical complications. In D. M. Garner & P. E. Garfinkel (Eds.), *Handbook of treatment for eating disorders* (2nd ed., pp. 383–393). New York: Guilford.

Neumarker, K.-J. (1997). Mortality and sudden death in anorexia nervosa. *International Journal of Eating Disorders, 21*, 205–212.

Neumarker, K.-J. (2000). Mortality rates and causes of death. *European Eating Disorders Review, 8*, 181–187.

Nielsen, S., Moller-Madsen, S., Isager, T., Jorgensen, J., Pagsberg, K., & Theander, S. (1998). Standardized mortality in eating disorders—A quantitative summary of previously published and new evidence. *Journal of Psychosomatic Research, 44*, 413–434.

Pavela, G. (1985). *The dismissal of students with mental disorders: Legal issues, policy considerations and alternative responses*. Asheville, NC: College Administration Publications.

Ramsay, R., Ward, A., Treasure, J., & Russell, G. F. M. (1999). Compulsory treatment in anorexia nervosa. *British Journal of Psychiatry, 175*, 147–153.

Rathner, G. (1998). A plea against compulsory treatment of anorexia nervosa patients. In W. Vandereycken & P. J. V. Beumont (Eds.), *Treating eating disorders: Ethical, legal and personal issues* (pp. 179-215). New York: New York University Press.

Ratnasuriya, R. H., Eisler, I., Szmukler, G. I., & Russell, G. F. M. (1991). Anorexia nervosa: Outcome and prognostic factors after 20 years. *British Journal of Psychiatry, 158*, 495-502.

Richmond, J. (2001). Anorexia and involuntary commitment: A necessary approach? *Psychiatry, Psychology, and Law, 8*, 86-96.

Russell, G. F. M. (2001). Involuntary treatment in anorexia nervosa. *Psychiatric Clinics of North America, 24*, 337-349.

Schwartz, D. M., & Thompson, M. G. (1981). Do anorectics get well? Current research and future needs. *American Journal of Psychiatry, 138*, 319-323.

Serfaty, M., & McCluskey, S. (1998). Compulsory treatment of anorexia nervosa and the moribund patient. *European Eating Disorders Review, 6*, 27-37.

Stein, R. I., Saelens, B. E., Dounchis, J. Z., Lewszyk, C. M., Swenson, A. K., & Wilfley, D. E. (2001). Treatment of eating disorders in women. *The Counseling Psychologist, 29*, 695-732.

Sullivan P. F. (1995). Mortality in anorexia nervosa. *American Journal of Psychiatry, 152*, 1073-1074.

Tarasoff v. Regents of the University of California, 17 Cal.3d 425, 551 P.2d 334 (1976).

Theander, S. (1985). Outcome and prognosis in anorexia nervosa and bulimia: Some results of previous investigations, compared with those of a Swedish long-term study. *Journal of Psychiatric Research, 19*, 493-508.

Tiller, J., Schmidt, U., & Treasure, J. (1993). Compulsory treatment for anorexia nervosa: Compassion or coercion? *British Journal of Psychiatry, 162*, 679-680.

VandeCreek, L., & Knapp, S. (2001). *Tarasoff and beyond: Legal and clinical considerations in the treatment of life-endangering patients* (3rd ed.). Sarasota, FL: Professional Resource Press.

Viesselman, J. O., & Roig, M. (1985). Depression and suicidality in eating disorders. *Journal of Clinical Psychiatry, 46*, 118-124.

Vitiello, B., & Lederhendler, I. (2000). Research on eating disorders: Current status and future prospects. *Biological Psychiatry, 47*, 777-786.

Watson, T. L., Bowers, W. A., & Andersen, A. E. (2000). Involuntary treatment of eating disorders. *American Journal of Psychiatry, 157*, 1806-1810.

Werth, J. L., Jr. (2001). U.S. involuntary mental health commitment statutes: Requirements for persons perceived to be a potential harm to self. *Suicide and Life-Threatening Behavior, 31*, 348-357.

Werth, J. L., Jr., & Rogers, J. R. (2003). *Consistent application of the "duty to protect" when a client is a potential harm-to-self.* Manuscript submitted for publication.

World Health Organization (1992). *ICD-10 classification of mental and behavioral disorders: Clinical description and diagnostic guidelines.* Geneva, Switzerland: Author.

CHALLENGE QUESTIONS

Should Individuals with Anorexia Nervosa Have the Right to Refuse Life-Sustaining Treatment?

1. To what extent do you agree with Werth and his colleagues that medical providers have a duty to protect the patient when the individual's behaviors pose a serious threat to health? In what kind of situations, if any, should the medical professional put aside the obligation to protect?
2. Consider the situation in which an individual does not refuse treatment outright but expresses a resistance to intervention. If you were the treating clinician, how would you deal with such an individual?
3. Werth presents a fictional case about a college student named Jan who suffers from anorexia. If Jan were a friend of yours, at what point should you intervene if concerned about the possibility of this individual engaging in self-injurious behaviors related to anorexia nervosa? What "duty to protect" does a friend or relative have in such situations?
4. Draper makes the comparison between individuals with anorexia and individuals with breast cancer. She contends that a competent individual may base her decision to refuse therapy on arguments about the burden of therapy and the side effects of successful treatment. Just as a breast cancer patient may not want to undergo a mastectomy, an individual with anorexia may not want to live with a larger body. What similarities and differences pertain to these medical conditions?
5. How should one go about making the determination about a client's competency to make decisions about treatment options? Who should make the assessment about competency—clinicians, lawyers, or judges?

Suggested Readings

Daniels, D., & Jenkins, P. (2000). *Therapy with children: Children's rights, confidentiality and the law.* Thousand Oaks, CA: SAGE Publications.

Giordano, S. (2003). *Understanding eating disorders: Conceptual and ethical issues in the treatment of anorexia and bulimia nervosa.* New York: Oxford University Press.

MacDonald, C. (2002). "Treatment resistance in anorexia nervosa and the pervasiveness of ethics in clinical decision making." *Canadian Journal of Psychiatry,* 47(3): 267–270.

Vandereycken, W., & Beumont, P. J. V. (1998). *Treating eating disorders: Ethical, legal, and personal issues.* New York: NYU Press.

ISSUE 3

Is Psychological Debriefing a Harmful Intervention for Survivors of Trauma?

YES: Grant J. Devilly and Peter Cotton, from "Psychological Debriefing and the Workplace: Defining a Concept, Controversies and Guidelines for Intervention," *Australian Psychologist* (July 2003)

NO: J. T. Mitchell, from "A Response to the Devilly and Cotton Article, 'Psychological Debriefing and the Workplace . . .'," *Australian Psychologist* (March 2004)

ISSUE SUMMARY

YES: Psychologists Grant J. Devilly and Peter Cotton assert that critical incident stress debriefing (CISD) is poorly defined and has been shown to do more harm than good. They propose alternative approaches for responding to trauma survivors, which they consider more effective.

NO: Jeffrey T. Mitchell of the International Critical Incident Stress Foundation (ICISF) argues that Devilly and Cotton have misrepresented important information about psychological debriefing and have confused several aspects of this system of responding to trauma survivors.

Immediately following the September 11th terrorist attacks, thousands of well-meaning people descended upon Ground Zero in New York with the intention of consoling and aiding the survivors of that harrowing trauma. Some of these helpers had the goal in mind of offering their "debriefing" services to traumatized individuals who had just barely escaped death. Psychological debriefing is an intervention process in which survivors are urged to recount and relive the incident in order to avoid long-term consequences and traumatic stress responses. Experts in the field of psychology and crisis intervention, however, debate the efficacy of psychological debriefing, and more specifically, critical incident stress debriefing (CISD). While some professionals insist that CISD can be greatly beneficial, others contend that this approach can do more harm than good.

Grant J. Devilly and Peter Cotton assert that CISD and critical incident stress management (CISM) are poorly defined responses to traumatized individuals, which at their worst are noxious and at their best are ineffective.

They cite examples of research suggesting that generic psychological debriefing has almost no effect on trauma victims and that CISD can actually provoke more negative symptoms in those who undergo the debriefing.

Jeffrey T. Mitchell criticizes the article by Devilly and Cotton, arguing that they have not done adequate research and contends that they make several glaring errors including the erroneous presentation of CISD and CISM as synonymous. Mitchell explains that CISD is a 7-step, small-group crisis intervention process, while CISM is a comprehensive, systematic, and multi-component system. Mitchell also asserts that the research studies upon which Devilly and Cotton rest their aguments involve instances in which the specifics of CISD are not properly applied, and do not reflect true efficacy of stress debriefing.

POINT

- The philosophy and techniques associated with psychological debriefing represent little more than "emotional first aid" for survivors of life-threatening trauma.

- Good intentions and the passion to help following a trauma may result in paradoxical effects, particularly if the tools being used to aid are cursorily understood, dogmatically applied, and the peer-reviewed research literature is ignored.

- Current expert consensus and meta-analytic reviews suggest that CISD is possibly noxious, that generic psychological debriefing is probably inert, and that more emphasis should be placed on the screening for, and providing of, early intervention to those who go on to develop pathological reactions.

- It appears that CISD and CISM are indistinguishable. We can only conclude that CISD may or may not be one component of CISM, or CISD may be equivalent to CISM, and CISM may or may not have a definite procedure.

- Debriefing is widely and routinely practiced, and is increasingly turned to as a first resort when disasters strike. Following harrowing experiences, psychological debriefing providers frequently advise organizations to use their services, asserting a number of claims about the effectiveness of debriefing.

COUNTERPOINT

- Crisis intervention is not intended to be a substitute for psychotherapy, but rather an effective provision of support following life-threatening trauma.

- There is ample justification for having unequivocal confidence in the group CISD process when it is properly applied according to acceptable standards of practice, and by people who have been properly trained in applying the model.

- Devilly and Cotton cannot legitimately state that "CISD is possibly noxious." The studies they use to support this comment never actually evaluated CISD processes that were provided by properly trained personnel adhering to acceptable standards of care.

- The most prominent of the many glaring errors of Devilly and Cotton is the treatment of a specific, structured, 7-step, small-group crisis intervention process called CISD as if it were one and the same as a comprehensive, systematic and multi-component program called CISM.

- Although Devilly and Cotton assert that psychological debriefing is the first resort when disasters strike, in fact, debriefings are not recommended for several weeks or longer after a disaster. The only people who would resort first to debriefing after a disaster are those who are untrained and apparently unaware of what is needed before debriefing.

YES ↵

**Grant J. Devilly and
Peter Cotton**

Psychological Debriefing and the Workplace: Defining a Concept, Controversies and Guidelines for Intervention

Critical incident stress debriefing (CISD), a specific form of psychological debriefing, has gained widespread acceptance and implementation in the few short years since it was first proposed (Mitchell, 1983). However, there has been recent doubt cast on this practice and confusion regarding the terminology used. This article explores the claims frequently made by proponents regarding its use, counterclaims of ineffectiveness by its detractors, and general consensus regarding its specific use and the use of more generic psychological debriefing. We conclude that the recently introduced critical incident stress management (CISM) and its proposed progenitor, CISD, are currently poorly defined and relatively indistinct in the treatment–outcome literature and should be treated similarly. Current expert consensus and meta-analytic reviews suggest that CISD is possibly noxious, generic psychological debriefing is probably inert and that more emphasis should be placed on screening for, and providing, early intervention to those who go on to develop pathological reactions. A set of generic guidelines for the minimisation and management of workplace traumatic stress responses is also proposed.

⋅⟨⊙⟩⋅

During times of organisational upheaval and personal and interpersonal crisis, organisations frequently access the services of psychologists to help mitigate the long-term consequences of these occurrences. Indeed, the provision of "debriefing" services to organisations is now a multi-million dollar industry. For example, after the tragedy of the World Trade Centre terrorist attacks in New York (2001) newspaper articles reported that thousands of "debriefers" attended the area, advocating and offering debriefing services (Kadet, 2002). This also involved many of the organisations associated with the World Trade

From *Australian Psychologist*, vol. 38, no. 2, July 2003, pp. 144–150. Copyright © 2003 by Taylor & Francis Journals. Reprinted by permission.

Center being contacted and offered such debriefing services. The primary aims of this article are to evaluate the need for "psychological debriefing," to define the terms currently being used and to determine whether such an intervention is useful or can, in fact, be counterproductive. Our secondary goal is to extrapolate from what we do know from the literature and provide some general guidelines for organisations and psychologists, based on our current state of knowledge.

Psychological debriefing has been recently placed under the scientific microscope (van Emmerik, Kamphuis, Hulsbosch, & Emmelkamp, 2002), and it has been argued that good intentions and the passion to help following a trauma may carry with it paradoxical effects, particularly if the tools being used to aid are cursorily understood, dogmatically applied and the peer-reviewed research literature left untouched (Gist & Devilly, 2002). Yet debriefing is widely and routinely practised and appears to be increasingly turned-to as a first resort when disasters strike. Following harrowing experiences psychological debriefing providers frequently advise organisations to utilise their services, asserting a number of claims about the effectiveness of debriefing. The rationale typically includes the following:

- Debriefing will be seen as a gesture of support by the employer, concerned with the psychological welfare of their employees.
- Psychological debriefing will help mitigate long-term poor functioning, which otherwise is "likely" to occur and is a "foreseeable" consequence of the event.
- This will, therefore, also protect the organisation from litigation for not fulfilling their workplace, health and safety obligations.
- And, lastly, with employees less likely to suffer long-term psychological consequences following the debriefing, the workforce will be healthier—and a healthy workforce is a more productive workforce.

With these claims in mind, it is fitting that we present working definition of our terms. Frequently, and particularly in applied contexts, terms are being used without operational definitions and are often used interchangeably. This makes inspecting the evidence behind the claims a murky and very difficult task.

Definitions

"Psychological debriefing" is a generic term that has been suitably equated with "emotional first-aid" following trauma. To our knowledge the term was first referenced in the Australian literature by Raphael (1984) who noted that some psychological debriefing programs "usually involved the rapid mobilisation of skilled staff to interview and work with the victims to assist them with the psychological response to the disaster and its aftermath, frequently in direct outreach to the disaster sites and the victims' homes" (p. 303). More recently, in a meta-analytic review of psychological debriefing (PD), Rose, Wessely, and Bisson (2001) defined PD as "any brief psychological intervention that involves some reworking/reliving/recollection of the trauma and subsequent emotional

YES / Devilly and Cotton

reactions." However, for the sake of being comprehensive, yet not at the price of specificity, Devilly, Gist, and Cotton (2002) describe PD as:

> . . . the generic term for immediate interventions following trauma (usually within 3 days) that seek to relieve stress with the hopeful intent of mitigating or preventing long term pathology . . . [and that . . . PD relies predominantly on ventilation/catharsis, normalisation of distress, and psycho-education regarding presumed symptoms (p. 4).

This is to be contrasted with the proprietary based term critical incident stress debriefing (and, more recently, critical incident stress management). This is a specific variety of PD, frequently utilised with groups, and developed by Mitchell (1983) as a structured approach with seven aspects. These steps include:

1. the introductory phase (where the rules, process and goals are outlined)
2. the fact phase (serial clarification of what the participants saw, did, heard etc.)
3. the thoughts phase (what the participants' first thoughts were/are following the event)
4. the reaction phase (exploration of individuals emotional reactions)
5. the symptoms phase (global assessment of physical or psychological symptoms)
6. the teaching/information phase (educating the participants about possible, common, or even "likely" stress responses)
7. the re-entry phase (referral information provided for future follow-up).

More recently, and with evidence against the use of CISD becoming more and more convincing, Everly and Mitchell (1999) proposed that CISD had been superseded by Critical Incident Stress Management (CISM) and these authors have since offered two reviews of CISM (Everly, Flannery, & Mitchell, 2000; Everly, Flannery, & Eyler, 2002). But what is CISM and does it significantly and operationally differ from CISD?

A review of the CISM literature offered by Everly et al. (2000) described it as "a new generation of intervention technologies" (p. 23) and, in keeping with a 7-step formula, offered the following definition:

> CISM represents seven core integrated elements: (a) pre-crisis preparation (both individual and organisational); (b) large scale demobilisation procedures for use after mass disasters; (c) individual acute crisis counselling; (d) brief small group discussions, called defusings, designed to assist in acute symptom reduction; (e) longer small group discussions, called Critical Incident Stress Debriefing (CISD), designed to assist in achieving a sense of psychological closure post-crisis and /or facilitate the referral process; (f) family crisis intervention techniques; and (g) follow-up procedures, and/or referral for psychological assessment or treatment (p. 24).

It would seem, therefore, that by 2000 CISD had been somewhat redefined and incorporated into a larger and more encompassing approach, although it should be stressed that there is no empirical support for any of the newly proposed steps. However, of interest in the review is that in support of CISM, studies which used only CISD were cited. It, therefore, begs the question of whether CISD and CISM are distinguishable.

In fact, in supporting the use of CISM, one of the studies Everly et al. (2000) cite is an Australian report (Leeman-Conley, 1990). This study details a management-wide intervention for dealing with trauma following violent bank hold-ups in the Commonwealth Banking Corporation. However, the term CISM is never referred to in this study, the procedure appears to differ significantly from that outlined by Everly et al. (2000), and outcome was assessed by comparing compensation costs and absenteeism in the year following the introduction of the intervention to the previous year's costs (i.e., not a randomised trial and open to untold influence from many other organisational and non-specific changes that may have occurred, e.g., improved security, improved health plans, fewer hold-ups, change in seasonal illnesses, changes in absenteeism practices).

By 2002 Everly et al. describe CISM as "an integrated multicomponent crisis intervention system"(p. 171, Everly et al., 2002). It is unclear exactly how to interpret this, but the authors claim that CISD "was designed to be only one component of a comprehensive multicomponent crisis intervention program referred to as Critical Incident Stress Management" (p. 174) and then cite Everly and Mitchell (1999) in support of this. It is difficult to see how this can be the case since the term CISM did not even enter the debriefing lexicon until the mid-1990s and CISD was advocated as a method for mitigating the effects of trauma back in the early 1980s (Mitchell, 1983).

The review by Everly et al. (2002) of CISM also needs further analysis. Firstly, the authors claimed that "CISD was never designed to be implemented as a single intervention outside of the multicomponent CISM program" (p. 174) and provide a 1999 reference to support this. As alluded to above, there appears to be an element of historical revisionism characterising this account, which is further weakened through citing such recent references. Notwithstanding, there are three further factors which are of even greater concern.

First, no operational definition of the facets integral to CISM, and necessary or sufficient to qualify as CISM, were incorporated into the review. Rather, studies were included which were "purporting to specifically assess interventions consistent with the CISM formulation" (p. 177). Second, of the eight studies that met this criteria, six were studies by the directors of the International Critical Incident Stress Foundation (ICISF) who are also the originators of CISD/M. This is important because meta-analyses typically draw on a range of studies delivering conclusions that are less likely to be disproportionately weighted by methodological weaknesses and/or researcher allegiance. Out of the two studies by other authors, one (Busuttil et al., 1995) had incorporated PD within a group therapy program aimed at *treating* posttraumatic stress disorder (PTSD) and no explicit mention of CISM is made, and the other (Richards, 1999) was a presentation at an ICISF conference and, therefore, not easily accessible for review.

Third, the authors of this review included into the same analysis studies using different domains of outcome measurement. Some of the studies were termed "Assault Staff Action Programs" and the outcome measure was the number of times staff (psychiatric hospital staff or community care staff) were assaulted following the intervention compared to before the intervention. Other studies utilised diagnostic interviews/psychometric assessment of distress levels of workers with PTSD and traumatic reactions. As mentioned, some of the studies were aimed at treating *trauma reactions* (and sometimes many months following the trauma; Busuttil et al., 1995; Mitchell, Schiller, Eyler, & Everly, 1999) and others were aimed at mitigating further distress or number of assaults (Flannery, Hanson, Penk, Flannery, & Gallagher, 1995; Flannery et al., 1998; Flannery, Penk, & Corrigan, 1999; Flannery, Anderson, Marks, & Uzoma, 2000). Such a fundamental methodological flaw undermines the validity of any conclusions based on the meta-analysis of this group of studies.

For now, we can only conclude that CISD may or may not be one component of CISM, or CISD may be equivalent to CISM, and CISM may or may not have a definite procedure. Until the necessary and sufficient conditions for what counts as CISD and/or CISM are clarified CISM must be regarded as an unfalsifiable intervention system, and the two terms should for now be treated synonymously.

More broadly, it is important to differentiate debriefing from early intervention. Devilly (2002) suggested that early intervention "is the provision of what could be called 'restorative treatment' to individuals who *request* psychological help following crime/trauma and have a *clinically significant* presentation" (p. 4). The notion here is that whilst the individuals report pathological functioning (2 days to 4 weeks following the event), the goal of early intervention is to prevent long-term, psychological and functional impairment. Interventions at this level are goal orientated, explicit and evidence-based. Such an example would be interventions for Acute Stress Disorder (ASD). Untreated, about 80% of individuals with ASD go on to develop PTSD by 6 months, and 75% maintain this presentation up to 2 years later (Bryant & Harvey, 2000). However, cognitive-behavioural treatments (CBT) based upon exposure principles have demonstrated efficacy to the point where only 8% at post-treatment (17% at 6 months) meet the criteria for PTSD, which is contrasted to supportive counselling strategies which show that 83% at posttreatment (and 67% at 6 months) meet criteria for PTSD (Foa, Hearst-Ikeda, & Perry, 1995; Bryant, Harvey, Dang, Sackville, & Basten, 1998; Bryant, Sackville, Dang, Moulds, & Guthrie, 1999). Likewise, CBT treatment for PTSD has shown exceptional efficacy with between 80 to 90% of those treated no longer meeting criteria at post-treatment and maintaining this presentation to 3 months and even 12 months follow-up (e.g., Devilly & Spence, 1999; Foa et al., 1999; Foa, Rothbaum, Riggs, & Murdoch, 1991). Current research in this paradigm is now focussing on improving the attrition rates during treatment and factors associated with treatment tolerance (see Devilly & Foa, 2001, and Tarrier, 2001, for a discussion of measurement issues relating to this and Foa, Zoellner, Feeny, Hembree, & Alvarez-Conrad, 2002, for a discussion of predictors of attrition during exposure therapy).

It should be clear that the basis of the distinction between CISD and early intervention goals appears to be that while the former aims to mitigate short and long-term negative reactions through preventative intervention immediately following an event, the latter aims to actively treat pathology with the goal of restoring the individual to pre-trauma functioning.

Consensus: Mitigation of Long-Term Poor Functioning?

At the beginning of this article we outlined some arguments frequently posited by those promoting the use of PD. Perhaps the most important of these from a psychologist's perspective is the promise that psychological debriefing will help mitigate poor long-term functioning, which otherwise may occur, or even worse is "likely" to occur, and is a "foreseeable" consequence of the event.

Turning to the second half of this statement first, while it can be convincingly argued that there is the *possibility* of poor long-term functioning following a trauma, this is not equivalent to claiming that it is *likely and foreseeable*. In the Australian National Morbidity Study, Creamer, Burgess, and McFarlane (2001) found an estimated 12-month, PTSD prevalence rate of 1.3% in the community, with 64.6% of males and 49.5% of females having ever experienced at least one traumatic event. However, of those who had experienced any trauma, 1.9% of men and 2.9% of women met criteria for PTSD over the previous 12 months. Notwithstanding specific categories of trauma, such as rape, which evidences a *12-month* PTSD prevalence rate of 9.2% in women (Creamer et al., 2001), lifetime prevalence rates of PTSD for the whole community is estimated at 7.8% (10.4% for women, 5.0% for men; Kessler, Sonnega, Bromet, Hughes, & Nelson, 1995). Hence, in the light of this epidemiological evidence, it is specious to assert that PTSD is likely and foreseeable following exposure to a specific stressful event.

Further, PTSD is not the only, or even the most likely pathological outcome from experiencing traumatic events. Studies have demonstrated that a history of trauma is in itself a risk factor for depression (Zlotnick, Warshaw, Shea, & Keller, 1997) with one study (Lopez, Piffaut, & Seguin, 1992) reporting that 71% of raped women suffered from major depression whilst 37.5% developed chronic PTSD that lasted from 1 to 3 years. Given that proponents of CISD have claimed that it aims to mitigate long-term distress, one needs to also investigate whether it has demonstrated potency in domains other than PTSD.

As part of the Cochrane Collaboration, Rose et al. (2001) conducted a meta-analytic review of the psychological debriefing literature. Their inclusion criteria were that the studies utilised psychological debriefing (which employed normalisation and ventilation), was administered as a single session within one month of the trauma, and relied upon a randomised design. This elicited only eight studies in all, two of which had uninterpretable statistics (Bunn & Clarke, 1979; Bordrow & Porritt, 1979). Unfortunately, the randomisation requirement, though scientifically rigorous and laudable, also meant that no group-based interventions were included in the review. This is problematic because group-based debriefing is the usual method of delivery for this type of intervention. Nevertheless, of the six studies that were interpretable, all either found no benefit of PD or—and worryingly—that PD increased the likelihood of developing PTSD compared to no intervention. Rose et al. (2001) concluded that compulsory debriefings should cease immediately and that resources would be better utilised by focusing on those individuals who develop recognisable disorders.

The thrust of this sentiment is shared in a recent meta-analysis by van Emmerik et al. (2002). These authors likewise conducted a literature search to find studies which had used debriefing within 1 month following a trauma, and where symptoms were assessed pre- and post-debriefing using psychometrically acceptable assessment instruments. Seven studies met their criteria, five of which used CISD as one intervention, six used no-intervention control conditions, and three used conditions of other PD interventions (i.e., "30 minute counselling," "education," and "historical group debriefing"). The results suggested that while people have a disposition to improve over time when they received no intervention (on both measures of PTSD and other trauma related domains), if they received non-CISD based interventions this made no significant difference to the outcome. However, those who received CISD did not improve over time on either PTSD symptoms or on other symptom dimensions. In summary, these authors found that while some generic PD made no significant difference to long-term outcome, CISD would seem to *hinder* recovery.

These findings and conclusions contrast dramatically with the review of CISD/CISM by Everly et al. (2000) and a statistical meta-analysis by Everly and Boyle (1997). The meta-analytic review stated that it only included studies that explicitly used CISD and group debriefings. They concluded that CISD achieved a treatment effect size of Cohen's $d = 0.86$ (i.e., a large, positive effect). However, when one looks at the studies included it is interesting to note that not one of them was included in either of the reviews outlined above (Rose et al., 2001; van Emmerik et al., 2002). It should also be stressed that none of the studies used a randomised, controlled design and some of the studies were unavailable for inspection. Furthermore, of those that were available, Devilly et al. (2002) were unable to equate the reported effect size in Everly and Boyle (1997) with the original data presented in two of the available three articles. Additionally, if CISD was never designed to be used as a stand-alone intervention, but rather as one aspect of a "multicomponent CISM program" (Everly et al., 2002), then it is puzzling why a meta-analysis of CISD was performed and acts as the bedrock to base claims for CISD/M effectiveness.

For now, one can only conclude that there has never been a randomly controlled trial of group CISD/M and, therefore, its effectiveness has not been demonstrated. On the other hand, a consensus of randomised controlled trials suggests that individual debriefings using the CISD/M system are noxious, and that generic PD has little or no prophylactic effect.

One anomaly characterising PD, though, is the replicated finding that people typically report high satisfaction ratings following involvement in PD (e.g., Matthews, 1998; Robinson & Mitchell, 1993). However, it has been argued that while this is one outcome domain, it is not necessarily the best upon which to make decisions regarding treatment implementation (Devilly, 2002). Additionally, Hart and Cotton (2003) have suggested an alternative explanation in terms of the possible impact of PD not on employee distress levels but on employee positive affective responses. In other words, PD may be more of a "morale maintenance" intervention qua gesture of employer support, rather than a clinical intervention influencing distress and clinical symptomatology. This line of enquiry is promising and warrants further investigation.

Of further interest are the findings that those who are offered PD yet decline to be involved are the most likely to be unaffected by the event in the long-term (Matthews, 1998), and those who are most distressed by the event are the very same people who are most likely to be adversely affected by debriefing (Mayou, Ehlers, & Hobbs, 2000). Such results do not make good bed-fellows with enforced practice following employee exposure to a major stressor.

Protection from Litigation

As mentioned above, an argument is frequently made for PD that reminds organisations that they have obligations under workplace health and safety commitments to provide for their staff when traumatic incidents occur in the workplace. Putting aside possible issues related to 'terminology slippage' and the definition of what could count as a traumatic event—which has been and is still an issue of great debate (e.g., see Bryant, 1996, and Dobson & Marshall, 1998)—the basis of this claim needs to be scrutinised. Perhaps the most famous case in Australia is that of *Howell v the State Rail Authority of New South Wales* (1997; S6/1997). On 4th December 1992 a female suicided by jumping in front of a train, the result of which was that some 42 different body parts lay on the track and surrounding area. A rail worker (Mr Howell) was called from a nearby station to secure the scene while emergency service workers were called for and during this time he witnessed the horrendous outcome of the suicide. A psychologist, contracted by the rail authority to follow-up on their worker, telephoned Mr Howell at home later that night and asked whether he would like to speak about how the event had affected him. Mr Howell reported that he did not wish to do so and the psychologist arranged to follow-up again a few days later. On the second contact Mr Howell again refused help and the psychologist submitted a report and remit for payment to the rail authority. In a case which came to a close in 1997, Mr Howell sued the rail authority for breach of duty, having developed PTSD as a result of the incident. Mr Howell was first awarded $514,000 ($130,000 damages for non-economic loss, $115,000 for past economic loss, $200,000 for future economic loss, $15,000 for superannuation loss, $16,000 in past medical expenses, $18,000 for future medical costs, and $20,000 relating to topping-up received workers compensation). However, after various presentations and appeals, this sum was eventually increased to $750,000.

Naturally, such a hefty award has made many employers anxious to mitigate the effects of trauma that occur in the workplace. Indeed, a cursory search of

Australian websites quickly demonstrates how this case is currently being used as a reason why debriefing should always be advocated, particularly by the providers of Employee Assistance Programs. Furthermore, in answer to Bledsoe (2002) who warns of possible liability *for providing* debriefing, the ICISF recently used this decision as further evidence for the use of CISD (Robinson, 2002). However, this decision needs to be inspected more closely.

First, it was implicitly accepted by the trial judge that debriefing would have improved the status of Mr Howell and acted as a mitigating force in long-term pathology. In light of hindsight and the more recent evidence, as cited above, such a decision would now seem ill-advised. Secondly, the rail authority handbook stipulated that Critical Incident Stress Debriefing (note that CISD was used and not generic PD) be provided in such cases within 48 hours. The fact that this was not followed leant heavily on the decision that the authority had breached their duty and acted negligently. Naturally, such practices need to be amended in keeping with the first point above. Thirdly, the trial judge decided that the psychologist either knew or should have known that "by 12.30 p.m. on Saturday 5th December 1992 . . . that the plaintiff was showing signs of Post-traumatic Stress Disorder." This is indeed a bold claim and in direct contradiction to research evidence and our current method of classification. Acute Stress Disorder (outlined above), as a method of early detection for PTSD, is sensitive but not specific as it currently stands (Harvey & Bryant, 1998) and even then cannot be diagnosed until at least 2 days following the event. However, and of further interest to psychologists, was the judge's explicitly declared low opinion of the psychologist. The judge decided that this psychologist was negligent in not conducting a face-to-face interview with Mr Howell and had:

> . . . seriously suggested in an initial report to the Railways that he had, in fact, had interviews, which would infer that he had conducted face to face interviews with the plaintiff at least on 7 December and 9 December . . . and [therefore] that there had been a misreporting by the psychologist as to what he had done.

It is thought that such a disparaged view of a psychologist may have tempered the final decision and detracted from the substantive point of whether the debriefing would have actually helped or not.

In an appeal that challenged this implicit assumption of debriefing as effective, the awarded sum was actually further increased to $750,000. However, it appears that this was mainly because it was testified by a prominent psychiatrist that had ASD been diagnosed, then early intervention could have been instituted based upon CBT procedures, which would increase the likelihood of recovery. This is a different argument to looking at debriefing effectiveness and appropriateness. Furthermore, this argument appears to be utilising information that was not available to either the organisation or the psychological community in 1992.

In fact, in light of the available evidence it is, in our opinion, more likely that at some point in the future a company may be litigated against where they compel employees to attend CISD rather than omit to provide it. This opinion is being taken more seriously in the literature (e.g., Bledsoe, 2002; in press) and one can only sympathise with organisations who must feel that they are trapped between a rock and a very hard place. Irrespective of vulnerability to litigation, expert traumatic stress panels have warned against such well intentioned care and, for example, after the World Trade Centre Terrorist attack on 11th September 2001, a letter signed by 14 eminent psychologists from around the world appeared in the New York Times and the American Psychiatric Association's newsletter, *The Monitor,* (Herbert et al., 2001) warning of the dangers of "debriefers" flocking to the area. In fact, this practice of armies of debriefers descending upon war-torn or devastated parts of the world has received the moniker, somewhat cynically, of "Trauma Tourism" (Gist & Lubin, 1999).

A Healthy Workforce Is a Productive Workforce

A review of the organisational behaviour and work psychology literature suggests that limited progress has been made in linking workplace-oriented clinical interventions to organisational performance outcomes (Hart & Cooper, 2001; Wright & Cropanzano, 2000). However, there are indications that increasing employee positive affective responses contributes towards increasing discretionary performance (Borman & Motowildo, 1993), as well as reducing absenteeism (George, 1989, 1996) and workers compensation costs (Hart & Cotton, 2003).

Accordingly, a healthy workforce may well be a more productive workforce, but the most reliable method of avoiding a sick workforce after a traumatic event is still open to debate. Nevertheless, given our current state of knowledge, it is possible to delineate some general guidelines to be used in organisational practice.

General Guidelines

Below we have outlined a very brief summary of suggested intervention principles:

Organisational policy.   An organisation's critical incident management policy should be regularly updated and be consistent with developments in the research literature. To facilitate this an organisation might contract a recognised expert in this field to review their policy documentation.

Facilitate access to immediate practical and social support.   It is not possible to specify all the kinds of practical support that are viable in all situations. For example, following mass trauma events, such as bushfires and floods, governments provide facilities such as access to information, places of safety, bedding, food and sanitation. Organisations after events, such as a workplace fatality, may provide such facilities as help with funeral arrangements, transport for work colleagues, and general changes in workplace conditions that may facilitate a sense that the employer cares about their plight. This may include making available a "veteran" in their area of work who has a wealth of experience and is willing to talk to those who witnessed the event or are concerned regarding how to cope. This use of a respected veteran that workers know and trust is discussed in greater detail by Bledsoe (in press) and Devilly et al. (2002). Contact from the exposed individuals' immediate manager to express concern and support is also helpful, as is the availability of contact with peers. The type of social support referred to here is the (non-clinical) everyday expression of care and listening to the individual's concerns.

Offer access to employee assistance services for those who request it.   In Australia organisations have a non-delegable duty of care in relation to workplace health. Providing access to appropriately qualified mental health service providers, for *face-to-face* emotional support and follow-up, also provides an important gesture of employer support. Additionally, accessing employee assistance programs provides an opportunity to screen for individuals who may go on to develop post-trauma reactions. The provision of "comfort" *may* also appease general and non-diagnosable distress. However, at this point it should not be regarded as a clinical intervention, but more as a socially supportive intervention and an opportunity to screen for individuals who may require more substantive support and treatment.

Provide factual information and normalise reactions (not "symptoms"). Without doubt, most frequently the first need of victims of crime or surviving members of a trauma (or related family and friends) is the need for information. This information can include the need to know who has been hurt, how far investigative processes have progressed, which documentation should be completed and when, and how to access facilities. At a national level this need is frequently met by the use of a well-informed telephone help-line, and at an organisational level this can be accomplished by regular, frequent and official meetings with all those involved.

Some authors recommend educating the client at various points about reactions to stressors (e.g., Litz, Gray, Bryant, & Adler, 2002) and others suggest that psycho-education regarding possible reactions should be done as a matter of course (e.g., Mitchell, 1983). However, we have argued elsewhere (Devilly et al., 2002) that this may in fact be counterproductive and may actually prime participating individuals to develop the very problems we wish them to avoid. However, educating people about *possible* reactions is very different to normalising problems that they report to be *already* experiencing. The latter is the more appropriate focus in post-incident follow-up. In the past, however, such intervention has been mandatory and did not take into account individual coping styles and reflect the wishes of the individuals involved. We suggest that this form of intervention can be conducted in either a group meeting or on an individual basis. The point, however, is that the delivery not be compulsory.

Terminology slippage.   Frequently the types of "critical events" that psychologists are brought in to provide services for are not of a "traumatic" nature.

"Debriefing" following, for example, workplace bullying or in reaction to a member of a team being dismissed, has become increasingly frequent and the terminology used during these interventions are often inappropriate. It is our view that the available evidence suggests that in these cases the responsible course is to recommend referral to a specialist in organisational psychology and, frequently, an expert in organisational change or mediation.

Promote proactive problem-solving.   Proactivity increases a sense of mastery over situations and increases a sense of self-efficacy. It is suggested that employees be encouraged to devise coping strategies that make sense to their specific situation. No specific coping strategies should be mandated (apart from discouraging counter-productive coping strategies such as increased alcohol consumption).

Monitor staff to identify at-risk individuals.   Following the provision of "comfort" and the facilitation of immediate needs being met, a follow-up for individuals of between 4 days and 2 weeks subsequent to the incident would offer the appropriate window of opportunity to screen for symptoms of depression, excessive arousal, avoidance behaviours, intrusive phenomena and dissociation.

Monitoring can be conducted collaboratively between employee assistance providers, managers and Human Resource professionals. The psychologist or EAP provider can consult with workplace personnel, to support them in identifying possible at-risk individuals, who can then be specifically followed up.

Provide access to early intervention for individuals who report enduring distress.   Access to early intervention psychological treatment has been shown to mitigate long-term pathology. More specifically, these interventions are specific and structured, and rely on cognitive-behavioural strategies, and predominantly on exposure treatment. These interventions should not be confounded with more generic supportive counselling which has no demonstrated impact on the course of post-traumatic incident recovery. Moreover, the effective delivery of these interventions requires specialised clinical training. Given the wide range of training and skill levels characterising employee assistance professionals, it is important for an organisation to ensure that any contracted Employee Assistance Providers possess the relevant specialist skills in this area. We note that in our own profession, a wide range of interventions are currently advocated, and not all of these are evidenced-based. Reliance on anecdotal reports or personal commitment to support the application of an intervention is inappropriate. Given that we know that early intervention cognitive-behavioural based interventions have demonstrated effectiveness, we suggest that we are now entering a time where serious ethical concerns may arise in circumstances where exposed individuals are initially offered other types of interventions.

Ensure appropriate organisational liaison and feedback occurs.   This may also require that the psychologist feedback to the organisation ideas, concepts and remedies suggested by the employees. However, caution should be taken during this process to ensure that the psychologist does not actively collude with any dissatisfaction with the organisation that may be expressed by the workers, but rather acts as a facilitative conduit between the organisational floor and management. It is important that service providers avoid confounding post incident distress with any pre-existing industrial discontent. In effect, the service provider should carefully balance "dual-client" considerations and not become an advocate for the individual, and should carefully differentiate incident related concerns from other industrial preoccupations.

The above guidelines should not be seen as prescriptive but rather suggestive of approaches that may act as a template to be adapted to the specific needs of the organisation and event.

Conclusion

What we hope to have highlighted in this paper is that claims of CISD/M being able to mitigate long-term pathology are not proven and this intervention system may, in fact, result in paradoxical outcomes. Specifically, this appears to be the case for individual CISD. To our knowledge there are currently no randomised group debriefing studies in existence and hence the efficacy of such approaches is unproven. We also conclude that CISD and CISM, as terms currently used in the research literature, have not been sufficiently differentiated to be used independently. Further, it is our opinion that research and practice in this area of psychological debriefing (or "psychological first-aid"), if not in its embryonic stage, has yet to reach adolescence.

References

Bledsoe, B.E. (2002). CISM: Possible liability for EMS services? *Journal Best Practices in Emergency Services, 5,* 66–67.

Bledsoe, B.E. (in press). Critical incident stress management (CISM): Benefit or risk for emergency services? Prehospital Emergency Care.

Bordrow S., & Porritt D. (1979). An experimental evaluation of crisis intervention. *Social Science and Medicine, 13,* 251–256.

Borman, W.C., & Motowildo, S.J. (1993). Expanding the criterion domain to include elements of contextual performance. In N. Schmitt & W.C. Borman and Associates (Eds.), *Personnel selection in organisations* (pp. 25–38). San Fransisco: Jossey-Bass.

Bryant, R.A. (1996). Atomic testing and post-traumatic stress disorder: Legally defining a stressor. *Australian Psychologist, 31,* 34–37.

Bryant, R.A., & Harvey, A.G. (2000). *Acute stress disorder.* Washington DC: American Psychological Association.

Bryant, R.A., Harvey, A.G., Dang, S.T., Sackville, T., & Basten, C. (1998). Treatment of acute stress disorder: A comparison of cognitive-behavioral therapy and supportive counseling. *Journal of Consulting and Clinical Psychology, 66,* 862–866.

Bryant, R.A., Sackville, T., Dang, S.T., Moulds, M., & Guthrie, R. (1999). Treating acute stress disorder: An evaluation of cognitive behavior therapy and supportive counseling techniques. *American Journal of Psychiatry, 156,* 1780–1786.

Bunn B., & Clarke A. (1979). Crisis intervention: An experimental study of the effects of a brief period of counselling on the anxiety of relatives of seriously injured or ill hospital patients. *British Journal of Medical Psychology, 52,* 191–195.

Busuttil, W., Turnbull, G., Neal, L., Rollins, J., West, A., Blanch, N., et al. (1995). Incorporating psychological debriefing techniques with a brief group therapy program for the treatment of posttraumatic stress disorder. *British Journal of Psychiatry, 167,* 495–502.

Creamer, M., Burgess, P., & McFarlane, A.C. (2001). Post traumatic stress disorder: Findings from the Australian National Survey of Mental Health and Well-being. *Psychological Medicine, 31,* 1237–1247.

Devilly, G.J. (2002). Clinical intervention, supportive counselling and therapeutic methods: A clarification and direction for restorative treatment. *International Review of Victimology, 9,* 1–14.

Devilly, G.J., & Foa, E.B. (2001). Commentary. The investigation of exposure and cognitive therapy: Comment on Tarrier et al. (1999). *Journal of Consulting and Clinical Psychology, 69,* 114–116.

Devilly, G.J., Gist, R., & Cotton, P. (2002). *Psychological debriefing and outcome.* Manuscript submitted for publication.

Devilly, G.J., & Spence, S.H. (1999). The relative efficacy and treatment distress of EMDR and a cognitive behavior Trauma Treatment Protocol in the amelioration of posttraumatic stress disorder. *Journal of Anxiety Disorders, 13,* 131–157.

Dobson, M., & Marshall, R.P. (1998). The stressor criterion and diagnosing posttraumatic stress disorder in a legal context. *Australian Psychologist, 31,* 219–223.

Everly, G.S., & Boyle, S. (1997). *A meta-analysis of the Critical Incident Stress Debriefing (CISD).* Paper presented at the fourth world congress on stress, trauma and coping in the emergency services professions, Baltimore.

Everly, G.S., Flannery, R.B., & Eyler, V.A. (2002). Critical Incident Stress Management (CISM): A statistical review of the literature. *Psychiatric Quarterly, 73,* 171–182.

Everly, G.S., Flannery, R.B., & Mitchell, J.T. (2000). Critical incident stress management (CISM): A review of the literature. *Aggression and Violent Behavior, 5,* 23–40.

Everly, G.S., & Mitchell, J.T. (1999). *Critical Incident Stress Management: A new era and standard of care in crisis intervention* (2nd ed.). Ellicott City, MD: Chevron.

Flannery, R.B., Anderson, E., Marks, L., & Uzoma, L. (2000). The Assault Staff Action Program and declines in rates of assault: Mixed replicated findings. *Psychiatric Quarterly, 71,* 165–175.

Flannery, R.B., Hanson, M.A., Penk, W., Flannery, G.J., & Gallagher, C. (1995). The Assaulted Staff Action Program: An approach to coping in the aftermath of violence in the workplace. In L. Murphy, R. Hurrell, S. Sauter, & G. Keita, (Eds.), *Job stress intervention.* Washington, DC: American Psychiatric Association.

Flannery, R.B., Hanson, M.A., Penk, W., Goldfinger, S., Pastva, G., & Navon, M. (1998). Replicated declines in assault rates after the implementation of the ASAP. *Psychiatric Services, 49,* 241–243.

Flannery, R.B., Penk, W., & Corrigan, M. (1999). Assault Staff Action Program (ASAP) and declines in the prevalence of assaults: Community-based replication. *International Journal of Emergency Mental Health, 1,* 19–22.

Foa, E.B., Dancu, C.V., Hembree, E., Jaycox, L.H., Meadows, E.A., & Street, G.P. (1999). The efficacy of exposure therapy, stress inoculation training and their combination in ameliorating PTSD for female victims of assault. *Journal of Consulting and Clinical Psychology, 67,* 194–200.

Foa, E.B., Hearst-Ikeda, D., & Perry, K.J. (1995). Evaluation of a brief cognitive-behavioral program for the prevention of chronic PTSD in recent assault victims. *Journal of Consulting and Clinical Psychology, 63,* 948–955.

Foa, E.B., Rothbaum, B.O., Riggs, D.S., & Murdoch, T.B. (1991). Treatment of post-traumatic stress disorder in rape victims: A comparison between cognitive-behavioral procedures and counseling. *Journal of Consulting and Clinical Psychology, 59,* 715–723.

Foa, E.B., Zoellner, L.A., Feeny, N.C., Hembree, E.A., & Alvarez-Conrad, J. (2002). Does imaginal exposure exacerbate PTSD symptoms? *Journal of Consulting and Clinical Psychology, 70,* 1022–1028.

George, J.M. (1989). Mood and absence. *Journal of Applied Psychology, 74,* 317–324.

George, J.M. (1996). Trait and state affect. In K.R. Murphy (Ed.), *Individual differences and behaviour in organisations* (pp. 145–171). San Francisco: Jossey-Bass.

Gist, R., & Devilly, G.J. (2002). Post-trauma debriefing: The road too frequently travelled. *The Lancet, 360,* 741–742.

Gist, R., & Lubin, B., (1999). *Response to disaster: Psychosocial, community, and ecological approaches.* Philadelphia: Bruner/Mazel.

Hart, P.M., & Cooper, C.L. (2001). Occupational Stress: Toward a more integrated framework. In N. Anderson, D.S. Ones, H.K. Sinangril, & C. Viswesvaran (Eds.), *Handbook of industrial, work and organisational psychology* (Vol. 2, pp. 93–114). Sage: London.

Hart P.M., & Cotton, P. (2003). Conventional wisdom is often misleading: Police stress within an organisational health framework. In M.F. Dollard, A.H. Winefield & H.R. Winefield (Eds.), *Occupational stress in the service professions* (pp. 103–140). London: Taylor & Francis.

Harvey, A.G., & Bryant, R.A. (1998). The relationship between acute stress disorder and posttraumatic stress disorder: A prospective evaluation of motor vehicle accident survivors. *Journal of Consulting and Clinical Psychology, 66,* 507–512.

Herbert, J.D., Lilienfeld, S.O., Kline, J., Montgomery, R., Lohr, J., Brandsma, L., et al. (2001). First do no harm: Treatment concerns in the aftermath of terrorist attacks [letter to the editor]. *Monitor On Psychology, 32* (p. 10).

Kadet, A. (2002). Good grief! *Smart Money, 11,* 108–14.

Kessler, R.C., Sonnega, A., Bromet, E., Hughes, M., & Nelson, C.B. (1995). Posttraumatic stress disorder in the national comorbidity survey. *Archives of General Psychiatry, 52,* 1048–1060.

Leeman-Conley, M. (1990). After a violent robbery . . . *Criminology Australia, April/May,* 4–6.

Litz B.T., Gray M.J., Bryant R.A., & Adler A.B. (2002). Early intervention for trauma: Current status and future directions. *Clinical Psychology: Science and Practice, 9,* 112–134.

Lopez, G., Piffaut, G., & Seguin, A. (1992). Psychological treatment of victims of rape. *Psychologie Medicale, 24,* 286–288.

Matthews, L.R. (1998). Effect of staff debriefing on posttraumatic symptoms after assaults by community housing residents. *Psychiatric Services, 49,* 207–212.

Mayou, R.A., Ehlers, A., & Hobbs, M. (2000). Psychological debriefing for road traffic accident victims: Three-year follow-up of a randomized controlled trial. *British Journal of Psychiatry, 176,* 589–593.

Mitchell, J.T. (1983). When disaster strikes . . . The critical incident stress debriefing process. *Journal of Emergency Services, 8,* 36–39.

Mitchell, J.T., Schiller, G., Eyler, V., & Everly, G. (1999). Community crisis intervention: The Coldenham tragedy revisited. *International Journal of Emergency Mental Health, 1,* 227–236.

Raphael, B. (1984). Psychiatric consultancy in major disaster. *Australian and New Zealand Journal of Psychiatry, 18,* 303–306.

Richards, D. (1999, April.). *A field study of CISD v. CISM.* Paper presented at the Fifth World Congress on Stress Trauma and Coping in the Emergency Services Professions, Baltimore.

Robinson, R. (2002). Points to ponder. *Newsletter of The Critical Incident Stress Management Foundation Australia, 4*(2).

Robinson, R., & Mitchell, J.T. (1993). Evaluation of psychological debriefings. *Journal of Traumatic Stress, 6,* 367–382.

Rose, S., Wessely, S., & Bisson, J. (2001). Brief psychological interventions ("debriefing") for trauma-related symptoms and prevention of post traumatic stress disorder: Review. *The Cochrane Library, Issue 2.*

Tarrier, N. (2001). What can be learned from clinical trials? Reply to Devilly and Foa. *Journal of Consulting and Clinical Psychology, 69,* 117–118.

van Emmerik, A.A.P., Kamphuis, J.H., Hulsbosch, A.M., & Emmelkamp, P.M.G. (2002). Single session debriefing after psychological trauma: A meta-analysis. *The Lancet, 360,* 766–771.

Wright, T.A., & Cropanzano, R. (2000). Psychological well-being and job satisfaction as predictors of job performance. *Journal of Occupational Health Psychology, 5,* 84–94.

Zlotnick, C., Warshaw, M., Shea, M.T., & Keller, M.B., (1997). Trauma and chronic depression among patients with anxiety disorders. *Journal of Consulting and Clinical Psychology, 65,* 333–336.

J. T. Mitchell

➡ **NO**

A Response to the Devilly and Cotton Article, "Psychological Debriefing and the Workplace . . ."

"Psychological Debriefing and the Workplace: Defining a Concept, Controversies and Guidelines for Intervention" appeared in *Australian Psychologist, 38*(2), 144–150. The article is replete with inaccuracies, misinterpretations and distortions. Furthermore, it gives the impression that both peer and editorial review processes were inadequate.

The most prominent of the many glaring errors in the article is the treatment of a specific, structured, 7-step, small group crisis intervention process called the Critical Incident Stress Debriefing (CISD) as if it were one and the same as a comprehensive, systematic and multi-component program called Critical Incident Stress Management (CISM).

The CISM program includes many tactics and techniques, but it is not limited to:

- crisis assessment services and strategic planning programs
- family support services
- individual, peer-provided crisis intervention services
- pre-crisis education programs
- large group crisis interventions
- the provision of food and fluids to work crews
- rotation and resting of work crews
- advice to command staff and supervisors
- small group crisis interventions
- follow up services and referral services
- post-crisis education
- and many other services.

The authors demonstrate a drastic lack of familiarity with the literature in the field of CISM. There is a substantial body of CISM literature not referred to by the authors. Even a cursory reading of these many publications would certainly have clarified the definitions in the CISM field and most likely would have eliminated the need for this confusing and inaccurate article.

The conclusion that a specific, 7-step group crisis intervention tool is equivalent to an entire multifaceted program defies logic and reason. Likewise, equating a broad spectrum of different crisis intervention tools and psychological counselling techniques, as if they were one and the same, is not only imprecise, it is clinically and academically illegitimate.

Crisis intervention is a support service, not psychotherapy or a substitute for psychotherapy. It is an opportunity for assessment to see if people need additional services including referrals for therapy such as cognitive-behavioral therapy. Comparing supportive "psychological first aid" with psychotherapy is a misguided endeavour which creates further confusion. Therapy does not substitute for crisis intervention. Likewise, crisis intervention does not substitute for psychotherapy.

On page 145 there is a colossal misrepresentation of the facts. Devilly and Cotton say, "More recently, and with evidence against the use of CISD becoming more and more convincing, Everly and Mitchell (1999) proposed that CISD has been superceded by Critical Incident Stress Management (CISM)." The statement is very far from the truth.

In 1983 I wrote the first article ever written on Critical Incident Stress Debriefing ("When Disaster Strikes . . . The Critical Incident Stress Debriefing Process," *Journal of Emergency Medical Services, 13*(11), 36–39). I stated then, "There are many methods to deal with a stress response syndrome" (p. 37). The following items were listed as part of a comprehensive systematic and multi-component program:

- ". . . strenuous physical exercise . . .
- . . . special relaxation programs . . .
- . . . individual or group meetings . . .
- . . . assessment by the facilitator of the intensity of the stress response in the workers . . .
- . . . support and reassurance from the facilitator. . .
- . . . information is provided . . .
- . . . a plan of further action may be designed . . .
- . . . referrals, if necessary, are made . . .
- The initial defusing . . .
- The *Formal CISD* . . .
- . . . *Follow-up.* . . ." (pp. 37–38)

Keep in mind that in the "When Disaster Strikes . . ." article the concepts were new, the thought processes were new and the wording may not have been perfect. A core of systematic interventions was present, however, and the specific CISD group process (then known at the "formal CISD") was not thought of as a stand alone intervention.

As in any field of human endeavour, imperfect initial efforts go through refinements and elaborations over time. More clearly defined systems and specific procedures emerge. This dynamic growth certainly occurred in the CISM field.

Shortly after the first article was published, it was recognised that "CISD" was being used as an umbrella term to cover the entire field as well as a label for a specific group crisis intervention process. The dual use of the term "CISD" was confusing. The error was corrected in numerous publications subsequent to the 1983 article. For example, the first issue of *Life Net,* the official publication of the International Critical Incident Stress Foundation, referred to "Critical Incident Stress Management Teams" (1990, pp. 1–2). In the same issue, the use of the term "Critical Incident Stress Management (CISM) teams was encouraged in an article entitled "CISM vs. CISD" (p. 5). Subsequent issues of *Life Net* contained articles that suggested a clarification and proper utilisation of the terms Critical Incident Stress Management (CISM) for the field and Critical Incident Stress Debriefing (CISD), previously known as the "formal CISD," for the specific group process. In 1998 the following quote appeared on the International Critical Incident Stress Foundation's website and in several of its training workbooks:

> Admittedly, some of the confusion surrounding this point was engendered by virtue of the fact that in the earlier expositions, the term CISD was used to denote the generic and overarching umbrella program/system, while the term "formal CISD" was used to denote the specific 7-phase group discussion process. The term CISM was later used to replace the generic CISD and serve as the overarching umbrella program/system . . . (Everly & Mitchell, 1997)

Again in 2001 the correction was made:

> Originally, Mitchell (1983) used the term Critical Incident Stress Debriefing, or CISD, as an overarching label to refer to a strategic multi-componential approach to crisis intervention . . . As can be imagined, the author's use of the term CISD to denote both the entire strategic approach to crisis intervention and the "formal" 6-phase small group discussion process that was part of it, led to significant confusion, which persists even today. In a direct effort to undo the confusion created by the dual usage of the term CISD and, more importantly, by the inferred, but erroneous, tacit endorsement of CISD (the small group discussion) as a stand-alone crisis intervention, the use of the term Critical Incident Stress Debriefing as the label for the cumulative strategic crisis intervention system was abandoned in favor of the term Critical Incident Stress Management. (Everly, Flannery, Eyler, & Mitchell, 2001)

Let me be perfectly clear, the change in terminology described in the paragraphs above had nothing to do with Devilly and Cotton's suggestion that "mounting evidence" against the use of CISD caused the change. In fact, we still have unequivocal confidence in the group CISD process when it is properly applied according to acceptable standards of practice and by people who have been properly trained in applying the model. Their perception of the reason for the change is, therefore, grossly mistaken.

On page 147 of their article, the authors make reference to an Australian legal case (*Howell v. the State Rail Authority of New South Wales, 1997*) and then state ". . . the ICISF recently used this decision as further evidence for the use of CISD." *This is a blatant misrepresentation of the facts.* ICISF *did not* and *would not* use such a case to support the utilisation of the group crisis inter-vention process known as CISD. First of all, ICISF is not a source of legal guid-ance. Second, ICISF is not knowledgeable about the case and would not choose to use it in recommending any kind of service. Third, the case was about an individual and ICISF would never recommend that a CISD be provided to an individual because the CISD is a group process. In any case, my personal opinion on the little I know of that particular legal case is that the CISD would, by commonly accepted standards of practice, have been the wrong intervention to apply.

It is troubling to see a disregard for studies that evaluate CISM and present positive results just because those studies do not refer to the "brand name" of CISM. Such is the case when the authors discuss Dr Raymond Flannery's studies. The authors say that his work is not about CISM because he calls his program the "Assaulted Staff Action Program (ASAP)." One does not have to look very far to see the misinformation that those authors are dis-tributing. On the back cover of Dr Flannery's 1998 book, *The Assaulted Staff Action Program: Coping with the Psychological Aftermath of Violence,* he states "ASAP is a Critical Incident Stress Management approach that includes indi-vidual crisis counseling, group debriefings, an employee victims' support group, employee victim family outreach, and professional referrals, when needed." On page 37 of his book, Flannery states:

> It was clear to me that no one intervention, no matter how effective in its own right, could address the differing needs of the employee victims in this facility. These differing situations suggested the need for a CISM approach (Everly & Mitchell, 1997), and led to my developing the *Assaulted Staff Action Program* (ASAP). (Flannery, 1998, p. 37)

Flannery defines his *Assaulted Staff Action Program* as ". . . a voluntary, system-wide, peer help, CISM crisis intervention program for employee victims of patient assault" (1999, pp. 103–108).

Furthermore, Devilly and Cotton say that Dr Flannery used the wrong dependent variable and that he only reports on violence reduction which is not a goal of CISM. They simply skip the other findings that Dr Flannery reports. Those findings demonstrate the effectiveness of his ASAP program which he clearly states is a CISM program. Take a look at what Dr Flannery actually says:

> ASAP, the most widely researched program of its kind in the world, is associ-ated with providing needed support to employee victims and with sharp reductions in the frequency of violence in many of the facilities, where it is fielded. ASAP programs pay for themselves by means of sustained produc-tivity, less medical and legal expense and reduced human suffering.

Again, this quote is on the back cover of his ASAP book. A reading of his actual articles will reveal greater details on the findings this eminent Harvard researcher and clinician has discovered which clearly demonstrate that CISM, even if called by another name, is a successful crisis intervention program.

The point about misinterpretation of Flannery's work has been made. However, I have found no less than eight other articles in peer reviewed journals in which he carefully defines CISM and then directly links CISM and his ASAP program (Flannery, 2001). Again Devilly and Cotton have demonstrated a significant lack of familiarity with the literature in the CISM field.

The authors cannot legitimately state that "CISD is possibly noxious" as they do in the first paragraph of their article (p. 144). The studies they use to support this comment never actually evaluated CISD processes that were provided by properly trained personnel who adhered to acceptable standards of care. In fact, there has never been a negative outcome study of the actual CISD when properly trained personnel adhered to the commonly accepted standards of practice that are used by 700 CISM teams in 28 countries around the world.

The majority of criticisms against debriefing have been levelled at a process called "single session debriefing" which *in no way resembles* the specific group crisis intervention process of CISD. This is so even in light of the fact that some of studies evaluating the single session debriefing erroneously use the term "CISD." The studies were not measuring the same things. Yet the authors glibly intermingle the terms throughout the article as if they were one and the same. ICISF has never recommended the single session debriefings. They are considered a clear violation of the standards of CISM practice. It should be noted that no other organisation which provides crisis services has ever recommended the "single session debriefings." That includes the International Red Cross, the American Red Cross, the National Organisation of Victim Assistance, the American Academy of Experts in Traumatic Stress, the Salvation Army or the Association of Traumatic Stress Specialists. When primary victims are receiving truncated, poorly designed and badly executed services that call themselves "debriefings," "psychological debriefings," or "CISD," but do not follow the standards of care in the CISM field, it is of no surprise that they would generate negative outcomes. But the authors cannot, with legitimacy, say that those studies are evaluating the same things as a study on the specific group crisis process of CISD.

As a point of fact, the negative outcome studies represent a hodgepodge of different types of interventions which do not equate to the actual CISD but which loosely use the terminology "CISD." Each of those studies is seriously flawed. Such a prejudicial statement about CISD being possibly noxious so early on in an article without substantiating evidence implies an author bias. It is suggested that the readers of this response review the "Crisis Intervention and CISM Research Summary" which appears on the International Critical Incident Stress Foundation website. . . . That article outlines both sides of the controversy and counteracts the unsubstantiated comments of the authors of the article under discussion here.

On page 144 Devilly and Cotton state that psychological debriefing is "first resort when disasters strike." The only people who would resort first to debriefing after a disaster are those who are untrained and apparently unaware that many other things need to be done before a debriefing is provided. Debriefings are not recommended for several weeks or longer after a disaster. The reader should be aware that disaster response is only a tiny percentage of the activity of a CISM team. Most of the Devilly and Cotton argument against CISM seems to be focused on disaster response. At least that is the most sensational (and erroneous) material they bring out in their article.

In proportion to stress management education, individual peer support, family support, defusings, referrals, planning, protocol development, consultation with administration and supervisor staff, and responses to daily small scale emergencies, the number of times that CISM services are used at a disaster is rather small.

Likewise, the number of small group, 7-phase CISD processes actually utilised by any CISM team is minute. The proportion of one-on-one peer support services to CISDs is about 1000 to 1. We have witnessed among the many CISM teams a decline in the number of CISDs when stress education, defusing services and one-on-one crisis intervention services are pursued by CISM teams. Much of that work is provided by trained para-professionals called "peer support personnel."

I would question whether administrations of emergency services organisations are willing to substitute expensive therapy programs run exclusively by mental health professionals when trained peer support personnel have been very successful running these programs for nearly 30 years. My personal experience and that of the nearly 7000 members of the International Critical Incident Stress Foundation which includes over 2500 mental health professionals, is that peer support personnel are absolutely vital to the success of a CISM program and mental health professionals are usually kept at an arm's length from the operations personnel even when they are known and trusted people who have provided valuable services in the past.

The following items are of further concern within the Devilly and Cotton article:

- Paragraph number 2 on page 144 is sensational but not backed up by the actual numbers. The term "multimillion dollar industry" is very questionable. ICISF coordinates over 700 CISM teams and they almost all offer their services free of charge and largely on a "by request" basis. The average call out for a team is less than once a month. No fees are charged for services provided to emergency services personnel. So where is the "multimillion dollar industry?"
- Reports about the World Trade Center that thousands of "'debriefers' attended the area, advocating and offering debriefing services" (p. 144) are greatly exaggerated. First, who were they? Did they come in under some official body designated to provide disaster support services or by themselves? If they came in by themselves, then why would Devilly and Cotton attempt to lay the blame for this abnormal and inappropriate response in the CISM camp? Second, what did they offer? Third what is the definition of a "debriefing?" It seems that many unauthorised people may have offered a plethora of good and bad services. But these people were not functioning under auspices of a CISM team or any official disaster response organisation such as the Red Cross and the field of CISM should not be blamed for their poor behavior.

- At *the request* of the New York Police Department, ICISF coordinated a response of 1500 CISM trained police officers, police psychologists and police chaplains. It took over *a year and a half* to cycle these people through New York. They went in 7 to 12 at a time, depending on specific local needs and they stayed for a 7-day commitment. Critical Incident Stress Debriefings (specific, 7-stage, group process provided by a trained team of personnel and following well publicised standards of practice) were rarely held. They were only provided when homogeneous groups with roughly equal exposure to specific traumatic events were finished with their long term disaster assignments. For some that was months after the event. The greatest emphasis in New York was on individual crisis intervention support. Does this organised, appropriate, free of charge, and requested level of support need to be painted with the same brush that Devilly and Cotton use to condemn the thousands who descended like an army of "trauma tourists" on New York City? Professional articles should, in my opinion, stick to verifiable facts and not degenerate into name calling and fantastic, but unsubstantiated rhetoric.
- On page 145 the authors state that two of the authors of some of the studies in one of the meta-analyses are "directors" of the International Critical Incident Stress Foundation. *That is not the truth.* Dr. Everly and I are not the directors of ICISF. Please, let's everyone stick to the facts. The innuendo, of course, is that the authors of the meta-analyses cannot be trusted because they developed the program. It disregards their professional credentials and status and their actual qualifications to evaluate material with which they are most familiar. That is a rather bizarre position to hold and it smacks of an ad hominem argument.
- Toward the end of the article they describe a program that offers many of the same types of services that a CISM program offers. I must ask "Why is their program any more acceptable than a program that has been functioning well for nearly 30 years?" It appears inappropriate to criticise one program only to offer a similar program with the exception that theirs is based in psychotherapy and mental health professional control instead of crisis intervention with peer support personnel in control. If the Devilly and Cotton are recommending a therapy program, such as cognitive-behavioral therapy, that is just fine. It would appear to me that they would make better progress by extolling the benefits of their program without trying to diminish the value of another program. Should their program not stand on its own without attacking another?

Scientific articles should serve to clear up confusion and misunderstandings. The Devilly and Cotton article, unfortunately, only adds to the cacophony of misinformation about crisis intervention and the field of Critical Incident Stress Management.

References

Devilly, G.D., & Cotton, P. (2003). Psychological debriefing and the workplace: Defining a concept, controversies and guidelines for intervention. Australian *Psychologist, 38,* 144–150.

Everly, G.S., Jr. & Mitchell, J.T. (1997). *Critical incident stress management: Assisting Individuals in crisis: A workbook.* Ellicott City, MD: International Critical Incident Stress Foundation.

Everly, G.S., Jr., & Mitchell, J.T. (1999). *Critical incident stress Management: A new era and standard of care in crisis intervention.* Ellicott City, MD: Chevron Publishing Corp.

Everly, G.S. Jr., Flannery, R.B., Eyler, V., Mitchell, J.T. (2001). Sufficiency analysis of an integrated multicomponent approach to crisis intervention: Critical incident stress management. *Advances in Mind-Body Medicine, 17*(3), 174–183.

Flannery, R.B. (1998). *The Assaulted Staff Action Program: Coping with the psychological aftermath of violence.* Ellicott City, MD: Chevron Publishing.

Flannery, R.B. (1999). Critical incident stress management and the Assaulted Staff Action Program. *International Journal of Emergency Mental Health, 2,* 103–108.

Flannery, R.B. Jr. (2001). Assaulted Staff Action Program (ASAP): Ten years of empirical support for Critical Incident Stress Management (CISM). *International Journal of Emergency Mental Health, 3*(1), 5–10.

Mitchell, J.T. (1990). Critical incident stress management teams. *Life Net* (the official publication of the International Critical Incident Stress Foundation), *1*(1), 1–2.

Mitchell, J.T. (1983). When disaster strikes . . . The critical incident stress debriefing process. *Journal of Emergency Medical Services, 13*(11), 36–39.

Mitchell, J.T. (2001). *Crisis intervention and critical incident stress management (CISM) research summary.* Retrieved from. . . .

CHALLENGE QUESTIONS

Is Psychological Debriefing a Harmful Intervention for Survivors of Trauma?

1. Mitchell claims that only untrained people would resort to psychological debriefing as a first resort after a disaster. Why is it important to wait as long as several weeks or months before using psychological debriefing services?
2. Imagine that you are a clinician who is treating a person who has survived a life-threatening trauma. How would you go about assessing the extent to which you would have the client relive the details of the trauma?
3. If you were a researcher interested in studying the extent to which psychological debriefing helps or harms survivors of trauma, how would you go about studying this question?
4. Some would argue that following the experience of trauma, it makes more sense to try to avoid recollections of the harrowing event. What arguments would support this viewpoint, and how realistic is it to put such troubling memories out of mind?
5. The positions regarding psychological debriefing taken by the authors in the two pieces you read are quite vehement. What are your thoughts about the reasons such strong viewpoints are expressed on this topic?

Suggested Readings

Doka, K. J. (2003). *Living with grief: Coping with public tragedy.* New York: Brunner-Routledge.

Litz, B. T. (2003). *Early intervention for trauma and traumatic loss.* New York: The Guilford Press.

Mitchell, J. T., & Everly, George S. (2001). *Critical incident stress debriefing: An operations manual for CISD, defusing and other group crisis intervention services.* Ellicott, MD: Chevron Publishing Company.

Precin, P. (Ed.) (2004). *Surviving 9/11: Impact and experiences of occupational therapy practitioners.* Binghamton, NY: The Haworth Press.

Prince, M. (2004). *Trauma: Treatment and transformation.* Lincoln, Nebraska: Universe, Inc.

Thompson, R. (2004). *Crisis intervention and crisis management: Strategies that work in schools and communities.* New York: Brunner-Routledge.

ISSUE 4

Are Blocked and Recovered Memories Valid Phenomena?

YES: David H. Gleaves, Steven M. Smith, Lisa D. Butler, and David Spiegel, from "False and Recovered Memories in the Laboratory and Clinic: A Review of Experimental and Clinical Evidence," *Clinical Psychology: Science and Practice* (Spring 2004)

NO: John F. Kihlstrom, from "An Unbalanced Balancing Act: Blocked, Recovered, and False Memories in the Laboratory Clinic," *Clinical Psychology: Science and Practice* (Spring 2004)

ISSUE SUMMARY

YES: Psychologist David Gleaves and his colleagues assert that for some people, memories of traumatic events are blocked but may subsequently be recovered.

NO: Psychologist John Kihlstrom disputes the validity of blocked and recovered memories. He views the phenomenon of "false memories" as a serious problem in contemporary society.

Most people have had an experience in life that has been so traumatic that they strive to avoid any memories of the harrowing event. In such instances, this response is a coping strategy that enables people to move on with life despite a horrible event. There is no controversy about the process associated with active efforts to suppress or avoid intrusive recollections of the trauma. But, are there instances in which a survivor unconsciously "blocks" the memory of the traumatic event? And, can these blocked memories at some point be "recovered"? For decades, clinicians and researchers have engaged in vigorous debate about the validity of the phenomena of blocked and recovered memories.

David Gleaves and his colleagues assert that under certain circumstances, severe distress can lead to suppression or blocking of memory, and then to a reemergence or recovering of the memory. These scholars reject the notion of a "false memory syndrome" in which individuals reportedly experience memories of a traumatic event that did not occur. They acknowledge that, while researchers have reported that some individuals do indeed believe that they have memories of events that did not occur, these "memories" usually pertain to ordinary and non-stressful topics that can be experimentally "implanted."

John Kihlstrom systematically refutes the claims of Gleaves regarding the validity of blocked and recovered memories. Rather, he points to the impact of persuasive therapists and popular culture in perpetuating myths that memories of trauma are commonly blocked and can be recovered. He rejects the assertion that there is a history of recovered memories that gives the concept credibility, and he cites methodological inconsistencies and flaws associated with claims that these are valid phenomena.

POINT

- Clinicians have recognized the phenomena of blocked and recovered memories for two centuries in soldiers, holocaust survivors, and victims of civilian violence or childhood abuse.

- Memories that are blocked, and subsequently recovered, are often a response to what the DSM characterizes as an event "usually of a traumatic or stressful nature"; furthermore, the inability to remember is "too extensive to be explained by normal forgetfulness."

- While it has been proven that false memories about ordinary and non-stressful topics can be successfully implanted, people are unlikely to develop false memories about traumatic situations.

- Attempts to substantiate claims of false memories come not from empirical data, but from anecdotal reports, often from those who assert that they were wrongly accused of perpetrating sexual abuse or from "retractors" (persons who once reported memories of sexual abuse that they subsequently came to recognize as false).

- While there is support for the phenomenon of false memories, there is little professional support for the notion of "false memory syndrome," a concept that is primarily used in efforts to discredit those who make accusations of sexual abuse.

COUNTERPOINT

- Claims of blocked and recovered memories emerge primarily from "clinical folklore" rather than scientific studies and evidence. While memory loss is not disputed, the assertion that its cause is trauma has not been proven.

- Given that emotional arousal leads to the release of stress hormones that actually improve memory, it follows that trauma should result in a more vivid memory—not a repressed one.

- Therapists who believe in both the traumatic etiology of syndromes and the theory of repression will likely communicate these ideas to the patient, who may already share them because of exposure to the popular media. The result may be beliefs about unsubstantiated trauma that seem quite plausible.

- While much of the evidence supporting false memories comes in the form of anecdotal case reports published in the popular press, that is not a reason to discount them. "Anecdotal" does not mean invalid. In fact, journalists or other lay-people who report incidents of false memory are held to a higher level of corroborative accountability than psychotherapists who claim to assist in recovering blocked memories.

- False memory syndrome involves more than a person's individual false memory. Instead, it occurs when a person uses a false memory to construct an entirely different identity and personality based on that memory. There have been several documented cases of the false memory syndrome.

YES

David H. Gleaves, Steven M. Smith, Lisa D. Butler, and David Spiegel

False and Recovered Memories in the Laboratory and Clinic: A Review of Experimental and Clinical Evidence

Blocked and recovered memories of traumatic events have long been regarded as real phenomena by the mental health profession, our legal system, and the public at large. These phenomena originally were studied by Pierre Janet and Sigmund Freud, and Freud's (1896/1962) "Aetiology of Hysteria" is perhaps the best known early discussion of this topic. In this now famous 1896 address, Freud presented his "Seduction Theory" in which he argued that "hysteria" resulted from repressed memories of childhood sexual trauma. Freud further argued that bringing these memories into consciousness would lead to the alleviation of the hysterical symptom.

Freud subsequently abandoned his seduction theory in favor of his theory of childhood sexual fantasy at a time when he was trying to develop a more general theory of psychopathology designed to account for disorders other than hysteria such as obsessive-compulsive neurosis (Freud, 1955) and schizophrenia. However, the concept of repressed memories of trauma continued to receive attention, particularly in the literature on wartime trauma. For example, Sargant and Slater (1941) described a World War II account of 1000 consecutive admissions to a neurological unit. Over 14% of the sample exhibited amnesia, with the severity of amnesia appearing to be associated with the severity of trauma (e.g., 35% of those exposed to severe stress exhibited significant amnesias). Retrieval of these memories of trauma was seen as essential to recovery and was accomplished through the use of psychotherapy, hypnosis (Kardiner & Spiegel, 1947), or even drugs such as sodium pentothal (see also Grinker & Spiegel, 1945).

More recently, reported amnesia and/or subsequent recovery of memories have been found to be relatively common in studies of clinical populations that experienced childhood sexual and physical abuse (e.g., Briere & Conte, 1993; Feldman-Summers & Pope, 1994; Herman & Schatzow, 1987; Loftus,

From *Clinical Psychology: Science and Practice*, vol. 11, issue 1, 2004. Copyright © 2004 by Oxford University Press Journals. Reprinted by permission.

Polonsky & Fullilove, 1993; L. Williams, 1994, 1995; for a recent review, see D. Brown, Scheflin, & Whitfield, 1999).

Despite these clinical data, other researchers, clinicians, or journalists have questioned the existence of repressed and recovered memories (e.g., Holmes, 1994; Loftus, 1993; Ofshe & Watters, 1993; H. Pope & Hudson, 1995), challenging the academic community to provide objective evidence of these phenomena and at times going so far as to claim that there is no scientific support for the phenomena (e.g., Ofshe & Watters, 1993). Some have also questioned whether "recovered" memories might actually be confabulated or false memories (e.g., Lindsay & Read, 1993; Loftus, 1993). Empirical evidence from controlled laboratory studies of nonpatient populations reliably demonstrates the reality of false memories (e.g., Brewer & Treyens, 1981; Loftus, Miller, & Burns, 1978; McDermott, 1996; Loftus & Palmer, 1974; Payne, Elie, Blackwell, & Neuschatz, 1996; Read, 1996; Roediger & McDermott, 1995), providing support for this alternative explanation.

The debate over false and recovered memories has polarized the academic and mental health communities into camps that endorse one phenomenon or the other (see Pezdek & Banks, 1996 for a balanced review). The controversy also affects the legal system in that it has seen lawsuits based on alleged repressed and recovered memory as well as lawsuits based on alleged implantation of false memories of abuse (see Bowman & Mertz, 1996a, 1996b; D. Brown et al., 1999; Lipton, 1999; M. R. Williams, 1996).

In the present paper we take the position described by Pezdek and Banks (1996) as well as others (e.g., Brewin, 1996; Butler & Spiegel, 1997; J. J. Freyd, 1996; Knapp & VandeCreek, 2000; Smith, 1995a). We acknowledge that under certain circumstances both false and genuine recovered memories may exist. We describe laboratory analogues for both types of experiences. Assuming that both types of phenomena are possible, we suggest that the critical questions are (a) how common is each type of memory phenomenon, (b) what factors lead to the occurrence of each (including under what conditions are each possible and/or likely to occur), and perhaps most importantly, (c) can these two types of memories be distinguished from each other? Toward these goals, we review experimental and clinical data relevant to answering these questions and propose and describe an empirical research protocol that can not only demonstrate both phenomena, but that can also compare the two. Such comparisons can help to determine the causes of these phenomena, discover factors that influence the two, and hopefully reveal signature variables that could provide telltale signs differentiating false memories from recovered ones.

Theoretical Accounts and Evidence of False Memories

The Logic of False Memories

A number of researchers have found evidence of "false memories," defined as experiences that to rememberers seem to be memories of events that took place within experiments, but which do not correspond to experimentally presented stimuli (e.g., McDermott, 1996; Payne et al., 1996; Read, 1996; Robinson & Roediger, 1997; Roediger & McDermott, 1995). A false memory is not simply any memory error. The term refers to cases in which one appears to experience a memory of an event that did not occur. Memory errors that do not constitute false memories include, for example, retrieval failures, omission errors in recall, and recognition failures. Rather than the absence of memory that is characteristic of omission errors, a false memory involves an experience of remembering a relatively complete episode that did not in fact occur. The difference between accurate and false memories is in the correspondence or noncorrespondence of the memory with objective reality.

Human memories constitute evidence of prior experiences, but currently there may be no guarantee of accuracy, however authentic the memories may seem to the rememberer. Studies of the relation between subjective metacognitive assessments of one's memory accuracy and objective measures of accuracy have often shown weak or even nonexistent correlations (e.g., Wells & Loftus, 1984). Even when such correlations are strong, they are by no means perfect, indicating that the accuracy of memories can be misjudged (Lindsay, Read, & Sharma, 1998).

Clinical Evidence for False Memories

Despite recent claims that false memories of sexual abuse and a false-memory syndrome reached epidemic proportions in the 1990s (e.g., P. Freyd, 1999; Goldstein & Farmer, 1992; Pendergrast, 1995), we found no empirical clinical research to support such a claim (for further discussion of this topic see K. S. Pope, 1996, 1997; for a critique, see Kihlstrom, 1997). The primary clinical evidence for the existence of false memories of trauma comes mainly from anecdotal reports by either persons who claim to have been falsely accused of sexual abuse or from persons known as "retractors" or "recantors," persons who once reported having had memories of sexual abuse that they now believe to be false. In addition, there are clinical reports (particularly with respect to dissociative identity disorder) that describe admixtures of true and false traumatic memories being recounted by the same patient (e.g., Kluft, 1998). Reports of the first type have appeared as books published in the popular literature (e.g., Goldstein & Farmer, 1992; Pendergrast, 1995) and have been described in review papers published in the scientific literature. For example, Loftus (1993) described having received numerous letters from persons claiming to have been falsely accused of sexual abuse. Anecdotal and case reports of recantors have also recently been published in the popular and scientific literature (de Rivera, 1997, 2000; Gavigan, 1992; Lief & Fetkewicz, 1995; McElroy & Keck, 1995; Nelson & Simpson, 1994; Pasley, 1994).

In addition, there have been published discussions of "high profile" cases in which persons claimed that false memories of abuse had been suggested or implanted. One such case occurred in *Ramona v. Ramona* (also *Ramona v. Isabella;* see Bowman & Mertz, 1996a; H. Pope & Hudson, 1996) in which a man whose daughter allegedly recovered memories of abuse by him successfully sued his daughter's therapist (against the daughter's wishes) for suggesting or reinforcing false memories. Another often cited case is that of

Paul Ingram, a man serving time after confessing to raping his daughters repeatedly. Writers who have cited his case as an example of false memories (e.g., Loftus, 1993; Ofshe, 1992) argue that Ingram's confessions were based on false memories created during interrogation (see Kassin, 1997 for a discussion of "internalized false confession"). Thus, in this case, both the alleged victim and the alleged perpetrator are said to have had false memories of nonexistent sexual abuse.

Experimental Evidence of False Memories

Despite the lack of clinical evidence for a false-memory syndrome epidemic, several lines of experimental research support the conclusion that subjects can be made to report remembering events that did not occur. These include studies of the misinformation effect (e.g., Loftus & Palmer, 1974), hypnotic pseudomemory (e.g., Laurence & Perry, 1983), failures of reality monitoring (e.g., Johnson & Raye, 1981), intrusions in schema-guided recall (e.g., Brewer & Treyens, 1981), and intrusions in recall of list words (e.g., Roediger & McDermott, 1995). The putative causes of the false memories in these studies have included overwriting of the original memory trace, which inextricably integrates accurate and inaccurate information, and source monitoring failures that involve such factors as misattributions of familiarity or failures to distinguish perceived events from imagined ones.

The misinformation effect, similar to retroactive interference effects, is generated in three basic steps that include presentation of the original events, intervening events intended to mislead the participant, and a memory test. For example, the participant might witness a videotaped sequence of events, followed by a postevent question that contained a misleading inference. On a later test many participants remember the inferred events as having actually occurred.

In a particularly interesting example of the misinformation effect, the subject is convinced by family members that a fabricated event occurred during the subject's childhood, at which point the subject may report remembering details of what is a fabricated event (e.g., Hyman, Husband, & Billings, 1995; Loftus & Ketchum, 1994). Although the validity of Loftus' "lost in the mall study" has been seriously questioned (e.g., D. Brown, 1995), in part because the misinformation was of a relatively common, plausible, and non-traumatic experience, Pezdek and colleagues (Pezdek, Finger, & Hodge, 1997) replicated the finding to the extent that three of 20 subjects accepted a similar suggestion. However, when a suggestion of a more unusual and possibly traumatic memory analogous to sexual abuse (a rectal enema) was given, none of the subjects adopted the suggestion.

The original explanation of misinformation effects was based upon the notion that related events are not stored faithfully, independently, and veridically, but rather the individual events are used to construct an integrated memory trace that represents the gist or general meaning of the episode (e.g., Bransford & Franks, 1972). This constructed memory supposedly includes inferences, not only from the original events, but potentially from intervening misleading suggestions. Furthermore, according to this explanation, original events cannot be distinguished from the potentially false inferences in a memory representation. In this view, false memories could include retrieval of false suggestions or inferences, or retrieval of blends of original and intervening (false) information (e.g., Loftus & Hoffman, 1989). Alternative explanations of misinformation effects are based upon the presumption that parallel and independent memory traces of original and intervening events are both stored in memory, thereby allowing at least the possibility of later distinguishing original events from inaccurate suggestions and inferences (e.g., Estes, 1997; Zaragoza & Koshmider, 1989). This theoretical debate has not yet been resolved.

Another experimental methodology for creating and demonstrating false memory, which is a variant of the misinformation approach, involves hypnotically created pseudomemory (Barnier & McConkey, 1992; Laurence & Perry, 1983; Lynn, Weekes, & Milano, 1989). In Laurence and Perry's experiment, they hypnotically regressed subjects to a night during the previous week and suggested their having awakened from sleep upon hearing a loud noise. Approximately half of the highly hypnotizable subjects reported the suggested memory as real (although some reported being unsure; also see below discussion for alternative interpretations from Spanos & McLean, 1985–1986, of these results). Barnier and McConkey (1992) extended this line of research by determining that it was hypnotizability rather than induction of a hypnotic trance that better predicted the report of pseudomemory. Dywan and Bowers (1983) illustrated another nonhypnotic component that affects findings in studies of hypnotic "misinformation." They found that the use of hypnosis increased conviction that recalled information was correct, but not its accuracy. Accuracy was a product of recall effort: the more information produced, the less likely it was to be accurate, indicating that the increase in productivity occurs at the expense of the strictness of the response criterion (Erdelyi & Goldberg, 1979). On the one hand, the best recollection is usually not the first one; repeated recall trials produce more accurate information (Erdelyi & Kleinbard, 1978), meaning that at least some accurate information is not immediately available to conscious recall. On the other hand, pressure to recall more information about an event may result in lower overall accuracy of recall.

Another experimental methodology that has been used to demonstrate false memory effects is the reality-monitoring paradigm (e.g., Johnson & Raye, 1981). Reality monitoring refers to the ability (or inability) to distinguish between memories that were generated from internal and those from external events. In this procedure, participants might be asked to view a mixed list of pictures and words and to form mental images of the referents of the words. On a later memory test the participants are often unable to distinguish between pictures they were shown and those that they generated through mental imagery (although see Johnson & Raye, 1981 for a discussion of the conditions under which participants *are* able to discriminate the two). This phenomenon has its corollary in the hypnotic phenomenon of "source amnesia," in which an individual will recall some information implanted during hypnosis but will be unable to recall, or will misrepresent, the source, for example it as coming from a prior store of information rather than the recent hypnotic suggestion (Evans, 1988).

Johnson, Hashtroudi, and Lindsay (1993) have explained failures of reality monitoring as examples of more general source-monitoring failures. Source monitoring refers to the ability to correctly attribute the source of a memory. A number of attributes of memories, including contextual, semantic, or perceptual features, potentially can be used to discriminate among different sources of the memories. Johnson et al. claimed that most memory illusions, such as misattributed familiarity (e.g., Jacoby, 1991), cryptamnesia (e.g., A. S. Brown & Murphy, 1989), and confabulation (e.g., Loftus & Palmer, 1974) are due to source monitoring failures. Jacoby's (1991) explanation of misattributed familiarity is based upon a distinction between two types of memory, an automatic, unconscious familiarity response, and an intentional, deliberate type of remembering that is under conscious control. When a memory is automatically stimulated without an accompanying conscious respecification of its source, the resultant familiarity might be attributed to an inappropriate source.

Another approach to the study of false memories has been to observe schema-guided recall and recognition (e.g., Brewer & Treyens, 1981; Rabinowitz & Mandler, 1983). For example, Brewer and Treyens (1981) examined false recognition of objects that fit an episodic schema. They found that schema-consistent memories were more likely to be falsely recalled and recognized than schema-inconsistent responses. This is similar to Pezdek et al.'s (1997) finding that plausibility and script-relevant knowledge determine the extent to which events can be suggestively implanted in memory.

List-learning techniques have also been used to study false memories (e.g., McDermott, 1996; Payne et al., 1996; Read, 1996; Robinson & Roediger, 1997; Roediger & McDermott, 1995). Participants in these paradigms are typically presented with a list of words that are all associatively related to a single nonpresented target word. The critical nonpresented target word is often falsely recalled even though it does not appear on the memorized list. For example, a list might have words associated with the word *spider,* such as *web, insect,* and *arachnid,* but not the word *spider.* Participants often claim to recall *spider* even when they are admonished not to report words that were not on the list. In one variant of this procedure, participants are given a categorized list that contains the most common members of a category except for the most typical category member, which is omitted from the list. Participants often falsely recall the nonpresented category member, and the effect is even stronger if the number of associates is increased (Robinson & Roediger, 1997) or the critical nonpresented word is primed on an unrelated task (Smith et al., 1996).

Theoretical accounts of false memories generated in list-learning paradigms include explanations involving implicit associative responses, misattributed source memory, and fuzzy memory traces. The first of these explanations is that when people study a list of words they implicitly think of associates of those words, and memories of the implicit associates are later mistaken for memories of actual list members (e.g., Kirkpatrick, 1894; Roediger & McDermott, 1995). This explanation is related to the source-monitoring explanation of false memories in that it supposes that memories of implicit associative responses are not adequately distinguished from memories of physical stimuli. The source monitoring explanation is also useful for explaining primed false memories (Smith et al., 1996); memories of primed words are not adequately distinguished from memories of correct list words.

Another theory, the fuzzy-trace explanation of false memories in list-word recall, is that both verbatim and gist memory traces are stored during learning, and false recall can result if memory relies on the inaccurate memory trace representing the gist of the event (e.g., Reyna & Brainerd, 1995). Reliance on fuzzy-gist memory traces rather than veridical verbatim traces, according to this theory, is increased by longer retention intervals, a prediction supported by the results of list-learning studies of false memories (e.g., McDermott, 1996). In addition, when memory tests emphasize memory for substance (i.e., meaning), then things that were not previously studied may be easier to endorse on recognition tests than things that were (Brainerd & Reyna, 1998).

Conclusions and Limitations of Conclusions about False Memory Research

The clinical and experimental research on false memory each has its own strengths and limitations. The most glaring limitation of some *clinical* reports on false memory is that they provide no way of determining if the memories are in fact false. In many cases, the credibility of the source of information needs to be considered. For example, Rubin (1996) noted that when the source of information is the parent accused of the abuse, there are numerous alternative interpretations of what may have actually occurred. Rubin noted that "Denial, dynamics of secrecy in incestuous families, behavioral reenactments of childhood victimization, alcohol-induced blackouts, and outright lying" (p. 447) may explain some claims that persons have been falsely accused of abuse. When the data come from a "retractor" they may be more convincing. However, persons with verifiable histories of abuse are known to vacillate between accepting and denying the reality of their memories of abuse and may be vulnerable to suggestions (by family members or lawyers) that their memories are false (Gleaves, 1994). It is inconsistent to assume that a memory is credible when someone claims not to have been abused, and to assume that a memory is not credible when someone claims the opposite (Schooler, 1996). However, there are reports in which the history of abuse has been documented, such as L. M. Williams' study in which the episodes were identified through hospital emergency room records of assessment and treatment for abuse (L. M. Williams, 1994, 1995).

There are also severe limitations regarding the "high profile" cases that have been presented in the scientific literature. Numerous authors (Gleaves, 1994; Olio, 1994; Olio & Cornell, 1994, 1998; Peterson, 1994) have noted that claims regarding the Ingram case are contradicted by the actual facts. For example, there is testimony from those who initially interviewed Ingram, that he confessed to the sexual abuse the first time he was confronted with the charges, rather than after months of interrogation, suggestions, and pressure, as some commentators (e.g., Loftus, 1993; Kassin, 1997) have suggested. Olio and Cornell (1998) have recently observed that the uncritical acceptance and parroting of the alleged facts of the Ingram case has become "an academic version of an urban legend" (p. 1195). Similarly, regarding the *Ramona v. Isabella* case, we refer the reader to Bowman and Mertz's (1996a) indepth discussion of the case to determine to what degree it should be regarded as evidence supporting the reality of false memories of abuse. This type of data suffer from the same limitation as the clinical data described above; there is not convincing evidence that the memories in question are in fact false.

Another limitation of the clinical data on false memories is that the possible occurrence of such phenomena does not imply the existence of a false-memory syndrome (FMS). The current *Diagnostic and Statistical Manual of Mental Disorders* (*DSM-IV;* American Psychiatric Association, 1994) defines a syndrome as "a grouping of signs and symptoms, based on their frequent co-occurrence, that may suggest a common underlying pathogenesis, course, familial pattern, or treatment selection" (p. 771). Currently there are few or no empirical data supporting the claim that false-memory syndrome exists (Gleaves & Freyd, 1997; K. Pope, 1996, 1997), mainly because so little research on this issue has been conducted. In one published empirical study that we found, Hovdestad and Kristiansen (1996) concluded that, "In sum, the weak evidence for the construct validity of the phenomenon referred to as FMS, together with the finding that few women with recovered memories satisfied the criteria and that women with continuous memories were equally likely to do so, lends little support to the FMS theory" (p. 330). More recently, Dallam (2001) concluded that "in the absence of any substantive scientific support, 'False memory Syndrome' is best characterized as a pseudoscientific syndrome that was developed to defend against claims of child abuse" (p. 10).

Although these conclusions illustrate that data in support of false-memory syndrome are still lacking, objection to the term is not new among the scientific community. As early as 1993, numerous researchers published a formal objection to the term being used in this context arguing that the term false-memory syndrome was really "a non-psychological term originated by a private foundation whose stated purpose is to support accused parents." They urged, "For the sake of intellectual honesty, let's leave the term 'false memory syndrome' to the popular press" (Carstensen et al., 1993, p. 23).

Kihlstrom (1998) has more recently attempted to defend the use of the term. Basically his argument was that numerous other writers have used the term "syndrome" in nonscientific context (e.g., the "Lolita syndrome," "sissy boy syndrome," and "China syndrome," p. 17); thus there is no reason to question its use in this case. A related defense (noted by a reviewer of this article) is that criticism of use of the term "syndrome" is simply a red herring, and the critical matter is whether memories are accurate or inaccurate. Although we in general agree with the justification here (that accuracy per se is what is critical), the issue is not a red herring because clearly FMS is being described (a) *as if* it is a scientific diagnosis and form of psychopathology, and (b) as being an entity above and beyond the simple issue of the accuracy of a memory. One needs to look no further than the definition from Kihlstrom quoted on the False Memory Syndrome Foundation web site. He described FMS as a form of psychopathology above and beyond the simple issue of the accuracy of memory. Kihlstrom wrote:

> Note that the syndrome is *not* characterized by false memories as such. We all have memories that are inaccurate. Rather, the *syndrome* may be *diagnosed* when the memory is so deeply ingrained that it orients the individual's entire personality and lifestyle, in turn disrupting all sorts of other adaptive behavior. The analogy to *personality disorder* is intentional. [emphasis added]

Clearly false-memory syndrome is being described as if it is a form of psychopathology much above and beyond the issue of the accuracy of memory. The fact that mental health professionals have even testified in court that plaintiffs in sexual abuse cases suffered from "FMS" is further evidence that the term is being misused. Although research may someday suggest that FMS actually exists, current data do not. Thus, it is at best premature to use the term "false memory syndrome" and we recommend that the term not be used. To thoroughly discuss this issue is beyond the scope of the present paper (see Dallam, 2001; K. S. Pope, 1996, 1997 for a more detailed discussion).

Regarding the experimental research on false memories, these studies make it clear that some persons can be made to report remembering events that did not occur (or objects that were not observed), in settings in which the consequences of a mistake are relatively minor. Reported false memories can be reliably and predictably evoked and studied with a variety of laboratory procedures. Furthermore, the occurrence of false memories does not appear to rely on extraordinary affective states or special cognitive processes; rather, they seem to be produced by the same cognitive mechanisms that produce accurate remembering. However, there are a number of limitations to the conclusions and inferences that can be made from experimental research on false memories. One limitation concerns the degree to which reported false memories reflect genuine alterations in memory (or belief in memory) versus reporting biases (Barnier & McConkey, 1992; Murrey, Cross, & Whipple, 1992; Spanos & McLean, 1985–1986). That is, do research participants reporting false memories really believe that what they are reporting are memories, or are their reports due to the demand characteristics of the research? In their study of hypnotizability and pseudomemory, Lynn, Weekes, and Milano (1989) asked subjects about reported pseudomemories in more than one way. When asked in open-ended style 11.5% of subjects reported actually remembering the suggested event (a phone ringing). However, when actually required (in a forced-choice format) to indicate whether they had heard an actual phone ring or if the ring was suggested, none of the participants exhibited pseudomemory. The findings led the authors to conclude that "Although hypnotic suggestions produce shifts in awareness and attention, subjects are not deluded by suggestions into confusing fantasy with reality" (p. 143).

Similar results were obtained by Barnier and McConkey (1992), who showed participants slides of a purse snatching and then suggested false aspects of the event in the slides (that the attacker wore a scarf and helped the victim pick up flowers). The authors tested for false memories in both formal and informal contexts using high- and low- hypnotizable subjects. Although a sizeable number of the highly hypnotizable subjects reported remembering the false aspects of the events when tested in a formal setting, the majority

(13 out of 15 for one memory and 14 out of 15 for another) did *not* exhibit pseudomemory when tested in an informal setting. The authors also collected qualitative data regarding participants' behaviors. Some indicated behavioral compliance. For example, one noted: "I knew he didn't have a scarf. I felt pressured, so I put a scarf on him to give an answer" (p. 525). Response bias does not seem to explain all of the experimental research on false memory, but the degree to which it does should not be minimized and has not been completely determined.

Another limitation of published empirical work concerns the degree to which this research can be generalized and applied to cases of false memories of child sexual abuse (Butler & Speigel, 1997; J. J. Freyd & Gleaves, 1996) or naturally occurring traumatic events. The reliability of producing certain laboratory phenomena, such as optical illusions, is no assurance that the phenomena are common, naturally occurring events. Indeed, Mook (1983; see also Butler & Spiegel, 1997) suggests that laboratory research best illuminates "what *can* happen, rather than what typically *does*" (p. 384). When the purpose is to predict or explain behavior in the real world, then the generalizability concerns as to the comparability of populations, settings, manipulations, and measurement must be considered (Butler & Spiegel, 1997; Campbell & Stanley, 1967). At issue is the fact that the vast majority of the laboratory research on false memories has involved suggesting memories of schema-consistent, mundane events or objects to nonclinical subjects—events which are, in many cases, corroborated by family members—and eliciting false reports with no long-term personal consequences, such as family disruption or a jail term for a family member. In the only study with adult subjects in which the investigators attempted to implant a memory remotely similar to child sexual abuse (Pezdek et al., 1997), they were unsuccessful in doing so.

There are also many ways in which false memory research fails to parallel what may happen in psychotherapy, thus limiting the generalizability of the results. For example, in Loftus's "lost in the mall" study, it was actually the family member, rather than the experimenter, who convinced the subjects of the false childhood memories. The generalizability depends on what this finding actually demonstrates. Is it that therapists can have powerful influence over clients or that parents or other family members can deceive their children? If it is the latter, such results do not support the position that false memories frequently occur in therapy.

In another line of recent laboratory research that more closely mimics a possible psychotherapy situation, Loftus and Mazzoni (1998) exposed subjects to a 30-min brief-therapy simulation in which an expert clinician analyzed a dream report that the subject offered. The clinician proposed an interpretation (an "expert personalized suggestion") that the dream indicated that the subject had probably experienced a given event in early childhood (either being lost or being in a dangerous situation). The theme of the interpretation was determined by random assignment, however the interpretation was personalized to build on the dream material that the subject had provided. Results indicated that the majority of subjects were more confident at four-week follow-up that they had experienced these childhood events. It is unknown, however, whether participants also developed false memories of the events that corresponded to their increased confidence.

This distinction between increasing confidence that something has happened and increasing the production of false memories of the event is a potential limitation to the relevance of the recent "imagination inflation" literature to the understanding of false-memory creation. In these studies, having subjects simply imagine events increases their confidence that the events have indeed occurred (e.g., Garry, Manning, Loftus, & Sherman, 1996; reviewed in Garry & Polaschek, 2000). However, changing beliefs about the likelihood of the events does not necessarily create memories of the event. In one false-memory study, however, coupling imagination with authoritative suggestion (for an event confirmed by family members) increased false-memory creation over authoritative suggestion alone (Hyman & Pentland, 1996), confirming that imagination can facilitate false-memory creation.

For a different reason, laboratory research may *underestimate* the degree of influence and suggestion that may occur in therapy. Contact between experimenter and research participant is generally brief compared to therapist-client contact. In Hyman et al.'s (1995) study of false childhood memories, participants only reported false memories after two or three sessions but never did in the first. In the Loftus and Mazzoni study (1998) only one experience was interpreted. The possible effects of several weeks or even months of suggestion, or of multiple converging suggestions/interpretations, have not been studied experimentally. Of relevance to the former possible effect, Zaragoza and Mitchell (1996) found that repeated exposure to suggestion can increase confidence in and conscious recollections of false memories of witnessing an event.

Experimental studies have not yet determined whether false memories could occur for bizarre or affectively charged events, important concerns to clinical psychologists. It is not yet known whether bizarreness in a memory identifies it as a false memory or an accurate one. The limitation of our understanding of false memories that is most relevant to the present paper is whether accurate and false memories can be distinguished from one another, either by the subject who is remembering, or by an observer. Whether or not there are experiential or behavioral "signatures" that indicate the likelihood that a memory is false or accurate is a critical question that has not been thoroughly addressed by empirical research. To date, findings suggest that memories for true events tend to be described with more words, contain greater clarity of perceptual details, and are held with greater confidence than are false memories (for reviews see Oakes & Hyman, 2000; Pezdek & Taylor, 2000). The sensory detail results are similar to those found when experimenters compare remembered versus imagined autobiographical childhood events (Johnson, Foley, Suengas, & Raye, 1988) or childhood events that subjects *remember* happening rather than simply *know* happened (Hyman, Gilstrap, Decker, & Wilkinson, 1998).

To summarize, the empirical findings of false memories provide an alternative explanation for memories recovered in therapy, casting some doubt as to the accuracy or reality of the memories. However, the circumstances under which false memories can or are likely to occur have yet to be determined. Furthermore, the existence of false memories does not imply the existence of a syndrome nor does it contradict the possibility that blocked and accurately recovered memories can also occur. We now consider evidence concerning blocked and recovered memories.

Empirical Evidence and Theories of Memory Blocking and Recovery

Defining Blocked and Recovered Memories

What we refer to as blocked and recovered memories are cases in which established memories are rendered inaccessible for some period of time, after which the essentially intact memories are retrieved. Memory blocks and the potential recovery of memories are directly relevant to clinical disorders such as post-traumatic stress disorder and the dissociative disorders. Our operational definition of blocked and recovered memories specifies three criteria: (a) There must be corroborating evidence that the event in question was actually experienced by the person, (b) At some later time it must be found that the event cannot be recalled, and (c) After the period of inaccessibility, it must be found that the event can be successfully recalled. Criteria similar to these have also been used by Haber and Haber (1996) and Schooler and colleagues (Schooler & Fiore, 1995; Schooler, Ambadar, & Bendiksen, 1997).

Clinical Evidence of Blocked and Recovered Memories: Dissociative Amnesia

In the current *DSM* (APA, 1994), dissociative amnesia is defined as "a reversible memory impairment in which memories of personal experience cannot be retrieved in verbal form" (p. 478). The events that cannot be recalled are "usually of a traumatic or stressful nature" (p. 478) and the inability to remember is "too extensive to be explained by normal forgetfulness" (p. 478) (see also Gleaves, 1996; Loewenstein, 1991; or van der Hart & Nijenhuis, 1995 for more extensive reviews).

Although there have been claims that dissociative amnesia is a recently recognized (or invented) phenomenon (e.g., Ofshe & Singer, 1994), it has been recognized by clinicians since the beginning of the 19th century (Nemiah, 1979; Prince 1906). Dissociative (or psychogenic or hysterical) amnesia was studied and described extensively by Pierre Janet in the 1880s as well as by Freud in some of his early writings. There are also numerous descriptions of dissociative amnesia in the early and recent literature on combat and war trauma (e.g., Bremner, Steinberg, Southwick, Johnson, & Charney, 1993; Grinker & Spiegel, 1945; Kardiner & Spiegel 1947; Kolb, 1988; Sargant & Slater, 1941) and civilian violence (e.g., Kaszniak, Nussbaum, Berren, & Santiago, 1988). Modai (1994) also described total amnesia for childhood in a survivor of the holocaust. In many of these reports, the authors also described how memory for the traumatic experiences of war could be retrieved through therapy, hypnosis, or even narcosynthesis. These authors did sometimes caution that what was retrieved was often a mixture of accurate memory and fantasy (e.g., Kolb, 1988; Sargant & Slater, 1941).

More recent research has focused on the presence of amnesia and/or recovered memory for experiences of child sexual abuse (CSA). Recently reported anecdotal, legal, and clinical cases (e.g., Bull, 1999; Cheit, 1998; Corwin & Olafson, 1997; Dalenberg, 1996, 1997; Duggal & Sroufe, 1998; Schooler et al., 1997) of amnesia and memory recovery offer compelling "existence proof" for these phenomena. D. Brown, Scheflin, and Whitfield (1999) recently reviewed the clinical research in this area. They concluded that "In just this past decade alone, 68 research studies have been conducted on naturally occurring dissociative or traumatic amnesia for childhood sexual abuse. Not a single one of the 68 data-based studies failed to find it" (p. 126). Similar conclusions were reached by van der Hart and Nijenhuis (1995) and Scheflin and D. Brown (1996) in their earlier review of the literature. Critics of these conclusions may point to the report of H. G. Pope, Hudson, Bodkin, and Oliva (1998), who reviewed 63 different studies of victims of non-CSA types of trauma and claimed that they "could not find any clear and unexplained occurrences of amnesia for the traumatic events" (p. 213), though some of the evidence and conclusions presented in this review were disputed by D. Brown et al. (1999). More recently, some of D. Brown and colleagues' own evidence and conclusions have also been vigorously challenged (Piper, Pope, & Borowiecki, 2000). Nonetheless, collectively the clinical evidence does seem to suggest that varying degrees of amnesia for traumatic experiences and subsequent recovery of memory are real phenomena.

Experimental Evidence for Blocked and Recovered Memory

Critics or skeptics of the concept of recovered memory (e.g. Ofshe & Watters, 1993; Wakefield & Underwager, 1994) often claim that there is no experimental (or laboratory) evidence for the concept of recovered memory. Almost invariably, the reference cited for such statements is a literature review by Holmes (1990) who concluded that "despite over sixty years of research . . . at the present time there is no controlled laboratory evidence supporting the concept of repression" (p. 96). To thoroughly discuss Holmes's conclusions and the relevance to the recovered memory/false memory controversy would be beyond the scope of this article (see Gleaves, 1996 or Gleaves & Freyd, 1997 for more extensive discussions). The critical point is that Holmes only reviewed evidence for one possible mechanism of memory blocking and recovery (repression), defined in a very specific form.

In reality, empirical evidence of memory blocking (or inhibition) and recovery has come from several experimental paradigms, including spontaneous recovery from retroactive interference (e.g., Wheeler, 1995), tip-of-the-tongue (TOT) research (e.g., Jones, 1989; Read & Bruce, 1982; Smith, 1994b), blocking in implicit memory (e.g., Lustig & Hasher, 2001; Smith & Tindell, 1997), recovery from posthypnotic amnesia (e.g., Kihlstrom, 1987), output interference and recovery (e.g., J. Brown & Smith, 1992; Roediger, 1974; Smith & Vela, 1991), retrieval-induced forgetting (e.g., Anderson, Bjork & Bjork, 1994), directed forgetting and recovery (e.g., Bjork & Bjork, 1996), and memory inhibition through executive control (Anderson & Green, 2001). In each of these cases the memory blocks are more enduring than a few seconds, as is the case with many other empirical findings of temporary inaccessibility, such as negative priming effects (e.g., Tipper, 1985), Stroop interference tasks (e.g., MacLeod, 1991), or inhibitory orthographic priming (e.g., Grainger, 1990). We will briefly review each of these areas of empirical research that documents memory blocking and recovery (for a more extensive review of interference and inhibition effects in memory retrieval see Anderson & Bjork, 1994; Anderson & Neely, 1996).

Retroactive interference and spontaneous recovery. Retroactive interference has been one of the longest standing topics of interest in the experimental study of human memory. When experiences similar to an event in question are stored in memory after the target event, the resultant forgetting of the target event is referred to as retroactive interference. Lengthening the retention interval, however, causes recovery of the forgotten material (e.g., A. S. Brown, 1976), suggesting either that associations weakened by retroactive interference somehow recover their strength, or that original associations remain intact and interference only causes temporary inaccessibility. Consistent with the notion that original memories remain intact after retroactive interference are findings from associative-matching tests that show retention of original memories (e.g., Postman, Stark, & Fraser 1968), as well as evidence that original and interfering memories are independent entities (e.g., Martin, 1971). Spontaneous recovery effects in verbal learning and memory have been found with paired associate learning tasks, serial recall, and free recall (Wheeler, 1995). These findings show that whatever the mechanisms involved, it is nonetheless clear that learned associations can become temporarily inaccessible and can be recovered at a later time.

Output interference and reminiscence. Memory blocking and recovery can be used to explain another interesting conundrum, the question of what causes hypermnesia and reminiscence (Payne, 1987). Hypermnesia is a net improvement in recall when repeated recall tests are given without extra practice sessions. Reminiscence, a very similar concept, refers to the recovery of unrecalled material, independently of the amount forgotten from one test to the next. These phenomena defy the notion that forgetting increases over time, because more is remembered on later tests.

Hypermnesia and reminiscence can be explained as recovery from initial blocking in recall. That is, when people recall a list of words or pictures, the act of recalling some of the items on the list has the effect of blocking other items that have not yet been recalled (e.g., Roediger, 1974). This inhibition or interference has been termed *output interference* (e.g., Rundus, 1973). Thus, hypermnesia and reminiscence may occur on a later test because blocks caused by output interference weaken over time, in accordance with predictions of stimulus fluctuation theory (e.g., Estes, 1955; Mensink & Raaijmakers, 1988). The theory predicts that delaying a second recall test should allow more time for output interference to weaken, and therefore should increase recovery.

This prediction was supported by the finding of incubated reminiscence and hypermnesia effects (Smith & Vela, 1991).

Output interference is caused not only by one's own recall efforts, but also by experimenter-provided items from a learned list. The procedure in which the experimenter provides some of the list items as cues on a recall test is called part-list or part-set cueing. Surprisingly, part-list cueing inhibits or interferes with recall of the remainder of the list (e.g., Rundus, 1973; Nickerson, 1984).

If part-list cueing causes output interference, and if greater initial output interference leads to greater recovery and hypermnesia, then using part-list cues on an initial recall test should increase the hypermnesia observed on a retest. Experiments reported by Basden and Basden (1995), Basden, Basden, and Galloway (1977), and J. M. Brown and Smith (1992) supported this prediction; part-list cues caused memory blocking on an initial recall test, and increasing recovery (reminiscence) on a later recall test. An exaggerated version of this part-list cueing procedure constitutes an essential component of the comparative memory paradigm that we report in the present study.

Directed forgetting. The directed forgetting paradigm (e.g., Bjork, 1972) has been used successfully to impair the accessibility of experimentally presented materials. In one version of the directed forgetting paradigm, the list method, experimental participants are told that they can forget the list of words they had just been trying to memorize because, they are told, they will not need to remember that list on a later memory test (e.g., Basden, Basden, & Gargano, 1993; Bjork & Bjork, 1996). Instead, participants are told, they should concentrate on memorizing a second list of words, which are then presented. In the control condition, participants are not given this *forget* instruction. The typical directed forgetting effect is evidenced by two results: (a) the first list is recalled more poorly if forget instructions are given, and (b) the second list is recalled better if the forget instruction is given, presumably due to decreased proactive interference from the forgotten first list.

Bjork and Bjork (1996) found that the inaccessibility caused by directed forgetting can be eradicated if experimental participants are re-exposed to some of the forgotten material on a recognition test. In this study Bjork and Bjork found that if they included a few forgotten list-1 words on an intervening recognition test, then directed forgetting effects were not seen on a final recall test. This result constitutes another finding of recovery of memories that had been made inaccessible.

Posthypnotic amnesia and hypermnesia. Perhaps the strongest experimental support for blocked and recovered memories comes from the research on hypnotic (or posthypnotic) amnesia and hypermnesia (e.g., Clemes, 1964; Evans, 1988; Kihlstrom, 1979; Kihlstrom & Evans, 1979). This body of research shows that when hypnotizable participants are given suggestions during hypnosis to forget some events they have already experienced, memories of those events appear to be blocked or inaccessible. Although the degree of forgetting induced by hypnotic suggestion is often great, it has also been found that the "lost" memories can be largely recovered if the participant is given a prearranged signal to cancel the suggested amnesia. As noted by Evans (1988), "When the experimenter administers a prearranged cue, the critical memories appear to flood back into awareness, and the hitherto amnesic subject is now able to remember the events and experiences clearly and without difficulty" (p. 161).

It is this reversibility of amnesia that makes the hypnotic phenomenon most analogous to blocked and recovered memories of naturally occurring traumatic events (for an examination of the parallels between formal hypnotic and pathological dissociative states, see Butler, Duran, Jasiukaitus, Koopman, & Spiegel, 1996). Furthermore, experimental tests of implicit memory suggest that during their period of inaccessibility, memories may indirectly affect experiences and behavior (Kihlstrom & Barnhardt, 1993) in the same sense that dissociated memories are allegedly assumed to affect behavior even though one may have no explicit memory of the events.

Another aspect of posthypnotic amnesia that makes it a good laboratory model for dissociative amnesia concerns Bowers and Woody's (1996) study of hypnotic amnesia and the "paradox of intentional forgetting." This paradox refers to the fact that, in many instances, when someone tries to forget some learned material, the result is an intrusion of the to-be-forgotten material (see Wegner's 1989 study of forgetting white bears). As noted by Bowers and Woody and known by many clinicians, the very intention to *not* think about something paradoxically can bring the material to mind (cf. Anderson & Green, 2001).

This paradox of intentional forgetting in some ways parallels what is observed with victims of psychological trauma. That is, most put great effort into not thinking about the events in question (Koutstaal & Schacter, 1997), but frequently still (or perhaps consequently) experience intrusive thoughts (Horowitz, 1986). In fact, the *DSM-IV* (APA, 1994) diagnostic criteria for post-traumatic stress disorder include both avoidance (e.g., trying to avoid thinking about the event, amnesia for the experience) and re-experiencing/intrusive symptoms (e.g., intrusive thoughts, nightmares, flashbacks). The fact that many persons with PTSD seem to exhibit this paradoxical inability to forget has led some critics of dissociative amnesia to argue that it is totally inconsistent with what is observed in actual victims of trauma (i.e., actual trauma victims cannot forget). For example, in describing her experiences at a conference for the False Memory Syndrome Foundation, Wylie (1993) wrote, "People remember their traumas, speakers point out again and again; their problem is not that they've lost their memories, but that they can't get rid of them—they intrude relentlessly into their daily lives and always have" (p. 22). However, this analysis suggests a fundamental lack of understanding of the clinical phenomenon. The problem in PTSD is not simply a paucity *or* a flooding of memories. Rather it is poor modulation of these emotionally charged memories, such that they are sometimes overwhelming and at other times avoided (Horowitz, 1986). Their intrusive strength invites withdrawal, and their reappearance is experienced as an unbidden re-inflicting of the trauma, analogous to the effect of the traumatic event itself, now recapitulated through the nature of its reappearance in memory (Horowitz, 1986; Spiegel, 1997). As Widiger and Sankis (2000) noted, explaining why PTSD is more similar to the dissociative disorders than the anxiety disorders, "difficulty forgetting (or letting go of) a horrifying experience may simply be the opposite side of the same coin of difficulty remembering (accepting or acknowledging) a horrifying experience" (p. 391).

In Bowers and Woody's (1996) study, however, they found that hypnotic amnesia was *not* associated with paradoxical effects. They noted that the majority of high-hypnotizable individuals showed no intrusions when administered suggestions for amnesia and concluded that "thought suppression and hypnotic amnesia represent quite different processes" (p. 381). This distinction may be the laboratory analogue of what happens to some victims of trauma. The clinical data on dissociative disorders, some of which we reviewed above, suggest that some persons *are* able to block out trauma memories to varying degrees. Furthermore, the diagnostic criteria for PTSD actually include amnesia. Thus, the above assertion that all trauma victims cannot "get rid of" their traumatic memories appears inaccurate. It would be more accurate to say that victims of trauma experience varying degrees of intrusive memories versus amnesias for the events. A diathesis-stress model has been proposed in which the level of hypnotizabilty (or a related trait) interacts with the nature of the traumatic event to the degree to which memories intrude or are blocked at any given point in time (Butler, et al., 1996). The level of motivation and the forgetting strategy the person uses (Bower, 1990; L. M. Williams, 1995) may also be factors in determining memory accessibility. . . .

Theoretical Explanations for Blocked and Recovered Memories

Our brief review of theoretical mechanisms that could cause memory blocking and recovery reveals a number of potential causes of these phenomena that can occur even in simple laboratory situations. Although we make no definitive claims as to which of these mechanisms are at work in naturally occurring cases, it is nonetheless clear that there already exist several possible explanations of blocking and recovery that have been used to explain experimental findings. Theoretical mechanisms that could be used to explain blocked and recovered memories include explanations of hypermnesia, recovery from retrieval inhibition, state-dependent memory, arousal effects, and a special emotion mechanism.

Repression and hypermnesia.   Erdelyi and Goldberg (1979) defined repression as a tendentious rejection from awareness of aversive memories for the purpose of avoiding the painful feelings associated with the rejected memories. This rejection from awareness may or may not occur as a result of unconscious mechanisms, depending upon one's theoretical outlook. The best evidence of the existence of repression, according to Erdelyi and Goldberg, is hypermnesia, a lifting or recovery from the amnesia that is symptomatic of repression. Citing evidence from a broad array of clinical and nonclinical sources, they conclude that most people experience such hypermnesias, recalling events that had previously excluded from consciousness to avoid psychic pain. An alternative explanation, that hypermnesia effects are due not to memory, but rather to a reporting bias, was not supported by the results of Roediger and Payne (1985), who found that the observed level of hypermnesia was not affected by a relaxed reporting criterion, or even by "forced recall" instructions that required experimental participants to guess at to-be-recalled memories once intentional attempts to recall had been exhausted. Although the cognitive mechanisms that give rise to hypermnesia have not yet been conclusively determined, it is conceivable that laboratory-induced and clinically observed hypermnesias have the same causes.

State dependence.   Mood-dependent memory, sometimes seen as a type of contextual dependence (e.g., Smith, 1988, 1995c), refers to findings that show that memory of events can be enhanced by reinstating the affective state present when the events were initially experienced (e.g., Bower, 1981; Eich, 1989, 1995). Mood-dependence could be one of the reasons that traumatic memories become blocked from conscious awareness. That is, if the critical events were associated with an extreme or unusual affective state, then dissociation could occur, or become exacerbated, by the low likelihood of reentering that mood state. Bower (1994) has proposed this as a possible model of how some memories and identity information could remain inaccessible at times for patients with dissociative identity disorder.

Interference, inhibition, and spontaneous recovery.   Interference, a classic issue of interest in the experimental study of memory (e.g., McGeoch, 1933; Melton & Irwin, 1940; Postman & Underwood, 1973), is forgetting caused by the presence of material in memory that is similar to the target of one's memory search. Mechanisms that have been proposed as underlying interference effects include response competition, occlusion, inhibition, and unlearning. Whereas unlearning (Melton & Irwin, 1940) refers to a loss of material from memory, response competition, occlusion, and inhibition refer to temporary memory failures. Response competition (e.g., McGeoch, 1942) occurs when the retrieval of one associated response impedes or delays retrieval of another associated response. Occlusion (e.g., Anderson & Bjork, 1994; Anderson, Bjork, & Bjork, 1994) is similar to competition, and refers to forgetting that depends upon the strength of competing associations.

Inhibition, a theoretical mechanism analogous to neural inhibition, refers to a temporary deficiency in one's ability to retrieve material stored in memory. Retrieval inhibition has been suggested as the mechanism responsible for a number of forgetting phenomena, including post-hypnotic amnesia, directed forgetting (e.g., Geiselman et al., 1983; but see Kihlstrom, 1983; Kihlstrom & Barnhardt, 1993), retrieval induced forgetting, part-list cueing effects (e.g., Anderson & Bjork, 1994), and memory suppression (e.g., Anderson & Green, 2001). In the Anderson and Green study, both associative interference and unlearning of the cue-target association were ruled out as the mechanisms underlying the observed retrieval impairment, providing strong support in this case for the existence of an inhibitory control mechanism inhibiting the unwanted memory itself.

Recovery from interference (or inhibition), sometimes called spontaneous recovery, constitutes the best evidence that interference does not necessarily render memories permanently inaccessible. A theoretical model that explains recovery from retroactive interference originated with Estes' (1955) stimulus-sampling theory, and has been developed by several other theoreticians, including Bower (1972), Glenberg (1979), and Mensink and Raaijmakers (1987). The general form of this model states that interfering memories, which are cue-dependent, are rendered inaccessible over time or with contextual changes because temporal/contextual change leads to altered encodings of memory cues. Decreasing the accessibility of competing memories makes the originally blocked memories less inaccessible, thereby increasing the chances of recovering the original memories (see Smith, 1994a). This research is consistent with the notion that conflicting memories regarding abusive parents that emerge from victimization and continued dependence on the same people may hamper episodic memory retrieval (Freyd, 1996). This type of model can also be used to explain recovery of memories in other experimental paradigms (Smith, 1995b).

Mechanisms related to emotion and arousal.   Approaches to repression as forgetting of emotionally traumatic experiences focus more on the traumatic aspects of the phenomenon rather than the resultant amnesia. Experimental evidence of such a putative emotional mechanism is understandably sparse. However, in studies by Loftus and Burns (1982) and Christianson and Nilsson (1984), both of which used material that was perhaps as stressful as ethically possible, both found that amnesia was associated with trauma. Although Loftus and Burns concluded that their results suggested that "mentally shocking episodes" (p. 318) possibly disrupt processes related to storage of information in memory (p. 318), Christianson and Nilsson found amnesia on tests of recall but not recognition, indicating that retrieval rather than storage was affected by the traumatic experience.

Conclusions and Limitations of Conclusions Regarding Blocked and Recovered Memory

As with the reviewed research on false memory, there are many limitations associated with the clinical and experimental research on blocked and recovered memory. Many of the clinical reports suffer from limitations of retrospective research. In many instances, the alleged events of abuse were not corroborated. When they were, the type of corroborating evidence was sometimes not described (e.g., Feldman-Summers & Pope, 1994) and thus is not open to objective evaluation. In some of the research, especially the report by L. M. Williams (1994), one cannot be certain that failure to report memory is due to failure to remember or that failure to remember is due to anything other than normal forgetting, although the documented intensity of the trauma and resulting injury make this explanation less plausible.

Nonetheless, there is an accumulating, if small, store of corroborated and well-documented case studies (e.g., Bull, 1999; Cheit, 1998; Corwin &

Olafson, 1997; Dalenberg, 1996, 1997; Duggal & Sroufe, 1998; Schooler et al., 1997; L. M. Williams, 1995) that may help illuminate the phenomena and inform future research. In fact, in one clinical case study (Corwin & Olafson, 1997) the initial memory recovery event was videotaped and has been examined and evaluated by a variety of commentators (e.g., Ekman, 1997; Neisser, 1997; Putnam, 1997). Additionally, clinical studies of the circumstances and triggers of memory recovery (e.g., Andrews et al., 2000; Herman & Harvey, 1997) have helped to further describe the nature of amnesia and memory recovery in the case of real traumatic memories.

Some of the laboratory research also suffers from limitations. For the same ethical reason that one cannot try to induce false memories of actual sexual trauma, one cannot subject participants to truly traumatic experiences to determine the degree to which persons can block or "repress" these memories. Thus, the degree to which research on blocking and recovery of memory can be generalized to memories of trauma cannot be directly determined.

Some researchers (e.g., Coe, 1978; Spanos, 1986) have argued that findings of posthypnotic amnesia are limited no less than are findings of hypnotic pseudomemories. It is not clear to what degree reports of amnesia are due to compliance, role playing, or strategic enactment, although these studies rarely take hypnotizability into account and overemphasize subjects' motivation to "behave like a hypnotized person." As with the research on hypnotically induced false memory, these factors do not appear to account for all of the findings of posthypnotic amnesia (Evans, 1988). . . .

Conclusions and Future Directions

When memories of traumatic events appear to be recovered, do such experiences reflect truly recovered memories that are essentially accurate, or are such events likely to be false memories of events that never happened? Although no immediate resolution of this important question is at hand, in the present paper we acknowledge and demonstrate the reality of both recovered and false memories. That is, the conclusion that we want to convey is that there is a wealth of data related to both sides of this controversial coin. Recurrent claims that no data exist that support either of these phenomena are, in our opinion, contradicted by the actual data. Furthermore, we believe that it is also inaccurate to paint this debate (as has been done both in the popular and scientific media) as being the academics against the clinicians with only the clinical data supporting the recovered memory position and the experimental data supporting the false memory position. Research from numerous bodies of experimental research supports the reality of memory blocking and recovery.

The issues that are truly debatable concern what inferences can be drawn from the available data. All of the data are limited to some degree. For ethical reasons, research that would perhaps definitively resolve this controversy cannot be conducted. It is noteworthy that the same ethical limitation applies to both aspects of this topic. That is, it would be unethical to subject research participants (particularly children) to the types of events allegedly associated with dissociative amnesia (i.e., physical and/or sexual traumas).

However, it would also be unethical to attempt to create false memories of horrific events in research participants. We are then left with different bodies of research that, each in its own way, is limited in terms of what inferences can be drawn.

Pezdek and Banks (1996) described the unavoidable dialectic of "control versus applicability" (p. 1) or that of internal versus external validity. Often the research that has the highest of the former has the least of the latter (or vice-versa), and this appears to be the case when it comes to false versus recovered memory research. We urge researchers to exercise appropriate cautions and to consider seriously both types of validity when interpreting research. We also suggest that there is much room for improvement in terms of finding a balance of the different types of validity. That is, we believe that the external validity of research can be improved without necessarily sacrificing internal validity. Pezdek et al.'s (1997) study of the limits of what types of memory can be suggested is an example of a step in the correct direction. Applying controlled experimental paradigms to clinical samples (rather than simply undergraduate students) is another.

Another step in the correct direction was Smith et al.'s (2003) attempt to study both false and recovered memories within a single experimental procedure, allowing for the possibility of directly comparing the two phenomena. We believe that the greatest advancements will be made by researchers with interests in studying both phenomena. Unfortunately, few researchers seem interested in doing so. Smith et al. (2003) were indeed able to discriminate between false and recovered memories on the basis of metacognitive reports, including confidence ratings (Experiments 1 and 2) and remember/know judgments (Experiment 2). To our knowledge, this was the first experimental attempt to make such a discrimination. Two variables measuring response latencies did not prove to be useful in discriminating the two types of memories. One of the major goals of future research on this topic should be to experimentally test other variables (e.g., emotionality of events, affective states, retention intervals, and personality factors) that might discriminate the two types of memory phenomena.

By exploring these naturalistic phenomena in controlled experimental settings we can learn more about the mechanisms that underlie them. The same signatures that occur in experimental paradigms could be investigated in naturally occurring cases. Retrospective accounts of individuals with histories of memory dissociation and of therapists who have treated such individuals could be examined as a function of evidence that corroborates or falsifies the reality of the recovered memories (similar to the methodology of Dalenberg, 1996, 1997). The clearest cases of recovered and false memories, as determined by corroborating evidence, would hopefully display the same signatures that can be observed in controlled laboratory studies. Thus, only by returning our attention to those naturalistic contexts, looking for the same patterns identified experimentally, will we learn whether or not the mechanisms we identify in the laboratory are relevant to real life cases of memory blocking and recovery.

References

American Psychiatric Association. (1994). *Diagnostic and statistical manual of mental disorders* (4th ed.). Washington, DC: Author.

Anderson, M. C., & Bjork, R. A. (1994). Mechanisms of inhibition in long-term memory: A new taxonomy. In D. Dagenbach & T. Carr (Eds.), *Inhibition in attention, memory and language.* New York: Academic Press.

Anderson, M. C., Bjork, R. A., & Bjork, E. L. (1994). Remembering can cause forgetting: Retrieval dynamics in long-term memory. *Journal of Experimental Psychology: Learning, Memory & Cognition, 20,* 1063–1087.

Anderson, M. C., & Green, C. (2001). Suppressing unwanted memories by executive control. *Nature, 410,* 366–369.

Anderson, M. C., & Neely, J. (1996). Interference and inhibition in memory retrieval. In E. Bjork & R. A. Bjork (Eds.), *Memory: Handbook of perception and cognition,* (2nd ed., pp. 237–313). San Diego: Academic Press.

Andrews, C., Brewin, C. R., Ochera, J., Morton, J., Bekerian, D. A., Davies, G. M., et al. (2000). The timing, triggers and qualities of recovered memories of therapy. *British Journal of Clinical Psychology, 39,* 11–26.

Barnier, A. J., & McConkey, K. M. (1992). Reports of real and false memories: The relevance of hypnosis, hypnotizability, & context of memory test. *Journal of Abnormal Psychology, 101,* 521–527.

Basden, D. R., & Basden, B. H. (1995). Some tests of the strategy disruption interpretation of part-list cueing inhibition. *Journal of Experimental Psychology: Learning, Memory, & Cognition, 21,* 1656–1669.

Basden, D. R., Basden, B. H., & Galloway, B. C. (1977). *Journal of Experimental Psychology: Human Learning & Memory, 3,* 100–108.

Basden, B. H., Basden, D. R., & Gargano, G. J. (1993). Directed forgetting in implicit and explicit memory tests: A comparison of methods. *Journal of Experimental Psychology: Learning, Memory, and Cognition, 19,* 603–616.

Bjork, R. A. (1972). Theoretical implications of directed forgetting. In A. W. Melton & E. Martin (Eds.), *Coding processes in human memory* (pp. 217–236). Washington, DC: Winston.

Bjork, R. A., & Bjork, E. L. (1996). Continuing influences of to-be-forgotten information. *Consciousness and Cognition, 5,* 176–196.

Bower, G. H. (1972). Stimulus-sampling theory of encoding variability. In A. W. Melton and E. Martin (Eds.), *Coding processes in human memory* (pp. 85–124). Washington, DC: Winston.

Bower, G. H. (1981). Mood and memory. *American Psychologist, 36,* 129–148.

Bower, G. H. (1990). Awareness, the unconscious, and repression: An experimental psychologist's perspective. In J. L. Singer (Ed.), *Repression and dissociation: Implications for personality theory, psychopathology, and health.* Chicago: University of Chicago Press.

Bower, G. H. (1994). Temporary emotional states act like multiple personalities. In R. M. Klein & B. K. Doane (Eds.), *Psychological concepts and dissociative disorders* (pp. 207–234). Hillsdale, NJ: Erlbaum.

Bowers, K. S., & Woody, E. Z. (1996). Hypnotic amnesia and the paradox of intentional forgetting. *Journal of Abnormal Psychology, 105,* 381–390.

Bowman, C. G., & Mertz, E. (1996a). A dangerous direction: Legal interventions in sexual abuse survivor therapy, *Harvard Law Review, 109,* 549–639.

Bowman, C. G., & Mertz, E. (1996b). What should the courts do about memories of sexual abuse: Toward a balanced approach. *The Judges Journal, 35*(4), 6–17.

Brainerd, C. J., & Reyna, V. F. (1998). When things that were never experienced are easier to "remember" than things that were. *Psychological Science, 9,* 484–489.

Bransford, J. D., & Franks, J. J. (1972). The abstraction of linguistic ideas: A review. *Cognition, 1,* 211–249.

Bremner, J. D., Steinberg, M., Southwick, S. M., Johnson, D. R., & Charney, D. S. (1993). Use of the Structured Clinical Interview for DSM-IV-Dissociative Disorders for systematic assessment of dissociative symptoms in posttraumatic stress disorder. *American Journal of Psychiatry, 150,* 1011–1014.

Brewer, W. F., & Treyens, J. C. (1981). Role of schemata in memory for places. *Cognitive Psychology, 13,* 207–230.

Brewin, C. R. (1996). Scientific status of recovered memories. *British Journal of Psychiatry, 169,* 131–134.

Briere, J., & Conte, J. (1993). Self-reported amnesia for abuse in adults molested as children. *Journal of Traumatic Stress, 6,* 21–31.

Brown, A. S. (1976). Spontaneous recovery in human learning. *Psychological Bulletin, 83,* 321–338.

Brown, A. S., & Murphy, D. R. (1989). Cryptomnesia: Delineating inadvertent plagiarism. *Journal of Experimental Psychology: Learning, Memory, & Cognition, 15,* 432–442.

Brown, D. (1995). Pseudomemories: The standard of science and the standard of care in trauma treatment. *American Journal of Clinical Hypnosis, 3,* 1–24.

Brown, D., Scheflin, A. W., & Whitfield, C. L. (1999). Recovered memories: The current weight of the evidence in science and in the courts. *Journal of Psychiatry & Law, 27,* 5–156.

Brown, J. M., & Smith, S. M. (1992, April). *Recovery from part-list cueing inhibition.* Paper presented at the meeting of the Midwestern Psychological Association, Chicago, IL.

Bull, D. L. (1999). A verified case of recovered memories of sexual abuse. *American Journal of Psychotherapy, 53,* 221–224.

Butler, L. D., Duran, R. E. F., Jasiukaitus, P., Koopman, C., & Spiegel, D. (1996). Hypnotizability and traumatic experience: A diathesis-stress model of dissociative symptomatology. *American Journal of Psychiatry, 153*(7, suppl.), 42–63.

Butler, L. D., & Spiegel, D. (1997). Trauma and memory. In L. J. Dickstein, M. B. Riba, & J. M. Oldham (Eds.), *Review of Psychiatry* (Vol. 16, pp. II-13–II-53). Washington, DC: American Psychiatric Press.

Campbell, D. T., & Stanley, J. C. (1967). *Experimental and quasi-experimental designs for research.* Chicago: Rand McNally.

Carstensen, L., Gabrieli, J., Shepard, R., Levenson, R., Mason, M., Goodman, G., et al. (1993, March). Repressed objectivity. *APS Observer,* p. 23.

Cheit, R. E. (1998). Consider this, skeptics of recovered memory. *Ethics & Behavior, 8,* 141–160.

Christianson, S., & Nilsson, L. (1984). Functional amnesia as induced by a psychological trauma. *Memory & Cognition, 12,* 142–155.

Clemes, S. (1964). Repression and hypnotic amnesia. *Journal of Abnormal and Social Psychology, 69,* 62–69.

Coe, W. C. (1978). The credibility of posthypnotic amnesia: A contextualist's view. *International Journal of Clinical and Experimental Hypnosis, 26,* 218–245.

Corwin, D. L., & Olafson, E. (1997). Videotaped discovery of a reportedly unrecallable memory of child sexual abuse: Comparison with a childhood interview videotaped 11 years before. *Child Maltreatment, 2,* 91–112.

Dalenberg, C. J. (1996). Accuracy, timing and circumstances of disclosure in therapy of recovered and continuous memories of abuse. *Journal of Psychiatry and Law, 24,* 229-276.

Dalenberg, C. J. (1997). The prediction of accurate recollections of trauma. In J. D. Read & D. S. Lindsay (Eds.), *Recollections of trauma—Scientific evidence and clinical practice* (pp. 449-453). New York: Plenum Press.

Dallam, S. J. (2001). Crisis or creation? A systematic examination of "false memory syndrome." *Journal of Child Sexual Abuse, 9,* 9-36.

de Rivera, J. (1997). The construction of False Memory Syndrome: The experience of retractors. *Psychological Inquiry, 8,* 271-292.

de Rivera, J. (2000). Understanding persons who repudiate memories recovered in therapy. *Professional Psychology: Research and Practice, 31,* 378-386.

Duggal, S., & Sroufe, L. A. (1998). Recovered memory of childhood sexual trauma: A documented case from a longitudinal study. *Journal of Traumatic Stress, 11,* 301-321.

Dywan, J., & Bowers, K. (1983). The use of hypnosis to enhance recall. *Science, 222,* 184-185.

Ekman, P. (1997). Expressive behavior and the recovery of a traumatic memory: Comments on the videotapes of Jane Doe. *Child Maltreatment, 2,* 113-116.

Eich, E. (1989). Theoretical issues in state-dependent memory. In H. L. Roediger and F. I. M. Craik (Eds.), *Varieties of memory and consciousness: Essays in honour of Endel Tulving* (pp. 331-354). Hillsdale, NJ: Erlbaum.

Eich, E. (1995). Mood as a mediator of place-dependent memory. *Journal of Experimental Psychology: General, 124,* 293-308.

Erdelyi, M. H., & Goldberg, B. (1979). Let's not sweep repression under the rug: Towards a cognitive psychology of repression. In J. F. Kihlstrom & F. J. Evans (Eds.), *Functional disorders of memory* (pp. 355-402). Hillsdale, NJ: Erlbaum.

Erdelyi, M. H., & Kleinbard, J. (1978). Has Ebbinghaus decayed with time? The growth of recall (hypermnesia) over days. *Journal of Experimental Psychology: Human Learning and Memory, 4,* 275-289.

Estes, W. K. (1955). Statistical theory of spontaneous recovery and regression. *Psychological Review, 62,* 369-377.

Estes, W. K. (1997). Processes of memory loss, recovery, and distortion. *Psychological Review, 104,* 148-169.

Evans, F. J. (1988). Posthypnotic amnesia: Dissociation of content and context. In H. M. Pettinati (Ed.), *Hypnosis and memory* (pp. 157-192). New York: Guilford.

Feldman-Summers, S., & Pope, K. S. (1994). The experience of "forgetting" childhood abuse: A national survey of psychologists. *Journal of Consulting & Clinical Psychology, 62,* 636-639.

Freud, S. (1955). Notes upon a case of obsessional neurosis. In J. Strachey (Ed. & Trans.), *The standard edition of the complete psychological works of Sigmund Freud* (Vol. 10, pp. 153-249). London: Hogarth Press (original work published 1909).

Freud, S. (1962). The aetiology of hysteria. In J. Strachey (Ed. & Trans.), *The standard edition of the complete psychological works of Sigmund Freud* (Vol. 3, pp. 191-221). London: Hogarth Press. (Original work published 1896).

Freyd, J. J. (1996). *Betrayal trauma: The logic of forgetting childhood abuse.* Cambridge, MA: Harvard University Press.

Freyd, J. J., & Gleaves, D. H. (1996). Remembering words not presented in lists: Relevance to the current recovered/false memory controversy. *Journal of Experimental Psychology: Learning, Memory, and Cognition, 22,* 811-813.

Freyd, P. (1999). About the False Memory Syndrome Foundation. In S. Taub (Ed.), *Recovered memories of child sexual abuse—Psychological, social, and legal perspectives on a contemporary mental health controversy* (pp. 17–39). Springfield, IL: Charles C. Thomas.

Garry, M., Manning, C. G., Loftus, E. F., & Sherman, S. J. (1996). Imagination inflation: Imagining a childhood event inflates confidence that it occurred. *Psychonomic Bulletin & Review, 3,* 208–214.

Garry, M., & Polaschek, D. L. L. (2000). Imagination and memory. *Current Directions in Psychological Science, 9,* 6–10.

Gavigan, M. (1992). False memories of childhood sexual abuse: A personal account. *Issues in Child Abuse Accusations, 4,* 246–247.

Geiselman, R. E., Mackinnon, D. P., Fishman, D. L., Jaenicke, C., Larner, B. R., Schoenberg, S., et al. (1983). Mechanisms of hypnotic and nonhypnotic forgetting. *Journal of Experimental Psychology: Learning, Memory, and Cognition, 9,* 626–635.

Gleaves, D. H. (1994). On the reality of repressed memories. *American Psychologist, 49,* 440–441.

Gleaves, D. H. (1996). The evidence for "repression": An examination of Holmes (1990) and the implications for the recovered memory controversy. *Journal of Child Sexual Abuse, 5,* 1–19.

Gleaves, D. H., & Freyd, J. J. (1997). Questioning additional claims about the "False memory syndrome" epidemic. *American Psychologist, 52,* 993–994.

Glenberg, A. M. (1979). Component-levels theory of the effects of spacing of repetitions on recall and recognition. *Memory & Cognition, 7,* 95–112.

Goldstein, E., & Farmer, K. (1992). *Confabulations: Creating false memories, destroying families.* Boca Raton, Florida: SIRS.

Grainger, J. (1990). Word frequency and neighborhood frequency effects in lexical decision and naming. *Journal of Memory and Language, 29,* 228–244.

Grinker, R. R., & Spiegel, J. P. (1945). *War neuroses.* Philadelphia: Blakiston.

Haber, R. N., & Haber, L. (1996). *Antecedent conditions and operational definitions for recovered memory effects.* Paper presented at the meeting of the Psychonomic Society, Chicago, IL.

Herman, J. L., & Harvey, M. R. (1997). Adult memories of childhood trauma: A naturalistic study. *Journal of Traumatic Stress, 10,* 557–571.

Herman, J. L., & Schatzow, E. (1987). Recovery & verification of memories of childhood sexual trauma. *Psychoanalytic Psychology, 4,* 1–14.

Holmes, D. S. (1990). The evidence for repression: An examination of sixty years of research. In J. L. Singer (Ed.), *Repression and dissociation: Implications for personality theory, psychopathology, and health* (pp. 85–102). Chicago: University of Chicago Press.

Holmes, D. S. (1994). Is there evidence for repression? Doubtful. *The Harvard Mental Health Newsletter,* June, 4–6.

Horowitz, M. J. (1986). *Stress response syndromes.* New York: Aronson.

Hyman, I. E., Gilstrap, L. L., Decker, K. L., & Wilkinson, C. L. (1998). Manipulating remember versus know judgments in autobiographical memories. *Applied Cognitive Psychology, 12,* 371–386.

Hyman, I. E., Husband, T. H., & Billings, J. F. (1995). False memories of childhood experiences. *Applied Cognitive Psychology, 9,* 181–197.

Hyman, I. E., & Pentland, J. (1996). The role of mental imagery in the creation of false childhood memories. *Journal of Memory and Language, 35,* 101–117.

Jacoby, L. L. (1991). A process dissociation framework: Separating automatic from intentional uses of memory. *Journal of Memory & Language, 30,* 513–541.

Johnson, M. K., Foley, M. A., Suengas, A. G., & Raye, C. L. (1988). Phenomenal characteristics of memories for perceived and imagined autobiographical events. *Journal of Experimental Psychology: General, 117,* 371–376.

Johnson, M. K., Hashtroudi, S., & Lindsay, D. S. (1993). Source monitoring. *Psychological Bulletin, 114,* 3–28.

Johnson, M. K., & Raye, C. L. (1981). Reality monitoring. *Psychological Review, 88,* 67–85.

Jones, G. V. (1989). Back to Woodworth: The role of inter-lopers in the tip of the tongue phenomenon. *Memory & Cognition, 17,* 69–76.

Kardiner, A., & Spiegel, H. (1947). *War stress and neurotic illness.* New York: Hoeber.

Kassin, S. M. (1997). The psychology of confession evidence. *American Psychologist, 52,* 221–233.

Kaszniak, A. W., Nussbaum, P. D., Berren, M. R., & Santiago, J. (1988). Amnesia as a consequence of male rape: A case report. *Journal of Abnormal Psychology, 97,* 100–104.

Kihlstrom, J. F. (1979). Hypnosis and psychopathology: Retrospect and prospect. *Journal of Abnormal Psychology, 88,* 459–473.

Kihlstrom, J. F. (1983). Instructed forgetting: Hypnotic and nonhypnotic. *Journal of Experimental Psychology: General, 112,* 73–79.

Kihlstrom, J. F. (1987). The cognitive unconscious. *Science, 237,* 1445–1452.

Kihlstrom, J. F. (1997). Memory, abuse, and science. *American Psychologist, 52,* 994–995.

Kihlstrom, J. F. (1998). Exhumed memory. In S. J. Lynn & K. M. McConkey (Eds.), *Truth in memory* (pp. 3–31). New York: Guilford.

Kihlstrom, J. F., & Barnhardt, T. M. (1993). The self-regulation of memory, for better and for worse, with and without hypnosis. In D. B. Wegner & J. J. Pennebaker (Eds.), *Handbook of mental control* (pp. 88–125). Englewood Cliffs, NJ: Prentice-Hall.

Kihlstrom, J. F., & Evans, F. J. (1979). Memory retrieval processes during post-hypnotic amnesia. In J. F. Kihlstrom & F. J. Evans (Eds.), *Functional disorders of memory* (pp. 179–218). Hillsdale, NJ: Erlbaum.

Kirkpatrick, E. A. (1894). An experimental study of memory. *Psychological Review, 1,* 602–609.

Kluft, R. P. (1998). Reflections on the traumatic memories of dissociative identity disorder patients. In S. J. Lynn & K. M. McConkey (Eds.), *Truth in memory* (pp. 304–322). New York: Guilford.

Knapp, S., & VandeCreek, L. (2000). Recovered memories of childhood abuse: Is there an underlying professional consensus? *Professional Psychology: Research and Practice, 31,* 365–371.

Kolb, L. C. (1988). Recovery of memory and repressed fantasy in combat-induced post-traumatic stress disorder of Vietnam veterans. In H. M. Pettinati (Ed.), *Hypnosis and memory* (pp. 265–274). New York: Guilford.

Koutstaal, W., & Schacter, D. L. (1997). Intentional forgetting and voluntary thought suppression: Two potential methods for coping with childhood trauma. In L. J. Dickstein, M. B. Riba, & J. M. Oldham (Eds.), *Review of psychiatry* (Vol. 16, pp. II-55–II-78). Washington, DC: American Psychiatric Press.

Laurence, J. R., & Perry, C. (1983). Hypnotically created memory among highly hypnotizable subjects. *Science, 222,* 523–524.

Lief, H. I., & Fetkewicz, J. M. (1995). Retractors of false memories: The evolution of pseudomemories. *Journal of Psychiatry & Law, 23,* 411–435.

Lindsay, D. S., Read, J. D., & Sharma, K. (1998). Accuracy and confidence in person identification: The relationship is strong when witnessing conditions vary widely. *Psychological Science, 9,* 215–218.

Lipton, A. (1999). Recovered memories in the courts. In S. Taub (Ed.), *Recovered memories of child sexual abuse—Psychological, social, and legal perspectives on a contemporary mental health controversy* (pp. 165–210). Springfield, IL: Charles C. Thomas.

Loewenstein, R. J. (1991). Psychogenic amnesia and fugue: A comprehensive review. In D. Spiegel (Ed.), *Dissociative disorders: A clinical review* (pp. 45–78). Lutherville, MD: Sidran Press.

Loftus, E. F. (1993). The reality of repressed memories. *American Psychologist, 48,* 518–537.

Loftus, E. F., & Burns, T. E. (1982). Mental shock can produce retrograde amnesia. *Memory & Cognition, 10,* 318–323.

Loftus, E. F., & Hoffman, H. G. (1989). Misinformation and memory: The creation of new memories. *Journal of Experimental Psychology: General, 118,* 100–104.

Loftus, E. F., & Ketcham, K. (1994). *The myth of repressed memory: False memories and allegations of sexual abuse.* New York: St. Martin's Press.

Loftus, E. F., & Mazzoni, G. A. L. (1998). Using imagination and personalized suggestion to change people. *Behavior Therapy, 29,* 691–706.

Loftus, E. F., Miller, D. G., & Burns, H. J. (1978). Semantic integration of verbal information into a visual memory. *Journal of Experimental Psychology: Human Learning and Memory, 4,* 19–31.

Loftus, E. F., & Palmer, J. C. (1974). Reconstruction of automobile destruction: An example of the interaction between language and memory. *Journal of Verbal Learning and Verbal Behavior, 13,* 585–589.

Loftus, E. F., Polonsky, S., & Fullilove, M. T. (1994). Memories of childhood sexual abuse: Remembering & repressing. *Psychology of Women Quarterly, 18,* 67–84.

Lustig, C., & Hasher, L. (2001). Implicit memory is vulnerable to proactive interference. *Psychological Bulletin, 127,* 618–628.

Lynn, S. J., Weekes, J. R., & Milano, M. J. (1989). Reality versus suggestion: Pseudomemory in hypnotizable and simulating subjects. *Journal of Abnormal Psychology, 98,* 137–144.

MacLeod, C. M. (1991). Half a century of research on the Stroop effect: An integrative review. *Psychological Bulletin, 109,* 163–203.

Martin, E. (1971). Verbal learning theory and independent retrieval phenomena. *Psychological Review, 78,* 314–332.

McDermott, K. B. (1996). The persistence of false memories in list recall. *Journal of Memory & Language, 35,* 212–230.

McElroy, S. L., & Keck, P. E., Jr. (1995). The formation of false memories. *Psychiatric Annals, 25,* 720–725.

McGeoch, J. A. (1933). Studies in retroactive inhibition: The temporal course of the inhibitory effects of interpolated learning. *Journal of General Psychology, 9,* 24–43.

McGeoch, J. A. (1942). *The psychology of human learning.* New York: Longmans, Green.

Melton, A. W., & Irwin, J. (1940). The influence of interpolated learning on retroactive inhibition and the overt transfer of specific responses. *American Journal of Psychology, 53,* 175–203.

Mensink, G.-J. & Raaijmakers, J. G. (1988). A model of interference and forgetting. *Psychological Review, 95,* 434–455.

Modai, I. (1994). Forgetting childhood: A defense mechanism against psychosis in a Holocaust survivor. *Clinical Gerontology, 14*(3), 67–71.

Mook, D. G. (1983). In defense of external invalidity. *American Psychologist, 38,* 379–387.

Murrey, G. J., Cros, H. J., & Whipple, J. (1992). Hypnotically created pseudomemories: Further investigation into the "Memory distortion or response bias" question. *Journal of Abnormal Psychology, 101,* 75–77.

Nelson, E. L., & Simpson, P. (1994). First glimpse: an initial examination of subjects who have rejected their visualizations as false memories. *Issues in Child Abuse Accusations, 6,* 123–133.

Neisser, U. (1997). Jane Doe's memories: Changing the past to serve the present. *Child Maltreatment, 2,* 123–125.

Nemiah, J. C. (1979). Dissociative amnesia: A clinical and theoretical reconsideration. In J. F. Kihlstrom & F. J. Evans (Eds.), *Functional disorders of memory* (pp. 303–324). Hillsdale, NJ: Erlbaum Associates.

Nickerson, R. S. (1984). Retrieval inhibition from part-set cueing: A persisting enigma in memory research. *Memory & Cognition, 12,* 531–552.

Oakes, M. A., & Hyman, I. E. (2000). The changing face of memory and self. In D. F. Bjorklund (Ed.), *False-memory creation in children and adults* (pp. 45–67). Mahwah, NJ: Erlbaum.

Ofshe, R. J. (1992). Inadvertent hypnosis during interrogation: False confession due to dissociative state, misidentified multiple personality and the satanic cult hypothesis. *International Journal of Clinical and Experimental Hypnosis, 40,* 125–156.

Ofshe, R., & Singer, M. T. (1994). Recovered-memory therapy and robust repression: Influence and psuedomemories. *International Journal of Clinical and Experimental Hypnosis, 42,* 391–410.

Ofshe, R., & Watters, E. (1993, March/April). Making monsters. *Society,* 4–16.

Olio, K. (1994). Truth in memory. *American Psychologist, 49,* 442–443.

Olio, K., & Cornell, W. (1994). The Paul Ingram case: Pseudomemory or pseudo-science? *Violence Update, 3,* 4.

Olio, K. A., & Cornell, W. F. (1998). The facade of scientific documentation. A case study of Richard Ofshe's analysis of the Paul Ingram case. *Psychology, Public Policy, and Law, 4,* 1182–1197.

Pasley, L. (1994). Misplaced trust: A first-person account of how my therapist created false memories. *Skeptic, 2,* 62–67.

Payne, D. G. (1987). Hypermnesia and reminiscence in recall: A historical and empirical review. *Psychological Bulletin, 101,* 5–27.

Payne, D. G., Elie, C. J., Blackwell, J. M., & Neuschatz, J. S. (1996). Memory illusions: Recalling, recognizing, and recollecting events that never occurred. *Journal of Memory & Language, 35,* 261–285.

Pendergrast, M. (1995). *Victims of memory: Incest accusations and shattered lives.* Hinesburg, VT: Upper Access.

Pezdek, K., & Banks, W. P. (Eds.). (1996). *The Recovered memory/false memory debate.* San Diego: Academic Press.

Pezdek, K., Finger, K., & Hodge, D. (1997). Planting false childhood memories: The role of event plausibility. *Psychological Science, 8,* 437–441.

Pezdek, K., & Taylor, J. (2000). Discriminating between accounts of true and false events. In D. F. Bjorklund (Ed.), *False-memory creation in children and adults* (pp. 69-91). Mahwah, NJ: Erlbaum.

Piper, A., Pope, H. G., & Borowiecki, J. J. (2000). Custer's last stand: Brown, Scheflin and Whitfield's latest attempt to salvage "dissociative amnesia." *Journal of Psychiatry & Law, 28,* 149-213.

Pope, H. G., & Hudson, J. I. (1996). "Recovered memory" therapy for eating disorders: Implications of the Ramona verdict. *International Journal of Eating Disorders, 19,* 139-146.

Pope, H. G., Hudson, J. A., Bodkin, J. A., & Oliva, P. (1998). Questionable validity of 'dissociative amnesia' in trauma victims. *British Journal of Psychiatry, 172,* 210-215.

Pope, K. S. (1996). Memory, abuse, and science: Questioning claims about the false memory syndrome epidemic. *American Psychologist, 51,* 957-974.

Pope, K. S. (1997). Science as careful questioning: Are claims of a False Memory Syndrome epidemic based on empirical evidence? *American Psychologist, 52,* 99-1006.

Postman, L., Stark, K., & Fraser, J. (1968). Temporal changes in interference. *Verbal Learning and Verbal Behavior, 7,* 672-694.

Postman, L., & Underwood, B. J. (1973). Critical issues in interference theory. *Memory & Cognition, 1,* 19-40.

Prince, M. (1906). *The dissociation of a personality.* New York: Longmans, Green.

Putnam, F. W. (1997). Commentary. *Child Maltreatment, 2,* 117-120.

Rabinowitz, M., & Mandler, J. M. (1983). Organization and information retrieval. *Journal of Experimental Psychology: Learning, Memory & Cognition, 9,* 430-439.

Read, J. D. (1996). From a passing thought to a false memory in 2 minutes: Confusing real and illusory events. *Psychonomic Bulletin & Review, 3,* 105-111.

Read, J. D., & Bruce, D. (1982). Longitudinal tracking of difficult memory retrievals. *Cognitive Psychology, 14,* 280-300.

Reyna, V. F., & Brainerd, C. J. (1995). Fuzzy-trace theory: An interim synthesis. *Learning & Individual Differences, 7,* 1-75.

Robinson, K. J., & Roediger, H. L., III. (1997). Associative processes in false recall and false recognition, *Psychological Science, 8,* 231-237.

Roediger, H. L., III. (1974). Inhibition in recall from cueing with recall targets. *Journal of Verbal Learning and Verbal Behavior, 12,* 644-657.

Roediger, H. L., III & McDermott, K. B. (1995). Creating false memories: Remembering words not presented in lists. *Journal of Experimental Psychology: Learning, Memory, & Cognition, 21,* 803-814.

Roediger, H. L., III & Payne, D. (1985). Recall criterion does not affect recall level or hypermnesia: A puzzle for generate/recognize theories. *Memory & Cognition, 13,* 1-7.

Rubin, L. J. (1996). Childhood sexual abuse: False accusations of "False memory"? *Professional Psychology: Research and Practice, 27,* 447-451.

Rundus, D. (1973). Negative effects of using list items as recall cues. *Journal of Verbal Learning & Verbal Behavior, 12,* 43-50.

Sargant, W., & Slater, E. (1941). Amnestic syndromes of war. *Proceeding of the Royal Society of Medicine, 34,* 757-764.

Scheflin, A. W., & Brown, D. (1996). Repressed memory or dissociative amnesia: What the science says. *Journal of Psychiatry & Law, 24,* 143-188.

Schooler, J. W., & Fiore, S. M. (1995). *Toeing the middle line: Evidence for both recovered and fabricated memories of abuse.* Paper presented at the meeting of the Psychonomic Society, Los Angeles, CA.

Schooler, J. W., Ambadar, Z., & Bendiksen, M. (1997). A cognitive corroborative case study approach for investigating discovered memories for sexual abuse. In J. D. Read & D. S. Lindsay (Eds.), *Recollections of trauma—Scientific evidence and clinical practice* (pp. 379–387). New York: Plenum Press.

Smith, S. M. (1988). Environmental context-dependent memory. In G. Davies and D. Thomson (Eds.), *Memory in context: Context in memory* (pp. 13–33). New York: Wiley.

Smith, S. M. (1994a). Theoretical principles of context-dependent memory. In P. Morris and M. Gruneberg (Eds.) *Aspects of memory: Theoretical aspects* (2nd ed., pp. 168–195). Routledge Press.

Smith, S. M. (1994b). Frustrated feelings of imminence: On the tip-of-the-tongue. In J. Metcalfe & A. Shimamura (Eds.), *Metacognition: Knowing about knowing* (pp. 27–45). Cambridge, MA: MIT Press.

Smith, S. M. (1995a). *Recovery from memory blocks: Experimental evidence.* APA Division 3 Invited Address. Presented at the meeting of the American Psychological Association, New York, NY.

Smith, S. M. (1995c). Mood is a component of mental context: Comment on Eich (1995). *Journal of Experimental Psychology: General, 124,* 309–310.

Smith, S. M, Gleaves, D. H., Pierce, B. H., Williams, T. L., Gilliland, T. & Gerkins, D. R. (2003). Eliciting and comparing false and recovered memories: An experimental approach. *Applied Cognitive Psychology, 17,* 251–279.

Smith, S. M., & Tindell, D. R. (1997). Memory blocks in word fragment completion caused by involuntary retrieval of orthographically similar primes. *Journal of Experimental Psychology: Learning, Memory and Cognition, 23,* 355–370.

Smith, S. M., & Vela, E. (1991). Incubated reminiscence effects. *Memory and Cognition, 19,* 168–176.

Smith, S. M., Ward, T. B., Sifonis, C. M., Tindell, D. R., Wilkenfeld, M. J., & Pierce, B. H. (1996). *Priming and category structure in created memories.* Paper presented at the meeting of the Psychonomic Society, Chicago, IL.

Spanos, N. P. (1986). Hypnotic behavior: A social psychological interpretation of amnesia, analgesia, and "trance logic." *Behavioral and Brain Sciences, 93,* 449–467.

Spanos, N. P., & McLean, J. (1985–1986). Hypnotically created pseudomemories: Memory distortions or reporting bias? *British Journal of Experimental & Clinical Hypnosis, 3,* 155–159.

Spiegel, D. (1997). Trauma, dissociation, and memory. In R. Yehuda & A. McFarlane (Eds.), *Psychobiology of post-traumatic stress disorder* (pp. 225–237). New York: New York Academy of Sciences.

Tipper, S. P. (1985). The negative priming effect: Inhibitory priming by ignored objects. Quarterly *Journal of Experimental Psychology: Human Experimental Psychology, 37A,* 571–590.

Van der Hart, O., & Nijenhuis, E. (1995). Amnesia for traumatic experiences, *Hypnosis, 22,* 73–86.

Wakefield, H., & Underwager, R. (1994). *Return of the furies: An investigation into recovered memory therapy.* Chicago: Open Court.

Wegner, D. M. (1989). *White bears and other unwanted thoughts.* New York: Viking.

Wells, G. L., & Loftus, E. F. (1984). *Eyewitness testimony: Psychological perspectives.* Cambridge, England: Cambridge University Press.

Wheeler, M. A. (1995). Improvement in recall overtime without repeated testing: Spontaneous recovery revisited. *Journal of Experimental Psychology: Learning, Memory, and Cognition, 10,* 733–744.

Widiger, T. A., & Sankis, L. M. (2000). Adult psychopathology: Issues and controversies. *Annual Review of Psychology, 51,* 377–404.

Williams, L. M. (1994). Recall of childhood trauma: A prospective study of women's memories of child sexual abuse. *Journal of Consulting and Clinical Psychology, 52,* 1167–1176.

Williams, L. M. (1995). Recovered memories of abuse in women with documented child sexual victimization histories. *Journal of Traumatic Stress, 8,* 649–674.

Williams, M. R. (1996). Suits by adults for childhood sexual abuse: Legal origins of the "repressed memory" controversy. *Journal of Psychiatry & Law, 24,* 207–228.

Wylie, M. S. (1993). The shadow of a doubt. *Family Therapy Networker, 17,* 18–29, 70–73.

Zaragoza, M. S., & Koshmider, J. W., III. (1989). Misled subjects may know more than their performance implies. *Journal of Experimental Psychology: Learning, Memory and Cognition, 15,* 246–255.

Zaragoza, M. D., & Mitchell, K. J. (1996). Repeated exposure to suggestion and the creation of false memories. *Psychological Science, 7,* 294–300.

John F. Kihlstrom

NO

An Unbalanced Balancing Act: Blocked, Recovered, and False Memories in the Laboratory and Clinic

In their paper, Gleaves, Smith, Butler, and Spiegel (this issue) draw on clinical and laboratory research to persuade the reader that traumatic memories can be repressed, that recovered memories of trauma are valid, and that false memories of trauma are not too important, thus supporting both the trauma-memory argument and recovered-memory therapy. Although the authors adopt an ostensibly balanced position that "both false and genuine recovered memories may exist" (p. 4), their actual presentation is seriously unbalanced. As a result, the reader is encouraged to discount laboratory evidence of false memories while accepting laboratory evidence of repression and recovered memories, and to discount clinical evidence of false memories while accepting clinical evidence of repression and recovered memories.

Clinical Studies of False Memories

With respect to false memories, Gleaves et al. (2004) discuss the clinical evidence in a little over a page of text. While it may be true that much of this evidence comes in the form of anecdotal case reports published in the popular press, that is no reason to discount them. Journalists, lawyers, judges, and other "laymen" can read and reason too, as exemplified by Frederick Crews, the literary critic whose articles on the "memory wars" did so much to bring our attention to the problems raised by the recovered memory movement (Crews, 1995), and Dorothy Rabinowitz, the *Wall Street Journal* columnist who won a 2001 Pulitzer Prize in part for her critical commentaries on the "Kelly Michaels" and "Amirault" cases of preschool child sex-abuse allegations (Rabinowitz, 2003). At least responsible journalists are required to confirm their sources before their stories are published. Psychotherapists—or at least psychotherapists of a certain kind—are content with "narrative" or "personal" truth, regardless of the fact of the matter (Spence, 1982, 1994). It took a journalist interviewing a psychiatrist for a literary journal to expose Sybil as, shall we say, misdiagnosed (Borch-Jacobsen, 1997).

From *Clinical Psychology: Science and Practice*, vol. 11, issue 1, 2004, pp. 34–41. Copyright © 2004 by Oxford University Press Journals. Reprinted by permission.

What really matters, of course, is not the professional affiliation of the investigator, or the means by which the investigation was published, but the actual evidence produced by the investigation. On this score, Gleaves et al. (2004) have remarkably little to say. They do not confront Moira Johnston's (1997) account of the Ramona case, a landmark court decision in which practitioners paid heavy penalties and lost their licenses for implanting false memories and which established the precedent, entirely new in tort law, that third parties can sue practitioners for damages caused by malpractice. And although we can quibble about the details of who said what, when, and under what circumstances, can anyone read Lawrence Wright's (1994) account of the Paul Ingram case and not come away wondering whether he really participated in hundreds of episodes of ritual infanticide and cannibalism, including the rape of his own children by his poker buddies while their mother watched? Unfortunately, neither of these book-length analyses is even cited by the authors, much less discussed.

Turning to the "professional" literature, Gleaves et al. (2004) cite Williams' (1994) study as evidence that self-reports of abuse have been independently "documented" (p. 8). But this is something of a red herring because the issue is not whether Williams' survey respondents had been abused. The issue is whether any of them showed trauma-induced amnesia for their abuse. On that matter, Williams' study is simply unconvincing (Kihlstrom, 1995, 1996, 1997, 1998). It is more likely that the events in question were subject to normal forgetting processes or to infantile and childhood amnesia. It is also likely that many informants were simply unwilling to disclose their histories to the interviewer, a common and well-known problem with crime reports of any type (Widom & Morris, 1997; Widom & Shepard, 1996).

To my knowledge, nobody has ever claimed that all adult memories of childhood sexual abuse are false, so it should come as no surprise that some such memories can be corroborated. But what are we to do with those self-reports that are not corroborated? Should we simply accept them at face value? Just because some memories are valid does not mean that all memories are valid. But that seems to be the implication of the authors' argument. When therapists speculate that their patients' current problems are causally linked to events in childhood, it would seem that they incur some obligation to determine whether the alleged events actually occurred. But apparently therapists rarely seek independent corroboration of their patients' autobiographical narratives (Shobe & Kihlstrom, 2002). If indeed there is an absence of clinical literature bearing on the problem of false memory, to a great extent this may be attributed to a sort of "pact of ignorance" between patients, who do not wish to have their self-narratives challenged, and therapists, who have no wish to challenge them.

People can also quibble forever about the scientific status of "false memory syndrome," but no one who uses such concepts as "battered woman syndrome" (Walker, 1988, 1991) or "Stockholm syndrome" (Graham, Rawlings, & Rimini, 1988; Graham et al., 1995) in clinical discourse should have any principled objection to the term. Still, Gleaves et al. (2004) are quite right that the essence of the syndrome is not merely the existence of a false memory.

Rather, the syndrome refers to the re-orientation of an individual's identity and personality around a mental representation of his or her personal past—in other words, a memory—that is objectively false. Consider, for example, the well-documented case of Binjamin Wilkomirski, author of the award-winning Holocaust "memoir" *Fragments* (Eskin, 2002; Gourevitch, 1999; Lappin, 1999; Mächler & Wilkomirski, 2001). *Fragments* now appears to have been the work of an author who was actually born in neutral Switzerland to an unmarried Protestant woman and raised and schooled there by foster parents who died before he published his book. Apparently, Wilkomirski incorporated details of the Holocaust gleaned from his voluminous reading into what is essentially a work of the imagination, but one in which he himself devoutly believed. Following a detailed investigation, Wilkomirski's publisher withdrew *Fragments* from publication. Yet, when confronted with the facts, the author angrily replied, "I *am* Binjamin Wilkomirski!" In an interesting twist, at one point a woman who claimed to have been in the camps as a child herself, and to have known Wilkomirski there ("He's my Binje!"), was found to have been born in Tacoma in 1941 and raised in Washington as a foster child by devout Presbyterians.

Laboratory Studies of False Memories

In stark contrast to their relatively brief overview of the clinical evidence of false memories, Gleaves et al. (2004) provide a detailed analysis of laboratory studies of false memories—but one that is written in such a way as to blunt the impact of the laboratory findings and convey the impression that they are not too important for clinicians. For example, the reader is informed that there are several different explanations for both the postevent misinformation effect (Loftus & Palmer, 1974) and the associative-memory illusion (Roediger & McDermott, 1995)—as if that mattered, given that both effects are so robust that they can be demonstrated under classroom conditions. In the final analysis, it is the robust nature of these and similar effects that should give clinicians pause, because the effects are created by the very forces that go on in recovered-memory therapy: the presentation and discussion of themes related to incest, sexual abuse, and the like (Shobe & Kihlstrom, 2002). In fact, the clinical situation may be even more conducive to the formation of illusory memories than the laboratory.

Instead, we are reassured that because laboratory phenomena do not necessarily occur in the real world, we do not have to worry about them after all. The authors barely mention studies indicating that people with histories of self-reported childhood sexual abuse and other traumas show elevated levels of the associative-memory illusion (Bremner, Shobe, & Kihlstrom, 2000; Clancy, Schacter, McNally, & Pitman, 2000). Moreover, they push the conclusion that false memories for unusual or infrequent events are difficult to implant (Pezdek, Finger, & Hodge, 1997), without any mention of later studies that show otherwise (Mazzoni, Loftus, & Kirsch, 2001; Porter, Yuille, & Lehman, 1999). In a psychotherapeutic context, a therapist who believes in both the traumatic etiology of syndromes like anxiety, depression, and eating disorders, as well as the theory of repression, will very likely communicate these ideas to the patient, who may already share them by virtue of exposure to the popular media. Under such circumstances, repressed childhood sexual abuse may become quite plausible indeed.

Despite the authors' efforts to blunt the impact of the laboratory evidence, everything we know about memory from laboratory research suggests that false memories can be a real problem in the clinic, and in the courtroom as well, as indicated, for example, by the extensive literature on false eyewitness identification (Loftus, 1979; Wells & Olsen, 2003). This body of memory research is supplemented by a wealth of literature on persuasion, conformity, and other aspects of social influence that are relevant to the therapeutic situation (Forgas & Williams, 2001; Zanna, Olson, & Herman, 1987). Psychotherapy, including psychiatry and clinical psychology, must be the only part of healthcare where basic laboratory research is routinely dismissed when inconvenient. Maybe that's why psychotherapy is in the shape it's in.

Clinical Studies of "Blocked" and "Recovered" Memories

Turning to clinical evidence for "blocked and recovered" memories, Gleaves et al. (2004) begin by offering an argument from authority that blocked memories have been recognized by clinicians since the beginning of the 19th century. Unfortunately, they fail to distinguish between clinical folklore, which indeed contains abundant references to repression and other forms of trauma-induced amnesia, and the evidentiary basis for this folklore. While it is true that functional (psychogenic, dissociative) amnesia, fugue, and multiple personality disorder (dissociative identity disorder) have long been recognized in the psychiatric nosology, the evidence for a traumatic etiology in these rarely observed syndromes is remarkably thin (Kihlstrom, 2001a; Kihlstrom & Schacter, 2000). The term "dissociative," as applied to these disorders, is better construed as a descriptive label (referring to loss of conscious access to memory) than any pathological process instigated by trauma.

Gleaves et al. (2004) also make reference to the clinical literature on combat trauma—a good rhetorical device, because amnesia has been part of the folklore of war neurosis, and a staple of many movies, since World War I. But this evidence is totally unanalyzed. How well were the clinicians able to rule out brain insult, injury, and disease as causal factors? How well were the clinicians able to independently corroborate the combat memories ostensibly recovered by their patients after hypnosis or narcosynthesis? They also cite the widely discussed case study of Jane Doe (Corwin & Olafson, 1997) as a compelling "existence proof" of recovered memory, despite subsequent evidence that the alleged abuse might not have occurred at all and that Jane Doe's alleged recovery of abuse memories may have been nothing more than her remembering *what she said,* rather than what she experienced, 11 years previously (Loftus & Guyer, 2002a, 2002b).

Going beyond anecdotal case evidence, Gleaves et al. (2004) attempt to bolster their case for trauma-induced amnesia by referring to studies of amnesia for childhood sexual abuse (CSA) reviewed by Brown, Scheflin, and Whitfield

(1999), and they quote approvingly those authors' statement that "Not a single one of the 68 databased studies failed to find it" (manuscript, pp. 19–20). Unfortunately, re-examination of this body of evidence, as well as of studies of trauma other than CSA, shows the facts to be otherwise (Piper, Pope, & Borowiecki, 2000; Pope, Hudson, Bodkin, & Oliva, 1998; Pope, Oliva, & Hudson, 2000). All too often, researchers in the area of trauma and memory fail to obtain independent corroboration of the traumatic event in question. Or, when the trauma has been satisfactorily documented, they fail to distinguish memory failure from reporting failure. Or, in cases of genuine forgetting, they fail to distinguish functional amnesia induced by psychological trauma, and presumably mediated by processes such as repression and dissociation, from other causes of forgetting, including normal forgetting over a long retention interval, the effects of infantile and childhood amnesia, and "organic" amnesia associated with brain insult, injury, or disease. Nor, in cases where trauma was forgotten and subsequently remembered, do they distinguish memories recovered by the lifting of repression or breaching of dissociation from other causes of remembering, including the normal effects of shifting retrieval cues, reminiscence, and hypermnesia. Nor is there any distinction drawn between the recovery of a forgotten memory of trauma and a reinterpretation of an event that had always been remembered.

These are serious methodological problems, and one or more of them infect every one of the studies in this body of literature. In a particularly revealing exchange, Brown et al. (1999) offered nine studies "in favor of the existence of traumatic amnesia" (p. 28), only to have each of these studies systematically dismantled by Piper et al. (2000). Nevertheless, Gleaves et al. (2004) conclude that, "collectively the clinical evidence does seem to suggest that varying degrees of amnesia for traumatic experiences and subsequent recovery of memory are real phenomena" (p. 12). It would be more accurate to say that this entire body of research has failed to uncover even a single convincing instance of repressive or dissociative amnesia for trauma.

Laboratory Studies of "Blocked" and "Recovered" Memories

Turning to laboratory evidence for "blocked and recovered" memory, Gleaves et al. (2004) attempt to bolster clinical claims of repression and recovered memory by listing a number of experimental paradigms that show either the blocking or the recovery of memory or both, including spontaneous recovery from retroactive inhibition and the tip-of-the-tongue phenomenon. The fact is that nobody has ever argued that people cannot intentionally forget things, nor has anybody ever argued that people cannot forget something they once remembered and then remember it again later. The real question is whether the laboratory evidence of "blocked and recovered" memories cited by Gleaves et al. (2004) supports the idea that traumatic memories can be blocked by such psychological processes as repression and dissociation (however broadly defined), or that recovered-memory therapy can generate valid memories of traumatic events.

Consider, for example, the authors' statement that studies by Loftus and Burns (1982) and Christianson and Nilsson (1984) "both found that amnesia was associated with trauma" (p. 17). In fact, they found nothing of the sort. In the Loftus and Burns study, for example, subjects in the violent condition showed an average recall of 75.6% correct across the 17 items tested, compared to 80.9% in the nonviolent control group. Both studies did find impairments of memory for peripheral details of an event, in line with the Yerkes-Dodson law (Anderson, 1990; Revelle & Loftus, 1992). But none of the subjects forgot central details, just as no trauma victim who was old enough to remember (and not brain damaged) was amnesic for his or her experiences in the clinical studies reviewed earlier (Piper et al., 2000; Pope et al., 2000).

Omitted from this discussion is the wealth of laboratory research, including studies of nonhuman animals employing more stressful conditions than can be used with humans, showing conclusively that emotional arousal leading to the release of stress hormones actually improves memory, at least so far as the central details of the arousing event are concerned (e.g., Cahill & McGaugh, 1998). The well-known relation between arousal and memory can easily account for the "un-forgettable" memories suffered by those with post-traumatic stress disorder, but it cannot account for the repressive and dissociative amnesias claimed by some patients and their therapists (Kihlstrom, 2001b; Shobe & Kihlstrom, 1997).

Consider, too, the authors' favorable discussion of the study by Anderson and Green (Anderson & Green, 2001), which has also been touted elsewhere as evidence for Freud's concept of repression (Anderson & Levy, 2002; Conway, 2001; Levy & Anderson, 2002). In fact, it is woefully inadequate for this purpose (Kihlstrom, 2002). The memories in this study were pairs of innocuous words, deliberately suppressed by the subjects at the request of the experimenter. But even after 16 suppression trials, the average subject still recalled more than 70% of the targets. There was no evidence presented of persisting unconscious influence of the suppressed items, and there was no evidence that the "amnesia" could be "reversed." Moreover, it is extremely doubtful that any of the subjects were induced to forget that they had participated in a laboratory experiment. The fact is, as the clinical research cited above documents convincingly, the vast majority of trauma victims remember what happened to them all too well. The Anderson and Green study is an interesting contribution to an already extensive literature on the self-regulation of memory (Kihlstrom & Barnhardt, 1993), but as support for Freudian repression its reach far exceeds its grasp.

Gleaves et al. (2004) also review a laboratory study that combined the Anderson and Green (Anderson & Green, 2001) retrieval-inhibition paradigm with the Roediger and McDermott (Roediger & McDermott, 1995) false-memory paradigm in an attempt to uncover features that might discriminate between continuously remembered, blocked but accurately recovered, and false-created memories (S. M. Smith et al., 2003). Of course, the clinically important issue is not the nomothetic question of how these classes of memories might be distinguished statistically in the aggregate. Rather, it is the idiographic question of whether any discriminanda are reliable enough to be used to evaluate individual memories in the absence of independent corroboration. In this respect, previous attempts to distinguish memories that are the product of experience from those that are the product of imagination (e.g., Johnson, Hashtroudi, & Lindsay, 1993; Johnson & Raye, 1981) hold out little hope. In any event, the principal conclusion from this research was that continuous and recovered memories were associated with higher confidence levels than false memories (dichotomous remember-know judgments are highly correlated with confidence). But surely the authors cannot be suggesting that clinicians use confidence levels as a proxy for accuracy in memory. The weakness of the relationship between accuracy and confidence is one of the best-documented phenomena in the 100-year history of eyewitness memory research (Bothwell, Deffenbacher, & Brigham, 1987; Busey, Tunnicliff, Loftus, & Loftus, 2000; Read, Lindsay, & Nicholls, 1998; V. L. Smith, Kassin, & Ellsworth, 1989; Sporer, Penrod, Read, & Cutler, 1995; Wells & Lindsay, 1985; Wells & Murray, 1984). If confidence were an adequate criterion for validity, Binjamin Wilkomirski might have gotten a Pulitzer Prize for history.

The irony of this last section should not go unnoticed: Gleaves himself was among the first to complain (Freyd & Gleaves, 1996) when Roediger and McDermott (1995) suggested that their laboratory paradigm had any bearing on the problem of recovered memories in the clinic (for a reply, see Roediger & McDermott, 1996). If Gleaves et al. (2004) are going to discount and dismiss laboratory evidence of false memories, as they seek to do earlier in their paper, why are they so ready to accept laboratory evidence of "blocked and recovered" memories later? The bottom line is that, more than 100 years after Janet and Freud, the proponents of the trauma-memory argument and recovered-memory therapy can point to only a handful of clinical cases to support their views, and even these cases are ambiguous. Theirs is a laboratory model in search of a clinical phenomenon. The irony goes even further, because Gleaves et al. (2004) call on researchers and theorists to "[return] our attention to . . . naturalistic contexts" and "real life cases of memory blocking and recovery" (p. 39), as if the laboratory research they have reviewed at such length, including their own, is irrelevant after all.

Memory in Science and in Practice

The fact is, there has been plenty of attention to naturalistic contexts in research on trauma and memory (McNally, 2003). Unfortunately, the clinical research purporting to demonstrate the blocking and recovery of traumatic memories is fatally flawed, in many cases due to a failure to demonstrate either that the events in question actually occurred or that the person was actually amnesic. Moreover, research on actual trauma victims has produced hardly a shred of evidence for psychogenic amnesia covering the traumatic event itself. Perhaps, after more than 100 years, we should simply declare the trauma-memory argument bankrupt and recovered-memory therapy passé. This would allow us to break the Freudian death-grip on clinical practice once and for all and move psychotherapy into the here and now, where patients' problems actually exist, and where their problems must be resolved. Because the status and autonomy of clinical psychology rests on the assumption that its principles and methods are scientifically validated, continued reliance on clinical folklore with respect to trauma, memory, and repression can only serve to undermine the profession.

References

Anderson, K. J. (1990). Arousal and the inverted-U hypothesis: A critique of Neiss's "Reconceptualizing arousal." *Psychological Bulletin, 107,* 96–100.

Anderson, M. C., & Green, C. (2001, March 15). Suppressing unwanted memories by executive control. *Nature, 410,* 366–369.

Anderson, M. C., & Levy, B. (2002). Repression can (and should) be studied empirically. *Trends in Cognitive Sciences, 6,* 502–503.

Borch-Jacobsen, M. (1997, April 24). Sybil—The making of a disease: An interview with Dr. Herbert Spiegel. *New York Review of Books, 44,* 60–64.

Bothwell, R. K., Deffenbacher, K. A., & Brigham, J. C. (1987). Correlation of eyewitness accuracy and confidence: Optimal hypothesis revisited. *Journal of Applied Psychology, 72,* 691–695.

Bremner, J. D., Shobe, K. K., & Kihlstrom, J. F. (2000). False memories in women with self-reported childhood sexual abuse: An empirical study. *Psychological Science, 11*(4), 333–337.

Brown, D., Scheflin, A. W., & Whitfield, C. L. (1999). Recovered memories: The current weight of the evidence in science and in the courts. *Journal of Psychiatry & Law, 27,* 5–156.

Busey, T. A., Tunnicliff, J., Loftus, G. R.,& Loftus, E. F. (2000). Accounts of the confidence-accuracy relation in recognition memory. *Psychonomic Bulletin & Review, 7,* 26–48.

Cahill, L., & McGaugh, J. L. (1998). Mechanisms of emotional arousal and lasting declarative memory. *Trends in Neurosciences, 21,* 294–299.

Christianson, S. A., & Nilsson, L. G. (1984). Functional amnesia as induced by a psychological trauma. *Memory and Cognition, 12,* 142–155.

Clancy, S. A., Schacter, D. L., McNally, R. J., & Pitman, R. K. (2000). False recognition in women reporting recovered memories of sexual abuse. *Psychological Science, 11*(1), 26–31.

Conway, M. A. (2001). Repression revisited. *Nature, 410,* 319–320.

Corwin, D. L., & Olafson, E. (1997). Videotaped discovery of a reportedly unrecallable memory of child sexual abuse: Comparison with a childhood interview videotaped 11 years before. *Child Maltreatment, 2,* 91–112.

Crews, F. (1995). *The memory wars: Freud's legacy in dispute.* New York: New York Review of Books.

Eskin, B. (2002). *A life in pieces: The making and unmaking of Binjamin Wilkomirski.* New York: Norton.

Forgas, J. P., & Williams, K. D. (Eds.). (2001). *Social Influence: Direct and indirect processes.* Philadelphia: Psychology Press.

Freyd, J. J., & Gleaves, D. H. (1996). "Remembering" words not presented in lists: Relevance to the current recovered/ false memory controversy. *Journal of Experimental Psychology: Learning, Memory, & Cognition, 22,* 811–813.

Gleaves, D. H., Smith, S. M., Butler, L. D., & Spiegel, D. (2004). False and recovered memories in the laboratory and clinic: A review of experimental and clinical evidence. *Clinical Psychology: Science & Practice, 11*(1), 3–28.

Gourevitch, P. (1999, June 14). The memory thief. *The New Yorker,* 48–68.

Graham, D. L. R., Rawlings, E. I., Ihms, K., Latimer, D., Foliano, J., Thompson, A., et al. (1995). A scale for identifying "Stockholm Syndrome" reactions in young dating women: Factor structure, reliability, and validity. *Violence & Victims, 10,* 3–22.

Graham, D. L. R., Rawlings, E., & Rimini, N. (1988). Survivors of terror: Battered women, hostages, and the Stockholm Syndrome. In K. Ylloe & M. Bograd (Eds.), *Feminist perspectives on wife abuse* (pp. 217–233). Thousand Oaks, CA: Sage.

Johnson, M. K., Hashtroudi, S., & Lindsay, D. S. (1993). Source monitoring. *Psychological Bulletin, 114*(1), 3–28.

Johnson, M. K., & Raye, C. L. (1981). Reality monitoring. *Psychological Review, 88,* 67–85.

Johnston, M. (1997). *Spectral evidence: The Ramona case: Incest, memory and truth on trial in Napa Valley.* Boston: Houghton-Mifflin.

Kihlstrom, J. F. (1995). The trauma-memory argument. *Consciousness & Cognition: An International Journal, 4*(1), 63–67.

Kihlstrom, J. F. (1996). The trauma-memory argument and recovered memory therapy. In K. Pezdek & W. P. Banks (Eds.), *The recovered memory/false memory debate* (pp. 297– 311). San Diego, CA, USA: Academic Press, Inc.

Kihlstrom, J. F. (1997). Suffering from reminiscences: Exhumed memory, implicit memory, and the return of the repressed. In M. A. Conway (Ed.), *Recovered memories and false memories* (pp. 100–117). Oxford: Oxford University Press.

Kihlstrom, J. F. (1998). Exhumed memory, *Truth in memory* (pp. 3–31). New York: The Guilford Press.

Kihlstrom, J. F. (2001a). Dissociative disorders. In P. B. Sutker & H. E. Adams (Eds.), *Comprehensive handbook of psychopathology* (3rd ed.; pp. 259–276). New York: Plenum.

Kihlstrom, J. F. (2001b). *Traumatic memory: Not so very special after all?* Retrieved May 20, 2003, from . . .

Kihlstrom, J. F. (2002). No need for repression. *Trends in Cognitive Sciences, 6,* 502.

Kihlstrom, J. F., & Barnhardt, T. M. (1993). The self-regulation of memory: For better and for worse, with and without hypnosis. In D. M. Wegner & J. W. Pennebaker (Eds.), *Handbook of mental control* (pp. 88–125). Englewood Cliffs, NJ: Prentice-Hall.

Kihlstrom, J. F., & Schacter, D. L. (2000). Functional amnesia. In F. Boller & J. Grafman (Eds.), *Handbook of neuropsychology: Vol. 2* (2nd ed., pp. 409–427). Amsterdam: Elsevier.

Lappin, E. (1999). The man with two heads. *Granta, 66,* 7–65.

Levy, B. L., & Anderson, M. C. (2002). Inhibitory processes and the control of memory retrieval. *Trends in Cognitive Sciences, 6,* 299–305.

Loftus, E. F. (1979). *Eyewitness testimony.* Cambridge, MA: Harvard University Press.

Loftus, E. F., & Burns, T. E. (1982). Mental shock can produce retrograde amnesia. *Memory and Cognition, 10,* 318–323.

Loftus, E. F., & Guyer, M. J. (2002a, May/June). Who abused Jane Doe? Part 1. *Skeptical Inquirer, 26*(3), 24–32.

Loftus, E. F., & Guyer, M. J. (2002b, July/August). Who abused Jane Doe? Part 2. *Skeptical Inquirer, 26*(4), 37–40.

Loftus, E. F., & Palmer, J. C. (1974). Reconstruction of automobile destruction: An example of the interaction between language and memory. *Journal of Verbal Learning & Verbal Behavior, 13,* 585–589.

Mächler, S., & Wilkomirski, B. (2001). *The Wilkomirski affair: A study in biographical truth.* New York: Schocken Books.

Mazzoni, G. A. L., Loftus, E. F., & Kirsch, I. (2001). Changing beliefs about implausible autobiographical events: A little plausibility goes a long way. *Journal Of Experimental Psychology—Applied, 7,* 51–59.

McNally, R. J. (2003). *Remembering trauma.* Cambridge, MA: Harvard University Press.

Pezdek, K., Finger, K., & Hodge, D. (1997). Planting false childhood memories: The role of event plausibility. *Psychological Science, 8,* 437–441.

Piper, A., Pope, H. G., & Borowiecki, B. S. (2000). Custer's last stand: Brown, Scheflin, and Whitfield's latest attempt to salvage "dissociative amnesia." *Journal of Psychiatry & Law, 28,* 149–213.

Pope, H. G., Jr., Hudson, J. I., Bodkin, J. A., & Oliva, P. (1998). Questionable validity of "dissociative amnesia" in trauma victims: Evidence from prospective studies. *British Journal of Psychiatry, 172,* 210–215.

Pope, H. G., Oliva, P. S., & Hudson, J. I. (2000). Repressed memories: B. Scientific status. In D. L. Faigman, D. H. Kaye, M. J. Saks, & J. Sanders (Eds.), *Modern scientific evidence: The law and science of expert testimony: Vol. 1* (pp. 154–195). St. Paul, MN: West Publisher.

Porter, S., Yuille, J. C., & Lehman, D. R. (1999). The nature of real, implanted, and fabricated memories for emotional childhood events: Implications for the recovered memory debate. *Law and Human Behavior, 23,* 517–537.

Rabinowitz, D. (2003). *No crueler tyrannies: Accusation, false witness, and other terrors of our times.* New York: Free Press.

Read, J. D., Lindsay, D. S., & Nicholls, T. (1998). The relation between confidence and accuracy in eyewitness identification studies: Is the conclusion changing? In C. P. Thompson, D. J. Herrmann, J. D. Read, D. Bruce, D. G. Payne & M. P. Toglia (Eds.), *Eyewitness memory: Theoretical and applied perspectives* (pp. 107–130). Mahwah, NJ: Erlbaum.

Revelle, W., & Loftus, D. A. (1992). The implications of arousal effects for the study of affect and memory. In S-A. Christianson (Ed.), *Handbook of emotion and memory: Research and theory* (pp. 113–149). Hillsdale, NJ: Erlbaum.

Roediger, H. L., & McDermott, K. B. (1996). False perceptions of false memories. *Journal of Experimental Psychology: Learning, Memory, & Cognition, 22,* 814–816.

Roediger, H. L., & McDermott, K. B. (1995). Creating false memories: Remembering words not presented in lists. *Journal of Experimental Psychology: Learning, Memory, & Cognition, 21,* 803–814.

Shobe, K. K., & Kihlstrom, J. F. (1997). Is traumatic memory special? *Current Directions in Psychological Science, 6*(3), 70–74.

Shobe, K. K., & Kihlstrom, J. F. (2002). Interrogative suggestibility and "memory work". In M. L. Eisen, J. Quas, & G. S. Goodman (Eds.), *Memory and suggestibility in the forensic interview* (pp. 309–327). Mahwah, NJ: Erlbaum.

Smith, S. M., Gleaves, D. H., Pierce, B. H., Williams, T. L., Gilliland, T. R., & Gerkens, D. R. (2003). Eliciting and comparing false and recovered memories: An experimental approach. *Applied Cognitive Psychology, 17,* 251–279.

Smith, V. L., Kassin, S. M., & Ellsworth, P. C. (1989). Eyewitness accuracy and confidence: Within- versus between-subjects correlations. *Journal of Applied Psychology, 74,* 356–359.

Spence, D. P. (1982). *Narrative truth and historical truth.* New York: Norton.

Spence, D. P. (1994). *The rhetorical voice of psychoanalysis: Displacement of evidence by theory.* Cambridge, MA: Harvard University Press.

Sporer, S. L., Penrod, S. L., Read, J. D., & Cutler, B. L. (1995). Choosing, confidence, and accuracy: A meta-analysis of the confidence-accuracy relation in eyewitness identification studies. *Psychological Bulletin, 118,* 315–327.

Walker, L. E. (1988). The battered woman syndrome. In G. T. Hotaling & D. Finkelhor (Eds.), *Family abuse and its consequences: New directions in research* (pp. 139–148). Thousand Oaks, CA: Sage.

Walker, L. E. (1991). Post-traumatic stress disorder in women: Diagnosis and treatment of battered woman syndrome. *Psychotherapy: Theory, Research, Practice, Training, 28,* 21–29.

Wells, G. L., & Lindsay, R. C. L. (1985). Methodological notes on the accuracy-confidence relation in eyewitness identification. *Journal of Applied Psychology, 70,* 413–419.

Wells, G. L., & Murray, D. M. (1984). Eyewitness confidence. In G. L. Wells & E. F. Loftus (Eds.), *Eyewitness testimony: Psychological perspectives* (pp. 155–170). New York: Cambridge University Press.

Wells, G. L., & Olsen, E. A. (2003). Eyewitness testimony. *Annual Review of Psychology, 54,* 277–295.

Widom, C. S., & Morris, S. (1997). Accuracy of adult recollections of childhood victimization. Part 2: Childhood sexual abuse. *Psychological Assessment, 9,* 34–46.

Widom, C. S., & Shepard, R. L. (1996). Accuracy of adult recollections of childhood victimization: Part 1. Childhood physical abuse. *Psychological Assessment, 8,* 412–421.

Williams, L. M. (1994). Recall of childhood trauma: A prospective study of women's memories of child sexual abuse. *Journal of Consulting & Clinical Psychology, 62,* 1167–1178.

Wright, L. (1994). *Remembering Satan: A case of recovered memory and the shattering of an American family.* New York: Knopf.

Zanna, M. P., Olson, J. M., & Herman, C. P. (Eds.). (1987). *Social Influence: Vol. 5.* Hillsdale, NJ: Erlbaum.

CHALLENGE QUESTIONS

Are Blocked and Recovered Memories Valid Phenomena?

1. Both articles accept that examples of false memories most often emerge anecdotally and from the popular press, rather than through clinical experiments. Gleaves and his colleagues use this information to discredit those who say there is a prevalence of false memories in today's world. Kihlstrom, however, asserts that anecdotal evidence can be just as compelling as statistically significant research. What are the strengths of an argument that relies on anecdotal evidence? What are the weaknesses?

2. Gleaves and his colleagues assert that while mundane false memories are relatively easy to create, it is much more difficult to convince a person that a trauma of an event occurred, when in fact it has not. Thus, these authors contend that those who recover memories of trauma can usually be viewed as truthful. To what extent to you agree with this notion? What are your thoughts about the possibility that popular culture has pushed people to accept the phenomenon of false memories?

3. How would you develop a research study that would shed more light on the validity of blocked and recovered memories? What ethical challenges would you face in conducting this kind of research?

4. What recommendations would you make to clinicians treating clients who report that they have recovered a formerly blocked memory?

5. Usually it is not possible to confirm the reality or accuracy of memories that have been blocked and then recovered. In a clinical situation, how should therapists proceed with clients who reportedly recover memories that would implicate another person in criminal behavior, such as perpetrating the abuse of children?

Suggested Readings

Arnold, M., & Lindsay, D. (2002). Remembering remembering. *Journal of Experimental Psychology: Learning, Memory and Cognition, 28,* 521–529.

Lindsay, D., Hagen, L., Read, J., Wade, K., & Garry, M. (2004). True photographs and false memories. *Psychological Science, 15,* 149.

Loftus, E. (2004). Memories of things unseen. *Current Directions in Psychological Science 13,* 145–147.

McNally, R. (2004). Is traumatic amnesia nothing but psychiatric folklore? *Cognitive Behaviour Therapy, 33,* 97–101.

Peace, K., & Porter, S. (2004). A longitudinal investigation of the reliability of memories for trauma and other emotional experiences. *Applied Cognitive Psychology,* 18, 1143–1159.

Schacter, D. L. (2001). *The seven sins of memory: How the mind forgets and remembers.* Boston: Houghton Mifflin.

ISSUE 5

Is Attention-Deficit/Hyperactivity Disorder (ADHD) a Real Disorder?

YES: National Institute of Mental Health, from *Attention Deficit Hyperactivity Disorder* (NIH Publication No. 3572) (U.S. Department of Health and Human Services, 2006)

NO: Rogers H. Wright, from "Attention Deficit Hyperactivity Disorder: What It Is and What It Is Not," in Rogers H. Wright and Nicholas A. Cummings, *Destructive Trends in Mental Health: The Well Intentioned Path to Harm* (Routledge 2005)

ISSUE SUMMARY

YES: The National Institute of Mental Health concurs with the *DSM-IV-TR* in viewing ADHD as a valid disorder which warrants thoughtful diagnosis and effective intervention.

NO: Psychologist Rogers H. Wright argues that ADHD has vague diagnostic criteria that lead to over-diagnosis and overmedication.

Some children who show a constellation of behaviors characterized by inattention and hyperactivity are referred to by teachers and special educators as having attention-deficit/hyperactivity disorder (ADHD), as described in *DSM-IV-TR*. Their inattention is evidenced by a range of behaviors including carelessness, distractibility, forgetfulness, and difficulty following through on tasks or organizing themselves. Their hyperactivity is characterized by restlessness, running around, difficulty playing with others, excessive talk, and other behaviors.

In the following section, the National Institute of Mental Health (NIMH) takes a stand in endorsing ADHD as a biologically caused condition affecting between 3 and 5 percent of American children. Between 30 and 70 percent of children with ADHD continue to exhibit symptoms in their adult years. In differentiating ADHD from commonplace forms of heightened activity, inattention, or impulsivity, NIMH contends that a valid diagnosis must take into consideration the extent to which the behavior is inappropriate for the person's age, and the degree to which the behaviors cause a real handicap. Diagnosis and treatment of people with ADHD should be done by specialists who understand the causes, symptom picture, and most effective interventions.

In the second selection, Rogers H. Wright asserts that ADHD is a fad diagnosis, which has moved beyond the confines of childhood and adolescence, and is now a diagnosis that has invaded adulthood as well. Wright points out that the diagnostic criteria for the "so-called" disorder include symptoms that normal children and adults experience on a day-to-day basis. He acknowledges that there are some extreme cases for which a comprehensive evaluation by several specialists might provide evidence of neurological involvement; in such cases, if medication is indicated, it would be of a type quite different from what is so widely prescribed to people with the condition known as ADHD.

POINT

- Scientists are finding more and more evidence that ADHD is a diagnosable condition which stems from biological causes. Studies indicate that ADHD is strongly influenced by genetics, and that children with ADHD show brain differences compared with children who do not have ADHD.
- Although all children can experience hyperactivity, distractibility, poor concentration, or impulsivity, for children with ADHD, such behaviors often affect their performance in school, social relationships or their life at home.
- To assess whether someone has ADHD, specialists compare the person's pattern of behavior against a set of criteria and characteristics of the disorder as listed in the DSM-IV-TR.

- Research shows that medication, ideally in combination with behavioral treatment, is the most effective remedy for ADHD. While the brains of non-medicated ADHD children have abnormally small volumes of white matter, once medicated, the white matter brain volume in these children does not differ from that in non-ADHD children.
- People who believe that they may have ADHD should consult with a professional with expertise in the diagnosis of this condition.

COUNTERPOINT

- ADHD is just another fad diagnosis that doesn't exist, not unlike the former fad label "minimal brain syndrome."

- Hyperactivity and distractibility are behaviors that are most commonly symptoms of excessive fatigue or stress, rather than signs of a psychological disorder.

- A major disservice caused by the elevation of nonspecific symptoms, and then diagnoses of ADHD, is that we lump together individuals with very different needs and problems, and then attempt to treat the problems with a single entity, resulting in a one-pill-fits-all response.
- Treatment interventions focused primarily on medication, and based on such ethereal and universal symptoms, promise an instant "cure" for a patient who now does not have to confront possible unhappiness or stress.

- Whether or not someone has ADHD is a judgment that is best made only after exhaustive study by pediatrics, psychology, neurology, and perhaps, last of all, psychiatry, which so often seems too eager to overmedicate.

Attention Deficit Hyperactivity Disorder

Attention Deficit Hyperactivity Disorder (ADHD) is a condition that becomes apparent in some children in the preschool and early school years. It is hard for these children to control their behavior and/or pay attention. It is estimated that between 3 and 5 percent of children have attention deficit hyperactivity disorder (ADHD), or approximately 2 million children in the United States. This means that in a classroom of 25 to 30 children, it is likely that at least one will have ADHD.

A child with ADHD faces a difficult but not insurmountable task ahead. In order to achieve his or her full potential, he or she should receive help, guidance, and understanding from parents, guidance counselors, and the public education system.

Symptoms

The principle characteristics of ADHD are inattention, hyperactivity, and impulsivity. These symptoms appear early in a child's life. Because many normal children may have these symptoms, but at a low level, or the symptoms may be caused by another disorder, it is important that the child receive a thorough examination and appropriate diagnosis by a well qualified professional. Symptoms of ADHD will appear over the course of many months, often with the symptoms of impulsiveness and hyperactivity preceding those of inattention that may not emerge for a year or more. Different symptoms may appear in different settings, depending on the demands the situation may pose for the child's self-control. A child who "can't sit still" or is otherwise disruptive will be noticeable in school, but the inattentive daydreamer may be overlooked. The impulsive child who acts before thinking may be considered just a "discipline problem," while the child who is passive or sluggish may be viewed as merely unmotivated. Yet both may have different types of ADHD. All children are sometimes restless, sometimes act without thinking, sometimes daydream the time away. When the child's hyperactivity, distractibility, poor concentration, or impulsivity begin to affect performance in school, social relationships with other children, or behavior at home, ADHD may be suspected. But because the symptoms vary so much across settings, ADHD is not easy to diagnose. This is especially true when inattentiveness is the primary symptom.

From National Institute of Mental Health, 2006.

According to the most recent version of the Diagnostic and Statistical Manual of Mental Disorder (DSM-IV-TR), there are three patterns of behavior that indicate ADHD. People with ADHD may show several signs of being consistently inattentive. They may have a pattern of being hyperactive and impulsive far more than others of their age. Or they may show all three types of behavior. This means that there are three subtypes of ADHD recognized by professionals. These are the predominantly hyperactive-impulsive type (that does not show significant inattention); the predominantly inattentive type (that does not show significant hyperactive-impulsive behavior) sometimes called ADD—an outdated term for this entire disorder; and the combined type (that displays both inattentive and hyperactive-impulsive symptoms).

Hyperactivity-Impulsivity

Some signs of hyperactivity-impulsivity are:

- Feeling restless, often fidgeting with hands or feet, or squirming while seated
- Running, climbing, or leaving a seat in situations where sitting or quiet behavior is expected
- Blurting out answers before hearing the whole question
- Having difficulty waiting in line or taking turns.

Inattention

The DSM-IV-TR gives these signs of inattention.

- Often becoming easily distracted by irrelevant sights and sounds
- Often failing to pay attention to details and making careless mistakes
- Rarely following instructions carefully and completely losing or forgetting things like toys, or pencils, books, and tools needed for a task
- Often skipping from one uncompleted activity to another.

Is It Really ADHD?

Not everyone who is overly hyperactive, inattentive, or impulsive has ADHD. Since most people sometimes blurt out things they didn't mean to say, or jump from one task to another, or become disorganized and forgetful, how can specialists tell if the problem is ADHD?

Because everyone shows some of these behaviors at times, the diagnosis requires that such behavior be demonstrated to a degree that is inappropriate for the person's age. The diagnostic guidelines also contain specific requirements for determining when the symptoms indicate ADHD. The behaviors must appear early in life, before age 7, and continue for at least 6 months. Above all, the behaviors must create a real handicap in at least two areas of a person's life such as in the schoolroom, on the playground, at home, in the community, or in social settings. So someone who shows some symptoms but whose schoolwork or friendships are not impaired by these behaviors would not be diagnosed with ADHD. Nor would a child who seems overly active on the playground but functions well elsewhere receive an ADHD diagnosis.

To assess whether a child has ADHD, specialists consider several critical questions: Are these behaviors excessive, long-term, and pervasive? That is, do they occur more often than in other children the same age? Are they a continuous problem, not just a response to a temporary situation? Do the behaviors occur in several settings or only in one specific place like the playground or in the schoolroom? The person's pattern of behavior is compared against a set of criteria and characteristics of the disorder as listed in the DSM-IV-TR.

Diagnosis

Professionals Who Make the Diagnosis

If ADHD is suspected, to whom can the family turn? What kinds of specialists do they need?

Ideally, the diagnosis should be made by a professional in your area with training in ADHD or in the diagnosis of mental disorders. Child psychiatrists and psychologists, developmental/behavioral pediatricians, or behavioral neurologists are those most often trained in differential diagnosis. Clinical social workers may also have such training. The family can start by talking with the child's pediatrician or their family doctor. Some pediatricians may do the assessment themselves, but often they refer the family to an appropriate mental health specialist they know and trust. In addition, state and local agencies that serve families and children . . . can help identify appropriate specialists.

Within each specialty, individual doctors and mental health professionals differ in their experiences with ADHD. So in selecting a specialist, it's important to find someone with specific training and experience in diagnosing and treating the disorder.

Whatever the specialist's expertise, his or her first task is to gather information that will rule out other possible reasons for the child's behavior. Among possible causes of ADHD-like behavior are the following:

- A sudden change in the child's life—the death of a parent or grandparent; parents' divorce; a parent's job loss.
- Undetected seizures, such as in petit mal or temporal lobe seizures
- A middle ear infection that causes intermittent hearing problems
- Medical disorders that may affect brain functioning
- Underachievement caused by learning disability
- Anxiety or depression

Next the specialist gathers information on the child's ongoing behavior in order to compare these behaviors to the symptoms and diagnostic criteria listed in the DSM-IV-TR. This also involves talking with the child and, if possible, observing the child in class and other settings.

The child's teachers, past and present, are asked to rate their observations of the child's behavior on standardized evaluation forms, known as behavior rating scales, to compare the child's behavior to that of other children the same age.

The specialist interviews the child's teachers and parents, and may contact other people who know the child well, such as coaches or baby-sitters. Parents are asked to describe their child's behavior in a variety of situations. They may also fill out a rating scale to indicate how severe and frequent the behaviors seem to be.

In most cases, the child will be evaluated for social adjustment and mental health. Tests of intelligence and learning achievement may be given to see if the child has a learning disability and whether the disability is in one or more subjects.

The specialist then pieces together a profile of the child's behavior.

A correct diagnosis often resolves confusion about the reasons for the child's problems that lets parents and child move forward in their lives with more accurate information on what is wrong and what can be done to help. Once the disorder is diagnosed, the child and family can begin to receive whatever combination of educational, medical, and emotional help they need. This may include providing recommendations to school staff, seeking out a more appropriate classroom setting, selecting the right medication, and helping parents to manage their child's behavior.

What Causes ADHD?

One of the first questions a parent will have is "Why? What went wrong?" "Did I do something to cause this?" There is little compelling evidence at this time that ADHD can arise purely from social factors or child-rearing methods. Most substantiated causes appear to fall in the realm of neurobiology and genetics. This is not to say that environmental factors may not influence the severity of the disorder, and especially the degree of impairment and suffering the child may experience, but that such factors do not seem to give rise to the condition by themselves.

The parents' focus should be on looking forward and finding the best possible way to help their child. Scientists are studying causes in an effort to identify better ways to treat, and perhaps someday, to prevent ADHD. They are finding more and more evidence that ADHD does not stem from home environment, but from biological causes. Knowing this can remove a huge burden of guilt from parents who might blame themselves for their child's behavior.

Genetics. Attention disorders often run in families, so there are likely to be genetic influences. Studies indicate that 25 percent of the close relatives in the families of ADHD children also have ADHD, whereas the rate is about 5 percent in the general population. Many studies of twins now show that a strong genetic influence exists in the disorder.

Researchers continue to study the genetic contribution to ADHD and to identify the genes that cause a person to be susceptible to ADHD. Since its inception in 1999, the Attention-Deficit Hyperactivity Disorder Molecular

Genetics Network has served as a way for researchers to share findings regarding possible genetic influences on ADHD.

Recent Studies on Causes of ADHD. Some knowledge of the structure of the brain is helpful in understanding the research scientists are doing in searching for a physical basis for attention deficit hyperactivity disorder. One part of the brain that scientists have focused on in their search is the frontal lobes of the cerebrum. The frontal lobes allow us to solve problems, plan ahead, understand the behavior of others, and restrain our impulses. The two frontal lobes, the right and the left, communicate with each other through the corpus callosum, (nerve fibers that connect the right and left frontal lobes).

The basal ganglia are the interconnected gray masses deep in the cerebral hemisphere that serve as the connection between the cerebrum and the cerebellum and, with the cerebellum are responsible for motor coordination. The cerebellum is divided into three parts. The middle part is called the vermis.

All of these parts of the brain have been studied through the use of various methods for seeing into or imaging the brain. These methods include functional magnetic resonance imaging (fMRI), positron emission tomography (PET), and single photon emission computed tomography (SPECT). The main or central psychological deficits in those with ADHD have been linked through these studies. By 2002 the researchers in the NIMH Child Psychiatry Branch had studied 152 boys and girls with ADHD, matched with 139 age-and gender-matched controls without ADHD. The children were scanned at least twice, some as many as four times over a decade. As a group, the ADHD children showed 3-4 percent smaller brain volumes in all regions—the frontal lobes, temporal gray matter, caudate nucleus, and cerebellum.

This study also showed that the ADHD children who were on medication had a white matter volume that did not differ from that of controls. Those never-medicated patients had an abnormally small volume of white matter. The white matter consists of fibers that establish long-distance connections between brain regions. It normally thickens as a child grows older and the brain matures.

The Treatment of ADHD

Every family wants to determine what treatment will be most effective for their child. This question needs to be answered by each family in consultation with their health care professional. To help families make this important decision, the National Institute of Mental Health (NIMH) has funded many studies of treatments for ADHD and has conducted the most intensive study ever undertaken for evaluating the treatment of this disorder. This study is known as the Multimodal Treatment Study of Children with Attention Deficit Hyperactivity Disorder (MTA).

The MTA study included 579 (95-98 at each of 6 treatment sites) elementary school boys and girls with ADHD, randomly assigning them to one of four treatment programs: (1) medication management alone; (2) behavioral treatment alone; (3) a combination of both; or (4) routine community care.

In each of the study sites, three groups were treated for the first 14 months in a specified protocol and the fourth group was referred for community treatment of the parents' choosing. All of the children were reassessed regularly throughout the study period. An essential part of the program was the cooperation of the schools, including principals and teachers. Both teachers and parents rated the children on hyperactivity, impulsivity, and inattention, and symptoms of anxiety and depression, as well as social skills.

The children in two groups (medication management alone and the combination treatment) were seen monthly for one-half hour at each medication visit. During the treatment visits, the prescribing physician spoke with the parent, met with the child, and sought to determine any concerns that the family might have regarding the medication or the child's ADHD-related difficulties. The physicians, in addition, sought input from the teachers on a monthly basis. The physicians in the medication-only group did not provide behavioral therapy but did advise the parents when necessary concerning any problems the child might have.

In the behavior treatment-only group, families met up to 35 times with a behavior therapist, mostly in group sessions. These therapists also made repeated visits to schools to consult with children's teachers and to supervise a special aide assigned to each child in the group. In addition, children attended a special 8-week summer treatment program where they worked on academic, social, and sports skills, and where intensive behavioral therapy was delivered to assist children in improving their behavior.

Children in the combined therapy group received both treatments, that is, all the same assistance that the medication-only received, as well as all of the behavior therapy treatments.

In routine community care, the children saw the community-treatment doctor of their parents' choice one to two times per year for short periods of time. Also, the community-treatment doctor did not have any interaction with the teachers.

The results of the study indicated that long-term combination treatments and the medication-management alone were superior to intensive behavioral treatment and routine community treatment. And in some areas—anxiety, academic performance, oppositionality, parent-child relations, and social skills—the combined treatment was usually superior. Another advantage of combined treatment was that children could be successfully treated with lower doses of medicine, compared with the medication-only group.

Medications

For decades, medications have been used to treat the symptoms of ADHD.

The medications that seem to be the most effective are a class of drugs known as stimulants.

Some people get better results from one medication, some from another. It is important to work with the prescribing physician to find the right medication and the right dosage. For many people, the stimulants dramatically reduce their hyperactivity and impulsivity and improve their ability to focus, work, and learn. The medications may also improve physical coordination, such as that needed in handwriting and in sports.

The stimulant drugs, when used with medical supervision, are usually considered quite safe. . . . [T]o date there is no convincing evidence that stimulant medications, when used for treatment of ADHD, cause drug abuse or dependence. A review of all long-term studies on stimulant medication and substance abuse, conducted by researchers at Massachusetts General Hospital and Harvard Medical School, found that teenagers with ADHD who remained on their medication during the teen years had a lower likelihood of substance use or abuse than did ADHD adolescents who were not taking medications.

The stimulant drugs come in long- and short-term forms. The newer sustained-release stimulants can be taken before school and are long-lasting so that the child does not need to go to the school nurse every day for a pill. The doctor can discuss with the parents the child's needs and decide which preparation to use and whether the child needs to take the medicine during school hours only or in the evening and weekends too.

About one out of ten children is not helped by a stimulant medication. Other types of medication may be used if stimulants don't work or if the ADHD occurs with another disorder. Antidepressants and other medications can help control accompanying depression or anxiety.

Side Effects of the Medications

Most side effects of the stimulant medications are minor and are usually related to the dosage of the medication being taken. Higher doses produce more side effects. The most common side effects are decreased appetite, insomnia, increased anxiety and/or irritability. Some children report mild stomach aches or headaches.

When a child's schoolwork and behavior improve soon after starting medication, the child, parents, and teachers tend to applaud the drug for causing the sudden changes. Unfortunately, when people see such immediate improvement, they often think medication is all that's needed. But medications don't cure ADHD; they only control the symptoms on the day they are taken. Although the medications help the child pay better attention and complete school work, they can't increase knowledge or improve academic skills. The medications help the child to use those skills he or she already possesses.

Behavioral therapy, emotional counseling, and practical support will help ADHD children cope with everyday problems and feel better about themselves.

Facts to Remember about Medication for ADHD

- Medications for ADHD help many children focus and be more successful at school, home, and play. Avoiding negative experiences now may actually help prevent addictions and other emotional problems later.
- About 80 percent of children who need medication for ADHD still need it as teenagers. Over 50 percent need medication as adults.

The Family and the ADHD Child

Medication can help the ADHD child in everyday life. He or she may be better able to control some of the behavior problems that have led to trouble with parents and siblings. But it takes time to undo the frustration, blame, and anger that may have gone on for so long. Both parents and children may need special help to develop techniques for managing the patterns of behavior. In such cases, mental health professionals can counsel the child and the family, helping them to develop new skills, attitudes, and ways of relating to each other. In individual counseling, the therapist helps children with ADHD learn to feel better about themselves. The therapist can also help them to identify and build on their strengths, cope with daily problems, and control their attention and aggression. Sometimes only the child with ADHD needs counseling support. But in many cases, because the problem affects the family as a whole, the entire family may need help. The therapist assists the family in finding better ways to handle the disruptive behaviors and promote change. If the child is young, most of the therapist's work is with the parents, teaching them techniques for coping with and improving their child's behavior.

Several intervention approaches are available. Knowing something about the various types of interventions makes it easier for families to choose a therapist that is right for their needs.

Psychotherapy works to help people with ADHD to like and accept themselves despite their disorder. It does not address the symptoms or underlying causes of the disorder. In psychotherapy, patients talk with the therapist about upsetting thoughts and feelings, explore self-defeating patterns of behavior, and learn alternative ways to handle their emotions. As they talk, the therapist tries to help them understand how they can change or better cope with their disorder.

Behavioral therapy (BT) helps people develop more effective ways to work on immediate issues. Rather than helping the child understand his or her feelings and actions, it helps directly in changing their thinking and coping and thus may lead to changes in behavior. The support might be practical assistance, like help in organizing tasks or schoolwork or dealing with emotionally charged events. Or the support might be in self-monitoring one's own behavior and giving self-praise or rewards for acting in a desired way such as controlling anger or thinking before acting.

Social skills training can also help children learn new behaviors. In social skills training, the therapist discusses and models appropriate behaviors important in developing and maintaining social relationships, like waiting for a turn, sharing toys, asking for help, or responding to teasing, then gives children a chance to practice. For example, a child might learn to "read" other people's facial expression and tone of voice in order to respond appropriately. Social skills training helps the child to develop better ways to play and work with other children.

Attention Deficit Hyperactivity Disorder in Adults

Attention Deficit Hyperactivity Disorder is a highly publicized childhood disorder that affects approximately 3 to 5 percent of all children. What is much less well known is the probability that, of children who have ADHD, many will still have it as adults. Several studies done in recent years estimate that between 30 percent and 70 percent of children with ADHD continue to exhibit symptoms in the adult years.

Typically, adults with ADHD are unaware that they have this disorder—they often just feel that it's impossible to get organized, to stick to a job, to keep an appointment. The everyday tasks of getting up, getting dressed and ready for the day's work, getting to work on time, and being productive on the job can be major challenges for the ADD adult.

Diagnosing ADHD in an Adult

Diagnosing an adult with ADHD is not easy. Many times, when a child is diagnosed with the disorder, a parent will recognize that he or she has many of the same symptoms the child has and, for the first time, will begin to understand some of the traits that have given him or her trouble for years—distractability, impulsivity, restlessness. Other adults will seek professional help for depression or anxiety and will find out that the root cause of some of their emotional problems is ADHD. They may have a history of school failures or problems at work. Often they have been involved in frequent automobile accidents.

To be diagnosed with ADHD, an adult must have childhood-onset, persistent, and current symptoms. The accuracy of the diagnosis of adult ADHD is of utmost importance and should be made by a clinician with expertise in the area of attention dysfunction. For an accurate diagnosis, a history of the patient's childhood behavior, together with an interview with his life partner, a parent, close friend or other close associate, will be needed. A physical examination and psychological tests should also be given. Comorbidity with other conditions may exist such as specific learning disabilities, anxiety, or affective disorders.

A correct diagnosis of ADHD can bring a sense of relief. The individual has brought into adulthood many negative perceptions of himself that may have led to low esteem. Now he can begin to understand why he has some of his problems and can begin to face them.

References

DSM-IV-TR workgroup. *The Diagnostic and Statistical Manual of Mental Disorders,* Fourth Edition, Text Revision.Washington, DC: American Psychiatric Association.

Biederman J, Faraone SV, Keenan K, Knee D, Tsuang MF. Family-genetic and psychosocial risk factors in DSM-III attention deficit disorder. *Journal of the American Academy of Child and Adolescent Psychiatry,* 1990; 29(4): 526–533.

Faraone SV, Biederman J. Neurobiology of Attention-Deficit Hyperactivity Disorder. *Biological Psychiatry,* 1998; 44; 951–958.

The ADHD Molecular Genetics Network. Report from the third international meeting of the attention-deficit hyperactivity disorder molecular genetics network. *American Journal of Medical Genetics*, 2002, 114:272–277.

Castellanos FX, Lee PP, Sharp W, Jeffries NO, Greenstein DK, Clasen LS, Blumenthal JD, James RS, Ebens CI, Walter JM, Zijdenbos A, Evans AC, Giedd JN, Rapoport JL. Developmental trajectories of brain volume abnormalities in children and adolescents with attentiondeficit/hyperactivity disorder. *Journal of the American Medical Association*, 2002, 288:14:1740–1748.

Wilens TC, Faraone, SV, Biederman J, Gunawardene S. Does stimulant therapy of attention-deficit/hyperactivity disorder beget later substance abuse? A meta-analytic review of the literature. *Pediatrics*, 2003, 111:1:179–185.

Silver LB. Attention-deficit hyperactivity disorder in adult life. *Child and Adolescent Psychiatric Clinics of North America*, 2000:9:3: 411–523.

Wilens TE, Biederman J, Spencer TJ. Attention deficit/hyperactivity disorder across the lifespan. *Annual Review of Medicine*, 2002:53:113–131.

 **NO**

Attention Deficit Hyperactivity Disorder: What It Is and What It Is Not

It is almost axiomatic in the mental health field that fads will occur in the "diagnosis" and treatment of various types of behavioral aberrations, some of which border on being mere discomforts. Although the same faddism exists to some degree in physical medicine, its appearance is not nearly as blatant, perhaps in part because physical medicine is more soundly grounded in the physical sciences than are diagnoses in the mental health field. These fads spill over into the general culture, where direct marketing often takes place. One has to spend only a brief period in front of a television set during prime time to discover ADHD (Attention Deficit Hyperactivity Disorder), SAD (Social Anxiety Disorder), or IBS (Irritable Bowel Syndrome). Even when purporting to be informational, these are more or less disguised commercials, inasmuch as they posit a cure that varies with the drug manufacturer sponsoring the television ad.

The other certainty is that these "diagnoses" will fall from usage as other fads emerge, as was the case a decade or so ago with the disappearance of a once-common designation for what is now sometimes called ADHD. That passing fad was known as minimal brain syndrome (MBS) and/or food disorder (ostensibly from red dye or other food additives). From this author's perspective, these fad "diagnoses" don't really exist. Other writers in this volume (e.g., Cummings, Rosemond, and Wright) have commented on the slipperiness of these "diagnoses"—that is, the elevation of a symptom and/or its description to the level of a disorder or syndrome—and the concomitant tendency to overmedicate for these nonexistent maladies.

Children and ADHD

Certainly, there are deficiencies of attention and hyperactivity, but such behavioral aberrancies are most often indicative of a transitory state or condition within the organism. They are not in and of themselves indicative of a "disorder." Every parent has noticed, particularly with younger children, that toward the end of an especially exciting and fatiguing day children are literally "ricocheting off the walls." Although this behavior may in the broadest sense be classifiable as hyperactivity, it is generally pathognomonic of nothing more than excessive fatigue, for which the treatment of choice is a good night's sleep. Distractibility (attention deficit) is a frequent concomitant of excessive fatigue, particularly with children under five years of age, and can even be seen in adults if fatigue levels are extreme or if stress is prolonged. However, such "symptoms" in these contexts do not rise to the level of a treatable disorder.

Conversely, when distractibility and/or hyperactivity characterize the child's everyday behavior (especially if accompanied by factors such as delayed development, learning difficulties, impaired motor skills, and impaired judgment), they may be indicative of either a neurological disorder or of developing emotional difficulties. However, after nearly fifty years of diagnosing and treating several thousand such problems, it is my considered judgment that the distractibility and hyperactivity seen in such children is not the same as the distractibility and hyperactivity in children currently diagnosed as having ADHD. Furthermore, the hyperactivity/distractibility seen in the non-ADHD children described above is qualitatively and quantitatively different, depending on whether it is caused by incipient emotional maldevelopment (functional; i.e., nonorganic) or whether it is due to neurological involvement.

It is also notable that most children whose distractibility and/or hyperactivity is occasioned by emotional distress do not show either the kind or degree of learning disability, delayed genetic development, poor judgment, and impaired motor skills that are seen in children whose "distractibility/hyperactivity" is occasioned by neurological involvement. Only in children with the severest forms of emotional disturbance does one see the kind of developmental delays and impaired behavioral controls that are more reflective of neurological involvement (or what was known as MBS until the ADHD fad took hold). Differentiating the child with actual neurological involvement from the child that has emotionally based distractibility is neither simple nor easy to do, especially if the behavioral (as opposed to neurological) involvement is severe.

A major and profound disservice occasioned by the current fad of elevating nonspecific symptoms such as anxiety and hyperactivity to the level of a syndrome or disorder and then diagnosing ADD/ADHD is that we lump together individuals with very different needs and very different problems. We then attempt to treat the problem(s) with a single entity, resulting in a one-pill-fits-all response. It is also unfortunately the case that many mental health providers (e.g., child psychiatrists, child psychologists, child social workers), as well as many general care practitioners (e.g., pediatricians and internists), are not competent to make such discriminations alone. Therefore, it follows that such practitioners are not trained and equipped to provide ongoing care, even when an appropriate diagnosis has been made.

To add to an already complicated situation, the symptom picture in children tends to change with time and maturation. Children with neurological involvement typically tend to improve spontaneously over time, so that the symptoms of distractibility and hyperactivity often represent diminished components in the clinical picture. Conversely, children whose distractibility and hyperactivity are emotionally determined typically have symptoms that tend to intensify or be accompanied/replaced by even more dramatic indices of emotional distress.

Management of Children Exhibiting "ADHD" According to Etiology

It is apparent that somewhat superficially similar presenting complaints (i.e., distractibility and hyperactivity) may reflect two very different causative factors, and that the successful treatment and management of the complaint should vary according to the underlying causation. Neurological damage can stem from a number of causative factors during pregnancy or the birth process, and a successful remedial program may require the combined knowledge of the child's pediatrician, a neuropsychologist specializing in the diagnosis and treatment of children, and a child neurologist. In these cases appropriate medication for the child is often very helpful.

Psychotherapy for the child (particularly younger children) is, in this writer's experience, largely a waste of time. On the other hand, remedial training in visual perception, motor activities, visual–motor integration, spatial relations, numerical skills, and reading and writing may be crucial in alleviating or at least diminishing the impact of symptoms. Deficits in these skills can be major contributors to the hyperactivity and distractibility so frequently identified with such children. Counseling and psychotherapeutic work with the parents is very important and should always be a part of an integrated therapeutic program. Such children need to be followed by an attending pediatrician, a child neurologist, a child neuropsychologist, and an educational therapist, bearing in mind that treatment needs change throughout the span of remediation. For example, medication levels and regimens may need to be adjusted, and training programs will constantly need to be revised or elaborated.

It is also noteworthy that so-called tranquilizing medication with these children typically produces an adverse effect. This writer remembers a situation that occurred early in his practice, a case he has used repeatedly to alert fledgling clinicians to the importance of a comprehensive initial evaluation and ongoing supervision in the development of neurologically involved children.

John, a two-and-a-half-year-old boy, was referred by his pediatrician for evaluation of extreme hyperactivity, distractibility, and mild developmental delay. The psychological evaluation elicited evidence of visual perceptual impairment in a context of impaired visual motor integration, a finding suggestive of an irritative focus in the parietal-occipital areas of the brain. This finding was later corroborated by a child neurologist, and John was placed on dilantin and phenobarbital. A developmental training program was instituted, and the parents began participation in a group specifically designed for the parents of brain-injured children. Over the next couple of years, the patient's progress was excellent, and his development and learning difficulties were singularly diminished. The parents were comfortable with John's progress and with their ability to manage it, so they decided to have a long-wanted additional child. In the meantime, the father's work necessitated moving to another location, leading to a change of obstetrician and pediatrician.

The second pregnancy proceeded uneventfully and eventuated in the birth of a second boy. Shortly after the mother returned home with the new infant, John began to regress, exhibiting a number of prior symptoms such as hyperactivity and distractibility, as well as problems in behavioral control. The new pediatrician referred the family to a child psychiatrist, who promptly placed John on a tranquilizer. Shortly thereafter, John's academic performance began to deteriorate dramatically, and his school counseled the parents about the possibility that he had been promoted too rapidly and "could not handle work at this grade level."

At this point, the parents again contacted this writer, primarily out of concern for John's diminished academic performance. Because it had been more than two years since John had been formally evaluated, I advised the parents that another comprehensive evaluation was indicated. The parents agreed, and a full diagnostic battery was administered to John, the results of which were then compared to his prior performance. It immediately became apparent that he was not functioning at grade level, and that the overall level of his functioning had deteriorated dramatically.

In his initial evaluation, John's functional level had been in the Bright Normal range (i.e., overall IQ of 110 to 119), whereas his current functioning placed him at the Borderline Mentally Retarded level (IQ below 60). The history revealed nothing of significance other than the behavioral regression after the birth of the sibling and the introduction of the new medication. I advised the parents that I thought the child was being erroneously medicated, with consequent diminution of his intellectual efficiency, and that the supposition could be tested by asking the attending child psychiatrist to diminish John's medication to see if the child's performance improved.

The attending child psychiatrist was quite upset by the recommendations and the implications thereof and threatened to sue me for "practicing medicine without a license." I informed the physician that I was not practicing medicine but rather neuropsychology, along with deductive reasoning known as "common sense," which we could test by appropriately reducing John's dosage level for a month and then retesting him. Faced with the alternative of a legal action for slander or libel for having accused this neuropsychologist of a felony, the child psychiatrist agreed.

Upon retesting a month later, the child's performance level had returned to Bright Normal, and his academic performance and behavior in school had improved dramatically. By this time approximately six to eight months had elapsed since the birth of the sibling, and John had become accustomed to his new brother. All concerned agreed that the medication had not been helpful and that the child should continue for another three to six months without medication. Subsequent contact with the parents some six months later indicated that John was doing well at school. The parents were quite comfortable with the behavioral management skills they had learned, which enabled them to handle a child with an underlying neurological handicap.

As noted earlier, the marked distractibility and/or hyperactivity in children with neurological involvement tends to diminish through adolescence, especially after puberty, as do many of the other symptoms. As a consequence, these children present a very different clinical picture in adolescence and adulthood. Typically, they are characterized by impulsivity, at times poor judgment, and excessive fatigability. It is generally only under the circumstances of extreme fatigue (or other stress) that one will see fairly dramatic degrees of distractibility and hyperactivity. Thus, an appropriate diagnosis leading to productive intervention is difficult to make.

Conversely, children who exhibit the symptoms of distractibility and hyperactivity on an emotional basis typically do not show the diminution of symptomatology with increasing age. In fact, the symptoms may intensify and/or be replaced by even more dramatic symptoms, especially during puberty and adolescence (Myklebust, 1973). It should also be emphasized that the kind of distractibility and hyperactivity exhibited by the emotionally disturbed youngster is very different in quality and quantity from that of a youngster whose hyperactivity and distractibility has a neurological basis (Myklebust, 1973; Ochroch, 1979). Unfortunately, it is also frequently the case that a youngster with a neurological handicap may have significant emotional problems overlaying the basic neurological problems, making diagnosis even more complicated (Small, 1980). But the overriding problem confronting parents today is the misdiagnosis of emotionally-based symptoms that brings the recommendation of unwarranted medication.

In the largest study of its kind, Cummings and Wiggins (2001) retrospectively examined the records of 168,113 children and adolescents who had been referred and treated over a four-year period in a national behavioral health provider operating in thirty-nine states. Before beginning treatment, sixty-one percent of the males and twenty-three percent of the females were taking psychotropic medication for ADD/ADHD by a psychiatrist, a pediatrician, or a primary care physician. Most of them lived in a single-parent home, and lacked an effective father figure or were subjected to negative and frequently abusive male role models. Behavioral interventions included a compassionate but firm male therapist and the introduction of positive male role models (e.g., fathers, Big Brothers, coaches, Sunday school teachers, etc.) into the child's life. Counseling focused on helping parents understand what constitutes the behavior of a normal boy.

After an average of nearly eleven treatments with the parent and approximately six with the child, the percentage of boys on medication was reduced from sixty-one percent to eleven percent, and the percentage of girls on medication went from twenty-three percent to two percent. These dramatic results occurred despite very strict requirements for discontinuing the medication, which seems to point to an alarming overdiagnosis and overmedication of ADD/ADHD and greater efficacy of behavioral interventions than is generally believed to be the case by the mental health community.

Adult ADHD

The wholesale invasion of ADHD in childhood and adolescence is accompanied by a concurrent explosion of such diagnoses into adulthood. One cannot watch television without being bombarded by the direct marketing that asks:

"Do you find it difficult to finish a task at work? Do you frequently find yourself daydreaming or distracted? You may be suffering from ADD. Consult your physician or WebMD." Of course, adult ADD exists; children with real ADD will grow into adulthood. But the symptoms described in this aggressive TV marketing are more reflective of boredom, the mid-day blahs, job dissatisfaction, or stress than a syndrome or disorder requiring treatment.

Unfortunately, treatment interventions focused primarily on medication and based on such ethereal and universal symptoms promise an instant "cure" for the patient who now does not have to confront possible unhappiness or stress. Such simple solutions also find great favor with the insurers and HMOs that look for the cheapest treatment. Persons exhibiting "symptoms" are more likely to benefit from a variety of behavioral interventions ranging from vocational counseling for job dissatisfaction and marital counseling for an unhappy marriage, to psychotherapy for underlying emotional stress, anxiety, or depression. Such interventions tend to be time-consuming and costly, with the consequence that the patients may inadvertently ally themselves with managed care companies devoted to the principle that the least expensive treatment is the treatment of choice.

Distractibility and hyperactivity of the type that we have called the "real ADHD" does exist in adults. However, in general, symptoms are much more subtle and, in many if not most cases, overshadowed by other symptoms. Thus, if mentioned at all, distractibility and hyperactivity are rarely significant presenting complaints. Such things as poor judgment, behavioral difficulties, forgetting, difficulties in reading/calculating, and getting lost are typically pre-eminent in the adult patient's presenting complaints. These usually become apparent in adulthood after an accident, strokes (CVA), infections of the brain, and other such events. The very drama of the causative factor typically makes the diagnosis apparent, and treatment providers are "tuned in" to anticipate sequellae secondary to neurological damage: intellectual and/or judgmental deficits, behavioral change, impulsivity, and motor impairment.

It should be emphasized that hyperactivity and distractibility, although present, are less dramatic symptoms that are understandably of less concern to the patient. Furthermore, they often diminish rapidly in the first eighteen months following the neurological event. Even then, the major constellation of symptoms may not be sufficiently dramatic to alert attending medical personnel as to the primary cause of the patient's complaints. This is particularly true of contrecoup lesions occurring most frequently in auto accidents.

Although circumstances resulting in contrecoup damage are frequent and often missed, there are also other, even more significant, types of neurological involvement that may also pass unnoticed. These include early-onset Alzheimer's disease beginning at age fifty and cerebral toxicity resulting from inappropriate medication in the elderly, which is usually misdiagnosed as incipient Alzheimer's. Expectation can unfortunately contribute not only to a misdiagnosis, but also failure to order tests that might elicit the underlying condition. In addition, the converse may infrequently occur: Neurological involvement may be anticipated but is not demonstrable and does not exist. Three illustrative cases follow.

Case 1

Bill, a young construction worker, received notice of his imminent induction into the armed services. Right after lunch on a Friday afternoon, a large section of 2 × 4 lumber dropped from the second story of a work site, striking him butt-first in the right anterior temporal region of the head. He was unconscious for a short period of time, quickly recovered consciousness, and showed no apparent ill effects from the blow. He refused hospitalization, and was taken by his employer to his home.

On the following Monday, Bill phoned his employer saying that he was still "not feeling too good," and given the imminence of his induction into the Army, he "was just going to goof off" until he was "called up." The employer had no further contact with Bill, who was inducted into the Army, where he almost immediately began to have difficulty, primarily of a behavioral type. Throughout his basic training, he tended to be impulsive and to use poor judgment, and he was constantly getting into fights with his companions. He barely made it through training and was shipped overseas where he was assigned to a unit whose primary duty was guard duty.

Throughout his training and his subsequent duty assignment, Bill was a frequent attendee at sick call with consistent complaints of headache, earning him the reputation of "goof-off." His military career was terminated shortly after an apparently unprovoked attack on the officer in charge of the guard detail to which Bill was assigned. After a short detention in the stockade, he was discharged from the Army. His headaches and impulsivity continued into civilian life and prompted Bill to seek medical assistance through the Veterans Administration. The VA clinic's case study included neurological screening tests that were strongly suggestive of brain involvement. Consequently, he was given a full psychological work-up, which revealed intellectual impairment attendant to temporal lobe damage.

Subsequent neurological and encephalographic studies were consistent with the neuropsychological conclusions, and indicated a major focus in the anterior temporal area of the brain. A careful and detailed history was taken, and the incident of the blow to the head was elicited. This case suggests that even though Bill refused hospitalization, because of the severity of the blow it would have been prudent for the employer to insist on a thorough evaluation.

Case 2

James, a man in his late forties, was the son of a Southern sharecropper. Upon graduation from high school, he attended the Tuskegee Institute for a short period before he was drafted into the armed forces. James had a productive military career and upon his discharge moved to California, got married, and proceeded to raise his family. He had trained himself as a finish carpenter and cabinetmaker. His work was highly regarded, and his annual income was well above the average for his field. One of his three children was a college graduate, a second was well along in college, and the third was graduating from high school. James owned his own home and enjoyed a fine reputation as a contributing citizen of his community.

While at work installing a complicated newel post and banister, James became disoriented and tumbled from a stair landing, falling some five feet and landing primarily on his head and shoulders but experiencing no apparent loss of consciousness. He was taken to a hospital for evaluation but was released with no significant findings. Almost immediately thereafter, he began to have difficulty at work. He would become disoriented, could not tell left from right, and made frequent mistakes in measuring, sawing, and fitting even simple elements. Before the accident he seldom if ever missed work, but now he became a frequent absentee. The quality of his work deteriorated and his income plummeted. He sought medical advice and was given a small stipend under the Workers Compensation program.

Over several weeks, he demonstrated no progress, and the attending neurologist and neurosurgeon referred him for neuropsychodiagnostic evaluation as a possible malingerer. The neuropsychologist noted that James' current status was completely at odds with his prior history, and not at all consistent with malingering. For example, the evaluation revealed that this highly skilled cabinetmaker, to his embarrassment, could no longer answer the question, "How many inches are there in two and a half feet?" The neuropsychological finding of pervasive occipital-parietal involvement was subsequently corroborated by electroencephalographic study.

Case 3

An airline captain driving along Wilshire Boulevard in Los Angeles lost consciousness when he experienced a spontaneous cerebral hemorrhage. He was immediately taken to a nearby major hospital where he received immediate and continuing care. Subsequently, a subdural hematoma developed, requiring surgical intervention. The captain recovered and showed no clinically significant signs of neurological involvement. An immediate post-recovery issue was the possibility of being returned to flight status. The attending neurosurgeon referred the patient for a comprehensive neuropsychological evaluation that found no indication of residual neurological deficit. Consequently, the neuropsychologist and the attending neurosurgeon recommended return to flight status.

In summary, in none of the foregoing situations was attention deficit or hyperactivity a significant presenting complaint, although the presence of both was clinically demonstrable at various times in the posttraumatic period. Yet the failure to recognize their presence would not have had a negative impact on treatment planning and or management in any of the three cases. Conversely, if excessive focus on the possible "attention deficits and/or hyperactivity disorder" dictated the nature of the therapeutic intervention, a significant disservice to each of these patients would have resulted.

Traditionally when distractibility and/or hyperactivity are prominent parts of the presenting complaint, the mental health provider directs diagnostic energies toward ascertaining the underlying source of these dysphoric experiences. The distractibility and hyperactivity would have been viewed as secondary symptoms to be tolerated, if possible, until the resolution of the underlying problem resulted in their alleviation. In situations where the symptoms were so extreme as to be significantly debilitating, the mental health provider might reluctantly attempt to provide some symptom relief. However, in such cases this was done with the certain knowledge that it was an expedient, and was not addressing causation.

Times have changed dramatically, reflecting the interaction of a number of factors such as competition and cost controls. With the emergence of a plethora of mental health service providers, psychiatry opted to "remedicalize," essentially abandoning what it refers to as "talk therapy" in favor of medicating questionable syndromes and disorders. Psychology, pushed by its academic wing, could never decide what level of training was sufficient for independent mental health service delivery (i.e., master's versus doctoral degrees), and graduate-level training programs began to turn out hordes of master's-level providers in counseling, social work, education, and school psychology.

Meanwhile, the inclusion of mental health benefits in pre-paid health programs broadened consumption and brought about managed care as a means of reducing consumption of all kinds of health services, including behavioral health services. When the American public's impatience with time-consuming processes is added to managed care's limiting of services in the context of a glut of mental health providers the scene is set for considerable mischief. Add to this brew the fact that psychiatry holds a virtual medication-prescribing monopoly in mental health and that drug manufacturers are constantly developing and marketing new magic pills, it all adds up to an environment that encourages the "discovery" of yet another syndrome or disorder for which treatment is necessary.

Summary

When hyperactivity and/or distractibility is truly one of the presenting symptoms, it is indicative of a complex situation that warrants extensive and thoughtful evaluation, and, more often than not, complex and comprehensive treatment planning from the perspective of a variety of specialists. In situations where the attention deficit and/or hyperactivity reflects problems in parenting, chemotherapeutic intervention for the child is likely to be, at best, no more than palliative and, at worse, may succeed in considerably complicating the situation. In this writer's experience, chemotherapeutic intervention for emotionally disturbed children is a last resort and of minimal value in addressing the overall problem. Psychotherapeutic intervention with the parents, which may or may not include the child, is more often than not the treatment of choice. This is a judgment that is best made only after exhaustive study by pediatrics, psychology, neurology, and perhaps, last of all, psychiatry, which so often seems all too eager to overmedicate. . . .

Where the presenting complaints of hyperactivity and distractibility are in a context of delayed development, excessive fatigability, learning deficits, and other such signs, the complexity of the diagnostic problem is substantially increased. In such circumstances, it is absolutely not in the child's best interest to limit the diagnostic evaluation to a single specialty. With the increasing evidence that neurological involvement can follow any number of prenatal and postnatal exposures, wise and caring parents will insist on a comprehensive evaluation by specialists in pediatrics, child neurology, and child neuropsychology. More often than not, if medication is indicated, it will be of a type quite different than what is used in the management of so-called ADHD.

Furthermore, treatment intervention and case management will likely involve skilled educational training of the specialized type developed for use with the brain-injured child (see Myklebust, 1973, 1978; Ochroch, 1979; Small, 1980, 1982; Strauss & Kephart, 1955). In the case of a friendly pediatrician, a concerned psychologist, or a caring child psychiatrist, any or all attempting unilaterally to diagnose and/or manage the treatment regimen, the concerned and caring parent is well advised to promptly seek additional opinions. For a comprehensive description of the type of evaluation that is most productive in the management of children of this kind, see Small (1982).

References

Cummings, N.A. & Wiggins, J.G. (2001). A collaborative primary care/behavioral health model for the use of psychotropic medication with children and adolescents: The report of a national retrospective study. *Issues in Interdisciplinary Care, 3*(2), 121–128.

Myklebust, H.R. (1973). Identification and diagnosis of children with learning disabilities: An interdisciplinary study of criteria. *Seminars in Psychiatry, 5*(1), 74–93.

Myklebust, H.R. (Ed.) (1978). *Progress in Learning Disabilities.* New York: Grune & Stratton.

Ochroch, R.A. (1979). A review of the minimal brain dysfunction syndrome. In R. Ochroch (Ed.), *The Diagnosis and Treatment of Minimal Brain Dysfunction in Children: A Clinical Approach.* New York: Human Sciences.

Small, L. (1980). *Neuropsychodiagnosis in Psychotherapy,* (rev. ed.). New York: Brunner/Mazel.

Small, L. (1982). *The Minimal Brain Syndrome: Diagnosis and Treatment.* New York: Free Press.

Strauss, A. & Kephart, N. (1955). *The Psychotherapy and Education of the Brain Injured Child,* Vol. 2. New York: Grune & Stratton.

CHALLENGE QUESTIONS

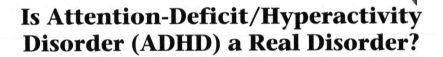

Is Attention-Deficit/Hyperactivity Disorder (ADHD) a Real Disorder?

1. To what extent should conditions involving inattention and hyperactivity be regarded as medical, as opposed to emotional, disorders?
2. What are the minimal behavioral criteria that should be met before recommending that an inattentive and easily distracted individual should be prescribed medication?
3. What might motivate some individuals to want to be diagnosed with the ADHD label?
4. How would you go about designing a research study aimed at differentiating normal characteristics such as occasional inattentiveness from diagnosable conditions such as ADHD?
5. A common style in contemporary society is to multitask, in which attention is divided among several simultaneous tasks (e.g., word processing, instant messaging, telephone conversations, and interpersonal chats). To what extent does multitasking cause people to believe that they have ADHD because they feel unable to process all the information coming their way?

Suggested Readings

O'Regan, F. (2008). *Understanding AD/HD: Frequently asked questions*. London: Jessica Kingsley Publishers.

Pauc, R. (2006). *The learning disability myth: Understanding and overcoming your child's diagnosis of Dyspraxia, Tourette's Syndrome of childhood, ADD, ADHD or OCD*. London: Virgin Books.

Phillips, C. B. (2006). Medicine goes to school: Teachers as sickness brokers for ADHD. *PLOS Medicine, 3(4)*, from http://medicine.plosjournals. org/perlserv/?request=get-document&doi=10.1371%2Fjournal.pmed.0030182.

Zeigler Dendy, C. A. (2006). *Teenagers with ADD and ADHD: A guide for parents and professionals* (2nd ed.). Bethesda: Woodbine House.

ISSUE 6

Should MDMA (Ecstasy) Be Prohibited, Even for Therapeutic Use?

YES: Robert Mathias and Patrick Zickler, from "NIDA Conference Highlights Scientific Findings on MDMA/Ecstasy," *NIDA Notes* (December 2001)

NO: June Riedlinger and Michael Montagne, from "Using MDMA in the Treatment of Depression," in Julie Holland, ed., *Ecstasy: The Complete Guide* (Park Street Press, 2001)

ISSUE SUMMARY

YES: Science writers Robert Mathias and Patrick Zickler argue that MDMA has skyrocketed in popularity and that insufficient attention has been paid to the physical and psychological risks associated with its use.

NO: June Riedlinger, an assistant professor of clinical pharmacy, and Michael Montagne, a professor of pharmacy, contend that the risks associated with MDMA use have been exaggerated and that there are legitimate therapeutic uses for this substance.

MDMA, popularly known as "Ecstasy," was first synthesized at the beginning of the twentieth century when a pharmaceutical company was trying to develop a medication to stop bleeding. However, this product was abandoned because of its dramatic psychoactive properties. MDMA resurfaced in the 1980s when some psychotherapists proposed that it be used to enhance communication in patients. The drug also began appearing on college campuses and in nightclubs, where users were enthralled by its euphoria-inducing effects. Although the Drug Enforcement Agency outlawed MDMA in 1985, the use of this substance continued to grow dramatically throughout the 1990s, as partygoers attending dance marathons known as raves craved MDMA as their recreational drug of choice.

By the late 1990s the rave party scene had caught the attention of the media and law enforcement authorities because of the increasing number of medical emergencies associated with the uncontrolled use of substances such as MDMA. For example, in 1994 there were 253 MDMA-related emergency room incidents, but by the year 2000 the number had risen to 4,511 individuals being rushed to hospitals because they were suffering from dehydration, hyperthermia, and seizures caused by MDMA. As Robert Mathias and Patrick Zickler assert in the following selection, in addition to the immediate physical risks associated with MDMA, there are long-term emotional and cognitive costs. For instance, chronic users of MDMA show evidence of impairment in learning and memory as well as an increased likelihood of developing serious psychological conditions later in life.

In the second selection, June Riedlinger and Michael Montagne acknowledge the potential for adverse effects and neurotoxicity associated with MDMA, but they urge more thoughtful attention to the haphazard ways in which MDMA has been taken by recreational users. They also argue that there are some potentially useful ways in which this substance might be prescribed to treat certain psychological problems, such as depression, for which traditional medications have considerable limitations and side effects. In responding to harsh criticisms of MDMA, Riedlinger and Montagne contend that the problems are attributable to the lack of pharmaceutical regulation; if MDMA were professionally manufactured such that samples of known purity were distributed, most adverse reactions would be avoidable.

POINT

- Even small doses of MDMA can greatly reduce the body's ability to metabolize the drug. Increased toxic effects can lead to harmful reactions, such as dehydration, hyperthermia, and seizures.
- In clinical studies, MDMA users have shown massive impairment on tests of learning, memory, and general intelligence when compared to nonusers.
- Exposure to MDMA is associated with damage to brain cells that release serotonin.
- Compared with nonusers, current and former users of MDMA have drastically higher measures of psychopathology, such as impulsivity, anxiety, and depression.
- Many Ecstasy-related emergencies occur because tablets are frequently laced with other drugs.

COUNTERPOINT

- Reports of adverse reactions have been sensationalized. Most adverse reactions and neurotoxicity can be avoided if the lowest effective therapeutic doses are used.
- Most clinical studies that allege neurotoxicity have recruited volunteers with histories of excessive and prolonged use. No study has been published that assesses individuals with histories of infrequent oral dosing.
- MDMA works to enhance serotonergic function and increase mood in a matter of hours.
- MDMA is, in fact, effective at treating psychopathology. It facilitates psychotherapy and helps to alleviate feelings of hopelessness.
- If MDMA were regulated and samples of known purity were used, most adverse reactions would be avoidable.

YES ⬅

Robert Mathias
and Patrick Zickler

NIDA Conference Highlights Scientific Findings on MDMA/Ecstasy

In the face of worldwide increases in the use of MDMA, or ecstasy, particularly among teens and young adults, NIDA convened an international array of scientists at the National Institutes of Health in Bethesda, Maryland, in July [2001] for a conference on "MDMA/Ecstasy Research: Advances, Challenges, Future Directions." MDMA researchers from Australia, Europe, and all regions of the United States detailed the latest findings on patterns and trends of MDMA abuse, its complex acute effects on the brain and behavior, and the possible long-term consequences of its use.

In opening remarks, Dr. Glen Hanson, director of NIDA's Division of Neuroscience and Behavioral Research, noted the tremendous interest of the scientific community and the general public in MDMA and its effects. The soldout conference drew an audience of 565 people with a broad range of interests and perspectives. They included scientists, drug abuse prevention and treatment practitioners, clinicians, educators, high school counselors, and representatives from Federal and local public health departments and agencies.

A public health perspective on MDMA by James N. Hall, of the Up Front Drug Information Center in Miami, Florida, provided a sharp contrast to the prevailing public view of MDMA as an innocuous drug. MDMA use began to expand rapidly in the United States in 1996 with "more pills going to younger populations," Mr. Hall said. This upsurge in use led to an increase in drug-related problems. For example, MDMA-related hospital emergency room incidents increased from 253 in 1994 to 4,511 in 2000, according to recent data from the Substance Abuse and Mental Health Services Administration's Drug Abuse Warning Network. "Most of these emergency room mentions are multiple-drug cases," Mr. Hall said, "as polydrug use has become the norm."

The common practice of using MDMA in conjunction with other drugs was just one of several recurring themes sounded during a conference session

From *NIDA Notes,* vol. 16, no. 5 (December 2001).

157

Figure 1

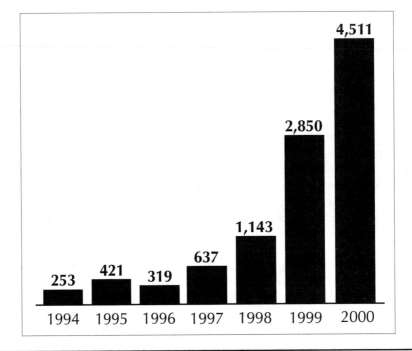

MDMA-Related Hospital Emergency Room Incidents—1994–2000

on current trends and patterns of MDMA use. Other significant themes were:

- MDMA now is being used in urban, suburban, and rural areas throughout the country;
- MDMA continues to be used in its traditional settings of all-night dance parties, called "raves," and nightclubs; use also is common now on college campuses and at small group gatherings, such as house parties;
- MDMA is used by all ages but still mainly by adolescents and young adults; use has increased sharply in this population in recent years;
- MDMA users are predominantly white, but ethnically and racially diverse groups of people are now using the drug; and
- MDMA's euphoric effects can lead to unplanned or unwanted sexual contact that increases the risk of transmitting HIV/AIDS and other infectious diseases.

Acute Effects of MDMA

A session on MDMA's acute effects presented the latest findings on how the drug works in the brain and body to produce its perceptual and physiological impact. The session explored the interaction of underlying biological and behavioral factors and mechanisms that may contribute to the possibly harmful effects of MDMA use.

Animal studies have indicated that MDMA increases extracellular levels of the chemical messengers serotonin and dopamine. In laboratory studies to understand how these increases affect humans, Dr. Manuel Tancer of Wayne State University in Detroit asked participants to compare MDMA's effects to those produced by compounds that stimulate serotonin alone and dopamine alone. MDMA's effects were reported to resemble some features of both compounds, noted Dr. Tancer. This indicates that both the dopamine and serotonin systems play a role in producing MDMA's subjective effects in humans.

MDMA also has powerful acute physiological effects in humans that increase with larger doses, according to several presentations. MDMA's cardiovascular effects include large increases in blood pressure, heart rate, and myocardial oxygen consumption, noted Dr. John Mendelson of the University of California, San Francisco. MDMA's elevations of heart rate and blood pressure were comparable to those produced by a maximal dose of dobutamine, a cardiovascular stimulant used in stress tests to evaluate patients for coronary artery disease, he said. However, unlike dobutamine, MDMA did not increase the heart's pumping efficiency. Thus, MDMA-induced heart rate and blood pressure increases may lead to an unexpectedly large increase in myocardial oxygen consumption, which can increase the risk for a cardiovascular catastrophe in people with preexisting heart disease, he said.

Even small increases in MDMA dose can greatly reduce the body's ability to metabolize the drug. This means MDMA is not processed and removed from the body quickly and remains active for longer periods. "As a result, plasma levels of the drug and concomitant increases in toxicity may rise dramatically when users take multiple doses over brief time periods. Increased toxic effects can lead to harmful reactions such as dehydration, hyperthermia, and seizures," Dr. Mendelson said. Drugs such as methamphetamine that are commonly abused in conjunction with MDMA also may increase the cardiovascular effects of MDMA, he said.

MDMA tablets often contain other drugs, such as ephedrine, a stimulant, and dextromethorphan, a cough suppressant that has PCP-like effects at high doses, that also can increase its harmful effects. In addition, drugs sold as MDMA may actually be substances that are much more dangerous, according to Dr. Rodney Irvine of the University of Adelaide in Australia. For example, the hallucinogen PMA (4-methoxyamphetamine), which is similar in some respects to MDMA, has even more severe toxic effects on the cardiovascular system, particularly as dosage increases. The drug has been sold as MDMA in Australia and has been associated with a number of deaths. PMA is now being distributed in the United States and has been linked to deaths in Chicago and Central Florida, according to the Federal Drug Enforcement Administration.

Long-Term Effects of MDMA

During the second day of the conference, researchers from the United States and other countries described current investigations of ecstasy's long-term effects. Introducing the day's program, Dr. Hanson summarized the mechanisms thought to be responsible for MDMA's toxic effects on the brain's serotonin system. In tests of learning and memory, he noted, MDMA users perform more poorly than nonusers on tasks associated with brain regions affected by MDMA. Higher doses of MDMA appear to be associated with more profound effects, and the consequences may be long-lasting.

Dr. Charles Vorhees of Children's Hospital Medical Center in Cincinnati, Ohio, has found that, in rats, exposure to MDMA during a period of brain development that corresponds to human brain development during the trimester before birth is associated with learning deficits that last into adulthood. "The impairment, which affects the rate at which the animals learn new tasks, increases in severity as the dose of MDMA increases and is more pronounced as the tasks become more complex," Dr. Vorhees said.

These findings of MDMA's effects on brain development are limited to studies involving rats, but there is a growing body of research suggesting that—in adult primates—MDMA can cause long-lasting damage. At the Johns Hopkins University School of Medicine in Baltimore, Drs. Una McCann, George Ricaurte, and other investigators have found that exposure to MDMA is associated with damage to brain cells that release serotonin; this damage persists for at least 7 years in nonhuman primates. In humans, the researchers have found that MDMA use is associated with verbal and visual memory problems in individuals who have not used the drug for at least 2 weeks. "We see a relationship between the dose of MDMA and the severity of the effects. In animals, MDMA-induced damage is extensive and long-lasting and we do not yet know if it is reversible," Dr. Ricaurte said. "A person who takes enough of the drug to feel its effects is taking enough to be at serious risk of similar damage to the brain and to memory and learning."

Dr. Linda Chang, a scientist at the Brookhaven National Laboratory in Upton, New York, reported on research using brain imaging techniques to evaluate the effects of occasional use of MDMA. She and her colleagues Dr. Charles Grob and Dr. Russell Poland at the University of California, Los Angeles, used single photon emission computed tomography to evaluate blood flow to the brain—which is regulated in part by serotonin—in 21 MDMA users who had taken the drug at least 6 times per year for more than 1 year (on average, a total of 75 times), but had not used the drug in at least 2 weeks (4 months average abstinence). The participants then were given MDMA in two sessions over the course of a week. Two weeks later, brain images showed decreased blood flow compared to the earlier images. The decrease was greater in those individuals who had higher total use of the drug.

Figure 2

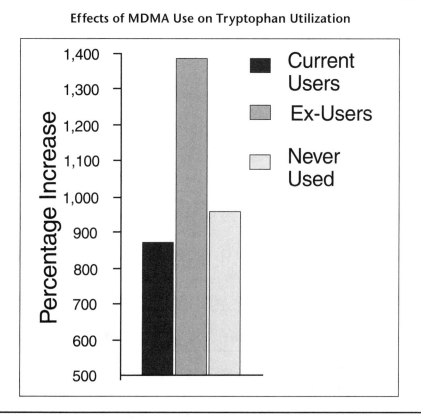

Effects of MDMA Use on Tryptophan Utilization

Note: MDMA disrupts brain processes that use the amino acid tryptophan to make the neurotransmitter seroto-nin, which affects memory and mood. Five hours after drinking a tryptophan supplement, ex-users of MDMA showed greater elevations of their blood tryptophan levels than did current users or non-users, indicating that less of the amino acid had been converted to serotonin.

MDMA Research in Europe

The popularity of MDMA as a "club drug" began in Europe in the late 1980s—roughly 5 years earlier than in the United States—and researchers there have studied the drug's effects in populations with a longer history of drug use. In Great Britain and Germany researchers have found that MDMA users—and even former users who have not taken the drug for at least 6 months—perform more poorly on some tests of memory and learning than do nonusers. MDMA also is associated with psychological problems such as anxiety and depression, this research suggests.

The learning and memory functions that appear to be impaired by MDMA in animal and human studies are associated with the brain's serotonin system. The specific effects of MDMA can be evaluated directly in animal studies, but in humans nearly all MDMA users also use other drugs such as marijuana, cocaine, and alcohol. In an effort to more fully understand

Figure 3

Effect of MDMA Use on Impulsivity

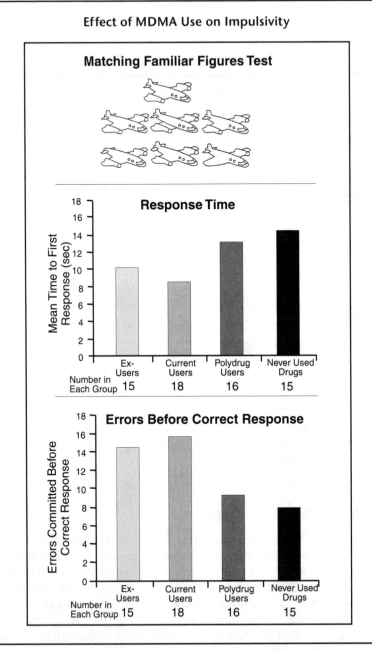

Note: The airplane figure at top is exactly matched by only one of six similar figures below. When asked to find the correct match, current and ex-users of MDMA made quicker choices and made more wrong choices before identifying the correct match than participants who used drugs other than MDMA or who used no drugs at all.

how MDMA affects polydrug users, Dr. Valerie Curran and her colleagues at University College London investigated the effect of MDMA use on the body's ability to use tryptophan, an amino acid that is one of the chemical building blocks for serotonin. The research involved three groups of polydrug users: some were current MDMA users, some had stopped using the drug, and some had never used it.

The researchers first measured blood levels of tryptophan and found that current and ex-users of MDMA had higher blood levels than did non-users and that the levels were elevated in proportion to the total amount of drug the participants had used. The investigators then gave participants drinks that contained augmented amounts of tryptophan in addition to all other necessary amino acids. Five hours later they measured blood levels of the amino acid. Ex-users of MDMA showed far higher levels of tryptophan in their blood than did nonusers or current users, Dr. Curran said. "Tryptophan should cross the blood-brain barrier to be incorporated into the biosynthesis of serotonin, but in ex-users, significantly higher levels of tryptophan remained in the blood," she said.

In memory tests, current users did more poorly than did nonusers; ex-users—who had not taken MDMA for an average of 2 years—had the poorest performance. The reason for such poor performance among the ex-users is uncertain, Dr. Curran said. One possibility is that these were people who developed particularly severe adverse effects and quit using the drug because of them. "Whatever the reason, there is a clear correlation between a biological marker (blood levels of tryptophan), a functional deficit (poor performance on tests of memory), and the total dosage and length of time these people used MDMA before they stopped," Dr. Curran said.

Dr. Euphrosyne Gouzoulis-Mayfrank of the University of Technology in Aachen, Germany, also described research involving MDMA's effects on polydrug users. She and her colleagues compared cognitive performance in three groups of participants age 18 to 30. One group included MDMA users with a typical pattern of recreational use (at least twice per month within the preceding 2 years) who also used marijuana (at least once per month over a 6-month period), a second group who did not use MDMA but whose marijuana use roughly matched that of the MDMA users, and a third group who had never used either drug. "Ecstasy users showed no impairment in tests of alertness," she said, "but performed worse than one or both control groups in more complex tasks of attention, in memory and learning tasks, and in tasks reflecting aspects of general intelligence."

Dr. Michael Morgan of the University of Sussex in Great Britain described research that suggests a relationship between marijuana use, MDMA use, and psychological problems and memory deficits. Dr. Morgan and his colleagues studied the effects among groups of current MDMA users, ex-users, polydrug users who did not use MDMA, and participants who had never used drugs.

The researchers found that the psychological measures were more closely associated in the polydrug population with current marijuana use than with past MDMA use. "Overall, however, current and ex-users of MDMA have dramatically higher measures of psychopathology such as impulsivity than nonusers," Dr. Morgan said. Like Dr. Curran, Dr. Morgan found cognitive deficits associated with rates of past MDMA use. In tests of memory, both current

Figure 4

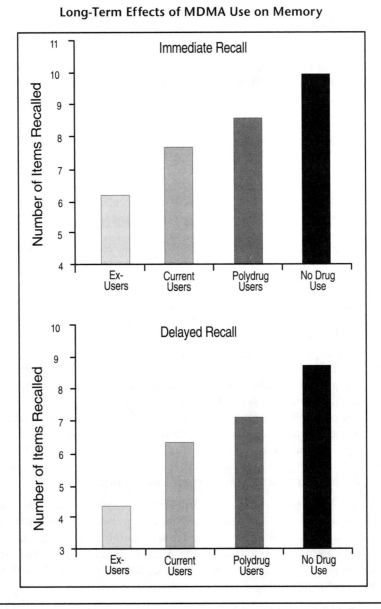

Long-Term Effects of MDMA Use on Memory

Note: In tests of MDMA effects on memory, ex-users and current users performed worse than participants who used drugs other than MDMA or used no drugs. Ex-users, in particular, showed greatly impaired memory.

and ex-users performed more poorly than nonusers. He also found that on some tests ex-users performed worse than did current users, although he noted that the reasons for poorer performance by ex-users could not clearly be linked exclusively to MDMA use. "Nonetheless, as a practical matter, ex-users show massively impaired memory. Not only had they not recovered, they were actually worse than current users," Dr. Morgan said.

June Riedlinger and
Michael Montagne

➔ **NO**

Using MDMA in the Treatment of Depression

Introduction

In this [selection] we discuss the use of the substance MDMA [ecstasy] for the treatment of depression. The first author's personal experience and work as a clinical pharmacist in psychiatry was the foundation for the hypothesis that MDMA could be a healing agent for the life-threatening illness of depression. Before discussing how MDMA may be beneficial in treating depression, a brief review of the medical criteria for the condition is warranted. . . .

Biochemical Basis of Depression

The possibility that some forms of human depression are based on central nervous system deficiencies of the neurotransmitter serotonin (5-hydroxytryptamine, or 5-HT), was first suggested by van Praag (1962) and then reinforced by the findings of other researchers (Coppen 1967; Lapin and Oxenburg 1969). Based on his later research, van Praag (1982) concluded that serotonin disorders are implicated most clearly in a subgroup of approximately 40 percent of patients afflicted with depression. He also emphasized that serotonin disorders probably play a causative, rather than a secondary, role in depression. This is suggested by the fact that serotonin-potentiating compounds, such as the precursors 5-hydroxytryptophan (5-HTP) and L-tryptophan, an essential amino acid, can have a therapeutic effect in depression (van Praag 1981).

It is significant that many of the drugs prescribed for treatment of depression have serotonergic activity. The newest class of antidepressants, the serotonin reuptake inhibitors (Prozac, Zoloft, Paxil, Celexa, and others) and, to varying degrees, the tricyclic antidepressants prevent the recycling of serotonin back into presynaptic nerve endings. Monoamine oxidase (MAO) inhibitors prevent the breakdown of serotonin by the enzyme MAO. In either case, more serotonin is available for binding to receptors (Spiegel and Aebi 1983). The specific mechanism of action of these drugs, however, is still not clear.

There is an entire class of psychoactive drugs that almost certainly derives its main effect from serotonin mediation (Freedman et al. 1970; Haigler and Aghajanian 1973; Anden et al. 1974; Winter 1975; Meltzer et al. 1978). These drugs, the psychedelics, are reported to have positive effects in the treatment of various psychological disorders, including depression. We present and discuss the value of psychedelic agents, with a focus on clinical reports and theoretical explanations for one specific drug, MDMA, that may become an efficacious treatment for depression in the future.

Psychedelic Psychotherapy

The possibility that psychedelic drugs could help facilitate the modern psychotherapeutic process was virtually ignored in the United States and Europe until about 1950. Between then and the mid-1960s, more than one thousand clinical papers describing forty thousand patients who had taken part in psychedelic therapy or other research trials were published, as well as several dozen related books; six international conferences on psychedelic drug therapy were held (Grinspoon and Bakalar 1983). Two different types of psychedelic psychotherapy were described (Grinspoon and Bakalar 1979). One emphasized a mystical or conversion experience and its after-effects (psychedelic therapy); using high doses of LSD (more than 200 mcg) was thought to be especially effective in reforming alcoholics and criminals. The other type explored the unconscious in the manner of psychoanalysis (psycholytic therapy); it focused on the treatment of neuroses and psychosomatic disorders using low doses of LSD (100–150 mcg) as well as other psychedelic drugs.

By the mid-1950s, it was recognized that psychedelics function as nonspecific amplifiers, drugs that project into consciousness (amplify) memories, fears, and other subjectively varying (nonspecific) psychological material that had been repressed, or was unconscious. Among the first announcements of this highly significant finding was a report entitled "Ataractic and Hallucinogenic Drugs in Psychiatry," written by a team of international experts convened by the World Health Organization. This report challenged the prevailing idea that psychedelic drugs are psychotomimetic, that is, capable of inducing a model of temporary psychosis. Instead, the team concluded, "It may be a gross oversimplification to speak of drug-specific reactivity patterns. On the contrary, experience suggests that the same drug, in the same dose, in the same subject may produce very different effects according to the precise interpersonal and motivational situation in which it was given" (World Health Organization 1958). Thus, it was made clear that the issues of set (the users' expectations) and setting (the environment for the drug experience) . . . must be taken into account when using psychedelics.

Another important issue to consider in a discussion of drug-assisted psychotherapy is this: at present, psychiatrists prescribe doses of mood elevators or stabilizers with which patients must comply on a daily basis. There is no currently accepted model of one-time or infrequent dosing of medications to alleviate psychic suffering. Thus, Grinspoon and Bakalar (1986) have emphasized: "It is a misunderstanding to consider psychedelic drug therapy as a form of chemotherapy, which must be regarded in the same way as prescribing lithium or phenothiazines." Instead, it is more like "a hybrid between pharmacotherapy and psychotherapy" (Grinspoon and Bakalar 1990) that incorporates features of both. . . .

MDMA's Role in the Treatment of Depression

That MDMA is apparently serotonergic was first noted by Nichols and associates (1982), who introduced it in vitro to homogenized rat brains and then measured the release of serotonin from the synaptosomes (vesicles in the synapses that store neurotransmitters). Elevated levels were detected, suggesting that serotonin release may play a role in MDMA's pharmacological activity. Subsequent research described in Peroutka (1990) appears to confirm the drug's serotongenicity. As with serotonergic antidepressant drugs, however, the specific mode of action is uncertain. . . .

In any case, MDMA's use in psychotherapy to stimulate positive feelings, such as openness and empathy, would seem to recommend it for a possible clinical role in treating depression. Riedlinger (1985) first proposed this in a discussion of MDMA's positive isomer activity and consequent release of serotonin in the brain. Because it is a potent releaser of serotonin into the synapse, and because of its short duration of effect, MDMA seems to be both effective and efficient as a drug for the medical treatment of depression. It works to enhance serotonergic function and mood in a matter of hours instead of weeks (as is the case for most prescription antidepressants), and it is effective when administered infrequently, perhaps in weekly or monthly dosing intervals. This compares favorably to the multiple daily dosing required for most of the currently available drugs that can be prescribed for treating depression (such as tricyclic antidepressants, MAO inhibitors, serotonin reuptake inhibitors). The other drugs often take several days or even weeks to produce antidepressant effects and frequently cause lasting troublesome side effects (appetite and sleep changes, sexual dysfunction, sweating, nausea, and headaches). Compassion for the victims of depression, in addition to the evidence of MDMA's serotonin-releasing effect, should compel further research to establish clearly whether MDMA is indeed an alternative antidepressant.

Treating Suicidal Depression with MDMA

The notion that MDMA might be useful in treating suicidal depression is based on a comparison of psychological patterns in suicidal people and MDMA's psycoactive effects. Psychological characteristics of suicidal people tend to vary between different age groups, cultures, economic classes, and gender (Hendin 1982; American Psychiatric Association 1994). Many cases seem to be manifestations of alienation. The anguish of the suicidal person is frequently that of a person in exile. He or she feels totally isolated, singled out by fate to suffer hardships and endless frustrations alone. Such people often find it hard to deal with the conflicts and demands of interpersonal relationships. They withdraw into a private, lonely world. Their justification might be that they feel unworthy of love or that others have abandoned them unfairly.

In either case, the isolation typically starts to feel irreversible. There seems to be no possibility of ever establishing meaningful contact with other human beings.

According to the *Harvard Medical School Mental Health Letter* ("Suicide," 1986), "Among the immediate motives for suicide, not surprisingly, despair is most common. In one long-term study, hopelessness alone accounted for most of the association between depression and suicide, and a high level of hopelessness was the strongest signal that a person who had attempted suicide would try again. Intense guilt, psychotic delusions, and even the severity of the depression were much less adequate indicators." The study referred to in the *Mental Health Letter,* by Beck and colleagues (1985), reported that high ratings on the Beck Hopelessness Scale successfully predicted 90.9 percent of eventual cases of suicide in a sample of 165 hospitalized suicide ideators (people who initially went to the doctor with thoughts of suicide) who were followed for five to ten years after taking the test. A subsequent report regarding the study affirmed that "because hopelessness can be reduced fairly rapidly by specific therapeutic interventions . . . the assessment of hopelessness can potentially improve the prevention as well as the prediction of suicide" (Beck et al. 1989). Hopelessness itself might mediate the relationship between dysfunctional attitudes and psychopathology, especially depression.

Interpersonal attitudes related to depression, not hopelessness per se, also may be the root cause of suicide. To that extent, suicide might be considered an act of interpersonal frustration that seeks to communicate misery and break out of isolation ("Suicide," 1986). This goal may be reached, alternatively and more safely, by means of guided psychotherapy. The recalcitrance of suicidal people, however, is a problem for conventional psychotherapy. For therapy to work, a positive, dynamic interaction must take place between the patient and the therapist (Henry et al. 1990; Talley et al. 1990; Strupp 1993). The patient must be willing to communicate what is going on inside. Someone who is consumed by strong feelings of alienation and hopelessness is likely to resist interpersonal contact and open discussion. Of course, it is frequently true that patients hesitate to talk about personal problems at the start of psychotherapy and need several sessions before they warm up to the therapist. Time is often a luxury that suicidal patients cannot afford, however. They may be treatable over the long term with conventional psychotherapy, but first they must be stabilized or otherwise prevented from taking their own lives. Usually this means hospitalization, keeping a suicide watch on such patients, and even actively restraining them if necessary.

Here is where MDMA can perhaps play a viable role, based on certain effects and ramifications for guided psychotherapy succinctly described in an issue of the *Harvard Medical School Mental Health Letter* (Grinspoon and Bakalar 1985): Although MDMA has no officially approved medical or psychiatric application, a few psychiatrists and other therapists had been using it as an aid to psychotherapy for more than fifteen years, in the 1970s and '80s. It has now been taken in a therapeutic setting by hundreds, if not thousands, of people with few reported complications. It is said to fortify the therapeutic alliance by inviting self-disclosure and enhancing trust. Some patients also report changes that last several days to several weeks or longer—improved mood, greater relaxation, heightened self-esteem, and enhanced relations with others. Psychiatrists who have used MDMA with patients suggest that it might be helpful, for example, in marital counseling, in diagnostic interviews, or as a catalyst for insight in psychotherapy. Reports of therapeutic results are so far unpublished and anecdotal and cannot be properly evaluated without more systematic study.

Anecdotal reports by the hundreds of people who have taken MDMA in therapeutic settings are not irrelevant. Their testimonies indicate that certain psychological effects occur consistently across a broad spectrum of usage. This is evident in Adamson's (1985) collection of about fifty such testimonies. The forward, by Ralph Metzner, observes that these firsthand accounts include such words as "ecstasy, empathy, openness, acceptance, forgiveness, and emotional bonding" in reference to MDMA's effects. These are the opposite terms often used to describe the psychological distress of suicidal people: anguish, alienation, recalcitrance, rejection, blame, guilt, and emotional withdrawal. Eisner (1989) also describes several cases of MDMA-assisted psychotherapy in which depression is mentioned specifically as one of the symptoms that is alleviated.

The value of MDMA is that it does not make its users feel better by transporting them into a naive state of bliss. They are aware of the fact that their lives have been burdened by negative thinking, have been based on fears and anxieties. MDMA seems to lend them a different perspective for several hours by minimizing their defensiveness and fear of emotional injury (Greer 1985; Greer and Tolbert 1986, 1990). It stimulates a process by which they are able to look at their problems more objectively and thus transcend a feeling of hopeless entrapment. At the same time, they feel more in touch with their positive emotions. This sustains them as the therapeutic process takes its course. The drug gives them the courage to confront their emotional problems and the strength to work them out, often by enhancing their desire to communicate constructively. Numerous examples of this process are described in Adamson's book (1985).

The particular value of MDMA for suicidal patients and, by extension, for patients with less severe forms of depression is twofold. First, it might be useful as an interventional medicine. By providing the relief from overwhelmingly dark emotions, MDMA likely can help forestall the act of suicide or otherwise alleviate the patient's sense of hopelessness. This buys time for the drug's second major effect, facilitating psychotherapy by helping to enhance the patient's trust and by inviting self-analysis and disclosure. As previously noted, the result is a fortifying of the therapeutic alliance between patient and therapist. Furthermore, MDMA does so in a relatively short time. According to Metzner in Adamson's book (1985): "One therapist has estimated that in five hours of one Adam [MDMA] session clients could activate and process psychic material that would normally require five months of weekly sessions." Needless to say, such accelerated therapeutic healing can mean the difference between life and death for people in imminent danger of suicide.

Risks of MDMA Use

There has been concern about neurotoxicity and other possible health risks from MDMA use. Most of these adverse reactions appear to be avoidable, if samples of known purity are administered in the lowest effective therapeutic dose range and frequency, after carefully screening patients for risk factors. This is consistent with the view of Grob and colleagues (1990) that fears of MDMA neurotoxicity may have been exaggerated and that rigorous clinical trials of the drug in psychotherapy should be resumed.*

Animal research with MDMA seems to indicate that even its high-dose neurotoxic effects can be minimized by the concurrent administration of flu-oxetine (Schmidt 1987; Schmidt et al. 1987). One report by McCann and Ricaurte (1993) suggested that fluoxetine pretreatment, at doses of 20 to 40 mg, does not compromise MDMA's therapeutic effects and, furthermore, decreases postsession insomnia and fatigue. A cautionary editorial by Price and colleagues (1990) maintains that it is premature to pursue clinical trials of MDMA in conditions that are not life-threatening. Both sides would be served by exploring the possible use of MDMA as an intervention drug for the stabili-zation and subsequent treatment of patients afflicted with severe and perhaps suicidal depression.

Conclusions

Central nervous system deficiency of 5-hydroxytryptamine (serotonin) has been implicated as a biochemical basis of at least some forms of depression. Existing drug treatments for depression include some with serotonergic effects. Studies suggest that psychedelic drugs are also serotonergic, which may indicate that there is a role for psychedelics in the treatment of depres-sion. Such treatment has been attempted using psychedelic drugs in both the indoleamine and phelylalkylamine categories. Encouraging results recom-mend further research, with special emphasis on drugs in the group called entactogens or empathogens, which cause substantially less distortion of nor-mative consciousness than classic psychedelics, such as LSD or mescaline. They could be assimilated more easily into existing psychotherapy approaches, where their function would be to accelerate and enhance the nor-mal psychotherapeutic process rather than to serve as a maintenance medica-tion. Their usefulness in such an application would be mainly at the start of psychotherapy. The goals would be to reduce the client's fear response, which often inhibits the ability to deal with repressed traumatic material; to facili-tate the client's interpersonal communications with the therapist, spouse, or significant others; and to accelerate the formation of a therapeutic alliance between client and therapist.

---

* [Most articles that allege neurotoxicity have recruited volunteers with histories of excessive and prolonged use. No study has been published that examines infrequent, single oral dosing.—Ed.]

CHALLENGE QUESTIONS

Should MDMA (Ecstasy) Be Prohibited, Even for Therapeutic Use?

1. As spokespersons for the federal government, Mathias and Zickler present compelling arguments against the use of MDMA based on extensive research. What are some of the social issues associated with the government's aggressive efforts to reduce MDMA use?

2. Riedlinger and Montagne object to anti-MDMA arguments, which they view as biased and exaggerated. How could one justify the regulated production of MDMA by pharmaceutical companies?

3. Concerns about the detrimental side effects of MDMA use have been downplayed by those who say that such problems are found only in chronic heavy users, rather than occasional recreational users. How could researchers investigate the validity of this argument?

4. Some social critics assert that it is the right of the individual to make choices about substance use and that such choices should not be the concern of the government. What are your thoughts about this viewpoint?

5. Much controversy has emerged in recent years about the medical use of substances such as marijuana to alleviate chronic pain. What are some arguments for and against the use of MDMA for the alleviation of psychological distress such as depression?

Suggested Readings

Cohen, R. S. (1998). *The love drug: Marching to the beat of Ecstasy.* New York: Haworth Medical Press.

Collin, M., and Godfrey, J. (1998). *Altered state: The story of Ecstasy culture and acid house.* New York: Serpent's Tail.

Eisner, B. (1994). *Ecstasy: The MDMA story.* Berkeley, CA: Ronin Publishing.

Holland, J. (Ed.). (2001). *Ecstasy: The complete guide: A comprehensive look at the risks and benefits of MDMA.* South Paris, ME: Park Street Press.

Levert, S. (2004). *The facts about Ecstasy (drugs).* New York: Benchmark Books.

Parrott, A. C. (Ed.). (2000). *MDMA (Methylenedioxymethamphetamine).* Farmington, CT: S. Karger Publishing.

ISSUE 7

Should Abstinence Be the Goal for Treating People with Alcohol Problems?

YES: Patricia Owen, from "Should Abstinence Be the Goal for Alcohol Treatment," *The American Journal of Addictions* (Fall 2001)

NO: Anne M. Fletcher, from *Sober for Good: New Solutions for Drinking Problems—Advice from Those Who Have Succeeded* (Houghton Mifflin Company, 2001)

ISSUE SUMMARY

YES: Psychologist Patricia Owen asserts that abstinence is the safest and most honest treatment goal for most people who are dependent on alcohol.

NO: Health and medical writer Anne Fletcher contends that many people with alcohol problems can be successful in their efforts to control their drinking, particularly if they are given professional guidance and support.

Each year countless millions of dollars are spent on alcohol, a substance that alters human behavior, cognition, and emotion. The costs to society associated with alcohol abuse are inestimable in terms of health expenses, lost productivity, accidents, and violence. The costs on the intrapsychic and interpersonal level are similarly tremendous. Lives are destroyed, and families are disrupted as a result of the profound addiction with which millions of people struggle. Despite the potential for it to be so destructive, alcohol is a legal substance that most people regard as an acceptable agent for easing tension, facilitating social interaction, and inducing pleasant feelings. The conflictual view of alcohol as being either an acceptable beverage or a harmful toxin is reflected in the debate about whether people with alcohol problems are capable of using this substance in a controlled manner. For decades, Alcoholics Anonymous (AA) has been regarded as one of the most effective interventions for people struggling with alcohol problems. According to the AA philosophy, abstinence is essential. In contrast, however, others have proposed that abstinence is not necessarily the goal for all problem drinkers.

Psychologist Patricia Owen, who has conducted extensive research on alcoholism, believes that abstinence is indeed the safest and the most honest goal for people with alcohol dependence problems. She also asserts that it is much easier for alcohol-dependent people to abstain than to moderate their drinking.

Health writer Anne Fletcher takes issue with the assertion that abstinence is the only path for people with alcohol problems. She points out drinking problems vary considerably in degree; consequently, it makes sense that interventions should be responsive to the varying levels of maladaptive behavior. Fletcher notes that many problem drinkers can be taught to drink in moderation, and in fact will fare better than they would in their attempts to abstain completely from alcohol use.

POINT

- Abstinence is logical as a treatment goal for problem drinkers because it is the most direct approach.

- Many studies have shown that about half of individuals presenting for treatment are able to achieve abstinence.

- People who are dependent on alcohol find that their attempts at controlled drinking are extremely difficult and typically unsuccessful.

- Experts cannot precisely determine what kinds of people are capable of moderating their alcohol use.

- As is the case in the treatment of medical problems such as diabetes and hypertension, it is the professional's role to state the treatment goal (i.e., abstinence) even if it is at odds with the patient's own ideas about the best course of treatment.

COUNTERPOINT

- Pressuring all people with drinking problems to abstain ignores the fact that drinking problems exist on a continuum, from mild to life-threatening.

- Some studies have shown that people who are offered controlled-drinking approaches at the outset may fare better than those offered abstinence approaches (page 184).

- People can achieve some success in controlling their drinking if they are given professional guidance and help establishing safeguards to monitor their progress.

- Experts have defined a set of characteristics of people who succeed with moderate drinking (e.g., being psychologically stable, well-educated, steadily employed).

- Experts believe that more people would do something about their drinking problem at an earlier point if they were offered a choice between abstinence and a moderated drinking program.

YES

Patricia Owen

Should Abstinence Be the Goal for Alcohol Treatment?

For most people who are dependent on alcohol, abstinence is the safest course and most honest treatment goal. For this subset of drinkers, a goal of abstinence is logical, possible, and, in the end, easier than sustaining moderation. I will take each of these points in turn.

First, abstinence as a treatment goal is logical. If a person presents with problems related to alcohol, the most direct approach is to eliminate the offending behavior, ie, drinking alcohol. By the time they have reached treatment, most people have tried in numerous ways to change their drinking behavior: they've changed the time of day they drink, the setting, the type of beverage, or have made an entire geographical relocation. By simply discontinuing the common source of the problems (ie, alcohol), a person has laid the foundation for change. It should be noted that abstinence is the goal of treatment for models other than Twelve Step approaches. In community reinforcement or voucher programs, cumulative abstinence is reinforced as much or more than daily abstinence. One reason for this approach is that researchers using these strategies have found that in cocaine dependent outpatients, early continuous abstinence predicts longer-term abstinence.[1]

Second, abstinence is possible. Many studies have shown that about half of individuals presenting for treatment are able to achieve abstinence.[e.g., 2] Although results vary with setting and sample, there is no question that individuals can succeed in achieving abstinence. Further, abstinence does not produce a life of sad deprivation. Quality of life indicators (emotional health, relationship with spouse and friends, higher power, performance on the job, legal and health status) generally improve with abstinence. Because of the relapsing nature of alcoholism, several treatments may be needed to achieve abstinence; however, this phenomenon is more an indication of its similarity to other chronic illnesses rather than a reason to abandon the treatment goal itself.[3]

Third, and perhaps most critical to the argument for abstinence as the preferred goal for alcohol treatment, is the issue of control over drinking. If a person is dependent on alcohol, attempts at control are extremely difficult and generally unsuccessful. In the end, it may take individuals as much emotional time and energy (often referred to as obsession or preoccupation) *not*

From *The American Journal of Addiction,* Fall 2001, pp. 289–295. Copyright © 2001 by American Academy of Addiction Psychiatry. Reprinted by permission.

to use as they once expended in planning to use. "Loss of control" in this context refers specifically to the inability for an individual to not drink or reliably quit drinking once the first drink is taken.[4] Recent research on neuroadaptation, the brain's adjustment to the effect of repeated alcohol intake, is providing a scientific understanding of the phenomenon of loss of control.[5(p112)] Robinson and Berridge[6] provide a compelling model of loss of control. Repeated use of alcohol can lead to neuronal sensitization to future exposure to alcohol. This sensitization occurs in the very structures of the brain most powerfully associated with what these researchers refer to as incentive salience, or "wanting" rather than "liking." In other words, the alcohol-dependent individual relapses not simply because of the rewarding properties of the substance but because of an intense compulsion, often against all reason. The effect of the ethanol occurs in the mesolimbic structure of the brain, in the dopaminergic systems. Robinson and Berridge note that "the persistence of neural sensitization is hypothesized to leave addicts susceptible to relapse even long after the discontinuation of drug use"[6(pS94)] and that this susceptibility, in animal studies, has been shown to last "months or years."[6(pS96)] Leshner[7] has also observed that "prolonged drug use causes pervasive changes in brain function that persist long after the individual stops taking the drug."[7(p46)] From their review of over 200 studies on the effect of ethanol on the brain, Robinson and Berridge conclude that "Sadly, the persistence of neural sensitization may mean, to paraphrase Alcoholics Anonymous, that in a neurobiological sense once an addict always an addict."[6(pS109)] In fact, they point out that until medication development targets neuroadaptation (of which sensitization is a manifestation), even these approaches will have limited success when compared with abstinence.

There are other compelling reasons for abstinence as a treatment goal beyond those stated above. For example, for people who are dependent on both alcohol and cocaine, drinking after treatment increases the probability of relapsing into cocaine.[8]

Some people incorrectly assume that disease model or Twelve-Step model programs dogmatically insist that all problem drinkers must abstain from alcohol. Nothing is farther from the truth. In fact, in the source book for Alcoholics Anonymous,[9] the writers assert several times that some people are able to moderate or control their use:

> Moderate drinkers have little trouble in giving up liquor entirely if they have good reason for it. They can take it or leave it alone. Then we have a certain type of hard drinker. He may have the habit badly enough to gradually impair him physically and mentally. It may cause him to die a few years before his time. If a sufficiently strong reason, ill health, falling in love, change of environment, or the warning of a doctor becomes operative, this man can also stop or moderate, although he may find it difficult and troublesome and may even need medical attention.[9(p20, 21)]

In other words, the authors and founders of AA repeatedly acknowledge that moderation or relatively easy cessation is possible for some types of drinkers.

The crux of the issue then is two-fold: (1) who is capable of moderating his or her alcohol use? and (2) for those people who cannot, what is the best treatment goal? In terms of the first question, the diagnostic criteria for alcohol abuse and dependence are far from perfect.[10] Someday, using biological or other indicators, we may be able to identify prospectively those heavy drinkers who can moderate their drinking. However, until we can make that distinction or have a biological method to reverse neuroadaptation, abstinence is the best treatment goal. . . .

. . . Periods of use preceding abstinence do not make the ultimate goal of abstinence any less important or achievable. Abstinence-based models generally accept the fact that some people may need to "collect more experience" about their use before attaining abstinence.

Individuals are free to make their own choice about how to deal with problematic use of alcohol. But when they seek help from a professional, it is the professional's role to make an accurate diagnosis and clearly state the treatment goal and plan, even though that plan may be at odds with the patient's own ideas about the best course of treatment. This is not so different from approaches used to treat other chronic diseases. If an out-of-control diabetic comes to a physician's office and says, "my insulin is a little off, but I really want to have a chocolate milkshake and two candy bars every day," the physician doesn't say, "I'm happy to work with you whatever your goals." If a hypertensive says "I won't change my diet, I refuse to take my meds, but I will take a walk around the block once a day for exercise," the physician doesn't say, "well that's a place to start; let me know how it goes and come back in a month." Rather, in both these cases, the physician explains the diagnosis and treatment plan and goal, offers ancillary help, and may bring in the family for reinforcement. Although not all patients will immediately comply,[11] the physician does not use this as a cue to abandon the goal.

We can be respectful, realistic, and compassionate, and cheer people on as they slip and slide their way to abstinence. But, at this point in our understanding about alcohol dependence, we need to be clear about the goal of abstinence and help people obtain it as soon and as successfully as they can.

References

1. Higgins, S. T., Badger, G. J., and Budney, A. J. Initial abstinence and success in achieving longer term cocaine abstinence. *Exp Clin Psychoparmacol.* 2000; 8:377–386.

2. Stinchfield, R., and Owen, P. Hazelden's model of treatment and its outcome. *Addict Behav.* 1998; 23:669–683.

3. McLellan, A. T., Lewis, D. C., O'Brien, C. P., and Kleber, H. D. Drug dependence, a chronic medical illness. *JAMA.* 2000; 284:1689–1695.

4. Erickson, C. K. Voices of the Afflicted [commentary]. *Alcohol Clin Exp Res.* 1998; 22:132–133.

5. National Institute on Alcohol Abuse and Alcoholism. *Tenth Special Report to Congress on Alcohol and Health: Highlights from Current Research.* Bethesda, Md.: U.S. Dept of Health and Human Services; 2000.

6. Robinson, T. E., and Berridge, K. C. The psychology and neurobiology of addiction: an incentive-sensitization view. *Addiction*. 2000; 95:S91–S117.

7. Leshner, A. I. Addiction is a brain disease, and it matters. *Science*, 1997; 278:45–47.

8. McKay, J. R., Alterman, A. I., Rutherford, M. J., Cacciola, J. S., and McLellan, A. T. The relationship of alcohol use to cocaine relapse in cocaine dependent patients in an aftercare study. *J Stud Alcohol*. 1999; 60:176–180.

9. Alcoholics Anonymous World Services. *Alcoholics Anonymous*. New York, NY: Alcoholics Anonymous World Services; 1976.

10. Dawson, D. H. Drinking patterns among individuals with and without DSM-IV alcohol use disorders. *J Stud Alcohol*. 1998; 61:111–120.

11. McLellan, A. T., Lewis, D. C., O'Brien, C. P., and Kleber, H. D. Drug dependence, a chronic medical illness: implications for treatment, insurance, and outcomes evaluation. *JAMA*. 2000; 284(13):1689–1695.

One Drink Does Not a Drunk Make: How the Masters Determined Whether They Could Ever Drink Again

One drink for a recovered "alcoholic" and she'll pick up drinking right where she left off–isn't that a fact? While it is true that the vast majority of the masters feel they cannot have any alcohol, a handful have found that they are able to drink moderately. Another dozen or so have a small amount of alcohol on rare occasions without getting into any trouble. I am not suggesting that moderate or even occasional drinking is a workable goal for most people with serious drinking problems. But this select group of masters is living proof that at least for some people, one drink does not necessarily a drunk make. . . .

Nolan H.'s Story

Always the kind of guy who liked to walk on the wild side, Nolan H. was addicted to both alcohol and cocaine by the time he was in his mid-twenties. Now a churchgoing forty-six-year-old father and responsible married man, he still rides a motorcycle and jetskis at speeds of more than sixty miles per hour–new highs that have taken the place of drugs and alcohol in his life. His alcohol problem has been resolved for twelve years now, but not in the stereotypical way. He's one of the small number of masters who have been able to return to nonproblematic drinking.

More than a decade ago, after the birth of his second child, Nolan knew he was in trouble when he stayed out partying with the boys until the morning's wee hours. "At two A.M., high on cocaine and beer, I was pacing in my living room, with my heart racing–still going one hundred miles an hour. I realized that what I was doing wasn't normal," he says. Not prone to expressing his emotions openly, Nolan slipped his wife a note that morning announcing that he was going to go into treatment and making it clear that he didn't want to back out. After taking about a month to get his business affairs in order (and having a few final flings with drugs and alcohol), he checked in for a one-month stay at a residential treatment center. Aside from attending AA meetings for the first six months after treatment, he has maintained sobriety on his own since then.

At first it wasn't easy to stay away from his drug-using friends and from bars, but the six-foot-one-inch Nolan soon discovered the joy of running. "When I quit drinking, my weight was up to 237. So I started running, lost weight, and began to feel good." He adds, "The up side of not drinking began far to outweigh the down side. The down side was giving up a couple of hours pleasure, if that. The up side was that I would get up in the morning and feel so good about myself, my body, and my family. I felt good about abstaining." And abstain he did—for eight years.

"I Don't Let Situations Control Whether I Have a Drink"

Then, four years ago, Nolan started wondering whether he could have a glass of wine or a beer now and then and proceeded to try it. Since that time he has been able to drink moderately, but does so only in social situations, never at home. He might have two to three beers twice in one week, then go several weeks with no alcoholic beverages at all. Nolan has no desire to drink unless he's in a restaurant or out with the guys, such as after a sporting event. He admits that he has gotten intoxicated—which for him means having a blood alcohol level above the legal limit for driving—but rarely, maybe once in an entire summer. He adds, "If I know I'm getting a little looped, I usually quit. I just don't want to get drunk."

How does he keep himself from going overboard? Nolan explains, "I've been labeled an alcoholic, and all the men on my father's side were alcoholics. So I always keep an awareness in the back of my mind. If enough people tell you you have a tail, sooner or later you'd better turn around and take a look. I don't take it lightly. I'll say to myself, 'Gee, buddy, you've had some drinks twice this week—that's pushing it.'" He adds, "Sometimes when I have an urge to drink, I think of my wife and kids and ask myself, 'Is this the right thing to do?'" Nolan also mentioned that he never allows a circumstance, like being angry, attending a party, or having someone push a drink on him, dictate whether he drinks. "I don't use excuses for having a drink—if I want one, I have it. But I don't let situations control whether I have a drink," he explains.

For those who might doubt that a former alcohol abuser can return to moderate drinking, I spoke to Nolan's wife (with his permission) to confirm that he is now able to manage his alcohol intake. She is not usually with him when he drinks, but her estimation of how much alcohol he consumes is consistent with his description. Although it worries her that he drinks at all because of his history, his current drinking habits have had no negative consequences and no impact on their family.

When I asked Nolan how he is able to exert control over his drinking, he replied, "I never want to go back to feeling that way again—that terrible feeling of regularly coming home drunk and high on drugs, the way I felt the next morning, the guilt." He added, "Tell me I can't do something, and I'll show

WHO CAN DRINK MODERATELY AFTER HAVING A DRINKING PROBLEM?

Experts are virtually unanimous in agreeing that moderate or controlled drinking is not apt to work for the vast majority of people with very serious drinking problems. So what kind of person is most likely to succeed with being able to drink moderately? Studies involving both people who have quit drinking on their own and those who have been through treatment indicate that most alcohol abusers who are able to return to controlled drinking have relatively less serious drinking problems or are people (like college binge drinkers) who "mature out" of heavy alcohol abuse as they become responsible adults. In general, research suggests that successful controlled drinkers tend to be women and people under forty. Also, they typically have alcohol problems of shorter duration (fewer than ten years).

Finally, individuals who are successful with moderate drinking tend to have the following characteristics:

Are psychologically stable

Are well educated

Are steadily employed

Don't regard themselves as "alcoholic" or "problem drinkers"

Don't subscribe to the disease concept of alcohol problems

Believe controlled drinking is possible

Develop alternatives to drinking as a means of coping with stress

---

you that I can. If you want success in life, you don't want alcohol and drugs to control you.". . .

The Problem with Abstinence for All

Pressuring all people with drinking problems to abstain ignores the fact that drinking problems exist on a continuum, from mild to life-threatening. Consider the case of Enrico J., a three-time drunk driving offender who was required to take part in a several-month abstinence-oriented treatment program, followed by weekly AA attendance for a year, when he was a young adult. When he protested that he was not an "alcoholic" but instead was part of a carousing crowd that abused alcohol, he was told he was in denial. He says, "I wasn't ready to quit drinking, and didn't really need to—I needed to learn to be more responsible with my drinking." Now, ten years later, he can take or leave alcohol. He occasionally has a beer or two, but he enjoys it as a beverage rather than using it to get high. In fact, according to the alcohol expert and attorney Stanton Peele, "Most drunk driving offenders are not 'alcoholics,' yet they represent one of the largest groups of people coerced into abstinence-based programs in the United States."

Indeed, a number of experts at the forefront of alcohol research believe that more people would do something about their alcohol problem at an earlier point if at the outset they were offered a choice between abstinence and a moderate drinking approach. Heather F. admits that although she knew that she would probably be better off electing abstinence, she was not ready to make a permanent commitment to it when she first tackled her drinking problem. "If the therapists who allowed me to try drinking moderately had required abstinence from the start, I would have walked right out the door. Because I was able to experiment and make my own decision, I eventually came to see that abstinence is the best option for me."

Dr. Alan Marlatt points out that Canada, Australia, and some European countries routinely offer formal controlled drinking programs, which are likely to attract problem drinkers uninterested in abstinence. As a *U.S. News & World Report* feature stated, "By calling abstinence the only cure, we ensure that the nation's $100 billion alcohol problem won't be solved." If someone elects moderate drinking and it doesn't work out, then he or she can step up to an abstinence-based approach.

Some studies suggest that people who are offered controlled drinking approaches at the outset may actually fare better than those who are offered abstinence-oriented approaches. Perhaps the most famous of these studies was conducted by the psychologists Mark and Linda Sobell in the 1970s. It involved chronic male "alcoholics" who were randomly assigned to either controlled drinking treatment or a traditional abstinence-oriented program. According to Dr. Mark Sobell, "Three years after treatment, it was found that those who received the moderation approach did much better all around. Surprisingly, they even had more abstinent days than those who had been told to be abstinent."

Moderate drinking can also be part of a plan for recovery that starts out with a period of abstinence, goes on to a moderation trial, and involves a return to abstinence if moderate drinking doesn't work. Heather F. recalls, "My first chemical dependency counselor had me start out with three months of abstinence, followed by a trial of moderate drinking. When my drinking crept back up again, I realized that someday I would probably have to give up alcohol completely."

If people *are* allowed to choose whether they want to try moderate drinking or abstinence, won't they all flock to the option that still allows them to drink? Interestingly, studies suggest that even when they are trained in controlled drinking, many alcohol-dependent people wind up choosing abstinence. The psychologist Marc Kern says that a number of participants in the Moderation Management group he directs do just that after following a recommended thirty-day break from alcohol. "Some people find that after a month of no alcohol, it's just easier that way, and they stay with abstinence," he notes.

Dr. Sobell concurs: "Most people whose problems are serious will say, 'I want to stop drinking altogether,' because they just don't want to risk further consequences." He adds, "Occasionally someone will opt for a goal that is clearly not in his best interest, but the frequency of this occurring is far less than one would expect." Dr. Kern's and Dr. Sobell's remarks are echoed by other experts who conclude that when given a choice, people tend to elect goals that are right for their situations.

How the Masters of Moderate Drinking Set Limits

The masters who choose to drink from time to time use various strategies to make sure their drinking doesn't get out of hand: Their experiences support the observation of experts that former problem drinkers who achieve stable moderation not only drink less but make changes in their drinking practices. For instance, they switch to an alcoholic beverage that is not their favorite, they no longer hang around with a drinking crowd, and they drink in different locations or under different circumstances. Nolan H. changed his circle of friends and leisure activities so he was less influenced by the bar and drug culture. He also keeps careful mental track of how often he drinks within a given time period. Bill L., who in the past "abused alcohol in private," states, "Now I drink only in public, where I am very careful about my appearance and behavior. But my most important strategy is planning ahead. Being older and more aware, I now actively plan on not drinking much or at all. I set limits both on time spent drinking and the number and type of drinks I have. I also visualize how I appear to others when I am drinking."

Ed Shaw, a moderate drinker and master who is the cohost and producer of the worldwide radio program *The Ruth and Ed Shaw Show,* has a number of set conditions for drinking. He explains, "I plan when I will drink; it's conscious, not accidental. I normally don't drink any more than once a week, and I never have beer, because for me, 'just one' is bullshit. Also, I try to avoid big drunks who need company, as well as stay away from St. Patrick's Day parties where all they do is drink."

Not only do the masters who drink moderately rely on certain strategies to limit the amount of alcohol they consume, but they also take care of their emotional well-being in order to prevent themselves from going back to their old ways. For instance, Nolan H. has vowed not to drink because of "circumstances" such as being angry. He has found new ways of feeling good through exercising, coaching his sons' athletic teams, enjoying leisure activities, and pursuing his career. More than a decade into sobriety, four years of which he has spent drinking moderately, Nolan still takes stock of the pluses and minuses of drinking. He explains, "Just recently I passed up a day out with the guys because I knew it would be a whole day of drinking. I really didn't want to feel bad the next morning. The joy of drinking in a situation like this just doesn't outweigh the down side for me anymore."

Moderate drinker Pat A. not only attends Moderation Management meetings and keeps alcohol out of her home, but she's involved in professional counseling to resolve problems that initially led her to drink too much. She tries to deal with anger by exercising rather than drinking and has learned to speak up for herself. "I don't let a drink take care of something that does not sit well with me," she declares.

Finally, it's quite clear that even though they are not abstinent, these masters *have* made a long-term commitment to changing their relationship with alcohol—just as other masters have made a commitment to abstinence. Fifteen years into resolving his drinking problem, Jack B., who now has a beer or glass of wine each day, revisited the bar culture with its "various characters," which he sorely missed in the beginning of sobriety. He says, "After I returned to bars in a much more limited way, I came to see the people I had once viewed as fascinating as damaged, broken, beaten-down persons—a painful revelation, yet one that reinforced my commitment *not* to go down that road again."

Getting Help with Moderate Drinking

"The problem," Dr. Marlatt points out, "is that most people who try moderate drinking attempt it on their own, without any tools. If they were offered some professional guidance and had safeguards in place for monitoring their progress, then moderate drinking wouldn't have to end in disaster." Indeed, few masters indicated that they had had any formal help when they tried to drink moderately. That kind of help may be difficult to find in the United States. A study in the mid-1990s found that more than three quarters of two hundred randomly selected treatment programs saw controlled drinking as an unacceptable goal. Outpatient programs were less likely to object to this option than residential programs, according to the same study, but still, about half of them found controlled drinking unacceptable. In describing this study, the U.S. government publication *Alcohol and Health* says, "In general, program respondents indicated an unwillingness to negotiate treatment goals with their clients."

If you want to try moderate drinking, you would be advised to do so as part of a recognized program like Moderation Management or another [similar program] and/or under the guidance of a professional who has experience in assessing the severity of alcohol problems as well as in moderation approaches. That way, you can get some sense of whether you are a candidate for moderate drinking, have access to helpful tools, and receive guidance if moderate drinking fails. . . .

CHALLENGE QUESTIONS

Should Abstinence Be the Goal for Treating People with Alcohol Problems?

1. Owen concurs with the notion that abstinence is indeed the most appropriate goal for people with alcohol dependence, a viewpoint that is promoted by Alcoholics Anonymous (AA). Based on what you know about the approach of AA, discuss whether there are certain personality characteristics that respond especially well with the AA philosophy.
2. Fletcher contends that controlled drinking may work better than abstinence for some people. Consider some of the characteristics (e.g., personality, education, socioeconomic level, emotional stability) that would contribute to effectiveness of a controlled-drinking strategy.
3. Some social critics express alarm about the fact that our society recognizes the extraordinary costs associated with alcohol abuse yet permits and reinforces the omnipresent marketing of alcohol. Discuss the reasons for this seeming contradiction.
4. Imagine that you are a clinician who is treating a man who has been mandated by the court to seek professional help because of his history of legal problems associated with alcohol abuse. He states that he now understands the seriousness of his problem, but insists that he will control his drinking rather than abstain. What approach would you take in treating such an individual?
5. Imagine that you are a researcher who has been given a grant to compare different interventions for college students who have been arrested for alcohol-related problems on campus. What research design would you use to compare the relative effectiveness of abstinence and controlled drinking in this group?

Suggested Readings

Alcoholics Anonymous: The story of how many thousands of men and women have recovered from alcoholism (4th edition). (2001). New York: Alcoholics Anonymous World Services, Inc.

DeSena, J. et al. (2003). *Overcoming your alcohol, drug & recovery habits: An empowering alternative to AA and 12-step treatment.* Tucson, AZ: James DeSena.

Ellis, A., and Velten, E. (1992). *When AA doesn't work for you: Rational steps to quitting alcohol.* Fort Lee, NJ: Barricade Books.

Marlatt, G. A., Dimeff, L. A., Baer, J. S., & Kivlahan, D. R. (1999). *Brief alcohol screening and intervention for college students (BASICS): A harm reduction approach*. New York: The Guilford Press.

Newhouse, E. (2001). *Alcohol: cradle to grave*. Center City, MN: Hazelden Information and Educational Services, 2001.

Tatarsky, A. (2002). *Harm reduction psychotherapy: A new treatment for drug and alcohol problems*. Northvale, NJ: Jason Aronson.

Internet References . . .

The Post Traumatic Stress Disorder Psychophysiology Laboratory at Massachusetts General Hospital

The Post Traumatic Stress Disorder Psychophysiology Laboratory is a division of Massachusetts General Hospital's Psychiatric Neuroscience Research and Neurotherapeutics.

http://www.massgeneral.org/allpsych/PsychNeuro/ptsdpsycholab.asp

Neuroethics & Law Blog

This website, maintained by University of San Diego law professor Adam Kolber, is "an interdisciplinary forum for legal and ethical issues related to the brain and cognition".

http://kolber.typepad.com/

Internet Mental Health

This Web site povides extensive coverage of topics in the field of mental health, including consideration of various issues pertaining to medication.

http://www.mentalhealth.com

The Treatment Advocacy Center

This Web site focuses on the problems associated with the failure of treatments for people with schizophrenia and other mental illnesses.

http://www.psychlaws.org

The Mental Health Forum: Archive of Electroconvulsive Therapy Questions

This Web site contains various forums including mental health forums discussing topics such as electroconvulsive therapy.

http://www.medhelp.org

National Alliance on Mental Illness

This website, maintained by NAMI, presents an overview of the issues pertaining to prescription privileges for psychologists.

http://www.nami.org/Template.cfm?Section=Issue_Spotlights&template=/ ContentManagement/ContentDisplay.cfm&ContentID=8375

Psychology Today

This Web site from the magazine *Psychology Today* gives a brief summary of the reorientation discussion today and highlights the key psychologists and organizations involved in the debate.

http://cms.psychologytoday.com/articles/pto-20000901-000004.html

Center for Media Literacy (CML)

The CML is a nonprofit educational organization, with the mission of supporting and promoting media literacy education.

http://www.medialit.org

The Trend Toward Biological Interventions

*A*lthough *the medical model has been prominent in the field of mental health for the past century, in recent years the trend toward biological explanations and interventions for psychological problems has been more evident. The field of psychopharmacology has mushroomed to such an extent that billions of dollars are spent each year on medications for a wide array of emotional and behavioral problems. Medications are being tried in ways that would have been regarded as quite unlikely only a decade ago, as is the case in the use of drugs to dampen the memories of a traumatic experience and thereby reduce the likelihood of developing post-traumatic stress disorder. In addition to recommending medications, some mental health professionals have advocated more extreme medical interventions such as electroconvulsive treatment or psychosurgery. Many psychologists have expressed interest in becoming more central players in the medical sphere by pursuing the right to prescribe medications, an option regarded as objectionable by many physicians and of questionable wisdom by many psychologists.*

- Should Memory-Dampening Drugs Be Used to Alleviate the Symptoms of Trauma?

- Are Antipsychotic Medications the Treatment of Choice for People with Psychosis?

- Is Ritalin Overprescribed?

- Should Psychologists Prescribe Medication?

- Is Electroconvulsive Therapy Ethical?

ISSUE 8

Should Memory-Dampening Drugs Be Used to Alleviate the Symptoms of Trauma?

YES: Adam J. Kolber, from "Therapeutic Forgetting: The Legal and Ethical Implications of Memory Dampening," *Vanderbilt Law Review* (2006)

NO: The President's Council on Bioethics, from *Beyond Therapy: Biotechnology and the Pursuit of Happiness* (October 2003)

ISSUE SUMMARY

YES: Law professor Adam Kolber supports the use of memory-dampening drugs for survivors of trauma in the belief that some experiences are so horrific that they can stand in the way of traumatized people moving toward happier and healthier levels of functioning.

NO: The President's Council on Bioethics, chaired by Dr. Leon Kass, criticizes memory-dampening drugs because they could falsify a person's perception and understanding of the world, making terrible acts seem less terrible than they are.

It is understandable that people who have survived a trauma would go to great lengths to reduce their symptoms and alleviate their profound distress. Preliminary research has pointed to the possibility that the drug propranolol can dampen the memory of trauma, and thereby make life more bearable for some trauma survivors. Controversy has arisen about whether this intervention is really as beneficial as it sounds.

Law professor Adam Kolber asserts that a memory-dampening drug such as propranolol can alleviate the suffering of millions of people, and that government restriction is inappropriate. Kolber contends that people have the right to control their own memories, and believes that the debate about memory dampening raises fundamental questions about who owns memories. Rather than representing an unfortunate loss of one's life narrative through the process of memory dampening, trauma survivors can make life transformations that they would have otherwise been incapable of making.

The President's Council on Bioethics, chaired by Dr. Leon Kass, criticizes the use of memory-dampening drugs to treat the symptoms of trauma by asking, "What kind of society are we likely to have when the powers to control memory, mood, and mental life through drugs reach their full maturity?" The Council asserts that identities are formed by what people do and what they undergo or suffer. Escaping painful memories would necessarily result in a change in the identity of who the person is, as well as the person's perception and understanding of significant life events.

POINT

- So long as physicians who prescribe propranolol explain to their patients the potential costs and benefits of the treatment, the fact that the treatment involves making a decision based on the probability (as opposed to certainty) of different outcomes is otherwise irrelevant.
- It seems quite plausible that one could craft a coherent life narrative that is punctuated by periods of dampened memories, and it is open to debate how important it is that one's life story be coherent or otherwise neatly packaged.
- Memory-dampening drugs may enable traumatized people to make life transformations that they would be incapable of making without these drugs.

- What makes the retention of a traumatic, socially relevant memory significant is that the person who bears the traumatic memory has chosen to identify with it in some way. In fact, memory-dampening drugs, by giving us the opportunity to consciously choose to keep a memory intact, may actually facilitate our identification with it.
- If memory dampening does make some trauma *seem* less horrible, this happens in part because memory dampening can *actually make* trauma less horrible. That is, much of what is bad about traumatic experience is that it traumatizes those who survive it.

COUNTERPOINT

- Since the drugs in question appear to be effective only when administered during or shortly after a traumatic event, we would have to make a prospective judgment as to which traumatized individuals should be treated.

- As we reminisce from greater distance and with more experience, even our painful experiences can often acquire for us a meaning that we did not foresee when the experiences occurred.

- Our identities are formed both by what we do and by what we undergo or suffer. Though we may regret the shadows that unchosen memories cast over our pursuit of happiness, we cannot simply escape them while remaining who we really are.
- Those who endure bad memories should not use the new biotechnical powers to ease the psychic pain of bad memories. Using such medications does not preserve the memories' truth, but attempts instead to make the problem go away, and with it the truth of the experience in question.

- Altering the formation of emotionally powerful memories risks falsifying our perception and understanding of the world, making shameful acts seem less shameful, or terrible acts less terrible.

YES ↵

Therapeutic Forgetting: The Legal and Ethical Implications of Memory Dampening

In this article, . . . I describe the ethical concerns raised by the President's Council on Bioethics and argue that they are insufficient to justify broad government interference with our ability to dampen memories.[1]

If I am right that memory dampening has the potential someday to ease the suffering of millions of people and that heavy-handed government restriction of memory dampening is inappropriate, it follows that we should have some limited right to therapeutically forget. I will suggest that this right is just a small part of a larger bundle of rights to control our own memories that I call our "freedom of memory." This bundle of rights will become increasingly important as neuroscientists develop more powerful ways to manipulate human memory.

I. Memory-Dampening Technology

In this Part, I provide background on PTSD, the disorder that has sparked the quest for a means of therapeutic forgetting. I describe how traumatic experiences are believed to generate the painful, recurrent memories that characterize PTSD and how drugs like propranolol may prevent these memories from imprinting as strongly as they would in the absence of the drug. By weakening the emotionality of our reactions to arousing experiences, drugs like propranolol may, in effect, dampen emotional, and perhaps even factual, aspects of memory.

According to a recent, large-scale study, approximately 7% of Americans are expected to develop PTSD within their lifetimes.[2] It is estimated that "a person with PTSD will endure 20 years of active symptoms and will experience almost 1 day a week of work impairment, perhaps resulting in a $3 billion annual productivity loss in the United States."[3] Rates of attempted suicide among those with PTSD have been reported to be "as high as 19%."[4] According to the DSM, rates of PTSD are particularly high among survivors of rape, combat, and genocide.[5] Approximately one-third to one-half of those in these at-risk populations have or will develop the disorder.[6]

From *Vanderbilt Law Review*, vol. 59, 2006, pp. 1521–1626 (edited by Kolber). Copyright © 2006 by Vanderbilt University Law School. Reprinted by permission.

PTSD can be quite debilitating. Those with PTSD have been described as "stuck" on their trauma, "reliving it in thoughts, feelings, actions, or images."[7] They may become physiologically hyperaroused or develop a sense of helplessness, symptoms that can "permanently change how a person deals with stress, alter his or her self-concept, and interfere with his or her view of the world as a manageable place."[8] Usually, PTSD is associated with "vivid intrusions of traumatic images and sensations,"[9] although some upsetting experiences can lead to a loss of recall.[10]

Current treatments for PTSD rely on antidepressants[11] and a variety of forms of psychotherapy.[12] A common form of therapy gradually exposes patients to stimuli associated with their traumatic experiences in a controlled manner in hopes of easing their responses.[13] Despite such efforts, however, PTSD is difficult to treat, and the search continues for new therapies. Treatments under investigation include d-cycloserine,[14] MDMA (commonly known as "ecstasy"),[15] transcranial magnetic stimulation,[16] and memory-dampening drugs that are the subject of this article.[17]

II. Legal Issues

[M]emory dampening using propranolol is currently thought most likely to be effective in the first six hours after a traumatic event while the memory is still in the process of consolidating.[18] During this period, however, we cannot accurately predict whether a given patient will eventually develop PTSD or otherwise develop severe traumatic memories. This means that doctors would have to prescribe propranolol and seek informed consent to the treatment before they can predict with confidence whether a particular patient would go on to develop PTSD in the absence of the drug.

Despite these concerns, . . . we frequently use preventative medicines on people who are unlikely to develop the illnesses we seek to prevent. We make such decisions by weighing expected costs and benefits, even when these decisions dramatically alter people's lives. For example, some women with a known genetic predisposition to develop breast cancer opt for preventative mastectomies even though many of them would never have actually developed the disease.[19] Part of the role of physicians is to inform patients of the costs and benefits of medical interventions, particularly when the outcome of a proposed intervention is uncertain. Thus, physicians prescribing propranolol have obligations to obtain their patients' consent after describing the probabilistic costs and benefits of treatment. Assuming they do so, the fact that the treatment involves probabilistic decisionmaking is otherwise irrelevant.

Furthermore, while it is true that many of those asked to consent to memory dampening, having just recently suffered emotional trauma, will not have the full benefit of their faculties of contemplative reflection, we ordinarily require no such thing before commencing serious medical treatments. For example, suppose a person is severely injured in a motor vehicle accident and is rushed to the emergency room, conscious and aware but emotionally shaken. Suppose further that the patient must decide whether to have part of a limb amputated to reduce the probability of amputating the entire limb later on. Despite the patient's emotional turmoil, both from the accident itself and the prospect of amputation, if the patient satisfies rather minimal standards of competence,[20] health professionals will seek the patient's consent to the operation.[21]

Assume now that this same patient must decide not only whether to amputate but also whether to dampen his memory of the accident. If he can consent to the amputation by making a probabilistic determination after recently suffering trauma, then he can make the same sort of determination about memory dampening.[22]

III. Ethical Issues

The President's Council on Bioethics was established by executive order in November 2001 to "advise the President on bioethical issues that may emerge as a consequence of advances in biomedical science and technology."[23] In October 2002 and again in March 2003, the Council held hearings on ethical issues raised by memory-altering drugs.[24] Not surprisingly, part of these hearings concerned efforts to increase memory retention, either to help those with memory disorders, like Alzheimer's disease, or to give healthy people extraordinary powers of recall.[25] More importantly for our purposes, the Council also heard testimony concerning the current state of research on memory dampening and the direction it may take in the future.[26]

By and large, however, the tone of the Council's report is skeptical of the benefits of technologies that go beyond therapy, including memory dampening.[27]

1. Specific Responses to the Prudential Concerns

a. The Tough Love Concern

The Council claims that memory dampening, by offering us a solution in a bottle, allows us to avoid the difficult but important process of coming to terms with emotional pain. There are two ways to understand the concern. The first is that there is something false or undeserved about the manner in which memory dampening eases distress. Gilbert Meilaender makes this point in his essay on memory dampening where he claims that, rather than erasing traumatic experiences, "it might still be better to struggle—with the help of others—to fit them into a coherent story that is the narrative of our life."[28] "Our task," according to Meilaender, "is not so much to erase embarrassing, troubling, or painful moments, but, as best we can and with whatever help we are given, to attempt to redeem those moments by drawing them into a life whose whole transforms and transfigures them."[29]

People have divergent views, however, about what it means to transform and transfigure our experiences into "a coherent story."[30] It seems quite plausible that one could craft a coherent life narrative that is punctuated by periods of dampened memories. Moreover, it is open to debate how important it is that one's life story be coherent or otherwise neatly packaged.

Furthermore, even if one shares Meilaender's preference to redeem and transform our experiences without memory dampeners, two additional responses are suggested. First, many experiences are simply tragic and terrifying, offering virtually no opportunity for redemption or transformation. For example, after a 1978 plane crash in San Diego, desk clerks and baggage handlers were assigned to retrieve dead bodies and clean up the crash site.[31] Emotionally unprepared for this task, many of them were so distraught that they were unable to return to work.[32] In such cases, it seems unlikely that the traumatized employees should, in Meilaender's words, "redeem those moments by drawing them into a life whose whole transforms and transfigures them."[33] Most would agree that such employees should not have participated in the cleanup in the first place, and, hence, they should not be required or expected to bear the emotional burden of having done so.[34]

Second, even if it is better to weave traumatic events into positive, life-affirming narratives, many people are never able to do so. Memory-dampening drugs may enable such people to make life transformations that they would be *incapable* of making in the absence of the drugs. For others, pharmaceuticals may drastically shorten the time it takes to recover from a traumatic experience. Suppose a person spends ten years coming to terms with a traumatic event that he could have come to terms with in two years with pharmaceutical assistance. While he might be viewed as heroic by Meilaender, others might view him as extremely obstinate. Therefore, even in those instances when positive human transformation should accompany traumatic experience, there may well be a role for memory dampening to facilitate the process.

As the Council acknowledges, "individuals 'naturally' edit their memory of traumatic or significant events—both giving new meaning to the past in light of new experiences and in some cases distorting the past to make it more bearable."[35] In fact, such selective reconstruction of our lives seems to be at the very heart of the creation of a coherent life story that Gilbert Meilaender advocates.[36] Nevertheless, we do not worry whether our better-feeling naturally reconstructed selves remain the same as before.

It is, thus, not at all clear why we ought to revere the selective rewriting of our lives that we do without pharmaceuticals, yet be so skeptical of pharmaceutically-assisted rewriting.[37] In fact, memory dampening may strengthen our sense of identity. By preventing traumatic memories from consuming us, memory dampeners may allow us to pursue our own life projects, rather than those dictated by bad luck or past mistakes. As David Wasserman has noted, "pharmacologically-assisted authorship may strengthen rather than reduce narrative identity,"[38] by allowing one to "edit his autobiography, instead of having it altered only by the vagaries of neurobiology."[39] Thus, to the extent that people voluntarily make changes to their mental processes, such changes may be perceived as bolstering self-identity. In fact, many people who begin taking antidepressants report feeling like themselves for the first time.[40] This suggests that some deliberate shifts in identity may not seem alienating at all.

c. The Genuine Experiences Concern

The Council also worries that a memory-dampened life, chemically-altered as it is, is somehow a less genuine life.[41] According to the Council, "we might often be tempted to sacrifice the accuracy of our memories for the sake of easing our pain or expanding our control over our own psychic lives. But doing so means, ultimately, severing ourselves from reality and leaving our own identity behind."[42] This, according to the Council, "risks making us false, small, or capable of great illusions."[43] It also risks making us "capable of great decadence or great evil."[44]

Unfortunately, the Council never explains what makes a life genuine and truthful (nor how leading a life that is otherwise makes us capable of great evil). Is a memory-dampened life thought less genuine simply because some of the memories associated with it decay at a faster rate than they otherwise would have? Given that memories never precisely replicate our past experiences, do undampened memories provide a standard of genuineness? How important is it to lead a "genuine" life, whatever that means?[45]

In the case of those who are emotionally traumatized, memories of the trauma can be overwhelming and trigger exaggerated responses to harmless stimuli associated with a traumatic memory. Such overreactions are themselves divorced from reality. Memory dampeners, by preventing people from being overtaken by trauma, may actually make them more genuine, more true to what they take their lives to be, than they would be if they were gripped by upsetting memories.

Furthermore, we are not always troubled by discrepancies between our perceptions and the world as it "genuinely" is.

At a March 2003 hearing, then-Council member Michael Sandel raised a related example.[46] At a class on child-bearing, Sandel was told that the memory women have of the pain of childbirth is dulled through natural processes and that because of this, women are less likely to be deterred from having children in the future.[47] Whether or not this folklore is true,[48] Sandel suggested (and most would agree) that if it were true, we would not be troubled by this natural process of memory dampening, even if the memory of the pain were, in some sense, less representative of the pain as it was actually experienced.[49]

No doubt, as a general life strategy, we do well to firmly commit ourselves to reality and to discovering the truth about ourselves and the world around us. Yet, such a strategy might, at times, be worse for us all things considered; or, at least, the Council has not shown otherwise. To make the case that memory-dampening drugs will harmfully affect our lives, the Council must be much more specific about what makes a life genuine, how these drugs make lives less genuine, and why that should matter so much to us that we ought to suffer in distress to preserve our unadulterated memories.

Each of the concerns presented reflects a bias for our natural, pharmaceutical-free mechanisms of responding to trauma. The Council implicitly or explicitly defended: (1) our natural ability to surmount difficult life obstacles, (2) our natural memories as the desirable basis for our sense of identity, and (3) our natural memories as more genuine and more desirable than those that are pharmaceutically altered.

[W]e clearly hold people responsible for failing to remember. For example, we blame those who forget an important birthday or anniversary, and we penalize those who forget to file a timely tax return.[50] Some of the most tragic instances of failed memory occur when parents unintentionally cause the death of their young children by leaving them stranded in the backseats of automobiles on hot days,[51] sometimes leading to criminal punishment.[52]

Even if we can have obligations to remember, however, it is easy to overestimate the strength of these obligations. Perhaps the Council does so when it states that it may have been inappropriate for those with firsthand experiences of the Holocaust to dampen their traumatic memories:

> Consider the case of a person who has suffered or witnessed atrocities that occasion unbearable memories: for example, those with firsthand experience of the Holocaust. The life of that individual might well be served by dulling such bitter memories, but such a humanitarian intervention, if widely practiced, would seem deeply troubling: Would the community as a whole—would the human race—be served by such a mass numbing of this terrible but indispensable memory? Do those who suffer evil have a duty to remember and bear witness, lest we all forget the very horrors that haunt them?[53]

There is something harsh about expecting trauma sufferers to bear the additional burden of carrying forward their traumatic memories for the benefit of others. The Council, recognizing this, goes on to soften its perspective somewhat, stating that "we cannot and should not force those who live through great trauma to endure its painful memory *for the benefit of the rest of us.*"[54] Yet, even for those who suffer from the most tragic of memories, the Council is ambivalent about the ethics of pharmaceutical dampening:

> [A]s a community, there are certain events that we have an obligation to remember—an obligation that falls disproportionately, one might even say unfairly, on those who experience such events most directly. What kind of people would we be if we did not "want" to remember the Holocaust, if we sought to make the anguish it caused simply go away? And yet, what kind of people are we, especially those who face such horrors firsthand, that we can endure such awful memories?[55]

According to the Council, we are sometimes obligated to remember some person or set of events because doing so pays respect to that person or set of events.[56] For example, we may have obligations to remember great sacrifices that others make on our behalf, not because these memories will guide our actions, but rather because retaining the memory demonstrates a kind of respect or concern for these others.

The case for legally restricting memory dampening is particularly weak when it comes to such "homage" memories. What makes the retention of a traumatic homage memory significant is that the person who bears the traumatic memory has chosen to identify with it in some way. In fact, memory-dampening drugs, by giving us the opportunity to consciously choose to keep a memory intact, may actually facilitate our identification with it. On the other hand, if an individual retains an homage memory simply because he has no choice—because the tragic memory was indelibly imprinted into his brain by stress hormones or because memory dampening has been prohibited—the holding of the homage memory loses much of its significance. Such memories are not truly homages at all.[57]

d. Coarsening to Horror

The Council also expressed concern that memory dampening will coarsen our reactions to horror and tragedy. If we see the world from a chemically-softened, affect-dulled perspective, we may grow inured to trauma and its associated distress, "making shameful acts seem less shameful, or terrible acts less terrible, than they really are."[58] As an example, the Council describes a hypothetical witness to a violent crime who dampens his memory and eventually perceives the crime as less severe than he would have without pharmaceutical assistance:

> Imagine the experience of a person who witnesses a shocking murder. Fearing that he will be haunted by images of this event, he immediately takes propranolol (or its more potent successor) to render his memory of the murder less painful and intrusive. Thanks to the drug, his memory of the murder gets encoded as a garden-variety, emotionally neutral experience. But in manipulating his memory in this way, he risks coming to think about the murder as more tolerable than it really is, as an event that should not sting those who witness it. For our opinions about the meaning of our experiences are shaped partly by the feelings evoked when we remember them. If, psychologically, the murder is transformed into an event our witness can recall without pain— or without any particular emotion—perhaps its moral significance will also fade from consciousness.[59]

One concern . . . is that memory dampening will coarsen our feelings and make us less willing to respond to tragic situations. Along these lines, one can imagine a would-be-famous civil rights leader in the 1960s who, in order to combat the memory of childhood injustices, would have gone on to revolutionize our social institutions but, due to his use of memory dampeners, instead pursues a more mundane life plan and is never so much as mentioned in the history books.

Not only might our coarsened emotions disincline us to take positive action, it has been suggested that memory dampeners could reduce our inhibitions to engage in socially destructive action. Thus, violent criminals could use memory dampeners to ease feelings of guilt, making them more likely to recidivate.[60] In addition, it has been claimed, memory-dampened soldiers, freed from burdens of conscience, may be more effective at killing.[61] Council member Paul McHugh asks, "If soldiers did something that ended up with children getting killed, do you want to give them beta blockers so that they can do it again?"[62] The question is lacking in some important details but, more importantly, these examples suggest that fear and remorse or expectations of fear and remorse inhibit certain antisocial behaviors and that memory dampening may interfere with this desirable control mechanism. While this concern is far from universal,[63] it may warrant studying whether any proposed memory-dampening agent actually has such effects.

Even if there is some empirical basis for these concerns, however, it is important not to overstate their importance. For even if memory dampening does make some trauma *seem* less horrible, this happens in part because memory dampening can *actually make* trauma less horrible. That is, much of what is bad about traumatic experience is that it traumatizes those who survive it. So, for example, to the extent that we can ease the traumatic memories of those involved in military conflict (without leading to a significant increase in total military conflict), then memory dampening makes combat somewhat better than it would otherwise be. Furthermore, when soldiers are injured in battle, we heal their physical wounds using advanced technology, even if doing so makes war seem less horrible; so it is unclear why their emotional wounds should be treated any differently.[64]

While the coarsening concern is far from overwhelming, it at least shows how the widespread use of memory dampeners can potentially affect the lives of those who do not use them. Nevertheless, this concern cannot alone justify broad restrictions on memory dampening, at least not if such restrictions are consistent with our typical policies of drug regulation. For example, people consume alcohol to relieve themselves of the pain of traumatic events. Whether or not this leads to some general inurement to tragedy in society (which seems doubtful), most would not address the problem with a comprehensive prohibition of alcohol. Similarly, even if antidepressants are used for relief from the pain of traumatic experiences, we would not generally prohibit them for fear that society will be less compassionate. Likewise, the world may benefit from the inspired artwork of a Vincent van Gogh, yet few would deprive a tortured soul of antidepressants in order to foster artistic creation.

We likely permit the use of such drugs, despite whatever minimal effects they may have on our reactions to tragedy, because their costs are outweighed by other benefits. So even if data someday support the Council's concern that memory-dampening drugs can have negative effects on soldiers' battlefield reactions or on societal reactions more generally, we can surely tailor limits on their use in particular contexts.

While memory dampening has its drawbacks, such may be the price we pay in order to heal intense emotional suffering.

e. Freedom of Memory

I have argued that concerns over memory dampening are insufficient to justify broad restrictions on the therapy. Furthermore, having the choice to dampen memories supports our interests in self-determination and in avoiding mental illness and upset, and, as noted, enables us to identify more strongly with memories that we decide to keep. Given the potential that memory dampening has to ease the pain of so many people, and that, at a minimum, memory dampening ought not be entirely prohibited, it follows that we should have some right to dampen our memories.

Conclusion

The mere possibility of memory dampening raises fundamental questions about who owns our memories and how we should balance the rights of memory-holders against society as a whole.

Notes

1. Because our understanding of memory dampening is still in its early stages, I do not attempt to draw the line between a broad restriction on memory dampening, which I disfavor, and more narrow restrictions on its use in particular contexts, which I readily entertain. Prohibiting any kind of possession of memory-dampening drugs is an example of the former, but requiring that such drugs be prescribed by a physician is an example of the latter. I am content to allow finer gradations to be determined in the future.

2. Ronald C. Kessler et al., *Lifetime Prevalence and Age-of-Onset Distributions of DSM-IV Disorders in the National Comorbidity Survey Replication*, 62 ARCHIVES OF GEN. PSYCHIATRY 593, 595 (2005); *cf.* Davidson, *supra* note 32, at 584 ("In the US population, lifetime prevalence rates are in the range of 8%, with women affected twice as often as men. However, studies from other countries and studies of high-risk populations have reported widely ranging prevalence rates from a low of 1.3% in Germany to 37.4% in Algeria."). *But cf.* RICHARD J. MCNALLY, REMEMBERING TRAUMA 282-85 (2003) (discussing controversy as to whether PTSD is, in part, a "social construction"); Benedict Carey, *Most Will Be Mentally Ill at Some Point, Study Says*, N.Y. TIMES, June 7, 2005, at A18 (noting that some experts believe that the data cited in the text rely on overly-inclusive diagnostic standards).

3. Davidson, *supra* note 32, at 584.

4. *Id.*

5. DSM IV-TR, *supra* note 33, at 466.

6. *Id.*; *see also* Ronald C. Kessler et al., *Posttraumatic Stress Disorder in the National Comorbidity Survey*, 52 ARCHIVES OF GEN. PSYCHIATRY 1053 (1995) ("Sixty-five percent of men and 45.9% of women who reported [being raped] as their most upsetting trauma developed PTSD.").

7. Bessel A. van der Kolk et al., *A General Approach to Treatment of Posttraumatic Stress Disorder* [hereinafter Bessel A. van der Kolk et al., *A General Approach*], *in* TRAUMATIC STRESS: THE EFFECTS OF OVERWHELMING EXPERIENCE ON MIND, BODY, AND SOCIETY 417, 419 (Bessel A. van der Kolk et al. eds., 1995) [hereinafter TRAUMATIC STRESS].

8. *Id.*

9. Bessel A. van der Kolk, *Trauma and Memory*, *in* TRAUMATIC STRESS, *supra* note 39, at 279, 283.

10. *Id.*; *see also* MCNALLY, *supra* note 34, at 186–228 (discussing the nature of traumatic amnesia); Alison Motluk, *Memory Fails You After Severe Stress*, 182 NEW SCIENTIST 14, 14 (2004) (reporting a study finding that military personnel subject to intense physiological stress during mock interrogations had great difficulty identifying their mock interrogators a day after the exercise). Though I know of no research on the matter, if drugs like propranolol can help patients avoid extreme forgetting (or perhaps extreme repression), then propranolol could actually have a memory-enhancing effect. For the time being, I disregard this possibility.

11. Jonathan R. Davidson & Bessel A. van der Kolk, *The Psychopharmacological Treatment of Posttraumatic Stress Disorder*, *in* TRAUMATIC STRESS, *supra* note 39, at 510, 516–20.

12. Bessel A. van der Kolk et al., *A General Approach*, *supra* note 39, at 417–18.

13. *See id.* at 430, 434-35 (describing controlled exposure methods of treatment).

14. U. Heresco-Levy et al., *Pilot-Controlled Trial of D-Cycloserine for the Treatment of Post-Traumatic Stress Disorder*, 5 INT'L J. NEUROPSYCHOPHARMACOLOGY 301, 301-07 (2002).

15. The FDA has approved use of MDMA (methylenedioxymethamphetamine) in medical experiments investigating PTSD treatment. David Adam, *Ecstasy Trials for Combat Stress*, GUARDIAN, Feb. 17, 2005, at 6; *see also* National Institutes of Health, *A Test of MDMA-Assisted Psychotherapy in People with Posttraumatic Stress Disorder. . . .*

16. Miller, *supra* note 12, at 35.

17. Whether we should treat or seek to prevent PTSD with memory dampening will, of course, depend on the relative efficacy, financial costs, and side effects of the technology compared to the alternatives.

18. *See supra* note 87 and accompanying text.

    [87. *See* MCGAUGH, *supra* note 54, at 68 ("Immediately after learning, the brain is in a state that allows either disruption (retrograde amnesia) or enhancement of the consolidation of the long-term memory."); *see also* Janine Rossato et al., *Retrograde Amnesia Induced by Drugs Acting on Different Molecular Systems*, 118 BEHAVIORAL NEUROSCIENCE 563, 563 (2004) (recognizing research in animals demonstrating that "[m]emories can be modified by pharmacological treatments not only in the immediate posttraining period, but also several hours after training" (citations omitted)).]

19. Timothy R. Rebbeck et al., *Bilateral Prophylactic Mastectomy Reduces Breast Cancer Risk in* BRCA1 *and* BRCA2 *Mutation Carriers: The PROSE Study Group*, 22 J. CLINICAL ONCOLOGY 1055, 1055 (2004); *see also* Carl T. Hall, *Surgery Cuts Risk of Breast Cancer: Study Supports Use of Preventive Mastectomies*, S.F. CHRON., Feb. 24, 2004, at A2 ("The first major study of preventive breast-removal surgery in women with a high genetic risk for breast cancer showed the radical step may reduce cancer risk by 90 percent.").

20. "[N]o general agreement exists concerning the appropriate legal standard for ascertaining competency to provide informed consent." WINICK, *supra* note 96, at 349. "Some courts simply describe a valid choice as 'informed,' 'reasoned,' or 'rational,' without specifying any particular decisionmaking process. Most courts, however, do indicate that the patient must understand essential information." Elyn R. Saks, *Competency to Refuse Treatment*, 69 N.C. L. REV. 945, 978 (1991) (footnotes omitted); *see also In re Schiller*, 372 A.2d 360, 367 (N.J. Super. Ct. Ch. Div. 1977) (stating that "[t]he mental capacity to give consent to a surgical procedure is the same as that required to enter into a contract," requiring examination of whether a patient "possesses sufficient mind to understand, in a reasonable manner, the nature, extent, character, and effect of the act or transaction in which he is engaged.").

21. Similarly, parents who are emotionally traumatized from witnessing their children's traumatic injuries can ordinarily still give informed consent to their children's medical treatment.

22. As Bruce Winick has noted:

    [I]f the decision process is sufficiently free of coercion and undue influence, a patient . . . who receives sufficient information concerning the possible risks and side effects of a proposed therapy and alternative approaches, and who is sufficiently competent and intelligent to comprehend the information, may choose whether to participate in the proposed treatment. Such an informed consent allows treatment to be administered and constitutes a defense to any subsequent legal action asserting violation of the right to refuse treatment. WINICK, *supra* note 96, at 346.

23. Exec. Order No. 13237, 66 Fed. Reg. 59851 (Nov. 28, 2001), *available at. . . .*

24. *See supra* note 17 and accompanying text.

25. *See* Hearings, Part 1, *supra* note 17.

26. *See id.*; Hearings, Part 2, *supra* note 17; Hearings, Part 3, *supra* note 17.

27. *See id.* at 299–300 (summarizing the Council's concerns about enhancement technologies and stating that our efforts to obtain human perfection "may turn out to be at best but passing illusions, at worst a Faustian bargain that could cost us our full and flourishing humanity").

28. Meilaender, *supra* note 11, at 21–22.

29. *Id.* at 22.

30. *Id.* at 21.

31. This example was raised by James McGaugh at the Council's Hearing. *See* Hearings, Part 2, *supra* note 17, at 23-24; *see also* James N. Butcher & Chris Hatcher, *The Neglected Entity in Air Disaster Planning*, 43 AM. PSYCHOLOGIST 724, 728 (1988) (describing the incident).

32. Hearings, Part 2, *supra* note 17, at 23 (comments of James McGaugh).

33. Meilaender, *supra* note 11, at 22.

34. The Council acknowledges that if "bitter memories are so painful and intrusive as to ruin the possibility for normal experience of much of life and the world," the "impulse" to dampen those memories is "fully understandable." BEYOND THERAPY, *supra* note 97, at 230. The Council quickly retreats, however, adding: "And yet, there may be a great cost to acting compassionately for those who suffer bad memories, if we do so by compromising the truthfulness of how they remember." *Id.*

35. BEYOND THERAPY, *supra* note 97, at 217 n.*

36. *See supra* text accompanying notes 190–91.

37. *The Council's preference for natural changes in memory can be seen in the following:*

     [We] live through memorable experiences that we would never have chosen— experiences we often wish never happened at all. To some extent, these unchosen memories constrain us; though we may regret the shadows they cast over our pursuit of happiness, we cannot simply escape them while remaining who we really are. And yet, through the act of remembering—the act of discerning and giving meaning to the past as it really was—we can shape, to some degree, the meaning of our memories, both good and bad.

     BEYOND THERAPY, *supra* note 97, at 216.

38. Wasserman, *supra* note 11, at 14.

39. *Id.*

40. Peter Kramer quotes a patient who, after starting the SSRI antidepressant Prozac, said she felt "as if I had been in a drugged state all those years and now I am clearheaded." PETER KRAMER, LISTENING TO PROZAC 8 (1993). Eight months after beginning Prozac, the same patient stopped the treatment and said she felt like "I am not myself." *Id.* at 18. Some have argued that SSRI antidepressants have little, if any, efficacy that cannot be explained as a placebo effect. *See* Joanna Moncrieff & Irving Kirsch, *Efficacy of Antidepressants in Adults*, 331 BMJ 155, 157 (2005). Whatever personality changes Prozac patients experience, however, whether caused by placebo pathways or serotonin pathways, these patients frequently identify more closely with their pharmaceutically- or placebo-influenced new selves than their former selves.

41. *See* BEYOND THERAPY, *supra* note 97, at 213 ("[B]y disconnecting our mood and memory from what we do and experience, the new drugs could jeopardize the fitness and truthfulness of how we live and what we feel . . .").

42. *Id.* at 233–34.

43. *Id.* at 234.

44. *Id.*

45. Robert Nozick's famous "experience machine" thought experiment is often taken to show that we want our lives to be closely connected to reality. *See* ROBERT NOZICK, ANARCHY, STATE, & UTOPIA 42–45 (1974). Nozick asked us to imagine that:

    Superduper neuropsychologists could stimulate your brain so that you would think and feel you were writing a great novel, or making a friend, or reading an interesting book. All the time you would be floating in a tank, with electrodes attached to your brain. Should you plug into this machine for life, preprogramming your life's experiences? . . . Of course, while in the tank you won't know that you're there; you'll think it's all actually happening.

    Id. at 42-43. According to Nozick, we would not choose to spend our lives connected to such a machine because we value not just particular experiences but particular *genuine* experiences. *Id.* at 4–45. At best, however, Nozick's example only shows that we value *some* connection to the real world, not that we are opposed to having *any* illusory beliefs or perceptions (for example, the drug-induced, trauma-relieving perception that one has not witnessed some atrocity that, in fact, one has).

    Furthermore, even Nozick's limited conclusion that we value some connection to the real world is not robustly demonstrated by the thought experiment. The thought experiment would be more convincing if those already connected to an experience machine would also choose to disconnect from it in order to lead more genuine but substantially less enjoyable lives than they do while connected. Consistent with all available evidence, we might be connected to experience machines right now, yet I question whether we would choose to disconnect from the simulacra of our current lives, if given the choice. As I argue elsewhere, the fact that we are more willing to remain connected to an experience machine than to connect in the first place suggests that our initial intuitions about the experience machine may not be entirely trustworthy. *See* Adam Kolber, *Mental Statism and the Experience Machine*, 3 BARD J. SOC. SCI. 10 (Winter 1994/1995).

46. Hearings, Part 3, *supra* note 17, at 17.

47. *Id.*

48. *See* Catherine A. Niven & Tricia Murphy-Black, *Memory for Labor Pain: A Review of the Literature*, 27 BIRTH 244, 248–49, 252 (2000) (finding little scientific evidence to support folklore that memory of labor pain is quickly forgotten); C.A. Niven & E.E. Brodie, *Memory for Labor Pain: Context and Quality*, 64 PAIN 387, 388 (1996) (characterizing several studies as "reveal[ing] that the accuracy of memory for the intensity of labor pain is modest in accord with conclusions relating to memory for pain of diverse aetiology").

49. Sandel notes:

    [T]he objection to altering memory, whether to blot out traumatic memories or to increase our ability to remember certain things on either direction might be seen as part of what we do anyhow when we take in the world, and it might be odd to think that the way we just happen to take in the world unaltered from either direction is the past. . . . Why should we think that that's necessarily going to lead us to the truest life story?

    Hearings, Part 3, *supra* note 17, at 4.

50. *See* 26 U.S.C. § 6651 (2006) (setting forth penalties for failure to file a timely tax return). Of course, one may fail to file a timely tax return for reasons other than forgetfulness.

51. *See* Minerva Canto, *Kids' Death in Hot Cars Is a Curse for Parents*, ORANGE COUNTY REGISTER (Oct. 5, 2004). . . . Suzette Hackney, *County Won't Charge Father: Neglect Not Criminal in Son's Death in Van*, DETROIT FREE PRESS, July 28, 1999, at A1.

52. Before pursuing such cases, prosecutors generally require an extreme kind of forgetfulness that evidences gross negligence. *See, e.g.*, Kelly v. Commonwealth, 592 S.E.2d 353, 355-57 (Va. Ct. App. 2004) (affirming the manslaughter conviction of a father who left his 21-month-old daughter unattended in a hot van for approximately seven hours where there was evidence that the father had stranded children in automobiles in the past).

53. BEYOND THERAPY, *supra* note 97, at 230-31 (footnotes omitted).

54. *Id.* at 231.

55. *Id.* (footnotes omitted). The Council fears that memory dampening will encourage a shallow kind of human solidarity:

    [T]hose who suffer terrible things cannot or should not have to endure their own bad memories alone. If, as a people, we have an obligation to remember certain terrible events truthfully, surely we ought to help those who suffered through those events to come to terms with their worst memories. Of course, one might see the new biotechnical powers, developed precisely to ease the psychic pain of bad memories, as the mark of such solidarity. . . . But such solidarity may, in the end, prove false: for it exempts us from the duty to suffer-with (literally, to feel *com*-passion for) those who remember; it does not demand that we preserve the truth of their memories; it attempts instead to make the problem go away, and with it the truth of the experience in question.

    Id. at 231-32.

56. *See id.*

57. The analysis is complicated, however, by the inability to recover a previously dampened or erased memory. At one point in time, a particular memory could be merely homage-like, held only because one has no choice. With age and understanding, perhaps, the memory could become a genuine homage if the individual voluntarily identifies with the memory. By allowing people to erase homage-like memories, we cut off the subsequent opportunity to embrace the memory. This is a variation of the view described earlier by Gilbert Meilaender. *See supra* Part III.B.1.

58. *See supra* Part II.A.1.

58. BEYOND THERAPY, *supra* note 97, at 228.

59. *Id.* at 229.

60. *Cf.* BEYOND THERAPY, *supra* note 97, at 224 (noting that memory dampeners could be used "to dull the sting of one's own shameful acts").

61. *See id.* at 154 (describing the remorse-free soldier as a "killing machine"). At the Council's hearings, James McGaugh testified that "stimulants have been given to soldiers for years to make them implicitly, and I think explicitly in some cases, to make them better soldiers." Hearings, Part 1, *supra* note 17, at 13.

62. Mundell, *supra* note 5 (quoting McHugh).

63. *Id.* (quoting psychiatrist Margaret Altemus as saying, "I think Dr. McHugh may have been assuming that what prevents soldiers from committing atrocities is this overwhelming fear. . . . I've never been in a war, but my guess is that they do these things because they are really angry, or through some group attitude.").

64. James McGaugh, speaking of a hypothetical injured soldier who has killed during battle, asks: Do you just let him lie there and bleed to death because he needs to suffer the consequences of having killed another human being in battle? We give him first aid, pain medication, we do everything we can. But if he's having an emotional disturbance because of that trauma, we can't do anything about that because that would change the nature of who they are. Doesn't losing a leg change the nature of who they are? Jeanie Lerche Davis, *Forget Something? We Wish We Could*, WebMD, Apr. 9, 2004, . . . (quoting McGaugh).

Beyond Therapy: Biotechnology and the Pursuit of Happiness

Chapter Five

Who has not wanted to escape the clutches of oppressive and punishing memories? Or to calm the burdensome feelings of anxiety, disappointment, and regret? Or to achieve a psychic state of pure and undivided pleasure and joy? The satisfaction of such desires seems inseparable from our happiness, which we pursue by right and with passion.

In these efforts at peace of mind, human beings have from time immemorial sought help from doctors and drugs. In a famous literary instance, Shakespeare's Macbeth entreats his doctor to free Lady Macbeth from the haunting memory of her own guilty acts:

> *Macbeth.* Canst thou not minister to a mind diseas'd,
> Pluck from the memory a rooted sorrow,
> Raze out the written troubles of the brain,
> And with some sweet oblivious antidote
> Cleanse the stuff'd bosom of that perilous stuff
> Which weighs upon the heart?
>
> *Doctor.* Therein the patient
> Must minister to himself.

Ministering to oneself, however, is easier said than done, and many people have found themselves unequal to the task without some outside assistance. For centuries, they have made use of external agents to drown their sorrows or lift their spirits.

The burgeoning field of neuroscience is providing new, more specific, and safer agents to help us combat all sorts of psychic distress. Soon, doctors may have just the "sweet oblivious antidote" that Macbeth so desired: drugs (such as beta-adrenergic blockers) that numb the emotional sting typically associated with our intensely bad memories[.]

To be sure, these agents—and their better versions, yet to come—are, for now at least, being developed not as means for drug-induced happiness but rather as agents for combating major depression or preventing post-traumatic stress disorder (PTSD). Yet once available for those purposes, they could also be used to ease the soul and enhance the mood of nearly anyone.

From the President's Council on Bioethics, October 2003.

By using drugs to satisfy more easily the enduring aspirations to forget what torments us and approach the world with greater peace of mind, what deeper human aspirations might we occlude or frustrate? What qualities of character may become less necessary and, with diminished use, atrophy or become extinct, as we increasingly depend on drugs to cope with misfortune? How will we experience our incompleteness or understand our mortality as our ability grows to medically dissolve all sorts of anxiety? Will the availability of drug-induced conditions of ecstatic pleasure estrange us from the forms of pleasure that depend upon discipline and devotion? And, going beyond the implications for individuals, what kind of a society are we likely to have when the powers to control memory, mood, and mental life through drugs reach their full maturity and are widely used?

I. What are "Happy Souls"?

Because the happiness we seek we seek for *ourselves*—for *our* self, not for someone else's, and for our *self* or embodied soul, not for our bodies as material stuff—our happiness is bound up with our personhood and our identity. We would not want to attain happiness (or any other object of our desires) if the condition for attaining it required that we become someone else, that we lose our identity in the process.

The importance of identity for happiness implies necessarily the importance of memory. If experiencing our happiness depends upon experiencing a stable identity, then our happiness depends also on our memory, on knowing who we are in relation to who we have been.

But if enfeebled memory can cripple identity, selectively altered memory can distort it. Changing the content of our memories or altering their emotional tonalities, however desirable to alleviate guilty or painful consciousness, could subtly reshape who we are, at least to ourselves. With altered memories we might feel better about ourselves, but it is not clear that the better-feeling "we" remains the same as before. Lady Macbeth, cured of her guilty torment, would remain the murderess she was, but not the conscience-stricken being even she could not help but be.

[A]n unchecked power to erase memories, brighten moods, and alter our emotional dispositions could imperil our capacity to form a strong and coherent personal identity. To the extent that our inner life ceases to reflect the ups and downs of daily existence and instead operates independently of them, we dissipate our identity, which is formed through engagement with others and through immersion in the mix of routine and unpredictable events that constitute our lives.

II. Memory and Happiness

Our identity or sense of self emerges, grows, and changes. Yet, despite all the changes, thanks to the integrating powers of memory, our identity also, remarkably, persists *as ours*.

We especially want our memories to be not simply a sequence of discon-nected experiences, but a narrative that seems to contain some unfolding pur-pose, some larger point from beginning to end, some aspiration discovered, pursued, and at least partially fulfilled.

Memory is central to human flourishing, in other words, precisely because we pursue happiness in time, as time-bound beings. We have a past and a future as well as a present, and being happy through time requires that these be connected in a meaningful way. If we are to flourish as ourselves, we must do so without abandoning or forgetting who we are or once were. Yet because our lives are time-bound, our happiness is always incomplete—always not-yet and on-the-way, always here but slipping away, but also always possible again and in the future. Our happiest experiences can be revivified. And, as we reminisce from greater distance and with more experience, even our painful experiences can often acquire for us a meaning not in evidence when they occurred.

The place of memory in the pursuit of happiness also suggests some-thing essential about human identity, a theme raised in various places and in different ways throughout this report: namely, our identities are formed both by what we do and by what we undergo or suffer. We actively choose paths and do deeds fit to be remembered. But we also live through memorable expe-riences that we would never have chosen—experiences we often wish never happened at all. To some extent, these unchosen memories constrain us; though we may regret the shadows they cast over our pursuit of happiness, we cannot simply escape them while remaining who we really are. And yet, through the act of remembering—the act of discerning and giving meaning to the past as it really was—we can shape, to some degree, the meaning of our memories, both good and bad.

The capacity to alter or numb our remembrance of things past cuts to the heart of what it means to remember in a human way, and it is this biotech-nical possibility that we focus on here. Deciding when or whether to use such biotechnical power will require that we think long and hard about what it means to remember truthfully, to live in time, and to seek happiness without losing or abandoning our identity. The rest of this discussion of "memory and happiness" is an invitation to such reflection.

A. Good Memories and Bad

[T]he significance of past events often becomes clear to us only after much rumination in light of later experience, and what seems trivial at one time may appear crucial at another. Neither can an excellent memory be one that remembers only what we *want* to remember: sometimes our most valuable memories are of events that were painful when they occurred, but that on reflection teach us vital lessons.

B. Biotechnology and Memory Alteration

It is a commonplace observation that, while some events fade quickly from the mind, emotionally intense experiences form memories that are peculiarly vivid and long-lasting. Not only do we recall such events long after they happened, but the recollection is often accompanied, in some measure, by a recurrence of the emotions aroused during the original experience.

When a person experiences especially shocking or violent events (such as a plane crash or bloody combat), the release of stress hormones may be so intense that the memory-encoding system is over-activated. The result is a consolidation of memories both far stronger and more persistent than normal and also more apt, upon recollection, to call forth the intense emotional response of the original experience. In such cases, each time the person relives the traumatic memory, a new flood of stress hormones is released, and the experience may be so emotionally intense as to be encoded as a new experience. With time, the memories grow more recurrent and intrusive, and the response—fear, helplessness, horror—more incapacitating. As we shall see, drugs that might prevent or alleviate the symptoms of PTSD are among the chief medical benefits that scientists expect from recent research in the neurochemistry of memory formation.

In fact, the discovery of hormonal regulation of memory formation was quickly followed up by clinical studies on human subjects demonstrating that memory of emotional experiences can be altered pharmacologically. In one particularly interesting series of experiments, Larry Cahill and his colleagues showed that injections of beta-blockers can, by inhibiting the action of stress hormones, suppress the memory-enhancing effects of strong emotional arousal.

[T]aking propranolol appears to have little or no effect on how we remember everyday or emotionally neutral information. But when taken at the time of highly emotional experiences, propranolol appears to suppress the normal memory-enhancing effects of emotional arousal—while leaving the immediate emotional response unaffected. These results suggested the possibility of using beta-blockers to help survivors of traumatic events to reduce their intrusive—and in some cases crippling—memories of those events.

[A]lthough the pharmacology of memory alteration is a science still in its infancy, the significance of this potential new power—to separate the subjective experience of memory from the truth of the experience that is remembered—should not be underestimated. It surely returns us to the large ethical and anthropological questions with which we began—about memory's role in shaping personal identity and the character of human life, and about the meaning of remembering things that we would rather forget and of forgetting things that we perhaps ought to remember.

C. Memory-Blunting: Ethical Analysis

If we had the power, by promptly taking a memory-altering drug, to dull the emotional impact of what could become very painful memories, when might we be tempted to use it? And for what reasons should we yield to or resist the temptation?

At first glance, such a drug would seem ideally suited for the prevention of PTSD, the complex of debilitating symptoms that sometimes afflict those who have experienced severe trauma. These symptoms—which include persistent re-experiencing of the traumatic event and avoidance of every person, place, or thing that might stimulate the horrid memory's return[1] can so burden mental life as to make normal everyday living extremely difficult, if not impossible.[2] For those suffering these disturbing symptoms, a drug that could separate a painful memory from its powerful emotional component would appear very welcome indeed.

Yet the prospect of preventing (even) PTSD with beta-blockers or other memory-blunting agents seems to be, for several reasons, problematic. First of all, the drugs in question appear to be effective only when administered during or shortly after a traumatic event—and thus well before any symptoms of PTSD would be manifested. How then could we make, and make on the spot, the *prospective* judgment that a particular event is sufficiently terrible to warrant preemptive memory-blunting? Second, how shall we judge *which* participants in the event merit such treatment? After all, not everyone who suffers through painful experiences is destined to have pathological memory effects. Should the drugs in question be given to everyone or only to those with an observed susceptibility to PTSD, and, if the latter, how will we know who these are? Finally, in some cases merely witnessing a disturbing event (for example, a murder, rape, or terrorist attack) is sufficient to cause PTSD-like symptoms long afterwards. Should we then, as soon as disaster strikes, consider giving memory-altering drugs to all the witnesses, in addition to those directly involved?

If the apparent powers of memory-blunting drugs are confirmed, some might be inclined to prescribe them liberally to all who are involved in a sufficiently terrible event. After all, even those not destined to come down with full-blown PTSD are likely to suffer painful recurrent memories of an airplane crash, an incident of terrorism, or a violent combat operation. In the aftermath of such shocking incidents, why not give everyone the chance to remember these events without the added burden of painful emotions? This line of reasoning might, in fact, tempt us to give beta-blockers liberally to soldiers on the eve of combat, to emergency workers en route to a disaster site, or even to individuals requesting prophylaxis against the shame or guilt they might incur from future misdeeds—in general, to anyone facing an experience that is likely to leave lasting intrusive memories.

Yet on further reflection it seems clear that not every intrusive memory is a suitable candidate for prospective pharmacological blunting. As Daniel Schacter has observed, "attempts to avoid traumatic memories often backfire":

> Intrusive memories need to be acknowledged, confronted, and worked through, in order to set them to rest for the long term. Unwelcome memories of trauma are symptoms of a disrupted psyche that requires attention before it can resume healthy functioning. Beta-blockers might make it easier for trauma survivors to face and incorporate traumatic recollections, and in that sense could facilitate long-term adaptation. Yet it is also possible that beta-blockers would work against the normal process of recovery: traumatic memories would not spring to mind with the kind of psychological force that demands attention and perhaps intervention. Prescription of beta-blockers could bring about an effective trade-off between short-term

reductions in the sting of traumatic memories and long-term increases in persistence of related symptoms of a trauma that has not been adequately confronted.[3]

The point can be generalized: in the immediate aftermath of a painful experience, we simply cannot know either the full meaning of the experience in question or the ultimate character and future prospects of the individual who experiences it. We cannot know how this experience will change this person at this time and over time. Will he be cursed forever by unbearable memories that, in retrospect, clearly should have been blunted medically? Or will he succeed, over time, in "redeeming" those painful memories by actively integrating them into the narrative of his life? By "rewriting" memories pharmacologically we might succeed in easing real suffering at the risk of falsifying our perception of the world and undermining our true identity.

Finally, the decision whether or not to use memory-blunting drugs must be made in the absence of clearly diagnosable disease. The drug must be taken right after a traumatic experience has occurred, and thus before the different ways that different individuals handle the same experience has become clear. In some cases, these interventions will turn out to have been preventive medicine, intervening to ward off the onset of PTSD before it arrives—though it is worth noting that we would lack even post hoc knowledge of whether any particular now-unaffected individual, in the absence of using the drug, would have become symptomatic.[4] In other cases, the interventions would not be medicine at all: altering the memory of individuals who could have lived well, even with severely painful memories, without pharmacologically dulling the pain. Worse, in still other cases, the use of such drugs would inoculate individuals in advance against the psychic pain that *should* accompany their commission of cruel, brutal, or shameful deeds. But in all cases, from the defensible to the dubious, the use of such powers changes the character of human memory, by intervening directly in the way individuals "encode," and thus the way they understand, the happenings of their own lives and the realities of the world around them.

1. Remembering Fitly and Truly

Altering the formation of emotionally powerful memories risks severing what we remember from how we remember it and distorting the link between our perception of significant human events and the significance of the events themselves. It risks, in a word, falsifying our perception and understanding of the world. It risks making shameful acts seem less shameful, or terrible acts less terrible, than they really are.

Imagine the experience of a person who witnesses a shocking murder. Fearing that he will be haunted by images of this event, he immediately takes propranolol (or its more potent successor) to render his memory of the murder less painful and intrusive. Thanks to the drug, his memory of the murder gets encoded as a garden-variety, emotionally neutral experience. But in manipulating his memory in this way, he risks coming to think about the murder as more tolerable than it really is, as an event that should not sting those who witness it. For our opinions about the meaning of our experiences are shaped partly by the feelings evoked when we remember them. If, psychologically, the murder is transformed into an event our witness can recall without pain—or without *any* particular emotion—perhaps its moral significance will also fade from consciousness. If so, he would in a sense have ceased to be a genuine witness of the murder. When asked about it, he might say, "Yes, I was there. But it wasn't so terrible."

This points us to a deeper set of questions about bad memories: Would dulling our memory of terrible things make us too comfortable with the world, unmoved by suffering, wrongdoing, or cruelty? Does not the experience of hard truths—of the unchosen, the inexplicable, the tragic—remind us that we can never be fully at home in the world, especially if we are to take seriously the reality of human evil? Further, by blunting our experience and awareness of shameful, fearful, and hateful things, might we not also risk deadening our response to what is admirable, inspiring, and lovable? Can we become numb to life's sharpest sorrows without also becoming numb to its greatest joys?

There seems to be little doubt that some bitter memories are so painful and intrusive as to ruin the possibility for normal experience of much of life and the world. In such cases the impulse to relieve a crushing burden and restore lost innocence is fully understandable: If there are some things that it is better never to have experienced at all—things we would avoid if we possibly could—why not erase them from the memory of those unfortunate enough to have suffered them? If there are some things it is better never to have known or seen, why not use our power over memory to restore a witness's shattered peace of mind? There is great force in this argument, perhaps especially in cases where children lose prematurely that innocence that is rightfully theirs.

And yet, there may be a great cost to acting compassionately for those who suffer bad memories, if we do so by compromising the truthfulness of how they remember. We risk having them live falsely in order simply to cope, to survive by whatever means possible.

2. The Obligation to Remember

Having truthful memories is not simply a personal matter. Strange to say, our own memory is not merely our own; it is part of the fabric of the society in which we live. Consider the case of a person who has suffered or witnessed atrocities that occasion unbearable memories: for example, those with first-hand experience of the Holocaust. The life of that individual might well be served by dulling such bitter memories,[5] but such a humanitarian intervention, if widely practiced, would seem deeply troubling: Would the community as a whole—would the human race—be served by such a mass numbing of this terrible but indispensable memory? Do those who suffer evil have a duty to remember and bear witness, lest we all forget the very horrors that haunt them?

Surely, we cannot and should not force those who live through great trauma to endure its painful memory *for the benefit of the rest of us.* But as a community, there are certain events that we have an obligation to remember—an obligation that falls disproportionately, one might even say unfairly, on those who experience such events most directly.[6] What kind of people would we be if we did not "want" to remember the Holocaust, if we sought to make the anguish it caused simply go away? And yet, what kind of people are we, especially those who face such horrors firsthand, that we can endure such awful memories?

The answer, in part, is that those who suffer terrible things cannot or should not have to endure their own bad memories alone. If, as a people, we have an obligation to remember certain terrible events truthfully, surely we ought to help those who suffered through those events to come to terms with their worst memories. Of course, one might see the new biotechnical powers, developed precisely to ease the psychic pain of bad memories, as the mark of such solidarity: perhaps it is our new way of meeting the obligation to aid those who remember the hardest things, those who bear witness to us and for us. But such solidarity may, in the end, prove false: for it exempts us from the duty to suffer-with (literally, to feel *com*-passion for) those who remember; it does not demand that we preserve the truth of their memories; it attempts instead to make the problem go away, and with it the truth of the experience in question.

4. The Soul of Memory, the Remembering Soul

[W]e might often be tempted to sacrifice the accuracy of our memories for the sake of easing our pain or expanding our control over our own psychic lives. But doing so means, ultimately, severing ourselves from reality and leaving our own identity behind; it risks making us false, small, or capable of great illusions, and thus capable of great decadence or great evil, or perhaps simply willing to accept a phony contentment. We might be tempted to alter our memories to preserve an open future—to live the life we wanted to live before a particular experience happened to us. But in another sense, such interventions assume that our own future is not open—that we cannot and could never redeem the unwanted memory over time, that we cannot and could never integrate the remembered experience with our own truthful pursuit of happiness.

To have only happy memories would be a blessing—and a curse. Nothing would trouble us, but we would probably be shallow people, never falling to the depths of despair because we have little interest in the heights of human happiness or in the complicated lives of those around us. In the end, to have only happy memories is not to be happy in a truly human way. It is simply to be free of misery—an understandable desire given the many troubles of life, but a low aspiration for those who seek a truly human happiness.

Notes

1. These symptoms are observed especially among combat veterans; indeed, PTSD is the modern name for what used to be called "shell shock" or "combat neurosis." Among veterans, PTSD is frequently associated with recurrent nightmares, substance abuse, and delusional outbursts of violence. There is controversy about the prevalence of PTSD, with some studies finding that up to 8 percent of adult Americans have suffered the disorder, as well as a third of all veterans of the Vietnam War. See Kessler, R. C., et al., "Post-Traumatic

Stress Disorder in the National Comorbidity Survey," *Archives of General Psychiatry* 52(12): 1048-1060, 1995; Kulka, R. A., et al., *Trauma and the Vietnam War Generation: Report of Findings from the National Vietnam Veterans Readjustment Study,* New York: Brunner/Mazel, 1990.

2. There is already ongoing controversy about excessive diagnosis of PTSD. Many psychotherapists believe that a patient's psychic troubles are generally based on some earlier (now repressed) traumatic experience which must be unearthed and dealt with if relief is to be found. True PTSD is, however, generally transient, and the search for treatment is directed against the symptoms of its initial (worst) phase—the sleeplessness, the nightmares, the excessive jitteriness.

3. Of course, many Holocaust survivors managed, without pharmacological assistance, to live fulfilling lives while never forgetting what they lived through. At the same time, many survivors would almost certainly have benefited from pharmacological treatment.

4. There is no definitive diagnostic criterion for PTSD, but the core symptoms are thought to include persistent re-experiencing of the traumatic event, avoidance of associated stimuli, and hyperarousal. See *Diagnostic and Statistical Manual of Mental Disorders, Fourth Edition, text revision*, Washington, D.C.: American Psychiatric Association, 2000, pp. 463–486.

5. Schacter, D., *The Seven Sins of Memory: How the Mind Forgets and Remembers*, New York: Houghton Mifflin, 2001, p. 183.

6. For a discussion of memory-altering drugs and the meaning of "bearing witness," see the essay by Cohen, E., "Our Psychotropic Memory," *SEED*, no. 8, Fall 2003, p. 42.

CHALLENGE QUESTIONS

Should Memory-Dampening Drugs Be Used to Alleviate the Symptoms of Trauma?

1. Assuming that memory-dampening drugs become available to the public, who should be given responsibility for determining the appropriateness of such a drug for an individual? For example, should it fall on the shoulders of a physician to make such a determination?

2. What specific criteria should be used in determining the appropriateness of such a drug prescription? Should prescriptions be limited to survivors of life-threatening traumas? What about victims of sexual assault? Those who have been psychologically terrorized? People who are distressed as a result of profound humiliation?

3. What would be the youngest age at which memory-dampening drugs could be considered, and why?

4. What kind of research study could be designed to assess the costs and benefits of taking memory-dampening drugs?

5. In recent years researchers have been investigating a phenomenon called "post-traumatic growth" in which trauma survivors speak about ways in which life became better for them as a result of having lived through a trauma. In what ways can the experience of a trauma be viewed as a beneficial event in a person's life? Give some examples.

Suggested Readings

Davis, J. L. (April, 2004). Forget Something? We Wish We Could: "Therapeutic Forgetting" Helps Trauma Victims Endure Their Memories. WebMD. http://www.medicinenet.com/script/main/art.asp?articlekey=52473/

Dupree, C. (2004). Cushioning Hard Memories. *Harvard Magazine,* 106 (6). http://www.harvardmagazine.com/on-line/070467.html/

Fletcher, T. (2005). A Case of Reemergent Post-Traumatic Stress Disorder Arrested by Propranolol Intervention: Does a Stitch in Time Save Nine? In Corales, T. A. (ed.), *Focus on Posttraumatic Stress Disorder Research* (37–49). Hauppauge, NY, U.S.: Nova Science Publishers.

Marvasti, J. A., & Pascal, B. (2004). Pharmacotherapy for Victims of Trauma. In Marvasti, J. A. (ed.), *Psychiatric Treatment of Victims and Survivors of Sexual Trauma: A Neuro-bio-psychological Approach* (113–131). Springfield, IL, U.S.: Charles C. Thomas Publisher.

Roberts, J. (2006). The Trauma Tamer: Easing the Emotional Strain of Crippling Memories. Headway, 2(1). http://www.mcgill.ca/headway/fall2006/newwave/

Rosenwald, M. (May, 2006). The Spotless Mind: A Routine Heart Drug Shows Promise as a Way to Blunt Bad Memories. Popsci.com. http://www.popsci.com/popsci/medicine/7001525ad18aa010vgnvcm1000004eecbccdrcrd.html/

ISSUE 9

Are Antipsychotic Medications the Treatment of Choice for People with Psychosis?

YES: **E. Fuller Torrey**, from *Surviving Schizophrenia: A Manual for Families, Consumers, and Providers,* 4th ed. (Quill, 2001)

NO: **Robert Whitaker**, from *Mad in America: Bad Science, Bad Medicine, and the Enduring Mistreatment of the Mentally Ill* (Perseus, 2002)

ISSUE SUMMARY

YES: Psychiatrist E. Fuller Torrey, an outspoken advocate for the needs of the mentally ill and their families, contends that antipsychotic medications play a centrally important role in alleviating psychotic symptoms and reducing the likelihood of rehospitalization.

NO: Journalist and social critic Robert Whitaker asserts that antipsychotic medications make people chronically ill, cause serious side effects, and increase the likelihood of rehospitalization; furthermore, reliance on these medical treatments for the mentally ill neglect important questions such as what it means to be human.

When antipsychotic medications were introduced in the 1950s and were popularized in the 1960s, at first, scientists and clinicians alike imagined that these medications would "cure" schizophrenia, or at the very least, help severely disturbed patients regain control. Little attention was given to the downside of powerful psychopharmacological interventions. As the years went by, however, disturbing evidence emerged regarding debilitating side effects such as tardive dyskinesia, a condition in which the individual experiences uncontrollable bodily movements. Pharmacological research continued in earnest as scientists looked for medications with minimal side effects that would treat not only the positive symptoms of psychosis (e.g., hallucinations), but also the negative symptoms (e.g., apathy and affective flattening). In recent years, many people have experienced tremendous improvement in their lives as a result of antipsychotic medications; at the same time, concerns have been raised about their widespread use.

Psychiatrist E. Fuller Torrey has established an international reputation as a professional devoted to educating the public about the nature of schizophrenia and appropriate ways for responding to and treating people. Torrey firmly believes that antipsychotic medications provide a safe method for treating debilitating psychotic symptoms by bringing about therapeutic changes in the brain; furthermore, they reduce the likelihood of rehospitalization.

Author and social critic Robert Whitaker expresses vehement alarm about the proliferation of antipsychotic medications. He contends that these agents make people chronically ill, cause worrisome side effects, and increase the likelihood of rehospitalization. He also criticizes such medical treatments as unfortunate reflections of warped societal and philosophical values.

POINT

- Research shows that taking antipsychotic drugs reduces the likelihood that people with schizophrenia will be rehospitalized.

- Antipsychotic drugs, as a group, are one of the safest groups of drugs in common use and are the greatest advance in the treatment of schizophrenia that has occurred to date.
- Studies show that the incidence of neuroleptic-related tardive dyskinesia has been overestimated, and in fact is a condition that affects less that 20% of those taking these drugs.

- Antipsychotic medication changes the brain in an effective way. Such changes include increased density of glial cells in the frontal cortex, an increase in synapses, and changes in the properties of synapses.
- The data on the effectiveness of drugs are so clear that any physician or psychiatrist who fails to try them on a person with schizophrenia is probably incompetent. It is not that drugs are the only ingredient, but they are the most essential.

COUNTERPOINT

- In the research study that launched the emptying of state hospitals in the 1960s, patients who took neuroleptics were more apt to be rehospitalized than those given a placebo.
- Research over the years has demonstrated that antipsychotic drugs make people chronically ill, a fact that psychiatry has cast aside.

- Antipsychotic drugs cause an increase in dopamine receptors, which is a change associated both with tardive dyskinesia and an increased biological vulnerability to psychosis; long-term outcomes are much better in countries where such medications are less frequently used.
- Antipsychotic drugs do not fix any brain abnormalities, nor do they put brain chemistry back into balance.

- History provides a lesson in understanding what is essential in treating people with psychosis: The Quakers viewed psychotic individuals as suffering "brethren" who needed comfort, and who had a God-given capacity for recovery. Humanitarian and optimistic caregivers could "assist Nature" in helping them heal.

YES ↵

E. Fuller Torrey

The Treatment of Schizophrenia: Medications

Once a competent doctor has been located and the intricacies of hospitalization have been mastered, then the treatment of schizophrenia becomes comparatively simple. Drugs are the most important treatment for schizophrenia, just as they are the most important treatment for many physical diseases of the human body. Drugs do not *cure,* but rather *control,* the symptoms of schizophrenia—as they do those of diabetes. The drugs we now have to treat schizophrenia are far from perfect, but they work for most of the people with the disease if they are used correctly.

The main drugs used to treat schizophrenia are usually called antipsychotics. They have also been called neuroleptics and major tranquilizers, but the best term is "antipsychotic" because that is what they are. They frequently do not produce tranquilization, so that term is a misnomer. The antipsychotic drugs were discovered in 1952 by French psychiatrist Pierre Deniker. He had heard about a new tranquilizer that his anesthesiology colleagues were using to sedate patients during surgery and decided to try it on psychiatric patients; the drug was chlorpromazine (Thorazine, Largactil).

Antipsychotics can be divided into two classes: first-generation and second-generation. Those are commonly referred to, respectively, as "typical" and "atypical," based on the previously widespread belief that the effectiveness of "typicals" was related to their ability to block dopamine receptors, whereas the effectiveness of the "atypicals" was related to their action on other neurotransmitter receptors. Associated with the dopamine blockade are certain side effects found commonly in first-generation antipsychotics but rarely in second-generation antipsychotics. These side effects are usually abbreviated EPS (extrapyramidal signs) and consist of Parkinsonian-like symptoms, acute dystonic reactions, and akathisia. Researchers are now less certain that dopamine blockade is the primary reason why the first-generation antipsychotics are effective, and in fact there is considerable overlap in receptor activity of "typical" and "atypical" antipsychotics. It is therefore more accurate simply to classify antipsychotics into first-generation (beginning with the introduction of chlorpromazine in 1952) and second-generation (beginning with the introduction of clozapine in the United States in 1990). Such a division is admittedly America-centric, since clozapine was used in some European countries in the 1970s and 1980s. . . .

Do They Work?

The efficacy of antipsychotic drugs is well established. Studies show that approximately 70 percent of patients with schizophrenia clearly improve on these drugs, 25 percent improve minimally or not at all, and 5 percent get worse. This is approximately the same level of effectiveness that penicillin exerts in pneumonia or streptomycin in tuberculosis. Antipsychotic drugs reduce symptoms of the disease, shorten the stay in the hospital, and reduce the chances of rehospitalization dramatically. Whereas persons with schizophrenia entering a psychiatric hospital used to stay for several weeks or months, the average stay with these drugs is now reduced to days. And the data on their preventing rehospitalization are even more impressive. John Davis, for example, reviewed 24 scientifically controlled studies testing whether antipsychotic drugs were effective. All 24 studies found that persons with schizophrenia who took antipsychotic drugs were less likely to have to return to the hospital than those who did not take these drugs. The differences between the two groups were highly significant, especially for persons with chronic schizo-phrenia. On the average, a person who takes the drugs has a 3-out-of-5 chance (60 percent) of not being rehospitalized by the end of one year, whereas the person who does not take the drugs has only a 1-out-of-5 chance (20 percent) of not being rehospitalized.

When studies have been done on the long-acting, injectable form of antipsychotics (where compliance in taking the drug is assured), the results are even more impressive. In one study of chronic patients, only 8 percent of the patients who were taking the drug relapsed within one year, but 68 percent of those not taking the drug relapsed. In another study of patients taking long-acting, injectable antipsychotics, 80 percent relapsed within two years when the drug was stopped. What all this means is that though taking the drugs does not guarantee you will *not* get sick again, and not taking the drugs does not guarantee you *will* get sick again, their use improves the odds toward stay-ing out of the hospital tremendously. The data on the effectiveness of drugs are so clear that any physician or psychiatrist who fails to try them on a person with schizophrenia is probably incompetent. It is not that drugs are the *only* ingredient necessary to treat schizophrenia successfully; they are just the most essential ingredient.

Antipsychotic drugs are not equally effective for all the symptoms of schizophrenia. They are most effective at reducing delusions, hallucinations, aggressive or bizarre behavior, thinking disorders, and the symptoms having to do with the overacuteness of the senses—the so-called "positive" symptoms. For example, against auditory hallucinations, one of the most common and disabling symptoms of schizophrenia, antipsychotic drugs are 80 to 90 percent effective in being able to relieve the hallucinations, usually making them disappear altogether. The drugs have less efficacy against symptoms such as apathy, ambivalence, poverty of thought, and flattening of the emotions—the "negative" symptoms.

Do They Change the Brain?

Some opponents of the use of antipsychotics have alleged that because these medications change the brain, that means they are dangerous and should not be used. Antipsychotic medications do, of course, change the brain—that is why they are effective. Medications used to treat epilepsy, Parkinson's disease, and other brain diseases also change the brain. And medications used to treat diseases in other organs, such as the heart and joints, may bring about structural changes to those organs as well.

The brain changes produced by antipsychotic drugs are relatively minor. The main changes that have been claimed to date are an increase in density of glial cells in the frontal cortex, an increase in synapses (connections between neurons), and changes in the properties of the synapses. There is no evidence that antipsychotic drugs cause the loss of neurons. Much research is ongoing in this area, since understanding the nature of these changes may help us understand how these drugs work, why they cause side effects, and who will respond to which drug. . . .

Does Early Treatment Help?

Some studies have suggested that early treatment may lead to a better clinical outcome in schizophrenia and, conversely, that delayed treatment may lead to a worse outcome. Dr. Richard Wyatt of the National Institute of Mental Health reanalyzed 22 studies on the course of schizophrenia and concluded that "early intervention with neuroleptics in first-break schizophrenic patients increases the likelihood of an improved long-term course." An analysis of the [Jeffrey] Lieberman et al. study of individuals undergoing their first episode of schizophrenia similarly concluded that "greater duration of illness [prior to beginning treatment] was found to predict increased time to remission" in younger but not in older patients. An Irish study of untreated patients with schizophrenia also found that "untreated psychosis in schizophrenia appears to have a progressive and, ultimately, a profoundly debilitating effect on long-term outcome." The implication of these studies is that the failure by mental illness professionals to treat individuals with schizophrenia with antipsychotic medications as early in the course of their illness as possible may produce a worse outcome. Other recent studies have not found this to be true, and this is an area of ongoing research. Until it is clarified, it should be assumed that treatment should begin as early in the course of the disease as possible.

Adverse Effects

"The antipsychotic agents," says Dr. Ross J. Baldessarini, "are among the safest drugs available in medicine." As one of the foremost experts on these drugs, Dr. Baldessarini should know, yet his claim is at variance with popular stereotypes of the drugs. It is widely believed that the first-generation antipsychotic drugs have terrible adverse effects, are dangerous, and almost invariably produce tardive dyskinesia (involuntary muscle movements) and other irreversible conditions that may be worse than the original schizophrenia.

Dr. Baldessarini is in fact correct, and the popular stereotype is wrong. Antipsychotic drugs, compared with drugs used to treat other diseases, are relatively safe. It is almost impossible to commit suicide with them by over-dosing, and their serious adverse effects are comparatively rare.

Then why is there such a strong misperception and fear of these drugs? Much of the reason can be traced to theories of causation of the disease. As we have noted, it is only in recent years that the evidence for schizophrenia's being a real biological disease has become clear. The resistance to this idea among mental illness professionals trained in the psychogenic belief systems has been impressive. And one of the ways this resistance is shown is by strongly opposing the use of drugs; implicitly, if the drugs are too dangerous to be used, then patients will again have to rely on psychotherapy and other nondrug modes of treatment. For this reason, occasional mental illness professionals—who should be better informed—still warn patients with schizophrenia about all kinds of ter-rible calamities that will befall them if they take antipsychotic drugs. Additional opposition to antipsychotic drug use comes from the Church of Scientology, whose founder, L. Ron Hubbard, was virulently anti-psychiatry. . . .

This is *not* to say that antipsychotic drugs are perfectly safe and have no adverse effects whatsoever. They do have adverse effects, sometimes so severe that the drug must be stopped. The adverse effects have on occasion even been fatal, but this is very rare. One of the main goals of the current search for second-generation antipsychotic drugs is to find effective compounds that will continue to suppress psychotic symptoms while producing minimal undesirable adverse effects. But it is important to repeat that the point to be remembered is that antipsychotic drugs, as a group, are one of the safest groups of drugs in common use and are the greatest advance in the treatment of schizophrenia that has occurred to date.

The adverse effects of first-generation antipsychotic drugs can be dis-cussed as a group. Some adverse effects are more common with particular drugs, but the differences are not great. And, like adverse effects to all drugs used in medicine, it is not possible to predict with any accuracy which person is likely to get which adverse effect. . . .

Tardive Dyskinesia

Tardive dyskinesia is the single most important adverse effect of first-generation antipsychotic drugs. Much of the fear of using these drugs is in fact linked to this adverse effect, and it has become a banner regularly waved by anti-psychiatry zealots. Tardive dyskinesia is certainly a serious problem, but it is not nearly as common as the apostles of hysteria have claimed.

Tardive dyskinesia consists of involuntary movements of the tongue and mouth, such as chewing movements, sucking movements, pushing the cheek out with the tongue, and smacking of the lips. Occasionally these are accom-panied by jerky, purposeless movements of the arms or legs or, rarely, even the whole body. It usually begins while the patient is taking the drug but, rarely, may begin shortly after the drug has been stopped. Occasionally it persists indefinitely, and no effective treatment has been found to date.

The incidence of tardive dyskinesia is difficult to ascertain because it may occur as part of the disease process as well as being a side effect of medication. A study of the records of over 600 patients admitted to an asylum in England between 1845 and 1890 found an "extraordinary prevalence of abnormal movements and postures. . . . Movement disorder, often equivalent to tardive dyskinesia, was noted in nearly one-third of schizophrenics." A recent study of spontaneous dyskinesia in individuals with schizophrenia who had never been treated with antipsychotic medication reported it to be present in 12 percent of individuals below age 30 and in 25 percent of individuals aged 30 to 50. Most estimates of the incidence of tardive dyskinesia have assumed that all such cases are drug-related when in fact a substantial percentage are not. In a study of this problem aptly titled "Not All That Moves Is Tardive Dyskinesia," Khot and Wyatt concluded that the true incidence of drug-related tardive dyskinesia was less than 20 percent. This also falls within the 10 to 20 percent range estimated by the American Psychiatric Association's 1980 task force on the subject.

Much current research is taking place in an attempt to identify which persons with schizophrenia are most likely to get tardive dyskinesia. It is clear that the older the person, the more susceptible he or she is. It is also clearly established that women are more susceptible than men and that patients with more affective symptoms (for example, depression or mania) are more susceptible. Many other risk factors are being investigated including ethnicity (higher in Jews, lower in Asians), dose of medication, duration of medication, use of depot injectable medication, use of anticholinergic drugs, concurrent diabetes, concurrent alcohol or drug abuse, concurrent evidence of organic brain disease, and concurrent Parkinsonian-like symptoms, but none of them has yet been clearly established. There is also no firm evidence that any particular first-generation antipsychotic is more or less likely to cause tardive dyskinesia.

Previously, most people believed that once the symptoms of tardive dyskinesia began they would almost always get worse if the person continued taking the antipsychotic medication. This put many individuals with schizophrenia into a cruel bind, needing the medication to remain well but not wishing to worsen the early symptoms of tardive dyskinesia. A 10-year follow-up of 44 patients with tardive dyskinesia who remained on the same antipsychotic medication found that in 30 percent the tardive dyskinesia got worse, in 50 percent it remained the same, and in 20 percent the tardive dyskinesia actually improved. In another 10-year follow-up study it was reported that approximately 5 percent of existing cases of tardive dyskinesia disappeared each year *even in individuals continuing to take their antipsychotic medications.*

According to Dr. Daniel Casey, a leading researcher on tardive dyskinesia, 20 patients out of every 100 with schizophrenia will get tardive dyskinesia; among these, five patients will have their tardive dyskinesia completely disappear and five others will have at least a 50 percent improvement. Casey then added: "Of the 10 remaining TD [tardive dyskinesia] patients, almost all of them will have mild to moderate symptoms. Severe TD is a very uncommon syndrome that probably occurs in approximately 1 in 100 to 1 in 1,000 TD patients."

The best treatment for tardive dyskinesia is to switch the person to a second-generation antipsychotic, especially clozapine. All patients taking first-generation antipsychotics should be watched for early signs such as tongue movements. The use of the Abnormal Involuntary Movement Scale (AIMS) is useful for measuring the progression of tardive dyskinesia. For fully developed cases of tardive dyskinesia there is no known effective treatment, although trials of levodopa, vitamin E, oxypertine, sodium valproate, and tiapride have shown some promise. . . .

The Medication-Savvy Consumer and Family

Smart consumers and their families quickly learn what Edward Francell teaches—that medication is "the foundation of recovery." Francell, a social worker who has been diagnosed at various times as having schizophrenia and manic-depressive illness, says that his improvement really began when he shifted from "passive recipiency" of whatever psychiatrists told him to do to active, informed involvement. "Recovery began," said Francell, "when I got off the bench and became an active player in the treatment game," shifting from spectator to player. . . .

Mad in America

My interest in this subject, the history of medical treatments for the mad, began in a simple manner. In the summer of 1998, I stumbled onto an unusual line of psychiatric research, which I reported on for the *Boston Globe.* In order to study the "biology" of schizophrenia, American scientists were giving the mentally ill chemical agents—amphetamines, ketamine, and methylphenidate—expected to heighten their psychosis. That seemed an unusual thing to do, particularly since some of the people recruited into the experiments had come stumbling into emergency rooms seeking help. Equally striking was the response of "ex-patients" to the experiments.

They were outraged, but not particularly *surprised.*

That seemed more than a little curious—why would they not be surprised?—and then I bumped into several studies in the medical literature that really struck me as odd. Over the past twenty-five years, outcomes for people in the United States with schizophrenia have *worsened.* They are now no better than they were in the first decades of the twentieth century, when the therapy of the day was to wrap the insane in wet sheets. Even more perplexing, schizophrenia outcomes in the United States and other developed countries today are much worse than in the poor countries of the world. The World Health Organization [WHO] has looked at this question repeatedly—initially, nobody could believe this disparity in outcomes—and each time it has come back with the same result. Suffer a psychotic break in a poor country like India or Nigeria, and chances are that in a couple of years you will be doing fairly well. But suffer a similar break in the United States or other developed countries, and it is likely that you will become chronically ill. Why should that be so? Why should living in a country with rich resources, and with advanced medical treatments for disorders of every kind, be so toxic to those who are severely mentally ill? Or to put it another way, why should living in countries where the poor struggle every day to find enough to eat and treatment for a mental disorder is likely to be provided by a shaman, whose armamentarium may consist of witch-doctor potions, be so helpful to recovery?

This medical failure is a profound one. More than 2 million Americans suffer from schizophrenia, and their difficult lives bring unimaginable heartache to their families, and to others who love them. Too many of the people so diagnosed end up in prison, homeless, or shuttling in and out of psychiatric hospitals. Our society as a whole is affected by this failure as well, and in a way that we don't normally appreciate. We usually think of the financial burden: Schizophrenia, it is said, is a "disease" that costs the United States more than $45 billion annually. But there is a much deeper cost. We, as a society, are *estranged* from the "mad" in our midst. We fear them and their illness. We read of occasional acts of violence committed by those said to be schizophrenic, and we respond by setting up programs that focus on keeping them medicated. But is that the best response? If the medications work so well, then why do "schizophrenics" fare so poorly in the United States?

The search to understand this therapeutic failure necessarily takes one deep into history. The past becomes a foil for understanding the present. It is a journey that begins with the founding of the first hospital in the colonies by Pennsylvania Quakers in 1751, and from there one can trace a path, however winding and twisted, to the poor outcomes of today. It is also a history that contains one surprise after another. For instance, we think of the 1800s as a time when the insane were routinely chained up and neglected, and yet, in the early nineteenth century, there arose a form of humanitarian care that has never been equaled since. Go forward one hundred years, however, and the path detours into one of the darkest chapters in America's history, one that, I believe, we have never dared to fully explore. Yet it is in that dark chapter that one finds the seeds for today's failure.

What one also quickly discovers is that a history of mad medicine reveals very little about what it is like to be "crazy" or "insane," or, as we say today, "ill with schizophrenia." However, it does reveal a great deal about the society that would "cure" these patients. Medical treatments for the severely mentally ill inevitably reflect the societal and philosophical values of the day. What is the nature of man? What does it mean to be human? Where is the line between "normals" and the "mad" to be drawn? What rights do the "mentally ill" have over their own minds? The medical treatments a society employs all arise from its answers to those questions. As such, mad medicine does provide a prism through which to view a society, and that is why the poor outcomes for those diagnosed with schizophrenia raise questions, I would think, for all of us. . . .

This book began with a straightforward goal, and that was to explore why schizophrenia outcomes are so poor in the United States today. It seemed like a simple question, and yet it quickly opened the door to a larger story—the story of how we as a society have historically treated those we call "mad." It clearly is a troubled history, one that begs to be better known. There are, perhaps, many lessons that can be drawn from it, but one seems to stand out above all others. Any hope of reforming our care of those "ill with schizophrenia" will require us to rediscover, in our science, a capacity for humility and candor.

There is one moment in the past where we can find such humility. It can be seen in moral therapy as practiced in its most ideal form, by the Quakers in York, England, or by Thomas Kirkbride at the Pennsylvania Hospital for the Insane in the mid-nineteenth century. In their writings, the York Quakers regularly confessed that they understood little about any possible physical causes of madness. But what they did see clearly was "brethren" who were suffering and needed comfort. That was the understanding that drove their care, and so they sought to run their asylum in a way that was best for their patients, rather than in a way that was best for them, as managers of the asylum. They put their patients' comforts and needs *first.* They also perceived of their patients as having a God-given capacity for recovery, and thus simply tried to "assist Nature" in helping them heal. It was care that was at once humanitarian and optimistic, and it did help many get well. But equally important, the York Quakers were quite willing to accept that many of their brethren would continue in their crazy ways. That was all right, too. They would provide a refuge for those who could not regain their mental health and at least make sure they had warm shelter and good food.

In the 1960s, as the United States set out to reform its care, it did look back to moral treatment for inspiration. President John Kennedy and the Joint Commission on Mental Illness and Mental Health spoke of the need for American society to see those who were distraught in mind as part of the human family, and deserving of empathy. Eugenics had stirred America to treat the severely mentally ill with scorn and neglect, and it was time to change our ways. We would welcome the mentally ill back into society. Asylums would be replaced with community care. But the design of that reform also rested on a medical notion of the most unusual sort, that neuroleptics "might be described as moral treatment in pill form." The confusion in that perception was profound: Neuroleptics were a medical treatment with roots in frontal lobotomy and the brain-damaging therapeutics of the eugenics era. Our vision for reform and the medical treatment that would be the cornerstone of that reform were hopelessly at odds.

Something had to give, and the moment of choice occurred very early on. The research study that launched the emptying of the state hospitals was the six-week trial conducted by the National Institute of Mental Health in the early 1960s, which concluded that neuroleptics were safe and antischizophrenic. But then, a very short while later, the NIMH found in a follow-up study that the patients who had been treated with neuroleptics were more likely than the placebo patients to have been rehospitalized. Something clearly was amiss. A choice, in essence, was presented to psychiatry. Would it hold to the original vision of reform, which called for the provision of care that would promote *recovery*? If so, it would clearly need to rethink the merits of neuroleptics. The drugs were apparently making people chronically ill, and that was quite apart from whatever other drawbacks they might have. Or would it cast aside questions of recovery and instead defend the drugs?

There can be no doubt today about which choice American psychiatry made. Evidence of the harm caused by the drugs was simply allowed to pile up and up, then pushed away in the corner where it wouldn't be seen. There was Bockoven's study that relapse rates were lower in the pre-neuroleptic era. Rappaport's study. Mosher's. Reports of neuroleptic malignant syndrome and tardive dyskinesia. Van Putten's report of medicated patients in boarding homes spending their days idly looking at television, too numbed in mind and spirit to even have a favorite program. Studies detailing the high incidence of akathisia, Parkinson's, and a myriad of other types of motor dysfunction.

Case reports of akathisia driving patients so out of their minds it made them suicidal or even homicidal. Harding's study and then the WHO studies. All of this research told of suffering, and of loss. And where were the studies showing that the drugs were leading people to *recovery*? Researchers studiously avoided this question. In 1998, British investigators reviewed the published results of 2,000 clinical trials of neuroleptics over the previous fifty years and found that only one in twenty-five studies even bothered to assess "daily living activities" or "social functioning." The trials again and again simply looked at whether the drugs knocked down visible symptoms of psychosis and ignored what was really happening to the patients as *people.*

It is not difficult today to put together a wish list for reform. An obvious place to start would be to revisit the work of Emil Kraepelin. Were many of his psychotic patients actually suffering from encephalitis lethargica, and has that led to an overly pessimistic view of schizophrenia? The next step would be to investigate what the poor countries are doing right. How are the "mad" treated in India and Nigeria? What are the secrets of care—beyond not keeping patients regularly medicated—that help so many people in those countries get well? Closer to home, any number of studies would be welcome. A study that compares neuroleptics to sedatives would be helpful. How would conventional treatment stack up against care that provided "delusional" people with a safe place to live, food, and the use of sedatives to help restore their sleep-wake cycles? Or how about an NIMH-funded experiment modeled on the work of Finnish investigators? There, physicians led by Yrjö Alanen at the University of Turku have developed a treatment program that combines social support, family therapy, vocational therapy, and the selective use of antipsychotics. They are picking apart differences in patient types and have found that some patients do better with low doses of antipsychotics, and others with no drugs at all. They are reporting great results—a majority of patients so treated are remaining well for years, and holding jobs—so why not try it here?

At the top of this wish list, though, would be a simple plea for honesty. Stop telling those diagnosed with schizophrenia that they suffer from too much dopamine or serotonin activity and that the drugs put these brain chemicals back into "balance." That whole spiel is a form of medical fraud, and it is impossible to imagine any other group of patients—ill, say, with cancer or cardiovascular disease—being deceived in this way.

In truth, the prevailing view in American psychiatry today is that there are any number of factors—biological and environmental—that can lead to schizophrenia. A person's genetic makeup obviously may play a role. Relatives of people with schizophrenia appear to be at increased risk of developing the disorder, and thus the thought is that they may inherit genes that make them less able to cope with environmental stresses. The genetic factors are said to *predispose* people to schizophrenia, rather than cause it. Another prominent theory is that complications during pregnancy or during delivery may affect the developing brain, and that this trauma leads to deficiencies in brain function once neuronal systems have matured. Yet another thought is that some people with schizophrenia have difficulty filtering incoming sensory data, and that this problem is due to abnormal function in brain cells known as interneurons. A number of investigators are still studying the role that different neurotransmitters may play in the disorder. The biological paths to schizophrenia may be many, but none is yet known for sure. It is also possible that the capacity to go mad, as it were, is in all of us. Extreme emotional trauma can clearly trigger psychosis, and some argue that psychosis is a mechanism for coping with that trauma. That view of the disorder is consistent with the fact that in the absence of neuroleptics, many people who suffer a schizophrenic break recover from it, and never relapse again.

Thus, if we wanted to be candid today in our talk about schizophrenia, we would admit to this: Little is known about what causes schizophrenia. Antipsychotic drugs do not fix any known brain abnormality, nor do they put brain chemistry back into balance. What they do is alter brain function in a manner that diminishes certain characteristic symptoms. We also know that they cause an increase in dopamine receptors, which is a change associated both with tardive dyskinesia and an increased biological vulnerability to psychosis, and that long-term outcomes are much better in countries where such medications are less frequently used. Although such candor might be humbling to our sense of medical prowess, it might also lead us to rethink what we, as a society, should do to help those who struggle with "madness."

But, none of this, I'm afraid, is going to happen. Olanzapine is now Eli Lilly's top-selling drug, surpassing even Prozac. There will be no rethinking of the merits of a form of care that is bringing profits to so many. Indeed, it is hard to be optimistic that the future will bring any break with the past. There is no evidence of any budding humility in American psychiatry that might stir the introspection that would be a necessary first step toward reform. At least in the public arena, all we usually hear about are advancements in knowledge and treatment, as if the march of progress is certain. Eli Lilly and Janssen have even teamed up with leaders of U.S. mental-health advocacy groups to mount "educational" missions to poor countries in East Asia, so that we can export our model of care to them. Hubris is everywhere, and in mad medicine, that has always been a prescription for disaster. In fact, if the past is any guide to the future, today we can be certain of only one thing: The day will come when people will look back at our current medicines for schizophrenia and the stories we tell to patients about their abnormal brain chemistry, and they will shake their heads in utter disbelief.

CHALLENGE QUESTIONS

Are Antipsychotic Medications the Treatment of Choice for People with Psychosis?

1. Psychiatrist E. Fuller Torrey has spent much of his career educating the public, patients, and their families about schizophrenia and its treatments. If you had the opportunity to interview Dr. Torrey, what would be the most challenging question that you would ask him about the treatment of people with schizophrenia?
2. Much has been written in recent years about the rights of patients to refuse medication. What issues should be considered in determining whether psychotic individuals should be forced to take antipsychotic medication against their expressed will?
3. Imagine that you are a clinician who is treating an individual with delusions, hallucinations, and disordered thought. What information would you want to gather in order to make a diagnosis? Assuming that you conclude that the individual has schizophrenia, what issues would you consider in making a recommendation regarding antipsychotic medication?
4. Imagine that you are a researcher who has just received a grant to compare the relative effectiveness of antipsychotic medication and herbal remedies for the treatment of psychotic symptoms. What kind of research design would you recommend?
5. Imagine that you have just been awarded a multi-million dollar grant to develop the most humane intervention for treating people with schizophrenia. Discuss the components that you would include in the treatment program.

Suggested Readings

Amador, X., & Johanson, A-L. (2000). *I am not sick: I don't need help!* Peconic, NY: Vida Press.

Amador, X. (Ed.)., & David, A. S. (Ed.). (2004). *Insight and psychosis: Awareness of illness in schizophrenia and related disorders.* New York: Oxford University Press.

Boyle, M. (2002). *Schizophrenia: A scientific delusion?* New York: Routledge.

Nasar, S. (1999). *A beautiful mind: A biography of John Forbes Nash, Jr., winner of the Nobel Prize in economics, 1994.* New York: Simon & Schuster.

Szasz, T. (2002). *Liberation by oppression: A comparative study of slavery and psychiatry.* New Brunswick, NJ: Transaction Publishers.

Weiden, P. J., Scheifler, P. L., Diamond, R. J., & Ross, R. (1999). *Breakthroughs in antipsychotic medications: A guide for consumers, families, and clinicians.* New York: W.W. Norton & Company.

ISSUE 10

Is Ritalin Overprescribed?

YES: Peter R. Breggin, from *The Ritalin Fact Book: What Your Doctor Won't Tell You about ADHD and Stimulant Drugs* (Perseus, 2002)

NO: Russell A. Barkley, from *Taking Charge of ADHD: The Complete, Authoritative Guide for Parents* (Guilford, 2000)

ISSUE SUMMARY

YES: Physician Peter R. Breggin asserts that Ritalin and similar stimulants are dangerous addictive medications that should not be prescribed to children because they suppress growth and lead to a number of worrisome physical and psychological symptoms.

NO: Psychologist and prominent ADHD researcher Russell A. Barkley objects to criticisms of Ritalin and similar stimulants, maintaining that these medications serve as important parts of interventions aimed at helping children increase their attention and concentration.

Fifteen years ago it would have been unfathomable to imagine a school-aged child entering a school and gunning down classmates; yet such images have become indelibly marked in the minds of Americans. Such alarming events have caused educators, parents, and mental health professionals to increasingly focus their attention on the behavior of young people, look for ways to help underachievers reach their potential, and make sure troubled youth get the help they need. Children with attention deficit hyperactivity disorder (ADHD) have been of particular concern because of the psychological problems they experience and also because of the disruption they cause at school, at home, and in the community.

ADHD is a disorder involving inattentiveness and hyperactivity-impulsivity, and it is a condition that is usually evident early in life. Even during the toddler years, children with this condition show a range of problematic behaviors, including defiance, resistance, and hostility. Many of them are incessant in their hyperactivity, incapable of paying attention even briefly. Their lives usually involve impaired relationships and serious inner distress. The most common interventions for ADHD involve behavioral techniques and medication, particularly stimulants such as Ritalin (methylphenidate). Proponents of medication express relief about the fact that such an effective intervention is available to help young people who need it; opponents are distressed by the increasing tendency to rely on a chemical for controlling active children rather than on methods that have been used for generations.

Peter Breggin, who is widely known and respected for his critical analysis of trends in psychiatry, is appalled by the extensive use of Ritalin-like medications. Breggin raises serious concerns about the physical dangers and psychological risks associated with these medications, and argues that the literature supporting their effectiveness is limited and biased.

Russell Barkley, who has established an international reputation as a researcher and expert on ADHD, views behavior disorders such as ADHD as serious conditions of brain dysfunction that warrant medical intervention; he asserts that stimulant medication helps ADHD children improve their attention and concentration, and therefore succeed academically.

POINT	COUNTERPOINT
• Like amphetamines, stimulants have a high potential for abuse and can cause potentially serious withdrawal symptoms.	• There are no reported cases of addiction or serious drug dependence on these medications; nor does research support the notion that children taking these drugs are at greater risk of abusing other substances during their teenage years.
• The growth of many children is suppressed or even stunted by stimulants.	• It is a myth to suggest that stimulant medications stunt children's growth; recent studies have shown that this is not as much of a problem as once thought.
• Drug-company propaganda has led the public to believe that psychiatric drugs correct biochemical imbalances; in fact, these drugs disrupt normal brain function.	• ADHD is largely a genetic disorder associated with deficiencies in brain functioning; stimulant medication helps normalize functioning in most cases.
• There is no evidence that stimulant drugs actually improve academic performance. Drug-induced impairments cannot make children wiser; they can only make children sit down, shut up, and do what they are told.	• Stimulant medication's ability to improve children's attention span, resistance to distraction, and concentration is beneficial to their academic performance.
• There are hundreds of cases documenting Ritalin-induced psychiatric reactions including agitation, hostility, depression, psychosis and other troubling conditions.	• Although stimulant medications can produce temporary symptoms of psychosis at very high doses, such reactions are very rare at low doses; such reactions occur in fewer than 1% of cases and last only until the dose wears off.

YES

Peter R. Breggin

The Ritalin Fact Book: What Your Doctor Won't Tell You about ADHD and Stimulant Drugs

Of Cages and Creativity— How Stimulants Work

If you are considering the use of stimulant drugs for yourself or your children, you probably want answers to the following questions:

> Do stimulants really help children?
> How do they work?
> Are they dangerous?

In response to these questions, too many doctors tell parents and patients that stimulants work well and have few if any serious risks. They may also explain that the drugs work by "correcting biochemical imbalances" or "improving focus and attention." . . .

Observing Children in the Classroom

The effectiveness of stimulant drugs is often "proven" by asking teachers to rate the behavior of children in a classroom setting. The teachers will be given checklists to fill out for the children containing items that are used in the official diagnostic manual to determine if a child has ADHD. This *Diagnostic and Statistical Manual of Mental Disorders, IV* is published by the American Psychiatric Association (1994). It contains items such as "often fidgets with hands or feet or squirms in seat," "often leaves seat in classroom," "often blurts out answers," "has difficulty awaiting turn," and "often does not seem to listen."

Teachers and parents almost always report a reduction of these kinds of behaviors in children given stimulants. The teachers and parents have not been told that this involves a suppression of spontaneous behavior with enforced submissiveness and so they fail to recognize that the drugs are suppressing or dulling the children.

Teachers are especially likely to find that the children are "improved" because they are asked to rate behaviors such as "blurts out answers" or "leaves seat" that are especially reduced when overall spontaneity is crushed. The reduction in spontaneous behavior, as well as the enforced submissiveness, makes the children less talkative, less likely to leave their seats, and less likely to social-ize with their neighbors. These reductions in overall spontaneous behavior make it easier for teachers to run their classrooms without having to pay atten-tion to the individual child.

Exactly as in the animal studies, stimulants also make children more compulsive. For the chimpanzees, this means sitting by themselves while they groom one small spot on the arm or play endlessly with a pebble. For our chil-dren, this drug-enforced compulsivity makes them focus on previously unen-durable boring tasks such as copying from the board or writing something down ten times. These children often become so compulsive that they bear down too hard on the paper as they write or persist at the task even when asked to stop. Studies describe them as abnormally over-focused. However, teachers and parents are likely to mistake such behavior for a genuine "buckling down" on schoolwork and homework.

Table 1 is entitled "Harmful Stimulant Drug Reactions Commonly Misi-dentified as 'Therapeutic' or 'Beneficial.'" When children are given Ritalin, Adderall, and other stimulant drugs, they frequently develop these kinds of reactions. Unfortunately, researchers, doctors, teachers, and parents routinely misinterpret these toxic effects as improvements in the children.

Do the children learn better? Are their scholastic abilities improved? Of course not. Drug-induced impairments cannot make a child wiser, more thoughtful, or better informed. They can only make children sit down, shut up, and do what they are told. As we shall see, there is no evidence that stimulant

Table 1

Harmful Stimulant Drug Reactions Commonly Misidentified as "Therapeutic" or "Beneficial," Selected from 20 Controlled Clinical Trials Involving Children Diagnosed with ADHD

Obsessive Compulsive Effects	Social Withdrawal Effects	Behaviorally Suppressive Effects
Compulsive persistence at meaningless activities (called stereotypical or perseverative behavior)	Social withdrawal and isolation	Compliant in structured environ-ment; socially inhibited, passive, and submissive
Increased obsessive-compulsive behavior (e.g., repeating chores endlessly and ineffectively)	General dampened social behavior	Somber, subdued, apathetic, lethargic, dopey, dazed, and tired
Mental rigidity (called cognitive perseveration)	Reduced communication and socialization	Bland, emotionally flat, humor-less, not smiling, depressed, and sad with frequent crying
Inflexible thinking	Decreased responsiveness to parents and other children	Lacking in initiative, spontaneity, curiosity, surprise, or pleasure
Overly narrow or excessive focusing	Increased solitary play and diminished overall play	

Modified from Breggin (1999b, 1999c). References to the 20 clinical trials provided in Breggin (1999b, 1999c).

drugs actually improve academic performance. But they do sometimes lead to improved grades because many teachers will reward more submissive, unobtrusive behavior with better grades.

Some of the staunchest advocates of stimulants for children have in effect admitted that the drugs work by enforcing blind obedience. Russell Barkley, one of the most widely published Ritalin/ADHD advocates, uses the term "compliance" to describe this improved behavior. Stimulant drugs do indeed tend to make children more compliant, that is, more manageable and obedient. They do so at the expense of their imaginations, their creativity, their capacity to generate activity, and their overall enthusiasm for life.

"Correcting Biochemical Imbalances"

Recently I gave a lecture to students and professionals at a medical center. Initially, some of them were surprised when I explained that all psychoactive drugs disrupt normal brain function. They, too, had been misled by drug-company propaganda to believe that psychiatric drugs correct biochemical imbalances. However, several were immediately able to see the truth once I reminded them about the facts.

Research on psychoactive drugs almost always begins with animal studies. As a first step, a series of animal brains will be examined to measure the normal activity of a specific function, such as the rate of firing of a particular type of brain cell (neuron). Tiny electrodes may be inserted into the brains to measure the activity of the cells. Or the animal brain may be removed in order to determine the normal amount of a specific chemical in the region.

Next, a new series of animals will be given the stimulant drug, such as Ritalin or Adderall. Then their brains will be examined to determine how the drug changes these normal functions. For example, the brain cells may begin to fire more rapidly than normal for a while and then, later on, more slowly than normal. Or the specific chemical messenger may increase above normal in amount for a while and then decrease below normal later on.

The pharmacological action of any psychoactive drug is demonstrated by how it disrupts the normal function of an animal's brain. That disruption is the basis of the psychoactive effect. The researchers, the drug company, the FDA, and everyone else involved in the field will then assume that the drug disrupts human brain function in exactly the same fashion. When textbooks or reviews discuss the drug's "mode of action," they will simply describe what has been learned from research on how the drug interferes with the functioning of the normal animal brain.

However, when the drug company and its experts get ready to present this information to the medical profession and the public, they will perform remarkable verbal sleights of hand. The known fact that the drug disrupts normal brain function will be ignored and instead the drug will be falsely promoted as correcting biochemical imbalances. The claim about correcting biochemical imbalances is a deliberate deception to make the drugs look positive. Similarly, the known fact that the drug suppresses behavior will be ignored, and in the case of the stimulants, nothing at all will be said about it. How the drug actually works will remain shrouded in mystery. . . .

How Stimulants Cause Psychiatric Disorders

Stimulants are powerful psychoactive substances that impact the brain and mind. We have already seen that their primary or therapeutic impact involves flattening all spontaneous behavior, enforcing submissiveness, and causing obsessive focus on rote activities. Therefore, it should be no surprise that they can cause a variety of other mental abnormalities.

In reviewing adverse drug reaction reports made to the FDA concerning Ritalin, I found hundreds of cases of Ritalin-induced psychiatric reactions. Children taking Ritalin were most commonly reported to develop—in the following order—agitation, hostility, depression and psychotic depression, abnormal thinking, hallucinations, psychosis, and emotional instability (called "lability"). There were many reports of overdose, intentional overdose, and suicide attempts, confirming the risk of depression and potential suicide. . . .

I have taken several approaches to summarizing the overall adverse effects of stimulants. Table 1 . . . uses data from twenty clinical trials to describe adverse psychiatric effects such as apathy, depression, and overfocusing that are commonly mistaken for improvements in children's behavior.

Table 2, "Toxic Reactions to Stimulants: Usually in Overdose and Occasionally at Low Doses," is drawn entirely from the "Overdose" sections of the

Table 2

Toxic Reactions to Stimulants: Usually in Overdose and Occasionally at Low Doses

Agitation	Elevated heart rate
Tremors	Palpitations
Increased neurologic reflexes	Cardiac arrhythmias
Muscle twitching	Hypertension
Convulsions	Enlarged pupils
Coma	Dry mouth, nose, and eyes
Euphoria	Increased respiration[a]
Confusion	Nausea, vomiting, diarrhea,
Hallucinations	and cramps[a]
Delirium	Muscle breakdown[a]
Sweating	Hypotension, shock, and
Flushing	circulatory collapse[a]
Headache	Panic states[a]
High fever	Assaultiveness[a]

[a]Indicates the item was taken from the FDA-approved overdose section of the labels for Dexedrine, Adderall, and Adderall XR, but not Ritalin. The remainder was taken from the Ritalin label with some overlap. The Dexedrine and Adderall labels both state that "individual patient response to amphetamines varies widely" and "toxic symptoms occasionally occur as an idiosyncrasy at doses as low as 2 mg." The Adderall XR label also states that patient responses "vary widely" and "toxic symptoms" may occur "at low doses." *Most of the symptoms can occur with any of the stimulants at routine clinical doses.*

official FDA-approved labels for Ritalin, Dexedrine, Adderall, and Adderall XR. Almost any adverse reaction that occurs in overdose can also occur at lower doses.

For an overview of stimulant effects taken from a broader variety of medical sources other than the drug labels, see Table 3, "Overview of Harmful Reactions to Stimulant Drugs: Ritalin, Dexedrine, Adderall, Concerta, and Metadate."

Tables 1, 2, and 3 cover most of the adverse effects of stimulants that are likely to show up in routine clinical use. They are compiled from standard or mainstream sources that tend to approve or advocate the use of stimulant drugs. There is a great tendency in the medical literature to minimize adverse drug effects in order to support or promote the use of medications in general. Therefore, the individual sources are not as comprehensive as the data that I have compiled in this book from all of the sources. *In addition, few if any*

Table 3

Overview of Harmful Reactions to Stimulant Drugs: Ritalin, Dexedrine, Adderall, Concerta, and Metadate

Brain and Mind Function	Gastrointestinal Function	Endocrine and Metabolic Function
Obsessive-compulsive behavior	Anorexia	Pituitary dysfunction, including growth hormone and prolactin disruption
Zombie-like (robotic) behavior with loss of emotional spontaneity	Nausea, vomiting, bad taste	
	Stomachache	Weight loss
Drowsiness, "dopey," reduced alertness	Cramps	Growth suppression
	Dry mouth	Disturbed sexual function
Abnormal movements, tics, Tourette's	Constipation, diarrhea	**Cardiovascular Function**
	Liver dysfunction	Hypertension
Nervous habits (picking at skin, pulling hair)	**Withdrawal and Rebound Reactions**	Abnormal heartbeat
Convulsions		Heart disease
Headache	Insomnia	Cardiac arrest
Stroke	Excessive sleep	**Other Functions**
Mania, psychosis	Evening crash	Blurred vision
Visual and tactile hallucinations	Depression	Hair loss
Agitation, anxiety, nervousness	Rebound worsening of ADHD-like symptoms	Dizziness
Insomnia	Overactivity and irritability	Hypersensitivity reaction with rash
Irritability, hostility, aggression		
Depression, suicide, easy crying, social withdrawal		
Confusion, mental impairments (decreased cognition and learning)		
Stimulant addiction and abuse		

Modified from Breggin (1999a, 1999c).

sources fully address the brain damage and dysfunction produced by these drugs, including strong evidence for stimulant-induced brain shrinkage, cell death, and persistent biochemical changes. . . .

Stimulants Commonly Cause Mental Disorders

Stimulants commonly cause a variety of serious emotional disturbances. I am not alone in drawing this conclusion. A handbook frequently used by physicians lists the . . . rates of adverse mental effects caused by stimulants [in Table 4].

The rates in [Table 4] are drawn from clinical studies. Not many parents would expose their children to these drugs if they were aware of the frequency with which the drugs can impair a child's mental life.

The studies are usually conducted by advocates for drugs and tend to minimize adverse drug reactions. Therefore, most of the rates are actually higher than reported in [Table 4]. While the rates for these adverse effects vary widely from study to study, the main point is inescapable: Stimulants frequently harm the brain and mind.

As a part of my scientific presentation at the NIH Consensus Development Conference on the Diagnosis and Treatment of Attention Deficit Hyperactivity Disorder in 1998, I reviewed eight representative controlled clinical trials to estimate the frequency of adverse effects. All of the studies were conducted by advocates of stimulants and aimed at proving that the drugs are safe and effective. I have reviewed them in the scientific literature and in *Talking Back to Ritalin* (rev. ed., 2001a). Based on these studies, I estimate that the reported rate of serious adverse reactions in children was as high as 10–20 percent or more. The real rate in clinical practice would be even higher.

In reviewing Table 4, it is important to realize that symptoms such as "irritability," "agitation," and "confused" are related to each other. They reflect gross underlying brain dysfunctions that then become manifested in varying ways. When brain function is disrupted in such a global or generalized way, almost any mental abnormality or mixture of abnormalities can result. . . .

Table 4

Rates of Adverse Mental Effects Reported in Stimulant Clinical Trials

Adverse Stimulant Effect	Amphetamines (Dexedrine, Adderall)	Methylphenidate (Ritalin, Concerta, Metadate ER)
Drowsiness, less alert	5.5%	5.7%
Confused, "dopey"	10.3% (8–12%)	3.9% (2–10%)
Depression	39%	8.7%
Agitation, restlessness	More than 10%	6.7% (3.3% to more than 10%)
Irritability, stimulation	25% (17–29%)	17.3% (11–19%)

The data are from Maxmen and Ward (1995, p. 366). The numbers are percentages of patients reported in studies to suffer from the adverse effects. Numbers in parentheses represent the range reported in studies.

My clinical experience confirms the data in Table 4: Children taking stimulants frequently become very depressed and even suicidal. Their doctors often fail to recognize the source of the depression. Instead of stopping the stimulant medication, they add an antidepressant, causing even greater emotional disturbances in the child.

How common is stimulant-induced depression? Very common! . . .

How Stimulants Harm the Child's Body

. . . From the heart to the skin, stimulants can also harm a variety of other organs of the body. By interfering with normal growth-hormone production, stimulants impair and even stunt the growth of the entire body.

Some harmful effects on the body result indirectly from the disruption of brain function, some result more directly from toxic effects on the organs themselves, and some result from both. . . .

Stunting Growth

In many cases, the growth of children is obviously suppressed or even stunted by stimulants. Some of the children look skinny and unhealthy as if starving, while others seem normal. Most will rebound with an unbelievably rapid growth in height and weight—if the drugs are stopped while the child is still growing. In one study, Ritalin reduced the expected monthly weight gain by 25 percent. When the drug was stopped, weight gain accelerated far above the normally expected rate.

When children seem to be growing well while taking stimulants, some doctors or parents will observe, "John's very big; the stimulants haven't hurt him." Unfortunately, we don't know how tall or large Johnny might have become without the drug, and the fact that he's achieved an even above-average size says little about the drug's actual effect on his unique genetic endowment for growth.

Too many doctors are misled into believing that growth suppression is a relatively harmless problem that results from a child losing his or her appetite. However, there's more to it than the mere loss of appetite. The stimulants cause marked dysfunction in the production of growth hormone. Specifically, they cause an abnormal increase in growth hormone during the day and then an abnormal compensatory suppression of the hormone at night, when it most significantly affects growth.

The impact on growth hormone is so dramatic that researchers have observed that growth-hormone levels can be used as a marker for whether or not children are taking their medication. If the growth-hormone cycle isn't disrupted, then the children are not taking the medication. Because stimulants always impair growth-hormone production, we should assume that there is always some impairment of growth, even if it remains grossly undetectable.

Some doctors used to tell parents not to worry about growth suppression because there is a compensatory growth spurt when the drugs are stopped. While the body does try to catch up when the stimulant is stopped, the phase of accelerated growth is abnormally rapid and not necessarily altogether healthy. In addition, there's no guarantee that irreversible harm hasn't been done along the way during weeks or months of stimulant treatment. Furthermore, nowadays children are kept on stimulants for months or years at a time, so the body is given no opportunity to go through a growth spurt.

The disruption of growth hormone should be viewed as an ominous finding. It means that all growth processes are being impaired, including the growth of the brain, heart, and lungs. The entire body relies on growth hormone to regulate its developmental processes. Citing many research reports, a respected research team wrote:

> Research reveals that methylphenidate stimulates daytime release of growth hormone, disrupting the usual nocturnal release. This is troublesome since disturbances in the normal release of growth hormone may not only influence height velocity but may also impair other critical aspects of physical development such as sexual maturation.

The researchers should also have emphasized the threat to the growth of the brain and hence the mind.

The authors of a medical textbook suggest that the growth lag caused by stimulants is temporary "in most cases." This assumes that the children are given regular drug vacations in order to catch up. Although these authors are staunch advocates of stimulants for children, they go on to recognize that "the effects on growth that the long-term use of stimulants has on children leads some physicians to believe that this drug should never be prescribed for children." This observation—like many others in this book—should give strength to parents who believe, as I do, that children should never be given these drugs for "ADHD" or the control of behavior.

Despite decades of sophisticated research demonstrating that stimulants disrupt growth hormone, cause growth suppression, and lead to accelerated growth spurts when stopped, some drug advocates have tried to demonstrate that there are no significant effects on growth. In my experience, the doctors who make these claims typically go to extremes in order to convince professionals and parents that it's safe to use these drugs. One such study was published in 1996 in an attempt to undermine a large, consistent body of research demonstrating growth suppression. However, the new study used only one measurement of height and weight for each child and attempted to draw conclusions from it. The researchers did not use consecutive measures on the same child to show the effect of the drug; they took one measure on every child and attempted to compare that one measurement to a similar measure in a control group of children who were not drug treated. Using these dubious methods as well as a badly flawed control group and questionable statistics, the authors leaped from one single measurement to a conclusion about the long-term effect of stimulants on growth. By contrast, many other studies have used multiple measurements to show a definite inhibition of growth.

As a result of disrupting pituitary function, stimulants also interfere with the normal cycles of prolactin production. Prolactin can be found throughout the body, but its functions are poorly understood. It does, however, participate in the regulation of sexual development, yet another fact that should raise caution in regard to giving stimulants to children and adolescents.

Causing Heart Problems

As already noted, stimulants produce a combined assault on the heart, first by overstimulating heart rate and blood pressure, and then by weakening the muscles of the overstressed organ. Palpitations are one signal that the heart is beating irregularly.

What's the result?

My review of spontaneous reports of adverse Ritalin effects made to the FDA disclosed a very large number of Ritalin-induced cases of cardiovascular disease. Many concerned the well-known problem of stimulant-caused hypertension. Most of them involved arrhythmias and conduction problems that sometimes cause sudden cardiac arrest. There were more than a dozen reports of cardiac arrest or heart failure. This was a relatively small portion of the 2,821 reports made during the period of time (1985 through early 1997) but presents an important signal of danger.

I have been consulted in several cases in which stimulant drugs have caused fatal cardiac arrhythmias in children. In one case, the child's heart on autopsy showed a pattern of deterioration that the coroner compared to changes he had observed in chronic cocaine addicts.

A number of animal studies confirm that stimulants such as Ritalin weaken heart muscle and reduce its function. Stimulants also cause high blood pressure, a special concern among African-American boys, who are especially prone to develop severe hypertension as relatively young adults. Weakened heart muscle combined with hypertension is, of course, a hazard for any human being.

Causing Strokes

Ritalin, Adderall, and all stimulants can cause strokes (cerebral vascular accidents). These potentially catastrophic events can result from bleeding or inflammation of the blood vessels in the brain. Hypertension probably plays a key role in many of these disasters. Physicians sometimes seem particularly unaware of stimulant-induced strokes, probably leading to underreporting of the problem.

Bleeding in the brain in association with oral amphetamine use has been reported in the literature since 1970. There are reports of strokes after a "single low dose exposure," but most reports have been made in association with stimulant abuse.

A report in *Lancet* in 1988 described the first published case of stroke involving Ritalin in a boy receiving the drug for hyperactivity. The author observed, "Physicians who prescribe methylphenidate [Ritalin] for long-term use should be aware of this potential complication and specifically question patients regarding symptoms of cerebral ischaemia [reduced blood flow], including headache." Remember that Ritalin and amphetamine both produce gross reductions in blood flow to the brain, thereby creating the conditions for stroke.

A report in 2000 in the *Journal of Child Neurology* describes the case of an eight-year-old boy who developed vasculitis and stroke after taking Ritalin for one and one-half years for hyperactivity. These authors also issue a warning: "We draw your attention to the risk of using methylphenidate [Ritalin] for a long period of time."

Overall, stimulants pose serious cardiovascular hazards. Individuals suffering from or at risk of experiencing hypertension, heart disease, or strokes should especially avoid stimulants. . . .

How Stimulants Cause Withdrawal, Addiction, and Abuse

The following remarkable warning appears in capital letters in a boxed section as the first item to be read in the Adderall and the Dexedrine labels:

> AMPHETAMINES HAVE A HIGH POTENTIAL FOR ABUSE. ADMINISTRATION OF AMPHETAMINES FOR PROLONGED PERIODS OF TIME MAY LEAD TO DRUG DEPENDENCE AND MUST BE AVOIDED.

Although it does not appear with the same strength in the Ritalin label, this statement is equally true for Ritalin and all of the other stimulants commonly used to treat children. It should also be taken as a warning that all of these drugs cause potentially severe withdrawal reactions.

Much of the medical profession acts as if it has never been admonished that stimulant administration for prolonged periods of time "must be avoided." Instead, long-term use of stimulants is often encouraged, and parents are told to keep their children on amphetamines for months and years.

If the medical profession were prescribing rationally, the forewarning to avoid long-term administration, and the lack of evidence for any long-term efficacy, would utterly prevent the prescription of stimulants to children or adults for more than a few weeks' duration.

Withdrawal Reactions and Worsening Behavior

Symptoms of withdrawal can take place a few hours after the last dose of a stimulant, so that children commonly begin to go into withdrawal by the evening or the next morning. If a child's behavior appears to get worse or to deteriorate in any way a few hours or more after taking a stimulant drug, there's a high probability that the child is undergoing a withdrawal reaction.

Teachers often observe, "I can tell when Johnny hasn't taken his medication," meaning that they can see his behavior become more distressed or distressing. They don't realize that this is typically caused by a withdrawal reaction rather than by Johnny's own problems.

Parents and teachers sometimes believe that a child needs stimulants because the child's behavior deteriorates when one or two doses are missed. Such abrupt changes in a child are more likely due to withdrawal symptoms than to a child's inherent need for the drug. If we thought of alcohol or narcotics in the same way, we would think that alcoholics and narcotics addicts "needed" their drugs in order to be normal. In fact, they need to get free of their drugs in order to have a hope of becoming normal or healthy human beings.

The Ritalin label confirms, however inadequately, the danger of serious withdrawal problems. In a boxed section labeled "Drug Dependence," it states, "Careful supervision is required during drug withdrawal, since severe depression as well as the effects of chronic overactivity can be unmasked." The sentence is marred by spin doctoring that suggests that the symptoms are somehow being "unmasked" rather than directly caused by the Ritalin withdrawal. The label then states, "Long-term follow-up may be required because of the patient's basic personality disturbances." Again, this is spin doctoring of the fact that long-term exposure to these drugs, followed by withdrawal, can leave the patient with "basic personality disturbances" that the individual never had before taking stimulants. . . .

Russell A. Barkley with George
J. DuPaul and Daniel Connor

 **NO**

The Stimulants

Medication is probably the most widely publicized, most hotly debated treatment for ADHD. As a whole, the hundreds of studies conducted indicate that stimulants, certain antidepressants, and clonidine (a drug used to treat high blood pressure in many adults) can be of great help to those with ADHD. The stimulants, the drugs most commonly used, have been shown to be effective in improving behavior, academic work, and social adjustment in anywhere from 50% to 95% of children with ADHD. How well your child responds may, however, depend on the presence of other problems, and the truth is that medication does not help everyone. For that reason—and because medication is no exception to the rule that misinformation about ADHD abounds—you should gather as much background knowledge as you can before agreeing to a trial of medication for your child. This article gives the most up-to-date information available on the stimulant medications. The brand names of these medications (with generic names in parentheses) include Ritalin (methylphenidate), Dexedrine (*d*-amphetamine), Adderall (*d*- and *l*-amphetamine combination), and Cylert (pemoline). . . .

Stimulant Drugs Are Dangerous and Should Not Be Taken by Any Child

During the 1980s and again in the mid- to late 1990s, an inaccurate and regrettably successful media propaganda campaign against the use of stimulants, particularly Ritalin (methylphenidate), with children was waged by a fringe religious group, causing a dramatic rise in media coverage of this medication. The 1990s campaign was fueled by the release of misleading, alarmist, and biased information about stimulant medication abuse in the United States by the Drug Enforcement Administration as part of an effort to prevent Ritalin from being reclassified as a nonaddictive drug—a change that would have made prescribing this medication more convenient for physicians. As a consequence, the use of these medications for children with ADHD continues to be controversial in the public's mind, although there is absolutely no controversy among the scientific community as to the safety and effectiveness of these medications.

Stimulants Just Cover Up the "Real Problem" and Do Not Deal Directly with the Root Causes of the Child's ADHD

Many parents come to us with the concern that stimulants do not treat the "real problems," but it is simply untrue. Critics of these medications mistakenly assume that a child's ADHD symptoms stem from purely social causes, such as poor discipline or lack of love at home. . . . [T]here is no scientific evidence that purely social causes are at the root of a child's ADHD. We now know that ADHD is largely a genetic disorder associated with deficiencies in the functioning of certain regions in the brain related to inhibition, attention, and self-control. The stimulants deal directly with the part of the brain that is underactive and gives rise to the outward symptoms of ADHD, as explained later in this [article]. In this sense, the stimulants are no different from using insulin for a child with diabetes. Unfortunately, like insulin, stimulants have only a temporary effect, which leads some people to believe they're masking the problem rather than helping it. Like a diabetic who needs insulin, your child may have to take stimulant medicine daily for a long time, but these drugs are a way of tackling the problem directly. *Stimulants are the only treatment to date that normalizes the inattentive, impulsive, and restless behavior in children with ADHD.* However, even though the stimulants do *improve* the behavior of 70–90% of all children with ADHD, the stimulants do not *normalize* the behavioral problems of all of these children who respond positively to medication. For approximately 30–45% of children with ADHD, their behavior will be significantly improved but not normalized by this medication.

Stimulants Make Children "High," as Other Drugs Do, and Are Addictive

You may have heard that adults who take stimulants often have a sense of elevated mood, euphoria, or excessive well-being. While this does happen, it is not common, and in children it is rare. Some children do describe feeling "funny," "different," or dizzy. Others actually become a little bland in their mood, and a few even report feelings of sadness. These mood changes occur a few hours after the medicine is taken and occur more often among children treated with higher doses. In most children, these changes are very minor.

Parents are often also quite concerned about the risk of addiction to stimulants and about an increased risk of abusing other drugs when the children become teenagers. There are no reported cases of addiction or serious drug dependence to date with these medications, and the several studies that have examined whether children on these drugs are more likely than those not taking them to abuse other substances as teenagers suggest that they are not. Indeed, several recent studies conducted by Dr. Timothy E. Wilens and colleagues at Massachusetts General Hospital (Harvard Medical School), and by Drs. Howard Chilcoat and Naomi Breslau at Henry Ford Hospital in Detroit, found that taking stimulants during childhood did not predispose children with ADHD to an increased risk of substance use or abuse as teenagers. In fact, Dr. Wilens's study found that adolescents with ADHD who had remained on their medication during the teen years had a significantly lower likelihood of substance use or abuse than did children with ADHD who were not taking medications during adolescence. Thus the scientific literature to date should reassure parents that they are not predisposing their children to the potential for later substance use or abuse by giving stimulants to their children for the management of ADHD. Parents should know that the most important factors in determining a child's risk for adolescent substance use or abuse are (1) early onset of conduct disorder or antisocial behavior in the child, (2) poor monitoring by parents of the child's or teen's whereabouts in the community, (3) the affiliation of the child or teen with other teens who are using or abusing illegal substances, and (4) the degree to which the parents may also be using alcohol or tobacco products or illegal substances.

Stimulant Medications Stunt Children's Growth, and Their Use Is Strictly Limited by Age

Some studies in the early 1970s seemed to suggest that children taking these medicines might be stunted in their height and weight gain. More recent and better studies have shown that this is not as much of a problem as was once thought. Your child's eventual adult height or skeletal size is not going to be affected by taking the medicine, and the effects on your child's weight are also likely to be minimal, resulting in a loss of one or two pounds during the initial year of treatment. Any weight lost should return by the second or later years of treatment. Keep in mind that children respond very differently to these medicines, some experiencing no weight change and others losing more than just a few pounds. Your child should be followed by your physician to make sure that any weight loss is not serious.

The initial belief in the 1970s that stimulants might stunt the growth of children with ADHD led to the common practice by physicians of recommending that children take these medications only for school days and stop taking them on weekends, on school holidays, and during summer vacations. Because we now know that the risk of growth problems arising from these medications is much less than was originally believed, it is not necessary that all children taking stimulants have such drug holidays. Many can continue to take medication throughout the weekends and summers. They will derive benefits from doing so in their relations with peers; their participation in organized clubs, sports, and summer programs; and their general behavior at home. Parents whose children experience significant behavioral problems during these and other weekend and summer activities, and whose children are not having growth problems from the medication, should discuss with the children's physicians the possible value of continuing the children's stimulant medication during these periods. . . .

Stimulants Do Not Result in Lasting Benefits to a Child's Academic Achievement

The argument that stimulants have no lasting positive effects on academic achievement is a misleading one, concocted as part of broader efforts to dissuade parents from considering the use of stimulants for their children with ADHD. If one takes a simplistic view of the term academic achievement and expects stimulants to directly increase the amount of academic knowledge and skill in a school subject matter that a child acquires, then of course the stimulants will disappoint. The pills do not contain any knowledge that is automatically placed in a child's brain when consumed. A child with ADHD who does not know her multiplication tables today, while not taking any medication, will not automatically know them tomorrow after taking a dose of stimulant medication. To expect this kind of change would be silly and demonstrates the flaws in this criticism of stimulants.

What the stimulants do is help the child with ADHD show what she knows during performance of school assignments by improving the child's attention span, concentration, resistance to distraction, and thoughtful, reflective behavior. They also make the child more available to learn what is being taught in school by reducing the child's off-task, disruptive, and otherwise inattentive behavior. Given these gains, several years of medication may very well leave the child with more academic knowledge than she would have had without medication, but unfortunately no studies have examined this issue beyond 14 to 18 months of medication use. We simply don't know about the long-term benefits to academic knowledge or skills from continued use of medication over several years or more of schooling.

If we view the term *academic achievement* more broadly, as how well the child is behaving at school, getting along with peers, following classroom rules and teacher directions, completing assignments, and completing them accurately, the evidence is overwhelming that the stimulant medications produce significant improvements. Even if the stimulants do not increase a child's academic knowledge, the fact that they result in improvements in many other areas of school functioning is sufficient justification for parents to consider the possible use of these medications with their children. Such changes not only can boost self-confidence and self-esteem in the classroom setting, but can make the child more likable to the peer group and therefore give him more opportunities to make or keep classmates as friends. They can also reduce the amount of censure, punishment, and rejection the child experiences at school from both peers and teachers, and may well preclude the child from needing to be retained in grade due to substandard academic achievement. For all of these reasons, the improvements in school adjustment and success that result from the stimulants are frequently the most common reasons for prescribing these medications for children with ADHD. . . .

The Side Effects

There are many side effects that children can experience when taking these medicines, but the vast majority are minor. Again, keep in mind that if any of these are bothersome enough to warrant stopping the medication, they will likely go away once the medicine "washes out" of a child's body—within 24 hours. Most of these side effects are clearly related to the dose of medicine the child is taking: Higher doses produce more side effects. It has been estimated, however, that from 1% to 3% of children with ADHD cannot tolerate *any* dose of *any* stimulant medication.

It's impossible to predict whether your child will have any of the side effects discussed here, but we do have some revealing test findings: Over half of children with ADHD we tested in our clinic showed decreased appetite, insomnia, anxiousness, irritability, or proneness to crying. *However many of these side effets (especially those associated with mood) were* present *when the children took a fake pill (called a placebo). This means that these side effects may represent problems that are associated with ADHD rather than with the medicine.* In most cases the actual side effects were quite mild. Stomachaches and headaches were reported in about a third of the children, but these were also mild. . . .

All of the stimulants seem to reduce a child's appetite to some degree—temporarily and mainly in the late morning or early afternoon, which explains why over half of all children on these drugs may eat little of their lunch while on the medicine. For many children their appetite comes back (sometimes with a vengeance!) by evening. That is why you should make sure that a child who is on this medicine has a chance to eat adequate types and amounts of food each day to grow well. . . .

Your physician may find that your child's heart rate and blood pressure increase a little while taking these medicines. These changes are minor and do not place most children with ADHD at any risk. However, if your child is one of the rare children who has high blood pressure already, you should make sure your doctor takes this into consideration. Cylert may be less likely to produce these effects on heart rate and blood pressure. . . .

Nearly half of all children placed on medication may notice that it is harder to fall asleep at bedtime after taking these medicines during the day. Most children fall asleep within an hour or so after their typical bedtime. If not, and this is a problem for your child, tell your physician so that the dose can be lowered. . . .

All of the stimulant medications can produce temporary symptoms of psychosis (thought disorganization, rapid speech, skin hallucinations, extreme anxiety, supersensitivity to noises, etc.) at very high doses. In very rare cases this can happen at low doses. Such reactions occur in fewer than 1% of the cases and last only until the dose wears off. . . .

CHALLENGE QUESTIONS

Is Ritalin Overprescribed?

1. Some people argue that parents and teachers play a prominent role in causing and maintaining problematic behaviors in children, because they fail to set limits or follow through with consequences for misbehavior. Taking this viewpoint, enumerate some dysfunctional styles that might contribute to children acting out of control.
2. Breggin contends that stimulants suppress spontaneous behavior with enforced submissiveness, thus dulling children. How would you go about differentiating spontaneous energy from disruptively annoying behaviors?
3. Some social critics have expressed alarm about the extent to which people are managing problems with medications such as Ritalin and Prozac. Discuss the extent to which medication provides a treatment for the basic problem (neurochemical dysfunction) or serves as a temporary method for alleviating symptoms of a more deeply rooted emotional nature.
4. Imagine that you are a psychiatrist being consulted by parents of a five-year-old boy who is reportedly "acting up" in kindergarten. They request a prescription of Ritalin for him. What kind of information would you want to have before making your decision about the prescription, and what kind of preliminary steps would you recommend before going along with the parents' request?
5. Imagine that you are a researcher who has been given research support to study different methods of intervening in a class composed of 20 "hyperactive" boys. What research methods would you use to compare the effectiveness of Ritalin to behavioral methods aimed at reducing the activity level of these boys?

Suggested Readings

DeGrandpre, R. (1999). *Ritalin nation: Rapid-fire culture and the transformation of human consciousness.* New York: W.W. Norton & Company.

Fowler, M. C. (1999). *Maybe you know my kid: A parent's guide to identifying, understanding, and helping your child with attention-deficit hyperactivity disorder* (3rd edition). Secaucus, NJ: Birch Lane Press.

Glasser, H. (2005). *101 reasons to avoid Ritalin like the plague.* Tucson, AZ: Nurtured Heart Publications.

Safer, D. J. (2000). Are stimulants overprescribed for youths with ADHD? *Annals of Clinical Psychiatry, 12*(1), 32–55.

Stein, D. B. (1999). *Ritalin is not the answer: A drug-free, practical program for children diagnosed with ADD or ADHD.* San Francisco: Jossey-Bass.

Taymans, J. M., West, L. L., & Sullivan, M. (Eds.). (2000). *Unlocking potential: College and other choices for people with LD and AD/HD.* Bethesda, MD: Woodbine House.

ISSUE 11

Should Psychologists Prescribe Medication?

YES: Robert Resnick, from "To Prescribe or Not To Prescribe—Is That the Question?" *The Psychologist* (April 2003)

NO: William N. Robiner, et al., from "Prescriptive Authority for Psychologists: A Looming Health Hazard?" *Clinical Psychology: Science and Practice* (Fall 2002)

ISSUE SUMMARY

YES: Psychologist Robert Resnick endorses the recommendation that psychologists be given prescription privileges in order to expand psychopharmacological availability to people needing medication.

NO: Psychologist William Robiner and his colleagues object to the notion of granting prescription privileges to psychologists, and express several concerns pertaining to training and competence.

During the past two decades, tremendous advances have been made in understanding biologically based causes and treatments for a wide array of emotional and behavioral disorders. The introduction of selective serotonin reuptake inhibitors in the 1980s began a revolution in the treatment of depression and several other serotonin-related conditions such as obsessive-compulsive disorder. During these past two decades, medications such as Ritalin and similar stimulants have become increasingly prescribed not only for children with attention-deficit/hyperactivity disorder, but also for adults with attentional problems. Psychopharmacological interventions have become so common and accepted in society that commercials and advertisements are found in all the media boasting about the effectiveness of these medications. As mental health professionals have increasingly endorsed the prescription of medications, questions have arisen about the possibility of permitting non-physician professionals to prescribe these medications for their patients.

Psychologist Robert Resnick asserts that there is ample justification for giving prescription privileges to psychologists. He cites the social benefit for patients in underserved areas of the United States who would be able to turn to professionals other than physicians for psychopharmacological prescriptions.

Resnick contends that well-trained psychologists would be able to provide a comprehensive service in which they offer a range of services including assessment, consultation, therapy, and medication.

Psychologist William Robiner and his colleagues express serious objections to the proposal to give prescription privileges to psychologists. Concern is expressed about the fact that the medically relevant training of psychologists differs markedly from that received by physicians and by other professionals with prescription privileges. Robiner and his colleagues criticize the arguments that have been put forth by those advocating prescription privileges for psychologists, noting that prescribing psychologists are not especially likely to relocate to underserved geographical regions; nor will they necessarily be able to respond to the needs of patients who seem to prefer obtaining their prescriptions from physicians.

POINT

- In many areas of the United States, people have urgent and unmet health needs that can be alleviated by professionals who can provide both psychotherapy, and when needed, medication.
- Prescribing psychologists will offer patients better options and more knowledgeable referrals. Of concern is the fact that 85% of prescriptions used to treat mental problems are written by physicians who have little or no training in psychiatry.

- As evidenced by a program initiated in 1991 by the U.S. Department of Defense, psychologists can be successfully trained to prescribe; after several years and thousands of prescriptions written by this small number of military psychologists, there has not been one inappropriate use, missed physical diagnosis or complication, or one untoward outcome.
- Giving psychologists prescribing privileges would make it easier for patients to obtain quality and accessible mental health care in a timely fashion and at the lowest cost; it is much more efficient to see one professional rather than two.

COUNTERPOINT

- There is little reason to believe that psychologists with prescriptive authority would relocate to areas lacking other prescribers, or would focus their practices to address the needs of underserved populations.
- There are several reasons why non-psychiatric physicians account for the majority of psychotropic prescriptions written including the fact that (1) some patients are more comfortable seeing their primary care physician than a mental health professional; and (2) managed care companies recommend such treatment by primary care physicians over referrals to specialist mental health professionals.
- It is not known how well the successes of these ten military prescribing psychologists, who were trained in a military medical setting, and whose care was confined to a patient population largely screened for health and other factors, would generalize to independently practicing psychologists working in a diversity of settings.
- As an alternative to giving psychologists prescription privileges, efficiency of service delivery in the mental health system can be enhanced by taking steps to improve collaboration between psychologists and medical personnel who prescribe medications.

YES ⬅

Robert Resnick

To Prescribe or Not To Prescribe— Is That the Question?

A patient is speaking to the doctor, relating several months of sadness, loss of appetite and sleep, irritability and just plain 'feeling lousy.' After further discussion the doctor concludes the patient is experiencing significant depression and decides upon a course of treatment: psychotherapy and the short-term use of an antidepressant. The doctor takes out a pad, writes a prescription for one of the newer antidepressant medications, and arranges to start psychotherapy with the patient next week while monitoring the response to the medication. A psychiatrist? No, a psychologist in the State of New Mexico. In March 2002 New Mexico became the first state in the United States to permit psychologists, with additional training, to prescribe medication for nervous, emotional and mental problems.

While New Mexico is the first of the 50 states to obtain the legal right to prescribe medications used in mental health practices, it is not alone. Eleven other states will be introducing proposed modifications in their state laws to permit psychologists to prescribe medications. An additional 20 states have groups of psychologists laying the groundwork to introduce such legislative change.

Why do psychologists want to prescribe? The answer is a bit complicated. Physicians have historically been the only professionals permitted to prescribe, but in the last 50 years, in addition to dentists and podiatrists (who can prescribe medications but are not medical doctors) many other healthcare professionals have added this service through changes in state law. Nurses and optometrists are permitted to prescribe medications in all states, physician assistants and pharmacists in many. For psychology it is not a case of 'me too' or 'monkey see, monkey do.' It is about quality care, and it is about accessible care.

To illustrate: I am a specialist in attention deficit disorder, and frequently medication is used as part of the overall treatment plan. Recently, a 10-year-old child was referred to me. Jason had significant problems with inattention and hyperactivity, and was failing in school. His parents had tried everything they could to get him to pay attention in school and complete homework. After the evaluation and a diagnosis of attention deficit hyperactivity disorder, I decided upon a four-part plan: work with Jason to develop better

From *The Psychologist*, vol. 16, no. 4, April 2003, pp. 184–186. Copyright © 2003 by British Psychological Society. Reprinted by permission.

coping mechanisms for his behaviour; help his parents develop different ways of parenting and relating to him; establish school-based strategies aimed at reducing classroom distraction and ensuring that homework and classwork was completed; and the use of a medication known to be effective in reducing the impulsivity and hyperactivity. The first three parts of the treatment plan were put in place within the first 24 to 48 hours. However, it took six weeks (with another report card grading period ending) before Jason and his parents were able to get an appointment with their paediatrician who would prescribe the medicine. Then, a four-week wait to see the paediatrician again for follow-up and adjustment of the medication towards the correct dose. If, as a psychologist, I had the right to prescribe medication, as I was seeing Jason and his parents weekly in psychotherapy, this part of the treatment plan would have been 'on board' within 24 hours as well. Lest the reader believe the paediatrician should have been involved earlier, the referral came from the paediatrician! This is not an uncommon experience among psychologists who see, and are referred, patients who need both psychotherapy and medication management. Frequently these referrals come from physicians who are ill equipped or trained to diagnose and treat psychological and mental issues.

There is clear evidence in the US that there are very grave and urgent unmet mental health needs. These needs could be met by professionals who can provide both psychotherapy and, when needed, medication. For example, there are over 450 counties in the United States with no psychiatrists in residence. An additional concern is that only about a third of the psychiatry training positions (residencies) are filled with American medical school graduates, with the majority of the remaining residency position being filled by physicians whose first language is not English. Language problems make it very difficult to work with minorities, inner-city families, Native Americans and rural communities. To illustrate the concern: A foreign-trained psychiatry resident whose English comprehension was passable but not extensive, admitted a man for 'being crazy,' 'because he talks to animals.' After I evaluated him the next morning, he was released with apologies. This was a African-American jazz musician who, when speaking about his band members told the resident 'I says to this cat, and the cat says to me.' Talks to animals! Right!

Also of concern is the fact that 85 per cent of prescriptions used to treat mental problems are written by physicians who have little or no training in psychiatry (Zimmerman & Wienckowski, 1991). The average psychiatric training is less than seven weeks and the average number of instructional hours in psychiatric medications is only 99 in the four years of US medical school training. . . . Thus another component of the complicated answer would include the ability of families to obtain quality and accessible mental health services in a timely fashion and at the lowest cost. It is much more efficient (in terms of time lost from work or school) and more cost-effective to see one professional rather than two.

Can psychologists be trained to be psychologist prescribers? They already have been! Many psychologists in medical schools and government agencies have either written prescriptions 'under the table' or did everything but sign them, seeking out a physician who would simply add his or her name. This has been going on for decades, though most of the training was self-taught and some by 'osmosis.' In 1991, however, the US Department of Defense began a four-year demonstration programme, to determine if psychologists who were in the military could be trained to prescribe medications. Several years later and thousands of prescriptions written, there has not been one inappropriate use, missed physical diagnosis or complication; nor has there been one untoward outcome. Clearly, psychologists can be trained to provide medication management at a very high level of competence as well as to provide high-quality psychotherapy.

The demonstration project was modified, over time, and evolved into a two-year postdoctoral programme. The first year is didactics, and the second on-the-job clinical experience. How is this training different from medical school? Prescribing psychologists embrace a more integrative or psychological model of prescribing. Psychological training is a health model focusing on strengths first then weaknesses, rather than the disease model of medical school. As a consequence psychologists are less likely to 'knee-jerk' a medication to treat symptoms. Indeed, the experience of the military psychologists has demonstrated this point over and over again.

We in the psychologist prescription movement acknowledge two truths that are—or should be—self-evident: medications are indeed effective for some patients, and current prescription writing practices are inadequate and dangerous, especially for underserved populations. We also recognise a very important 'treatment' given to prescribing psychologists: the authority to discontinue medications that have been prescribed by other professionals. Particularly with mental problems, there has been a tendency to practise 'polypharmacy'—prescribing more and more medications to treat newly created symptoms. In part, this is due to the problems cited earlier in psychiatric and medical training. A quick example: A depressed patient is given an antidepressant then gets the side-effect of sleep problems. Now a sedative is prescribed, but there are side-effects of morning drowsiness and fatigue. When a stimulant is added to provide 'alertness,' extrapyramidal symptoms such as severe dry mouth and lip-smacking develop and an anticholenergic drug is added. So the right to prescribe is also the right to *stop* inappropriate medications. You should note that over 7000 people a year die from legally prescribed medications (Kohn *et al.*, 2000: . . .

For almost a hundred years American psychology has debated the expansion of its competence and scope of practice. While never achieving unanimity, it has matured as a healthcare profession and will continue to do so. Clearly, a larger scope of practice will enable a psychologist to offer comprehensive services, including assessment, consultation, psychotherapy and, yes, when needed, medication. As psychology, like other professions, began the quest for independent prescriptive authority, organised medicine and some psychologists ominously warned of health hazards. In each instance the woeful predictions of wrongly treated patients flocking to hospitals and thousands of deaths never materialised.

Finally, I would argue that the best reason for psychologists having the ability to prescribe medication is not that it is good for psychology, but that it is good for the consumers. Psychologists have not entered this area of practice quickly or impulsively, but did so with deliberation and debate beginning in 1984. As a result, the additional training required for psychologists to prescribe medications has crucial differences from medical school training. Our training model is not disease-based. We include intensive and extensive training in the interaction of psychotherapy and medication, stressing when one is therapeutically superior to the other and when the use of both is in the best interest of the patient. In the final analysis, isn't this what this should be about? Isn't it what is best for the individuals, families and public we serve? It should be.

References

Kohn, L. T., Corrigan, J. M., & Donaldson, M. S. (Eds.) (2000). *To err is human: Building a safer health system.* Washington, DC: National Academy Press.

Zimmerman, M. A., & Wienckowski, L. A. (1991,Winter). Revisiting health and mental health linkages: A policy whose time has come . . . again. *Journal of Public Health Policy,* 510–524.

William N. Robiner, et al.

 **NO**

Prescriptive Authority for Psychologists: A Looming Health Hazard?

Advances in neuroscience, the development of safer, efficacious drugs such as the SSRIs, and changing realities in health care economics are transforming the delivery of mental health services. As these unfold, and as the use of psychotropics increases (Pincus et al., 1998), psychologists' interest in obtaining prescriptive authority for psychotropic medication has also increased (Ax, Forbes, & Thompson, 1997; Brentar & McNamara, 1991a, 1991b; Burns, DeLeon, Chemtob, Welch, & Samuels, 1988; Cullen & Newman, 1997; DeLeon, Folen, Jennings, Wilkis, & Wright, 1991; DeLeon, Fox, & Graham, 1991; DeLeon & Wiggins, 1996; Fox, 1988; Sammons, 1994). In this article we address a range of issues related to prescriptive authority for psychologists, including training, accreditation, regulation, and other topics raised by proponents of the prescriptive agenda, and discuss our concerns about it. . . .

Department of Defense Psychopharmacology Project

The controversy surrounding psychologists' prescription privileges was heightened by the Department of Defense (DoD) Psychopharmacology Demonstration Project (PDP). The PDP ultimately trained ten psychologists to prescribe in military health care settings (U.S. General Accounting Office, 1999). The initial PDP participants undertook some preparation in chemistry and biochemistry before completing a majority of first-year medical school courses. During their first full-time year at the Uniformed Services University of the Health Sciences, they worked with the Psychiatry-Liaison service and assumed night call with second-year psychiatry residents. In the second full-time year, they completed core basic science courses and continued psychopharmacology training and clinical work. After 2-day written and oral examinations, they had a third year of supervised clinical work at Walter Reed Army Medical Center or Malcolm Grow Medical Center. The PDP curriculum underwent subsequent iterations, streamlining training to 1 year of coursework and a year of supervised clinical practice (Sammons & Brown, 1997; Sammons, Sexton, & Meredith, 1996). For example, the didactic hours decreased by 48% in the second iteration. Most PDP graduates have functioned as prescribing psychologists in branches of the military. One graduate went on to medical school.

The PDP was discontinued after the first few years. Advocates of psychologist prescription privileges argue that the successes of the small sample of PDP participants justify extending prescriptive authority to other psychologists who undergo training consistent with the American Psychological Association (APA) (Council of Representatives [COR], 1996) model, even though that training model and the likely resources available for the training differ substantially from the PDP. It is not known how well the successes of the 10 PDP psychologists, who were trained within a military medical school and military hospital settings, and whose care was confined to a patient population largely screened for health and other factors, would generalize to the potentially thousands of psychologists who might wish to obtain psychopharmacology training and to practice independently across the spectrum of clinical or counseling settings with diverse populations (Bieliauskas, 1992a; Kennedy, 1998). If the clinical psychopharmacology training psychologists obtain elsewhere is less rigorous or is based on more limited access to medical populations than the PDP, the outcomes of the PDP potentially would overestimate outcomes of such training.

Additional skepticism seems warranted especially in light of the concerns about certain limitations of the PDP fellows' clinical proficiencies, such as in treating medically complex patients (Kennedy, 1998). The Final Report of the American College of Neuropsychopharmacology (1998) on the PDP assessed graduates as weaker medically and psychiatrically than psychiatrists. The report indicated that graduates only saw patients ages 18–65, some had limited formularies, and some continued to have dependent prescriptive practice (i.e., supervised by a physician). Moreover, the PDP graduates advised against "short-cut" programs and considered that a year of intensive full-time clinical experience, including inpatient care, was essential. Some of the program's psychiatrists, physicians, and graduates expressed doubts about the safety and effectiveness of psychologists prescribing independently outside of the interdisciplinary team of the military context. This latter concern has been echoed in a survey of military psychiatrists, nonpsychiatric physicians, and social workers (Klusman, 1998). Given the likelihood that other programs would lack some of the advantages of the PDP, and would provide less training than some of the PDP graduates received, we question how well the conditions of the PDP would be duplicated. Despite the positive experiences of PDP graduates, these concerns justify wariness about prescribing psychologists relative to other prescribers, especially for populations not included or emphasized in the PDP. We believe that more complete disclosure and consideration of the limitations and problems noted in the PDP are needed, both in the dialogue within the profession as well as in terms of public policy reviews of the prescriptive agenda. . . .

Quality of Care: The Central Concern about Psychologist Prescribing

Our primary concern is the risk of suboptimal care if psychologists undertake prescribing that could arise from their limited breadth and depth of knowledge about human physiology, medicine, and related areas. This risk would be compounded by psychologists' limited supervised physical clinical training experiences. Such knowledge and skills are fundamental to competent prescribing but have been limited or absent in training professional (i.e., clinical, counseling, school) psychologists. In one survey, more than two thirds of psychologists in independent practice described their training related to psychopharmacological issues as poor (APA, 1992b, p. 50). This is not surprising given the limited psychopharmacology training in doctoral programs and psychology internships (APA, 1992b).

Although advocates of prescription privileges readily acknowledge that additional training is needed to prepare psychologists to prescribe, the central questions are these. How much training is needed? Is it possible to attain adequate knowledge and skill through abbreviated training, such as proposed in models by the APA (CoR, 1996) or the California Psychological Association-California School of Professional Psychology Blue Ribbon Panel (1995)? How would psychologists who undergo the proposed training measure up to other prescribers? The concern is that abbreviated "crash courses" are inadequate to make up for psychologists' deficits in medical education (Bieliauskas, 1992a; Bütz, 1994).

At times, advocates for psychologist prescription privileges gloss over the complexity of knowledge sets inherent in competent prescribing (Kennedy, 1998; Kingsbury, 1992; Pies; 1991). For example, Patrick DeLeon, PhD, JD, Past President of the APA, contends that "prescription privileges is no big deal. It's like learning how to use a desk-top computer" (Roan, 1993). Related speculation that technological advances, such as computer-assisted learning (DeLeon & Wiggins, 1996), or prescriptive algorithms, could abbreviate the education necessary to prescribe competently strikes even proponents of prescription privileges as naïve (Pachman, 1996). Similarly, it seems unlikely that relying on more active roles of pharmacists or computerized systems for administration of drugs would compensate adequately for gaps in prescribers' medical knowledge. Ultimately, competence in prescribing demands adequate understanding not just of psychology and psychopharmacology but also of other domains of medical knowledge (e.g., human physiology, pathophysiology, biochemistry, clinical medicine) and clinical proficiencies (e.g., physical examination, interpretation of laboratory data) that historically have been excluded from the education and training of psychologists. More specifically, thorough understanding and proficiency related to two broad medical domains are required: understanding patients' medical status prior to and concurrent with prescribing and their medical status during and after treatment (i.e., their physiological responses to prescribed medications) (Pies, 1991; Robiner, 1999; see Table 1).

Table 1

Knowledge Base and Clinical Proficiencies Required for Prescribing

Psychopathology and Psychological Issues	Medical Status Prior to Prescribing	Response to Treatments
Primary psychiatric conditions	Comorbid medical conditions	Knowledge of adverse reactions 1. Side effects 2. Toxic effects
Comorbid psychiatric conditions Prevalence and course of psychiatric conditions	Contraindications Medical effects of concurrent treatments 1. Drug interactions 2. Other treatments (e.g., dialysis, plasmaphoresis)	Ability to recognize, diagnose, and treat adverse reactions Ability to differentiate between physical and psychiatric effects of psychoactive agents and concurrent medications
Knowledge of nonpharmacologic treatment options	Long-term effects of medications History of medication use	Other issues related to monitoring, titrating, or discontinuing prescribed medications

Note: The education of psychologists typically addresses column 1, but neglects columns 2 and 3.

There are scant data regarding how well prepared psychologists are to prescribe. Anecdotally, psychologists' confidence in diagnosing patients and providing other types of psychological treatment, combined with limited psychopharmacology training and informal exposure to medications, may provide some sense that they have much of the knowledge related to prescribing. Thus far, however, little is known about how well the combination of doctoral training in psychology and relatively brief, focused training in psychopharmacology would develop psychologists' knowledge base and clinical proficiency for managing patients' medications, especially long-term and in diverse settings. Noteworthy differences exist between pharmacotherapy and current aspects of psychologists' clinical practice. As one psychologist turned psychiatrist observes:

> The effects of medications on the kidney, the heart, and so forth is important for the use of many medications. Managing these effects is often crucial and has more to do with biochemistry and physiology than with psychology. I was surprised to discover how little about medication use has to do with psychological principles and how much of it is just medical. (Kingsbury, 1992, p. 5)

Training for Prescribing

Proponents have construed prescriptive authority for psychologists as an "evolutionary" or "logical" step (DeLeon, Folen, et al., 1991; Fox, 1988) or even a "right" (Brentar & McNamara, 1991a) that is consistent with the trend in other health care disciplines towards broadened scopes of professional practice, including prescribing.

The first premise is debatable, especially given its fundamental departure from psychology's historic training paradigms and conceptualizations of psychopathology and intervention. The education and training for a doctoral degree in psychology largely neglects key topics relevant to prescribing (i.e., the biological and physical sciences, physical examination). Also, psychology historically has questioned, de-emphasized, or even eschewed the "medical model" (Matthews, 1998; May & Belsky, 1992). Pursuing prescriptive authority reflects a profound change in the direction toward embracing the medical model. Adding prescribing to psychology's scope of practice might more realistically be characterized as "revolutionary" or "radical," requiring major shifts in focus; marked expansions of training and continuing education in key areas; reformulation of accreditation criteria; modification of regulatory structure, domains, and processes; expanded ethical guidelines; and uniform requirements that at least part of psychologists' training occur within health care settings.

The second premise, that psychologists' scope of practice should broaden because some nonphysicians such as physician assistants (PAs) and advanced practice nurses (APNs) prescribe also is dubious. This seems to be based on the notion that the overall length of doctoral training that psychologists undergo might justify prescribing despite the limited relevance to prescribing of much of their actual training. Disparities in training between psychology and other professions with prescriptive authority challenge the notion that those professions' scopes of practice justify expanding psychologists' scope of practice to incorporate prescription privileges. Other professions' training models are much closer to that of physicians than to that of psychologists, and their clinical practice is more focused on physical functioning, including medication effects. Comparing the boundaries of other professions' scope of practice with psychology's is inappropriate given the differences in training between those other disciplines and psychology. . . .

The comparisons that advocates draw between psychology's and other disciplines' scope of practice compel closer inspection of the entry requirements and training models for psychology and other prescribing disciplines (McCabe & Grover, 1999). As outlined below, the differences in emphasis and structure are noteworthy. Since prescribing psychologists would probably be compared most closely with psychiatrists, our emphasis is on these two groups.

Undergraduate Training

The APA task force (Smyer et al., 1993) noted that other health professions (e.g., nursing, allied health professions) require undergraduate preparation in anatomy, biology, inorganic and organic chemistry, pharmacology, human physiology, (and some require physics); undergraduate psychology degrees and admission to psychology graduate school do not. The biological sciences and related course work is the educational foundation for knowledge and conceptual understanding related to prescribing safely. Hence, the APA task force envisioned that students with strong undergraduate, postbaccalaureate, or early graduate biological backgrounds would be admitted to psychopharmacology training (Smyer et al., 1993). The problem is that such backgrounds are rare. A survey of psychology graduate students revealed that only 27% thought they had the undergraduate preparation to undertake training to prescribe (Tatman et al., 1997). Only 7% had completed the recommended undergraduate biology and chemistry prerequisites (APA, 1992b; Smyer et al., 1993). Robiner et al. (2001) found that psychologists generally had taken fewer than five courses in the biological and physical sciences during their undergraduate and graduate education. . . .

Unlike medical school applicants and medical students, whose mastery of these areas is reflected through a competitive selection process (e.g., based on grades in biological and physical science courses, MCAT scores) and screened again in objective measures (i.e., national board scores such as steps one, two, and three of the United States Medical Licensing Examination [USMLE]; specialty board examinations following residency), entry into proposed psychopharmacology training programs for psychologists would not require standardized, objective indices of applicants' understanding of the biological and physical sciences. It is not known whether competitive performance in biological and physical science courses with laboratory prerequisites would play any role in determining eligibility for psychologists' psychopharmacology training. In summary, the discrepancies between physicians' and psychologists' education in the biological and physical sciences, and objective mechanisms verifying that general scientific knowledge has been acquired (i.e., psychology has none), begin at the undergraduate level.

The APA College of Professional Psychology in conjunction with Professional Examination Services developed an examination for psychologists who have undergone training in clinical psychopharmacology, the Psychopharmacology Examination for Psychologists (PEP). Other groups have developed other tests (e.g., Veritas Assessment Systems). Within the APA (1996) model, psychologists seeking prescription privileges would be expected to pass one of these written tests. Such testing is an important safeguard, but may be limited, especially in an era when commercial courses have been designed to prepare individuals for tests. Whereas proponents would argue that passage of that examination demonstrates adequate knowledge for prescribing, it seems questionable that a single 3-hour, 150-item test on psychopharmacology could assure adequate knowledge of the broad spectrum of medical issues beyond clinical psychopharmacology per se that are relevant to prescribing safely or knowledge and clinical skill sets comparable to that of other prescribers (e.g., physicians, nurse practitioners).

Graduate Training

Educational discrepancies between psychologists and physicians widen at the graduate level. The training of physicians and other doctoral providers (e.g., dentists) entails coursework in anatomy, biochemistry, cell biology, immunology, microbiology, pathology, pharmacology, physiology, as well as laboratory experiences in the biological and physical sciences and physical, clinical training. Doctoral-level psychology education never has (see APA Office of Program Consultation and Accreditation, 1996). Rather, graduate education in psychology has been characterized as comprising "vastly differing models of study and practice" with "no effort to standardize the training of psychologists" (Klein, 1996). Programs vary in how much training is provided in the biological and physical sciences (Sammons et al., 1996), but it is generally quite limited for degrees in professional psychology. Some types of psychology degrees, (e.g., school psychology) have relatively limited exposure to psychopathology and psychological treatments, let alone the physical sciences (DeMers, 1994; Moyer, 1995) or medical environments. . . .

Surveys suggest that only 25% of psychology graduate students had courses in psychopharmacology (Tatman et al., 1997) and 36% of licensed psychologists indicated that their graduate programs offered psychopharmacology courses (Ferguson, 1997). Presumably fewer had courses in pharmacology or pathophysiology, which are intrinsic to prescribing safely (i.e., due to potential interactions and adverse effects). These limitations are of greater concern than the limitations identified in medical students' psychiatric training (Zimmerman & Wienckowski, 1991) or estimates that medical school students receive only approximately 100 hours of pharmacology instruction (Association for Medical School Pharmacology [1990] cited by the APA Task Force [APA, 1992b]); physicians' other didactics are relevant to prescribing and their lengthy supervised training across a continuum of settings and supervisors includes wide exposure to related topics and patient populations.

By the time psychologists obtain doctorates, most have obtained relatively little training that overlaps with that of physicians or other prescribers. Moreover, there are no objective quality assurance processes to ensure that the biological and physical sciences are well understood by entrants to psychology graduate school or by entrants to proposed postdoctoral psychopharmacology training programs. Even the Examination for the Professional Practice of Psychology (EPPP), the written test required for licensure in psychology, minimally queries knowledge of the biological and physical sciences (e.g., biochemistry) (Association of State and Provincial Psychology Boards, 2000).

Proposed Postdoctoral Level Psychopharmacology Training

. . . The APA (CoR, 1996) emphasizes that the proposed training is "unique to the needs of the practicing psychologist, and does not simply follow traditional medical practices." We question whether such condensed training overcomes current shortcomings to achieve knowledge and clinical proficiency equivalent to that of other prescribers, especially psychiatrists, and ensure competent prescribing that the public should reasonably expect of its doctors. Furthermore, it seems incumbent upon proponents of the prescriptive agenda to fully inform legislators and the public precisely how the psychopharmacology training proposed by the APA differs from "traditional medical practices." . . .

Proponents of prescription privileges recognize that the supervised practice in proposed psychopharmacology training "essential for effective, safe, ethical and practical incorporation of drugs into a psychological practice . . . is a substantive matter" (Fox et al., 1992, p. 218). Curiously, despite recognition of this substantiveness, the scope and requirements for supervised pharmacotherapeutic practice are not fully delineated in the APA model, so it is not possible to evaluate how adequate the supervised practice would be. Consistent with the APA model, training programs are designed for trainees to see a series of patients (e.g., ≥ 100) for psychopharmacologic management. The APA model fails to specify minimal criteria for (a) the breadth of patients' mental health conditions; (b) the duration of treatment (i.e., to allow for adequate monitoring and feedback) or requirements for outpatient or inpatient experiences; (c) exposure to adverse medication effects; or (d) exposure to patients with comorbid medical conditions and complex drug regimens. Also, the qualifications for supervisors are vague. Whereas the CPA-CSPP Panel (1995) recommended an 18-month practicum, the APA model does not specify any length. That the didactic and practical training would be abbreviated relative to the PDP, and less likely to occur in organized, academic health care settings with lengthy track records of providing medical or psychiatric training, raises questions about how comparable such programs would be to the PDP.

We doubt that the proposed models of training in psychopharmacology for psychologists (APA, 1996; CPA/CSPP, 1995; Fox et al., 1992) would prepare them to provide care equivalent to that provided by psychiatrists or other health professionals. Not only would they obtain less didactics in relevant areas, but the supervised pharmacologic care of patients would be considerably less comprehensive and less well organized than training within psychiatric residencies. . . .

Regulatory and Legal Issues

. . . A number of legal issues also would arise if psychologists were granted prescriptive authority. This includes the level of independence versus dependence of this authority, potential restrictions on their prescriptive practices (e.g., limited formulary and duration of treatment; specific settings), and the most appropriate standard of care to which psychologists would be held. Would psychologists be compared with other "reasonably prudent" psychologists who have undergone the proposed psychopharmacology training, or with other prescribers, such as psychiatrists, who have greater training and experience related to medication management and who have set the standard for prescribing psychoactive medications thus far? From the consumer's perspective, it seems likely that a standard of care closer to that provided by psychiatrists would promote accountability and afford greater protections and legal remedies than an unknown, less stringent, evolving standard based on psychologists who might gain prescriptive authority based on training that is less intensive than that of other prescribers. In addition, formulation of ethical guidelines relevant to prescribing, which are beyond the current APA (1992a) Ethical Principles of Psychologists and Code of Conduct, would be needed (Buelow & Chafetz, 1996) to address a range of ethical challenges associated with prescribing (Heiby, 1998).

Proponents' Focus on Peripheral Issues

In essentially waging a campaign for prescriptive authority, proponents tend to focus on certain provocative issues to promote their cause and divert attention away from the inadequacies in psychologists' education, knowledge, and skills in areas critical to prescribing. For example, DeLeon and Wiggins (1996) decry problems of current prescribers as if psychologists (who would have less extensive physical science backgrounds and more limited supervised prescriptive practical training) would avoid developing problematic patterns if they prescribe. Alternative strategies, such as enhancing the ability of current prescribers through such means as education and redesign of prescribing systems (Lesar, Briceland, & Stein, 1997), or enhancing psychologists' collaborative practices, as proposed in the APA task force's (Smyer et al., 1993) Level 2 training, might address such problems without requiring that psychologists prescribe.

Similarly, underserved populations (e.g., rural populations, the seriously and persistently mentally ill [SPMI], the elderly) have been invoked to frame prescriptive authority as a policy response to meet pressing societal needs (DeLeon, Sammons, & Sexton, 1995; Hanson et al., 1999). This line of reasoning is flawed in failing to consider the similar access patterns to psychologists and psychiatrists across the urban-rural continuum (Hendryx, Borders, & Johnson, 1995; Holzer, Goldsmith, & Ciarlo, 1998) and the APA task force's expectation that only "a small . . . minority of psychologists" (APA, 1992b, p. 106) would seek Level 3 psychopharmacology training. Such data and predictions, along with the virtual absence of any concrete plan to redistribute prescribing psychologists to meet the actual needs of underserved populations (May & Belsky, 1992), render broadening psychologists' scope of practice to include prescriptive authority an indirect, needlessly risky, and highly inefficient public policy response to rural areas' shortage of psychopharmacologic prescribers. . . .

Ultimately, there is little reason to assume that psychologists with prescriptive authority actually would relocate to areas lacking other prescribers, or would focus their practices to address the needs of other types of underserved populations (Adams & Bieliauskas, 1994; Bieliauskas, 1992a, 1992b). Even some proponents of prescriptive privileges concede that psychologists may not be more inclined than psychiatrists to work with underserved groups (Hanson et al., 1999).

Attempts to garner support for the prescriptive agenda on the basis of underserved populations also ignores efforts by the American Psychiatric Association to enhance psychiatric consultation to primary care providers ("APA board takes action," 1998) and the potential benefits of expanded use of telehealth technology to supplement the expertise of primary care practitioners in areas underserved by psychiatrists. Similarly, it ignores data that psychiatrists see significantly more SPMI and socially disadvantaged patients than do psychologists (Olfson & Pincus, 1996), which brings into question whether prescriptive authority would have a major impact in expanding care to SPMI populations. Pursuing prescriptive authority may distract focus from important opportunities for psychologists to improve their collaborations with primary care providers to collectively address needs as suggested by groups such as the National Depressive and Manic-Depressive Association (Hirschfeld et al., 1977) or the National Alliance for the Mentally Ill (NAMI). . . .

Another rationale of proponents of prescription privileges is that many mental health services, including prescriptions of psychotropic medications, are provided by nonpsychiatric physicians who have little psychiatric training (DeLeon & Wiggins, 1996). Indeed, the general medical sector is an essential component of the mental health system, serving an estimated 40–50% of people with mental disorders according to the utilization data of the Epidemiologic Catchment Area (ECA) study (Narrow, Regier, Rae, Manderscheid, & Locke, 1993). Similarly, data from the National Ambulatory Medicare Care Survey (NAMCS) reveal that outpatient appointments with primary care physicians and medical specialists account respectively for 48% and 19% of all appointments involving psychoactive prescription drugs: More than the appointments with psychiatrists (33%) (Pincus et al., 1998). General physicians provide somewhat more of the nation's outpatient mental health services (35%) than either psychologists (31%) or psychiatrists (27%) (Olfson & Pincus, 1996).

According to DeLeon and Wiggins (1996), an estimated 135.8 million prescriptions for psychoactive medications were written in 1991, of which only 17.3% were by psychiatrists. Such statistics, albeit interesting, do *not* indicate how many of these physician interactions for prescriptions are enhanced by consultations involving psychiatrists, psychologists, or other mental health professionals, or how many truly need mental health consultation. There are no benchmarks for how many prescriptions nonpsychiatric physicians should write or what percentage of them ought to be informed by collaborations with mental health professionals. It is possible that the large number of prescriptions written by nonpsychiatric physicians reflect that consultation with mental health professionals may be necessary only for subgroups of patients, or that adequate consultation already occurs related to many patients who might need medication. Moreover, despite focus on such patterns (DeLeon & Wiggins, 1996), the numbers neither reveal anything about problematic patterns of prescribing by physicians nor do they persuade that psychologists should prescribe. They probably do reflect several factors, such as (1) some people are more comfortable seeing their primary care physician than a mental health professional (Geller & Muus, 1997; Murstein & Fontaine, 1993), and (2) managed care organizations and capitated systems encourage primary care physicians to treat mental disorders rather than refer to specialist mental health professionals (Pincus et al., 1998). Such systems of health care delivery are similar to the service delivery models in other countries (e.g., Great Britain), where lower per capita rates of psychiatrists reflect psychiatrists' roles as specialist consultants to nonpsychiatric physicians who play primary roles in the psychopharmacological management of most patients' care (Scully, 1999).

The widespread prescription of psychoactive agents by nonpsychiatrist physicians reflects the significant opportunities for psychiatrists and psychologists (especially those with Level 2 training) to collaborate and consult about psychopharmacology. The data confirm the importance of continuing the ongoing efforts to enhance psychopharmacology training of nonpsychiatric physicians and other prescribers. Such trends do not, however, indicate a need or justification for psychologists to prescribe.

Medication Adverse Effects and Errors

Prescribers even of limited formularies necessarily assume some responsibility for the broader health status of their patients (Heiby, 1998; Kingsbury, 1992). Psychoactive medications have been described as presenting more complex drug interactions and adverse effects than any other class of drug (Hayes, 1998). Many people who take psychoactive medications also take other medications that complicate their care. Fewer than 30% who take an antidepressant take no other medications, so it is important to understand the comorbid conditions and other medications that patients concurrently experience (Preskorn, 1999). In primary care and psychiatric settings, more than 70% of patients prescribed an antidepressant take at least one other drug and a third take at least three other drugs (Preskorn, 1999). Polypharmacy rates are often higher with the elderly and medically ill, and in more specialized clinics (e.g., HIV). . . .

The timing of the intensification of psychologists' lobbying for prescriptive authority is ironic in light of growing national concern about errors in prescribing medication (Classen, Pestotnik, Evans, Lloyd, & Burke, 1997). Nationally, medication errors are estimated to lead to as many as 7,000 deaths annually (Phillips, Christenfeld, & Glynn, 1998). The Federal Drug Administration currently receives 235,000 reports per year about adverse drug events (Institute of Medicine Committee on Quality of Health Care in America, 1999). This could increase as medication options expand, requiring constant upgrades in knowledge of the entire pharmaceutical spectrum. In 1998, the FDA approved 90 new drugs, 30 new molecular entities, 124 new or expanded use of agents, and 344 generic drugs, not counting over the counter and orphan drugs (FDA, 1999). That nearly half of the drugs currently marketed have become available in the last decade (Shatin, Gardner, & Stergachis, 1999) suggests that the knowledge base for prescribing is becoming even more complex, requiring yet more extensive scientific understanding. Between 1970 and 1997, the annual number of publications on drug-drug interactions increased fivefold (Preskorn, 1999), reflecting factors such as increased use of medications for chronic conditions and an aging society with more medical problems and more complex medication regimens. Such trends underscore the need for strong basic education in medicine and pharmacology to prepare prescribers to understand medical conditions in integrating pharmacologic developments into their practice.

Among the many contributing factors to medication errors are *inadequate knowledge* and use of knowledge regarding drug therapy and *inadequate recognition* of important patient factors (e.g., impaired renal function, drug allergies) (Lesar et al., 1997). The influence of other factors that require more sophisticated scientific understanding, such as genetic variation in drug metabolism and uptake, is increasingly likely to affect prescribing. Along with other recommendations, Lesar et al. (1997) recommended *improved prescriber education*. There have not been calls from outside of psychology to create a new category of prescribers with relatively *less* training (as psychologist prescribers would be).

Given the paucity of education and training directly related to prescribing throughout undergraduate and graduate training in psychology (Robiner et al., 2001), the scant data about psychologists' proficiency in managing medications, which is limited to relatively few individuals, as well as inadequacies in psychologists' knowledge related to psychopharmacology (Robiner et al., 2001), we doubt that abbreviated psychopharmacology training for psychologists would be sufficient to ensure adequate competence in prescribing. Moreover, we are concerned that psychologists would lack the medical expertise to recognize, assess (e.g., all relevant hematological assays), and understand adverse effects and initiate proper medical care.

Short cuts in education seem likely to undermine patient care and contribute to medication errors along the patterns outlined by Lesar et al. (1997). Such training, especially if paired with independent prescriptive authority, risks generating a wave of suboptimal medication management and potentially avoidable adverse drug events. In addition to potentially hazardous consequences for patients, problems associated with psychologist prescribing would present regulatory conundrums, provide a new basis for litigation, and ultimately could detract from the public's esteem of psychologists in general.

Closing Considerations

We appreciate the important roles psychologists play within the delivery of health care broadly and mental health care in particular. Our findings and conclusions in no way belittle psychologists' knowledge or proficiencies in other areas. We agree with the APA task force (APA, 1992b) that it would be beneficial to promote psychologists' psychopharmacology knowledge so as to inform and enhance their collaborations with primary care providers and psychiatrists in providing care to patients who need medications. However, achieving the APA task force's goals for enhancing the care of patients needing medications does not require prescriptive authority for psychologists. Instead, we recommend that the APA refocus its energies to better educate psychologists about psychopharmacology to enhance the psychological services that psychologists provide and their collaborations with prescribers. This is a type of training that most psychology graduate students need and would welcome (Tatman et al., 1997). Also, survey data suggest that most (90%) licensed psychologists feel that psychologists should pursue a minimum of the collaborative practice level of training and most (79%) would be personally willing to pursue it (Ferguson, 1997). Moreover, most (85%) applied psychologists already consult regularly with physicians, so such training would enhance services that already are provided (Barkley, 1991).

Unfortunately, if psychologists prescribe, medically complex patients (e.g., older patients taking multiple medications) would probably be most vulnerable to the adverse consequences that potentially could derive from shortcomings in psychologists' scientific and medical training (Hayes & Heiby, 1996; Klein, 1996). Promoting psychologists' collaborative practices with prescribers rather than psychologists' prescription privileges would preclude new risks to patients associated with a potentially suboptimal level of care. Collaboration would avoid further confusion about psychologists' identities (Ax et al., 1997), skills, scope of practice, and the differentiation between psychology and psychiatry (Murstein & Fontaine, 1993; Wood, Jones, & Benjamin, 1986). . . .

As psychologists, educators of psychologists, and related health professionals, the authors have actively supported psychology's many other advances (e.g., Medicare reimbursement, licensure, provision of nonpharmacologic interventions), including appropriate, innovative roles of psychologists in health care (Schofield, 1969). We caution against framing the debate about prescription privileges as a chapter in the saga of struggles between psychology and psychiatry (DeLeon & Wiggins, 1996). Rather, at its core it is a controversy about the education and training necessary to promote safe and effective treatment that limits unnecessary risks to patients.

We have doubts that the shortcomings in psychologists' education and knowledge related to prescribing can be surmounted through abbreviated training, such as that currently advocated by the APA. Our skepticism that these gaps can be overcome within such a shorter time frame than is involved in the training of other prescribers leads us to urge psychologists to resist the temptation to venture into aspects of health care (i.e., prescribing and its related clinical activities) for which they would not be well-prepared. As legislators and regulators are lobbied about psychologists' prescriptive privileges agenda, they need to weigh judiciously any hoped-for benefits against the potential risks associated with the inadequacies in psychologists' preparation to prescribe, even after they may have obtained the psychopharmacology training in accordance with the model recommended by the APA (CoR, 1996).

Acknowledgment

The authors appreciatively acknowledge the editorial guidance and other contributions of William Schofield, PhD, and Irving I. Gottesman, PhD, in the preparation of this article.

References

Adams, K. M., & Bieliauskas, L. A. (1994). On perhaps becoming what you had previously despised: Psychologists as prescribers of medication. *Journal of Clinical Psychology in Medical Settings, 1,* 189–197.

American College of Neuropsychopharmacology. (1998, May). *Final report: DoD prescribing psychologists: External analysis, monitoring, and evaluation of the program and its participants.* Nashville, TN: Author.

American Psychological Association. (1992a). Ethical principles of psychologists and code of conduct. *American Psychologist, 47,* 1597–1611.

American Psychological Association (1992b). *Report of the ad hoc task force on psychopharmacology.* Washington, DC: Author.

American Psychological Association. (1996). *Model legislation for prescriptive authority.* Washington, DC: Author.

APA board takes action to provide consult services in certain areas. (1998, April 17). *Psychiatric News, 2.*

Association for Medical School Pharmacology. (1990, October). *Knowledge objectives in medical pharmacology* (2nd edition). Author.

Association of State and Provincial Psychology Boards. (2000). Psychology Licensure Exam (EPPP). Available online at . . .

Ax, R. K., Forbes, M. R., & Thompson, D. D. (1997). Prescription privileges for psychologists: A survey of predoctoral interns and directors of training. *Professional Psychology: Research and Practice, 28,* 509–513.

Barkley, R. A. (1991, Spring). Health Services Committee: Prescribing privileges for health psychologists: Implications from the Clinical Child Psychology Task Force. *Health Psychologist, 13*(1), 2.

Bieliauskas, L. A. (1992a). Prescription privileges for psychologists? Reality orientation for proponents. *Physical Medicine and Rehabilitation: State of the Art Reviews, 6,* 587–595.

Bieliauskas, L. A. (1992b). Rebuttal of Dr. Frank's position. *Physical Medicine and Rehabilitation: State of the Art Reviews, 6,* 584.

Brentar, J., & McNamara, J. R. (1991a). Prescription privileges for psychology: The next step in its evolution as a profession. *Professional Psychology: Research and Practice, 22,* 194–195.

Brentar, J., & McNamara, J. R. (1991b). The right to prescribe medication: Considerations for professional psychology. *Professional Psychology: Research and Practice, 22,* 179–187.

Buelow, G. D., & Chafetz, M. D. (1996). Proposed ethical practice guidelines for clinical pharmacopsychology: Sharpening a new focus in psychology. *Professional Psychology: Research and Practice, 27,* 53–58.

Burns, S. M., DeLeon, P. H., Chemtob, C. M., Welch, B. L., & Samuels, R. M. (1988). Psychotropic medication: A new technique for psychology? *Psychotherapy, 25,* 508–515.

Bütz, M. R. (1994). Psychopharmacology: Psychology's Jurassic Park? *Psychotherapy, 31,* 692–699.

California Psychological Association, Professional Education Task Force, California School of Professional Psychology. (1995, January). *Report of the Blue Ribbon Panel.* Los Angeles: Author.

Classen, D. C., Pestotnik, S. L., Evans, S., Lloyd, J. F., & Burke, J. P. (1997). Adverse drug events in hospitalized patients: Excess length of stay, extra costs, and attributable mortality. *Journal of the American Medical Association, 277,* 301–306.

Council of Representatives, American Psychological Association. (1996). *Recommended postdoctoral training in psychopharmacology for prescription privileges.* Washington, DC: Author.

Cullen, E. A., & Newman, R. (1997). In pursuit of prescription privileges. *Professional Psychology: Research and Practice, 28,* 101–106.

DeLeon, P. H., Folen, R. A., Jennings, F. L., Wilkis, D. J., & Wright, R. H. (1991). The case for prescription privileges: A logical evolution of professional practice. *Journal of Clinical Child Psychology, 20,* 254–267.

DeLeon, P. H., Fox, R. E., & Graham, S. R. (1991). Prescription privileges: Psychology's next frontier? *American Psychologist, 46,* 384–393.

DeLeon, P. H., Sammons, M. T., & Sexton, J. L. (1995). Focusing on society's real needs: Responsibility and prescription privileges? *American Psychologist, 50,* 1022–1032.

DeLeon, P. H., & Wiggins, J. (1996). Prescription privileges for psychologists. *American Psychologist, 51,* 225–229.

DeMers, S. (1994). Legal and ethical issues in school psychologists' participation in psychopharmacological interventions with children. *School Psychology Quarterly, 9,* 41–52.

Ferguson, V. V. (1997). *Prescription privileges for psychologists: A study of rural and urban licensed psychologists' opinions.* Unpublished doctoral dissertation, University of South Dakota, Vermillion, SD.

Food and Drug Administration. (1999, May). *Managing the risks from medical product use, Creating a risk management framework.* Report to the FDA Commissioner from the Task Force on Risk Management, U.S. Department of Health and Human Services. Washington, DC: Author.

Fox, R. E. (1988). Prescription privileges: Their implications for the practice of psychology. *Psychotherapy, 25,* 501–507.

Fox, R. E., Schwelitz, F. D., & Barclay, A. G. (1992). A proposed curriculum for psychopharmacology training for professional psychologists. *Professional Psychology: Research and Practice, 23,* 216–219.

Geller, J. M., & Muus, K. J. (1997). *The role of rural primary care physicians in the provision of mental health services* (Letter to the Field No. 5). Frontier Mental Health Services Resource Network. Available online at . . .

Hanson, K. M., Louie, C. E., Van Male, L. M., Pugh, A. O., Karl, C., Muhlenbrook, L., Lilly, R. L., & Hagglund, K. J. (1999). Involving the future: The need to consider the views of psychologists-in-training regarding prescription privileges for psychologists. *Professional Psychology: Research and Practice, 30,* 203–208.

Hayes, G. J. (1998). Diving into the chemical soup. In S. C. Hayes & E. M. Heiby (Eds.), *Prescription privileges for psychologists: A critical appraisal.* Reno, NV: Context Press.

Hayes, S. C., & Heiby, E. (1996). Psychology's drug problem: Do we need a fix or should we just say no? *American Psychologist, 51,* 198–206.

Heiby, E. (1998). The case against prescription privileges for psychologists: An overview. In S. C. Hayes & E. M. Heiby (Eds.), *Prescription privileges for psychologists: A critical appraisal.* Reno, NV: Context Press.

Hendryx, M. S., Borders, T., & Johnson, T. (1995). The distribution of mental health providers in a rural state. *Administration and Policy in Mental Health, 23,* 153–155.

Hirschfeld, R. M., Keller, M. B., Panico, S., Arons, B. S., Barlow, D., Davidoff, F., Endicott, J., Froom, J., Goldstein, M., Gorman, J. M., Guthrie, D., Marek, R. G., Maurer, T. A., Meyer, R., Phillips, K., Ross, J., Schwenk, T. L., Sharfstein, S. S., Thase, M. E., & Wyatt, R. J. (1997): The National Depressive and Manic-Depressive Association consensus statement on the undertreatment of depression. *Journal of the American Medical Association, 277,* 333–340.

Holzer, C. E., III, Goldsmith, H. F., & Ciarlo, J. A. (1998). Effects of rural-urban county type on the availability of health and mental health care providers. In R. W. Manderscheid & M. J. Henderson (Eds.), *Mental health, United States* (pp. 204–213). Rockville, MD: U.S. Department of Health and Human Services.

Institute of Medicine Committee on Quality of Health Care in America. (1999). In L. T. Kohn, J. M. Corrigan, & M. S. Donaldson (Eds.), *To err is human: Building a safer health system.* Washington, DC: National Academy Press.

Kennedy, J. (1998, April 3). Prescription privileges for psychologists: A view from the field. *Psychiatric News, 33*(7), 26.

Kingsbury, S. J. (1992). Some effects of prescribing privileges. *Professional Psychology: Research and Practice, 23,* 3–5.

Klein, R. (1996). Comments on expanding the clinical role of psychologists. *American Psychologist, 5,* 216–218.

Klusman, L. E. (1998). Military health care providers' views on prescribing privileges for psychologists. *Professional Psychology: Research and Practice, 29,* 223–229.

Lesar, T. S., Briceland, L., & Stein, D. S. (1997). Factors related to errors in medication prescribing. *Journal of the American Medical Association, 277,* 312–317.

Matthews, W. J. (1998, March 23). In opposition to prescription privileges for psychologists. GO Inside. Available online at. . . .

May, W. T., & Belsky, J. (1992). Response to "Prescription privileges: Psychology's next frontier?" or the siren call: Should psychologists medicate? *American Psychologist, 47,* 427.

Moyer, D. (1995). An opposing view on prescription privileges for psychologists. *Professional Psychology: Research and Practice, 26,* 586–590.

Murstein, B. I., & Fontaine P. A. (1993). The public's knowledge about psychologists and other mental health professionals. *American Psychologist, 7,* 838–845.

Narrow, W. E., Regier, D. A., Rae, D. S., Manderscheid, R. W., & Locke, B. Z. (1993). Use of services by persons with mental and addictive disorders: Findings from the National Institute of Mental Health Epidemiologic Catchment Area Program. *Archives of General Psychiatry, 50,* 95–107.

Office of Program Consultation and Accreditation, American Psychological Association. (1996). *Book 1: Guidelines and principles for accreditation of programs in professional psychology.* Washington, DC: Author.

Olfson, M., & Pincus, H. A. (1996). Outpatient mental health care in nonhospital settings: Distribution of patients across provider groups. *American Journal of Psychiatry, 153,* 1353–1356.

Pachman, J. S. (1996). The dawn of a revolution in mental health. *American Psychologist, 51,* 213–215.

Phillips, D. P., Christenfeld, N., & Glynn, L. M. (1998). Increase in US medication-error deaths between 1983 and 1993. *Lancet, 351,* 643–644.

Pies, R. W. (1991). The "deep structure" of clinical medicine and prescribing privileges for psychologists. *Journal of Clinical Psychiatry, 52,* 4–8.

Pincus, H. A., Tanielian, T. L., Marcus, S. C., Olfson, M., Zarin, D. A., Thompson, J., & Zito, J. M. (1998). Prescribing trends in psychotropic medications: Primary care, psychiatry, and other medical specialties. *Journal of the American Medical Association, 279,* 526–531.

Preskorn, S. H. (1999). *Outpatient management of depression: A guide for the practitioner* (2nd ed.). Caddo, OK: Professional Communications, Inc.

Roan, S. (1993, September 7). Tug-of-war over prescription powers; health: Pharmacists, nurses and other non-doctors want the authority to prescribe drugs. Others insist only physicians have the training to do so safely. *Los Angeles Times,* Part E, 1, 6.

Robiner, W. N. (1999, May). Why psychologists should not pursue prescription privileges. In J. Boyd, M. Chesney, R. Kollmorgen, J. L. Raymond, W. Robiner, & J. Boller, *Prescriptive authority for psychologists: Pros and cons.* Annual Meeting of the Minnesota Psychological Association, Minneapolis.

Robiner, W. N., Bearman, D. L., Berman, M., Grove, W., Colön, E., Armstrong, J., Mareck, S., & Tanenbaum, R. (2001). *Prescriptive authority for psychologists: Despite deficits in education and knowledge?* Manuscript submitted for publication.

Sammons, M. T. (1994). Prescription privileges and psychology: A reply to Adams and Bieliauskas. *Journal of Clinical Psychology in Medical Settings, 1,* 199–207.

Sammons, M. T., & Brown, A. B. (1997). The Department of Defense Psychopharmacology Demonstration Project: An evolving program for postdoctoral education in psychology. *Professional Psychology: Research and Practice, 28,* 107–112.

Sammons, M. T., Sexton, J. L., & Meredith, J. M. (1996). Basic science training in psychopharmacology: How much is enough? *American Psychologist, 51,* 230–234.

Schofield, W. (1969). The role of psychology in the delivery of health services. *American Psychologist, 24,* 565–584.

Scully, J. H., Jr. (1999). The psychiatric workforce. In S. Weissman, M. Sabshin, & H. Eist (Eds.), *Psychiatry in the new millennium* (pp. 273–283). Washington, DC: American Psychiatric Press.

Shatin, D., Gardner, J., & Stergachis, A. (1999). Letter. *Journal of the American Medical Association, 281*(4), 319–320.

Smyer, M. A., Balster, R. L., Egli, D., Johnson, D. L., Kilbey, M. M., Leith, N. J., & Puente, A. E. (1993). Summary of the report of the Ad Hoc Task Force on Psychopharmacology of the American Psychological Association. *Professional Psychology: Research and Practice, 24,* 394–403.

Tatman, S. M., Peters, D. B., Greene, A. L., & Bongar, B. (1997). Graduate students' attitudes toward prescription privileges training. *Professional Psychology: Research and Practice, 28,* 515–517.

U.S. General Accounting Office. (1999). *Prescribing psychologists: DOD demonstration participants perform well but have little effect on readiness or costs: Report to the Chairman and Ranking Minority Member, Committee on Armed Services, U.S. Senate.* Washington, DC: Author.

Wood, W., Jones, M., & Benjamin, L. T., Jr. (1986). Surveying psychology's public image. *American Psychologist, 41,* 947–953.

Zimmerman, M. A., & Wienckowski, L. A. (1991). Revisiting health and mental health linkages: A policy whose time has come . . . again. *Journal of Public Health Policy, 12,* 510–524.

CHALLENGE QUESTIONS

Should Psychologists Prescribe Medication?

1. Imagine that you are suffering from an intense degree of anxiety or depression for which medication has been shown to be an effective intervention. From whom would you want to seek a prescription, and what factors would influence your choice?
2. An argument has been made that giving psychologists the right to prescribe medications would address the fact that there are many regions in which prescribing mental health professionals are not available. Discuss the strengths and weaknesses of this argument.
3. In recent years, increased attention has been given to the aggressive marketing of psychotropic medications. Of particular concern are practices in which physicians are lavishly indulged with gifts or expensive dinners in order to "learn about" a pharmaceutical company's product. Discuss the ethical issues involved in such practices, and consider ways in which objectionable marketing practices could be changed.
4. Imagine that you are a researcher with a grant to evaluate effectiveness and satisfaction associated with psychologists being given prescription privileges. What factors would go into designing a study on this topic?
5. Consider the fact that the majority of prescriptions for mental health conditions are written by nonpsychiatric physicians. Discuss the benefits and problems associated with this practice.

Suggested Readings

Gutierrez, P. M., & Silk, K. R. (1998). Prescription privileges for psychologists: A review of the psychological literature. *Professional Psychology: Research and Practice, 29,* 213–222.

Hayes, S. C., & Heiby, E. M. (Eds.). (1998). *Prescription privileges for psychologists: A critical appraisal.* Reno, NV: Context Press.

Hobson, J. A., & Leonard, J. A. (2001). *Out of its mind: Psychiatry in crisis.* Boston: Perseus.

Johnstone, L. (2003). Back to basics. *The Psychologist, 16*(4), 186–7.

Long, J. E., Jr. (2005). Power to prescribe: The debate over prescription privileges for psychologists and the legal issues implicated. *Law and Psychology Review, 29,* 243–260.

Sternberg, R. J. (2001). Prescription privileges for psychologists: A view from academe. *The California Psychologist, 34*(10), 16–17.

ISSUE 12

Is Electroconvulsive Therapy Ethical?

YES: Max Fink, from *Electroshock: Restoring the Mind* (Oxford University Press, 1999)

NO: Leonard R. Frank, from "Shock Treatment IV: Resistance in the 1990s," in Robert F. Morgan, ed., *Electroshock: The Case Against* (Morgan Foundation, 1999)

ISSUE SUMMARY

YES: Physician Max Fink asserts that electroconvulsive therapy (ECT) is an effective intervention whose use has been limited as a result of social stigma and philosophical bias, which have been reinforced by intimidation from the pharmaceutical and managed care industries.

NO: Leonard R. Frank, editor and cofounder of the Network Against Psychiatric Assault, criticizes the use of ECT because of its disturbing side effects, some of which he personally has suffered, and asserts that its resurgence in popularity is economically based.

$\mathbf{F}$or more than six decades some psychiatrists have treated their patients with electroconvulsive therapy (ECT), an extreme intervention involving the administration of an electric shock with the aim of controlling disturbing emotional and behavioral symptoms. Most commonly used in cases of debilitating depression, ECT consists of a treatment in which electric shock is applied through electrodes attached to the head. The premise of ECT is that radical alterations in the brain's chemistry stimulate beneficial changes in neurons, thus reducing certain kinds of symptoms. ECT grew in popularity among American psychiatrists during the 1940s and 1950s, but so did criticisms of this procedure because it was so often abused as a means of disciplining and controlling disruptive patients in psychiatric hospitals. As a result of considerable controversy surrounding ECT, the method became infrequently used by the 1970s. In recent years, however, there has been renewed interest in this intervention, which some experts regard as an effective and efficient option, especially for severely symptomatic individuals who do not respond to medication or psychotherapy.

In the following selection, Max Fink asserts that ECT is an effective intervention whose use has been limited as a result of social stigma and philosophical bias against it. Fink views ECT as a safe treatment that has been demonstrated to be effective with a range of psychiatric disorders, including severe depression, mania, schizophrenia, and catatonia. In trying to explain the reluctance of American psychiatrists to recommend ECT, Fink contends that they are intimidated by the pharmaceutical industry, managed care companies, and political forces that have underfunded psychiatric care and research.

In the second selection, Leonard R. Frank speaks against ECT as a former patient who was given extensive treatments with ECT and its predecessor, insulin-induced coma treatments. Expressing alarm about the resurgence of ECT, he criticizes claims that it is effective and safe, and he contends that its current popularity is economically based. Highlighting a number of disturbing side effects, some of which he personally suffered, Frank speaks about this method as one that destroys "the memories and lives of those subjected to it."

POINT

- ECT is a safe and reliable form of treatment.

- ECT is not as widely used as it should be, because psychiatrists are intimidated by the pharmaceutical industry, managed care companies, and political forces that have underfunded psychiatric care and research.

- The antidepressant effects of ECT occur earlier and are more robust than those of antidepressant drugs.

- It is shameful that many agencies that are licensed to treat the mentally ill lack the facilities to give ECT.

- Many criticisms about ECT are based on references to problems that were associated with ECT when it was first introduced, which are wholly unwarranted today because modern practice has made ECT safe.

COUNTERPOINT

- The serious risks associated with ECT are consistently understated and overlooked.

- The increase in ECT, particularly in the psychiatric wards of general hospitals, has been due in part to the fact that costs are paid for by insurance companies, causing some hospitals to reap considerable financial benefits from their use of ECT.

- After 50 years of research on ECT, no methodologically sound study has shown beneficial effects of ECT lasting as long as four weeks.

- ECT is one of the most controversial treatments in psychiatry, and it has great potential for destroying the memories and lives of those who are subjected to it.

- The side effects associated with ECT are very serious and include amnesia, denial, euphoria, apathy, wide mood swings, helplessness, and submissiveness—effects that offset the problems that supposedly justified the use of ECT in the first place.

YES ⤶

Max Fink

Electroshock in the 1990s

Within the past decade, clinical and research interest in ECT [electrocon-vulsive therapy] has revived. The resurgence has been most marked in the United States, where the greatest efforts are under way to improve its safety and its efficacy. Psychiatrists in other countries have sought to reintroduce ECT, but its use varies widely. ECT is an accepted part of psychiatric practice in the Scandinavian countries, Great Britain, Ireland, Australia, and New Zealand, and usage is similar to that in the United States. A stigma attached to ECT limits its use in Germany, Japan, Italy, and the Netherlands to a few aca-demic medical centers. Low reimbursement rates hamper its use in Canada and Japan, and also affect its availability in the United States. The unavailabil-ity of modern equipment and the expense of the medicines for anesthesia pre-vent its use in Africa, Asia, and Eastern Europe, and many patients in these countries who do receive it are subjected to unmodified ECT, such as was delivered in the 1930s and 1940s.

ECT is mainly a treatment for hospitalized patients, although many institutions are developing programs for outpatient ECT. The equipment and trained personnel are, for the most part, in the academic hospitals. Academic leaders recognize the merits of the treatment; some even encourage research and teaching. ECT is ignored by the research scientists at the National Insti-tute of Mental Health. Few of the state, federal, or Veterans Administration hospitals provide ECT, and where it is available its use is infrequent. While 8 percent to 12 percent of adult inpatients at academic hospitals receive ECT, fewer than 0.2 percent of adults at nonacademic centers do. Such a discrep-ancy reflects the continuing social stigma and philosophical bias against elec-troshock. Before the federal Medicare and the Hill-Burton legislative acts of the 1960s opened access for all patients to any hospital facility, such discrep-ancies may have been common. But now that the nation has adopted an open-admission policy to its psychiatric facilities, the discrepancy is unjustified. It is shameful that many agencies licensed to treat the mentally ill lack the facilities to give the treatment.

Effects of Research on Practice

When ECT was revived in the late 1970s, the principal concern was its effects on cognition and memory. Unilateral ECT won favor with many practitioners after demonstrations that it reduced effects on memory. But other practitioners reported that unilateral ECT required more treatments than, and was not as effective as, bilateral ECT. The seizures in unilateral ECT were often brief, with poorly defined EEG seizure patterns. Studies of the interaction of electrode placement, energy dosing, and current form show that unilateral treatments, even with precise energy dosing, are less efficient than bilateral ECT. As a result, bilateral ECT is now preferred. When unilateral ECT is considered, its use includes precise energy dosing. Sinusoidal currents elicited unnecessarily high degrees of EEG and memory effects, compared with brief pulse square-wave currents, so the former have now been discarded.

We have learned that monitoring the motor seizure is not sufficient to measure the adequacy of an individual treatment, so we now look to EEG measures as more reliable indices. By recording and displaying the seizure EEG, we rely on the seizure characteristics as a guide to an effective treatment. Practitioners depend more on these characteristics than on criteria based on the motor convulsion and the change in heart rate as measures of beneficial treatment.

The interseizure EEG has stimulated research interest. Studies in 1957 had shown that a good clinical response in ECT depended on the slowing of the frequencies in the interseizure EEG. The observation was confirmed in 1972 and again in 1996, and the interseizure EEG is once again used as a guide to an effective course of treatment.

The indications for ECT have been broadened. As we have seen, it has gone from being a last resort for unresponsive depressed and suicidal patients to being a treatment option for patients with delusional depression, mania, schizophrenia, and catatonia. ECT can also be useful in patients with parkinsonism and those suffering from neuroleptic drug toxicity. Treatment can be safely given in the presence of complex systemic disorders and mental retardation.

Yet research on ECT is limited. Most of the research is directed at determining which treatment—medication or continuation ECT—can best maintain the benefits of a course of ECT in patients with severe depression. Some scientists still believe that sophisticated brain-imaging methods will find evidence of persistent brain dysfunction after ECT. So far, such studies have yielded no new information about mental illness or about ECT. Others seek the benefits of ECT without a seizure by the use of rapid magnetic pulses instead of electrical ones. The method, called "rapid transcranial magnetic stimulation" (rTMS), has yet to be proven of benefit.

Future of Electroshock

Psychiatric care in the United States is in such turmoil that the problem of restoring the availability of electroshock seems nearly insignificant. American psychiatry lacks the leaders to stand up to the pharmaceutical industry and the managed care executives who are taking ever larger portions of the financial resources allocated to treating mental illness. State legislatures are cutting funds for mental health care, urging their mental hospital administrators to reduce patient admissions and shorten durations of stay. The state mental hospitals, which served as the ultimate haven for the mentally ill, are being closed and patients are being consigned to a motley collection of inadequate substitutions. The nonthreatening and passive homeless are on the streets; those who are more ill go in and out of the revolving doors of community centers and emergency wards or to hospitals equipped only for short-term care. Those who fall between end up in halfway houses and adult homes.

At one time the states supported research centers that were the jewels of the nation's mental health activities. Few institutes are still supported by the states, and even these are forced to compete for larger portions of their budgets from federal resources and private charity.

Academic researchers depend on industry to support increasing portions of their salaries. Industry sponsorship has taken over major aspects of the training of psychiatric residents by providing funds for lectures and seminars at medical schools and hospitals, and for national and international meetings. Industry employees organize carefully crafted symposia, and the ensuing discussions are published as supplements to freely distributed psychiatric journals. The opportunity for independent assessment and open dialogue about the efficacy and safety of psychoactive drugs, and especially comparisons with other treatments such as electroshock, has been virtually eliminated.

The leaders of the lay agencies that speak for the mentally ill are confused, torn between the promises of an industry hawking its products, state mental health agencies seeking to self-destruct, and managed care companies striving to limit expenditures for the care of the mentally ill. The lay agencies are sensitive to the stigma of electroshock and avoid mention of it for fear of losing members and financial support. For that reason, they do not encourage state and municipal legislatures to provide the treatment.

In this turmoil, few psychiatrists speak up in behalf of electroshock for their patients. The two U.S. manufacturers who make modern ECT devices and support educational efforts are too small to do more than survive. Although their new devices have highly sophisticated EEG-recording capabilities that can monitor electroshock treatments with great precision, these manufacturers can do little to ensure that their instruments are properly used.

In the brouhaha over the revival of ECT in the 1970s, the anti-ECT lobby tried to persuade the FDA to limit the sale and use of ECT devices in the United States. Their claim was that the devices were unsafe. In the early 1980s the FDA ruled that the devices in use were safe and reliable. The devices delivered energies with a fixed maximum under standard conditions, a maximum that had been set arbitrarily. Patients' seizure thresholds, however, rise with age, and many of the elderly need higher energies for effective treatment. The device manufacturers developed such devices, but when they applied to the FDA for modification of the standards, they were turned down and could not sell their equipment. The devices now sold in the United States are inadequate for effective treatment of some patients. Since the higher-energy devices are sold in the rest of the world, we have the awkward situation that patients in Canada, Europe, and Australia are being effectively treated while we in this country fail in treating some patients with similar conditions.

There is one opportunity on the economic horizon for a broader recognition of the merits of electroshock. The duration of inpatient treatment for patients receiving electroshock seems to be longer than for those receiving other treatments. But patients come to ECT after drug trials, often many trials, have failed. If the duration of inpatient care of patients given ECT is estimated from the day of the decision to use ECT, it is shorter and the costs are lower than the costs for psychotropic drugs. In one academic general hospital, of 19 depressed patients treated with ECT alone, the average hospital stay averaged 41 days, and for the 55 patients treated with tricyclic antidepressants (TCA) alone, the average stay was 55 days. The longest stay was for patients first treated with TCA and, when those failed, with ECT—an average length of stay of 71 days. The estimated cost of the stay for ECT treatment was $20,000 and for TCA alone it was $26,500, a savings of $6,500 for ECT over TCA. The same financial advantage is found when outpatient ECT is prescribed.

A study of patients discharged from general hospitals with a principal diagnosis of depressive disorder found that the initiation of ECT within five days of admission leads to shorter and less costly inpatient treatment than for those treated with drugs alone or delayed ECT. Other studies found that the anti-depresssant effects of ECT occur earlier and are more robust than those of anti-depressant drugs.

For the present, few managed care insurers recognize the merits of ECT, either as a relief for their insured ill patients or as a financial benefit to their shareholders. Payment for ECT is rarely approved for a patient with schizophrenia, so that patient must endure one drug trial after another. The most specious arguments are made about patients seen as catatonic, where neuroleptic drug trials are required, despite the evidence that neuroleptic drugs may precipitate the more acute state of neuroleptic malignant syndrome (NMS).

As managed care organizations assume a greater role in medical care, they reduce costs by limiting the conditions for which payments will be made, cutting professional fees and negotiating cheaper hospital costs. Once these measures have squeezed out of the system all the "excess" costs they can, the demand for the most efficient treatments will gain support. The advantages of ECT over medication should promote its greater use. Such an effect is already apparent in the expanding number of institutions seeking to develop qualified ECT facilities, in the interest of practitioners in obtaining education credits for ECT, and in the overt inclusion of electroshock as a valid treatment in algorithms now recommended for depression.

Many object to the revival of ECT by reminding others of the problems with electroshock when it was first introduced; at the time it was virtually the only effective treatment for the mentally ill. Such criticism is wholly unwarranted today; it is no more reasonable than to speak of the excesses in tonsillectomy, hysterectomy, pallidotomy, insulin coma, and labotomy that marked the enthusiastic reception of those procedures in earlier decades. Our appreciation of electroshock must be based on its present practice. We call on it because it is effective, often more so than alternate treatments, and because modern practice has made it safe.

Shock Treatment IV:
Resistance in the 1990s

Electroshock: Death, Brain Damage, Memory Loss, and Brainwashing

Since its introduction in 1938, electroshock, or electroconvulsive therapy (ECT), has been one of psychiatry's most controversial procedures. Approximately 100,000 people in the United States undergo ECT yearly, and recent media reports indicate a resurgence of its use. Proponents claim that changes in the technology of ECT administration have greatly reduced the fears and risks formerly associated with the procedure. I charge, however, that ECT as routinely used today is at least as harmful overall as it was before these changes were instituted. I recount my own experience with combined insulin coma-electroshock during the early 1960s and the story of the first electroshock "treatment." I report on who is now being electroshocked, at what cost, where, and for what reasons. I discuss ECT technique modifications and describe how ECT is currently administered. I examine assertions and evidence concerning ECT's effectiveness. . . .

In October 1962, at the age of 30, I had a run-in with psychiatry and got the worst of it. According to my hospital records (Frank, 1976), the "medical examiners," in recommending that I be committed, wrote the following: "Reportedly has been showing progressive personality changes over past two or so years. Grew withdrawn and asocial, couldn't or wouldn't work, and spent most of his time reading or doing nothing. Grew a beard, ate only vegetarian food, and lived life of a beatnik—to a certain extent" (p. 63). I was labeled "paranoid schizophrenic, severe and chronic," denied my freedom for nine months, and assaulted with a variety of drugs and fifty insulin-coma and thirty-five electroshock "treatments."

Each shock treatment was for me a Hiroshima. The shocking destroyed large parts of my memory, including the two-year period preceding the last shock. Not a day passes that images from that period of confinement do not float into consciousness. Nor does the night provide escape, for my dreams bear them as well. I am back there again in the "treatment room;" coming out of that last insulin coma (the only one I remember); strapped down, a tube in my nose, a hypodermic needle in my arm; sweating, starving, suffocating, struggling to move; a group of strangers around the bed grabbing at me; thinking—Where am I? What the hell is happening to me?

Well into the shock series, which took place at Twin Pines Hospital in Belmont, California, a few miles south of San Francisco, the treating psychiatrist wrote to my father:

> In evaluating Leonard's progress to date, I think it is important to point out there is some slight improvement, but he still has all the delusional beliefs regarding his beard, dietary regime, and religious observances that he had prior to treatment. We hope that in continuing the treatments we will be able to modify some of these beliefs so that he can make a reasonable adjustment to life. (p. 77)

During the comatose phase of one of my treatments, my beard was removed—as "a therapeutic device to provoke anxiety and make some change in his body image," the consulting psychiatrist had written in his report recommending this procedure. He continued, "Consultation should be obtained from the TP [Twin Pines] attorney as to the civil rights issue—but I doubt that these are crucial. The therapeutic effort is worth it—inasmuch that he can always grow another" (p. 76).

Earlier, several psychiatrists had tried unsuccessfully to persuade me to shave off my beard. "Leonard seems to attach a great deal of religious significance to the beard," the treating psychiatrist had noted at the time. He had even brought in a local rabbi to change my thinking (p. 75), but to no avail. I have no recollection of any of this. It is all from my medical records.

> Genuine religious conversions are also seen after the new modified lobotomy operations. For the mind is freed from its old strait-jacket and new religious beliefs and attitudes can now more easily take the place of the old. (Sargant, 1957, p. 71)
>
> At the "Mental Health Center" [in Albuquerque] where I work, there is a sign on the wall near the inpatient wards that reads: "PATIENTS' RIGHTS: Patients have the right to religious freedom unless clinically contraindicated." (Jones, 1988, p. 2)

One day, about a week after my last treatment, I was sitting in the day room, which was adjacent to the shock-treatment wing of the hospital building. It was just before lunch and near the end of the treatment session (which lasts about five hours) for those being insulin-shocked. The thick metal door separating the two areas had been left slightly ajar. Suddenly, from behind the door, I heard the scream of a young man whom I had recently come to know and who was then starting an insulin course. It was a scream like nothing I had ever heard before, an all-out scream. Hurriedly, one of the nurses closed the door. The screams, now less audible, continued a while longer. I do not remember my own screams; his, I remember.

[The insulin-coma patient] is prevented from seeing all at once the actions and treatment of those patients further along in their therapy . . . As much as possible, he is saved the trauma of sudden introduction to the sight of patients in different stages of coma—a sight which is not very pleasant to an unaccustomed eye. (Gralnick, 1944, p. 184)

During the years since my institutionalization, I have often asked myself how psychiatrists, or anyone else for that matter, could justify shocking a human being. Soon after I began researching my book *The History of Shock Treatment* (1978), I discovered Gordon's (1948) review of the literature, in which he compiled fifty theories purporting to explain the "healing" mechanism of the various forms of shock therapy then in use, including insulin, Metrazol, and electroshock. Here are some excerpts:

Because prefontal lobotomy improves the mentally ill by destruction, the improvement obtained by all the shock therapies must also involve some destructive processes.
They help by way of a circulatory shake up . . .
It decreases cerebral function.
The treatments bring the patient and physician in closer contact. Helpless and dependent, the patient sees in the physician a mother.
Threat of death mobilizes all the vital instincts and forces a reestablishment of contacts with reality. . . .
The treatment is considered by patients as punishment for sins and gives feelings of relief.
Victory over death and joy of rebirth produce the results.
The resulting amnesia is healing.
Erotization is the therapeutic factor.
The personality is brought down to a lower level and adjustment is obtained more easily in a primitive vegetative existence than in a highly developed personality. Imbecility replaces insanity. (pp. 399–401)

One of the more interesting explanations I found was proposed by Manfred Sakel, the Austrian psychiatrist who, in 1933, introduced insulin coma as a treatment for schizophrenia. According to Sakel (cited in Ray, 1942, p. 250):

[W]ith chronic schizophrenics, as with confirmed criminals, we can't hope for reform. Here the faulty pattern of functioning is irrevocably entrenched. Hence we must use more drastic measures to silence the dysfunctioning cells and so liberate the activity of the normal cells. This time we must *kill* the too vocal dysfunctioning cells. But can we do this without killing normal cells also? Can we *select* the cells we wish to destroy? I think we can. [italics in original]

Electroshock may be considered one of the most controversial treatments in psychiatry. As I document below, the last decade has witnessed a resurgence of ECT's popularity, accompanied by assertions from proponents concerning its effectiveness and safety—assertions which deny or obscure basic facts about the historical origins of ECT, the economic reasons behind its current popularity, as well as its potential for destroying the memories and lives of those subjected to it. . . .

Electroshock Facts and Figures

Since 1938, between ten and fifteen million people worldwide have undergone electroshock. While no precise figure is available, it is estimated that about 100,000 people in the United States are electroshocked annually (Fink, cited in Rymer, 1989, p. 68). Moreover, the numbers appear to be increasing. Recent media accounts report a resurgence of ECT interest and use. One reason for this is the well-publicized enthusiasm of such proponents as Max Fink, editor-in-chief of *Convulsive Therapy,* the leading journal in the field. Fink was recently cited as saying that "[ECT should be given to] all patients whose condition is severe enough to require hospitalization" (Edelson, 1988. p. 3).

A survey of the American Psychiatric Association (APA) membership focusing on ECT (APA, 1978) showed that 22% fell into the "User" category. Users were defined as psychiatrists who had "personally treated patients with ECT" or "recommended to residents under their supervision that ECT be used on patients" during the last six months (p. 5). If valid today, this figure indicates that approximately 7,700 APA members are electroshock Users.

A survey of all 184 member hospitals of the National Association of Private Psychiatric Hospitals (Levy and Albrecht, 1985) elicited the following information on electroshock practices from the 153 respondents (83%) who answered a nineteen-item questionnaire sent to them in 1982. Fifty-eight percent of the respondents used electroshock (3% did not use electroshock because they considered it to be "inappropriate treatment for any illness").

The hospitals using ECT found it appropriate for a variety of diagnoses: 100% for "major depressive disorder," 58% for "schizophrenia," and 13% for "obsessive-compulsive disorder." Twenty-six percent of the ECT-using hospitals reported no contraindications in the use of the procedure.

Darnton (1989) reported that the number of private free-standing psychiatric hospitals grew from 184 in 1980 to 450 in 1988. In addition, nearly 2,000 general hospitals offer inpatient psychiatric service (p. 67). While the use of ECT in state hospitals has fallen off sharply over the last twenty years, the psychiatric wards of general hospitals have increased their reliance on ECT in the treatment of their adult inpatients (Thompson, 1986).

In cases of depression, an ECT series ranges from six to twelve seizures—in those of schizophrenia, from fifteen to thirty-five seizures—given three times a week, and usually entails four weeks of hospitalization. In 72% of the cases, according to the APA (1978, p. 8) survey cited above, electroshock costs are paid for by insurance companies. This fact led one psychiatrist to comment, "Finding that the patient has insurance seemed like the most common indication for giving electroshock" (Viscott, 1972, p. 356). The overall cost for a series of electroshock in a private hospital ranges from $10,000 to $25,000. With room rates averaging $500 to $600 a day, and bed occupancy generally falling, some hospitals have obtained considerable financial advantage from their use of ECT. A regular ECT User can expect yearly earnings of at least

$200,000, about twice the median income of other psychiatrists. *Electroshock is a $2–3 billion-a-year industry.*

More than two-thirds of electroshock subjects are women, and a growing number are elderly. In California, one of the states that requires Users to report quarterly the number and age categories of electroshock subjects, "the percentage 65 and over" being electroshocked increased gradually from 29% to 43% between 1977 and 1983 (Warren, 1986, p. 51). More recently, Drop and Welch (1989) reported that 60% of the ECT subjects in a recent two-year period at the Massachusetts General Hospital in Boston were over 60 years and 10% were in their eighties (p. 88).

There are published reports of persons over 100 years old (Alexopoulos, Young, and Abrams, 1989) and as young as $34^1/_2$ months (Bender, 1955) who have been electroshocked. In the latter case, the child had been referred in 1947 to the children's ward of New York's Bellevue Hospital "because of distressing anxiety that frequently reached a state of panic. . . . The child was mute and autistic." The morning after admission he received the first of a series of twenty electroshocks and was discharged one month later. "The discharge note indicated a 'moderate improvement' since he was eating and sleeping better, was more friendly with the other children, and he was toilet trained" (pp. 418–419).

Children continue to be electroshocked. Black, Wilcox, and Stewart (1985) reported on "the successful use of ECT in a prepubertal boy with severe depression." Sandy, 11 years old, received twelve unilateral ECTs at the University of Iowa Hospitals and Clinics in Iowa City. He "improved remarkably" and "was discharged in good condition. Follow-up over the next eight years revealed five more hospitalizations for depression" (p. 98).

Some of the better known people who have undergone shock treatment include: Antonin Artaud, Thomas Eagleton, Claude Eatherly, Frances Farmer, Zelda Fitzgerald, James Forrestal, Janet Frame, Ernest Hemingway, Vladimir Horowitz, Bob Kaufman, Seymour Krim, Vivien Leigh, Oscar Levant, Robert Lowell, Vaslav Nijinsky, Jimmy Pearsall, Robert Pirsig, Sylvia Plath, Paul Robeson, Gene Tierney, and Frank Wisner.

In the early 1970s electroshock survivors—together with other former psychiatric inmates/"patients"—began forming organizations aimed at regulating or abolishing electroshock and other psychiatric practices which they believed were harmful. In 1975, one group, the Network Against Psychiatric Assault (San Francisco/Berkeley), was instrumental in the passage of legislation that regulated the use of electroshock in California. Since then, more than thirty states have passed similar legislation.

In 1982, the Coalition to Stop Electroshock led a successful referendum campaign to outlaw ECT in Berkeley, California. Although the courts overturned the ban six weeks after it went into effect, this was the first time in American history that the use of any established medical procedure had been prohibited by popular vote.

The Committee for Truth in Psychiatry (CTIP), all of whose members are electroshock survivors, was formed in 1984 to support the Food and Drug Administration (FDA) in its original (1979) classification of the ECT device in the high risk category of medical devices, Class III, which earmarks a device of its related procedure for a safety investigation. To prevent an investigation of ECT, the APA had petitioned the FDA in 1982 for reclassification of the ECT device to Class II, which signifies low risk. After many years of indecision, the FDA proposed in 1990 to make this reclassification—but has not yet done so. . . .

Claims of Electroshock Effectiveness

Virtually all the psychiatrists who evaluate, write about, and do research on electroshock are themselves Users. This partially explains why claims regarding ECT's effectiveness abound in the professional literature—while the risks associated with the procedure are consistently understated or overlooked. User estimates of ECT's effectiveness in the treatment of the affective disorders (i.e., depression, mania, and manic-depression) usually range from 75% to 90%. Two important questions, however, need to be addressed: What is meant by effectiveness, and how long does it last?

Breggin (1979, p. 135; 1981, pp. 252–253) has proposed a "brain-disabling hypothesis" to explain the workings of electroshock. The hypothesis suggests that ECT "effectiveness" stems from the brain damage ECT causes. As happens in cases of serious head injury, ECT produces amnesia, denial, euphoria, apathy, wide and unpredictable mood swings, helplessness and submissiveness. Each one of these effects may appear to offset the problems which justified the use of ECT in the first place.

Amnesia victims, having forgotten their problems, tend to complain less. Denial serves a similar purpose. Because of their embarrassment, ECT subjects tend to discount or deny unresolved personal problems, as well as ECT-caused intellectual deficits. With euphoria, the subject's depression seems to lift. With apathy, the subject's "agitation" (if that had been perceived as part of the original problem) seems to diminish. Dependency and submissiveness tend to make what may have been a resistive, hostile subject more cooperative and friendly. In hailing the wonders of electroshock, psychiatrists often simply redefine the symptoms of psychiatrogenic brain damage as signs of improvement and/or recovery.

Electroshock advocates themselves unwittingly provide support for the brain-disabling hypothesis. Fink, Kahn, and Green (1958) offered a good example of this when describing a set of criteria for rating improvement in ECT subjects: "When a depressed patient, who had been withdrawn, crying, and had expressed suicidal thoughts, no longer is seclusive, and is jovial, friendly and euphoric, denies his problems and sees his previous thoughts of suicide as 'silly' a rating of 'much improved' is made" (p. 117). Two additional illustrations are given below; see Cleckley (cited in Thigpen, 1976) and Hoch (1948).

On the question of duration of benefit from ECT, Weiner (1984)—in one of the most important review articles on ECT published during the last decade—was unable to cite a single study purporting to show long-term, or even medium-term, benefits from ECT. Opton (1985) drew this conclusion from the Weiner review: "In this comprehensive review of the literature, after fifty years of research on ECT, no methodologically sound study was found that reported beneficial effects of ECT lasting as long as four weeks" (p. 2). Pinel (1984), in his peer commentary on the Weiner article, accepted Weiner's conclusion that "the risks of ECT-related brain damage are slight" and then added, "it is difficult to justify any risks at all until ECT has been shown unambiguously to produce significant long-term therapeutic benefits" (p. 31).

The following excerpt from an article in *Clinical Psychiatry News* reveals the short-range outlook of many ECT Users:

> The relapse rate after successful treatment for affective disorders is very high, from 20% to 50% within six months after a *successful* course of ECT, according to Dr. Richard Abrams [a well-known ECT proponent]. "I think it is reasonable and appropriate to always initiate maintenance in the form of a tricyclic [an antidepressant drug] or lithium" he said. For patients who relapse despite adequate drug therapy, maintenance ECT [periodic single electroshocks, spaced several weeks or months apart] has been used successfully. (Klug, 1984, p. 16) [italics added]

The underlying assumption of this approach is that affective disorders are for the most part chronic and irreversible. There is a popular saying among psychiatrists, "Once a schizophrenic, always a schizophrenic." While not a maxim, "Once a depressive, always a depressive" is nevertheless a core belief among many ECT Users. It "explains" so much for them. From this perspective, there are hardly any ECT failures, only patients with recurring depressive episodes who require ongoing psychiatric treatment, intensive and maintenance by turns.

Proponents also claim, but cannot demonstrate, that ECT is effective in cases of depression where there is a risk of suicide. They often cite a study by Avery and Winokur (1976) to support their position. But this study makes no such claim, as we can see from the authors' own conclusion: "In the present study, treatment [ECT and antidepressants] was not shown to affect the suicide rate" (p. 1033). Nevertheless, Allen (1978), in the very first paragraph of his article on ECT observed, "Avery and Winokur showed that suicide mortality in patients afflicted with psychotic depression was lower in patients treated with ECT than in those who were not" (p. 47). . . .

Electroshock Modifications

In recent years, to allay growing public fears concerning the use of electroshock, proponents have launched a media campaign claiming, among other things, that with the introduction of certain modifications in the administration of ECT, the problems once associated with the procedure have been solved, or at least substantially reduced. These techniques center around the use of anesthetics and muscle relaxants, changes in electrode placement, and the use of brief-pulse electrical stimulation.

However, investigation and common sense indicate that while these modifications may offer some advantages—for example, muscle relaxants prevent the subject's thrashing about, thereby greatly reducing the risk of bone and spinal fractures, and making the procedure less frightening to watch—the basic facts underlying the administration of electroshock have not changed at all. The nature of the human brain and that of electricity are the same today as they were more than fifty years ago when ECT was introduced. Whatever may be the ameliorating factors of the newer delivery techniques, when a convulsogenic dose of electricity is applied to the brain, there is going to be a certain amount of brain damage, some of which will be permanent.

There is even evidence that the drug modifications make ECT more destructive than ever because the central nervous system depressants, anesthetics and muscle relaxants raise the subject's convulsive threshold which, in turn, makes it necessary to apply a larger dose of electricity to set off the convulsion. And, the more current applied, the more amnesia and brain damage. As Reed (1988) noted, "The amnesia directly relating to ECT depends on the amount of current used to trigger the generalized convulsion" (p. 29).

Other problems are associated with the use of premedications in ECT. In his study of 254 ECT deaths, Impastato (1957) reported that thirteen of sixty-six persons from the "cerebral death" group had received muscle relaxants and that these "appear to play a major role in the death of some of these patients" (p. 42). There were also five other patients who died immediately after receiving muscle relaxants but before being given the electric shock. These figures are from a period when muscle relaxants were not widely used. More recently, Ulett (1972) concurred with Impastato on the danger of muscle relaxants in ECT: "The objection to the use of muscle relaxants is that, although decreasing the rate of fracture complication, they unquestionably increase the chance of fatal accident" (p. 284). Given the paucity of ECT-death studies in recent years, it is difficult to gauge the extent of this problem in current practice.

Another modification, unilateral ECT, has received much attention since its introduction in the late 1950s but has not replaced—and is not likely to replace—bilateral ECT as the standard technique. According to the APA survey on ECT (1978, p. 6), 75% of the Users reported using bilateral electrode placement exclusively. In bilateral ECT, the electrodes are placed on the subject's temples so that the current passes through the brain's frontal lobe area. In unilateral ECT, one electrode is placed on a temple and the other just above the back of the neck on the same (usually the nondominant) side of the head. Unilateral placement, proponents claim, results in less memory loss. But proponents of bilateral ECT assert that unilateral ECT is less effective and therefore requires more treatments (Gregory, Shawcross, and Gill, 1985).

Cleckley (cited in Thigpen, 1976) offered this explanation for the ineffectiveness of unilateral ECT: "My thought about unilateral stimulation is that it fails to cure. I think this failure to cure is in direct proportion to the avoidance of memory loss" (p. 40). During his interview with Abrams (1988b), Kalinowsky made this comment about unilateral ECT: "My experience is completely negative and if patients improve at all, it's probably due to the repeated anesthesia induction with methohexital" (p. 38).

Given the need for "somewhat more current to produce a seizure" in each treatment session (Fink, 1978, p. 79) and for more treatment sessions per series, unilateral ECT may be more brain damaging in some cases than bilateral ECT.

The problems associated with brief-pulse stimulation, another innovation in ECT administration, are similar to those associated with unilateral ECT. While brief-pulse stimulation may cause less amnesia than the routinely used sine-wave stimulation, the newer technique "may be insufficient to induce an adequate generalized seizure" (Reed, 1988, p. 29).

What Ulett (1972) wrote about unidirectional current stimulation—a supposed advance in ECT technology introduced by Liberson (1948)—may also apply to brief-pulse stimulation, and to unilateral ECT as well: "[I]t is often necessary to give a greater number of these milder treatments to achieve the desired therapeutic result" (p. 287). . . .

Conclusion

Mystification and conditioning have undoubtedly played an important role in shaping the public's tolerant attitude toward electroshock. But it is not only the uniformed and misinformed public that has stood by silently during the electroshock era. There has hardly been a voice of protest from the informed elite—even when one of its own has been victimized.

While undergoing a series of involuntary electroshocks at the famed Mayo Clinic in 1961, Ernest Hemingway told visitor A. E. Hotchner, "Well, what is the sense of ruining my head and erasing my memory, which is my capital, and putting me out of business? It was a brilliant cure but we lost the patient. It's a bum turn, Hotch, terrible." (cited in Hotchner, 1967, p. 308).

A few days after his release from the Mayo Clinic following a second course of ECT, Hemingway killed himself with a shotgun. With all that has been written about him since his death, no recognized figure from the world of literature, academia, law religion or science has spoken out against those responsible for this tragedy. As might have been expected, the psychiatric professional has also been silent. Not only did the psychiatrist who electroshocked Hemingway escape the censure of his colleagues, but a few years later they elected him president of the American Psychiatric Association.

Since ancient times, physicians have been trying to cure epilepsy. One might therefore think that they would object to the use of artificially-induced seizures as a method of treatment. But no such objection has been forthcoming. On the contrary, the medical profession's passive acquiescence to the use of electroshock has recently turned to active support:

The AMA [American Medical Association] has endorsed the use of electroconvulsive therapy (ECT) as an effective treatment modality in selected patients, as outlined by the American Psychiatric Association. . . . [The AMA] recognized ECT as a safe procedure in proper hands. (ECT, Animal Rights, 1989, p. 9)

ECT User Robert Peck titled his book *The Miracle of Shock Treatment* (1974). Antonin Artaud (cited in Sontag, 1976), the French actor and playwright, who was electroshocked in the early 1940s, wrote afterwards: "Anyone who has gone through the electric shock never again rises out of its darkness and his life has been lowered a notch" (p. 530). In which perspective—or at what point between these two perspectives—is the truth to be found? This is no trivia question. For some, it will be the gravest question they will ever have to answer.

References

Abrams, R. (1988b). Interview with Lothar Kalinowsky, M.D. *Convulsive Therapy, 4,* 25–39.

Alexopoulos, C. S., Young, R. C., and Abrams, R. C. (1989). ECT in the high-risk geriatric patient. *Convulsive Therapy, 5,* 75–87.

Allen, M. R. (1978). Electroconvulsive therapy: An old question, new answers, *Psychiatric Annals, 8,* 47–65.

American Psychiatric Association. (1978). *Electroconvulsive Therapy.* Task Force Report 14. Washington, D.C.: American Psychiatric Association.

Avery, D., and Winokur, O. (1976). Mortality in depressed patients treated with electroconvulsive therapy and antidepressants. *Archives of General Psychiatry, 33,* 1029–1037.

Bender, L. (1955). The development of a schizophrenic child treated with electric convulsions at three years of age. In C. Caplan (Ed.), *Emotional Problems of Early Childhood* (pp. 407–425). New York: Basic Books.

Black, D. W., Wilcox, J. A., and Stewart, M. (1985). The use of ECT in children: Case report. *Journal of Clinical Psychiatry, 46,* 98–99.

Breggin, P. R. (1979). *Electroshock: Its Brain-Disabling Effects.* New York: Springer.

Darnton, N. (1989, July 31). Committed youth. *Newsweek,* pp. 66–72.

Drop, L. J., and Welch, C. A. (1989). Anesthesia for electroconvulsive therapy in patients with major cardiovascular risk factors. *Convulsive Therapy, 5,* 88–101.

ECT, animal rights among topics discussed at AMA's Dallas meeting. (1989, January 20). *Psychiatric News,* p. 9; 23.

Edelson, E. (1988, December 28). ECT elicits controversy—and results. *Houston Chronicle,* p. 3.

Fink, M. (1978). Electroshock therapy: Myths and realities. *Hospital Practice, 13,* 77–82.

Fink, M., Kahn, R. L., and Green, M. (1958). Experimental studies of electroshock process. *Diseases of the Nervous System, 19,* 113–118.

Frank, L. R. (1976). The Frank papers. In J. Friedberg, *Shock Treatment is not Good for Your Brain* (pp. 62–81). San Francisco: Glide Publications.

Frank, L. R. (1978). *The History of Shock Treatment.* San Francisco: Frank.

Gordon, H. L. (1948). Fifty shock therapy theories. *Military Surgeon, 103,* 397–401.

Gralnick, A. (1944). Psychotherapeutic and interpersonal aspects of insulin treatment. *Psychiatric Quarterly, 18,* 177–196.

Gregory, S., Shawcross, C. R., and Gill, D. (1985). The Nottingham ECT study: A double-blind comparison of bilateral, unilateral and simulated ECT in depressive illness. *British Journal of Psychiatry, 146,* 520–524.

Hoch, P. H. (1948). Discussion and concluding remarks. *Journal of Personality, 17,* 48–51.

Hotchner, A. E. (1967). *Papa Hemingway.* New York: Bantam.

Impastato, D. (1957). Prevention of fatalities in electroshock therapy. *Diseases of the Nervous System, 18* (supplement), 34–75.

Jones, T. (1988, June). Letter. *Dendron* (Eugene, Oregon), p. 2.

Klug, J. (1984, June). Benefits of ECT outweigh risks in most patients. *Clinical Psychiatry News*, p. 16.

Levy, S. D., and Albrecht, E. (1985). Electroconvulsive therapy: A survey of use in the private psychiatric hospital. *Journal of Clinical Psychiatry, 46*, 125–127.

Liberson, W. T. (1948). Brief stimuli therapy: Physiological and clinical observations. *American Journal of Psychiatry, 105*, 28–39.

Opton, E. M., Jr. (1985, June 4). Letter to the members of the panel. National Institute of Health Consensus Development Conference on Electroconvulsive Therapy.

Peck, R. E. (1974). *The Miracle of Shock Treatment.* Jericho, New York: Exposition Press. Philadelphia Psychiatric Society. (1943). Symposium: Complications of and contraindications to electric shock therapy. *Archives of Neurology and Psychiatry, 49*, 786–791.

Pinel, J. PJ. (1984). After forty-five years ECT is still controversial. *Behavioral and Brain Sciences, 7*, 30–31.

Ray, M. B. (1942). *Doctors of the Mind: The Story of Psychiatry.* Indianapolis and New York: Bobbs-Merrill.

Reed, K. (1988). Electroconvulsive therapy: A clinical discussion. *Psychiatric Medicine, 6*, 23–33.

Rymer, R. (1989, March–April). Electroshock. *Hippocrates,* pp. 65–72.

Sargant, W. (1957). *Battle for the Mind: A Physiology of Conversion and Brainwashing.* Baltimore: Penguin.

Thigpen, C. H. (1976). Letter. *Convulsive Therapy Bulletin, 1*, 40.

Thompson, J. W. (1986). Utilization of ECT in U.S. psychiatric facilities, 1975 to 1980. *Psychopharmacology Bulletin, 22*, 463–465.

Ulett, G. A. (1972). *A Synopsis of Contemporary Psychiatry.* St. Louis: C. V. Mosby.

Viscott, D. (1972). *The Making of a Psychiatrist.* Greenwich, Connecticut: Faucett.

Warren, C. A. B. (1986). Electroconvulsive therapy: "new" treatment of the 1980s. *Research in Law, Deviance and Social Control, 8*, 41–55.

Weiner, R. D. (1984). Does electroconvulsive therapy cause brain damage? *Behavioral and Brain Sciences, 7*, 1–22 (peer commentary section, pp. 22–54).

CHALLENGE QUESTIONS

Is Electroconvulsive Therapy Ethical?

1. Fink views ECT as a safe intervention that has been underutilized partly because of ideological and financial pressures to use drugs instead. What kind of research study could be designed to compare the therapeutic effectiveness of ECT with the benefits of medication?
2. Frank criticizes ECT as an intervention that involves very serious and lasting side effects. Given the fact that this intervention is typically recommended for seriously impaired individuals, what steps should be taken to ensure that patients are protected from being given a treatment that involves considerable risk?
3. Imagine that you are a clinician treating a suicidal woman who is incapable of eating and for whom antidepressant medications have had no therapeutic effect. What arguments for and against ECT could be made with regard to the treatment of this client?
4. Psychopharmacological medications work by bringing about changes in brain chemistry. Consider the assumptions about what makes ECT effective. In what ways are the two interventions similar and different?
5. Fink contends that much of the negativity associated with ECT stems from its misuse in earlier decades and from the unfavorable presentation of ECT in the movie *One Flew Over the Cuckoo's Nest*. What aspects of these historical issues may account for the continuing negativity about ECT, even decades later?

Suggested Readings

Abrams, R. (2002). *Electroconvulsive therapy*. New York: Oxford University Press.

Breggin, P. R. (1997). *Brain disabling treatments in psychiatry: Drugs, electroshock, and the role of the FDA*. New York: Springer Publishing Company.

Dowman, J., Patel, A., & Rajput, K. (2005). Electroconvulsive therapy: Attitudes and misconceptions. *Journal of ECT*, 21(2), 84–87.

Fink, M. (1997). The decision to use ECT: For whom? When? In A. J. Rush (Ed.), *Mood disorders: Systematic medication management. Modern problems of pharmacopsychiatry, vol. 25* (pp. 203–214). Basel, Switzerland: Karger.

Fink, M. (1997). Prejudice against ECT: Competition with psychological philosophies as a contribution to its stigma. *Convulsive Therapy*, 13(4), 253–265.

Salzman, C. (1998). ECT, research, and professional ambivalence. *American Journal of Psychiatry,* 155(1), 1–2.

Taylor, M. A. (2005). Ethics in electroconvulsive therapy. *Cognitive and Behavioral Neurology,* 18(2), 137.

Internet References . . .

Body Integrity Identity Disorder (BIID)

The Body Integrity Identity Disorder Website is run by health professionals striving to both increase awareness of and determine the best treatment options for BIID.

http://www.biid.org/

Media Psychology: Division 46 of the American Psychological Association

This site provides information on the impacts and importance of the media.

http://www.apa.org/divisions/div46

National Feminist Antipornography Movement

This Web site contains information about the detrimental effects of pornography.

http://www.feministantipornographymovement.org/

The Anti-Pornography Activist Blog

This website offers numerous anti-pornography videos and a list of "101 Things You Can Do to Combat the Harms of Pornography," as well as links to related Websites.

http://antipornographyactivist.blogspot.com/

Men Can Stop Rape

This Web site addresses issues on the topics of rape and violence, with the goal of promoting gender equity.

http://www.mencanstoprape.org/

Oregon's Death With Dignity Act

This site contains an overview of the 1997 Oregon Death With Dignity Act.

http://www.oregon.gov/DHS/ph/pas/

Society for the Psychological Study of Lesbian, Gay, and Bisexual Issues: Division 44 of the American Psychological Association

This Web site focuses on gaining gay, lesbian, and bisexual issues in psychology.

http://www.apadivision44.org/

American Constitution Society for Law and Policy Blog

This nonprofit legal organization focusing on issues of human dignity, equality, individual rights, liberties, and access to justice.

http://www.acsblog.org/

Crime & Consequences

This website is dedicated to the goal of ensuring that criminals are punished quickly and in accord with the constitution.

http://www.crimeandconsequences.com/

Social Issues

*M*any issues in the field of abnormal psychology interface with social issues, with heated debate emerging about topics pertaining to balancing the protection of personal rights while also responding to societal concerns. For example, how much personal control is society willing to yield to individuals with extremely unusual or socially unacceptable wishes? Should society support (both ideologically and financially through insurance coverage) a person's wish to amputate a healthy limb? Should pornographic images of children that are generated by computers be protected by the First Amendment? How much psychological and social disturbance is attributable to out-of-control media images of violence? The role of mental health professionals in several of these debates is quite complex. Should clinicians agree to treat individuals seeking sexual orientation conversion therapy? What role should clinicians play in end-of-life decisions? What voice should be expressed in cases involving seriously mentally ill murderers who are sentenced to death, but who may not understand the rationale for their execution?

- Is It Ethical to Support the Wish for Healthy Limb Amputation in People with Body Integrity Identity Disorder?

- Is Sexual Orientation Conversion Therapy Ethical?

- Does Exposure to Media Violence Promote Aggressive Behavior?

- Would Legalization of Virtual Child Pornography Reduce Sexual Exploitation of Children?

- Does Evolution Explain Why Men Rape?

- Should Mental Health Professionals Serve as Gatekeepers for Physician-Assisted Suicide?

- Must Mentally Ill Murderers Have a Rational Understanding of Why They Are Being Sentenced to Death?

ISSUE 13

Is It Ethical to Support the Wish for Healthy Limb Amputation in People with Body Integrity Identity Disorder (BIID)?

YES: **Tim Bayne and Neil Levy**, from "Amputees by Choice: Body Integrity Identity Disorder and the Ethics of Amputation," *Journal of Applied Philosophy* (vol. 22, no. 1, 2005)

NO: **Wesley J. Smith**, from "Secondhand Smoke: Blog of Wesley J. Smith (2005)

ISSUE SUMMARY

YES: Authors Bayne and Levy contend that a person with BIID has the right to determine the structure of his or her body, and health professionals should be permitted to accommodate such a choice.

NO: Author Wesley Smith views people with BIID as severely mentally ill individuals who need treatment, not amputation.

Although millions of people undergo elective cosmetic surgery each year, very little controversy has arisen about the ethics. In contrast, a different response emerges when the topic turns to elective amputation of healthy limbs. People with body integrity identity disorder (BIID) have a form of body dysmorphic disorder so extreme that they feel compelled to seek amputation of a healthy body part, claiming that they are so psychologically pained by the discrepancy between their actual body and their body image that they live a life of torment. The question arises, then, about whether it is appropriate for health professionals to acquiesce to the wishes of people with BIID (who refer to themselves as "wannabes") to amputate a healthy limb, with the aim of satisfying the wish of these individuals to enhance psychological well-being.

Bayne and Levy argue that surgeons should accede to the requests of people with BIID requesting healthy limb amputation. These authors sympathize with the plight of people who have spent much of their lives with a non-standard sense of embodiment. Bayne and Levy believe that would-be amputees are likely to persist in their desire for amputation, and might actually take matters into their own hands, risking extensive injury or death in doing so.

Wesley Smith views would-be amputees as severely mentally disturbed individuals who need treatment, not amputation. In light of the fact that amputation is an irreversible procedure, insufficient thought is given to the likelihood of post-amputation regret. Smith contends that these individuals should be protected from harming themselves, and he critiques the notion of "choice" in such matters. Physicians who collude with emotionally unstable individuals in such situations are failing to adhere to their oath to do no harm.

POINT (Bayne & Levy)

- People with BIID have a non-standard sense of embodiment, and their experience of themselves has been built around this sense. To require them to change it is, to some extent, to require them to change who they are.
- Many would-be amputees will take matters into their own hands, risking extensive injury or death in doing so. Surgery may be the least of all evils.

- A would-be amputee can have a reasonable understanding of what life as an amputee would be like before becoming an amputee.
- An individual's conception of his or her own good should be respected in medical decision-making contexts.
- In the case of at least some would-be amputees the limb in question is not as healthy as it might appear: in an important sense, a limb that is not experienced as one's own is not in fact one's own.

COUNTERPOINT (Smith)

- Only a severely mentally disturbed person would want a healthy leg, arm, hand, or foot cut off. Such people need treatment, not amputation.

- Physicians are duty-bound to "do no harm," and thus should refuse to provide harmful medical services to patients—no matter how earnest the request. A physician who accedes to a patient's request to be mutilated would essentially be abandoning the patient.
- Once a limb is gone, it is gone for good. What if the patient has regrets?

- Would-be amputees need to be protected from harming themselves.

- If we allow doctors to remove healthy limbs, what is next? Helping people who want to cut themselves, slice themselves repeatedly? Or helping people who want to burn themselves do so safely?

YES ⬅

Tim Bayne and Neil Levy

Amputees by Choice: Body Integrity Identity Disorder and the Ethics of Amputation

In 1997, a Scottish surgeon by the name of Robert Smith was approached by a man with an unusual request: he wanted his apparently healthy lower left leg amputated. Although details about the case are sketchy, the would-be amputee appears to have desired the amputation on the grounds that his left foot wasn't part of him—it felt alien. After consultation with psychiatrists, Smith performed the amputation. Two and a half years later, the patient reported that his life had been transformed for the better by the operation.[1] A second patient was also reported as having been satisfied with his amputation.[2]

Smith was scheduled to perform further amputations of healthy limbs when the story broke in the media. Predictably, there was a public outcry, and Smith's hospital instructed him to cease performing such operations. At present, no hospital offers healthy limb amputations. Would-be amputees—or "wannabes", as they refer to themselves—would appear to number in the thousands. They have their own websites, and are the subject of a recent documentary.[3]

In this paper, we are concerned with two basic questions. First, what would motivate someone to have an apparently healthy limb amputated? Second, under what conditions is it reasonable for doctors to accede to such requests? We believe that the first question can shed significant light on the second, showing that, on the evidence available today, such amputations may be morally permissible.

What is It Like to Be a Wannabe?

What motivates someone to desire the amputation of a healthy limb? One possibility is that wannabes suffer from Body Dysmorphic Disorder (BDD), a condition in which the individual believes, incorrectly, that a part of their body is diseased or exceedingly ugly.[4] This belief can be a matter of intense concern for the individual, and is resistant to evidence against it. BDD appears to be closely akin to anorexia nervosa, in that both appear to be monothematic delusions that are sustained by misperceptions of one's own body.[5]

From *Journal of Applied Philosophy*, vol. 22, no. 1, 2005. Copyright © 2005 by Blackwell Publishing, Ltd. Reprinted by permission.

Perhaps wannabes desire amputation in order to rid themselves of a limb that they believe to be diseased or ugly.

A second explanation is that wannabes have a sexual attraction to amputees or to being an amputee.[6] On this account, the desire for amputation would stem from apotemnophilia, which is a kind of paraphilia—a psychosexual disorder. Apotemnophiles are sexually attracted to amputees, and sexually excited by the notion that they might become amputees themselves.

A third explanation is that there is a mismatch between the wannabe's experience of their body and the actual structure of their body. On this view there is a mismatch between their body and their body as they experience it— what we might call their phenomenal (or subjective) body. On this view, which is increasingly gaining favour, wannabes suffer from Body Integrity Identity Disorder (BIID), also known as Amputee Identity Disorder (AID).[7]

The BIID account can be developed in different ways depending on the type of bodily representation that is thought to be involved. On the one hand, one could conceive of BIID in terms of a mismatch between the patient's body and their body *schema*. The body schema is a representation of one's body that is used in the automatic regulation of posture and movement.[8] It operates subpersonally and sub-consciously, guiding the parts of one's body to successful performance of action. The body schema is a dynamic structure, providing a moment-by-moment sense of how one's body parts are articulated.

Mismatches between a person's body schema and their actual body are not uncommon. Individuals who lose (or have never had) a limb often experience a phantom limb: they feel as though the limb is still there, and in some cases attempt to employ it in order to carry out actions—such as answering the telephone. Whereas the body schema of individuals with phantom limbs includes body parts that they lack, other patients have no body schema for body parts they have. Patients who have undergone deafferentation from the neck down lose any proprioceptive sense of how their limbs are currently positioned, and rely on visual cues to control action.[9]

Perhaps wannabes also have a body schema that fails to incorporate the full extent of their bodies. Although we do not want to dismiss this suggestion, the evidence we have to date weighs against this account. As far as we know, wannabes do not exhibit any of the impairments in control of movement that one would expect in a person with a distorted or incomplete body schema. Further, wannabes who have had the amputation they desire seem, as far as we can tell, to be content to use a prosthesis. This suggests that the problem they suffer from is not primarily a conflict between their body and their body schema.

A more plausible possibility is that BIID involves a mismatch between the wannabe's body and their body *image*. One's body image is a consciously accessible representation of the general shape and structure of one's body. The body image is derived from a number of sources, including visual experience, proprioceptive experience, and tactile experience. It structures one's bodily sensations (aches, pains, tickles, and so on), and forms the basis of one's beliefs about oneself.[10]

Discrepancies between a person's body and their body image occur in a wide range of cases, known as asomatognosias. Asomatognosia can occur as a result of the loss of proprioception, in post-stroke neglect, and in the context of depersonalisation.[11] In many of these cases the patient in question has become delusional and denies either the existence of the affected limb or their ownership of it. In a condition known as somatoparaphrenia, patients will even ascribe ownership of their limbs to another person.[12]

Other forms of asomatognosia concern only the patient's perception of their body and leave the doxastic component of their body image intact. Oliver Sacks eloquently describes his own experience of this condition:

> In that instant, that very first encounter, *I knew not my leg*. It was utterly strange, not-mine, unfamiliar. I gazed upon it with absolute non-recognition [. . .] The more I gazed at that cylinder of chalk, the more alien and incomprehensible it appeared to me. I could no longer feel it as mine, as part of me. It seemed to bear no relation whatever to me. It was absolutely not-me—and yet, impossibly, it was attached to me—and even more impossibly, continuous with me.[13]

Sacks did not become delusional—he knew that the leg in question was his—but he no longer experienced it as his own. Perhaps BIID involves a similar form of nondelusional somatic alienation. If so, then there might be a very real sense in which the limb in question—or at least, the neuronal representation of it—is not healthy.

It is also tempting to draw parallels between BIID and the discrepancy between body image and the person's actual body that characterizes anorexia nervosa and bulimia nervosa.[14] Of course, there are also important differences between these conditions: Whereas the person with anorexia or bulimia fails to (fully) recognize the discrepancy between her body and her body image, the wannabe is all too aware of this discrepancy.

None of the three explanations of the desire for amputation that we have outlined attempts to provide *complete* models of the phenomenon: the BDD model does not attempt to explain why wannabes might regard the limb in question as diseased or ugly; the apotemnophilia model does not attempt to explain why wannabes might be sexually attracted to a conception of themselves as amputees; and the BIID model does not attempt to explain why wannabes might fail to incorporate the limb into their body image. Clearly these models can, at best, provide only a first step in understanding why someone might become a wannabe. Nevertheless, even though these models are incomplete, we can make some progress in evaluating them.

A first point to make is that these models may not be exclusive. It could be that there are two or three bases for the desire for amputation, with some patients suffering from BDD, others suffering from a paraphilia, and others suffering from a form of BIID. Some individuals might even suffer from a combination of these disorders. Perhaps, for example, the sexual element is better conceived of as a common, though not inevitable, element of asomatognosia. Sexuality is, after all, an essential ingredient in most people's sense of identity. Elliott reports that at least one wannabe (who is also a psychologist) characterizes their desire for amputation as indissolubly a matter of sex *and* identity.[15] Like

Gender Identity Disorder, BIID might be importantly sexual without ceasing to be essentially concerned with identity.

However, although each of the three models might play some role in accounting for the desire for healthy limb amputation, we can also ask which model best fits most wannabes. The initial media stories and a subsequent BBC documentary, *Complete Obsession*, identified Robert Smith's patients as suffering from BDD. However, there seems good reason to doubt whether any of these individuals suffered from BDD, strictly speaking. Neither of the two individuals featured in *Complete Obsession* appears to find their limbs diseased or ugly. Instead, they feel in some way alienated from them. Further evidence against the BDD hypothesis is provided by recent research by Michael First.[16] First conducted in-depth anonymous interviews with 52 wannabes, nine of whom had either amputated one of their limbs themselves or had enlisted a surgeon to amputate it. Only one of the 52 individuals interviewed cited the ugliness of the limb as a reason for wanting the amputation.

What about the suggestion that the desire for amputation stems from apotemphilia? First's study provides limited grounds for thinking that the desire for amputation might have a sexual basis in some cases. 15% (n = 8) of First's interviewees cited feelings of sexual arousal as their primary reason for desiring amputation, and 52% cited it as their secondary reason. Further, 87% of his subjects reported being sexually attracted to amputees. Additional support for the apotemenophilia hypothesis stems from the fact that there is a large overlap between the classes of devotees (acrotomophiles: people sexually attracted to amputees), pretenders (people who consciously fake a disability) and wannabes. More than 50% of devotees are also pretenders and wannabes, suggesting a common cause for all three syndromes.[17] Because of this overlap, the data researchers have gathered on devotees may be relevant to the desire for amputation.

Devotees are apparently more sexually attracted to the *idea* of amputation than to amputees themselves. Though many have had sexual relations with amputees, few go on to establish long-term relationships with particular individuals. As Riddle puts it, for the acrotomophile, 'No amputee is the right amputee'.[18] Bruno suggests that this fact is evidence that acrotomophilia essentially involves projection: the wannabe imagines themselves in place of the amputee. Acrotomophilia is apotemnophilia displaced, projected onto others. If apotemnophilia is essentially a body integrity disorder, Bruno seems to think, it could not be displaced so easily. But it seems just as plausible to interpret the acrotomophile's lack of interest in the individual amputee as evidence that it is a concern with his *own* body that motivates the devotee.

In any case, although First's study provides some support for thinking that the desire for amputation can have a sexual component in some instances, it offers little support for the paraphilia hypothesis as the best explanation of the disorder. After all, only 15% of wannabes identified sexual arousal as the primary motivation for amputation: this leaves 85% unaccounted for.

First's data provides equivocal support for the third model, on which the desire for amputation derives from the experience of a gulf between one's actual body and one's subjective or lived body. The leading primary reason First's subjects gave for wanting an amputation was to restore them to their true identity (63%, n = 33). Participants said such things as, "I feel like an amputee with natural prostheses—they're my legs, but I want to get rid of them—they don't fit my body image", and, "I felt like I was in the wrong body; that I am only complete with both my arm and leg off on the right side." First suggests that this data supports the view that most wannabes suffer from BIID, which he considers akin to Gender Identity Disorder.

There is reason for caution here. For one thing, only 37% (n = 19) of First's participants said that the limb in question felt different in some way, and only 13% (n = 7) said that the limb felt like it was not their own. In addition, we know of no evidence that wannabes suffer from the kinds of sensory and attentional impairments—such as neglect—that tend to accompany, and perhaps underlie, standard forms of asomatognosia.

Perhaps the notion of body image that First's subjects have in mind is closer to that of the self-image of the person who wants cosmetic surgery, say, for breast enlargement. She knows that she has small breasts, but her idealised image of herself is of someone with large breasts. She does not feel comfortable—at home—in her own body.

Although more research needs to be done about the nature and aetiology of the desire for amputation of a healthy limb, the foregoing suffices to put us in a position to make an initial foray into the ethical issues raised by such requests. We turn now to an examination of three arguments in favour of performing the requested amputations.

Harm Minimization

The first and perhaps weakest of the three arguments is familiar from other contexts. Whether wannabes are correct in thinking that their disorder requires surgery or not, we must recognize that a significant proportion of them will persist in their desire for amputation, even in the face of repeated refusals, and will go on to take matters into their own hands. The Internet sites run by wannabes often discuss relatively painless and safe ways of amputating limbs, or damaging them sufficiently to ensure that surgeons have no choice but to amputate. Six of the 52 participants in First's study had amputated a limb themselves, utilizing dangerous means including a shotgun, a chainsaw and a wood chipper. Other patients have turned to incompetent surgeons after competent doctors refused to treat them. In 1998 a seventy-nine year old man died of gangrene after paying $10,000 for a black-market amputation.[19]

Given that many patients will go ahead with amputations in any case, and risk extensive injury or death in doing so, it might be argued that surgeons should accede to the requests, at least of those patients who they (or a competent authority) judge are likely to take matters into their own hands. At least so long as no other treatments are available, surgery might be the least of all evils. This raises familiar practical and ethical issues to do with participation in a practice of which we might disapprove and our inability to confidently distinguish those patients for whom the desire for an amputation might be transient from those who will persist in their demand. Because these issues are familiar and have been extensively treated elsewhere, we will not dwell on them here.

Autonomy

It is well-entrenched maxim of medical ethics that informed, autonomous desires ought to be given serious weight. An individual's conception of his or her good should be respected in medical decision-making contexts. Where a wannabe has a long-standing and informed request for amputation, it therefore seems permissible for a surgeon to act on this request.

As an analogy, consider the refusal of life-saving treatment on religious grounds. Although such decisions might result in the death of the patient, they are accorded significant weight in the context of medical decision-making. If we ignore the informed and repeated wishes of the Jehovah's Witness who refuses the blood-transfusion needed to save her life, we fail to respect her as an autonomous moral agent who is living her life according to her conception of the good. If it is permissible (or even obligatory) to respect informed and autonomous rejections of life saving treatment, it is also permissible to act on informed and autonomous requests for the amputation of a healthy limb.

Of course, the parallel between the Jehovah's Witness who refuses life-saving treatment and the wannabe who requests the amputation of a limb is not exact: the first case involves an omission but the second case involves an action. This is a difference, but whether or not it is morally relevant depends on what one makes of the act/omission distinction. We are doubtful that the distinction can do much moral work in this context, but to make the case for this position would take us too far away from our present concerns.

We shall consider two objections to the argument from autonomy. The first is that wannabes are not fully rational, and that therefore their requests should not be regarded as autonomous. As Arthur Caplan put it: 'It's absolute, utter lunacy to go along with a request to maim somebody', because there is a real question whether sufferers 'are competent to make a decision when they're running around saying, "Chop my leg off".'[20]

It is clear that some individuals who might request the amputation of healthy limbs are not rational. Neither the schizophrenic patient who believes that God is telling her to amputate her leg, nor the patient with somatoparaphrenia who attempts to throw his leg out of bed because he thinks it is not his own, is rational. To what extent wannabes are also incompetent depends on what kinds of wannabes they are.

There is a prima facie case to be made for thinking that wannabes suffering from BDD are not competent to request surgery. There are grounds for regarding BDD as a monothematic delusion, akin to, say, Capgras' delusion (the delusion that a close relative has been replaced by an impostor) or Cotard's delusion (the delusion that one is dead). After all, individuals with BDD appear to satisfy the DSM definition of a delusion: they have beliefs that are firmly sustained despite what almost everyone else believes and despite incontrovertible and obvious proof or evidence to the contrary.[21]

Of course, the circumscribed and monothematic nature of this delusion problematizes the charge of incompetence. These patients are not globally irrational. One might argue that despite the fact that their beliefs about the affected limb have been arrived at irrationally, their deliberations concerning what to do in the light of these beliefs are rational, and hence ought to be respected. One might draw a parallel between the position of the person who requests amputation as a result of BDD and the person who refuses life-saving treatment on the grounds of strange religious beliefs. One might argue that in both cases the agent has arrived at their beliefs irrationally, but they may have chosen a reasonable course of action given their beliefs. And—so the argument continues—one might argue that competence is undermined only by unreasonable practical reasoning, not by impaired belief-fixation or theoretical reasoning.

There is obviously much more that could be said about whether or not individuals with BDD are competent to request surgery, but we will not pursue these issues, for—as we have already pointed out—First's data suggest that few wannabes are motivated by the belief that their healthy limb is diseased or exceedingly ugly. Instead, most wannabes appear to have some form of BIID: they appear to be motivated to achieve a fit between their body and their body image. Are wannabes with BIID delusional?

We have already suggested that they are not. Although wannabes seem not to experience parts of their body as their own, they do not go on to form the corresponding belief that it is alien. The wannabe with BIID clearly recognizes that the leg is hers: she does not identify it as someone else's leg, nor does she attempt to throw it out of bed, in the way that patients with somatoparaphrenia sometimes do.

One might argue that the wannabe's response to her somatic alienation demonstrates a form of irrationality. One might think that the rational response to a conflict between one's subjective experience of embodiment and one's body would be to change one's experience of embodiment rather than change the structure of one's body. The claim is correct but irrelevant: the wannabe's desire for amputation appears to be born out of an inability to change the way in which she experiences her body. Of course, it may be that some wannabes would rather change their actual body to fit their experienced body than vice-versa. Is someone with such a desire set competent to make a request for amputation? They certainly challenge our notions of autonomy and competency, but it is far from obvious that they ought to be regarded as incompetent. It is important to bear in mind that they have spent many years—perhaps even decades—with a non-standard sense of embodiment. (Most wannabes report having had a feeling of somatic alienation since childhood.) Their experience of themselves has been built around this sense, and to require them to change it is, to some extent, to require them to change who they are. The case is not dissimilar to a situation in which an elderly person, blind from an early age, is suddenly presented with the opportunity to regain her sight. The decision to decline such an offer can be understood as an exercise of rational agency.

A useful angle on the question of whether the requests of wannabes could be competent is provided by contrasting wannabes with people who desire cosmetic surgery (where the surgery is not for the treatment of disfigurement). While one can certainly argue on feminist grounds that such people are not fully competent, these arguments have left many people unmoved.[22] We allow individuals to mould their body to an idealized body type, even when we recognize that this body image has been formed under the pressure of non-rational considerations, such as advertising, gender-norms, and the like. If this holds for the individual seeking cosmetic surgery, what reason is there to resist a parallel line of argument for those seeking amputation? Of course, the latter individual is seeking to mould their body to an ideal that few of us aspire to, and one that has been formed under conditions that are far from perfect, but why should these facts cut any moral ice? In fact, one might think that the desire for cosmetic surgery (and gender-reassignment surgery) is *more* problematic than the desire for amputation. Men who believe that they are really women 'trapped in a man's body'—and the overwhelming majority of transsexuals are male-to-female—typically reinforce a stereotyped view of femininity, and contribute, however unwittingly and obliquely, to gender inequality.[23] The essential woman they seek to be is weak and helpless, obsessed by appearance, and so on.[24] There are related feminist grounds (and not only feminist grounds) on which to criticize cosmetic surgery: it reinforces a very unfortunate emphasis on appearance over substance. It is hard to see that the desire for amputation could be criticized upon grounds of these kinds, since it goes against the grain of our culturally endorsed ideals of the body.

A second objection to the argument from autonomy is that the wannabe is not in a position to give informed consent to the surgery, for he or she does not—and cannot—know what it is like to be an amputee without first becoming an amputee.

We think that this objection is weak. First, it is not at all obvious that the wannabe cannot know what it will be like to be an amputee without becoming an amputee. Arguably, there is a sense in which the wannabe *already* knows what it is like to be an amputee. We might also note that at least some wannabes pretend to be amputees—they spend their weekends in a wheelchair, and so on. To some degree, it seems that a wannabe can know what it is like to be an amputee.

But a more important point to be made here is that the objection appears to set the bar for autonomy too high.[25] Autonomy demands only that one have an adequate understanding of the likely consequences of an action, and one can have a reasonable understanding of what life as an amputee would be like without first becoming an amputee. Arguably, the wannabe is in a better position to appreciate the consequences of the desired surgery than is the person who seeks cosmetic surgery, the would-be surrogate mother, or the person desiring gender reassignment surgery.

Therapy

A third argument in favour of operating appeals to the therapeutic effects promised by such operations. The argument rests on four premises: (i) wannabes endure serious suffering as a result of their condition; (ii) amputation will—or is likely to—secure relief from this suffering; (iii) this relief cannot be secured by less drastic means; (iv) securing relief from this suffering is worth the cost of amputation. This argument parallels the justification for conventional amputations.

There is some reason to endorse (i). First, the lengths to which wannabes go in an effort to amputate their own limbs suggest that their desires are strong and unrelenting. Even when wannabes do not take active steps to secure an amputation, their feeling of bodily alienation seems to cause severe disruption to their everyday lives. 44% of First's subjects reported that their desire interfered with social functioning, occupational functioning, or leisure activities.

Some writers suggest that (ii) is problematic. Bruno and Riddle claim that the desire for amputation has its origins in attention-seeking sparked by the deprivation of parental love.[26] On this hypothesis, though it is *possible* that satisfying their wish for an amputation might give the wannabe the attention and kindness they seek, it is unlikely. Though amputees are treated with a certain degree of solicitude in many situations, the daily frustrations and difficulties caused by their condition almost certainly more than overbalance this care. Moreover, it is quite likely that the wannabe will not be satisfied with the solicitude of strangers. Instead she will seek ongoing commitment from particular individuals, and there is little reason to think that she is more likely to get this than are non-amputees. Finally, it might be that even the love of particular others will not suffice: it may be that literally nothing can stand in for the love of which she was deprived as a child. Bruno suggests that psychotherapy is the appropriate response to the disorder, not surgery. The patient needs to develop insight into the real source of her problems before she can solve them.

Bruno's proposal is empirically testable: we can evaluate whether the desire for amputation responds to psychotherapy, and whether amputation simply leads to the displacement of the patient's symptoms. What little data we have to date suggests that Bruno is wrong on both counts. We know of no systematic study of the effects of psychotherapy on the desire for amputation, but First's study suggests that it is not particularly effective. Of the 52 individuals he interviewed, 18 had told their psychotherapist about their desire for amputation, and none reported a reduction in the intensity of the desire following psychotherapy.

On the other hand, on the scant evidence available, wannabes who succeed in procuring an amputation seem to experience a significant and lasting increase in well-being. Both of Robert Smith's patients were reported as having been very happy with their operations, and the nine subjects in First's study who had had an amputation also expressed satisfaction with the results.[27] As far as we can tell, such individuals do not develop the desire for additional amputations (in contrast to individuals who have had cosmetic surgery). Nor, as far as we know, do such patients develop (unwanted) phantom limbs. Of course, it may be that the sample to which researchers have had access is self-selecting: adherents of the BIID account are motivated to come forward to adduce evidence in favour of their theory, while those who have had more unhappy experiences simply lose interest in the debate, or are too depressed to motivate themselves to take any further part. In any case, the sample sizes are too small to be statistically significant. Unfortunately, it is hard to see how it will be possible to collect sufficient data of the required sort. We can of course follow the fortunes of those who have arranged non-medical amputations for themselves, but a controlled study would presumably require medical amputations, and ethical approval for performing such operations is unlikely to be forthcoming without this very data.[28]

We turn now to (iii): can the wannabe secure relief from their suffering by less drastic means than amputation? Again, the jury is out on this. First's study suggests that psychotherapy is not a particularly effective form of treatment, but psychotherapy is not the only alternative to amputation. Some form of cognitive behavioural therapy might prove effective, perhaps in combination with psychotropic drugs. But it might also be that some wannabes cannot be helped by available drugs or talking therapy whatever the aetiology of the disorder. After all, the phantom limb phenomenon is resistant to these forms of treatment. For at least some patients, there may be no treatment available other than amputation.

Finally, we turn to (iv): is securing relief from this suffering worth the cost of amputation? This, of course, will depend on the degree of suffering in question and the costs of amputation. We have already noted that there is reason to think that wannabes often experience significant misery from their condition. But what should we say about the costs of amputation? These, of course, will vary from case to case, depending on the financial and social circumstances of the individual, and the nature of the amputation itself. The costs might be offset by the benefits of amputation in some cases but not in others. It is interesting to note that of the two would-be amputees featured in the *Complete Obsession* documentary, the person seeking amputation of a single leg was given psychiatric approval, while the person seeking to have both her legs amputated was denied psychiatric approval. And of course the costs are not always borne just by the patient; they are often also borne by the patient's family and by society as a whole.

There is ample room here for false consciousness. On the one hand, one can argue that wannabes have an overly rosy image of what life as an amputee involves. And certainly those wannabes who have become amputees have a motivation for thinking that their life is better than it really is. On the other hand, one could also argue that those of us who are able bodied have an overly pessimistic image of the lives of the disabled. As able-bodied individuals, we might be tempted to dwell on the harm that accompanies amputation and minimize what is gained by way of identification. Perhaps we are tempted to think that the effects of the surgery are worse than they are.

Repugnance

We believe that the arguments canvassed above establish a *prima facie* case for thinking that wannabes should have access to amputation, at least in those instances in which they suffer from BIID. However, we recognize that many people will continue to find the idea of voluntary amputation of a healthy limb objectionable, even when they acknowledge the force of these arguments. What motivates such reactions?

We suspect that much of this hostility derives from the sense of repugnance that is evoked by the idea that a person might wish to rid themselves of an apparently healthy limb. Dennis Canavan, the Scottish member of parliament who campaigned to prevent Robert Smith from carrying out such operations was quoted as saying: "The whole thing is repugnant and legislation needs to be brought in now to outlaw this".[29] Mr Canavan is surely not alone in having such a reaction. Wannabes evoke an affective response not dissimilar to that evoked by the prospect of kidney sales, bestiality, or various forms of genetic engineering. Even when a limb is severely diseased and must be removed in order to save the patient's life, the thought of amputation strikes many as distasteful at best.

Although they should not be dismissed, we think that such responses should be treated with a great deal of caution. A large number of morally benign practices—such as masturbation, inter-racial marriage, burial (and cremation) of the dead, organ selling, artificial insemination, tattooing and body piercing— have the ability to elicit disgust responses. Disgust responses can alert us to the possibility that the practices in question *might* be morally problematic, but they do not seem to be reliable indicators of moral transgression.[30]

Indirect Effects

We have explored three arguments for allowing self-demand amputation of healthy limbs: the argument from harm minimization, the autonomy argument and the therapeutic argument. We have suggested that these arguments have some force. But even if we are right about that, it does not follow that we ought to allow self-demand amputation of healthy limbs. One might hold that although these arguments are strong, their force is outweighed by reasons for not allowing such surgery.

In our view, the strongest such argument concerns the possible effects of legitimising BIID as a disorder. The worry is that giving official sanction to a diagnosis of BIID makes it available as a possible identity for people. To use Ian Hacking's term, psychiatric categories have a "looping" effect: once in play, people use them to construct their identities, and this in turn reinforces their reality as medical conditions.[31] Arguably, something like this has occurred in the case of Dissociative Identity Disorder (formerly multiple personality disorder): the explosion of diagnoses of DID might be due in part to the fact that people regard DID as a culturally sanctioned disorder. The very awareness of a disorder can contribute to its proliferation.

Could a similar effect occur for BIID? Is it likely that the inclusion of the disorder in the forthcoming DSM-V will generate an explosion of cases on the order of that seen in the study of dissociation? Perhaps, but there is reason to think that such fears are unwarranted. The desire for amputation of a healthy limb is at odds with current conceptions of the ideal body image. The preference for bodily integrity is deep-seated in normal human beings, and advertising does much to reinforce such norms. We therefore think it unlikely that the desire for amputation will proliferate.

Conclusion

In a world in which many are born without limbs, or lose their limbs to poisons, landmines, and other acts of man and God, it might seem obscene to legitimise the desire for the amputation of healthy limbs. But we have argued that, in the case of at least some wannabes, the limb in question is not as healthy as it might appear: in an important sense, a limb that is not experienced as one's own is not in fact one's own. Disorders of depersonalisation are invisible to the outside world: they are not observable from the third-person perspective in the way that most other disorders are. But the fact that they are inaccessible should not lead us to dismiss the suffering they might cause. Whether amputation is an appropriate response to this suffering is a difficult question, but we believe that in some cases it might be.[32]

Notes

1. K. SCOTT (2000) Voluntary amputee ran disability site. *The Guardian*, February 7.

2. G. FURTH and R. SMITH (2002) *Amputee Identity Disorder: Information, Questions, Answers, and Recommendations about Self-Demand Amputation* (Bloomington, IN. 1st Books).

3. M. GILBERT (2003) *Whole* U.S.A.

4. K. PHILLIPS (1996) *The Broken Mirror: Understanding and Treating Body Dysmorphic Disorder* (Oxford, Oxford University Press).

5. D. M. GARNER (2002) Body image and anorexia nervosa in T. F. CASH & T. PRUZINSKY (eds) *Body Image: A Handbook of Theory, Research, and Clinical Practice* (New York, The Guilford Press).

6. J. MONEY, R. JOBARIS, AND G. FURTH (1977) Apotemnophilia: Two cases of self-demand amputation as paraphilia, *The Journal of Sex Research*, 13, 2, 115–125.

7. Furth & Smith op. cit.

8. The term 'body schema' is used in different ways by different authors. We are following Shaun Gallagher's usage. See S. GALLAGHER (1995) Body schema and intentionality in J. BERMÚDEZ, N. EILAN and J. MARCEL (eds) *The Body and the Self.* (Cambridge MA, M.I.T. Press) pp. 225–44 and S. GALLAGHER (2001) Dimensions of embodiment: Body image and body schema in medical contexts in S. K. TOOMBS (ed) *Handbook of Phenomenology and Medicine* (Dordrecht, Kluwer Academic Publishers) pp. 147–75.

9. S. GALLAGHER, and J. COLE 1995 Body schema and body image in a deafferented subject, *Journal of Mind and Behavior*, 16, 369–90.

10. The term 'body image' is also used in different ways by different authors. Again, we follow Shaun Gallagher's usage of the term. See reference [8].

11. T. E. FEINBERG, L. D. HABER, and N. E. LEEDS (1990) Verbal asomatognosia, *Neurology*, 40, 1391–4; J. A. M. FREDERIKS (1985) Disorders of the body schema. In Clinical Neuropsychology in J. A. M. FREDERIKS (ed) *Handbook of Clinical Neurology*, rev. Series, No. 1 (Amsterdam, Elsevier); M. SIERRA and G. E. BERRIOS (2001) The phenomenological stability of depersonalization: Comparing the old with the new, *The Journal of Nervous and Mental Disorders*, 189, 629–636.

12. An account of such a case is described in O. SACKS (1985) The man who fell out of bed, in *The Man Who Mistook his Wife for a Hat* (New York, Touchstone).

13. O. SACKS (1991) *A Leg to Stand On* (London, Picador).

14. R. M. GARDNER and C. MONCRIEFF (1988) Body image distortion in anorexics as a non-sensory phenomenon: A signal detection approach, *Journal of Clinical Psychology*, 44, 101–107 and T. F. CASH and T. A. BROWN (1987) Body image in anorexia nervosa and bulimia nervosa: A Review of the literature, *Behavior Modification*, 11, 487–521.

15. C. ELLIOTT (2003) *Better Than Well: American Medicine Meets the American Dream* (New York, W.W. Norton & Company).

16. M. B. FIRST (unpublished) Desire for amputation of a limb: Paraphilia, psychosis, or a new type of identity disorder? Submitted.

17. R. BRUNO (1997) Devotees, pretenders and wannabes: Two cases of factitious disability disorder, *Journal of Sexuality and Disability*, 15, 243–260.

18. G. C. RIDDLE (1988) *Amputees and devotees: Made for each other?* (New York, Irvington Publishers).

19. C. E. ELLIOTT (2000) A new way to be mad, *The Atlantic Monthly*, 286, 6, December.

20. Quoted in R. DOTINGA (2000) Out on a limb, *Salon*, August 29, 1.

21. AMERICAN PSYCHIATRIC ASSOCIATION (2000) *Diagnostic and Statistical Manual of Mental Disorders, Text Revision.* Fourth Edition (Washington D.C., American Psychiatric Association).

22. For a feminist argument against the permissibility of cosmetic surgery see K. P. MORGAN (1991) Women and the knife: cosmetic surgery and the colonization of women's bodies, *Hypatia* 6, 3, 25–53.

23. H. BOWER (2001) The gender identity disorder in the DSM-IV classification: a critical evaluation, *Australian and New Zealand Journal of Psychiatry*, 35, 1–8.

24. M. GARBER (1993) *Vested Interests: Cross-Dressing & Cultural Anxiety* (London, Penguin).

25. See J. OAKLEY (1992) Altruistic surrogacy and informed consent, *Bioethics*, 6, 4, 269–287.

26. Bruno op. cit. and Riddle op. cit.

27. See also ELLIOTT (2000) and (2003) op. cit. and F. HORN (2003) A life for a limb: body integrity identity disorder, *Social Work Today*, Feb 24.

28. R. SMITHAND and K. FISHER (2003) Healthy limb amputation: ethical and legal aspects (letter), *Clinical Medicine*, 3, 2, March/April, 188.

29. Quoted in Dotinga op. cit.

30. See J. R. RICHARDS (1996) Nefarious goings on, *The Journal of Medicine and Philosophy*, 21, 375–416.

31. I. HACKING (1995) *Rewriting the Soul: Multiple Personality and the Sciences of Memory* (Princeton, Princeton University Press).

32. We are very grateful to Shaun Gallagher, Jonathan Cole, Michael First and an anonymous reviewer for their very useful comments on a previous version of this paper. We also thank Suzy Bliss for her valuable help.

Wesley J. Smith

NO

Should Doctors Be Allowed to Amputate Healthy Limbs?

If you want to see why Western culture is going badly off the rails, just read the drivel that passes for learned discourse in many of our professional journals. The most recent example is "Amputees by Choice: Body Integrity Identity Disorder and the Ethics of Amputation," published in the current issue of the Journal of Applied Philosophy (Vol. 22, No 1, 2005).

The question posed by the authors, Tim Bayne and Neil Levy, both Australian philosophy professors, is whether physicians should be permitted to amputate a patient's healthy limb because the patient is obsessed with becoming an amputee, an apparently newly discovered mental disorder that has been given the name "Body Integrity Identity Disorder" (BIID).

For people of common sense, the answer is obvious: NO! First, who but a severely mentally disturbed person would want a healthy leg, arm, hand, or foot cut off? Such people need treatment, not amputation. Second, physicians are duty bound to "do no harm," that is, they should refuse to provide harmful medical services to patients—no matter how earnestly requested. (Thus, if I were convinced that my appendix was actually a cancerous tumor, that would not justify my doctor acquiescing to my request for an appendectomy.) Finally, once the limb is gone, it is gone for good. Acceding to a request to be mutilated would amount to abandoning the patient.

But according to Bayne and Levy, and a minority of other voices in bioethics and medicine, the need to respect personal autonomy is so near-absolute that it should even permit doctors to cut off the healthy limbs of "amputee wannabes." After all, the authors write, "we allow individuals to mould their body to an idealized body type" in plastic surgery—a desire that is "more problematic than the desire for amputation" since cosmetic surgery "reinforces a very unfortunate emphasis on appearance over substance." Moreover, the authors claim in full post modernist mode, just because a limb is biologically healthy, does not mean that the leg is real. Indeed, they argue, "a limb that is not experienced as one's own is not in fact one's own."

That this kind of article is published in a respectable philosophical journal tells us how very radical and pathologically non judgmental the bioethics movement is becoming. And lest you believe that such advocacy could never reach the clinical setting: Think again. Such surgeries have already been performed in the

United Kingdom with no adverse professional consequence to the amputating physicians.

Even more worrisome, the current trends in American jurisprudence could one day legalize amputation as treatment for BIID. For example, in 1999, the Montana Supreme Court invalidated a law that required abortions to be performed in hospitals. But rather than limit the decision to that issue, the 6-2 majority opinion in James H. Armstrong, M.D. v. The State of Montana, imposed a radical and audacious medical ethic on the people of Montana, ruling: "The Montana Constitution broadly guarantees each individual the right to make medical judgments affecting her or his bodily integrity and health in partnership with a chosen health care provider free from government interference."

If indeed almost anything goes medically in Montana—so long as a patient wants it and a health care professional is willing to provide it—then it would seem that a physician could legally amputate a patient's healthy limbs upon request to satisfy a neurotic BIID obsession.

⌒

Yours Truly Taken to Task for Allegedly Inaccurate Article

I have heard from one of the authors of the journal article supporting the right of doctors to amputate healthy limbs for sufferers of a new mental health disorder known as Body Integrity Identity Disorder (BIID). He is unhappy with me. Neil Levy claims I misrepresented his and co-author Tim Bayne's work.

Levy wrote: "You write that we advocate 'abandoning the patient' by acceding to their request to amputate a healthy limb. First, as you fail to mention, we conclude that the question is difficult, but we think that 'in some cases' it 'might' be acceptable to accede. Second, you misrepresent our views by taking them out of context. You say that we write, 'in full post modernist mode, just because a limb is biologically healthy, does not mean that the leg is real.'" (Indeed, they argue, "a limb that is not experienced as one's own is not in fact one's own.") "If we had implied any such thing, we would deserve your mockery. But it should be clear, from even a cursory reading, that we intended to claim not that if the patient believes the limb is not theirs, it is not. We couldn't be claiming any such thing, because we distinguish between somatoparaphrenia, which is a delusion in which the patient denies ownership of the limb, and BIID, in which there are no false beliefs. The claim, rather, is that acknowledging ownership is normally a necesary condition for full ownership. Think of disowning a child. This is an act which does not alter the biological relationship, but alters the lived relationship. There is nothing 'postmodernist' about this. If you were familiar with norms in analytic philosophy you would hesitate to make such an accusation: no one is more vocal in denouncing facile relativism about truth. Third, we do not advocate abandoning the patient. Once again, a careful reading of the article would indicate that amputation is recommended only as a last resort: so long as there is genuine and significant suffering and there is no alternative treatment that is effective. If there is such an affective treatment developed, then it is obviously preferable."

My response was as follows:

"Thank you for writing.

It was a 550 word opinion piece. It is very clear that the term abandonment was mine and not yours, as was the opinion and interpretation that cutting off a healthy limb would be an act of abandonment. I never claimed you believed in abandoning a patient.

I quoted you accurately about the healthy limb not being the patient's, an amazing statement in my view. Whether or not a patient "owns" the limb, does not make it any less real. And the point I was making is that autonomy is getting recklessly out of control in bioethics advocacy, and in jurisprudence as well, ergo the quoting of the Montana court case. I probably should have said that "as a last resort," you would permit amputation. But you would still allow amputation.

I certainly had no intention of misrepresenting your article. I don't believe I did. I believe the essence of what I wrote is true."

(I would also note that the abstract of the article, which the authors wrote, states that they argue, "BIID sufferers meet reasonable standards for rationality and autonomy: so as long as no other effective treatment for their disorder is available, surgeons ought to be allowed to accede to their requests," in other words, cut off healthy limbs.)

⚜

"Choice" Gone Mad: Amputee Wannabes

We are witnessing the beginning of the public normalization of the profound mental illness known as Body Integrity Identity Disorder (BIID)—also known as "amputee wannabe" because its sufferers become obsessed with losing one or more limbs. A column published in *The Guardian* is an example: Susan Smith (not her real name) writes about wanting to have both legs amputated because **"the image I have of myself has always been one without legs."**

To achieve these ends, Susan harmed herself so that one leg would have to be removed. And now, she plans to do it again: **"Removing the next leg will not be any easier than the first; the pain will be horrendous. But I have no regrets about the path I have chosen. In fact, if I regret anything, it is that I didn't do this sooner. For the first time in my life, I can get on with being the real me."**

And here's the normalizing part: "I think BIID will stay taboo until people get together and bring it out. A hundred years ago, it was taboo to be gay in many societies, and 50 years ago the idea of transsexuals was abhorrent to most. I have tried to make the condition more understood but it is difficult to get a case out in the open by yourself. My psychiatrist went to a meeting last year in Paris, and many doctors there told her that they had operated on people who needed an amputation under mysterious circumstances, and how happy the person was when they woke up. It led them to believe that perhaps BIID is more prevalent than people think."

Something has gone terribly wrong with us at a profound and fundamental level. And deeper minds than mine need to figure out precisely what it is. Because, in the name of "being myself" we are moving toward normalizing mutilating surgery. Indeed, I have already attended a transhumanist conference where two Ph.D.s advocated that doctors be allowed to remove healthy limbs. And it has been suggested as worth considering in a professional journal article by Tim Bayne and Neil Levy. What next? Help people who want to cut themselves, slice themselves repeatedly? Or burn themselves, do it safely? Or what about kill themselves? Oh, that's right. It is already explicitly legal to help do that in Oregon, the Netherlands, Belgium, and Switzerland.

People like Susan need to be protected from harming themselves. We used to have the basic humanity and decency to understand that. But we have become so in the thrall of radical individualism, I wonder whether we still do. "Choice" is becoming a voracious monster.

CHALLENGE QUESTIONS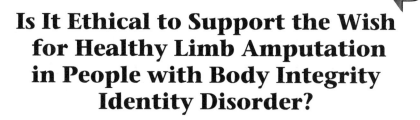

Is It Ethical to Support the Wish for Healthy Limb Amputation in People with Body Integrity Identity Disorder?

1. Tattooing and body piercing are regarded by some people, not as forms of bodily degradation, but rather as artistic personal expressions. What differentiates these procedures from the choice to undergo limb amputation in order to enhance one's sense of self and emotional well-being?
2. In some extreme cases of body integrity identity disorders, individuals have attempted to sever their own limbs. When such procedures fail, and the individual is left with a badly damaged limb, and possibly medically dangerous condition, how should physicians respond?
3. Some would argue that a person has the moral right to alter his or her body in any way desired. What are the arguments for and against this notion?
4. What kind of psychological assessment and intervention would you recommend for a person requesting limb amputation?
5. Assuming that a surgeon agrees to amputate a limb of a person with BIID, should health insurance cover this operation? Why or why not?

Suggested Readings

Elliott, C. & Kramer, P. D. (2004). Amputees by choice. In *Better than well: American medicine meets the American dream* (208–236). New York: W. W. Norton, & Company, Inc.

First, M. B. (2005). Desire for amputation of a limb: Paraphilia, psychosis, or a new type of identity disorder. *Psychological Medicine, 35*(6), 919–928.

Henig, S. S. (2005, March 22). At war with their bodies, they seek to sever limbs. *The New York Times.*

Schramme, T. (2007). Should we prevent non-therapeutic mutilation and extreme body modification? *Bioethics.* Retrieved from http://www.blackwell-synergy.com/toc/biot/0/0.

ISSUE 14

Is Sexual Orientation
Conversion Therapy Ethical?

YES: Christopher H. Rosik, from "Motivational, Ethical, and Episte-mological Foundations in the Treatment of Unwanted Homoerotic Attraction," *Journal of Marital and Family Therapy* (January 2003)

NO: Robert-Jay Green, from "When Therapists Do Not Want Their Clients to Be Homosexual: A Response to Rosik's Article," *Journal of Marital and Family Therapy* (January 2003)

ISSUE SUMMARY

YES: Psychologist Christopher Rosik asserts that many clients have valid reasons for pursuing sexual orientation conversion therapy, and mental health professionals have a responsibility to work with these clients toward their goals.

NO: Psychologist Robert-Jay Green expresses concern over therapy involving sexual reorientation, cautioning that clients must under-stand their motivations for seeking change. He contends that there is little evidence regarding the effectiveness of such therapy.

In 1973, the American Psychiatric Association removed homosexuality from the list of mental disorders in the third edition of the *Diagnostic and Statistical Manual of Mental Disorders.* Nevertheless, the debate regarding the issue of whether homosexuality should be considered a treatable condition continues in the mental health field, in part because of the emergence of sexual orientation conversion therapy. Professionals who provide sexual orientation conversion therapy assert that they are helping individuals who experience unwanted same-sex attraction to maximize their "heterosexual potential."

Psychologist Christopher Rosik contends that sexual orientation conver-sion therapy can be an effective tool for clients with unwanted homosexual tendencies, and therefore should not be overlooked as a therapeutic option. He cites several motivations that a client may have for seeking reorientation therapy, such as religious conflict, a desire to become or remain married, dis-satisfaction with sexual nonmonogamy, and concern about HIV infection. Rosik believes that a liberal sociopolitical frame of reference, which is prominent within the mental health field, is the reason that sexual orientation conversion therapy is looked upon with disapproval. He writes of the importance of inclusiveness, suggesting that if clinicians were more open to politically and religiously conservative individuals, they would have greater respect for sexual orientation conversion therapy.

Robert-Jay Green rejects the notion of bias in the mental health field and warns that a clinician's neutrality is paramount. He asserts that the existence of sexual orientation conversion therapy implies an underlying disapproval of homosexuality, a stance that is far from the neutrality that should characterize mental health professionals. Green rejects the notion that sexuality is alterable in the first place, and believes that desires and feelings are complex and deeply rooted from birth. Green writes that societal homophobia plays a large part in motivations to attempt change, and suggests that the most psychologically healthy clients accept their sexual orientation and feel supported and part of a larger community. Green refutes Rosik's claim that homosexuality leads to a greater prevalence of psychiatric illness and depression. Green also points to the high failure rate of sexual orientation conversion therapy and expresses concern about the ethical implications of unsuccessful therapy.

POINT

- Clients often have legitimate motivations for increasing heterosexual potential, such as an internal religious conflict, a desire to remain married, dissatisfaction with sexual nonmonogamy, and concern about HIV infection.

- Research on gender identity disorder suggests a developmental factor in the etiology of homosexuality, and indirectly supports the notion that heterosexual potential can be increased.

- There is a growing consensus that same-sex behavior is associated with elevated risk of certain forms of psychiatric disorder and with suicide when compared to heterosexual samples.

COUNTERPOINT

- A person's sexuality does not exist on one continuum of homosexual to heterosexual. Sexual orientation can best be conceptualized as encompassing several dimensions; the individual's functioning across those dimensions may or may not be consistent.

- Research on gender identity disorder actually demonstrates that sexual orientation is part of a continuous developmental process beginning early in life, manifesting as cross-gender behavior during childhood and as homosexual orientation in adulthood. Most researchers interpret this as evidence for the immutability of sexual orientation.

- Research shows that the experiences of discrimination and internalized homophobia are strong predictors of depression, suicidality, and HIV-risk behaviors among gay, lesbian, and bisexual persons. The solution to the mental health stresses faced by lesbians and gay men is a reduction in the prejudice to which they are subjected.

YES ↵

Christopher H. Rosik

Motivational, Ethical, and Epistemological Foundations in the Treatment of Unwanted Homoerotic Attraction

A recent special section of the *Journal of Marital and Family Therapy* (October, 2000) focusing on the mental health needs of gay, lesbian, and bisexual individuals neglected to address the clinical needs of homosexual persons who desire to increase their heterosexual potential. This article attempts to correct this omission by outlining common motivations for pursuing change, updating the current state of knowledge regarding the effectiveness of change efforts, and providing some ethical guidelines when therapists encounter clients who present with unwanted homoerotic attraction. Finally, to assist marriage and family therapists (MFTs) in more deeply understanding divergent perspectives about reorientation treatments, an examination of the role of moral epistemology is presented and some examples of its potential influence are described. MFTs are encouraged to recognize and accept, rather than ignore or deny the valid needs of clients who seek to modify their same-sex attraction.

There is a growing body of clinical literature that is designed to assist therapists in understanding and addressing the needs of gay, lesbian, and bisexual (GLB) clients. A recent issue of *Journal of Marital and Family Therapy* (October, 2000) dealt specifically with these issues. However, the series of articles failed to recognize an important subgroup of homosexual clients, namely those individuals who present for treatment with unwanted same-sex attractions. Understanding these individuals is an important step in being able to provide treatment that respects their cultural and religious values. Typically what little scholarly literature that exists on these men and women is presented within an evaluative framework that is far removed from how they actually perceive their circumstances. By examining these individuals within a more conservative value schema, MFTs can come to a greater appreciation of the worldview of these clients. This, in turn, can enable a greater tolerance of values and beliefs that are normative within this subgroup but may be foreign or disagreeable to the clinician.

Such analysis is vital for many reasons. Redding (2001) has noted that conservatives and conservative views are vastly underrepresented in mental health professions, and presumably MFT. He contends that without sociopolitical diversity, the therapeutic community undermines its credibility in several ways. Research hypotheses or interpretations from a conservative viewpoint go unasked or unrepresented. Scientific findings are rendered suspect or disregarded altogether among a large portion of society, seen only as the product of liberally dominated mental health guilds. A lack of conservative representation may also impede the ability of therapists to serve conservative clients and communities, as in the present case of homosexual persons who do not wish to self-identify as gay, lesbian, or bisexual.

This article will attempt to provide insight into clients who request treatment to further develop their heterosexual potential. Several motivations that lead individuals to seek such therapeutic goals will be presented and evidence will be outlined that appears to lend validity to these concerns. The issue of increasing heterosexual potential will be addressed and some guidelines for ethically conducting such treatment will be suggested. Finally, an analysis will be offered that makes sense of the controversies in this area of practice as representing a difference in moral epistemologies.

It should be mentioned at the outset that an increasingly vocal number of mental health professionals are on the record as favoring a complete prohibition of any therapeutic attempts to increase a client's heterosexual potential (Davison, 2001; Murphy, 1992). The perspective taken in this analysis is naturally more sympathetic to such a goal, provided that the therapy is conducted in accordance with well-recognized ethical standards. Ignoring the values and beliefs of these clients by prohibiting change-oriented therapies may lead these individuals to avoid the mental health system altogether. Time will tell as to whether our profession will risk precipitating such a large-scale form of client discrimination and abandonment.

Motivations for Pursuing Greater Heterosexual Potential

The limited studies of clients who seek therapeutic assistance in increasing heterosexual potential generally seem to converge around several motivational themes. As summarized most recently by Spitzer (2001a), these themes involve religious conflict, a desire to remain married, dissatisfaction with sexual nonmonogamy, and concern about HIV infection.

Religious/Moral Conflict

It appears that a significant majority of individuals with unwanted homoerotic attraction and who attempt to increase their heterosexual potential come from conservative religious backgrounds (Nicolosi, Byrd, & Potts, 2000; Schaeffer, Hyde, Kroencke, McCormick, & Nottebaum, 2000; Schaeffer, Nottebaum, Dech, & Drawczyk, 2000; Spitzer, 2001a). Spitzer (2001a) found that 79% of his sample of 200 men and women who claimed to have changed their sexual orientation were motivated by their religious beliefs. Moreover, 93% of the sample indicated that religion is "extremely" or "very" important in their lives. Many such individuals are well aware of efforts to revise their religious traditions in gay-affirmative ways, but they nonetheless maintain the conviction that their homoerotic feelings are not a part of who God created them to be. They instead see their homosexual behavior as falling short of the ideals for sexual conduct reflected in the sacred texts of their faith communities. Other individuals may seek to change same-sex attraction because of their moral beliefs and cultural values, which may or may not be connected to a religious worldview.

These concerns are aptly captured in the description of one client's statements about his choice to pursue change-oriented treatment:

> As a foster child, I was developing a coping mechanism of masturbation during which I fantasized about punishing men by beating them. I virtually had no male affirmation as a child. As an adult, I began to develop good relationships with men, which I did not have as a child. Later, under stress of the job and not dealing with my past, I allowed deep yearnings for affirmation from men to become mixed in with lust and finally immorality. It is my sincere desire to break with my sinful behavior and begin a process of healing and restoration.

Opportunity for or Maintenance of Marriage and Family

The desire to have or keep a traditional marriage and family is another powerful impetus for individuals to seek out therapy for unwanted homoerotic feelings. What few empirical studies that assessed this area found high levels of endorsement, especially for men. Spitzer (2001a) reported that 67% of men cited this reason as well as 35% of women. Nicolosi et al. (2000) indicated that 32% of their sample was married. Given the religiously conservative nature of these samples, it is not unexpected that the participants would desire to explore their heterosexual potential and, if possible, move toward the theologically sanctioned context for sexual expression within their faith community.

Marriage and family therapists have a particular expertise in addressing client concerns in a systemic context and should understand the validity of a values-based decision to attempt to increase heterosexual potential to maintain the integrity of a marriage and family. For example, one male client indicated that he sought treatment in order to "deal with my painful past properly and engage in a process of restoration in which I rebuild trust with my wife and family and a firm ability not to go back to my former sinful behaviors." Similarly, a young woman described the struggle between her values and her feelings:

> The big thing right now is my marriage. Am I happy? Why did I have an affair—and with a woman for god's sake? And how do I get over that. I feel so strongly about my lover—I feel like we have a connection that my husband and I never had—like we're soul mates. I want to do the right thing and stay in my marriage and not hurt my husband or my family—but I question— am I sacrificing my chance at true happiness?

Nonmonagomy

According to Spitzer (2001a), many individuals (especially men) who desire to modify homoerotic attraction strongly value monogamy and are motivated by dissatisfaction with their experience of a more sexually open homosexual culture. Statistics generally tend to confirm this, suggesting much higher levels of nonmonogamy and sexual partners, particularly as concerns gay and bisexual male couples in comparison to lesbian and heterosexual couples (Bepko & Johnson, 2000; Dworkin, 2001; Markowitz, 1993; Rust, 2001; Shernoff, 1999). More representative national studies appear to confirm this trend and achieve findings consistent with the research using less stringent sampling techniques (Gilman, Cochran, Mays, Hughes, Ostrow, & Kessler, 2001; Lauman, Gagnon, Michael, & Michaels, 1994). Even for self-identified closed-coupled gay men, nonmonogamy appears to be a frequent occurrence, possibly reflecting a tendency to define commitment in emotional rather than sexual terms (Appleby, Miller, & Rothspan, 1999; Blumstein & Schwartz, 1995; Bringle, 1995).

From the perspective of many GLB writers, failure to morally equate "polyamorous" or "polyfidelous" relationships with monogamous heterosexual ideals constitutes a heterosexist and sex-negative belief system (Dworkin, 2001, p. 674). Bepko and Johnson (2000) caution that it is important to avoid pathologizing what may be normative behavior for couples in the gay and lesbian community. This is equally valid advice for working with individuals who seek to increase their heterosexual potential and may have their normative religious values interpreted pathologically as internalized homophobia. One male client alluded to despondency over his homosexual behavior in his decision to pursue change.

> I was living a complete double life. Happy husband and father, church-goer and successful professional on the outside, rabid homosexual sex addict on the inside. While dating men, adopting a gay identity, and throwing myself into the gay lifestyle had been exhilarating at first, it had soon felt like it was killing my spirit, alienating myself from my goals in life, from God and a sense of higher purpose. I had realized then that I didn't want to be affirmed as gay; I wanted to be affirmed as a man.

Risky Sexual Behavior and Concern about HIV Infection

Some gay or bisexual men who seek change-oriented therapy are motivated in part out of a concern that risky sexual behavior may lead to HIV infection. Unprotected anal intercourse has been a particular focus in the medical literature, and recent studies suggest an upward trend in this practice, especially among young gay men (Catania et al., 2001; Ekstrand, Stall, Paul, Osmond, & Coates, 1999; Graham, Kirscht, Kessler, & Graham, 1998; Mansergh et al., 2001; Suarez & Miller, 2001; Wolitski, Valdiserri, Denning, & Levine, 2001). This practice raises the very real potential for HIV infection among these men. Wolitski et al. report that 260,000 American men who have sex with men (MSM) have died of AIDS, a total that is greater than for all other risk groups combined. They further estimate that 365,000-535,000 MSM in the United States are infected with HIV, representing more than one-half of those who live with HIV and 70% of HIV-infected men. Wolitski, et al. (2001) concluded that, "Given that only 5% to 7% of American men have sex with another man during adulthood, these figures are overwhelming" (p. 883). In the mid-1990s one epidemiological analysis reported that 30% of all 20-year-old homosexual males would be dead by the time they reached 30 years of age (Goldman, 1994). More recently, Strathdee et al. (2001) found that men who reported recently engaging in homosexual activity were four times more likely to become infected with HIV. In another recent nationally representative sample, Gilman et al. (2001) reported HIV positive prevalence rates to be 2.3% in their same-sex sexual partner subsample and 0.2% in the opposite-sex subsample. Similarly, Wolitski et al. found that 18% of MSM participants compared to less than 1% of the overall population reported being HIV positive.

Fortunately, the advent of highly active antiretroviral therapy (HAART) has improved the lives and decreased the mortality of HIV positive individuals in recent years. This wonderful advancement in medical treatment is not, however, without a significant downside (Catania et al., 2001; Wolitski et al., 2001). Highly active antiretroviral therapy typically has multiple unpleasant side effects and can lead to drug-resistant strains of HIV that can be transmitted to others. In addition, this treatment is costly, lifelong, and medical compliance is difficult to maintain. In fact, one study found that one-third of HIV cases had foregone medical care because they could not afford the time or the expense (Landsberg, 1999). Even under the best conditions, data suggest that nearly 25% of newly infected individuals are resistant to all three current classes of medications, and nearly 80% display resistance to at least one class of antiretrovirals (Voelker, 2000). This appears to place significant limits on current and future treatment options. Preventive measures such as safer sex practices are also a necessary component of combating HIV, although rates of condom failure with anal sexual activity appear to be alarmingly high (Kalichman, Kelly, & Rompa, 1997; Rosser, Metz, Bockting, & Buroker, 1996).

Researchers have suggested many reasons for the apparent increases in risk behavior (Appleby, Miller, & Rothspan, 1999; Dilley, Woods, & McFarland, 1997; Vanable, Ostrow, McKirnan, Taywaditep, & Hope, 2000; Wolitski, et al., 2001). In spite of its limitations, improved medical management of HIV through HAART has caused many gay men to reevaluate their adherence to safer sex practices. The eroticism of HIV, fed by images of persons living with the virus as healthy, virile, and physically fit, may also change perceptions of risk and lead to increasing risk behavior. Years of coping with HIV, changing desired sexual behavior patterns, and exposure to prevention messages may result in "AIDS burnout." Young MSM may feel pessimistic about aging as gay men, and may view HIV as a means to escape a dreaded future. Finally, for some gay men risky sex may be seen as symbolizing trust, love, and commitment. It appears reasonable that some individuals involved in such practices, particularly those with emergent health concerns and newly found or rediscovered traditional religious faith, may grow dissatisfied with their circumstances and desire to increase their heterosexual potential. Such was the case with one religiously oriented male client involved in change-oriented intervention. He decided not to go further into the gay lifestyle after watching his brother die from AIDS and later mistaking as his own HIV infection what eventually was diagnosed to be the symptoms of chronic fatigue syndrome.

The Possibility of Increasing Heterosexual Potential

To evaluate the ethics of therapeutic attempts to assist clients toward greater heterosexual functioning, evidence suggesting that change is possible for at least some people needs to be presented. In spite of a sociopolitical climate that is generally hostile to such analyses, some of the relevant research is indirectly supportive, whereas a few more recent studies have looked directly at the outcomes of change efforts.

Indirect support can be found in the literature concerning Gender Identity Disorder (GID), defined in the DSM-IV as involving "a strong and persistent cross-gender identification" accompanied by the child's "persistent discomfort with his or her sex or sense of inappropriateness in the gender role of that sex" (American Psychiatric Association, 1994). This diagnosis is increasingly coming under attack, in large part because a significant number of adult homosexual men and women report histories of early cross-gender behavior that would fall within the description of GID (Bradley & Zucker, 1997, 1998). An inherent tension thus exists in the DSM, as GID is a childhood mental disorder that is often a developmental precursor to a sexual orientation declassified for adults. Consequently, there is mounting sociopolitical pressure to remove GID in the next DSM revision (Isay, 1997).

In spite of this, research on GID does suggest a developmental factor in the etiology of homosexuality and indirectly supports the potential for increasing heterosexual potential (Bradley & Zucker, 1997; Zucker et al., 1999). Bradley and Zucker (1997) indicate that therapy can be effective in modifying cross-gender feelings. They also describe treatment for GID as involving the discouragement of cross-gender behavior and increasing opportunities to develop same-sex skills and friendships, interventions not unlike those reported as helpful by adults who claim to have changed homoerotic attraction (Spitzer, 2001a).

Another indirect indicator of the potential for development of heterosexual potential is found in the literature on the relative malleability of erotic attraction for lesbians (Baumeister, 2000; Diamond, 1998; Dworkin, 2001; Peplau & Garnets, 2000; Venigas & Conley, 2000). Studies have reported 31% to 50% of lesbians sampled consider their sexual orientation to be the result of a conscious, deliberate choice (Rosenbluth, 1997; Whisman, 1996). The findings that 25%–50% of lesbians report previous heterosexual marriage and that 77% have had one or more long-term male sexual partners also suggest some degree of malleability (Bridges & Croeau, 1994; Diamant, Schuster, McGuigan, & Lever, 1999). Moreover, religious beliefs appear to be an important element in maintaining or returning to heterosexual functioning (Baumeister, 2000; Rosenbluth, 1997). Baumeister's fascinating account posits a brief period of plasticity in childhood for males followed by a relatively more fixed orientation, whereas females retain plasticity throughout adulthood. Overall, these data suggest that increasing heterosexual potential may take less effort for lesbians and bisexual women than for gay and bisexual men.

The limited number of recent studies on change of homosexual feelings and behavior are consistent with the potential for increasing heterosexual functioning. Self-report information by clients and their therapists strongly suggest that some individuals can and do make significant modifications in their homoerotic attractions (Macintosh, 1994; Throckmorton, 1998).

Research by Schaeffer, Hyde, Kroencke, McCormick, and Nottebaum (2000; Schaeffer, Nottebaum et al., 2000) examined religiously motivated attempts to change sexual orientation. They described a sample of 248 adults surveyed at a conference of Exodus International, a religiously oriented organization that assists individuals with unwanted homoerotic attraction. These participants reported experiencing significantly more heterosexuality than they recalled experiencing at age 18. At a 1-year follow-up, 140 of these subjects were reinterviewed and 60.8% of males and 71.1% of females indicated behavioral success, defined as abstaining from homosexual contact. These results did not support the short-term benefit of change-oriented therapy and speak more to modification of homosexual behavior, rather than feelings. However, they did indicate that even when some level of homoerotic attraction persists, change efforts could promote positive mental health and religious experience.

Nicolosi, Byrd, and Potts (2000) surveyed 882 individuals who underwent psychological treatment, in the form of conversion therapy and self-help groups, to modify same-sex attraction. Of the 318 clients who rated themselves as having exclusively same-gender sexual orientation prior to treatment, posttreatment results indicated that 18% rated themselves as exclusively heterosexual, and 17% felt almost entirely heterosexual. Individual pastoral and professional counseling, group therapy, and personal spirituality and faith were identified as key ingredients in the process of change. Self-report information revealed significant improvement in self acceptance, emotional stability, depression, and spirituality. Finally, 30–4% of the respondents spontaneously reported frustration with previous therapists who had dismissed their desire to change homoerotic feelings and had attempted to impose gay-affirmative therapy on them.

Spitzer's (2001a) study marked an improvement over previous research in that he carefully assessed for the affective components of homosexual experience (e.g., subjective ratings of sexual attraction, and sexual fantasies during masturbation and heterosexual sex) and limited his subject pool to individuals reporting at least 5 years of sustained change from a homosexual to a heterosexual orientation. Using reasonably stringent criteria, Spitzer found that 66% of male participants and 44% of female subjects had achieved good heterosexual functioning. Of the 33 men who rated most extreme on the homosexual indicators, a surprising 67% achieved good heterosexual functioning. Although 20% of the sample reported being heterosexually married prior to change attempts, 76% of the men and 47% of the women reported being married at the time of the interview. Even though 42% of the men and 46% of the women reported their sexual attraction to be exclusively homosexual before change attempts, 17% of the men and 55% of the women indicated exclusive heterosexual attraction upon interview. Depression was indicated as a problem prior to change efforts by 43% of the men and 47% of the women, whereas these statistics had fallen to posttreatment levels of 1% and 4%, respectively.

Most of Spitzer's subjects reported a gradual diminution of homosexual feelings and a gradual emerging or intensification of heterosexual feelings, with the completion of the change effort occurring after approximately 5 years. This is consistent with other studies that suggest the benefits of change-oriented therapies may be most fully experienced well into the treatment process (Nicolosi et al., 2000; Schaeffer, Nottebaum et al., 2000). Spitzer excluded 74 subjects from his study because they only reported change in their identity or overt homosexual behavior. However, even these individuals experienced their degree of change as substantially improved, albeit less than desired. Finally, Spitzer also documented reports of earlier change efforts that were not helpful, including many involving therapists who told clients that they had no choice but to accept their homosexuality. Spitzer concludes from his research that change for some individuals is possible along a multidimensional continuum.

Spitzer's (2001a) study has sparked a heated and overdue debate about the possibility of changing homoerotic attraction, especially in light of the fact that he was a primary architect of the 1973 decision to remove homosexuality from the DSM. Much of the criticism has focused on the issue of sample bias, as most of the participants were religiously conservative and were often referred from organizations known to promote and assist in change efforts (Ritter, 2001). However, in actuality this is a strength of the research, given that the vast majority of studies relevant to the issue of change have utilized convenience samples solicited through GLB-affirmative organizations, support groups, and media. This suggests the presence of skew in the existing literature as a whole, the degree of which can only be determined through a closer examination of individuals such as those in Spitzer's study.

In the short term, the more strident elements on both sides of this debate are likely to continue with opposing anecdotal horror stories. However, it appears increasingly certain that at least some highly motivated individuals can significantly increase their heterosexual potential. If the sociopolitical pressures to prohibit such treatment can be withstood, a growing recognition of the possibility for change will hopefully lead to more collaborative research endeavors that can identify criteria associated with the success or failure of reorientation treatments.

Ethical Considerations for Working with Clients Pursuing Change

When a client who experiences unwanted homoerotic attraction first presents to the MFT, the controversial nature of the presenting problem mandates extra care to insure ethical practice. Some therapists, such as Murphy (1992), who view the practice of therapy to increase heterosexual potential (sometimes referred to as reorientation or conversion therapy) as inherently unethical, will need to avoid involvement altogether. However, MFTs who assume a less extreme stance will have to consider several ethical guidelines, including consent, nonexploitation, and respecting client autonomy and diversity.

Consent

The American Association for Marriage and Family Therapy code of ethics (AAMFT; 2001) is clear about the need for informed consent (1.2). In the context of a client requesting assistance for change in homoerotic feelings, some specific areas need to be addressed. The client needs to be informed about the different types of treatment related to sexual orientation that exist along with the potential risks and benefits of each (Yarhouse, 1998a, 1998b). Broadly speaking, the client can be informed that some professionals provide gay-affirmative therapy with the goal of acceptance of a GLB identity, whereas others provide reorientation therapies that assist in increasing heterosexual potential. Assuming the client wishes to pursue change-oriented treatment, several potential risks and benefits can be discussed consistent with the research outlined above. Potential risks include the very real possibility of no change in homoerotic feelings and accompanying religious distress, disappointment with the degree of change achieved, and the likelihood of any change being a slow and gradual experience over a prolonged period of time. Benefits may include increased ability to live within normative religious sexual ideals, subsequently enhanced spiritual and emotional functioning, a decrease in certain health risks, and an increased ability to have or maintain heterosexual marriage and family.

It is wise for the clinician to have clients seeking change articulate what criteria for success they envision. This can allow for identification of unrealistic expectations, education regarding potential outcomes (e.g., behavioral and/or affectional change), and discussion of how failure to achieve the desired degree of change would be experienced. An acknowledgement of the experimental nature of reorientation therapy is also in order, in that a large body of rigorous empirical studies confirming treatment efficacy does not yet exist. Criticisms of reorientation therapies on these grounds have been widely aired, often with the recommendation to refrain from such interventions until supportive research is available (American Psychiatric Association, 2000; Haldeman, 1994). However, these position statements and resolutions, often drafted by GLB committees (American Psychiatric Association, 1999, 2000; American Psychological Association, 2000), risk being perceived as somewhat self serving unless they are also willing to call for funding to support collaborative outcome research among opponents and proponents of change efforts.

Noncoercion

It is essential that MFTs assess the extent to which a client presenting for change-oriented treatment may be motivated by some degree of coercion from others and thus insure that an autonomous decision is being made (AAMFT Code of Ethics, 2001, 1.2, 1.8). This is especially important when adolescent clients are referred by their parents. Great caution must be exercised to avoid exploitation of the client's vulnerability (AAMFT, 2001, 1.3,

3.9). Therapists need to guard against any impulse to exert pressure on clients to continue in a therapy they no longer wish to pursue. Marriage and family therapists who engage in reorientation treatment must respect a client's decision to leave treatment and pursue gay-affirmative therapy, just as MFTs who operate from a gay-affirmative approach must allow a client who becomes dissatisfied with the gay lifestyle to seek change-oriented intervention. When MFTs feel unable clinically, ethically, or morally to provide either one of these treatments, they should provide referral sources that can assist clients accordingly (AAMFT, Code of Ethics, 2001, 1.10, 3.4, 3.11; Bernstein, 2000; Yarhouse, 1998b). . . . . A more exhaustive description and listing of such resources has been published quite recently (Yarhouse, Burkett, & Kreeft, 2002).

Some professionals have claimed that the decision to attempt to increase heterosexual potential can never be ultimately volitional because of societal homophobia (Haldeman, 1994). This hypothesis is stated in such extreme terms as to make it scientifically untestable and classifiable as ideological posturing (Yarhouse, 1998a). It appears to reflect a perspective that assumes personal identity will always be fundamentally organized around sexual feelings. However, for many people, religious belief forms the primary organizing principle of personal identity and, in the case of conservative religious sentiment, a desire to increase heterosexual potential can legitimately result from such self-identification.

Respecting Client Autonomy and Diversity

Assuming clients are provided with informed consent in a noncoercive environment, the recognition that some individuals with homoerotic attraction will still want to pursue change-oriented therapy upholds the ethical assumption that clients make autonomous choices that MFTs must respect (AAMFT Code of Ethics, 2001, 1.8). In addition, because many of these clients are motivated to attempt change because of deeply held religious convictions, allowing them to pursue such therapy supports the AAMFT (Code of Ethics, 2001, 1.1) ethical pledge not to discriminate on the basis of religion, respecting religious diversity even when members may hold different moral beliefs regarding homosexual behavior and sexual identity (Rosik, 2001; Yarhouse, 1998b; Yarhouse & VanOrman, 1999). As Dworkin (2001) affirmed, "Sexual identity is defined by the client, and it is important for therapists to respect that" (p. 674). Similarly, Bernstein (2000) rightly contended, "it is vital that therapists defer to clients in defining their therapeutic goals" (p. 452).

Bernstein (2000) offered many important considerations for straight therapists who work with GLB clients. Primary among them was the need for MFTs to understand cultural backgrounds different from their own. Given that a generally liberal sociopolitical frame of reference dominates the mental health field (Redding, 2001), it may be even more pressing for MFTs to educate themselves about the cultural background, heritage, and normative belief systems of religious conservatives (Yarhouse & VanOrman, 1999). Applying Bernstein's suggestions to this population of clients, MFTs from different cultural backgrounds are encouraged to develop personal relationships with religiously conservative acquaintances, colleagues, and students. Visiting a conservative church, synagogue, or mosque would also provide important insights into the normative beliefs and practices of this population. Such efforts can greatly assist MFTs in examining and challenging their religious prejudices and enable therapeutic sensitivity with religiously conservative clients who present for therapy with the goal of increasing heterosexual potential (Gartner, 1985, 1986). Akin to the need for awareness of heterocentric bias, MFTs working with religious clients should examine their value assumptions regarding sexual behavior and determine whether they can comfortably assist clients whose conservative moral perspective may motivate the pursuit of change in homoerotic attraction.

In fact, it may well be that differences in underlying moral visions provide a framework for understanding the tensions that often arise over attempts to change unwanted homoerotic attraction both within the therapeutic relationship and the mental health profession at large. What follows is an examination of the potential impact of moral epistemology in this arena intended to assist MFTs in the generally accepted mandate to know their own biases (Bernstein, 2000). . . .

Homophobia

Homophobia has generally been defined to denote any negative belief, attitude, or behavior toward gay and lesbian persons (Bernat, Calhoun, Adams, & Zeichner, 2001; O'Donohue & Caselles, 1993; Sanders & Kroll, 2000). More recently, the term biphobia has been coined with reference to negative views of bisexuality (Dworkin, 2001; Mohr & Rochlen, 1999). In an important contribution to this literature, O'Donohue and Caselles observe that homophobia has been operationalized using many scale items referring to debatable value positions and moral judgments. Moral disapproval and avoidance may not be irrational or phobic within a specific religious or ideological subculture, and this distinction needs to be taken into account. O'Donahue and Casettes suggest that a valid use of the term homophobia would only refer to the emotional reaction of fear, plus the behavioral reaction of avoidance, in the absence of negative moral or aesthetic arguments. The authors thus contend that, "there are certain value, moral, aesthetic, and political questions and positions that, in a free society, should not be closed and suppressed by mental-health professionals and behavioral science research, and the moral status of homosexuality is one of these" (p. 190).

Recent research suggests the legitimacy and utility of distinguishing between religious belief that is homonegative in evaluating the moral status of homosexual behavior but homopositive in affirming the value of GLB persons versus religious belief that is uniformly homonegative (Bassett, Baldwin, et al, 2001; Bassett, Hodak, et al., 2000; Fulton, Gorsuch, & Maynard, 1999). Such nuances are important to consider when assessing religiously conservative clients who request assistance in increasing heterosexual potential; yet, our current scales of homophobia and biphobia (including internalized versions) are simply unable to take them into account (e.g., Johnson, Brems, & Alford-Keating, 1997). This, in turn, may compromise the usefulness and validity of these terms when applied to this population.

Examining these concerns through the lens of Haidt and Hersh's (2001) findings, it appears that homophobia, biphobia, and related terms (such as heterosexism) derive from and make perfect sense within the EOA adopted by liberalism. The trouble lies in attempts to carry this understanding into conservative groups that do not define their moral domain primarily in terms of autonomy, but also maintain social and religious concerns found in the EOC and EOD. Conservatives within the broader moral domain may thus experience their being labeled homophobic as an attempt to force them to embrace an alien evaluative framework. Indeed, O'Donahue and Caselles (1993) warn that the ambiguity surrounding the construct of homophobia may allow it to be used as a means of influencing individuals to react differently toward homosexuals and homosexuality by condemning certain sets of negative reactions.

Marriage and family therapists who encounter conservative religious individuals struggling with homoerotic attractions need to be very cautious about applying value-laden terms, such as homophobia, to these individuals or their families and support networks. In fact, an uncritical use these terms may actually risk increasing homonegative sentiment should conservatively religious clients and their families perceive their normative beliefs about sexual morality to be globally characterized as homophobic.

Given all the aforementioned considerations, it seems advisable for MFTs dealing with religiously conservative clients to limit the use of the term homophobia to individuals whose moral disapproval of homosexuality is expressed in a way that is inconsistent with the well-accepted values of traditional religious ideology. Thus, incivility, demeaning speech, and any type of aggression toward GLB persons are likely to be forms of behavior for which the term homophobic would be widely endorsed within religious communities and not perceived in an antagonistic manner. Forms of disapproval that appear consistent with the normative values of the religious subculture might preferably be characterized as stemming from a "nonequivalency" position that does not view sexual behavior outside of heterosexual marriage as the moral equivalent of sexual activity within such bounds. This would be a much less pejorative and value-laden term that could facilitate more meaningful dialogue and understanding about reorientation treatment for therapists and clients who operate out of different moral domains.

Causal Attributions for Psychopathology

There is a growing consensus that same-sex behavior is associated with elevated risk of certain forms of psychiatric disorder and with suicide when compared to heterosexual samples (Cochran, 2001; Cochran & Mays, 2000a, 2000b; Diamant, Wold, Spritzer, & Gelberg, 2000; Gilman et al., 2001; Herrell et al., 1999; Hughes & Eliason, 2002; Sandfort, de Graaf, Biji, & Schnabel, 2001; Valanis, Bowen, Bassford, Whitlock, Charney, & Carter, 2000). . . .

Hypothesized biological factors are more commonly minimized or interpreted as signaling constitutional malfunction. This undergirds both the viability of change-oriented therapy and the suspicion that there is something unnatural or sinful in homosexual or bisexual sexual activity. Conservatives are thus more skeptical of the benefits of normalizing homosexual and bisexual sexual behavior in reducing psychological distress. They may point to studies in regions with considerably long histories of tolerance, such as San Francisco or the Netherlands, where elevated emotional and behavioral health risks for GLB individuals persist (Page-Shafer et al., 1999; Sandfort et al., 2001).

The differing emphases in moral vision suggest that both conservative and liberal MFTs may need to look beyond the boundaries of their immediate evaluative frameworks to maintain a balanced attributional perspective. On the one hand, conservative therapists may not sufficiently recognize the impact of stigmatization and discrimination experiences on the psychological distress of GLB clients (Mays & Cochran, 2001). On the other hand, liberally oriented clinicians may be inclined to underestimate or overlook the etiological significance of developmental experience for GLB identity and sexual behavior, such as childhood sexual abuse (Doll et al., 1992; Paul, Catania, Pollack, & Stall, 2001; Tomeo, Templer, Anderson, & Kotler, 2001). . . .

Conclusions

The clinical treatment of unwanted homoerotic attraction continues to be a controversial practice. It is important that MFTs educate themselves on this subject in a manner that includes information and perspectives sensitive to clients who seek such care, the majority of whom have conservative religious backgrounds. This analysis has attempted to provide an initial foray into the issue, utilizing a conservative evaluative framework that is likely to resonate with many of these clients. As such, evidence for the validity of their motivations and efforts toward increasing heterosexual potential has been presented, along with some guidelines for ethical practice that allow for change efforts. Finally, by digging deeper into the divergent moral epistemologies likely to be covertly fueling the debate, it is hoped that the viewpoints of both proponents as well as opponents of reorientation treatment will be regarded as having something important to contribute. Surely, clients who seek to change unwanted homoerotic attraction deserve to have scholarly representation that reflects their experiences, interests, and aspirations. Without this input, the authoritative conclusions about change efforts put forth by mental health associations may merely reflect suppression, rather than consensus, of opinion among therapists and their clients.

References

American Psychiatric Association (1994). Diagnostic and statistical manual of mental disorders. Washington, DC: Author.

American Psychiatric Association (1999). Position statement on psychiatric treatment and sexual orientation. *American Journal of Psychiatry, 156,* 1131.

American Psychiatric Association (2000). Position statement on therapies focused on attempts to change sexual orientation (reparative or conversion therapies). *American Journal of Psychiatry, 157,* 1710–1721.

American Psychological Association (2000). Guidelines for psychotherapy with lesbian, gay, and bisexual clients. *American Psychologist, 55,* 1440–1451.

Appleby, P. R., Miller, L. C., & Rothspan, S. (1999). The paradox of trust for male couples: When risking is a part of living. *Personal Relationships, 6,* 81–93.

Bassett, R. L., Baldwin, D., Tammaro, J., Mackmer, D., Mundig, C., Wareing, A., & Tschorke, E. (2001). Reconsidering intrinsic religion as a source of universal compassion. *Journal of Psychology and Theology, 30,* 131–143.

Bassett, R. L., Hodak, E., Allen, J., Bartos, D., Grastorf, J., Sittig, L., & Strong, J. (2000). Homonegative Christians: Loving the sinner but hating the sin. *Journal of Psychology and Christianity, 19,* 258–269.

Baumeister, R. F. (2000). Gender differences in erotic plasticity: The female sex drive as socially flexible and responsive. *Psychological Bulletin, 126,* 347–374.

Bepko, C., & Johnson, T. (2000). Gay and lesbian couples in therapy: Perspectives for the contemporary family therapist. *Journal of Marital and Family Therapy, 26,* 409–419.

Bernstein, A. C. (2000). Straight therapists working with lesbians and gays in family therapy. *Journal of Marital and Family Therapy, 26,* 443–454.

Bernat, J. A., Calhoun, K. S., Adams, H. E., & Zeichner, A. (2001). Homophobia and physical aggression toward homosexual and heterosexual individuals. *Journal of Abnormal Psychology, 110,* 179–187.

Blumstein, P, & Schwartz, P. (1990). Intimate relationships and the creation of sexuality. In D. P. McWirter, S. A. Sanders & J. M. Reinisch (Eds.), *Homosexuality/ heterosexuality: Concepts of sexual orientation* (pp. 307–320). New York: Oxford University Press.

Bradley, S. J., & Zucker, K. J. (1997). Gender identity disorder: A review of the past 10 years. *Journal of the American Academy of Child and Adolescent Psychiatry, 36,* 872–880.

Bradley, S. J., & Zucker, K. J. (1998). [Letter to the Editor]. *Journal of the American Academy of Child and Adolescent Psychiatry, 37,* 244–245.

Bridges, K. L., & Croteau, J. M. (1994). Once-married lesbians: Facilitating changing life patterns. *Journal of Counseling and Development, 73,* 134–140.

Bringle, R. G. (1995). Sexual jealousy in the relationships of homosexual and heterosexual men: 1980 and 1992. *Personal Relationships, 2,* 313–325.

Catania, J. A., Osmond, D., Staff, R. D., Pollack, L., Paul, J. P., Blower, S., Binson, D., Canchola, J. A., Mills, T. C., Fisher, L., Choi, K., Porco, T., Turner, C., Blair, J., Henne, J., Bye, L. L., & Coates, T. J. (2001). The continuing HIV epidemic among men who have sex with men. *American Journal of Public Health, 91,* 907–914.

Cochran, S. D. (2001). Emerging issues in research on lesbians' and gay men's mental health: Does sexual orientation really matter? *American Psychologist, 56,* 931–947.

Cochran, S. D., & Mays, V. M. (2000a). Relation between psychiatric syndromes and behaviorally defined sexual orientation in a sample of the U.S. population. *American Journal of Epidemiology, 151,* 516–523.

Cochran, S. D., & Mays, V. M. (2000b). Lifetime prevalence of suicidal symptoms and affective disorders among men reporting same-sex sexual partners: Results from NHANES Ill. *American Journal of Public Health, 90,* 573–578.

Davison, G. C. (2001). Conceptual and ethical issues in therapy for the psychological problems of gay men, lesbians, and bisexuals. *Journal of Clinical Psychology, 57,* 695–704.

Diamant, A. L., Schuster, M. A., McGigan, K., & Lever, J. (1999). Lesbians' sexual history with men. *Archives of Internal Medicine, 159,* 2730–2736.

Diamant, A. L., Wold, C., Spritzer, K., & Gelberg, L. (2000). Health behaviors, health status, and access to health care: A population-based study of lesbian, bisexual, and heterosexual women. *Archives of Family Medicine, 9,* 1043–1051.

Diamond, L. M. (1998). Development of sexual orientation among adolescent and young adult women. *Developmental Psychology, 34,* 1085–1095.

Dilley, J. W., Woods, W. J., & McFarland, W. (1997). Are advances in treatment changing views about high-risk sex? *New England Journal of Medicine, 337,* 501–502.

Doll, L. S., Joy, D., Bartholow, B. N., Bolan, G., Douglas, J. M., Saltzman, L. E., Moss, P. M., & Delgado, W. (1992). Self-reported childhood and adolescent sexual abuse among adult homosexual and bisexual men. *Child Abuse and Neglect, 16,* 855–864.

Dworkin, S. H. (2001). Treating the bisexual client. *Journal of Clinical Psychology, 57,* 671–680.

Ekstrand, M. L., Stall, R. S., Paul, J. P., Osmond, D. H., & Coates, T. J. (1999). Gay men report high rates of unprotected anal sex with partners of unknown or discordant HIV status. *AIDS, 13,* 1525–1533.

Fulton, A. S., Gorsuch, R. L., & Maynard, E. A. (1999). Religious orientation, antihomosexual sentiment, and fundamentalism among Christians. *Journal for the Scientific Study of Religion, 38,* 14–22.

Gartner, J. D. (1985). Religious prejudice in psychology: Theories of its cause and cure. *Journal of Psychology and Christianity, 4,* 16–23.

Gartner, J. D. (1986). Antireligious prejudice in admissions to doctoral programs in clinical psychology. *Professional Psychology: Research and Practice, 17,* 473–475.

Gilman, S. E., Cochran, S. D., Mays, V. M., Hughes, M., Ostrow, D., & Kessler, R. C. (2001). Risk of psychiatric disorders among individuals reporting same-sex sexual partners in the national comorbidity survey. *American Journal of Public Health, 91,* 933–939.

Goldman, E. L. (1994, October). Psychological factors generate HIV resurgence in young gay men. *Clinical Psychiatry News, 29,* 5.

Graham, R. P, Kirscht, J. P., Kessler, R. C., & Graham, S. (1998). Longitudinal study of relapse from AIDS-preventive behavior among homosexual men. *Health Education and Behavior, 25,* 625–639.

Haidt, J., & Hersh, M. A. (2001). Sexual morality: The cultures and emotions of conservatives and liberals. *Journal of Applied Social Psychology, 31,* 191–221.

Haldeman, D. C. (1994). The practice and ethics of sexual orientation conversion therapy. *Journal of Consulting and Clinical Psychology, 62,* 221–227.

Herrell, R., Goldberg, J., True, W. R., Ramakrishnan, V., Lyons, M., Eisen, S., & Tsuang, M. T. (1999). Sexual orientation and suicidality. A co-twin control study in adult men. *Archives of General Psychiatry, 56,* 867–874.

Hughes, T. L., & Eliason, M. (2002). Substance use and abuse in lesbian, gay, bisexual, and transgender populations. *Journal of Primary Prevention, 22,* 263–298.

Isay, R. A. (1997). Remove gender identity disorder in DSM. *Psychiatric News, 32,* 13.

Johnson, M. E., Brems, C., & Alford-Keating, P. (1997). Personality correlates of homophobia. *Journal of Homosexuality, 34,* 57–69.

Kalichman, S. C., Kelly, J. A., & Rompa, D. (1997). Continued high-risk sex among HIV seropositive gay and bisexual men seeking HIV prevention services. *Health Psychology, 16,* 369–373.

Lauman, E. O., Gagnon, J. H., Michael, T., & Michaels, S. (1994). *The social organization of sexuality.* Chicago: University of Chicago Press.

Mansergh G., Colfax, G. N., Marks, G., Rader, M., Guzman, R., & Bookbinder, S. (2001). The circuit party men's health survey: Findings and implications for gay and bisexual men. *American Journal of Public Health, 91,* 953–958.

Macintosh, H. (1994). Attitudes and experiences of psychoanalysts in analyzing homosexual patients. *Journal of the American Psychoanalytic Association, 42,* 1183–1205.

Markowitz, L. M. (1993, March/April). Understanding the differences: Demystifying gay and lesbian sex. *Family Networker, 17,* 50–59.

Mays, V. M., & Cochran, S. D. (2001). Mental health correlates of perceived discrimination among lesbian, gay, and bisexual adults in the United States. *American Journal of Public Health, 91,* 1869–1876.

Mohr, J. J., & Rochlen, A. B. (1999). Measuring attitudes regarding bisexuality in lesbian, gay male, and heterosexual populations. *Journal of Counseling Psychology, 46,* 353–369.

Murphy, T. F. (1992). Redirecting sexual orientation: Techniques and justifications. Journal of Sex Research, 29, 501–523. Nicolosi, J., Byrd, A. D., & Potts, R. W. (2000). Retrospective self-reports of changes in homosexual orientation: A consumer survey of conversion therapy clients. *Psychological Reports, 86,* 1071–1088.

O'Donohue, W., & Caselles, C. E. (1993). Homophobia: Conceptual, definitional, and value issues. *Journal of Psychopathology and Behavioral Assessment, 15,* 177–195.

Page-Shafer, K. A., McFarland, W., Kohn, R., Klausner, J., Katz, M. H., Wohlfeiler, D., & Gibson, S. (1999). Increases in unsafe sex and rectal gonorrhea among men who have sex with men—San Francisco, California, 1994-1997. *Journal of the American Medical Association, 281,* 696–697.

Paul, J. P., Catania, J., Pollack, L., & Stall, R. (2001). Understanding childhood sexual abuse as a predictor of sexual risk-taking among men who have sex with men: The urban men's health study. *Child Abuse and Neglect, 25,* 557–584.

Peplau, L. A., & Garnets, L. D. (2000). A new paradigm for understanding women's sexuality and sexual orientation. *Journal of Social Issues, 56,* 267–282.

Redding, R. E. (2001). Sociopolitical diversity in psychology. *American Psychologist, 56,* 205–215.

Ritter, M. (2001, May 9). Study: Some gays can go straight. *Washington Post.* Retrieved on 5/12/01 from. . . .

Rosenbluth, S. (1997). Is sexual orientation a matter of choice? *Psychology of Women Quarterly, 21,* 595–610.

Rosik, C. H. (2001). Conversion therapy revisited: Parameters and rationale for ethical care. *Journal of Pastoral Care, 55,* 47–69.

Rosser, B. R. S., Metz, M. E., Bockting, W. O., & Buroker, T. (1996). Sexual differences, concerns, and satisfaction in homosexual men: An empirical study with implications for HIV prevention. *Journal of Sex and Marital Therapy, 23,* 61–73.

Rust, P. (2001). Two many and not enough: The meanings of bisexual identity. *Journal of Bisexuality, 1,* 31–68.

Sanders, G. L., & Kroll, I. T. (2000). Generating stories of resilience: Helping gay and lesbian youth and their families. *Journal of Marital and Family Therapy, 26,* 433–442.

Sandfort, T. G., de Graaf, R., Bijl, R. B., & Schnabel, P. (2001). Same-sex sexual behavior and psychiatric disorders. *Archives of General Psychiatry, 58,* 85–91.

Schaeffer, K. W., Hyde, R. A., Kroencke, T., McCormick, B., & Nottebaum, L. (2000). Religiously-motivated sexual orientation change. *Journal of Psychology and Christianity, 19,* 61–70.

Schaeffer, K. W., Nottebaum, L., Dech, P., & Drawczyk, J. (2000). Religiously-motivated sexual orientation change: A follow-up study. *Journal of Psychology and Theology, 27,* 329–337.

Shernoff, M. (1999, March/April). Monogamy and gay men. *Family Networker, 23,* 63–71.

Spitzer, R. L. (2001a). 200 subjects who claim to have changed their sexual orientation from homosexual to heterosexual. Paper presented at the meeting of the American Psychiatric Association, New Orleans, LA.

Spitzer, R. L. (2001b, May 23). Psychiatry and homosexuality. *The Wall Street Journal,* A26.

Strathdee, S. A., Galai, N., Safaiean, M., Celentano, D. D., Vlahov, D., Johnson, L., & Nelson, K. E. (2001). Sex differences in risk factors for HIV seroconversion among injection drug users. *Archives of Internal Medicine, 161,* 1281–1288.

Suarez, T., & Miller, J. (2001). Negotiating risks in context: A perspective on unprotected anal intercourse and barebacking among men who have sex with men—where do we go from here. *Archives of Sexual Behavior, 30,* 287–300.

Temeo, M. E., Templer, D. L, Anderson, S., & Kotler, D. (2001). Comparative data of childhood and adolescence molestation in heterosexual and homosexual persons. *Archives of Sexual Behavior, 30,* 535–541.

Throckmorton, W. (1998). Efforts to modify sexual orientation: A review of outcome literature and ethical issues. *Journal of Mental Health Counseling, 20,* 283–304.

Valanis, B. G., Bowen, D. J., Bassford, T., Whitlock, E., Chamey, P., & Carter, R. A. (2000). Sexual orientation and health: Comparisons in the Women's Health Initiative sample. *Archives of Family Medicine, 9,* 843–853.

Vanable, P. A., Ostrow, D. G., McKirnan, D. J., Taywaditep, K. J., & Hope, B. A. (2000). Impact of combination therapies on HIV risk perceptions and sexual risk among HIV-positive and HIV-negative gay and bisexual men. *Health Psychology, 19,* 134–145.

Venigas, R. C., & Conley, T. D. (2000). Biological research on women's sexual orientation: Evaluating the scientific evidence. *Journal of Social Issues, 56,* 267–282.

Voelker, R. (2000). HIV drug resistance. *Journal of the American Medical Association, 12,* 169.

Whisman, V. (1996). *Queer by choice: Lesbians, gay men, and the politics of identity.* New York: Routledge.

Wolitski, R. J., Valdiserri, R. O., Denning, R. H., & Levine, W. C. (2001). Are we headed for a resurgence of the HIV epidemic among men who have sex with men? *American Journal of Public Health, 91,* 883–888.

Yarhouse, M. A. (1998a). When clients seek treatment for same-sex attraction: Ethical issues in the "right to choose" debate. *Psychotherapy, 35,* 248–259.

Yarhouse, M. A. (1998b). When families present with concerns about an adolescent's experience of same-sex attraction. *American Journal of Family Therapy, 36,* 321–330.

Yarhouse, M. A., Burkett, L. A., & Kreeft, E. M. (2002). Paraprofessional Christian ministries for sexual behavior and same-sex identity concerns. *Journal of Psychology and Theology, 30,* 208–227.

Yarhouse, M. A., & VanOrman, B. T. (1999). When psychologists work with religious clients: Applications of the general principles of ethical conduct. *Professional Psychology: Research and Practice, 30,* 557–562.

Zucker, K. J., Bradley, S. J., Kuksis, M., Pecore, K., Birkenfeld-Adams, Doering, R. W., Mitchell, J. N., & Wild, J. (1999). Gender constancy judgments in children with gender identity disorder: Evidence for a developmental lag. *Archives of Sexual Behavior, 28,* 475–502.

Robert-Jay Green

→ **NO**

When Therapists Do Not Want Their Clients to Be Homosexual: A Response to Rosik's Article

This commentary is a response to Rosik's "Motivational, Ethical, and Episte-mological Foundations in the Treatment of Unwanted Homoerotic Attraction" (this issue). Such treatment raises complex questions that cannot be resolved by focusing on the therapist's conservative versus liberal values. Most such clients are deeply ambivalent about their homosexual attractions. The degree to which their homosexuality is "unwanted" is highly variable among them and some-times within them over time. Clients who are exclusively homosexual are very unlikely to be able to change their sexual attractions, whereas some clients who are bisexual may be more able to "manage" their homoerotic attractions (acting only on their heterosexual feelings). Marriage and family therapists should be able to support a client along whatever sexual orientation path the client ulti-mately takes, and the client's sense of integrity and interpersonal relatedness are the most important goals of all.

Although the value of therapeutic "neutrality" has been challenged in the field of family therapy, it is preferable to strive toward neutrality rather than take a partisan position when it comes to the treatment of unwanted homosexuality. If a therapist is not able to support a client's explorations and decisions initially or over the course of treatment to live as heterosexual, homosexual, or bisexual, then I believe that the therapist should excuse her/himself from treating such clients. In contrast to the frame Rosik (this issue) suggests, the treatment of clients' "unwanted homosexuality" should not be approached as mostly a matter of therapists' politics with equal pro and con (liberal vs. conservative) positions or reduced to a matter of religious debate.

There is a crucial difference between religious exhortation/proselytizing and psychotherapy, and that difference lies primarily in whose needs and beliefs are at the center of attention. I do not believe that clients can resolve any major internal conflict in therapy when the continuation of treatment is contingent on the client accepting the therapist's preferred resolution. For example, although he does not state so explicitly, Rosik seems to believe (based on his personal interpretation of the Bible) that homosexuality is a sin, and he seems willing to agree with clients who assert that homosexuality is a sin. Thus, it is unclear how he would treat clients who decided over the course of treatment that they wanted to embrace their homosexuality, as many clients seeking reorientation therapy later do (Shidlo & Schroeder, 2001). Would Rosik reject these clients and refer them elsewhere at such a juncture? Or do these clients leave treatment without explanation, sensing that he would be unable to support their new direction?

Although Rosik (this issue)—in one of the more inflammatory remarks in his article—accuses our profession of risking "a large scale form of client discrimination and abandonment" (p. 14) toward gay or bisexual clients who wish to become heterosexual, this claim is unjustified. Gay-affirmative couple and family therapists such as myself (Green & Mitchell, 2002; Laird & Green, 1996) believe just as strongly that clients should set the goals of their treatment. For example, in my practice, I personally have helped lesbian/gay clients stay in heterosexual marriages, and I am comfortable with this goal if clients approach it with integrity (i.e., honesty with their spouse, rather than deception). Also, more than half of my clients at any given time tend to be heterosexuals, and I fully support their being so. In contrast, Rosik seems not to feel that homosexuality is a legitimate moral choice and presumably would have a hard time or find it impossible to work with clients who start out and wish to remain lesbian or gay or wish to increase their self-acceptance. Ironically (borrowing his words), it seems that Rosik and other conversion therapists advocate "discrimination and abandonment" of gay/lesbian clients who wish to remain gay-identified.

Thus, although Rosik would have us believe that his approach is the moral or political equivalent of a "prochoice" position, he is actually communicating a rather confusing double message. If he views the choice of homosexuality as a sin and believes that homosexuality can only to lead to unhappiness and a morally inferior life, it becomes impossible to accept his claim of giving clients any "choice" in therapy other than to adopt his views of homosexuality if they wish to remain in therapy with him. He states, for example: "MFTs who engage in reorientation therapy must respect a client's decision to leave treatment and pursue gay-affirmative therapy" (p. 19). Clearly, the implication of the phrase "leave treatment" is that such clients would be terminated and have to seek treatment elsewhere. Presumably this is because Rosik believes there is only one mentally healthy choice that could bring happiness and ethical fulfillment: heterosexuality.

Despite his pronouncements to that effect, the research literature on lesbian/gay psychology shows clearly that acceptance of one's sexual orientation and finding social support within the lesbian/gay community are the strongest predictors of mental health (Diplacido, 1998; Herek, 1998; Meyer & Dean, 1998). The majority of lesbian/gay people are as happy and mentally healthy as heterosexuals, even if the overall group means differ slightly in large population rates of substance use, depression, and attempted suicide (Bell & Weinberg, 1978; Cochran, 2001; Gonsiorek, 1991). The researchers attribute these small (but statistically significant) differences in group averages to the greater minority stress experienced by lesbian/gay people in society, whereas Rosik implies that these differences are endemic to homosexual orientation itself. If the latter were true, however, how would he explain that the vast majority of lesbian/gay people do not differ from the majority of heterosexuals in terms of substance abuse and mental health? In light of this research, it seems highly inappropriate for a therapist to support a client's jaundiced view that homosexuality is antithetical to psychological well-being and happiness, which is exactly what Rosik appears to do in his article.

Motivations for Seeking Conversion Therapy

The notion of "unwanted homoerotic attraction" is much more complex than Rosik implies in his article, particularly in his section on "motivations for pursuing greater heterosexual potential" (p. 14). Clients with these concerns run the gamut from having no same-sex experiences at all to having exclusive same-sex experiences over many years. In addition, many such clients are bisexual in attractions and/or behavior (Fox, 1996; Klein, 1993). Some of these "bisexual" clients fantasize only homosexual activity even when they are having heterosexual sex.

Many clients who are seeking treatment for unwanted homoerotic attraction are actually rather ambivalent about it. They say they do not want to be homosexual, yet they continue homosexual behavior and do not show serious intent to change. Others seem to be saying something like "I'm okay with being homosexual, but I'm afraid my parents, employers, children, or friends will find out and reject or discriminate against me." It is essential to help clients examine what is motivating their desire to change at the time treatment is started and whether their motivation is externalized or internalized, temporary in response to some precipitating event (e.g., a breakup of a same-sex relationship, or an attempt to appease a heterosexual spouse who discovered an affair), or persistent over time. As every therapist knows, almost no presenting problem or treatment is quite as simple and straightforward as it might appear to be at the outset, and many attempts to change that are begun "under duress" (due to external pressures) meet with initial success but are not sustained over time.

There are many minority human traits that may be "unwanted" by their holders in our society (e.g., ethnic appearance, body shapes that do not match the cultural ideal, foreign accents), but these attributes are undesired because someone (or some group) defines them as undesirable, not because they are problematic in and of themselves (Green, 1998). In addition to facing external prejudice and discrimination, members of minority groups frequently internalize society's irrational views of their group traits and suffer various levels of psychological distress as a result (DiPlacido, 1998; Meyer & Dean, 1998). However, often their internalization of society's prejudice is highly conflicted because they simultaneously understand that prejudice is arbitrary, irrational, and can be resisted. Although some of these minority group traits might be changeable (e.g., plastic surgery to reshape a nose, or surgery to remove epicanthic folds in eyelids), it is valuable to inquire what motivates such clients to seek change, whether change in that trait is possible, what obstacles exist to accepting one's "differentness," rather than trying to eliminate it, and what advantages/disadvantages might follow from embracing one's individuality and minority status versus trying to conform to the dominant social norms of the majority group.

Clearly, there are some therapeutic goals (for example, an anorectic's goal to become even thinner; an abusive husband's desire to increase his dominance over his wife) that therapists may not be able to support because the achievement of those goals would severely threaten the well being of the client or another family member. For these reasons, the first steps in the treatment of "unwanted homoerotic attraction" should include efforts to understand with the client why he/she does not want homoerotic attraction. I do not mean that one should dismiss or refute the client's stated goals. Rather, that it is important to try to understand the basis of the client's motivation to change and whether it is internalized and stable (versus externalized and ambivalent) or based on negative stereotypes about homosexuality (such as the false ideas that gay people are invariably unhappy, lonely in old age, promiscuous, unable to establish lasting relationships, afflicted with HIV, etc.), some of which Rosik actually endorses in his article.

For example, Rosik suggests in his "motivations" section that many male clients justifiably want to rid themselves of homoerotic desire because of the heightened risk of contracting HIV in sex with gay men. However, most of the people in the world with AIDS now are heterosexuals (in Africa), and lesbians have the lowest rates of HIV infection. By using Rosik's logic (that homosexual clients should seek to become heterosexual to lessen their risks of contracting HIV), one could argue just as easily that heterosexual women should be encouraged to become lesbians to reduce their chances of contracting HIV. The fact is that homosexuality does not cause AIDS. Unsafe sex with HIV-positive partners (heterosexual or homosexual) causes AIDS. Obviously, the solution in HIV prevention is safer sex, not sexual orientation conversion therapy for heterosexual women and gay men.

Likewise, the solution to the unique mental health stresses faced by lesbians and gay men is a reduction in the prejudice to which they are subjected. Research shows quite clearly that external discrimination (homophobia) and internalized homophobia (Malyon, 1982; Shidlo, 1994) are strong predictors of depression, suicidality, and HIV-risk behaviors among gay, lesbian, and bisexual persons. Lesbians and gay men who are more self accepting of their sexual orientations, who receive more acceptance of their sexual orientation from family, friends, or coworkers, and who are more involved in the gay community have lower rates of mental health problems and HIV risk behaviors than do lesbians/gay men who are less self accepting and less identified with the gay community (Green & Mitchell, 2002; Herek, 1998; Meyer & Dean, 1998). Rosik seems to have gotten these results backwards in his "motivations" section. He seems to be arguing that gay/lesbian persons who accept and live out their sexual orientations will have greater mental health problems, but the research shows the opposite to be true.

The Possibility of Eliminating Homoerotic and Increasing Heteroerotic Potential

At the outset, we need to clarify that the terms heterosexual, bisexual, and homosexual are much more complicated than their casual usage by Rosik and most authors writing on these topics imply. As readers may know, Kinsey (Kinsey, Pomeroy, & Martin, 1948; Kinsey, Pomeroy, Martin, & Gebhard, 1953) counterposed heterosexuality and homosexuality on a single bipolar continuum, which ranged from exclusive heterosexuality (0) to exclusive homosexuality (6):

0 = Exclusively heterosexual
1 = Predominantly heterosexual, only incidentally homosexual
2 = Predominantly heterosexual, but more than incidentally homosexual
3 = Equally heterosexual and homosexual
4 = Predominantly homosexual, but more than incidentally heterosexual
5 = Predominantly homosexual, only incidentally heterosexual
6 = Exclusively homosexual

However, in this rating system, Kinsey did not distinguish the person's overt sexual behavior from underlying feelings, attractions, or fantasies, nor did he distinguish either of these dimensions from the person's self-labeling or presentation to others (as heterosexual, bisexual, or gay/lesbian). By putting heterosexuality and homosexuality on a single bipolar continuum, Kinsey created a kind of "zero sum game," in which it was assumed that the more one was heterosexual, the less one was homosexual, and vice versa.

More recently, theorists such as Klein (1993) have suggested that several other theoretical continua are needed to understand a person's sexual orientation. Revising Klein's framework, I would suggest that it is most important to take into account the person's attractions, behavior, self-identification, and self-presentation, as follows:

1. Degree of heterosexual attractions (from high to low)
2. Degree of heterosexual behavior (from high to low)
3. Degree of homosexual attractions (from high to low)
4. Degree of homosexual behavior (from high to low)
5. Self-identity (self-labeling) as heterosexual, bisexual, or gay/lesbian
6. Self-presentation to others as heterosexual, bisexual, or gay/lesbian

In contrast to Kinsey, there is no reason to believe that the strength of one's heterosexual attractions diminishes one's homosexual attractions or vice-versa. That is, one may have a high degree of attraction to persons of both sexes; or a low degree of attraction to persons of both sexes; or be highly attracted to one sex and not to the other at all; or have all other possible combinations of levels of attractions to males and females. Likewise, for behavior, some people are high in heterosexual activity and simultaneously high in homosexual activity and others are low in both, with most people higher in heterosexual attractions and behavior.

In this framework, sexual orientation can best be conceptualized as encompassing several dimensions, and the person's functioning across those dimensions may or may not be consistent. For example, Ms. Smith may be strongly attracted to women but only have sex with men (while fantasizing only about women); and she may inwardly label herself as "bisexual" but present herself to others as exclusively heterosexual. In general, greater levels of incongruity among the dimensions are associated with greater levels of internal conflict, relationship dissatisfaction, and potential dissolution of relationships over time.

It is not clear whether Rosik believes that all clients seeking treatment for unwanted homoerotic attraction stand an equal chance of success at conversion. For example, in his review of the developmental research, Rosik erroneously stated that the link between gender nonconformity in childhood and homosexual orientation in adulthood "indirectly supports the potential for increasing heterosexual potential" (p. 16). However, this whole line of scientific evidence actually does the opposite. It shows that sexual orientation in these cases is part of a continuous developmental process that begins quite early in life, manifesting as cross-gender behavior during childhood and manifesting as homosexual orientation later, in adulthood (Bailey & Zucker, 1995; Bell, Weinberg, & Hammersmith, 1981; D'Augelli & Patterson, 1995; Green, Bettinger, & Zacks, 1996). Most researchers interpret this finding as evidence for the immutability of sexual orientation, concluding that it must be highly resistant to change, given the enormous social sanctions that gender nonconforming children and lesbian/ gay adults encounter throughout life.

Thus, most sexologists tend to believe that sexual attractions are relatively fixed early in life, whereas sexual behavior, self labeling, and self presentation can vary dramatically according to situational and personality factors. Some of the sex therapy literature indicates that clients who start out as truly bisexual in their attractions may be able to suppress their homosexual activity and increase their heterosexual activity at least temporarily during the treatment period or beyond (Masters & Johnson, 1979). However, clients who are exclusively homosexual (in terms of attractions) are very unlikely to succeed in developing enduring heterosexual attractions. Some proportion of the latter clients may be able to engage in temporary heterosexual behavior while utilizing homosexual fantasies. However, most of them would not find this mode of sexual expression sufficiently fulfilling emotionally over the long term. As one might imagine, the maintenance of changes after treatment in these different subgroups of clients may be quite variable depending on their degree of initial bisexual versus homosexual attractions.

Lastly, it is worth noting that women seem to be somewhat more fluid in their sexual orientation than are men, and the reasons for this difference are not entirely known (Peplau & Garnets, 2000). One may speculate, however, than women are aroused sexually more by emotional and interactional aspects of a romantic relationship, whereas men are more aroused by visual stimuli alone. Also, for obvious anatomical reasons, men require a relatively higher degree of attraction and physical arousal to participate in sexual intercourse, whereas woman can often participate at much lower levels of arousal or in its absence. This enables women to move more easily from heterosexual to lesbian relationships or vice-versa, regardless of their degree of sexual arousal in those relationships.

Research on Conversion Therapy

Rosik's entire article seems based on the premise that unwanted homoerotic attraction could be eliminated and heterosexual responsiveness developed through reorientation therapy. To support this contention, he presents a selective review of the research on this topic, emphasizing studies conducted by religiously based researchers whose findings are consistent with his point of view, while omitting the most significant research (e.g., Shidlo & Schroeder, 2001) that throws those findings into question. However, even the research he emphasizes shows that a majority of participants in conversion therapies fail to attain their goals.

For example, Rosik cites the survey by Nicolosi, Byrd, and Potts (2000) showing that 18% of participants in conversion therapy changed to becoming exclusively heterosexual and 17% almost entirely heterosexual. But this leaves two-thirds of clients who failed to attain or nearly attain the sought-after changes. Rosik also touts research by Shaeffer, Hyde, Kroencke, McCormick, and Nottebaum (2000) but then advises that: "These results did not support the short-term benefit of change-oriented therapy and speak more to modification of homosexual behavior rather than feelings" (p. 17).

With more fanfare, Rosik then presents the results of a recent study by Spitzer (2001a), who specifically sought research subjects who claimed to have changed their sexual orientations as a result of conversion therapy. This research design cannot yield information on what percentage of attempters succeed or fail to convert. Rather, it reveals only what self-described converters have to say about their experiences. Many, if not most, of Spitzer's research participants were religious conservatives and were referred by religious ex-gay groups. Although Rosik selectively reports some of Spitzer's data to buttress his contention that lesbian/gays can change their sexual orientations, it is interesting that Spitzer (2001b) himself draws a much more cautious conclusion from the study:

> Complete change was uncommon. . . . In reality, change should be seen as complex and on a continuum. Some homosexuals appear able to change self-identity and behavior, but not arousal and fantasies; others can change only self-identity; and only a very few, I suspect, can substantially change all four. Change in all four is probably less frequent than claimed by therapists who do this kind of work; in fact, I suspect the vast majority of gay people would be unable to alter by much a firmly established homosexual orientation (Spitzer, 2001b).

Furthermore, there is reason to doubt the veracity of research participants who were referred by religion-oriented conversion treatment programs (as was the case in the studies by Shaeffer et al., 2000; Nicolosi et al., 2001; and Spitzer, 2001a). For example, Exodus (which is listed in the appendix to Rosik's article and is the largest of the ex-gay religious groups) was founded in 1976 by Michael Bussee, Gary Cooper, and others. Bussee became one of Exodus's main leaders and spokespersons. However, even as they claimed to be ex-gays and worked to convert others to heterosexuality, Bussee and Cooper secretly were involved with each other romantically and sexually, and they subsequently left Exodus together in 1979. In interviews later, Bussee stated:

> "The desires never go away. . . . The confrontations begin and the guilt gets worse and worse." Bussee recalled that some people who went through the Exodus program had breakdowns or committed suicide. "One man slashed his genitals with a razor and poured Drano on his wounds. Another man impulsively underwent an incomplete sex-change operation because he believed his sexual desires might receive divine approval were he biologically a woman." After dealing with hundreds of people, Bussee concluded that he and his partner had not "met one who went from gay to straight. Even if you manage to alter someone's sexual behavior, you cannot change their true sexual orientation. . . . If you got them away from the Christian limelight . . . and asked them, 'Honestly now, are you saying that you are no longer homosexual and you are now heterosexually oriented?' . . . not one person said, 'Yes, I am actually now heterosexual.'" (Mills, 1999).

More recently, John Paulk, a gay man who undertook conversion therapy with Exodus and claimed to have converted to heterosexuality, was appointed Chairman of the Board of Exodus North America. He married an "ex-lesbian" and frequently was described at the time as the "poster child" of the ex-gay movement, becoming its main public spokesman and appearing very frequently on television and other news media. However, in September 2000, Paulk was spotted in a gay bar in Washington, DC. He claimed initially that he did not realize that he had walked into and was sitting in a gay bar. However, he later recanted this story and was put on probation by the Exodus North America board of directors for what the board described as Paulk's "lapse" in judgment (Exodus North America, 2000).

These episodes among the leaders of Exodus throw into serious doubt the statements religious "ex-gays" make about their sexual orientations to the media and to researchers. For obvious reasons, members of fundamentalist religious groups have very strong incentives to be in denial or to hide their sexual orientations from researchers who are studying their group's treatment outcomes. Spitzer's follow-back sample of ex-gays was made up mainly of such persons. Given the history of duplicity among the leadership of Exodus as described above, it is difficult to determine whether self-reports given over the telephone by religious "ex-gay" research participants in the studies cited by Rosik were valid.

In contrast to Spitzer's (2001a) study of self-described "ex-gays," Shidlo and Schroeder (2001) undertook a survey of all clients who had attempted sexual orientation conversion treatment, regardless of whether or not they had succeeded in changing their sexual orientation. These authors found that the attempt to convert was itself severely damaging psychologically to many clients; that it reflected and contributed to their self-hatred; and that it delayed the ultimate acceptance of their sexual orientation later in life. Furthermore, Shidlo and Schroeder found that many clients involved in such treatments had lied to their therapists about continuing homosexual activity. Their conversion therapists never learned of the longer-term outcomes, which usually involved more therapy later on and ultimate acceptance of homosexuality.

Of the 202 participants in Shidlo and Schroeder's (2001) study who had participated in some form of conversion therapy, only eight participants (about 4%) reported having achieved the goal of being in a heterosexual relationship and not struggling with homoerotic desires/behavior. Of these eight participants, seven provided ex-gay counseling, and four of the seven had paid positions as ex-gay or conversion counselors. In other words, this shift in sexual orientation may have been sustained partially by work involvements as well as by participation in treatment. But even if these eight successful cases (out of 202 attempts) are genuine and permanent conversions, the generally high failure rate of conversion therapy (96%) found by Shidlo and Schroeder has to be addressed in terms of the ethical implications for clients who are seeking to eliminate homoerotic attractions.

Given the above studies, it is probably fair to conclude from the existing research that only a very small percentage of exclusively gay/lesbian people could undertake a significant degree of heterosexual involvement and feel reasonably content in doing so. Mostly, the changes that could be achieved would be behavioral and in terms of identity, rather than in terms of underlying attractions. These "ex-gays" could engage in heterosexual relationships and present themselves as heterosexual despite predominant homosexual attractions and despite using homosexual fantasies during heterosexual encounters. For some strongly religious clients or clients with few relationship alternatives, this adaptation may be adequately satisfying and workable, especially if their partner/spouse were aware and willing to accommodate the situation, as is sometimes the case.

However, for most other predominantly homosexual clients, the large discrepancy between their attractions and their behavior would become intolerable over time, and they would feel that a deeper love and emotional fulfillment was missing in their lives. The fact remains that most homosexual (as opposed to bisexual) clients seeking conversion therapy are simply unable to make a sustained shift to heterosexuality, especially in underlying attractions, rather than in overt behavior or self-presentation. Many of these clients continue to engage in homosexual activity during and/or after treatment, and the vast majority of them are likely to accept a lesbian/gay identity later in their lives, after conversion therapy ends (see Duberman, 2002, and Moor, 2001, for very poignant case examples).

Ethical Issues

Given the high likelihood of failure in the treatment of unwanted homoerotic attraction, serious ethical issues arise regarding informed consent and the possibility that such failed therapy will be harmful to clients. If, as even the religion-motivated research cited by Rosik shows, the vast majority of clients who undertake conversion therapy do not succeed at suppressing their homosexuality and converting to heterosexuality, then therapists have an ethical obligation to so inform clients at the outset of treatment.

In addition, there is much documentation of the destructive effects that certain sexual orientation conversion treatments have had on lesbian/gay/bisexual people. These treatments often exacerbate internalized homophobia and all of its correlates, such as self-hatred, depression, suicidality, drug abuse, and HIV-risk behaviors (Garnets, Hancock, Cochran, Godchilds, & Peplau, 1991; Schroeder & Shidlo, 2001; Shidlo, Schroeder, & Drescher, 2001). Clients need to be informed of these risks at the start of therapy and advised to discuss with their therapists any signs that the therapy is making things worse, rather than better.

Obviously, no psychotherapeutic treatments are 100% successful. However, conversion therapy appears to fail such a significant amount of the time and to be harmful such a large proportion of the time that this issue of informed consent seems essential to raise with a client. The most ethical stance is to: (a) present the information on conversion therapy outcomes as it currently exists in the scientific literature as summarized above; (b) inform the client that this literature is still not definitive; (c) indicate one's willingness to continually review the client's progress toward goals as therapy progresses and to stop therapy if it is unhelpful or harmful; (d) indicate that the continuation of therapy is not contingent on the client selecting any particular sexual orientation; and (e) emphasize that the main concern of therapy will be the client living his or her life with the greatest degree of interpersonal relatedness (connection and compassion) and with integrity (differentiation of a "whole self" based on lived experience, rather than a "pseudo-self"). This stance allows the client to fully utilize his/her religious values in deciding whether and how to express sexuality with integrity. It also leaves the client free to attempt heterosexuality and still provides a safety net and psychological help if the client does not achieve that goal or changes goals along the way.

What Is Rosik's "Treatment of Unwanted Homoerotic Attraction?"

Although the title of Rosik's article refers to a "treatment," it is noteworthy that there is almost no description of that treatment. Instead, the author focuses almost exclusively on the polemics of liberal versus conservative therapists' acceptance of the client's initial goal to become heterosexual. In addition, while claiming that his approach is grounded in religion, Rosik overlooks other religious perspectives and interpretations of the Bible that help clients incorporate their religious beliefs into a positive gay identity (see the website of PFLAG—Parents, Families, & Friends of Lesbians and Gays—for a continually updated reading list on "Homosexuality and Religion," . . .). Thus, Rosik's article remains rather abstract throughout, tending toward caricatures of liberal and conservative therapists, but avoiding the nitty-gritty information about how to conduct this treatment with real people.

For example, Rosik states: "Conservatives, in contrast, tend to grapple with a broader and more multifaceted moral domain that extends beyond the EOA to include two other influential dimensions in their evaluative framework: the ethics of community (EOC), and the ethics of divinity (EOD)" (p. 20). He then explains that this larger domain goes beyond the "ethics of autonomy (EOA)" (which are supposedly the only ethics embraced by liberal therapists) to include the "ethics of community (EOC)" and the "ethics of divinity (EOD)," the latter referring to Biblical and other religious precepts. However, it is completely arbitrary to state that liberal therapists are concerned only with the ethics of autonomy and not with the ethics of community or divinity, and to anoint conservative therapists the keepers of a "larger" (presumably superior) morality compared to the rest of the professional and academic community. There simply is no basis for claiming that the bulk of therapists are dealing with a smaller moral domain than conservative therapists or for assuming that conservative religious therapists' applications of the Bible are superior to those of other, less conservative therapists with religious affiliations. Yet this is the kind of ad hoc reasoning that makes much of Rosik's writing about moral epistemology so polemical at the core.

The omission of a treatment method description is quite worrisome, because many religious conversion programs seem to use techniques that are ethically questionable from the standpoint of mainstream psychological treatments. In addition, readers are unable to evaluate the merits of Rosik's treatment techniques even on theoretical or logical grounds, because these techniques were never described. For example, does Rosik engage in various combinations of Biblical study, prayer groups, and pastoral counseling? Exorcisms or other rituals based on a sin-based conception of homosexuality? Aversion therapy to decrease homosexual attractions, or classical conditioning techniques to increase heterosexual attractions? Does the treatment use fear-based tactics with references to Satan and punishment in the afterlife?

Frequently, conversion therapists authoritatively attribute the cause of homosexuality to factors that research has shown are completely unrelated to the development of sexual orientation. Such attributions seem unethical in light of the existing research. For example, that old psychodynamic saw of blaming "overinvolved mothers and/or distant fathers" for a child's homosexual orientation (and for almost every other psychological problem) is still frequently used by conversion therapists, even though research findings have long since put that notion to rest (Bell et al., 1981). In fact, no family patterns have been found to bear a causal relationship to the development of homosexuality. Nor has child physical or sexual abuse been found to bear a relationship with homosexuality. No longitudinal studies on this question have been conducted, and some studies show that the rates of such prior abuse are identical for heterosexual and lesbian women (Herman, 1992), yet this is another frequent interpretation offered to clients by conversion therapists.

Because he does not give us specifics, we are left with many more questions than answers when it comes to understanding Rosik's clinical treatment for unwanted homoerotic attraction. I invite Dr. Rosik to provide in his rejoinder a more tangible description of the treatment, however briefly. We need to know what sorts of interpretations, homework assignments, suggestions, adjunctive treatments, referrals, religious activities, and sequences of interventions are typically used in his method of therapy. We need to know what information about sexual orientation the clients are advised to disclose to their spouses or dating partners, and whether and how spouses or partners are involved in the treatment. We also need to know how therapists working in Rosik's framework would respond if a client changed goals and decided to try to accept his/her homosexuality during the course of treatment. Lacking such basic information, it is impossible for readers to adequately evaluate Rosik's treatment methods or his ethics.

References

Bailey, J. M, & Zucker, K. J. (1995). Childhood sex-typed behavior and sexual orientation: A conceptual analysis and quantitative review. *Developmental Psychology, 31,* 43–55.

Bell, A. P, & Weinberg, M. (1978). *Homosexualities: A study of diversity among men and women.* New York: Simon and Schuster.

Bell, A. P, Weinberg, M. S., & Hammersmith, S. K. (1981). *Sexual preference: Its development in men and women.* Bloomington, IN: Indiana University Press.

Cochran, S. D. (2001). Emerging issues in research on lesbians' and gay men's mental health: Does sexual orientation really matter? *American Psychologist, 56,* 931–947.

D'Augelli, A. R., & Patterson, C. J. (Eds.). (1995). *Lesbian, gay, and bisexual identities over the lifespan: Psychological perspectives.* New York: Oxford University Press.

DiPlacido, J. (1998). Minority stress among lesbians, gay men and bisexuals. In G. M. Herek (Ed.), *Stigma and sexual orientation: Understanding prejudice against lesbians, gay men, and bisexuals* (pp. 138–159). Thousand Oaks, CA: Sage.

Duberman, M. J. (2002). *Cures: A gay man's odyssey* (10th anniversary ed.). Boulder, CO: Westview Press.

Exodus North America (October 3, 2000). Chairman Disciplined for Gay Bar Visit (Press release). Retrieved July 31, 2002, from. . . .

Fox, R. (1996). Bisexuality in perspective: A review of theory and research. In B. Firestein (Ed.), *Bisexuality: The psychology and politics of an invisible minority* (pp. 3–50). Thousand Oaks, CA: Sage.

Garnets, L., Hancock, K. A., Cochran, S. D., Godchilds, J., & Peplau, L. A. (1991). Issues in psychotherapy with lesbians and gay men: A survey of psychologists. *American Psychologist, 46,* 964–972.

Gonsiorek, J. C. (1991). The empirical basis for the demise of the illness model of homosexuality. In J. C. Gonsiorek & J. D. Weinrich, J. D. (Eds.), *Homosexuality: Research implications for public policy* (pp. 115–136). Thousand Oaks, CA: Sage.

Green, R.-J., (1998a). Race and the field of family therapy. In M. McGoldrick (Ed.), *Revisioning family therapy: Race, culture, and gender in clinical practice* (pp. 93–110). New York: Guilford Press.

Green, R.-J., Bettinger, M., & Zacks, E. (1996). Are lesbian couples fused and gay male couples disengaged? Questioning gender straightjackets. In J. Laird & R-J. Green (Eds.), *Lesbians and gays in couples and families: A handbook for therapists* (pp. 185–230). San Francisco: Jossey-Bass.

Green, R.-J., & Mitchell, V. (2002). Gay and lesbian couples in therapy: Homophobia, relational ambiguity, and social support. In A. S. Gurman & N. S. Jacobson, (Eds.), *Clinical handbook of couple therapy* (3rd ed., pp. 546-568). New York: Guilford Press.

Herek, G. M. (Ed.) (1998). *Stigma and sexual orientation: Understanding prejudice against lesbians, gay men, and bisexuals.* Thousand Oaks, CA: Sage.

Herman, J. L. (1992). *Trauma and recovery.* New York: Basic Books.

Klein, E. (1993). *The bisexual option.* New York: Haworth Press.

Kinsey, A. C., Pomeroy, W. B., & Martin, C. E. (1948). *Sexual behavior in the human male.* Philadelphia: W. B. Saunders.

Kinsey, A. C., Pomeroy, W. B., Martin, C. E., & Gebhard, P. H. (1953). *Sexual behavior in the human female.* Philadelphia: W. B. Saunders.

Laird, J., & Green, R.-J. (Eds.). (1996). *Lesbians and gays in couples and families: A handbook for therapists.* San Francisco: Jossey-Bass.

Malyon, A. K. (1982). Psychotherapeutic implications of internalized homophobia in gay men. In J. Gonsiorek (Ed), *Homosexuality and psychotherapy: A practitioner's handbook of affirmative models* (pp. 59-69). New York: Haworth Press.

Masters, W., & Johnson, V. (1979). *Homosexuality in perspective.* Boston: Little, Brown.

Meyer, I. H., & Dean, L. (1998) Internalized homophobia, intimacy, and sexual behavior among gay and bisexual men. In G. M. Herek (Ed.), *Stigma and sexual orientation: Understanding prejudice against lesbians, gay men, and bisexuals* (pp. 160-186). Thousand Oaks, CA: Sage.

Mills, K. I. (February, 1999). Mission impossible: Why reparative therapy and ex-gay ministries fail. Retrieved July 31, 2002 from. . . .

Moor, P. (2001). The view from Irving Bieber's couch: "Heads I win, tails you lose." In A. Shidlo, M. Schroeder, & J. Drescher (Eds.), *Sexual conversion therapy: Ethical, clinical, and research perspectives* (pp. 25-36). New York: Haworth Press.

Nicolosi, J., Byrd, A. D., & Potts, R. W. (2000). Retrospective self-reports of changes in homosexual orientation: A consumer survey of conversion therapy clients. *Psychological Reports, 86,* 1071-1088.

Peplau, L. A., & Garnets, L. D. (2000). A new paradigm for understanding women's sexuality and sexual orientation. *Journal of Social Issues, 56,* 267-282.

Rosik, C. H. (2002). Motivational, ethical, and epistemological foundations in the treatment of unwanted homoerotic attraction. *Journal of Marital & Family Therapy, 29,* pp. 13-28.

Schaeffer, K. W., Hyde, R. A., Kroencke, T., McCormick, B., & Nottebaum, L. (2000). Religiously-motivated sexual orientation change. *Journal of Psychology & Christianity, 19,* 61-70.

Schroeder, M., & Shidlo, A. (2002). Ethical issues in sexual orientation conversion therapies. In A. Shidlo, M. Schroeder, & J. Drescher (Eds.), *Sexual conversion therapy: Ethical, clinical, and research perspectives* (pp. 131-166). New York: Haworth Press.

Shidlo, A. (1994). Internalized homophobia: Conceptual and empirical issues in measurement. In B. Greene & G. Herek (Eds.), *Lesbian and gay psychology: Theory, research, and clinical applications* (pp. 176-205). Thousand Oaks, CA: Sage.

Shidlo, A., & Schroeder, M. (2001). Conversion therapy: A consumers report. *Professional Psychology: Research & Practice, 33,* 249-259.

Shidlo, A., Schroeder, M., & Drescher, J. (2001). (Eds.). *Sexual conversion therapy: Ethical, clinical, and research perspectives.* New York: Haworth Press.

Spitzer, R. L. (2001a). Two hundred subjects who claim to have changed their sexual orientation from homosexual to heterosexual. Paper presented at the meeting of the American Psychiatric Association, New Orleans, LA.

Spitzer, R. L. (May 23, 2001b). Commentary: Psychiatry and Homosexuality. Wall Street Journal. Retrieved July 31, 2002 from. . . .

CHALLENGE QUESTIONS

Is Sexual Orientation Conversion Therapy Ethical?

1. Green argues that the very nature of sexual orientation conversion therapy demonstrates that homophobia has permeated the culture to the detriment of society. Rosik views this form of therapy as acceptable because it is respectful of religious diversity. How might a clinician reconcile these two opposing views?
2. Rosik and Green each use the condition gender identity disorder (GID) as support for his viewpoint. In your opinion, to what extent does GID provide support for the notion that sexual orientation is changeable?
3. Both Rosik and Green argue that it is important for clients to understand their motivations when requesting sexual orientation conversion therapy. Once the motivation is clarified, the next step is to determine the extent to which it is psychologically legitimate and healthy. How would you go about helping clients to evaluate their motivations?
4. Green argues that the strongest predictor of mental health can be found in those people who accept their sexual orientation and surround themselves with others who are accepting as well. Sometimes, though, a client's family and community refuse to be supportive. How might a therapist help a client cope with such a situation?
5. Since sexual orientation conversion therapy seeks to alter behavior and feelings that are inherently personal, an evaluation of the effectiveness of therapy can be very difficult. Rosik relies primarily on self-reports of clients to validate effectiveness. How much credence should be given to self-reports, and why might they be problematic?

Suggested Readings

Ford, J. G. (2002). Healing homosexuals: A psychologist's journey through the ex-gay movement and the pseudo-science of reparative therapy. *Journal of Gay and Lesbian Psychotherapy, 5,* 69–86.

Haldeman, D. C. (2002). Gay rights, patient rights: The implications of sexual orientation conversion therapy. *Professional Psychology: Research and Practice, 33,* 260–264.

Nicolosi J., Byrd, A. D., & Potts, R. W. (2000). Beliefs and practices of therapists who practice sexual reorientation psychotherapy. *Psychological Reports, 2,* 689–702.

Yarhouse, M. A., & Throckmorton, W. (2002). Ethical issues in attempts to ban reorientation therapies. *Psychotherapy: Theory/Research/Practice/ Training, 39,* 66–75.

Zucker, K. J. (2003). The politics and science of "reparative therapy." *Archives of Sexual Behavior, 32,* 399–402.

ISSUE 15

Does Exposure to Media Violence Promote Aggressive Behavior?

YES: Nancy Signorielli, from *Violence in the Media: A Reference Handbook* (ABC-CLIO, 2005)

NO: Jonathan L. Freedman, from *Media Violence and Its Effect on Aggression: Assessing the Scientific Evidence* (University of Toronto Press, 2002)

ISSUE SUMMARY

YES: Professor of communication Nancy Signorielli asserts that research supports the position that media violence affects viewers by fostering aggression, causing desensitization to violence, and promoting fear.

NO: Psychologist Jonathan L. Freedman argues that the scientific evidence does not support the notion that exposure to TV and film violence causes aggression, desensitization, or fear.

In recent years, video games have caught the attention of the public because of various reports about violent and sexually explicit imagery contained in products sold to young people. The debate about the potential impact of exposure to aggressive or sexually explicit media has raged for decades, with social critics expressing great concern about the impact on movies and television shows in which violence has become almost normative. The question has been raised about whether such imagery desensitizes viewers, and possibly even promotes a tolerance for the most unacceptable of interpersonal behaviors.

Nancy Signorielli asserts that there is a large body of research that delineates three ways in which media violence may affect viewers; she contends that exposure to such imagery fosters aggression, desensitizes viewers to violence, and causes people to develop a "mean world syndrome" in which they come to believe that the world is a scary place. Signorielli discusses research that points to the fact that exposure to media violence leads to aggressive behavior in children, teens, and adults.

Jonathan L. Freedman claims that scientific evidence does not support the notion that exposure to media violence leads to aggression in children or adults. Freedman contends that far fewer than half the research studies have found a causal connection between exposure to media violence and aggression, and that the research may be interpreted as showing that there is no causal effect. Freed-man points out other factors relevant to this debate, such as the major decline in violent offenses over the past 10 years, the notion that violent media may just be exciting and arousing to people, that the impact of exposure to real violence hasn't been sufficiently considered, and that several of the studies conducted on media violence and its effects on aggression are methodologically flawed.

POINT

- Numerous controlled laboratory studies provide strong evidence that there is a causal relation between seeing violent media portrayals and the expression of subsequent aggression in children's behavior.

- Researchers have documented some compelling findings about childhood exposure to media violence and the development of aggression several years later. One longitudinal study of boys found that the amount of violence seen on television at age 8 was related to aggressiveness at age 18, as well as involvement in antisocial behavior (fights and spouse abuse) and criminal acts at age 30.

- In many representations of media violence, there is a lack of adequate context, as well as a failure to convey the message that "crimes does not pay." This may transmit the lesson that violence is not necessarily immoral, and that those characters who commit violence are not sorry for their actions and they may not be punished for their transgressions. These messages could lead viewers, especially children, to learn and even accept aggressive behaviors.

- Exposure to media violence may cause desensitization; that is, viewers may become less sensitive to the violence they see and thus become willing to tolerate a more violent society.

- Research shows a solid and consistent base of evidence supporting the relationship between watching media violence and subsequent aggressive behavior for children, teens, and adults.

COUNTERPOINT

- When considering laboratory experiments, there is an important difference between violent and non-violent media, in that violent media are generally more arousing and exciting. People who are aroused by provocative imagery tend to perform any activity more strongly than those less aroused. Thus, when viewers of violent films punch a punching bag more vigorously, this does not necessarily reflect heightened aggression.

- The pattern of evidence from research fails to support the hypothesis that exposure to media violence at a young age causes aggressive behavior later in life. Longitudinal and cross-national studies have produced more non-supportive results than supportive ones.

- Films and television programs that contain violence are not designed to convey the message that violence is good or that people should engage in violent acts. They do not contain information that is likely to convince anyone of anything; they do not contain explicit messages in favor of aggression or violence. They are just entertainment. So it should not be surprising that they have no effect on aggressive behavior or on attitudes toward violence.

- There is little or no evidence for a desensitization effect, and there is some evidence that directly contradicts it.

- Perhaps it is not exposure to fictional media violence, but rather exposure to real-world violence that children, as well as adults, may then imitate.

YES

Nancy Signorielli

What We Know about Media Violence

Who Is Involved?

. . . Any discussion of the amount of violence on television must examine the characters who are involved in violence—those who do the hurting and killing or are hurt and killed. CI [Cultural Indicators project] has shown that television violence illustrates and provides lessons about power. Violence shows who's on top and who's on the bottom, who gets hurt and who does the hurting, and who wins and who loses. These studies consistently find a power structure related to character demographics, with earlier studies showing women and minorities more likely to be hurt than to hurt others.

Research in the CI tradition consistently shows that during prime time, men are more likely than women to be hurt (victimized) or hurt others (commit violence) (Signorielli 1990). There have been some changes in these patterns, however, in the past thirty-five years. In the programs of the 1980s, men were slightly less likely to be involved in violence than in the programs of the 1970s. Fewer characters still were involved in violence between 1993 and 2002 (Signorielli 2003). Only one-third of the major and supporting characters were involved in violence during that period, and although more men than women were involved (38 percent of the men, compared to 27 percent of the women), whites and minorities were equally likely to be victimized or commit violence (about a quarter of both whites and minorities). During the 1990s, the ratios of hurting to being hurt changed from the patterns seen in the 1970s and 1980s for women but not for men. Today, for every ten male characters who hurt or kill, eleven are victimized, the same ratio found in the earlier analysis. For women, however, instead of sixteen women being victimized for each woman who hurts or kills, the odds are even—women are equally likely to hurt or kill as to be hurt or killed. Moreover, although whites are a little more likely to be victimized than hurt others, the odds for minority characters are even.

Although the NTVS [National Television Violence Study] did not generate a profile of all characters on television, it did examine the demographic characteristics of perpetrators (those who commit) and targets (victims) of violence. Most of the perpetrators (close to three-quarters) were men; only one in ten was a woman. Few perpetrators were categorized as heroes, and most were white. Similarly, most of the targets were men (71 percent)—only 10 percent were women—and most were white (Smith, et al. 1998). W. James Potter and colleagues (1995), in looking at a composite week of evening programming (6 PM to midnight) on four networks, also found that television typically presents an unrealistic picture of serious aggression in regard to the race of those who commit the acts as well as those who are victimized. In short, television over-represents both white perpetrators and white victims of aggression. Although the study by Potter and colleagues, the NTVS, and the CI reports differ in how they isolate characters' involvement in violence, the patterns are similar—more men than women and more whites than minorities. Similarly, studies con-ducted in the United Kingdom found that women were much less likely to be involved in violence and that the onscreen time devoted to female violence was considerably less than that devoted to male violence (Gunter et al. 2003).

Overall, it appears that the consensus of findings from studies of media content indicated that contemporary television programs may not adequately support or reinforce the lesson that "crime does not pay." The lack of ade-quate contexts for violent behaviors may transmit the lesson that violence is "sanitary," that it is not necessarily immoral, and that those characters who commit violence are not sorry for their actions and may not be punished for their transgressions—in short, there are few, if any, consequences for committing violence. From a social learning perspective, these messages could lead viewers, particularly children, to learn and even accept aggressive behaviors. Thus, the environment of violent entertainment in which many people, including children, spend most of their free time may be potentially harmful. Moreover, television's lack of realistic contexts for violence may signal that aggression and violence are acceptable modes of behavior. . . .

How Media Violence Affects Us

There are numerous ways media violence affects us. Potter (2003) differentiates effects that are immediate or short-term from those that are long-term. Researchers, including John Murray (2003) and Potter (2003), further delineate three ways in which media violence may affect viewers: fostering aggression, becoming desensitized to violence, and becoming fearful. Each of these effects, in turn, may have both short- and long-term consequences.

Aggression and Aggressive Behavior

One of the biggest concerns about media violence is that exposure to violent images will result in aggression and aggressive behavior. There is a sizable body of research that supports this position. Although . . . there is some disagreement with this statement, the number of researchers in this camp is rather small, and some have ties to the broadcast industry. The strength of the evidence led the American Psychological Association (1985) to conclude that one factor in the development of aggressive and/or antisocial behavior in children is a steady diet of real and/or mediated violence. Similarly, the 1982 report by the

National Institute of Mental Health concluded that children and teens who watch violence on television tend to exhibit more aggressive behavior. The research evidence on which these conclusions were based comes from experimental studies, longitudinal studies, and meta-analyses (a particular type of analysis that simultaneously compares the statistical results from a large number of existing studies on the same topic).

Some of the earliest research on mediated violence was experimental in nature and found that filmed or televised (mediated) images affected behavior. Glenn Ellis and Francis Sekyra (1972) and O. Ivar Lovaas (1961) found that children exposed to media violence behaved aggressively shortly after seeing violence. Another study comparing violent and prosocial (positive messages) programs (Stein and Friedrich 1972) found that children who saw positive or prosocial programs (e.g., *Mister Roger's Neighborhood*) increased their helping behaviors, whereas those who saw violent images behaved more aggressively. Overall, numerous studies have found a causal relation between seeing violent portrayals and later aggressive behavior. L. Rowell Huesmann and Laurie Miller conclude: "In these well-controlled laboratory studies there can be no doubt that it is the children's observation of the scenes of violence that is *causing* the changes in behavior" (1994, 163).

Another strong line of evidence of long-term effects comes from studies conducted over several years (longitudinal studies), specifically the research of Leonard Eron and L. Rowell Huesmann. One study of young boys begun in the 1970s in New York state that was able to control for intelligence quotient (IQ), initial levels of aggressiveness, and social class found that the amount of violence seen on television at age eight was related to aggressiveness at age eighteen, as well as involvement in antisocial behavior (fights and spouse abuse) and criminal acts at age thirty (Huesmann and Miller 1994). Similar results were found in samples of youngsters in Chicago as well as children from other countries, including Finland, Poland, and Israel. These studies found that more aggressive children, compared to less aggressive children, watched more television, preferred programs that were more violent, and perceived mediated violence as closer to real life. The most recent study in this tradition (Huesmann, Moise-Titus, Podolski, and Eron 2003) found that watching violence, identification with same-sex aggressive characters, and a perception that television violence is realistic were related to adult aggression, regardless of how much aggression was exhibited as a child.

A particularly interesting and important longitudinal study (Joy, Kimball, and Zabrack, 1986) was conducted in the late 1970s in three communities in Canada as part of a larger study by Tannis MacBeth (formerly Williams). While vacationing in Canada, MacBeth visited an area in which a new and more powerful transmission tower was being built that would have a major impact on television reception in the area. One town located in the valley, Notel, would receive television for the first time. Unitel, a town about 50 miles away that had been receiving one television channel, would increase its reception by a second channel with the new transmitter. The third community, Multitel, was located close to the U.S. border and received numerous television channels originating both in Canada and the United States. The researchers gathered data relating to aggression, gender roles, and academic achievement both before and two years after the installation of the more powerful transmitter. The results showed that the children in Notel exhibited more aggressive behavior (both verbal and physical) after the introduction of television. Aggressive behavior increased for both boys and girls, for children of different ages, and for those who had different initial levels of aggressiveness. Interestingly, this comprehensive study also found that after the introduction of television, children's gender role stereotyping increased and measures of academic success (e.g., reading levels) decreased (Williams 1986).

A recent cross-cultural study of twelve-year-old children (2,788 boys and 2,353 girls) from twenty-three different countries (funded by the United Nations Education, Scientific, and Cultural Organization, or UNESCO) found an interactive relationship between media violence and real violence such that "media can contribute to an aggressive culture" (Groebel 2001, 265). In short, these studies found that aggressive people, particularly those who live in more aggressive environments, use the media to confirm their attitudes and beliefs, which are then reinforced by media content. For example, the study found that one of the messages of aggressive content is that aggression is a good way to solve conflicts and that it is fun and provides status. Moreover, the study found that successful media figures, such as the Terminator (Arnold Schwarzenegger) and Rambo (Sylvester Stallone), had become cross-cultural heroes.

Another line of naturalistic research is the work of Brian Centerwall, MD (1989a; 1989b). Using an epidemiological approach, Centerwall examines relationships between the introduction of television in a society (e.g., the United States, Canada, and South Africa) and changes in homicide rates among the white population in these countries. In comparison with South Africa, where television was banned until 1975, Centerwall found that the white homicide rates in both the United States and Canada increased 90 percent between 1945 and 1975, whereas homicide rates for the white population in South Africa remained stable. These increases held despite the implementation of statistical controls for economic growth, urbanization, alcoholism, gun ownership, and so on. Moreover, in South Africa homicide rates in South Africa's white population increased by 56 percent between 1975, when television was introduced in the country, and 1983. Although most social scientists find Centerwall's research compelling, Elizabeth Perse (2001) notes that South Africa may not have been a good choice for comparison because it was a highly controlled and repressed society and had a higher homicide rate before the introduction of television. Moreover, Perse notes that Centerwall's method, a simple bivariate graphical analysis, does not dispel the possibility that the relationships may be due to a third, unmeasured, variable. Nevertheless, many find that these data are very compelling in that they show convincing, statistically significant increases in homicide rates of the white population over time.

Another solid base of evidence about the detrimental effects of media violence comes from a number of meta-analyses, a statistical technique that analyzes findings from a large number of studies about a particular topic. The first meta-analysis (Andison 1977) examined sixty-seven separate studies (experiments, surveys, longitudinal) conducted between 1956 and 1996 that examined over 30,000 participants. This analysis found strong support for a relationship between watching media violence and subsequent aggression. An analysis of samples of children, teens, and adults in 230 separate studies found a positive relationship between antisocial behavior (behaving aggressively, rule breaking, etc.) and exposure to violent media in most of the studies (Hearold 1986). Similarly, Haejung Paik and George Comstock's (1994) meta-analysis of 217 studies found statistically significant and positive correlations between viewing and subsequent aggression in samples of adults, children, and teens. Meta-analyses thus show a solid and consistent base of evidence supporting the relationship between watching media violence and behaving aggressively.

Desensitization

A second major concern is that media violence may be related to increased desensitization; that is, viewers may become less sensitive to the violence they see and thus become willing to tolerate a more violent society (Murray 2003). Laboratory studies have shown that adults and children become callous and even punitive after watching violent images. Children in the third grade, for example, who either did not see mediated violence or were shown a short clip from a violent western, were then asked to monitor two younger children by listening to the noise of them playing through an intercom. As they listened to the children, it became apparent that their play had become physically aggressive (Drabman and Thomas 1974). The children who saw the violent episode took considerably longer to get adult help than those who did not see violence. Similarly, Daniel Linz, Edward Donnerstein, and Steven Penrod (1984) found that a group of college men who viewed violent "slasher" films for five consecutive days rated the films as less violent and degrading to women at the end of the week. Moreover, after watching these films and then watching a documentary about a trial for sexual assault, these young men were less sympathetic toward the rape victim than the group of young men who had not seen the slasher films. Similarly, Stacy Smith and Edward Donnerstein (1998) note that the more viewers see graphic media violence, the more they rate material they originally perceived as offensive or degrading as less offensive or degrading.

Desensitization is particularly a concern as the amount of viewing increases. Several studies have shown that those who watch more violent programming may become more desensitized. Victor Cline, Roger Croft, and Steven Courrier (1973) found that those who saw more graphic violent portrayals were more likely to become physiologically desensitized—in short, the images stopped having an impact. In some situations, however, desensitization may have positive outcomes. Repeated exposure to an initially frightening or threatening image or character (e.g., the Incredible Hulk, the Wizard of Oz) can reduce children's fears (Cantor and Wilson 1984). Humor also contributes to desensitization (Potter 1999). Emotionally disturbed children (e.g., those with attention deficit hyperactivity disorder) are especially vulnerable to media violence and desensitization. Tom Grimes, Eric Vernberg, and Teresa Cathers (1997) found that after watching television violence, children with emotional problems (compared to a matched group of children without these disorders) showed less concern for the victims of violence and believed that the media violence they saw characters commit was justified.

Fear

Media violence may be related to fear, in both the short and long terms. Joanne Cantor (2002) has studied fright as both a physiological and emotional reaction and found that children may become fearful after seeing violent media images. These reactions typically do not last very long, but it is possible for some to last for several days, months, or even longer. For example, Kristen Harrison and Cantor (1999) found that nine out of ten college students said that they had an intense fear reaction to a media depiction that lasted for a long time. Some of the things that evoke fear responses include injuries and dangers as well as deformities and/or distortions, such as monsters or ghosts. Several factors are likely to induce fear or fright reactions. Viewers who identify and/or empathize with the target of violence are likely to feel more fearful. Similarly, viewers who think the violence could happen to them often become more fearful. Although these reactions may be immediate and short-lived, there may be some long-term consequences. For example, children may become scared while watching a movie or program and perhaps hide their eyes or scream and have nightmares. Fear, however, differs by age. Young children typically are more fearful of images that are fantastic, threatening, and just look scary; older, children, however, are more fearful of more realistic dangers, things that could possibly happen to them.

There is also evidence of a generalized fear effect—the result of long-term exposure to violent media. Cultivation theory posits a positive relationship between watching more television and being fearful and exhibiting the "mean world syndrome." Studies testing this theory show that those who watch more television believe that there are more people employed in law enforcement, exaggerate the numbers of people involved in violence in a given week, overestimate their own chances of being a victim of violence, are more likely to believe they need more protection, and believe that, in general, the world is a mean and scary place in that most people "cannot be trusted" and are "just looking out for themselves" (Gerbner et al. 2002, 52). Although there is some criticism of this approach . . ., it is a position that takes into consideration the fact that the media are an ongoing facet of day-to-day life and that the influence of the media (cultivation) is "a continual, dynamic, ongoing process of interaction among messages, audiences, and contexts" (Gerbner et al. 2002, 49).

Cultivation, however, may be culturally determined. There is less evidence of fear-related cultivation effects in the United Kingdom. Mallory Wober (1978) reports no relationship between television viewing and notions of fear and violence. There are, however, several cultural differences that may explain the lack of relationship. First, as noted above, U.K. television is considerably less violent and U.S. imports make up only a small portion of available programming. Second, programming in the United Kingdom must follow the government's family viewing policy requirements. This policy ensures that programs with potentially objectionable content are scheduled later in the evening and that programs unsuitable for children cannot be shown before 9 PM. Moreover, in the United Kingdom televised films are given age-based ratings (Gunter, Harrison, and Wykes 2003). Similarly, in the Netherlands, Harry Bouwman (1984) found only weak associations between viewing and perceptions of violence, mistrust, and victimization. Even though the Netherlands imports a considerable amount of U.S. programming and Dutch and U.S. programming provides similar messages about violence, many viewers choose to watch programs that are more "informational" in nature.

Nevertheless, some cultures have shown cultivation effects. For example, students in Australia who watched more U.S. crime/adventure programs had higher scores on the "mean world" and "violence in society" indices (Pingree and Hawkins 1981). Other analyses have found evidence of the cultivation of conceptions of sex roles and political orientations as well as violence. For example, in South Korea, watching U.S. television was related, for women, to more liberal perspectives about gender roles and family values. Among the male students, however, seeing more U.S. programming was related to exhibiting greater protectiveness of Korean culture and more hostility toward the United States (Kang and Morgan 1988). Overall, the findings from numerous studies conducted in the cultivation tradition show that if televised images are less homogeneous and repetitive than those seen in the United States, the results of cultivation analyses are less consistent and predictable (Gerbner et al. 2002).

Who Will Be Influenced?

The research discussed in this section can be interpreted in three different ways: (1) that media violence is inconsequential and people, including children, are not affected by these images, particularly what they see on television (e.g., Fowles 1999); (2) that media violence will affect some people some of the time (Potter 2003); and (3) that media violence will always have a very negative impact (as believed, for example, by grassroots groups such as the National Coalition on Television Violence).

The evidence from numerous research studies indicates that the first and third interpretations are too extreme. The position that media violence is inconsequential has only a few supporters. For example, during the 1970s, when NBC was actively involved in a research program, Ronald Milavsky and others (1982) conducted a three-year longitudinal study (1970–1973) of 2,400 elementary school children and 800 teenage boys and reported no evidence of a relationship between television violence and aggressive behavior. A re-analysis of this data set, however, found a relationship between television violence and aggression (Turner, Hesse, and Peterson-Lewis 1986). Huesmann and Miller (1994) also interpret the NBC data as consistent with other research findings that support a relationship.

Similarly, the position that television violence always has a negative impact on people, particularly impressionable children, is also too extreme and again has very few supporters. The one group that has supported this outcome, the National Coalition on Television Violence . . . was founded in 1980 and has been active in both rating television programs for violence and assessing which companies advertise on the most violent programs. Although the lion's share of the research shows a relationship between viewing and behaving aggressively, media violence is only one of many potential causes of aggression and/or violence in people. For example, child abuse or living in an excessively violent neighborhood may also play a critical role in subsequent aggressive behavior. Consequently, it is unreasonable to say that television violence will always have negative effects on viewers.

The most reasonable argument to make in understanding the effects of violent media content is to say that not everyone is affected in the same way; indeed, the same person may respond to violence differently on different occasions. Violent media content may have large effects on a small number of adults and/or children or small effects on large numbers of viewers. The large, consistent body of literature points to a positive relationship between television violence and aggressive behavior. Moreover, even though findings may be modest in size, the relationship must be taken seriously because of the large numbers of children who watch television each day, largely unsupervised. Even though their aggressive behavior may not put society at risk, it still may have negative social and cognitive consequences, such as the alienation of their peers and teachers (Singer and Singer 1988).

There is, however, another potentially important consequence. Although many people are reluctant to admit that they or their children could be affected by media violence, they believe that others are affected. This perspective, called "third-person effects" (Davison 1983), is particularly illusionary because it allows people to believe that they (and their children) are immune from the effects of media, but their neighbors (and their children) are not. People tend to overestimate the media's effects on others while underestimating its effects on themselves. An example might be the person who claims not to pay attention to advertising and states that advertising does not influence his or her purchasing decisions, yet won't buy anything but brand-name products and typically wears brand-name clothing such as T-shirts from the Gap or Abercrombie and Fitch.

Potter (2003) believes that third-person effects constitutes one of the "myths of television violence" mentioned in the title of his book. This myth is troublesome because people do not understand how they may be affected by media violence. Although most people do not copy violent behavior they see in the media (and if they did with any regularity, the world would be extremely chaotic), that violence has numerous long-term effects, including physiological and/or emotional habituation and the cultivation of fear and the belief that the world is mean. Another of Potter's myths is that "children are especially vulnerable to the risks of negative exposure to media violence" (2003, 67). Classifying this statement as a myth does not mean that children are not vulnerable, for indeed they may be particularly influenced by media violence. Rather, this myth underscores the third-person effects because it diminishes the fact that people of all age groups may be negatively influenced by media violence.

Finally, as cultivation theory postulates, the ultimate long-term effects of watching television violence may post threats for civil liberties and freedom. Cultivation studies have found that those who watch more television, compared to those who watch less, are more likely to overestimate their chances of being involved in violence, believe that fear of crime is an important personal problem, and assume that crime is rising. Those who spend more time watching television tend to believe that they are living in a mean and dangerous world and express feelings of alienation and gloom (Gerbner et al. 2002). Because violent images are almost impossible to avoid, those who watch more television may express sentiments of dependency and be willing to accept deceptively simple, strong, and hard-line political and religious postures, if these beliefs seem to promise to relieve existing insecurities and anxieties. From the perspective of cultivation theory, the overall long-term effects of television violence may be the ready acceptance of repressive political and social environments that could translate into a loss of personal liberties.

Conclusion

This large and solid body of research about media violence shows generally stable levels of violence on television and interesting relationships between media use and violence, particularly aggression. As in any field of research, throughout the years there have been numerous controversies about different findings and ways of conducting research. Chapter 3 addresses some of the major controversies relating to media violence and offers some possible solutions to the problem of media violence.

Note

1. Although recent surveys (Kaiser Family Foundation 1999; Annenberg Policy Research Center 2000) focused only on children ages eighteen and under, my personal experience (my college-age children, their friends, and students in my classes at the University of Delaware) indicates that video game playing does not end with graduation from high school and that earlier gender differences still prevail.

References

American Psychological Association. 1985. *Violence on Television*. Washington, DC: APA Board of Social and Ethical Responsibility for Psychology.

Andison, F. S. 1977. "TV Violence and Viewer Aggression: A Cumulation of Study Results, 1956–1976." *Public Opinion Quarterly* 41: 314–331.

Bouwman, H., and N. Signorielli. 1985. "A Comparison of American and Dutch Programming." *Gazette* 35: 93–108.

Cantor, J. 2002. "Fright Reactions to Mass Media." In J. Bryant and D. Zillmann, eds., *Media Effects: Advances in Theory and Research*, pp. 287–306. Mahwah, NJ: Lawrence Erlbaum Associates.

Cantor, J., and B. J. Wilson. 1984. "Modifying Fear Responses to Mass Media in Preschool and Elementary School Children." *Journal of Broadcasting* 28: 431–443.

Centerwall, B. S. 1989a. "Exposure to Television as a Cause of Violence." In G. Comstock, ed., *Public Communication and Behavior,* pp. 1–58. Vol. 2, Orlando, FL: Academic.

——. 1989b. "Exposure to Television as a Risk Factor for Violence." *American Journal of Epidemiology* 129: 643–652.

Cline, V. B., R. G. Croft, and S. Courrier. 1973. "Desensitization of Children to Television Violence." *Journal of Personality and Social Psychology* 27: 260–265.

Davison, W. P. 1983. "The Third-Person Effect in Communication." *Public Opinion Quarterly* 47: 1–15.

Drabman, R. S., and M. H. Thomas. 1974. "Does Media Violence Increase Children's Toleration of Real-Life Aggression?" *Developmental Psychology* 10: 418–421.

Ellis, G. T., and F. Sekyra III. 1972. "The Effect of Aggressive Cartoons on the Behavior of First Grade Children." *Journal of Psychology* 81: 7–43.

Fowles, J. 1999. *The Case for Television Violence.* Thousand Oaks, CA: Sage.

Gerbner, G., L. Gross, M. Morgan, N. Signorielli, and J. Shanahan. 2002. "Growing Up with Television: The Cultivation Perspective." In J. Bryant and D. Zillmann, eds., *Media Effects: Advances in Theory and Research.* 2nd ed. Hillsdale, NJ: Lawrence Erlbaum Associates.

Grimes, T., E. Vernberg, and T. Cathers. 1997. "Emotionally Disturbed Children's Reactions to Violent Media Segments." *Journal of Health Communication* 2, no. 3: 157–168.

Groebel, J. 2001. Media Violence in Cross-Cultural Perspective." In D. G. Singer and J. L. Singer, eds., *Handbook of Children and the Media*, pp. 25–268. Thousand Oaks, CA: Sage.

Gunter, G., J. Harrison, and M. Wykes. 2003. *Violence on Television: Distribution, Form, Context, and Themes.* Mahwah, NJ: Lawrence Erlbaum Associates.

Harrison, K. and J. Cantor. 1999. "Tales from the Screen: Enduring Fright Reactions to Scary Media." *Media Psychology* 1, no. 2: 97–116.

Hearold, S. 1986. "A Synthesis of 1043 Effects of Television on Social Behavior." In G. Comstock, ed., *Public Communications and Behavior*, pp. 65–133. *Vol. 1.* New York: Academic.

Huesmann, L. R., and L. S. Miller. 1994. "Long-Term Effects of Repeated Exposure to Media Violence in Childhood." In L. R. Huesmann, ed., *Aggressive Behavior: Current Perspectives*, pp. 153–186. New York: Plenum.

Huesmann, L. R., J. Moise-Titus, C. Podolski, and L. D. Eron. 2003. "Longitudinal Relations between Children's Exposure to TV Violence and Their Aggressive and Violent Behavior in Young Adulthood, 1977–1992." *Developmental Psychology* 39, no. 2: 201–221.

Joy, L. A., M. M. Kimball, and M. L. Zabrack. 1986. "Television and Children's Aggressive Behavior." In T. M. Williams. ed., *The Impact of Television: A Natural Experiment in Three Communities*, pp. 303–360. Orlando, FL: Academic.

Kaiser Family Foundation. 1999. *Kids and Media @ the New Millennium: A Comprehensive National Analysis of Children's Media Use.* Menlo Park, CA: Kaiser Family Foundation.

Kang, J. G., and M. Morgan. 1988. "Culture Clash: U.S. Television Programs in Korea." *Journalism Quarterly* 65, no. 2: 431–438.

Linz, D., E. Donnerstein, and S. Penrod. 1984. "The Effects of Multiple Exposures to Filmed Violence against Women." *Journal of Communication* 34, no. 3: 130–147.

Lovaas, O. I. 1961. "Effects of Exposure to Symbolic Aggression on Aggressive Behavior." *Child Development* 32: 37–44.

Milavsky, J. R., R. Kessler, H. Stipp, and W. S. Rubens. 1982. "Television and Aggression: Results of a Panel Study." In D. Pearl, L. Bouthilet, and J. Lazar, eds., *Television and Behavior: Ten Years of Scientific Progress and Implications for the 80s*, pp. 138–157. Vol. 2. Washington, DC: U.S. Government Printing Office.

Murray, J. P. 2003. "The Violent Face of Television: Research and Discussion." In E. L. Palmer and B. M. Young, eds., *The Faces of Televisual Media: Teaching, Violence, Selling to Children*. Mahwah, NJ: Lawrence Erlbaum Associates.

National Institute for Mental Health. 1982. *Television and Behavior: Ten years of Scientific Progress and Implications for the Eighties*. Vol. 1, *Summary Report*. Washington, DC: U.S. Government Printing Office.

Paik, H., and G. Comstock. 1994. "The Effects of Television Violence on Anti-social Behavior: A Meta-Analysis." *Communication Research* 21: 516–546.

Perse, E. 2001. *Media Effects and Society*. Mahwah, NJ: Lawrence Erlbaum Associates.

Pingree, S., and R. P. Hawkins. 1981. "U.S. Programs on Australian Television: The Cultivation Effect." *Journal of Communication* 31, no. 1: 97–105.

Potter, W. J. 1999. *On Media Violence*. Thousand Oaks, CA: Sage.

——. 2003. *The Eleven Myths of Media Violence*. Thousand Oaks, CA: Sage.

Potter, W. J., M. Vaughan, R. Warren, K. Howley, A. Land, and J. Hagemeyer. 1995. "How Real is the Portrayal of Aggression in Television Entertainment Programming?" *Journal of Broadcasting & Electronic Media* 39, 196–516.

Signorielli, N. 1990. "Television's Mean and Dangerous World: A Continuation of the Cultural Indicators Perspective. In N. Signorielli and M. Morgan, eds., *Cultivation Analysis: New Directions in Media Effects Research*, pp. 85–106. Newbury Park, CA: Sage.

——. 2003. "Prime-Time Violence, 1993–2001: Has the Picture Really Changed?" *Journal of Broadcasting and Electronic Media* 47, no. 1: 36–57.

Singer, J. L., and D. G. Singer. 1988. "Some Hazards of Growing Up in a Television Environment: Children's Aggression and Restlessness." In S. Oskamp, ed., *Television as a Social Issue*, pp. 171–188. Newbury Park, CA: Sage.

Smith, S. L., and E. Donnerstein. 1998. "Harmful Effects of Exposure to Media Violence: Learning of Aggression, Emotional Desensitization, and Fear." In R. G. Green and E. Donnerstein, eds., *Human Aggression: Theories, Research, and Implications for Social Policy*. San Diego: Academic.

Smith, S. L., B. J. Wilson, D. Kunkel, D. Linz, J. Potter, C. Colvin, and E. Donnerstein. 1998. "Violence in Television Programming Overall: University of California, Santa Barbara Study." In Center for Communication and Social Policy, University of California, Santa Barbara, ed. *National Television Violence Study, Vol. 3*. Thousand Oaks, CA: Sage.

Stein, A. H., and L. K. Friedrich, with F. Vondracek. 1972. "Television Content and Young Children's Behavior. In J. P. Murray, E. A. Rubinstein, and G. A. Comstock, eds., *Television and Social Behavior*. Vol. 2, *Television and Social Learning*, pp. 202–317. Washington, DC: U.S. Government Printing Office.

Turner, C. W., B. W. Hesse, and S. Peterson-Lewis. 1986. "Naturalistic Studies of the Long-Term Effects of Television Violence." *Journal of Social Issues* 42: 51–73.

William, T. M., ed. 1986. *The Impact of Television: A Natural Experiment in Three Communities*. Orlando, FL: Academic.

Wober, M. 1978. "Televised Violence and Paranoid Perceptions: The View from Great Britain." *Public Opinion Quarterly* 42, no. 3: 315–321.

Jonathan L. Freedman

NO

Summary and Conclusions

This review has considered in detail a great deal of research on the effects of exposure to media violence. Each study was described, analyzed, criticized, and evaluated. The previous sections summarized the results of each type of research. Several conclusions seem to be warranted.

First, the survey research, combined with the longitudinal studies, provides fairly good evidence that exposure to media violence—or perhaps only preference for more violent programs—is related to aggressiveness. Those who are exposed to more violence in the media and/or who prefer more violence in the media tend to be more aggressive than those who are exposed to or prefer less violence. The evidence for this is not entirely consistent, and the size of the relationship varies greatly from study to study. Nevertheless, most of the studies do find a correlation, and its magnitude seems to be between .1 and .2, although conceivably it is as high as .3. This means that between 1 percent and, at the very high end, 9 percent of the variation in aggression is predicted by exposure to media violence. This is not a big effect—especially at the low end—but it *is* a relationship, and if it were as high as 9 percent it would be a substantial one.

Of course, as explained in detail in this review, the existence of this relationship only raises the possibility that media violence causes aggression. There is a temptation to think that because there is a correlation, there must be a causal link. That is not correct. The correlation alone tells us nothing about causality: the relationship could be produced without any causal effect of media violence. All of the other research discussed in this review was designed to establish whether there is a causal link—whether exposure to violent media makes people more aggressive.

Second, the rest of the research does not demonstrate that exposure to media violence affects aggression. Some studies using each type of research have found some support for the causal connection, but far more have not found support. The largest group of studies are the laboratory experiments. Of these, 39 percent found results that were consistent with the causal hypothesis, and 41 percent obtained results that were not consistent with it and did not support it. Moreover, when studies that used questionable measures of aggression were eliminated, only 81 percent of the remaining experiments supported the hypothesis, whereas 55 percent did not and the rest produced mixed results. This is not a pattern of results that scientists expect when a hypothesis is correct, nor is it one that would cause them to accept the hypothesis.

There were some significant effects in the laboratory experiments; however, this should not be interpreted to mean that exposure to media violence does cause aggression but not always. The significant effects that did occur were probably due to factors other than the violent content of the programs used in the experiments. In particular, I suggest that the violent programs were almost always much more interesting and more arousing than the non-violent programs. Few of the experiments even tried to equate the two types of films, even though it should have been clear that this was a crucial problem that had to be solved. You cannot show one group a film of a prizefight and another group a film of canal boating and argue that the only difference between the two films is the amount of violence. Almost all the laboratory experiments suffered from this problem; this casts doubt on the interpretation of the results in terms of the amount of violence in the films.

The most obvious difference between the violent and non-violent films was that the former were usually more arousing and exciting. This presents a very serious problem, because it is well established that differences in arousal affect behaviour. People who are more aroused tend to perform any activity more strongly than those who are less aroused. Given a bag to punch, they will punch it harder; given something to squeeze, they will squeeze it harder; and given almost any activity, they will do more of it. In the experiments at hand, subjects were often given a doll to punch or a button to press or a dial to turn. If we knew nothing about the subjects except their level of arousal, we would certainly expect those who were more aroused to punch the doll, press the button, or turn the dial more than those who were less aroused. Since the violent film produced more arousal, that alone could explain the effects of the films.

Perhaps an even more important problem with the laboratory experiments is that almost all of them had strong demand factors that, in essence, gave the subjects permission to behave aggressively or even instructed them to behave aggressively. When people are brought into a laboratory, they are very sensitive to what the experimenter does. If he shows them a film, they will wonder why that film was chosen. If no good explanation is provided, they will assume that the experimenter has a reason. And if the film is a violent film, many if not most people will infer that the experimenter likes the film, or approves of violence, or wants them to behave aggressively. This inference will be strengthened when they are later given a chance to behave aggressively—not something they would ordinarily expect to do in a laboratory. Having drawn that inference, they will be more likely to behave aggressively (since that is apparently what the experimenter wants). In other words, simply because of demand pressures, subjects shown violent films are more likely to behave aggressively than those shown non-violent films.

Psychologists are well aware of the problem of demand factors and usually make great efforts to eliminate or at least minimize them in laboratory research. Yet for some reason, in this group of experiments very little effort was made to do so. As a result, demand factors alone could explain the differences in aggressiveness that sometimes occurred.

In sum, the laboratory experiments produced inconsistent results, with more of them being non-supportive than supportive. And the results that were obtained were, in my opinion, more likely due to factors other than the violence in the programs. In any case, I firmly believe that the laboratory experiments tell us little about how exposure to violence in the media affects people in the real world—which is presumably our main concern.

The field experiments were in some sense the strongest test of the causal hypothesis. They involved relatively long-term effects, and full-length movies or actual television programs rather than short excerpts. Also, they were conducted in more natural settings: the programs were viewed and the behaviours were observed in locations that were familiar to the subjects. Perhaps most important, they were experiments, so any significant effects would have causal implications. For all these reasons, the field experiments were the best hope of getting evidence to support the causal hypothesis.

The results were, in fact, even less supportive of the hypothesis than were the results of the laboratory experiments. Only three of eleven field experiments obtained even slightly supportive results—three of twenty-four if one counts all the separate experiments. Those who favour the causal hypothesis often cite the research by the Leyens/Parke group as providing strong support. I agree that two of these studies (but not the third) produced results that are consistent with the hypothesis. However, as I discussed earlier, these studies suffered from having too few independent groups and from employing statistical procedures that were without question inappropriate (as admitted by Leyens). Yet even if these studies had produced strong, consistent results supporting the causal hypothesis, they would have been swamped by those that found either no effect of media violence on aggression, or a reverse effect, or a mixture of effects with most being inconsistent with the causal hypothesis. Moreover, the studies that obtained supportive results involved very small samples of subjects, whereas many of those that obtained non-supportive results had quite large samples. Even more so than with the laboratory experiments, this is an extremely discouraging pattern of results for the causal hypothesis.

The rest of the research related to the causal hypothesis is non-experimental. This means that regardless of the results, it could never provide terribly strong evidence that exposure to media violence causes aggression. Nevertheless, since the ideal experiment cannot he conducted, scientists can try to build a case for a causal effect using other methods. In this context, I consider longitudinal studies extremely important. They provide information relevant to two predictions from the causal hypothesis. First, they show whether the correlations between exposure to violent media and aggression change with age. If the causal hypothesis is correct, the correlations should probably increase as children get older. Even if this is not absolutely required by the hypothesis, there is little question that increasing correlations with age would be consistent with the hypothesis and provide some support for it. However, the longitudinal studies found no evidence for such a pattern. I consider this to be inconsistent with the hypothesis. In any case, it certainly does not support it.

An even more important aspect of these studies is that they provide evidence as to whether early exposure to media violence is associated with increased aggression at a later age after early aggression is held constant. The reasoning underlying this prediction and the statistical analyses have been discussed earlier. The basic point is that if children are equally aggressive at age eight but watch different amounts of media violence, those who watch more should become more aggressive than the others two or seven years later. As noted before, this spreading apart in terms of aggressiveness is the major prediction from the causal hypothesis. This prediction is tested with multiple regression analyses (or similar statistical analyses) that hold aggression constant at age eight and look at the remaining relationship between violence exposure at age eight and aggression at the later age. If this relationship is positive and significant, it is consistent with and to some extent supports the causal hypothesis. If it is not significant, it is inconsistent with the causal hypothesis.

As with all of this research, the results have been mixed. The supportive results were for males on one measure in the twenty-two-year study; from the cross-national study, for boys and girls in the Israeli city sample, and considerably weaker effects for boys and girls in Poland and for girls in the United States; and for boys and girls combined in the later phase of the nursery school study. Some of these results are open to serious criticisms, so they are less clear than they might appear. Moreover, both the twenty-two-year study and the cross-national study produced more non-supportive results than supportive ones. So considering only the results that are most consistent with the causal hypothesis, they are not impressive.

But even if one were to accept these supportive results entirely, there are many more studies that obtained results that are inconsistent with the causal hypothesis. The twenty-two-year study found no effect for girls or for boys on two other measures; the cross-national study found no effect for boys or girls in Australia, for boys or girls in the Netherlands, for boys or girls in Finland, for boys or girls in the Israeli kibbutz sample, or for boys in the United States. The nursery school study found no effect in the first phase. And none of the other studies found any support for the hypothesis. Although this body of research provides some supportive evidence, it obviously did not produce the kind of consistent support that would give one confidence in the hypothesis. Rather, the pattern of evidence generally fails to support the hypothesis.

Some studies compared communities that had television with those that did not and looked for differences in aggression. This research is perhaps the most discouraging for the causal hypothesis. One study reported an increase in aggression after television was introduced, but it is a flawed study, the results were inconsistent, and there are many possible explanations for the result. None of the other studies provided any evidence in favour of the causal hypothesis; in fact, they provided some quite strong evidence against it.

Finally, there was a small group of studies using a variety of methods. These studies offer no support at all for the causal hypothesis, and several of them provide quite convincing evidence against it.

It should be obvious from the individual reviews that the results of the research have been generally non-supportive of the causal hypothesis. Some studies of each type found results that could be considered as supporting the hypothesis, but more found results that did not support it. What should we make of this pattern of results?

Science depends on consistency. Before a theory or hypothesis can be considered correct, the research testing it must produce results that support it with great consistency. Ideally, every single study will support the hypothesis. More realistically—especially when dealing with complex hypotheses and situations—we would probably consider a hypothesis to be supported as long as the great majority of the studies support it. If 90 percent of the studies obtain the results predicted by the hypothesis, we can be reasonably confident that the hypothesis is correct. We may wish to know why the others failed, but even if we cannot establish why, we will still accept the hypothesis. If the results are less consistent than that—if, say, only 70 percent support the hypothesis and 30 percent do not—we will be considerably less confident. We may feel that the hypothesis is probably correct, but we will have serious concerns about the failures. And if only 50 percent support the hypothesis, we will be very unlikely to believe the hypothesis is correct. We may still think there is some slight truth to the hypothesis, but it will be clear that the effects are unreliable, probably very weak, and perhaps not there at all. In fact, if the results are this inconsistent, our focus may well shift to explaining why there were any positive results. We may then look for problems in the research that produced the effects even though the hypothesis is incorrect. If we still believe in the hypothesis despite the inconsistency and the lack of support, that belief is based on faith and hope rather than on the scientific results.

Turning to the research on media violence and aggression, it should be clear that not one type of research provided the kind of supportive evidence that is ordinarily required to support a hypothesis. Not one found 90 percent supportive or 80 percent or 70 percent or even 50 percent. In fact, regardless of the method used, fewer than half the studies found results that supported the hypothesis—sometimes considerably fewer than half. The results of this research have sometimes been described as overwhelmingly supportive of the causal hypothesis. That is not correct. Rather, the research is discouraging for the hypothesis, with most of the research not supporting it. I conclude that the scientific research does not support the hypothesis that exposure to violent media causes aggression.

Third, the small body of research on desensitization has tested two quite different effects. There is some evidence that exposure to media violence causes habituation and therefore reduced responsiveness to further media violence. The results are rather weak and inconclusive, but the effect may be real. Regarding the more important effect on actual violence, three small-scale studies found some support for this, but the effect failed to replicate and other studies did not support it. I conclude that there is little or no evidence for a desensitization effect and there is some evidence that directly contradicts it.

Where does this leave us? On the one hand, we have considerable justification for rejecting the hypotheses. If they were correct, we should expect to see a pattern of results that consistently support them. We do not get that pattern, so the hypotheses are almost certainly incorrect. On the other hand, those who continue to believe in them can argue that the research is flawed, or that one should not expect perfect consistency, or even that the existence of some supportive results shows that the hypotheses are correct. This is not very good science, but it cannot easily be rejected.

However, those who believe in the hypotheses cannot argue that the research provides overwhelming or even strong support for them. I hope it is clear that the research does not support either hypothesis. After so much research, with many of the studies being of very high quality, if the hypotheses were correct, I believe that we would have found the evidence to support them.

Accordingly, this comprehensive review of the scientific evidence leads to two clear conclusions. First, despite the way it has sometimes been described, the research does not provide overwhelming support for either the causal hypothesis or the desensitization hypothesis. On the contrary, the evidence for both hypotheses is weak and inconsistent, with more non-supportive results than supportive results. Second, following from the first conclusion, exposure to media violence does not cause aggression, or if it does the effects are so weak that they cannot be detected and must therefore be vanishingly small. I would not make such a strong statement about the desensitization hypothesis, because there has been too little relevant research. Instead I would conclude that it is probably not true, but the case is not yet closed. . . .

Films and television programs that contain violence are not designed to convey the message that violence is good or that people should engage in violent acts. They do not contain information that is likely to convince anyone of anything; they do not contain explicit messages in favour of aggression or violence. They are just entertainment. The programs are not meant to be persuasive, just popular. So it should not be surprising that they have no effect on people's aggressive behaviour or on their attitudes toward violence.

What about *implicit* messages? Though most people would agree that the media almost never deliver a message that explicitly encourages violence, some people argue that violence in the media carries the implicit message that violence is acceptable. When Batman punches the bad guy, perhaps the message is that one must resort to violence to solve problems. When the Roadrunner turns the tables on the Coyote and blows him up, perhaps children are being taught to use violence against their enemies rather than other means of settling disputes. When Bruce Willis or the police or the Power Rangers use violence against terrorists or criminals or evil monsters, perhaps the implicit message is that only violence will work and therefore you (the viewer) should also be violent. Or maybe the message is not so much that violence works as that violence is acceptable or even desirable. If all these nice, honest, good people are committing acts of violence, maybe this says to the viewer that this kind of behaviour is all right. These messages—that violence is the only way to settle disputes, that violence is acceptable—might influence attitudes and behaviours. If viewers who get these messages accept them, we can expect their own attitudes toward violence to become more positive, and that they will be likely to become violent themselves.

There are several responses to this idea. First, I do not think these programs carry the message that violence is the only way to settle disputes, or that violence is generally acceptable. To the extent they convey any messages about violence, those messages are quite different from these. One possible message is that when a bad person or a bad monster or a bad animal starts a fight or commits a crime or threatens you or those you love, those who are entrusted with protecting society may have to use violence in return. In the great majority of all films and television programs containing violence, all or most of the violence committed by the good guys is committed by police or crimefighters or others who are allowed to use violence. And they use violence only after it has been used by the bad guys; the good guys almost never (perhaps never) start the fight. While we would prefer a society without any violence, few of us would deny the police (and mythical protectors of society) the right to use violence when necessary. It would be nice if the police and other good guys could be shown trying a little harder to talk the bad guys out of the fight, convincing them to give up, and so on. Still, it is not realistic to expect many criminals, terrorists, monsters, and so on to be convinced by talk of this kind to give up their weapons and stop doing whatever bad stuff they are doing. The fact is that there is violence in our society and often it is dealt with by violence of some sort. I do not believe that those who watch these programs are getting the message that violence is the only way to deal with problems. If they get any message at all along these lines, it is that we should all be thankful that the good guys—those who are there to protect us—can also use violence when necessary. They are certainly not getting the message that they, the viewers, should engage in violence. So there is no reason to expect their behaviour to be affected.

A somewhat different concern of those who worry about the effects of media violence is that aggression is shown as effective. If so, viewers may come to believe this and may accordingly behave more aggressively themselves. The authors of the National Television Violence Study (NTVS) are especially adamant on this point. They assert that when violence is not punished—or even worse, when it is rewarded—it is especially likely to make viewers more aggressive. As we have seen, there is no scientific evidence to support this assertion. Despite that, it is repeated over and over as if it were a known fact. Scientific evidence of causation aside, the NTVS provides a highly useful picture of what occurs on television. It found that television programs often contain violent acts that are not punished immediately. However, the same study shows that bad characters in serious shows are almost always punished eventually. Although the authors of the study are concerned about the lack of immediate punishment, I think the viewers all know that punishment is coming. Much of the tension in the stories we watch on television comes from wondering when and how the bad guys will get punished, but there is no question that in almost every program, in almost every story, the bad people who start the violence will get what they have coming to them. One could argue that television presents an unrealistic picture in this respect: criminals on TV get caught and punished far more often than they do in the real world. So if viewers learn anything, if they get any message, it is that violence committed for a bad or illegal reason in a serious context will be punished.

The other possible message from most of the programs is that it is a bad idea, not a good one, to be the one who first uses violence. In almost every television program that has violence, and in most films, the person who starts the fight (the bad guy) eventually loses. The authors of the study are concerned that good characters are rarely punished after using violence. Naturally! They are allowed to use violence when it is necessary, so they should not get punished. When Batman punches a crook, should Batman get hurt? When Bruce Willis fights criminals, should Willis lose? When police officers get in a shootout with criminals, should the police get punished? Obviously not. In fact, to the extent that crime fighter shows have any message, it is not that police officers should get punished for using violence, but that it is dangerous to be a police officer or anyone who fights crime. This does not teach anyone that it is okay to use violence or that violence will be rewarded—if anything, it teaches the opposite.

Some have argued that the media glamorize violence. Certainly, some heroes are violent and glamorous. This is true of many of the comic book heroes (Batman, Superman, Power Rangers, Wonder Woman) and the non-cartoon versions of these characters. It is also true of some other characters, such as James Bond. But many violent heroes are anything but glamorous. Bruce Willis in *Die Hard,* most police officers in cop shows, and so on get dirty, are often hurt, and are typically shown doing their jobs, which are important but not at all glamorous. In fact, one theme that runs through many of the more realistic shows is that law enforcement people have tough, dangerous jobs and are not appreciated enough by the public or by politicians. Is there any evidence that the supposed glamour of these violent characters has caused more people to apply for jobs in law enforcement? I doubt it. So I do not accept that, in general, violence has been glamorized in the media. I agree that it is not made as awful and ugly as it really is, but not that it has been made especially attractive. Therefore, I am not surprised that children have not been influenced by the glamour of violence to engage in it.

I cannot prove that media violence carries no message or that it does not glamorize violence. But I ask those who believe it does to think seriously about whether the programs and films they know really urge people, explicitly or implicitly, to engage in violence; or suggest that violence is glamorous. A few films and programs may do this, but I think any reasonable view of the full range of programs would show that they do not encourage viewers to be violent themselves. They certainly do not directly try to sell violence the way ads for products try to sell those products. I cannot think of one television program that contains the explicit message that viewers should go out and commit violence.

One reason why some people are so convinced that media violence causes aggression is that they think they have seen it happen themselves. They know that children in schoolyards are imitating the Power Rangers and other television heroes who engage in martial arts. They see children watch a violent program and then get involved in fighting. Since they have witnessed it firsthand, they are totally convinced. At a congressional hearing, a congressman said he did not need any scientific evidence to prove that media violence causes aggression. The reason was that he had come home recently and been met at the door by his young son aiming a karate kick at him. Q.E.D. What more evidence does anyone need?

I understand the power of personal experience. However, it is important to step back and try to figure out what the experience means. The congressman's story is a perfect example. I did not get a chance to respond to him, but I would have said the following: Congressman, I assume that you and your son have a good relationship. I assume he did not harm you and that he did not mean to harm you. (If he meant to harm you, please get some professional help right away.) Congressman, your son was playing. He was not fighting; he did not hurt you; he was playing. He had probably seen someone on television doing karate kicks—or maybe he saw it in the schoolyard—and he was imitating them. Years ago, he might have pretended to punch you or to shoot you with a bow and arrow or with a gun. Would you have been as upset if he had put his fingers into the shape of a gun—as so many boys do—and said 'bang, bang'? Then I suppose you would have known he was playing, but it would have been the same thing. The precise behaviour is surely influenced by the media, but it is not aggression—it is play. You might not like that kind of play; you might prefer him to throw you a ball or do something really imaginative. If you want to complain that television does not foster imagination and creativity, you may have a point. But aggression? No.

Also, for those who have watched kids get into trouble after a violent program, maybe the effect is due entirely to the fact that they are excited. Violent programs tend to get kids aroused. When they are aroused, they engage in more active behaviour, and some of that may be aggressive. But it is the arousal that affects them, not the content of the show. Any show that aroused them would have had the same effect. There is even a study showing that kids are more aggressive after watching 'Sesame Street.' I can believe it. There is no aggression in the program. It is hard to imagine a more prosocial, educational, imaginative show. But it is a very active, lively, fast-paced show—that's one of the reasons children like it so much. If they are more aggressive after it, obviously it is not because of any aggressive content, but rather because of the arousal. Yes, children may be more aggressive after watching violent programs, but they may be equally aggressive after any action program or any program that is lively and exciting. You may prefer children to be quieter. I'm not so sure. I think it is probably good for them to get excited and aroused even if it sometimes leads to more trouble for the parents. Bored children can get into real trouble; interested, excited kids are probably better off in the long run. So don't blame media violence for increased action and sometimes increased aggression, unless you want to blame everything—movies, television programs, books, any arousing, exciting activity.

Another argument I hear is that since the advent of television, crime and aggression have increased. Supposedly the connection is obvious. I dealt with this at some length in my discussion of Centerwall's paper. The main point is that all sorts of things have changed since television was available, and these other changes are much more likely than television to have produced the increase in crime. I do not want to rehash these arguments, but I urge those who see a connection to keep in mind that there are explanations other than television violence. Let me add that both aggression and crime have been with us for a long time, since well before television and movies. There is no indication that in general, either aggressiveness or crime has increased since the invention of movies or television. Moreover, the homicide rates in the United States and Canada have gone through many cycles. What people tend to focus on is that the rate of violent crime—for homicide in particular—increased sharply from about 1965 to 1980. That's true. But the rate then levelled off, and has been dropping sharply since around 1992. The rate is now back to about what it was in the early 1970s, not much above its low point in the 1960s. It is the increase that makes some people think it must be due to television, because the increase came soon after the introduction and spread of television. However, an almost identical pattern—a sharp increase followed by a sharper decrease—occurred in the early part of this century, long before there was any television. The increase then was certainly not due to television, but rather to social factors of various kinds. If that earlier increase occurred in the absence of television, why think that the later increase was due to television? It makes no sense.

Then there is the recent decrease in violent crime. All of the studies indicate that television and films have just as much violence as they used to, or more, and that the violence is more graphic than ever. Also, violent video games started to become available and popular in the early 1990s and are now a major element in many children's lives. And I suppose the lyrics in popular music, especially rap music, are much more violent than they have ever been. Yet despite the continuing media violence, and the new violence in video games and music, the rates for homicide and other violent crimes have dropped seven years in a row. If media violence caused the increase, how can one explain the decrease? A more likely explanation is that media violence did not cause either the increase or the decrease; both of these were caused by major social forces.

Finally, it is important to remember that the research I have reviewed dealt almost exclusively with the effects of fictional or fictionalized programs and films. There has been almost no systematic research on the effects of exposure to real violence or to media coverage of real violence. Some ingenious work by Phillips (1979, 1983) suggests that watching prizefights may increase homicides and that hearing about suicides may cause an increase in suicides. This work has been criticized on methodological grounds, and in my earlier review I found many of the details of the results implausible. Phillips has answered the criticisms, and he may be right that highly publicized violent events of these kinds cause an increase in similar events. Although there is no systematic evidence to support it, many people believe that media coverage of horrific crimes causes some people to imitate those crimes. The killings at Columbine High School received an enormous amount of media attention and were followed by a number of similar attacks in other schools. It is possible that the later crimes were caused to some extent by coverage of the earlier one.

We do not know very much about the effects of coverage of actual violent events. However, I want to make it absolutely clear that this review does not deal with this issue. The lack of scientific support for the causal hypothesis relates entirely to fictional material. Indeed, I think it is likely that real violence and the coverage of real violence do affect aggression and crime. Children may imitate violence they observe directly. Both children and adults may be influenced by their knowledge that their society or their neighbourhood has a lot of violence. Moreover, it seems likely that repeated exposure to real violence, either directly or in the media, causes desensitization to subsequent real violence. I believe that when there is a murder on the front page of the newspaper every day or as the lead story on the television news every day, people are less shocked than when murders are rare events. Thus, both the causal hypothesis and the desensitization hypothesis may be correct with respect to real violence or media coverage of real violence, and perhaps that is what people should be worrying about.

Let me end by acknowledging again that to many people it seems self-evident that media violence causes aggression. I think I have shown in this comprehensive, detailed review that the scientific evidence does not support that view. Perhaps some of the arguments in this chapter will make it seems less obvious, and people will be willing to change their views. In any case, I hope that neither organizations nor individuals will ever again say that the evidence for a causal effect of media violence is overwhelming or that the case is closed. Perhaps people will even begin to accept the clear fact that the evidence does not support the notion that exposure to media violence causes aggression or desensitization to aggression.

References

Phillips, D. (1979). Suicide, motor vehicle fatalities, and the mass media: Evidence toward a theory of suggestion. *American Journal of Sociology, 87,* 1340–1539.

Phillips, D. (1982). The impact of mass media violence on U.S. homicides. *American Sociological Review, 48,* 560–568.

CHALLENGE QUESTIONS

Does Exposure to Media Violence Promote Aggressive Behavior?

1. Some people would suggest that a child emulating a Power Ranger by doing a karate-kick is an aggressive act. Others might see the act as playful. If you were conducting research in this area, how would you operationally define the difference between playful behavior and aggressive behavior?
2. To what extent do you believe that media violence encourages or glorifies violence? Provide an example or two of film images that might have led to subsequent violence in society.
3. If you were a clinician treating a child who enacts behaviors seen in violent media, what kind of intervention would you try to develop in an effort to reduce the child's aggressive behavior?
4. Imagine that you are a researcher studying the differential impact of exposure to media violence and exposure to real-world violence. How would you go about studying this difference?
5. It is well-known that video games have become increasingly violent in the past decade. How do you explain this trend?

Suggested Readings

Carter, C., & Weaver, C. K. (2003). *Violence and the media*. Philadelphia, PA: Open University Press.

Gentile, D. A. (Ed.). (2003). *Media violence and children: A complete guide for parents and professionals*. Westport, CT: Praeger.

Huesmann, L. R., Moise-Titus, J., Podolski, C., & Eron, L. D. (2003). Longitudinal relations between children's exposure to TV violence and their aggressive and violent behavior in young adulthood, 1977–1992. *Developmental Psychology*, 39(2), 201–221.

Potter, J. W. (2003). *The 11 myths of media violence*. Thousand Oaks, CA: Sage Publications.

ISSUE 16

Would Legalization of Virtual Child Pornography Reduce Sexual Exploitation of Children?

YES: Arnold H. Loewy, from "Taking Free Speech Seriously: The United States Supreme Court and Virtual Child Pornography," *UNC Public Law Research Paper No. 02-17* (November 2002)

NO: Diana E. H. Russell and Natalie J. Purcell, from "Exposure to Pornography as a Cause of Child Sexual Victimization," in Nancy E. Dowd, Dorothy G. Singer, and Robin Fretwell Wilson, *Handbook of Children, Culture, and Violence* (Sage Publications, 2006)

ISSUE SUMMARY

YES: Professor of Law Arnold Loewy contends that pornography involving children will continue to be marketed, and it therefore makes sense to permit virtual child pornography, because doing so would reduce the risk of real children being exploited.

NO: Authors Diana Russell and Natalie Purcell take a strong stand against all forms of pornography involving children, asserting that pornographic images involving children, even in cartoons or virtual media, undermine the societal prohibition against adult-child sex.

Some consumers of Internet pornography have pushed the limits farther and farther in their pursuit of images that will excite, and possibly shock their sensibilities. The ultimate taboo, sadly, involves pornography involving children. Few if any sane people would defend the exploitation of real children in order to serve the masturbatory fantasies of pornography consumers. However, some have argued that virtual forms of pornography might actually protect real children by accommodating the fantasies of adults who crave sexual images of children. Critics of child pornography in any form argue that permitting even virtual images of children in sexual situations violates a societal boundary and puts children at great risk of being victimized in real life.

Judicial decisions have come down on the side of the legality of virtual child pornography. In 2002 the U.S. Supreme Court (*Ashcroft v. The Free Speech Coalition*) ruled that virtual child pornography is speech that is protected under the First Amendment, and cannot be banned by child-pornography laws. The Ohio Supreme Court in 2007 which ruled that pornographic images which are wholly faked, no matter how realistic, are legal.

Professor of Law Arnold Loewy argues that pornography is a form of free speech that is constitutionally protected. Pragmatically speaking, Loewy acknowledges that child pornography is a reality that is here to stay; he believes that legalizing virtual child pornography may actually reduce the number of children that are currently being exploited by what he calls a "perverted industry."

Authors Diana Russell and Natalie Purcell advocate the implementation of legal sanctions against child pornography as critically important deterrents to the exploitation of children. They believe that allowing sexual images in any form that involve children undermines the prohibition against adult-child sex, and facilitates the proliferation of Internet sites on which such behaviors or desires are not considered deviant and where pedophiles and others interested in child pornography can feel more normal. The ultimate risk is that more children will be put at risk of sexual victimization.

POINT
(Loewy)

- Pedophiles most likely obtain child pornography because they are attracted to children, rather than becoming attracted to children by looking at the child pornography they already possess.
- Unless all speech is free, no speech is free. Virtual child pornography is speech that ought to be constitutionally protected.
- It is neither intuitively obvious, nor has it been proven, that eliminating all virtual pornography would significantly reduce the incidents of pedophilia. Even if it could be proven that virtual child pornography caused significant net harm, it would not follow that the law should permit its suppression.
- Many things can be misused. If virtual pornography is to be suppressed because of its capacity to seduce children, we might as well suppress cartoons, candy, puppy dogs, and vans.

- If virtual child pornography is (or can be made) nearly identical to real child pornography, and only real pornography is unlawful, why wouldn't pornographers and consumers view the virtual content? Legalizing virtual child pornography may actually reduce the number of children that are currently exploited by this perverted industry.

COUNTERPOINT
(Russell & Purcell)

- Internet users with no previous sexual interest in children may find themselves aroused by child pornography, which transforms children into sexual objects.
- Fear of legal sanctions is the most important factor in restraining potential and active molesters from abusing children.
- Some males who have never acted on their desire to have sex with a child may be ignorant or anxious about how to proceed with this. While such concerns could inhibit them from perpetrating such an act, child pornography removes this impediment by providing instructions for the sexual abuse of children.
- Many child molesters show pornography to children in order to arouse their sexual curiosity and to persuade children that they would enjoy certain sexual acts, and to convince them that what they are being asked to do is alright.
- Child pornography undermines the prohibition against adult-child sex. Even child pornography cartoons communicate its social acceptability.

YES ⤶

Arnold H. Loewy[1]

Taking Free Speech Seriously: The United States Supreme Court and Virtual Child Pornography

I. The Importance of Protecting Bad Speech

Few liberal democracies challenge freedom of speech in the abstract. Specific applications, however, are different. Many, who would never challenge freedom of speech in the abstract, balk at extending such protection to flag burners,[2] and Nazis.[3] Yet, the slightest reflection should reveal that unless all speech is free, no speech is free. No sensible government, including the most dictatorial, will ever prosecute good speech or even neutral speech.[4] Indeed, no democracy would even think of prosecuting ordinarily bad speech (*e.g.* vote Republican).[5] It is only when we get to very bad speech that the government even thinks about prosecution. Thus, it is in those situations in which free speech is needed most. Hence, protection for Nazis, flag burners, and virtual child pornographers logically follows if we want to take free speech seriously.

But should we want to take it seriously if the cost of doing so is to give added protection for speech that we would all be better off without? One's first intuition is to say "no," and indeed that is the result regularly reached in European courts[6] and too frequently in American courts.[7] The reason that this should bother us is that it gives government the power to decide which speech can compete in the marketplace and which speech is dead on arrival.

While some of us might be happy to relegate flag burning, Nazis, and virtual pornography to the scrapheap of dead on arrival speech, few would say that about speech urging racial integration. Yet speech urging racial integration fifty years ago would have been thought highly offensive to much of the citizenry of a large number of communities (including Charleston, South Carolina) and would have been subject to prohibition under a standard that protects the dignitary interest of some against the speech of others. Thus, even though government may be correct about some types of speech it is better to deny government the power to suppress that speech than it would be to allow it to suppress speech that may turn out to be valuable (such as civil rights speech).[8] . . .

UNC Public Law Research Paper No. 02-17, November 2002. First published in the First Amendment Law Review. Copyright © 2002 by Arnold H. Loewy. Reprinted by permission.

II. Distinguishing Real Child Pornography

Real child pornography is rightly subject to prosecution. But the reason that it is so treated has nothing to do with the abhorrent nature, or intrinsic worthlessness, of the material. It can be prosecuted for the same reason that employment of child labor can be prosecuted. Just as child labor harms the children that manufacture the goods to be sold, so does child pornography. It would not be a defense to a child labor prosecution that employment of children was necessary to enhance the quantity or quality of the product produced. Similarly, it should be no defense that the finished product had some kind of literary or artistic merit. It is the use of a child in an explicit sexual performance that is rightly forbidden.[9]

Similarly, as the United States Supreme Court has suggested, morphed child pornography, that is images of a real child morphed to appear to be engaging in sexual activity, is enough like real child pornography that it should be treated as though it were real.[10] A morphed image does not harm a real child by making the picture, but it does harm the child by providing an unauthorized permanent and false record of the child's engaging in sexual activity.[11]

Apart from pornography that displays the image of a real child, actual or morphed, the objections to the material are similar to the objections to any kind of distasteful speech, and should be subject to the same kind of scrutiny. In the remainder of this paper, I shall explain why none of the justifications generally advanced against virtual child pornography warrant its prohibition.

III. Virtual Pornography's Capacity to Harm Real Children

Proponents of criminalizing virtual pornography argue that there are two ways in which the material can harm real children. First, they argue that virtual child pornography can whet a pedophile's appetite, making it more likely that he will abuse real children. Second, it is argued that a pedophile can use a picture of what appears to be a real child enjoying her sexuality as a visual aid to persuade an innocent victim to engage in similar activity. I will treat these arguments separately.

As to the first argument, I question both its factual accuracy and its legal significance. As to its accuracy, it is undoubtedly true that many, if not most, pedophiles possess child pornography. It is quite another thing to assume that the pornography caused the pedophilia. More likely, it was the perpetrator's attraction to children that caused him to possess the pornography rather than vice-versa.[12] Indeed, one does not have to approach a "Clockwork Orange"[13] scenario to find behavioralists employing child pornography for the purpose of curing pedophiles?[14]

I do not mean to argue that there has never been a pedophile who but for the pornography would not have committed his crime. But, that can hardly be the relevant standard. For one to sustain this justification, it would be necessary to establish that virtual child pornography (as opposed to real child pornography) has significantly increased pedophilia. To prove that five people who viewed virtual pornography committed an act of pedophilia that they otherwise would not have committed (assuming one could establish causation, which I doubt) would only tell half of the story. We would also have to know how many potential pedophiles had their appetites satiated by virtual child pornography, and therefore left real children alone.

To illustrate, three of the most heinous crimes in history were inspired respectively by the holy Bible[15], an Anglican High Church Service[16], and the movie the Ten Commandments.[17] Obviously nobody measures the worth of these sources by the worst thing that they inspired. To be sure, child pornography, virtual or otherwise, has undoubtedly done far more harm and far less good than the aforementioned sources. Nevertheless, it is neither intuitively obvious, nor has it been proven, that eliminating all virtual pornography from the face of the earth would significantly reduce the incidents of pedophilia.

More importantly, even if it could be proven that virtual child pornography caused significant net harm, it would not follow that the law should permit its suppression. One of the costs of free speech is the recognition that sometimes speech will do more harm than good. Even so, for the reasons already given,[18] it is better to allow it to cause whatever harm it may rather than allow the government the power to decide whether the book can be published at all. For example, the Turner Diaries were said to have been the inspiration for Timothy McVeigh's massacre at Oklahoma City. It would not be hard for a court to conclude that on a cost/benefit basis that book should be condemned. Indeed, it is hard for me to believe that the Turner Diaries did not do significantly more harm than good. Yet, I would vehemently oppose the government's power to remove it from the marketplace of ideas.

To further illustrate the wrongness of allowing judges (or legislators) to condemn a book based on its net harm, imagine a claim in the United States that the Qur' an should be banned because it was said to inspire the 9/11 terrorists. Would anybody feel comfortable leaving a good versus harm standard to American judges, most of whom are Christian, in regard to Islam's holiest book? I certainly would not, and thus conclude that even if virtual child pornography were conclusively shown to do more harm than good, the Supreme Court was correct in not allowing it to be eliminated.[19]

As to the argument that virtual pornography can be used to seduce children, Justice Kennedy, for the Supreme Court, got it exactly right when he noted that if virtual pornography is to be suppressed because of its capacity to seduce children, we might as well suppress "cartoons, video games, and candy."[20] And, I might add that he could have included bicycles, puppy dogs, and vans. The point, of course, is that many things, including but not limited to literature, can be misused. But, as the Court once succinctly put it: "We cannot reduce the entire adult population to reading only that which is fit for children."[21]

IV. Distinguishing Virtual from Real Child Pornography

By far the most powerful argument for punishing virtual child pornography is the difficulty of distinguishing it from the real thing. The argument is that virtual and real pictures look so indistinguishable that a person marketing real child pornography might argue either that the material is virtual (and you can't prove beyond a reasonable doubt that it isn't) or at least that the defendant believed that it was virtual. To the extent that this argument rests on a factually sound premise, it presents a very serious problem. If real child pornography is punishable, but virtual isn't, and you can't tell the difference, what's a government to do?

The good news is that, at least for now, that does not seem to be an insurmountable problem. Although defendants have argued that the material was virtual, it has never been a successful defense.[22] Furthermore, there is technology available that allows the government to take a picture apart, pixel by pixel, to determine its origin.[23] Thus, as with the erstwhile nuclear arms race, detection appears to be keeping up with technology.

To the extent that technology outstrips detection and one really cannot tell the difference, some type of burden of proof shifting device might be appropriate. Surely, the government should be able to argue that a picture that appears real can be treated as real in the absence of evidence that it isn't. Such a rule would differ from the one at issue in *Ashcroft,* where the statute allowed punishment even when it was clear that the picture was virtual.

As for the *scienter* issue, presumably it would take more than the defendant's word that he intended to transmit virtual pictures to create a reasonable doubt. If the Government proves that the pictures are real, a simple statement from the defendant that he thought they were virtual would be very unlikely to create a reasonable doubt.

V. Decriminalizing Virtual Pornography May Protect Real Children

It is certainly not immediately obvious that real children would be *better* off by allowing the sale of virtual pornography, yet that may in fact be the case. In an ideal world, nobody would want child pornography, real or virtual. Unfortunately, the world we live in is not ideal. Despite the efforts of all civilized governments to suppress child pornography, it is still with us. Why? Simply because the demand is there. If one accepts the unfortunate truth that the demand for child pornography exists despite these governmental efforts, there is little reason to believe that we will totally stamp it out.

On the other hand, if virtual child pornography is (or can be made) nearly identical to real child pornography and only the latter is unlawful, why wouldn't the pornographer sell only the former? Certainly most pornographers would love to avoid the risk of prison if their anticipated profit would not be compromised. And, from the consumer's perspective, a virtual picture would also shield him from prosecution.[24] Thus, there is good reason to believe that legalizing virtual child pornography may reduce the number of children that are currently exploited by this perverted industry. And so, the United states Supreme Court may well have rendered a decision that will ultimately protect children as well as it protects freedom of speech.

Notes

1. Graham Kenan Professor of Law: University of North Carolina School of Law

2. See Chief Justice Rehnquist's impassioned dissent (joined by Justices White and O'Connor) in Texas v. Johnson 491 U.S. 397 at 421 (1989.) See also Justice Stevens dissent at 436. After *Johnson,* Congress and the President again attempted to ban flag burning with the "Flag Protection Act of 1989" which the Supreme Court again overturned by a bare 5-4 majority in U.S. v. Eichman 496 U.S. 310 (1990).

3. See dissenting opinion of Judge Sprecher in Collin v. Smith 578 F. 2d 1197 at 1210 (1978). A recent European example with strong ramifications in the United States has been the case of La Ligue Contra Le Racisme et L' Antisemitisme v. Yahoo (tried in America as Yahoo v. LICRA. 169 F. Supp. 2d 1181 N.D. Cal. 2001.) Here a French judge held that the act of displaying Nazi memorabilia itself violated French law (Article R645-1 Penal Code) and that the American web site Yahoo must comply with French law and not display Nazi memorabilia on its own, American site. Also see David Kretzmer, *Free Speech and Racism,* 8 Cardozo L. Rev. 445 (1987).

4. For example, "Blue is prettier then green." See Arnold H. Loewy, *Criminal Speech: Should Free Trade in Ideas be Absolute?,* 2 Crim. L. F. 117, 118 (1990).

5. Or if you don't like that one, try "Vote Democrat."

6. See, for example, Gay News, Ltd. v. United Kingdom 5 E. H. R. R. 123 (1982). Cf Jeremy Jones v. Fredrick Toben (No H97/120) dealing with section 18C of Australia's Racial Discrimination Act of 1975 that makes it a crime "to offend, insult, humiliate, or intimidate another person or group of people" based on "race, colour or national or ethnic origin."

7. See e.g. the Supreme Court's willingness to uphold obscenity laws such as in Miller v. California 413 U.S. 15 (1973). See Loewy, *"Obscenity, Pornography, and First Amendment Theory, supra* at note 2. See also the four justice dissent in Texas v. Johnson, *supra* at note 9. As I have said elsewhere " It is understandable that our President, Congress, legislators, and general populace who do not regularly study the First Amendment would initially condemn the *Johnson* decision. It is more difficult to rationalize the opinions of the Supreme Court dissenters who really ought to know better." Arnold H. Loewy, *The Flag-Burning Case: Freedom of Speech When We Need It Most,* 68 N.C. L. Rev. 165 at 172–173 (1989).

8. For a more detailed development of this point, see Arnold H. Loewy, *Freedom of Speech as a Product of Democracy,* 27 U. Rich. L. Rev. 427 (1993).

9. I put to one side the issue of whether the jurisdiction punishing the dissemination of child pornography is the one in which the pornography was made. I deal with the resolution of that issue elsewhere. See Arnold H. Loewy, *Obscenity, Pornography, and First Amendment Theory,* 2 Wm. & Mary Bill Rts. J. 471 at 480–482 (1993). Cited *supra* at note 2.

10. But did not hold. Justice Kennedy wrote that "Although morphed images may fall within the definition of virtual child pornography, they implicate the interests of real children and are in that sense closer to the images in *Ferber."* Ashcroft v. Free Speech Coalition 122 S. Ct. at 1397.

11. Any doubt that such pictures can be harmful, sometimes when least expected, was dispelled by the recent Miss North Carolina dispute in the Miss America contest. The winner's picture was taken unauthorizedly while she was changing clothes. The suggested presence of those pictures was enough to disqualify her.

12. See Eberhard Kronhausen & Phyllis Kronhausen, *Pornography and the Law,* (1959 and 1964 update.) Also see studies done in Denmark, Sweden and the

former West Germany concluding that the availability of sexually explicit material leads to less crime, not more. Reprinted in Marcia Pally, Sense and Censorship: The Vanity of Bonfires (Americans for Constitutonal Freedom 1991, vol. 2). Even opponents of pornography have long had to concede that there is "no substantial basis for the belief that erotic materials constitute a primary or significant cause or development of character defects or that they operate as a significant determanitive factor in causing crime and delinquency." President's Commission on Obscenity and Pornography (Bantam 1970) p. 243. See a similar concession in Lydia W. Lee, *Child Pornography Prevention act of 1996: Confronting the Challenges of Virtual Reality,* 8 S. Cal. Interdisc. L. J. 639 (1999).

13. A Clockwork Orange (Warner Brothers 1972) In this film a criminal is repeatedly shown images of horrific violence and given a drug that makes him associate it with strong feelings of nausea. The character is released into the world unable to commit any violent acts or even to think violent thoughts.

14. See Lobitz, W.C. and LoPiccolo, J., *New Methods in Behavioral Treatment of Sexual Dysfunction,* J. Behav. Ther. & Exp. Psychiat. Vol. 3 pp. 265–71. See generally, Patricia Gillan, *Therapeutic Uses of Obscenity,* reprinted in Dhavan and Davies, Censorship and Obscenity (Martin and Robertson 1978).

15. Albert Fish was inspired to castrate and 'sacrifice' young boys by reading about sacrifices in the Bible. See Earl Finbar Murphy, *The Value of Pornography,* 10 Wayne L. Rev. 655,668 (1964).

16. John George Haigh was inspired by the procedures of the Anglican High Church Service to drink his victims' blood through straws and dissolve their bodies in acid baths. *Id.*

17. Heinrich Pommerenke was prompted by Cecil B. DeMille's film The Ten Commandments to rape, abuse, and slay women. *Id.*

18. *Supra,* section I.

19. Anybody who doubts this would do well to see the Hollywood satire "Pleasantville," which recounts the story of a town from the fifties where only sweetness and light is allowed. Anybody who dares to deviate from the approved "everything is perfect" mantra is dealt with harshly.

20. 122 S. Ct. at 1402

21. Butler v. Michigan 352 U.S. 380 at 384

22. At least as of April 16, 2002 when *Ashcroft* was decided. See 122 S. Ct. at 1406 citing Brief for Petitioners 37.

23. The technique is called "digital pixel examination." Reported in ABC News "Detecting Real Child Porn: New software tools spot doctored pictures." (April 22, 2002) Available at. . . .

24. The only reason that this might not happen is the dollar cost of producing virtual child pronography. This, of course, is a reason for the law to keep the cost of exploiting real children high. It is also a reason to decriminalize virtual pornography as the Supreme Court has done.

Diana E. H. Russell and
Natalie J. Purcell

→ **NO**

Exposure to Pornography as a Cause of Child Sexual Victimization

Researchers almost universally agree that photographing children for child pornography constitutes child sexual victimization. We will argue in this chapter that a causal relationship exists between adult and juvenile males' exposure to child pornography—including computer-generated, written, and oral forms of pornography—and their perpetration of child sexual victimization. Because the theoretical work behind this model comes from the work of Diana Russell over decades, we describe this as "Russell's theory."

Because child pornography does not negatively affect all viewers to the same degree, some researchers conclude that mere exposure to this material cannot play a causal role in child sexual victimization. This is analogous to the tobacco industry's faulty claim that, since many smokers do not die of lung cancer, smoking does not cause lung cancer. Such reasoning is faulty. When there are multiple causes for a phenomenon, any one of them "may be a sufficient but not necessary condition for the occurrence of the effect or a necessary but not sufficient condition" (Theodorson & Theodorson, 1979, p. 40). In this sense of the term, we argue that exposure to child pornography causes child sexual victimization.

Although women have been known to sexually abuse both male and female children, males form the overwhelming majority of child pornography consumers and perpetrators of child sexual victimization. Therefore, Russell's three-factor causal theory focuses on male perpetrators. (The terms "man," "men," "male," or "males" in this chapter should be understood to include juvenile and adult males.)

Catharsus vs. Intensified Desire

According to the catharsis theory, the repeated exposure of males to pornography "leads to a steadily decreasing interest" in the material (Bart & Jozsa, 1980, p. 210). This exposure is frequently described as a "safety valve." As applied to child pornography, this theory assumes that repeated viewing of child pornography decreases viewers' desire for sex with children. Hence, according to this theory, viewers of child pornography should be less likely to sexually victimize children.

Zillmann and Bryant (1986) conducted an experiment based on 160 subjects.

These researchers found that the subjects' boredom after repeatedly viewing the same pornographic material motivated them to switch to viewing different and more extreme pornography, such as material involving the infliction of pain, violent pornography, and "uncommon or unusual sexual practices," including bondage, sadomasochism and bestiality (Zillmann & Bryant, 1986, p. 577).

Research aside, common sense and rationality unequivocally challenge the catharsis theory. Very few people would likely support a proposal to solve the problem of parents physically beating their children by having them watch movies that show parents battering and torturing their children. Why is it only in the case of misogynistic pornography that so many individuals—including a handful of researchers—believe that exposure dissipates the problem? The plain inconsistency and irrationality of the catharsis theory suffice to dismiss the notion that pornography serves as a "safety valve."

Pornography as a Cause of Child Sexual Victimization

The major objective of this chapter is to challenge the belief that exposure to child pornography is harmless and to demonstrate that exposure to child pornography can cause child sexual victimization in societies where this is proscribed.

Causal Factor IA: Viewing Child Pornography Predisposes Some Males, not Previously So Disposed, to Sexually Desire Children

It is commonly believed that exposure to child pornography cannot create a desire for sexual contact with children in males for whom it did not previously exist. Most people prefer to believe that any man who becomes sexually interested in children must have been predisposed to this interest. The following . . . points present ways in which exposure to child pornography can cause sexual arousal in some males who were not previously sexually interested in children. These points demonstrate that "normal" heterosexual males can become sexually aroused by depictions of children.

1. By Sexualizing/Sexually Objectifying Children

Child pornography transforms children into sexual objects designed to appeal to pedophiles and non-pedophilic child molesters.

Child pornographers often direct the girls they photograph to get into sexual poses or to engage in masturbation or sexual intercourse like women in adult pornography. These sexualized pictures of girls (often acting as mini-adults) evoke a sexual response in some males who previously had no interest in sex with girls.

3. By Application of the Laws of Learning

While some may believe that only males who are sexually aroused by child pornography would search for it, O'Connell (2001) maintains that "All the evidence is that many people [males] at least browse in this area [of child pornography], if not actively downloading" Web site pictures (p. 7).

A classic experiment by Rachman and Hodgson (1968) demonstrates that male subjects can learn to become sexually aroused by seeing a picture of a woman's boot after repeatedly seeing women's boots in association with sexually arousing slides of nude females. The laws of learning that created the boot fetish can also presumably teach males who previously were not sexually aroused by depictions of adult–child sex, to become aroused after exposure to child pornography.

Masturbation to child pornography during or following exposure to it, reinforces the association between these images and sexual gratification. This constitutes what McGuire, Carlisle, and Young (1965) refer to as "masturbatory conditioning" (p. 185). These researchers hypothesized that "an individual's arousal pattern can be altered by directly changing his masturbatory fantasies" (Abel, Blanchard, & Becker, 1978, p. 192). Abel et al. (1978) have treated violent sexual perpetrators by conditioning them to masturbate and ejaculate to nonviolent consensual portrayals of sex.

Presumably, it is equally possible to change males' non-deviant sexual fantasies and behavior to deviant ones. Hence, when male Internet users with no previous sexual interest in children inadvertently find themselves looking at child pornography, or when curiosity prompts such males to deliberately search out child pornography, they may be surprised to find themselves aroused by sexualized pictures of children. If these male viewers masturbate while viewing sexual pictures of children, this presumably can be the beginning of a growing interest in sex with children. For example, Jenkins (2001) notes that some posts on the Web "suggest that individuals were 'converted' after discovering the material [child pornography]" (p. 106) (emphasis added). Furthermore, repeated masturbation to these portrayals may result in increased arousal. The pleasurable experience of orgasm is an exceptionally potent reinforcer. Adult and child pornography are widely used by males as ejaculation material and thus are effective at constructing or reconstructing viewers' patterns of sexual arousal and expression.

4. By Males Who Have Become Habituated to Adult Pornography Seeking Different or More Extreme Forms of Pornography

It is important to recognize that males who frequently view adult pornography, persons Russell describes as pornophiles, can also become interested and sexually aroused by child pornography.

It seems reasonable to suppose that some of the males who become bored with ordinary adult pornography would opt to view child pornography since it qualifies as a "less commonly practiced sexual activity."

Causal Factor IB: Viewing Child Pornography Intensifies the Desire of Some Males Who Are Already Sexually Aroused by Children

1. By Increasing Males' Masturbatory Activity Thereby Reinforcing Their Desires for Sex with Children

When pedophiles and other males who desire sex with children are exposed to child pornography that corresponds to their specific preferences (e.g., the gender and age of the child), their sexual arousal intensifies.

Many males with a sexual interest in children deliberately use child pornography to intensify their sexual desire as a prelude to masturbation or the sexual abuse of children. Silbert and Pines (1993) report that a father in their study used to show "his friends pornographic movies to get them sexually aroused before they would rape" his 9-year-old daughter (p. 117–118).

In sum, the more pedophiles and child molesters masturbate to child pornography, the stronger their arousal to this material, and the more it reinforces the association between their fantasies and their desire to have sex with or sexually abuse children.

2. By Suggesting Exciting New Ideas for Having Sex with/Sexually Abusing Children

Jenkins (2001) notes that most pedophiles consider the old child pornography pictures still circulating on the Internet (which he refers to as "oldies") to be boring (p. 84). Consequently, "[a] common theme on the pedo boards is requests for material that is not readily available,"—that is, novel kinds of child pornography (p. 84). "The range of requests is bewilderingly perverse," according to Jenkins. "A few themes recur often and arouse real enthusiasm. By far the most common include calls for 'Black loli,' African or African American subjects. . . . Also in demand are incest pictures" (p. 85).

With regard to incestuous abuse, every conceivable relationship is portrayed in pictorial and written forms on the Internet—especially fathers having sex with their daughters. Rare forms of incestuous abuse are greatly overrepresented, including mother–son incest and female-on-female incestuous abuse. Many of the acts demonstrated or described in Internet pornography are portrayed as exciting and unconventional, providing viewers with new ideas for having sex with children.

3. By Providing Images and Models of Adult–Child Sex/Abuse for Males to Imitate

Child pornography provides models for males who already have a sexual interest in children. By seeing the different acts perpetrated on children (many of which elicit no negative responses and some of which appear to elicit positive responses or enjoyment), these "newbies" (a term used by many pedophiles) are provided with models that can shape and intensify their desires. Portrayals of child pornography showing only positive consequences for the perpetrators and the victims are particularly conducive to imitation. (However, for males who are sadistic, child pornography showing negative consequences for the victim is more likely to intensify sexual arousal and serve as a model to imitate.)

Several examples illustrate the use of pornography as a model for imitation. Consider also the young girl who testified in the 1985 Government Commission on Pornography:

> My father had an easel that he put by the bed. He'd pin a picture on the easel and like a teacher he would tell me this is what you're going to learn today. He would then act out the pictures on me. (Attorney General's Commission on Pornography: Final Report, Vol. 1, 1986, p. 782)

Tim Tate (1990) provides another example, quoting Len, a pedophile who had molested several hundred young boys during his lifetime:

> Child pornography became important to me because I enjoyed it, fantasized and masturbated to it. It wasn't a safety valve, though. At the time I was looking at the magazine it was OK, I was fine . . . but you're not going to look at a magazine all day. So when I went out in the open I would see another pretty boy and find myself chatting him up. In the end I would put into practice what I had seen in the magazines. (p. 110)

4. By Creating a Desire for Increasingly More Extreme Forms of Child Pornography

Jenkins (2001) maintains that some viewers of child pornography become addicted, with an increasing "hunger for ever more illegal material" (p. 109). Newcomers to child pornography on the Internet may be "amazed and stimulated by the first few softcore pornographic images" they see (p. 109). However, these images "are all too likely to become routine," motivating the more frequent downloaders to turn "avidly to the harder-core sites" (p. 109).

Habituation is clearly an intrinsic feature in the escalation described by viewers of child pornography. Some child pornography users acknowledge that "involvement thus becomes a cumulative process" (Jenkins, 2001, p. 109). For example, one pedophile explained, "With this hobby we get bored after a while with the usual and we risk a bit to get new stuff or get actual experience. It's a natural progression" (p. 109) (emphasis added).

In conclusion, it seems clear that exposure to child pornography often becomes an escalating problem; what may have begun as observation of seemingly nonviolent images of adult-child sexual abuse can lead to sexual interest in increasingly more hardcore and violent images of child sexual victimization.

Causal Factor II: Viewing Child Pornography Undermines Some Males' Internal Inhibitions against Acting Out Their Desires to Have Sex with/Sexually Victimize Children

Each component of Causal Factor II contributes to the undermining of moral beliefs that inhibit some males with a sexual interest in children from acting out their sexual desires.

1. By Sexualizing/Sexually Objectifying and/or Depersonalizing Girls

Exposure to child pornography plays a vital role in both creating a sexual interest in children in some males not previously so disposed and undermining some males' internal inhibitions against acting out their desire to have sex with children. Child pornography portraying girls in sexually provocative poses or happily engaged in sexual acts with other children or with adult men or women can convince those exposed to it that some children want and enjoy sex with adult males.

2. By Undermining the Prohibition against Adult–Child Sex/Victimization

Although legal ages of consent vary in different countries, adult–child sex is proscribed in most countries today.

Despite the prohibition in the United States, there are massive numbers of child pornography Web sites that promote adult–child sexual victimization through photographs, videos, or written stories. For example, an incest Web site titled "Golden Incest Sites!" lists 50 titles. . . . The pictures, stories, videos, and other material it makes accessible to interested Internet surfers can serve as highly suggestive models for viewers who may never before have thought of their daughters, sons, nieces, nephews, and other younger relatives in a sexual way. The ubiquity of incest pornography also conveys the popularity of such images, suggesting that large numbers of men must experience such desires.

The prevalence of child pornography sites, their content, and their positive portrayals of adult–child sexual abuse all serve to diminish the deviant nature of incestuous and extrafamilial child sexual abuse. This in turn enhances the likelihood that some men's internal inhibitions against acting out incestuous and extrafamilial child sexual victimization will be undermined.

It is also important to note two other ways in which the prohibition against adult–child sex is undermined by child pornography. First, the inclusion of many child pornography cartoons in mainstream men's magazines like Playboy and Penthouse communicates its social acceptability. Second, the boards on various sites allow visitors to form their own subcultural communities in which such behaviors or desires are not considered deviant and where pedophiles and others interested in child pornography can feel more normal. . . .

6. By Advocating, Legitimizing, and/or Normalizing Adult–Child Sex/ Victimization

The legitimatizing and normalizing of adults' sexual victimization of children in child pornography are two of the most frequently cited ways in which this material undermines some viewers' internal inhibitions. As Tate (1990) points out,

> All paedophiles need to reassure themselves that what they are doing or want to do is OK. It [child pornography] validates their feelings, lowers their inhibitions and makes them feel that their behaviour is pretty normal in the context of this pornography—they see other people doing it in the videos or the magazines and it reassures them. (p. 24)

Clearly, child pornography has the power "to reinforce both the paedophile's attraction to children and his self-justification process" (Tate, 1990, p. 110). Pedophiles also "use porn to convince themselves that their behavior is not abnormal, but is shared by others" (Calcetas-Santos, 2001, p. 59).

7. By Providing Specific Instructions on How to Sexually Victimize a Child

Some males who have never acted on their desire to have sex with a child may be ignorant or anxious about how to proceed with this. Such concerns can inhibit them from perpetrating such an act. Child pornography removes this impediment by providing instructions for the sexual abuse of children. Tyler, a detective sergeant in the San Bernardino, California, Sheriff's Department, testified in hearings on child pornography and pedophilia conducted by Senator Arlen Specter about a child pornography magazine that described "how to have sex with prepubescent children" (Child Pornography and Pedophilia, 1984, p. 33). During these hearings, Senator Specter also discussed a book titled How to Have Sex With Kids that described "how to meet children, how to entice them, how to develop a relationship with them, and how to have sex with them"(p. 30). Sexually explicit illegal material presumably demonstrates at what ages it is possible for adult males to penetrate young children anally and vaginally.

Presumably, pedophiles and child molesters in general find such instructions useful. Even when explicit instructions on how to sexually victimize a child are not provided in child pornography, this material always provides models that viewers may learn from and attempt to emulate.

Causal Factor III: Viewing Child Pornography Undermines Some Males' Social Inhibitions against Acting Out Their Desires to Have Sex with/Sexually Victimize Children

Child pornography undermines viewers' social inhibitions against sexually victimizing children. It does so in three distinct ways.

1. By Diminishing Fear of Disapproval

Potential or actual child molesters who look at or download child pornography on the Internet will quickly become cognizant of the enormous number of child pornography Web sites, videos, and chat rooms. This material makes it abundantly clear that there are many other viewers and collectors of child pornography, as well as many others who act out their sexual attraction to children. As Jenkins (2001) states it, "He [the pedophile viewer] finds that he is not alone in his deviant interests" (p. 106). This revelation "helps support the notion that the boards [where individuals post messages] are safe space that one can visit at will, [and] where like-minded friends can reliably be found," thereby diminishing viewers' fear of universal disapproval for their sexual interest in children (p. 108).

Crimmins (1995) testified at the Senate Judiciary Committee Hearings on Child Pornography on the Internet that, "People who may have never acted on such impulses before, are emboldened when they see that there are so many other individuals who have similar interests" (p. 2). Furthermore, Jenkins (2001) argues that, "The more pedophiles and pornographers are attacked by law enforcement agencies, mass media, and anti-pedos, the greater the sense of community against common enemies" (p. 114). The knowledge that they have a support group of like-minded colleagues contributes to undermining the fear of disapproval for sexually victimizing children.

2. By Diminishing Fear of Legal and Social Sanctions

Fear of legal sanctions is the most important factor in restraining potential molesters from abusing children. The more effective potential molesters perceive the social sanctions to be, the less likely they are to become perpetrators. Fear of legal sanctions also serves to restrain active child molesters.

However, child pornography consistently communicates the false message that those who violate children are in no danger of being apprehended or facing other negative consequences. We have not seen any pictorial child pornography that shows a sexual predator being apprehended by the police or ending up in prison. The same applies to written child pornography stories, fantasies, lists of Web sites and videos, as well as child pornography in men's magazines. The outcomes of child sexual abuse are always positive for the perpetrators. Hence, exposure to child pornography gives would-be child molesters a false sense of immunity from legal sanctions, thereby undermining their social inhibitions against acting out their desires.

Contributory Factor IV: Viewing Pornography Undermines Some Children's Abilities to Avoid, Resist, or Escape Sexual Victimization

Some perpetrators use force to accomplish their acts of child sexual victimization. In these cases, children's abilities to avoid, resist, or escape sexual victimization are irrelevant. There are, however, cases where children's exposure to pornography undermines these abilities and permits sexual abuse to occur where it otherwise would not.

1. By Arousing Children's Sexual Curiosity and/or Desire

Showing pornography to boys and girls is a common seduction strategy of pedophiles who hope thereby to arouse children's sexual curiosity or sexual desire.

Pedophiles posing as young teenagers in Internet teen chat groups often send pornographic pictures or e-mail messages containing pornographic language to children. These predators use pornographic pictures to arouse the children's curiosity or sexual interest and manipulate them into meeting. These meetings typically culminate in the sexual victimization of the child or children.

Thus we conclude that exposure to child or adult pornography can arouse children's sexual curiosity or desire and thereby undermine their abilities to avoid, resist, or escape being sexually abused.

2. By Legitimizing and/or Normalizing Child Sexual Victimization for Children

Many pedophiles and child molesters show pornography to children "in order to persuade them that they would enjoy certain sexual acts" (Kelly, 1992, p. 119). Another motive is "to convince them that what they are being asked to do is alright." Showing them a picture "legitimizes the abuser's requests" (p. 119).

In the following example, an incestuous father's attempts to use pornography to normalize and legitimize having sex with his daughter were unusually persistent.

> The incest started at the age of eight. I did not understand any of it and did not feel that it was right. My dad would try to convince me that it was ok. He would find magazines articles or pictures that would show fathers and daughters or mothers, brothers and sisters having sexual intercourse. (Mostly fathers and daughters.) He would say that if it was published in magazines that it had to be all right because magazines could not publish lies. . . . He would say, "See it's okay to do because it's published in magazines." (Attorney General's Commission on Pornography: Final Report, Vol. 1, 1986, p. 786)

Child molesters also send pornography to the children they have targeted for sexual victimization to convince them "that other children are sexually active" (Hughes, 1999, p. 28). Showing children child pornography thus normalizes and legitimatizes adult–child sexual encounters in the minds of some children.

3. By Desensitizing or Disinhibiting Children

A child molester's step-by-step "grooming" of a child serves to gradually desensitize her or him to the culminating act of sexual abuse, which is his goal. He moves from befriending a child, to touching her or him, to introducing her or him to an X-rated video, slowly showing more of it "until the child is able to sit and watch the videos without becoming too uncomfortable" (Whetsell-Mitchell, 1995, p. 201). Juliann Whetsell-Mitchell concludes, "Variations on the grooming ['seduction'] process are many but the end result is desensitizing the child to engaging in sexual acts with the perpetrator, other children, or other adults" (p. 201).

4. By Creating Feelings of Guilt and Complicity, Thereby Silencing Children

When child molesters expose targeted children to pornography, the children often feel guilty and complicit, particularly if they found the material sexually exciting or masturbated to it. According to Scotland Yard, one of the five major ways that pedophiles use pornography is to "ensure the secrecy of any sexual activity with a child who has already been seduced" (Tate, 1990, p. 24). Child molesters can often silence their victims by telling them that their parents would be very upset to learn that they had watched pornography. Even without such warnings, children often fear that their parents will blame and punish them for having looked at this material. Children who are sexually abused following the exposure may feel complicit in the abuse and thus become even more motivated to remain silent. Ultimately, this reduces the likelihood that abused children will disclose the sexual abuse to their parents or others.

Conclusion

Despite the relative dearth of research, we believe we have provided sufficient evidence to substantiate Russell's theory. This theory explains how exposure to child pornography can create a sexual interest in children in some males who previously had no such interest. When sexual interest in children exists, exposure to child pornography can intensify sexual desires and undermine internal and social inhibitions against acting them out. Thus, exposure to pornography induces some men, who otherwise would not sexually abuse children, to become child molesters.

References

Abel, G., Blanchard, E., & Becker, J. (1978). An integrated treatment program for rapists. In R. Rada (Ed.), Clinical aspects of the rapist (pp. 161–214). New York: Grune & Stratton.

Anderson, M. (1989, Summer). Iconoclast, 7.

Attorney General's Commission on Pornography: Final Report, Vol. 1. (1986). Washington, DC: United States Department of Justice.

Bart, P., & Jozsa, M. (1980). Dirty books, dirty films, and dirty data. In L. Lederer (Ed.), Take back the night: Women on pornography (pp. 188–217). New York: William Morrow.

Brady, K. (1979). Father's Days: A true story of incest. New York: Seaview Books.

Briere, J., & Runtz, M. (1989). University males' sexual interest in children: Predicting potential indices of "pedophilia" in a nonforensic sample. Child Abuse and Neglect, 13(1), 7, 65–75.

Bromberg, D. S., & Johnson, B. T. (2001, July). Sexual interest in children, child sexual abuse, and psychological sequaelae for children. Psychology in Schools 38(4), 343–355.

Burgess, A. W., & Hartman, C. R. (1987). Child abuse aspects of child pornography. Psychiatric Annals, 17(4), 248–253.

Burgess, A. W., Hartman, C. R., McCausland, M. P., & Powers, P. (1984). Response patterns in children and adolescents exploited through sex rings and pornography. American Journal of Psychiatry, 141(5).

Calcetas-Santos, O. (1996, Dec. 9–20). Rights of the Child: Report of the special rapporteur on the sale of children, child prostitution and child pornography. Addendum: Report on the mission of the special rapporteur to the United States of America on the issues of commercial sexual exploitation of children. New York: United Nations. Available at. . . .

Calcetas-Santos, O. (2001). Child pornography on the Internet. In C. Arnaldo (Ed.), Child abuse on the internet (pp. 57–60). New York: Berghahn Books.

Campagna, D. S., & Poffenberger, D. L. (1988). The sexual trafficking in children: An investigation of the child sex trade. Dover, MA: Auburn House.

Carey, C. A. (2005, January 31). Banishment is not the answer. San Francisco Chronicle, B5.

Check, J. (1995). Teenage training: The effects of pornography on adolescent males. In L. Lederer & R. Delgado (Eds.), The price we pay: The case against racist speech, hate propaganda, and pornography (pp. 89–91). New York: Hill and Wang. 04-Dowd-4799.qxd 11/18/2005 11:29 AM Page 80.

Check, J., & Maxwell, K. (1992a, June). Adolescents' rape myth attitudes and acceptance of forced sexual intercourse. Paper presented at the Canadian Psychological Association Meetings, Quebec.

Check, J., & Maxwell, K. (1992b, June). Children's consumption of pornography and their attitudes regarding sexual violence. Paper presented at the Canadian Psychological Association Meetings, Quebec. Child pornography and pedophilia (1984). United States Senate, 98th Congress, second session Sess. 30–37 (1984).

Cline, V. B. (Ed.). (1974). Where do you draw the line? Provo, UT: Brigham Young University Press.

Crimmins, B. (1995). Testimony before Congressional Hearing on Child Pornography on the Internet, Senate Judiciary Committee (104th Congress ed., pp. 1–15). Washington, DC: Government Printing Office.

Davies, N. (1994, November 26). Dirty business. Guardian, pp. 12–17.

Diamond, I. (1980). Pornography and regression: A reconsideration of who and what. In L. Lederer (Ed.), Take back the night: Women on pornography (pp. 187–203). New York: William Morrow.

Dietz, P., & Sears, A. (1987–1988). Pornography and obscenity sold in "Adult Bookstores": A survey of 5132 books, magazines, and films in four American cities. Journal of Law Reform, 21(1–2), 7–46.

Dines, G., Jensen, R., & Russo, A. (1998). Pornography: The production and consumption of inequality. New York: Routledge.

Ferguson, J. (1985). Effect of pornography on women and children (prepared statement). Subcommittee on Juvenile Justice of the Committee on the Judiciary (98h Congress, Second Session on Oversight on Pornography, Magazines of a

Variety of Courses, Inquiring into the Subject of Their Impact on Child Abuse, Child Molestation, and Problems of Conduct Against Women ed., pp. 281–288). Washington, DC: U.S. Government Printing Office.

Finkelhor, D. (1984). Child sexual abuse: New theory and research. New York: The Free Press.

Freund, K. (1981). Assessment of pedophilia. In M. Cook & K. Howells (Eds.), Adult sexual interest in children (pp. 137–180). New York: Academic Press.

Healy, M. (2002, February 27). Child pornography: An international perspective. Paper presented at the Second World Congress Against Commercial Sexual Exploitation of Children, Yokohama, Japan.

Howard, J., Reifler, C., & Liptzin, M. (1991). Effects of exposure to pornography. Washington, DC: Commission on Obscenity and Pornography.

Howells, K. (1981). Adult sexual interest in children: Consideration relevant to theories of aetiology. In M. Cook & K. Howells (Eds.), Adult sexual interest in children (pp. 55–94). New York: Academic Press.

Hughes, D. M. (1999). Pimps and predators on the Internet: Globalizing the sexual exploitation of women and children. Kingston, RI: The Coalition Against Trafficking in Women.

Itzin, C. (1996). Pornography and the organisation of child sexual abuse. In P. C. Bibby (Ed.), Organized abuse: The current debate (pp. 167–196). Hampshire, UK: Aldershot.

Jenkins, P. (2001). Beyond tolerance: Child pornography on the Internet. New York: New York University Press.

Katherine Brady's Testimony to the Senate Subcommittee on Juvenile Justice. (1984, August 8). 85 CIS S 52115 Testimony No: 1, pp. 28–117. Exposure to Pornography as a Cause of Child Sexual Victimization 81 04-Dowd-4799.qxd 11/18/2005 11:29 AM Page 81

Kelly, L. (1992). Pornography and child sexual abuse. In C. Itzin (Ed.), Pornography: Women, violence, and civil liberties (pp. 113–123). New York: Oxford University Press.

Kelly, L., Wingfield, R., & Regan, L. (1995). Splintered lives: Sexual exploitation of children in the context of children's rights and child protection. Ilford, Essex, UK: Barnardos.

Linz, D., & Imrich, D. (2001). Child pornography. In S. O. White (Ed.), Handbook of youth and justice (pp. 79–111). New York: Kluwer Academic/Plenum.

LoPiccolo, J. (1994). Acceptance and broad spectrum treatment of paraphilias. In S. C. Hayes, N. Jacobson, V. M. Follette, & M. Dougher (Eds.), Acceptance and change: Content and context in psychotherapy (pp. 149–170). Reno, NV: Context Press.

Mayne, A. (2000). Child pornography. In R. Barnes-September, I. Brown-Adam, A. Mayne, D. Kowen, & G. Dyason (Eds.), Child victims of prostitution in the Western Cape (p. 25). Cape Town, SA: Institute for Child and Family Development.

McGuire, R. J., Carlisle, J. M., & Young, B. G. (1965). Sexual deviation as a conditioned behavior: A hypothesis. Behavioral Research and Therapy, 2, 185–190.

Mohr, J., Turner, R., & Jerry, M. (1964). Pedophilia and Exhibitionism. Toronto: University of Toronto Press.

O'Connell, R. (2001). Paedophile networking and the Internet. In C. Arnaldo (Ed.), Child Abuse on the Internet: Ending the silence (p. 65). Paris: UNESCO Publishing/Berghahn Books.

Osanka, F. M., & Johann, S. L. (1989). Sourcebook on pornography. Lexington, MA: Lexington Books.

Rachman, S., & Hodgson, R. (1968). Experimentally-induced "sexual fetishism": Replication and development. Psychological Record, 18, 25–27.

Report of the Commission on Obscenity and Pornography (1970). Washington, DC: U.S. Government Printing Office.

Rush, F. (1980, May 17). Child pornography. Paper presented at the Pittsburgh Conference on Pornography: A Feminist Perspective, Pittsburgh, PA.

Russell, D. E. H. (1984). Sexual exploitation: Rape, child sexual abuse, and workplace harassment. Beverly Hills, CA: Sage.

Russell, D. E. H. (1999). The secret trauma: Incest in the lives of girls and women (Rev. ed.). New York: Basic Books/Perseus.

Russell, D. E. H., & Trocki, K. (1993). Evidence of harm. In D. E. H. Russell (Ed.), Making violence sexy: Feminist views on pornography (pp. 194–213). New York: Teachers College Press. Senn, C. (1993). Women's responses to pornography. In D. E. H. Russell (Ed.), Making violence sexy: Feminist views on pornography (pp. 179–193). New York: Teachers College Press. Silbert, M., & Pines, A. (1993). Pornography and sexual abuse of women. In D. E. H. Russell (Ed.), Making violence sexy: Feminist views on pornography (pp. 113–119). New York: Teachers College Press.

Sommers, E., & Check, J. (1987). An empirical investigation of the role of pornography in the verbal and physical abuse of women. Violence and Victims, 2(3), 189–209.

Stock, W. (1995). The effects of pornography on women. In L. Lederer & R. Delgado (Eds.), The price we pay: The case against racist speech, hate propaganda, and pornography (pp. 80–88). New York: Hill and Wang.

Swanson, D. (1968). Adult sexual abuse of children: The man and circumstances. Diseases of the Nervous System, 29, 677–683.

Tate, T. (1990). Child pornography: An investigation. London: Methuen.

Tate, T. (1992). The child pornography industry: International trade in child sexual abuse. In C. Itzin (Ed.), Pornography: Women, violence, and civil liberties (p. 213). New York: Oxford University Press.

Taylor, M., & Quayle, E. (2003). Child pornography: An Internet crime. New York: Brunner-Routledge.

Taylor, S. (2001, March 19). Is it sexual exploitation if victims are virtual? Newsweek, 137, 51.

Theodorson, G., & Theodorson, A. (1979). A modern dictionary of sociology. New York: Barnes & Noble.

Thimbleby, H. (1995, September 12). Problems in the global village. Presented at Discovery and Invention, The British Association Annual Festival of Science (Newcastle). Available: . . .

Whetsell-Mitchell, J. (1995). Rape of the innocent: Understanding and preventing child sexual abuse. Washington, DC: Accelerated Development.

Wyre, R. (1990). Why do men sexually abuse children? In T. Tate (Ed.), Child pornography: An investigation (pp. 281–288). London: Methuen.

Zillmann, D. (1989). Effects of prolonged consumption. In D. Zillmann & J. Bryant, (Eds.), Pornography: Research advances and policy considerations, pp. 127–157. Hillsdale, NJ: Lawrence Erlbaum.

Zillmann, D., & Bryant, J. (1986). Shifting preferences in pornography consumption. Communication Research, 12, 560–578. Exposure to Pornography as a Cause of Child Sexual Victimization 83 04-Dowd-4799.qxd 11/18/2005 11:29 AM Page 83 04-Dowd-4799.qxd 11/18/2005 11:29 AM Page 84.

CHALLENGE QUESTIONS

Would Legalization of Virtual Child Pornography Reduce Sexual Exploitation of Children?

1. For decades the United States Supreme Court has debated the definition of pornography. In light of dramatic changes in public attitudes during the past two decades, what would be a reasonable definition of pornography in contemporary American society?
2. Federal and state laws regard the production and procuring of pornography involving children as criminal. Should other groups of people be added to the category of individuals who should be protected from exploitation for the purposes of pornography (e.g., developmentally disabled people, psychiatrically disturbed individuals, senile or demented persons)?
3. Debate has arisen regarding the extent to which pedophiles should be viewed as criminals or as psychologically disturbed individuals. How might this same debate apply to adults who claim that they are addicted to child pornography?
4. What kind of research study could be developed to assess the extent to which virtual child pornography increases or reduces the likelihood of sexual victimization of children?
5. The treatment of pedophiles occasionally involves an aversive therapy in which shock is applied when the adult becomes sexually aroused at the sight of an inappropriate image involving a child. What are the pros and cons of using virtual images in such an intervention?

Suggested Readings

Carr, J. (2003). *Child abuse, child pornography, and the Internet.* London: NCH.

Kleinhans, C. (2004). Virtual child porn: The law and the semiotics of the image. *Journal of Visual Culture, 3*(1), 17–34.

Peters, R. (March, 2004). *The link between pornography and violent sex crimes.* From http://www.moralityinmedia.org/.

Seto, M. C., & Eke, A. W. (2005). The criminal histories and later offending of child pornography offenders. *Sexual Abuse: A Journal of Research and Treatment, 17*(2), 201–210.

ISSUE 17

Does Evolution Explain Why Men Rape?

YES: Randy Thornhill and Craig T. Palmer, from "Why Men Rape," *The Sciences* (January/February 2000)

NO: Susan Brownmiller, from *Against Our Will: Men, Women and Rape* (Simon & Schuster, 1975)

ISSUE SUMMARY

YES: Evolutionary biologist Randy Thornhill and evolutionary anthropologist Craig T. Palmer assert that the reasons why men rape are misunderstood. They contend that, rather than an act of gratuitous violence, rape can be understood as a biologically determined behavior in which socially disenfranchised men resort to this extreme act in order to gain access to women.

NO: Journalist Susan Brownmiller argues that rape is an exemplification of the male-female struggle in which men humiliate and degrade women in a blunt and ugly expression of physical power.

Rape is one of the most troubling and traumatizing of social problems, which is reflected in statistics that are almost unbelievable. It is estimated that in a given year, more than a quarter of a million individuals are the victims of rape, attempted rape, or sexual assault, and that the vast majority of these victims are females. More than one-third of all such cases involve completed rape. In addition to the horrendous physical harm associated with sexual assault, the psychological consequences are usually devastating, causing emotional havoc in the life of the rape victim for years or decades following the trauma. Despite the fact that increased attention has been given to the social problem of rape, controversy regarding explanations about why men commit this act continues.

In 1975 Susan Brownmiller caught the attention of the world with her harsh social commentary on rape. In *Against Our Will: Men, Women and Rape* (Simon & Schuster), Brownmiller assertively attacked widely held misconceptions about rape, such as the notion that victims of rape are somehow responsible for being assaulted or, worse yet, actually wanted to be attacked. In a compelling and straightforward presentation, Brownmiller discussed rape in such blunt terms that she sparked a dialogue that has lasted for decades.

In 2000 Randy Thornhill and Craig T. Palmer took a social and scholarly risk by discussing rape from a vantage point that they knew would be politically unpopular. Rather than viewing rape as representing a vicious, demeaning, and violent act against women, they argued that this behavior can be understood in evolutionary terms as representing the act of socially disenfranchised men who are desperate to gain access to women. Highlighting the fact that rape takes place among many species, Thornhill and Palmer asserted that this behavior is probably biologically rather than socially determined. Thornhill and Palmer further argued that society can only prevent rape by understanding male and female sexuality. Since publishing their theory, which is reprinted in the following selection, Thornhill and Palmer have been bombarded with criticism for what many view as flawed methodology and thinking. Nevertheless, they sparked a level of discussion that is heated and intense.

In the second selection, an excerpt from *Against Our Will,* Brownmiller asserts that rape is a process of intimidation by which women are kept in a state of fear by men who are motivated by a desire to exert control over women. She views rape as an act of violence committed by men who are socialized to devalue women. In explaining why rape continues to be so prevalent, Brownmiller acknowledges that most men do not rape but that they do benefit indirectly from the "rape system," a hierarchy that separates the genders, with men being on top. This chapter, first published in 1975 and reprinted almost two decades later, is considered one of the most important publications on the topic of rape.

POINT

- Females have evolved to carefully select mates who best support their offspring. That is why we understand that sex is "something females have that males want."

- Rape takes place not only among human beings but also among various other animal species.

- Men might resort to rape when they are socially disenfranchised and, thus, unable to gain access to women.

- The fact that men are able to maintain sexual arousal and copulate with unwilling women suggests that men have evolved psychological mechanisms that enable them to engage in forced copulation. This ability may reflect a "rape adaptation."

COUNTERPOINT

- The intent of rape is not merely to take but to humiliate and to degrade. Thus, men have always viewed sex as the "female treasure."

- Rape is a brief expression of physical power that exemplifies the male-female struggle.

- Access to women does not deter men from rape, as evidenced by the existence of officially sanctioned brothels for American soldiers during the Vietnam War.

- Rape is not a crime of irrational, impulsive, uncontrollable lust; it is a deliberate, hostile, violent act of degradation and possession on the part of a would-be conquerer, designed to intimidate and inspire fear.

YES ⤹

Randy Thornhill
and Craig T. Palmer

Why Men Rape

A friend of ours once told us about her rape. The details hardly matter, but in outline her story is numbingly familiar. After a movie she returned with her date to his car, which had been left in an isolated parking lot. She was expecting him to drive her home. Instead, the man locked the car doors and physically forced her to have sex with him.

Our friend was emotionally scarred by her experience: she became anxious about dating, and even about going out in public. She had trouble sleeping, eating and concentrating on her work. Indeed, like some war veterans, rape victims often suffer from post-traumatic stress disorder, in which symptoms such as anxiety, memory loss, obsessive thoughts and emotional numbness linger after a deeply disturbing experience. Yet gruesome ordeals like that of our friend are all too common: in a 1992 survey of American women aged eighteen and older, 13 percent of the respondents reported having been the victim of at least one rape, where rape was defined as unwelcome oral, anal or vaginal penetration achieved through the use or threat of force. Surely, eradicating sexual violence is an issue that modern society should make a top priority. But first a perplexing question must be confronted and answered: Why do men rape?

The quest for the answer to that question has occupied the two of us collectively for more than forty years. As a purely scientific puzzle, the problem is hard enough. But it is further roiled by strong ideological currents. Many social theorists view rape not only as an ugly crime but as a symptom of an unhealthy society, in which men fear and disrespect women. In 1975 the feminist writer Susan Brownmiller asserted that rape is motivated not by lust but by the urge to control and dominate. In the twenty-five years since, Brownmiller's view has become mainstream. All men feel sexual desire, the theory goes, but not all men rape. Rape is viewed as an unnatural behavior that has nothing to do with sex, and one that has no corollary in the animal world.

Undoubtedly, individual rapists may have a variety of motivations. A man may rape because, for instance, he wants to impress his friends by losing his virginity, or because he wants to avenge himself against a woman who has spurned him. But social scientists have not convincingly demonstrated that rapists are not at least partly motivated by sexual desire as well. Indeed, how

From *The Sciences*, January/February 2000, pp. 30–36 text only. Copyright © 2000 by Randy Thornhill. Reprinted by permission.

399

could a rape take place at all without sexual motivation on the part of the rapist? Isn't sexual arousal of the rapist the one common factor in all rapes, including date rapes, rapes of children, rapes of women under anesthetic and even gang rapes committed by soldiers during war?

⋅⟨◉⟩⋅

We want to challenge the dearly held idea that rape is not about sex. We realize that our approach and our frankness will rankle some social scientists, including some serious and well-intentioned rape investigators. But many facts point to the conclusion that rape is, in its very essence, a sexual act. Furthermore, we argue, rape has evolved over millennia of human history, along with courtship, sexual attraction and other behaviors related to the production of offspring.

Consider the following facts:

- Most rape victims are women of childbearing age.
- In many cultures rape is treated as a crime against the victim's *husband.*
- Rape victims suffer *less* emotional distress when they are subjected to *more* violence.
- Rape takes place not only among human beings but also in a variety of other animal species.
- Married women and women of childbearing age experience more psychological distress after a rape than do girls, single women or women who are past menopause.

As bizarre as some of those facts may seem, they all make sense when rape is viewed as a natural, biological phenomenon that is a product of the human evolutionary heritage.

Here we must hasten to emphasize that by categorizing a behavior as "natural" and "biological" we do not in any way mean to imply that the behavior is justified or even inevitable. *Biological* means "of or pertaining to life," so the word applies to every human feature and behavior. But to infer from that—as many of our critics assert that we do—that what is biological is somehow right or good, would be to fall into the so-called naturalistic fallacy. That mistake is obvious enough when one considers such natural disasters as epidemics, floods and tornadoes. In those cases it is clear that what is natural is not always desirable. And of course much can be, and is, done to protect people against natural threats—from administering antibiotics to drawing up emergency evacuation plans. In other words, the fact that rape is an ancient part of human nature in no way excuses the rapist.

⋅⟨◉⟩⋅

Why, then, have the editors of scholarly journals refused to publish papers that treat rape from a Darwinian perspective? Why have pickets and audience protesters caused public lectures on the evolutionary basis of rape to be canceled or terminated? Why have investigators working to discover the evolutionary causes of rape been denied positions at universities?

The reason is the deep schism between many social scientists and investigators such as ourselves who are proponents of what is variously called sociobiology or evolutionary psychology. Social scientists regard culture—everything from eating habits to language—as an entirely human invention, one that develops arbitrarily. According to that view, the desires of men and women are learned behaviors. Rape takes place only when men learn to rape, and it can be eradicated simply by substituting new lessons. Sociobiologists, by contrast, emphasize that learned behavior, and indeed all culture, is the result of psychological adaptations that have evolved over long periods of time. Those adaptations, like all traits of individual human beings, have both genetic and environmental components. We fervently believe that, just as the leopard's spots and the giraffe's elongated neck are the result of aeons of past Darwinian selection, so also is rape.

That conclusion has profound and immediate practical consequences. The rape-prevention measures that are being taught to police officers, lawyers, parents, college students and potential rapists are based on the prevailing social-science view, and are therefore doomed to fail. The Darwinian theory of evolution by natural selection is the most powerful scientific theory that applies to living things. As long as efforts to prevent rape remain uninformed by that theory, they will continue to be handicapped by ideas about human nature that are fundamentally inadequate. We believe that only by acknowledging the evolutionary roots of rape can prevention tactics be devised that really work.

◦◦◦

From a Darwinian perspective, every kind of animal—whether grasshopper or gorilla, German or Ghanaian—has evolved to produce healthy children that will survive to pass along their parents' genetic legacy. The mechanics of the phenomenon are simple: animals born without traits that led to reproduction died out, whereas the ones that reproduced the most succeeded in conveying their genes to posterity. Crudely speaking, sex feels good because over evolutionary time the animals that liked having sex created more offspring than the animals that didn't.

As everyone knows all too well, however, sex and the social behaviors that go with it are endlessly complicated. Their mysterious and tangled permutations have inspired flights of literary genius throughout the ages, from *Oedipus Rex* to *Portnoy's Complaint*. And a quick perusal of the personal-growth section of any bookstore—past such titles as *Men Are from Mars, Women Are from Venus* and *You Just Don't Understand*—is enough to show that one reason sex is so complicated is that men and women perceive it so differently. Is that the case only because boys and girls receive different messages during their upbringing? Or, as we believe, do those differences between the sexes go deeper?

Over vast periods of evolutionary time, men and women have confronted quite different reproductive challenges. Whereas fathers can share the responsibilities of child rearing, they do not have to. Like most of their male counterparts in the rest of the animal kingdom, human males can reproduce successfully with a minimal expenditure of time and energy; once the brief act of sexual intercourse is completed, their contribution can cease. By contrast, the minimum effort required for a woman to reproduce successfully includes nine months of pregnancy and a painful childbirth. Typically, ancestral females also had to devote themselves to prolonged breast-feeding and many years of child care if they were to ensure the survival of their genes. In short, a man can have many children, with little inconvenience to himself; a woman can have only a few, and with great effort.

That difference is the key to understanding the origins of certain important adaptations—features that persist because they were favored by natural selection in the past. Given the low cost in time and energy that mating entails for the male, selection favored males who mated frequently. By contrast, selection favored females who gave careful consideration to their choice of a mate; that way, the high costs of mating for the female would be undertaken under circumstances that were most likely to produce healthy offspring. The result is that men show greater interest than women do in having a variety of sexual partners and in having casual sex without investment or commitment. That commonplace observation has been confirmed by many empirical studies. The evolutionary psychologist David M. Buss of the University of Texas at Austin, for instance, has found that women around the world use wealth, status and earning potential as major criteria in selecting a mate, and that they value those attributes in mates more than men do.

Remember, none of the foregoing behavioral manifestations of evolution need be conscious. People do not necessarily have sex because they want children, and they certainly do not conduct thorough cost-benefit analyses before taking a partner to bed. As Darwin made clear, individual organisms merely serve as the instruments of evolution. Men today find young women attractive because during human evolutionary history the males who preferred prepubescent girls or women too old to conceive were outreproduced by the males who were drawn to females of high reproductive potential. And women today prefer successful men because the females who passed on the most genes, and thereby became our ancestors, were the ones who carefully selected partners who could best support their offspring. That is why, as the anthropologist Donald Symons of the University of California, Santa Barbara, has observed, people everywhere understand sex as "something females have that males want."

⋈⊙⋊

A dozen roses, romantic dinners by candlelight, a Tiffany engagement ring: the classic courtship ritual requires lots of time, energy and careful attention to detail. But people are far from unique in that regard: the males of most animal species spend much of their energies attracting, wooing and securing sexual partners. The male woodcock, for instance, performs a dramatic display each spring at mating time, soaring high into the air and then tumbling to the ground. Male fireflies are even flashier, blinking like neon signs. The male bowerbird builds a veritable honeymoon cottage: an intricate, sculpted nest that he decorates with flowers and other colorful bric-a-brac. Male deer and antelope lock antlers in a display of brute strength to compete for females.

Once a female's interest is piqued, the male behaves in various ways to make her more sexually receptive. Depending on the species, he dances, fans his feathers or offers gifts of food. In the nursery web spider, the food gift is an attempt to distract the female, who otherwise might literally devour her partner during the sex act. The common thread that binds nearly all animal species seems to be that males are willing to abandon all sense and decorum, even to risk their lives, in the frantic quest for sex.

But though most male animals expend a great deal of time and energy enticing females, forced copulation—rape—also occurs, at least occasionally, in a variety of insects, birds, fishes, reptiles, amphibians, marine mammals and nonhuman primates. In some animal species, moreover, rape is commonplace. In many scorpionfly species, for instance—insects that one of us (Thornhill) has studied in depth—males have two well-formulated strategies for mating. Either they offer the female a nuptial gift (a mass of hardened saliva they have produced, or a dead insect) or they chase a female and take her by force.

A remarkable feature of these scorpionflies is an appendage that seems specially designed for rape. Called the notal organ, it is a clamp on the top of the male's abdomen with which he can grab on to one of the female's forewings during mating, to prevent her escape. Besides rape, the notal organ does not appear to have any other function. For example, when the notal organs of males are experimentally covered with beeswax, to keep them from functioning, the males cannot rape. Such males still mate successfully, however, when they are allowed to present nuptial gifts to females. And other experiments have shown that the notal organ is not an adaptation for transferring sperm: in unforced mating, the organ contributes nothing to insemination.

Not surprisingly, females prefer voluntary mating to mating by force: they will approach a male bearing a nuptial gift and flee a male that does not have one. Intriguingly, however, the males, too, seem to prefer a consensual arrangement: they rape only when they cannot obtain a nuptial gift. Experiments have shown that when male scorpionflies possessing nuptial gifts are removed from an area, giftless males—typically, the wimpier ones that had failed in male-male competitions over prey—quickly shift from attempting rape to guarding a gift that has been left untended. That preference for consensual sex makes sense in evolutionary terms, because when females are willing, males are much more likely to achieve penetration and sperm transfer.

Human males obviously have no external organ specifically designed for rape. One must therefore look to the male psyche—to a potential mental rape organ—to discover any special-purpose adaptation of the human male to rape.

⋘◉⋙

Since women are choosy, men have been selected for finding a way to be chosen. One way to do that is to possess traits that women prefer: men with symmetrical body features are attractive to women, presumably because such features are a sign of health. A second way that men can gain access to women is by defeating other men in fights or other kinds of competitions—thereby gaining power, resources and social status, other qualities that women find attractive.

Rape can be understood as a third kind of sexual strategy: one more way to gain access to females. There are several mechanisms by which such a strategy could function. For example, men might resort to rape when they are socially disenfranchised, and thus unable to gain access to women through looks, wealth or status. Alternatively, men could have evolved to practice rape when the costs seem low—when, for instance, a woman is alone and unprotected (and thus retaliation seems unlikely), or when they have physical control over a woman (and so cannot be injured by her). Over evolutionary time, some men may have succeeded in passing on their genes through rape, thus perpetuating the behavior. It is also possible, however, that rape evolved not as a reproductive strategy in itself but merely as a side effect of other adaptations, such as the strong male sex drive and the male desire to mate with a variety of women.

Take, for instance, the fact that men are able to maintain sexual arousal and copulate with unwilling women. That ability invites inquiry, according to the psychologist Margo Wilson of McMaster University in Hamilton, Ontario, and her coworkers, because it is not a trait that is common to the males of all animal species. Its existence in human males could signal that they have evolved psychological mechanisms that specifically enable them to engage in forced copulation—in short, it could be a rape adaptation. But that is not the only plausible explanation. The psychologist Neil M. Malamuth of the University of California, Los Angeles, points out that the ability to copulate with unwilling women may be simply a by-product of men's "greater capacity for impersonal sex."

⋅⟨⊙⟩⋅

More research is needed to decide the question of whether rape is an adaptation or merely a by-product of other sexual adaptations. Both hypotheses are plausible: one of us (Thornhill) supports the former, whereas the other (Palmer) endorses the latter. Regardless of which hypothesis prevails, however, there is no doubt that rape has evolutionary—and thus genetic—origins. All traits and behaviors stem from a complex interplay between genes and the environment. If rape is an adaptation, men must possess genes that exist specifically because rape increased reproductive success. If rape turns out to be merely a side effect of other adaptations, then the genes involved exist for reasons that have nothing to do with rape. Either way, however, the evolutionary perspective explains a number of otherwise puzzling facts about the persistence of rape among human males.

For example, if rape is evolutionary in origin, it should be a threat mostly to women of childbearing age. And, in fact, young adult women are vastly overrepresented among rape victims in the female population as a whole, and female children and post-reproductive-age women are greatly underrepresented.

By the same token, if rape has persisted in the human population through the action of sexual selection, rapists should not seriously injure their victims—the rapist's reproductive success would be hampered, after all, if he killed his victim or inflicted so much harm that the potential pregnancy was compromised. Once again, the evolutionary logic seems to predict reality. Rapists seldom engage in gratuitous violence; instead, they usually limit themselves to the force required to subdue or control their victims. A survey by one of us (Palmer), of volunteers at rape crisis centers, found that only 15 percent of the victims whom the volunteers had encountered reported having been beaten in excess of what was needed to accomplish the rape. And in a 1979 study of 1,401 rape victims, a team led by the sociologist Thomas W. McCahill found that most of the victims reported being pushed or held, but that acts of gratuitous violence, such as beating, slapping or choking, were reported in only a minority of the rapes—22 percent or less. A very small number of rape victims are murdered: about .01 percent (that figure includes unreported as well as reported rapes). Even in those few cases, it may be that the murder takes place not because the rapist is motivated by a desire to kill, but because by removing the only witness to the crime he greatly increases his chance of escaping punishment.

⋅⟨⊙⟩⋅

Rape is more distressing for women than are other violent crimes, and evolutionary theory can help explain that as well. In recent years research on human unhappiness informed by evolutionary theory has developed substantial evidence about the functional role of psychological pain. Such pain is thought to be an adaptation that helps people guard against circumstances that reduce their reproductive success; it does so by spurring behavioral changes aimed at preventing future pain [see "What Good Is Feeling Bad?" by Randolph M. Nesse, *The Sciences*, November/December 1991]. Thus one would expect the greatest psychological pain to be associated with events that lower one's reproductive success, and, indeed, emotionally traumatic events such as the death of a relative, the loss of social status, desertion by one's mate and the trauma of being raped can all be interpreted as having that effect.

Rape reduces female reproductive success in several ways. For one thing, the victim may be injured. Moreover, if she becomes pregnant, she is deprived of her chance to choose the best father for her children. A rape may also cause a woman to lose the investment of her long-term partner, because it calls into question whether the child she later bears is really his. A variety of studies have shown that both men and women care more for their genetic offspring than for stepchildren.

One of us (Thornhill), in association with the anthropologist Nancy W. Thornhill, has conducted a series of studies on the factors that contribute to the emotional pain that women experience after a rape. Those studies confirmed that the more the rape interfered with the women's reproductive interests, the more pain they felt. The data, obtained from the Joseph J. Peters Institute in Philadelphia, came from interviews with 790 girls and women who had reported a sexual assault and who were subsequently examined at Philadelphia General

Hospital between 1973 and 1975. The subjects, who ranged in age from two months to eighty-eight years, were asked a variety of questions designed to evaluate their psychological responses to the rape. Among other things, they were asked about changes in their sleeping habits, in their feelings toward known and unknown men, in their sexual relations with their partners (children were not asked about sexual matters), and in their eating habits and social activities.

Analysis of the data showed that young women suffered greater distress after a rape than did children or women who were past reproductive age. That finding makes evolutionary sense, because it is young women who were at risk of being impregnated by an undesirable mate. Married women, moreover, were more traumatized than unmarried women, and they were more likely to feel that their future had been harmed by the rape. That, too, makes evolutionary sense, because the doubt a rape sows about paternity can lead a long-term mate to withdraw his support.

Among the women in the study, psychological pain rose inversely to the violence of the attack. In other words, when the rapist exerted less force, the victim was more upset afterward. Those findings, surprising at first, make sense in the evolutionary context: a victim who exhibits physical evidence that sexual access was forced may have less difficulty convincing her husband or boyfriend that what took place was rape rather than consensual sex. In evolutionary terms, such evidence would be reassuring to a pair-bonded male, because rape is a one-time event, whereas consensual sex with other partners is likely to be frequent, and thus more threatening to paternity.

Finally, women of reproductive age reported more emotional distress when the assault involved sexual intercourse than when it involved other kinds of sexual behavior. Among young girls and older women, however, penile-vaginal intercourse was no more upsetting than other kinds of assaults. Again, the possibility of an unwanted pregnancy may be a key factor in the degree of trauma the victim experiences.

For all those reasons, the psychological pain that rape victims suffer appears to be an evolved defense against rape. The human females who outreproduced others—and thus became our ancestors—were people who were highly distressed about rape. Their distress presumably served their interests by motivating them to identify the circumstances that resulted in the rape, assess the problems the rape caused, and act to avoid rapes in the future.

❧

If women today are to protect themselves from rape, and men are to desist from it, people must be given advice that is based on knowledge. Insisting that rape is not about sex misinforms both men and women about the motivations behind rape—a dangerous error that not only hinders prevention efforts but may actually *increase* the incidence of rape.

What we envision is an evolutionarily informed program for young men that teaches them to restrain their sexual behavior. Completion of such a course might be required, say, before a young man is granted a driver's license. The program might start by inducing the young men to acknowledge the power of their sexual impulses, and then explaining why human males have evolved in that way. The young men should learn that past Darwinian selection is the reason that a man can get an erection just by looking at a photo of a naked woman, why he may be tempted to demand sex even if he knows that his date truly doesn't want it, and why he may mistake a woman's friendly comment or tight blouse as an invitation to sex. Most of all, the program should stress that a man's evolved sexual desires offer him no excuse whatsoever for raping a woman, and that if he understands and resists those desires, he may be able to prevent their manifestation in sexually coercive behavior. The criminal penalties for rape should also be discussed in detail.

Young women also need a new kind of education. For example, in today's rape-prevention handbooks, women are often told that sexual attractiveness does not influence rapists. That is emphatically not true. Because a woman is considered most attractive when her fertility is at its peak, from her midteens through her twenties, tactics that focus on protecting women in those age groups will be most effective in reducing the overall frequency of rape.

Young women should be informed that, during the evolution of human sexuality, the existence of female choice has favored men who are quickly aroused by signals of a female's willingness to grant sexual access. Furthermore, women need to realize that, because selection favored males who had many mates, men tend to read signals of acceptance into a woman's actions even when no such signals are intended.

❦

In spite of protestations to the contrary, women should also be advised that the way they dress can put them at risk. In the past, most discussions of female appearance in the context of rape have, entirely unfairly, asserted that a victim's dress and behavior should affect the degree of punishment meted out to the rapist: thus if the victim was dressed provocatively, she "had it coming to her"—and the rapist would get off lightly. But current attempts to avoid blaming the victim have led to false propaganda that dress and behavior have little or no influence on a woman's chances of being raped. As a consequence, important knowledge about how to avoid dangerous circumstances is often suppressed. Surely the point that no woman's behavior gives a man the right to rape her can be made without encouraging women to overlook the role they themselves may be playing in compromising their safety.

Until relatively recently in Europe and the United States, strict social taboos kept young men and women from spending unsupervised time together, and in many other countries young women are still kept cloistered away from men. Such physical barriers are understandably abhorrent to many people, since they greatly limit the freedom of women. But the toppling of those barriers in modern Western countries raises problems of its own. The common practice of unsupervised dating in cars and private homes, which is often accompanied by the consumption of alcohol, has placed young women in environments that are conducive to rape to an extent that is probably unparalleled in history. After studying the data on the risk factors for rape, the sex investigators Elizabeth R. Allgeier and Albert R. Allgeier, both of Bowling Green State University in Ohio, recommended that men and women interact only in public places during the early stages of their relationships—or, at least, that women exert more control than they generally do over the circumstances in which they consent to be alone with men.

⁊◉⁊

An evolutionary perspective on rape might not only help prevent rapes but also lead to more effective counseling for rape victims. A therapy program explaining that men rape because they collectively want to dominate women will not help a victim understand why her attacker appeared to be sexually motivated, why she can no longer concentrate enough to conduct her life effectively, or why her husband or boyfriend may view the attack as an instance of infidelity. In addition, men who are made aware of the evolutionary reasons for their suspicions about their wives' or girlfriends' claims of rape should be in a better position to change their reactions to such claims.

Unlike many other contentious social issues, such as abortion and homosexual rights, everyone has the same goal regarding rape: to end it. Evolutionary biology provides clear information that society can use to achieve that goal. Social science, by contrast, promotes erroneous solutions, because it fails to recognize that Darwinian selection has shaped not only human bodies but human psychology, learning patterns and behavior as well. The fact is that men, relative to women, are more aggressive, sexually assertive and eager to copulate, and less discriminating about mates—traits that contribute to the existence of rape. When social scientists mistakenly assert that socialization alone causes those gender differences, they ignore the fact that the same differences also exist in all the other animal species in which males offer less parental investment than females and compete for access to females.

In addressing the question of rape, the choice between the politically constructed answers of social science and the evidentiary answers of evolutionary biology is essentially a choice between ideology and knowledge. As scientists who would like to see rape eradicated from human life, we sincerely hope that truth will prevail.

Women Fight Back

To a woman the definition of rape is fairly simple. A sexual invasion of the body by force, an incursion into the private, personal inner space without consent—in short, an internal assault from one of several avenues and by one of several methods—constitutes a deliberate violation of emotional, physical and rational integrity and is a hostile, degrading act of violence that deserves the name of rape.

Yet by tracing man's concept of rape as he defined it in his earliest laws, we now know with certainty that the criminal act he viewed with horror, and the deadly punishments he saw fit to apply, had little to do with an actual act of sexual violence that a woman's body might sustain. . . .

Man's historic desire to maintain sole, total and complete access to woman's vagina, as codified by his earliest laws of marriage, sprang from his need to be the sole physical instrument governing impregnation, progeny and inheritance rights. As man understood his male reality, it was perfectly lawful to capture and rape some other tribe's women, for what better way for his own tribe to increase? But it was unlawful, he felt, for the insult to be returned. The criminal act he viewed with horror and punished as rape was not sexual assault *per se,* but an act of unlawful possession, a trespass against his tribal right to control vaginal access to all women who belonged to him and his kin.

Since marriage, by law, was consummated in one manner only, by defloration of virginity with attendant ceremonial tokens, the act man came to construe as criminal rape was the illegal destruction of virginity outside a marriage contract of his making. Later, when he came to see his own definition as too narrow for the times, he broadened his criminal concept to cover the ruination of his wife's chastity as well, thus extending the law's concern to nonvirgins too. Although these legal origins have been buried in the morass of forgotten history, as the laws of rape continued to evolve they never shook free of their initial concept—that the violation was first and foremost a violation of *male* rights of possession, based on *male* requirements of virginity, chastity and consent to private access as the female bargain in the marriage contract (the underpinnings, as he enforced them, of man's economic estate).

To our modern way of thinking, these theoretical origins are peculiar and difficult to fully grasp. A huge disparity in thought—male logic versus female logic—affects perception of rape to this very day, confounding the analytic processes of some of the best legal minds. Today's young rapist has no thought of capturing a wife or securing an inheritance or estate. His is an act of impermanent conquest, not a practical approach to ownership and control. The economic advantage of rape is a forgotten concept. What remains is the basic male-female struggle, a hit-and-run attack, a brief expression of physical power, a conscious process of intimidation, a blunt, ugly sexual invasion with possible lasting psychological effects on all women.

When rape is placed where it truly belongs, within the context of modern criminal violence and not within the purview of ancient masculine codes, the crime retains its unique dimensions, falling midway between robbery and assault. It is, in one act, both a blow to the body and a blow to the mind, and a "taking" of sex through the use or threat of force. Yet the differences between rape and an assault or a robbery are as distinctive as the obvious similarities. In a prosecutable case of assault, bodily damage to the victim is clearly evident. In a case of rape, the threat of force does not secure a tangible commodity as we understand the term, although sex traditionally has been viewed by men as "the female treasure"; more precisely, in rape the threat of force obtains a highly valued sexual service through temporary access to the victim's intimate parts, and the intent is not merely to "take," but to humiliate and degrade.

This, then, is the modern reality of rape as it is defined by twentieth-century practice. It is not, however, the reality of rape as it is defined by twentieth-century law. . . .

Since the beginning of written history, criminal rape has been bound up with the common law of consent in marriage, and it is time, once and for all, to make a clean break. A sexual assault is an invasion of bodily integrity and a violation of freedom and self-determination wherever it happens to take place, in or out of the marriage bed. I recognize that it is easier to write these words than to draw up a workable legal provision, and I recognize the difficulties that juries will have in their deliberations when faced with a wife who accuses her husband of forcing her into copulation against her will, but the principle of bodily self-determination must be established without qualification, I think, if it is to become an inviolable principle on any level. . . .

In a sexual assault physical harm is much more than a threat; it is a reality because violence is an integral part of the act. Body contact and physical intrusion are the purpose of the crime, not appropriation of a physically detached and removable item like money. Yet the nature of the crime as it is practiced does bear robbery a close resemblance, because the sexual goal for the rapist resembles the monetary goal of the robber (often both goals are accomplished during the course of one confrontation if the victim is a woman), and so, in a sex crime, a bargain between offender and victim may also be struck. In this respect, a sexual assault is closer in victim response to a robbery than it is to a simple case of assault, for an assaultive event may not have a specific goal beyond the physical contest, and furthermore, people who find themselves in an assaultive situation usually defend themselves by fighting back.

Under the rules of law, victims of robbery and assault are not required to prove they resisted, or that they didn't consent, or that the act was accomplished with sufficient force, or sufficient threat of force, to overcome their will, because the law presumes it highly unlikely that a person willingly gives away money, except to a charity or to a favorite cause, and the law presumes that no person willingly submits to a brutal beating and the infliction of bodily harm and permanent damage. But victims of rape and other forms of sexual assault do need to prove these evidentiary requirements—that they resisted, that they didn't consent, that their will was overcome by overwhelming force and fear—because the law has never been able to satisfactorily distinguish an act of mutually desired sexual union from an act of forced, criminal sexual aggression.

Admittedly, part of the law's confusion springs from the normal, biologic, male procedural activity in an act of *unforced* copulation, but insertion of the penis (a descriptive phrase less semantically loaded than penetration, I think) is not in itself, despite what many men think, an act of male dominance. The real reason for the law's everlasting confusion as to what constitutes an act of rape and what constitutes an act of mutual intercourse is the underlying cultural assumption that it is the natural masculine role to proceed aggressively toward the stated goal, while the natural feminine role is to "resist" or "submit." And so to protect male interests, the law seeks to gauge the victim's behavior during the offending act in the belief that force or the threat of force is not conclusive *in and of itself.*

According to Menachem Amir's study, the assailant actually displays a dangerous weapon in no more than one-fifth of all police-founded cases of rape. Clearly, these are the cases a jury would most likely believe. But most rapes are not accomplished by means of a knife, a gun, a lead pipe or whatever. The force that is employed more often consists of an initial stranglehold, manhandling, beating, shoving, tearing at clothes, a verbal threat of death or disfigurement, the sheer physical presence of two, three, four, five assailants, etc. Without doubt, any of these circumstances can and does produce immobilizing terror in a victim, terror sufficient to render her incapable of resistance or to make her believe that resistance would be futile. . . .

The theory of aggressive male domination over women as a natural right is so deeply embedded in our cultural value system that all recent attempts to expose it—in movies, television commercials or even in children's textbooks—have barely managed to scratch the surface. As I see it, the problem is not that polarized role playing (man as doer; woman as bystander) and exaggerated portrayals of the female body as passive sex object are simply "demeaning" to women's dignity and self-conception, or that such portrayals fail to provide positive role models for young girls, but that cultural sexism is a conscious form of female degradation designed to boost the male ego by offering "proof" of his native superiority (and of female inferiority) everywhere he looks. . . .

Once we accept as basic truth that rape is not a crime of irrational, impulsive, uncontrollable lust, but is a deliberate, hostile, violent act of degradation and possession on the part of a would-be conqueror, designed to intimidate and inspire fear, we must look toward those elements in our culture that promote and propagandize these attitudes, which offer men, and in particular, impressionable, adolescent males, who form the potential raping population, the ideology and psychologic encouragement to commit their acts of aggression *without awareness, for the most part, that they have committed a punishable crime,* let alone a moral wrong. The myth of the heroic rapist that permeates false notions of masculinity, from the successful seducer to the man who "takes what he wants when he wants it," is inculcated in young boys from the time they first become aware that being a male means access to certain mysterious rites and privileges, including the right to buy a woman's body. When young men learn that females may be bought for a price, and that acts of sex command set prices, then how should they not also conclude that that which may be bought may also be taken without the civility of a monetary exchange?

That there *might* be a connection between prostitution and rape is certainly not a new idea. Operating from the old (and discredited) lust, drive and relief theory, men have occasionally put forward the notion that the way to control criminal rape is to ensure the ready accessibility of female bodies at a reasonable price through the legalization of prostitution, so that the male impulse might be satisfied with ease, efficiency and a minimum of bother. . . . To my mind the experience of the American military in Vietnam, where brothels for GI's were officially sanctioned, even incorporated into the base-camp recreation areas, should prove conclusively that the availability of sex for a small price is no deterrent to the decision to rape, any more than the availability of a base-camp shooting range is a deterrent to the killing of unarmed civilians and children.

But my horror at the idea of legalized prostitution is not that it doesn't work as a rape deterrent, but that it institutionalizes the concept that it is man's monetary right, if not his divine right, to gain access to the female body, and that sex is a female service that should not be denied the civilized male. Perpetuation of the concept that the "powerful male impulse" must be satisfied with immediacy by a cooperative class of women, set aside and expressly licensed for this purpose, is part and parcel of the mass psychology of rape. Indeed, until the day is reached when prostitution is totally eliminated (a millennium that will not arrive until men, who create the demand, and not women who supply it, are fully prosecuted under the law), the false perception of sexual access as an adjunct of male power and privilege will continue to fuel the rapist mentality.

Pornography has been so thickly glossed over with the patina of chic these days in the name of verbal freedom and sophistication that important distinctions between freedom of political expression (a democratic necessity), honest sex education for children (a societal good) and ugly smut (the deliberate devaluation of the role of women through obscene, distorted depictions) have been hopelessly confused. . . .

[H]ard-core pornography is not a celebration of sexual freedom; it is a cynical exploitation of female sexual activity through the device of making all such activity, and consequently all females, "dirty." . . .

The gut distaste that a majority of women feel when we look at pornography, a distaste that, incredibly, it is no longer fashionable to admit, comes, I think, from the gut knowledge that we and our bodies are being stripped, exposed and contorted for the purpose of ridicule to bolster that "masculine esteem" which gets its kick and sense of power from viewing females as anonymous, panting playthings, adult toys, dehumanized objects to be used, abused, broken and discarded. . . .

There can be no "equality" in porn, no female equivalent, no turning of the tables in the name of bawdy fun. Pornography, like rape, is a male invention, designed to dehumanize women, to reduce the female to an object of sexual access, not to free sensuality from moralistic or parental inhibition. The staple of porn will always be the naked female body, breasts and genitals exposed, because as man devised it, her naked body is the female's "shame," her private parts the private property of man, while his are the ancient, holy, universal, patriarchal instrument of his power, his rule by force over *her*.

Pornography is the undiluted essence of anti-female propaganda. Yet the very same liberals who were so quick to understand the method and purpose behind the mighty propaganda machine of Hitler's Third Reich, the consciously spewed-out anti-Semitic caricatures and obscenities that gave an ideological base to the Holocaust and the Final Solution, the very same liberals who, enlightened by blacks, searched their own conscience and came to understand that their tolerance of "nigger" jokes and portrayals of shuffling, rolling-eyed servants in movies perpetuated the degrading myths of black inferiority and gave an ideological base to the continuation of black oppression—these very same liberals now fervidly maintain that the hatred and contempt for women that find expression in four-letter words used as expletives and in what are quaintly called "adult" or "erotic" books and movies are a valid extension of freedom of speech that must be preserved as a Constitutional right.

. . . The majority report of the President's Commission on Obscenity and Pornography tried to pooh-pooh the opinion of law enforcement agencies around the country that claimed their own concrete experience with offenders who were caught with the stuff led them to conclude that pornographic material is a causative factor in crimes of sexual violence. The commission maintained that it was not possible at this time to scientifically prove or disprove such a connection.

But does one need scientific methodology in order to conclude that the anti-female propaganda that permeates our nation's cultural output promotes a climate in which acts of sexual hostility directed against women are not only tolerated but ideologically encouraged? A similar debate has raged for many years over whether or not the extensive glorification of violence (the gangster as hero; the loving treatment accorded bloody shoot-'em-ups in movies, books and on TV) has a causal effect, a direct relationship to the rising rate of crime, particularly among youth. Interestingly enough, in this area—nonsexual and not specifically related to abuses against women—public opinion seems to be swinging to the position that explicit violence in the entertainment media does have a deleterious effect; it makes violence commonplace, numbingly routine and no longer morally shocking. . . .

Men are not unmindful of the rape problem. To the contrary, their paternalistic codes reserved the harshest penalties for a violation of their property. But given an approach to rape that saw the crime as an illegal encroachment by an unlicensed intruder, a stranger come into their midst, the advice they gave (and still try to give) was all of one piece: a set of rules and regulations designed to keep their property penned in, much as a sheep-herder might try to keep his flock protected from an outlaw rustler by taking precautions against their straying too far from the fold. By seeing the rapist always as a stranger, never as one of their own, and by viewing the female as a careless, dumb creature with an unfortunate tendency to stray, they exhorted, admonished and warned the female to hide herself from male eyes as much as possible. In short, they told her not to claim the privileges they reserved for themselves. Such advice—well intentioned, solicitous and genu-inely concerned—succeeded only in further aggravating the problem, for the message they gave was to live a life of fear, and to it they appended the dire warning that the woman who did not follow the rules must be held responsible for her own violation.

Clinton Duffy, the famous warden of San Quentin, couldn't understand why women didn't imprison themselves under maximum security conditions for their own protection. He wrote, "Many break the most elementary rules of caution every day. The particularly flagrant violators, those who go to bar-rooms alone, or accept pickups from strangers, or wear unusually tight sweat-ers and skirts, or make a habit of teasing, become rape bait by their actions alone. When it happens they have nobody to blame but themselves." . . .

A fairly decent article on rape in the March, 1974, issue of *The Reader's Digest* was written by two men who felt obliged to warn,

> Don't broadcast the fact that you live alone or with another woman. List only your last name and initial on the mailbox and in the phone book. Before entering your car, check to see if anyone is hiding on the rear seat or on the rear floor. If you're alone in a car, keep the doors locked and the windows rolled up. If you think someone is following you . . . do not go directly home if there is no adult male there. Possible weapons are a hat-pin, corkscrew, pen, keys, umbrella. If no weapons are available, fight back physically only if you feel you can do so with telling effect.

What immediately pops into mind after reading the advice of Warden Duffy and *The Reader's Digest* is the old-time stand-up comedian's favorite fig-ure of ridicule, the hysterical old maid armed with hatpin and umbrella who looks under the bed each night before retiring. Long a laughable stereotype of sexual repression, it now appears that the crazy old lady was a pioneer of sound mind after all.

But the negative value of this sort of advice, I'm afraid, far outweighs the positive. What it tells us, implicitly and explicitly, is:

1. A woman alone probably won't be able to defend herself. Another woman who might possibly come to her aid will be of no use whatsoever.

2. Despite the fact that it is men who are the rapists, a woman's ultimate security lies in being accompanied by men at all times.
3. A woman who claims to value her sexual integrity cannot expect the same amount of freedom and independence that men routinely enjoy. Even a small pleasure like taking a spin in an automobile with the windows open is dangerous, reckless behavior.
4. In the exercise of rational caution, a woman should engage in an amazing amount of pretense. She should pretend she has a male protector even if she hasn't. She should deny or obscure her personal identity, life-style and independence, and function on a sustained level of suspicion that approaches a clinical definition of paranoia.

Of course I think all people, female and male, child and adult, must be alert and on guard against the warning signs of criminal violence and should take care in potentially hazardous situations, such as a dark, unfamiliar street at night, or an unexpected knock on the door, but to impose a special burden of caution on women is no solution at all. There can be no private solutions to the problem of rape. A woman who follows this sort of special cautionary advice to the letter and thinks she is acting in society's interest—or even in her own personal interest—is deluding herself rather sadly. While the risk to one potential victim might be slightly diminished (and I even doubt this, since I have known of nuns who were raped within walled convents), not only does the number of potential rapists on the loose remain constant, but the ultimate effect of rape upon the woman's mental and emotional health has been accomplished *even without the act.* For to accept a special burden of self-protection is to reinforce the concept that women must live and move about in fear and can never expect to achieve the personal freedom, independence and self-assurance of men.

That's what rape is all about, isn't it? And a possible deep-down reason why even the best of our concerned, well-meaning men run to stereotypic warnings when they seek to grapple with the problem of rape deterrence is that they *prefer* to see rape as a woman's problem, rather than a societal problem resulting from a distorted masculine philosophy of aggression. For when men raise the spectre of the unknown rapist, they refuse to take psychologic responsibility for the nature of his act. . . .

Unthinkingly cruel, because it is deceptive, is the confidential advice given from men to women (it appears in *The Reader's Digest* article), or even from women to women in some feminist literature, that a sharp kick to the groin or a thumb in the eye will work miracles. Such advice is often accompanied by a diagram in which the vulnerable points of the human anatomy are clearly marked—as if the mere knowledge of these pressure spots can translate itself into devastating action. It is true that this knowledge has been deliberately obscured or withheld from us in the past, but mere knowledge is not enough. What women need is systematic training in self-defense that begins in childhood, so that the inhibition resulting from the prohibition may be overcome.

It would be decidedly less than honest if at this juncture I did not admit that my researches for [my] book included a three-month training program in jujitsu and karate, three nights a week, two and a half hours a night. . . . I learned I had natural weapons that I didn't know I possessed, like elbows and knees. I learned how to kick backward as well as forward. I learned how to fight dirty, and I learned that I loved it.

Most surprising to me, I think, was the recognition that these basic aggressive movements, the sudden twists, jabs and punches that were so foreign to my experience and ladylike existence, were the stuff that all little boys grow up learning, that boy kids are applauded for mastering while girl kids are put in fresh white pinafores and patent-leather. Mary Janes and told not to muss them up. And did that early difference in rearing ever raise its draconic head! At the start of our lessons our Japanese instructor freely invited all the women in the class, one by one, to punch him in the chest. It was not a foolhardy invitation, for we discovered that the inhibition against hitting was so strong in each of us that on the first try none of us could make physical contact. Indeed, the inhibition against striking out proved to be a greater hindrance to our becoming fighting women than our pathetic underdeveloped muscles. (Improvement in both departments was amazingly swift.)

Not surprisingly, the men in our class did not share our inhibitions in the slightest. Aggressive physical grappling was part of their heritage, not ours. And yet, and yet . . . we women discovered in wonderment that as we learned to place our kicks and jabs with precision we were actually able to inspire fear in the men. We *could* hurt them, we learned to our astonishment, and hurt them hard at the core of their sexual being—if we broke that Biblical injunction.

Is it possible that there is some sort of metaphysical justice in the anatomical fact that the male sex organ, which has been misused from time immemorial as a weapon of terror against women, should have at its root an awkward place of painful vulnerability? Acutely conscious of their susceptibility to damage, men have protected their testicles throughout history with armor, supports and forbidding codes of "clean," above-the-belt fighting. A gentleman's agreement is understandable—among gentlemen. When women are threatened, as I learned in my self-defense class, "Kick him in the balls, it's your best maneuver." How strange it was to hear for the first time in my life that women could fight back, *should* fight back and make full use of a natural advantage; that it is *in our interest* to know how to do it. How strange it was to understand with the full force of unexpected revelation that male allusions to psychological defeat, particularly at the hands of a woman, were couched in phrases like emasculation, castration and ball-breaking because of that very special physical vulnerability.

Fighting back. On a multiplicity of levels, that is the activity we must engage in, together, if we—women—are to redress the imbalance and rid ourselves and men of the ideology of rape.

Rape can be eradicated, not merely controlled or avoided on an individual basis, but the approach must be long-range and cooperative, and must have the understanding and good will of many men as well as women.

CHALLENGE QUESTIONS

Does Evolution Explain Why Men Rape?

1. Some view the arguments of Thornhill and Palmer as steps toward excusing men who rape by explaining their behavior as biologically determined. What are some of the social costs and benefits of such dialogue?
2. The theory proposed by Thornhill and Palmer is quite speculative. How might a researcher go about studying the validity of their argument?
3. For three decades Brownmiller has kept rape in the consciousness of society. What impact has the work of Brownmiller and other feminist theorists had on societal attitudes about rape?
4. The phenomenon of "acquaintance rape" has been surrounded by legal controversy in recent years. How would Thornhill and Palmer view the behavior of men who initiate unwanted sexual activity with women in a casual or dating context? How would Brownmiller view such behavior?
5. Imagine that you are a clinician treating a man who has raped women. Based on the arguments of Thornhill/Palmer and Brownmiller, how would you go about trying to understand this man's behavior and treating him psychotherapeutically?

Suggested Readings

Koss, M. P. (2000, April). Evolutionary models of why men rape: Acknowledging the complexities. *Trauma, Violence, and Abuse: A Review Journal.*

Koss, M. P., Goodman, L., Browne, A., Fitzgerald, L., Keita, G. P., & Russo, N. F. (1994). *No safe haven: Violence against women at home, work, and in the community.* Washington, DC: American Psychological Association Press.

Low, B. (1999). *Why sex matters: A Darwinian look at human behavior.* Princeton, NJ: Princeton University Press.

Raine, N. V. (1998). *After silence: Rape and my journey back.* New York: Crown Publishers.

Russell, D. (1994). *Against pornography: The evidence of harm.* Berkeley, CA: Russell Publications.

Thornhill, R., & Palmer, C. T. (2000). *A natural history of rape: Biological bases of sexual coercion.* Cambridge, MA: MIT Press.

ISSUE 18

Should Mental Health Professionals Serve as Gatekeepers for Physician-Assisted Suicide?

YES: Rhea K. Farberman, from "Terminal Illness and Hastened Death Requests: The Important Role of the Mental Health Professional," *Professional Psychology: Research and Practice* (vol. 28, no. 6, 1997)

NO: Mark D. Sullivan, Linda Ganzini, and Stuart J. Youngner, from "Should Psychiatrists Serve as Gatekeepers for Physician-Assisted Suicide?" *The Hastings Center Report* (July–August 1998)

ISSUE SUMMARY

YES: Rhea K. Farberman, director of public communications for the American Psychological Association, makes the case that mental health professionals should be called upon to assess terminally ill people who request hastened death in order to ensure that decision making is rational and free of coercion.

NO: Psychiatrists Mark D. Sullivan, Linda Ganzini, and Stuart J. Youngner argue that the reliance on mental health professionals to be suicide gatekeepers involves an inappropriate use of clinical procedures to disguise society's ambivalence about suicide itself.

Most mental health professionals are drawn to their careers out of a desire to help people live happier and healthier lives. Few ever give a thought to the possibility that they might be called upon to help people take their own lives. In recent decades, however, increasing attention has been given to the legal and ethical right of an individual to choose suicide, particularly in cases in which the person has a terminal disease. Michigan physician Jack Kevorkian brought the issue into public awareness because he facilitated the deaths of dozens of seriously ill individuals throughout the 1990s.

The professional assessment of seriously ill individuals wanting to commit suicide is complex primarily because it is difficult to determine the extent to which profound depression about being sick propels these individuals to make impulsive decisions. As Americans have grown increasingly accepting of the right of seriously ill people to take their own lives, they have also turned more and more to mental health professionals to play a role in this process. Mental health professionals have been called upon to help protect the sick person's rights, provide support to loved ones, and evaluate whether or not the sick person has the capacity to make a rational decision.

In the following selection, Rhea K. Farberman argues that a mental health assessment by a qualified mental health professional is imperative for any ill person requesting a hastened death. She contends that the professional should first work to separate clinical depression from the patient's grief, fear of dying, fear of the unknown, and fear of pain. Farberman urges professionals to put aside their personal beliefs on the issue and to strive to ensure that the patient's decision-making process is rational, well reasoned, and free of coercion.

Taking a much more cautious stand on the issue, Mark D. Sullivan, Linda Ganzini, and Stuart J. Youngner argue in the second selection that the reliance on mental health professionals to be suicide gatekeepers is associated with an inappropriate use of clinical procedures to disguise society's ambivalence about suicide itself. They assert that society is shifting responsibility for a troubling moral decision to an outside specialist, rather than relying on shared decision making involving the patient, family, and physician. Sullivan, Ganzini, and Youngner offer several points of caution about using mental health professionals in this context.

POINT

- A mental health assessment by a qualified mental health professional is imperative for any ill person requesting a hastened death.
- A mental health professional helps to evaluate if the patient has the capacity to make a rational decision about dying.

- In light of extensive clinical and research experience, psychologists and other mental health professionals are an underused resource when patients and their significant others are forced to deal with end-of-life care issues.
- Competent mental health professionals recognize the importance of basing recommendations on data derived from several sources, including the involvement of significant others and family members.

COUNTERPOINT

- Mental health professionals should not have the social authority to use themselves as the measure of when it is the right time for a person to die.
- The determination of adequate decision-making capacity is difficult because competence is a complex social, rather than scientific, construct.
- The relevant expertise in this area is limited in light of the fact that so few mental health professionals regularly work with seriously ill and dying patients in hospital, nursing home, and hospice settings.
- There is a risk that, in the absence of robust independent standards, mental health professionals may resolve the ethical dilemmas concerning physician-assisted suicide in an ad hoc fashion, using themselves as the "reasonable person" standard by which to judge the patient's decision to die.

YES ⤺   Rhea K. Farberman

Terminal Illness and Hastened Death Requests

Do terminally ill individuals have the right to decide the timing of their death and to have assistance in a hastened death? This article is based on an American Psychological Association briefing paper prepared for the media regarding the June 1997 Supreme Court decision on physician-assisted suicide. The Court's decision clarified the role medical doctors can play in caring for the terminally ill, but the role of mental health professionals is still evolving. It is clear, however, that on the basis of behavioral research and clinical experience, a mental health assessment by a qualified mental health professional is imperative for any ill person requesting a hastened death.

Becoming ill is unfortunately a part of living. The number of terminally ill persons who decide to hasten their death is difficult to define and estimate, but several recent studies have found a fairly large number of requests for assistance in dying as well as a high rate of acquiescence to these requests by physicians. In addition, public opinion polls consistently show that at least 60% of those surveyed are in favor of physician-assisted suicide for terminally ill patients.

New technologies have given health care professionals more effective ways to treat and retard serious illness and therefore sustain life. We can all agree that this medical progress has lengthened life and changed the end-of-life process. However, there is disagreement as to whether this progress is beneficial for the patient. Has the end-of-life process been changed in a way that is harmful to human dignity and self-determination? Or, is every day worth living regardless of the quality of that existence? These are complex questions that involve our fundamental values about life and liberty. They elude easy answers.

In June 1997, the U.S. Supreme Court ruled that terminally ill people do *not* have a constitutional right to doctor-assisted suicide, but the Court gave states the option of enacting their own assistance-in-dying statutes (*Vacco v. Quill,* 96-10, 1997; *Washington v. Glucksberg,* 95-1858, 1997). The Court's decision lent some greater clarity to the role that medical doctors can play in providing care and comfort to the terminally ill; still evolving, however, is the role of the mental health professional in working with terminally ill people. What is

From *Professional Psychology: Research and Practice,* vol. 28, no. 6, 1997, pp. 544–547. Copyright © 1997 by American Psychological Association. Reprinted by permission.

clear is that there is still much controversy and difference of opinion about the end-of-life process and, therefore, end-of-life care. Further court challenges about the right of dying people are likely. Because of this uncertainty, it is altogether likely that medical teams and families will still have to deal with hastened death requests from dying patients.

There are several concerns about such a request for a hastened death from a terminally ill person. One such concern is that depression and suicidal thoughts in seriously ill people are common. A 1994 study found that the prevalence rates for both major and minor depression among terminally ill cancer patients receiving palliative (relief of pain and discomfort) care ranged from 13% to 26%. At the same time, the capacity of physicians untrained in psychiatry to diagnose depression is alarmingly low. On the basis of numerous studies, it is estimated that depression is correctly diagnosed by physicians in only 20% to 60% of the cases presented. It is important to remember that the reasoning on which a terminally ill person (whose judgments are not impaired by mental disorders) bases a decision to end his or her life is fundamentally different from the reasoning a clinically depressed person uses to justify suicide.

Depression in Seriously Ill People

Although many people consider depression normal in a seriously ill person, depression is a diagnoseable illness and is highly treatable. The first task of a mental health professional when dealing with a terminally ill person is to separate the patient's prospective grief, fear of dying, fear of the unknown, and fear of pain from clinical depression.

It is often assumed, but not correctly so, that the most pain-ridden, physically distressed terminally ill patients are more likely to become depressed or suicidal when compared to other less afflicted patients. In reality, a person's lifelong values, temperament, and behavior are often better indicators of who is at risk for suicide thoughts when ill. In fact, the importance of terminal illness, physical decline, or chronic pain as a reason for suicide has been seriously questioned by the behavioral science research on end-of-life decisions.

Ill people and elderly people are often concerned about becoming a burden to their families. Some research has in fact shown that control, quality of life, and loss of independence are weightier issues for terminally ill patients than is actual pain. However, pain lessens the patient's ability to do things for him or herself, which in turn adds to the patient's concern about the loss of independence and about burdening loved ones.

In short, there is no simple formula explaining what motivates an ill person to want to end his or her life. Most research points to multiple causes, including anxiety, fear, desire for control and dignity, a lack of information or an inability to get questions answered, depression, and cognitive losses. Although pain management is at times a problem for terminally ill patients (research shows that terminal cancer patients are particularly at risk for insufficient pain control), pain, in and of itself, is not the single most important factor in suicide ideation. Much of this research suggests that what is needed for the terminally ill patient is improved palliative care and more psychosocial support at the end of his or her life.

The Role of Mental Health Professionals in End-of-Life Decisions

In the absence of mental illness, a terminally ill person can be capable of rational thinking and an informed choice. However, separating sadness brought on by the loss of ability and the loss of the persona the patient once was from clinical depression brought on by a mental disorder is a complex clinical judgment. One critical factor is the patient's self-esteem. The self-esteem of a person who is grieving or is terminally ill is not affected by the illness; however, the self-esteem of a clinically depressed person is.

Attempting to determine to what degree, if any, a terminally ill person is experiencing depression or other cognitive impairments is extremely difficult. The mental health professional who is called on to make such an evaluation should have specific training and clinical experience working with that population group, be it elderly persons, cancer patients, AIDS patients, and so forth.

Today, psychologists and other mental health professionals are an underused resource when patients and their significant others are forced to deal with end-of-life care issues. Psychologists not only have clinical experience on this issue, but also have conducted much of the research from which we have learned a great deal about depression, the diagnosis of depressive illness, patients' coping with end of life, and support of significant others during the end-of-life process.

Some health professionals who work in hospitals and hospice settings say that in reality, hastened death is already a relatively common occurrence—the opening of the morphine drip to allow for a lethal dose of the pain killer, for example. The role of the psychologist working with a terminally ill patient who wishes to end his or her life is not to control the patient's decision but to attempt to ensure that the patient's decision-making process is rational, well-reasoned, and free of coercion.

Mental health professionals who work in this area must approach their work in a neutral manner. Their personal beliefs on the issue should not influence the process. The role of the mental health professional is (a) to attempt to ensure that the end-of-life decision-making process includes a complete assessment of the patient's ability to make a rational judgment and (b) to help protect the patient's right to self-determination. The mental health professional attempts to bring the pertinent issues to the patient and his or her family and significant others and to assist the patient and significant others in understanding and working through those issues.

The American Psychological Association (APA) does not advocate for or against assisted suicide. What psychologists do support is high-quality end-of-life care and informed end-of-life decisions that are based on the correct assessment of the patient's mental capacity, social support systems, and degree of self-determination.

Surveys of mental health professionals have found that most (as high as 81% in the case of a survey of members of APA's Division of Psychotherapy) believe that assisted suicide *can be* a rational choice within the following parameters: (a) The patient is acting under his or her own free will, (b) the patient is competent to make an informed and reasonable judgment, (c) the patient's physical condition is hopeless, and (d) the patient is under no outside pressure (financial pressure, pressure from family, and so forth) to make the choice.

The Psychologist's Role

In helping terminally ill patients make end-of-life decisions, psychologists should do the following:

1. Protect the client's rights.
2. Support the family.
3. Don't allow physicians to affix a mental illness diagnosis if it is inappropriate.
4. Help evaluate if the patient has the capacity to make a rational decision, that is, does not have a mental disorder that significantly impairs his or her ability to reason, is fully informed of all treatment options, understands all treatment options, is not being coerced, and is using a rational, reasoned process to reach his or her decision.

Early referral of a terminally ill patient to a mental health professional can help prevent premature deterioration in the quality of life for the patient and allows for the teaching of coping skills to both the patient and his or her family. In addition, research has shown that psychological interventions with both cardiac and cancer patients can help in the recovery process by strengthening medical compliance and by helping the patient make healthful lifestyle choices. Another reason for having a mental health professional available to a person who has been diagnosed with a serious illness is that research has shown that a person with such an illness is at greatest risk for suicide when he or she first learns of the diagnosis.

The analysis of end-of-life care by a psychologist or other competent mental health professional would typically include the assessment of data from multiple interviews with the patient as well as multiple contacts with the family or significant others, a full review of the patient history, and a full cognitive and depression assessment. The psychologist should bring to this work a thorough understanding of the pertinent psychological literature and data on end-of-life issues.

Furthermore, because end-of-life decisions have family and social consequences, significant others and family members should be involved in the decision-making process if at all possible. In fact, there is research that shows that survivors who are involved in end-of-life decisions do better after the death than those who were not part of the decision-making process.

In determining whether a person is competent to make a reasoned end-of-life decision, most psychologists like to see convergent validity across a number of different measures of the patient's mental health and capacity (i.e., multiple assessments that point to the same conclusion). If significant symptoms of a mood disorder or depression are present, treatment should be attempted before any request for assistance in dying is considered. With resolution of the depression, the patient's capacity to weigh the available options may improve and his or her attitude toward death may change.

The Dilemma for Physicians

Adequate pain control is critical for terminally ill patients, but it is often problematic for physicians. Fear of the patient's addiction affects the physician's willingness to prescribe the strong pain drugs required and also interferes with the patient's willingness to take the prescribed medications. Physicians also worry about how state and federal regulatory agencies will interpret their writing such prescriptions.

In addition, as discussed before, most primary care and internal medicine doctors are not trained in the assessment and treatment of psychiatric illness. They cannot be expected to accurately diagnose a depressive disorder.

Public Policy Questions

Additional public discourse and legislative action on the question of end-of-life care are expected. Already some state legislatures are looking at proposed legislation that would mandate certain pain control procedures for terminally ill people.

What continues to be critical for the courts, legislatures, and the public to recognize is the importance of ensuring that an appropriately trained and licensed mental health professional is involved in the end-of-life decision process. Having a terminal illness is a stressful, sad, and painful experience for any human being. However, terminal illness, in and of itself, is not typically the cause of suicide ideation. The important clinical assessment is whether the patient is fearful, is not receiving the correct treatment for pain, and is concerned about the emotional or financial stress he or she feels is being inflicted on the family or whether the patient is suffering from a clinical depression or a cognitive deficit.

Concern does exist within the psychological community that if some states do move to legalize assisted suicide, this could present a slippery slope equation for our society. That is, if hastened death becomes an option for the terminally ill, will society's attitude toward those people with other types of health or physical challenges be affected? How will legalized assisted suicide affect the position within our society of elderly people, people with chronic debilitating illness, or people with disabilities? In short, every American has a stake in whatever course this country takes vis-à-vis end-of-life issues, because the direction taken will affect whole communities. Psychological research has proven without question that behavior is often modeled.

An added caution: At a time when the population is aging (elderly people are disproportionately represented in the national suicide statistics), where there exist extreme financial pressures on the provision of medical care, and when the social safety net is at risk, many mental health professionals worry that physician-assisted suicide may become legal *without* the added requirement of a mental health assessment by a qualified mental health professional.

More Research Needed

Suicidal thoughts are complex and difficult to study. More research about what motivates a person with a terminal illness to want to hasten his or her death is needed. For example, answers are needed to the following questions:

1. What effect do improved social–psychological supports have on the hastened death ideation of terminally ill patients?
2. What effect does improved palliative care have on the hastened death ideation of terminally ill patients?
3. How do the issues of race, age, ageism, disabilities, religious beliefs, and gender play into the risk factors of an individual for end-of-life decisions?

Complicating the issue is the fact that no definitive data exist on the prevalence (with terminally ill patients) of suicide ideation caused by a depressive illness. Studies have shown that about 5% of the total U.S. population will at any one time suffer from a major depression with some level of suicidal thinking. From this figure, it may be assumed that some fraction of terminally ill patients will suffer from clinical depression that coincides with their illness but did not arise from it.

Conclusion

Any discussion about the ending of a life is controversial and highly charged because it involves our most personal value systems. In the final analysis, we may be called on, both individually and as a society, to balance the important and yet competing interests of preserving human life versus the desire to die peacefully and with dignity. This is a vexing equation for all health care professionals, for the ill and their families, for religious institutions, and for society as a whole. What the state-of-the-art behavioral research and clinical experience of mental health professionals can tell us to date is that a mental health assessment of any ill person who is requesting assistance in hastening his or her death is imperative.

Mark D. Sullivan, Linda Ganzini,
and Stuart J. Youngner

→ **NO**

Should Psychiatrists Serve as Gatekeepers for Physician-Assisted Suicide?

As our society debates the legalization of physician-assisted suicide for terminally ill persons, mandatory psychiatric evaluation has been suggested as a safeguard against abuse. This is to guarantee that the patient choosing physician-assisted death is mentally competent to do so. As psychiatrists who have provided both psychiatric and ethics consultation for dying patients, we believe there are serious unacknowledged problems with this "safeguard."

Our arguments do not depend on a moral position for or against physician-assisted suicide. Nor do we deny that psychiatry has a great deal to offer in the evaluation and treatment of patients who request assistance in dying. Rather, we argue that due to the lack of applicable objective standards of decisionmaking capacity and the inevitable distortion of the mental health professional's role as a clinician, we should think carefully before requiring psychiatric certification of competence in every case. We are concerned that this "safeguard" inappropriately uses a technical clinical procedure to disguise our society's ambivalence about suicide itself. By making every patient who requests physician-assisted suicide jump the hurdle of psychiatric evaluation, we shift responsibility for a troubling moral decision from the therapeutically directed and socially embedded context of shared decisionmaking of patient, family, and primary physician to an outside specialist. As this specialist, the consultant psychiatrist becomes a secular priest dressed in the clothes of a medical expert.

The Question of Safeguards

Health professionals who believe assisted suicide may sometimes be appropriate have called for safeguards to ensure that suffering patients who are assisted to die are choosing suicide freely and autonomously. To address these concerns, recent initiatives for the legalization of assisted suicide have incorporated specific restrictions to assure autonomous decisionmaking. Some initiatives have included the requirement that the request be expressed consistently over a specified period of time in order to prevent impulsive decisions and allow time for ambivalence to be manifested. A delay of fifteen days in Oregon and nine days in Northern Australia (the only other region in which physician-assisted suicide was legal, until overturned by the Australian Parliament in March 1997) is required between a request for assisted suicide and its implementation.[1]

The most important safeguard of autonomous choice is the restriction of access to physician-assisted suicide to those whose decisionmaking capacity is above a threshold that qualifies them as "competent" to make the choice of suicide. Expert discussion of safeguards in the implementation of physician-assisted suicide frequently includes a call for mandatory psychiatric consultation.[2] The Oregon initiative requires that a psychiatric consultation be completed in just those cases where the primary physician believes that the patient has a mental disorder affecting his or her judgment, but the injunction mentioned this safeguard as inadequate.[3] The Northern Australia statute required psychiatric consultation in all cases, and a "Model State Act to Authorize and Regulate Physician-Assisted Suicide" recently published in the United States mandates that "a professional mental health provider (psychiatrist, psychologist, or psychiatric social worker) evaluate the patient to determine that his or her decision is fully informed, free of undue influence, and not distorted by depression or any other form of mental illness."[4] There is thus widespread support for mandatory psychiatric evaluation to verify the competence of all those who request physician-assisted suicide.

How Our Society Understands and Copes with Suicide

Psychiatrists who have cared for suicidal patients can describe how deeply ambivalent these patients can be about suicide. What is not as apparent from the clinical perspective is the ambivalence of psychiatrists and our culture about the morality of suicide. Talcott Parsons described how societies inevitably institutionalize expectations for their members and how "deviance" from these roles is considered a threat to the social fabric.[5] Suicide is a wonderful object for Parsonian analysis because societies have employed a variety of models, sometimes conflicting and sometimes complementary, to understand and manage suicide. Traditionally, suicide has been viewed as a choice. Reflecting this, for many years our society used the legal model to manage suicide. Suicide was a crime, punishable by the criminal justice system. It was considered not simply an assault on the self, but an assault on the community as well. While suicide is no longer a criminal offense in any state, assisting the suicide of another is in many. The religious/moral model also viewed suicide as a choice, but emphasized an individual's violation of core human values rather than laws that protect the social fabric. The Catholic Church and Orthodox Judaism, for example, are adamantly opposed to all suicide, even if it appears rationally chosen.[6] While Protestant fundamentalists are generally opposed to suicide, some Protestant denominations take a more tolerant stance.[7] Many nonreligious persons also find suicide immoral.

The modern medical model considers suicide to be, not the choice of a rational agent, but a symptom of mental illness. Epidemiological studies have overwhelmingly linked suicide to treatable psychiatric disorders. "Psychological autopsy" studies have documented that up to 90 percent of completed suicides had some psychiatric disorder at the time of death.[8] Treatment studies have shown that identification and treatment of psychiatric disorders can result in a substantial decrease in risk of suicide. Depression, and to a lesser extent medical illness, have been identified as the primary risk factors for suicide in the elderly.[9] This fact has been codified into diagnostic systems (e.g., DSM-IV, ICD-10) that consider suicidal ideas as one of the diagnostic criteria of mental disorder. It has also been codified into law, where danger to self is justification for involuntary mental health treatment.

On balance, this medicalization of suicide has substantially benefited the mentally ill by removing legal and moral sanctions and promoting effective treatment. Over the past few years, however, the hegemony of this medical/psychiatric view has been challenged. Many in our society now see some suicides among those who are terminally ill as the product of rational choice while continuing to see most suicides in other contexts as the product of mental illness.[10] However, a valid method for determining which suicides are rational and which are not has never been developed by psychiatrists, psychologists, or any other profession.

In summary, our society currently uses all three models—legal, religious/moral, and medical—to cope with physician-assisted suicide. Different jurisdictions, communities, institutions, and individuals may rely on different models. Acceptance of the conclusions of one model does not necessarily imply agreement with the conclusions of another. One person might believe that suicide is rational in some situations, but always morally unacceptable. Another might believe truly rational suicide would be morally acceptable, but that suicide is nearly always the irrational product of a diagnosable and treatable psychiatric condition. It is likely that many persons, including psychiatrists and other mental health professionals, are not always aware of which model they are employing to analyze a particular case. For example, a recent survey of Oregon psychologists revealed that those who objected to physician-assisted suicide for religious reasons were also more concerned about the mental health and social consequences of the legalization of physician-assisted suicide.[11] Although the concept of competence is intended to sort out rational from irrational decisions, it may blur the lines between the moral and medical models for a highly contentious issue such as assisted suicide.

Competence in the Clinical Setting

Clinical assessment of decisionmaking capacity is ethically important because of the central role that "adequate decisionmaking capacity" or competence plays in valid consent, the cornerstone in the protection of patient autonomy. This makes it inevitable that adequate decisionmaking capacity becomes a key issue in evaluating patients' requests for physician-assisted death. However, requiring that a psychiatrist control access to physician-assisted suicide is problematic for the following reasons. First, competence is a complex social, rather than scientific construct. In fact, psychiatrists use a sliding scale to determine when decisionmaking capacity is adequate, and the scale slides according to the values of the psychiatrists themselves. Second, the relationship of mental illness and decisionmaking capacity in dying patients is not as clear as is implied by some initiatives, statutes, and court decisions. Third, although psychiatrists have a great deal to offer in the assessment and enhancement of patient decisionmaking, casting them in the role of gatekeeper poses risks for patients, society, and the psychiatric profession itself. These risks should not be overlooked in shaping public policy.

Competence as a Social Construct A "scientific" or purely objective definition of competence is unattainable because thresholds for adequate decisionmaking capacity are in fact socially established. Indeed, competence is not well measured by standardized instruments, but "is a malleable entity that is inevitably molded to fit the particular interpersonal, emotional, clinical, and cultural context."[12] "Competence" is used clinically to resolve situations in which two extremely important social goals come into conflict—that is, the promotion of self-determination (autonomy) and the promotion of patient welfare (beneficence or nonmaleficence).[13] As the consequences of physician-patient disagreement grow more serious, the tension between the principles of autonomy and beneficence also grows. It is important to recognize that this tension originates beyond the bounds of the physician-patient relationship. The growing visibility of patient requests for physician-assisted suicide has inspired calls for mandatory psychiatric evaluations of competence precisely because many citizens believe that suicide and assisting suicide are often great harms.

Tests of decisionmaking capacity have been traditionally ranked on a continuum of increasing stringency, with more stringent standards used for treatment refusals with more serious consequences. Simply making a choice or agreeing with the physician's recommendation are examples of more lenient standards. More stringent standards demand an examination of the process of reasoning underlying the patient's decision, such as the ability to understand, appreciate, or reason about one's clinical situation.[14] For example, when a patient refuses an invasive intervention with little chance of success, the physician rarely challenges his or her reasoning process. However, when the patient makes a choice that appears to be harmful, more rigorous tests of decisionmaking capacity are brought to bear. By employing this sliding scale, physicians gain flexibility to balance concerns about patient autonomy and patient welfare.

The malleability of competence is a two-edged sword. It allows competence to be used as a socially viable compromise between the conflicting values of respect for autonomy and prevention of harm, but it vests tremendous power in the expert who assesses decisionmaking capacity. The employment of a sliding scale for the determination of adequate decisionmaking capacity blurs the line between the process and product of decisionmaking. Without a truly independent standard for decisionmaking capacity, psychiatrists may apply standards derived from their own opinion of the harms associated with decisions such as requests for assisted suicide.

In the absence of robust independent standards, psychiatrists may resolve the ethical dilemmas concerning physician-assisted suicide in an ad hoc fashion, using themselves as the "reasonable person" standard by which to judge the patient's decision. Do I agree that this patient has an intolerable quality of life? Would I consider such a quality of life intolerable for myself? Would I consider suicide morally acceptable in this situation? Too often, to ask what a competent person would do in such a dire situation comes down to asking ourselves what we would do. In one survey psychiatrists' support for legalized physician-assisted suicide was highly correlated to desire for physician-assisted suicide for themselves in the case of terminal illness.[15] A survey of Oregon psychologists revealed that the conditions under which respondents would consider assisted suicide for themselves are highly correlated to conditions under which they believe it should be allowed for other people.[16]

While psychiatrists have skills relevant to the understanding and evaluation of patients' decisions, they should not have the social authority to use themselves as the measure of when it is right to die. In a society that is as confused and conflicted about physician-assisted death as ours is, allowing such individual discretion will result in arbitrary and unfair practices. Society is unsure about how to honor patients' choices to die, as are individual physicians. Deep disagreement exists about what constitutes an intolerable quality of life and whether suicide is ever an acceptable alternative to suffering. We question whether the clinical apparatus of competence assessment can resolve this tension.

Competence and Psychiatric Disorders   One reason psychiatrists have been selected to perform competence evaluations in the terminally ill is that the prevalence of psychiatric disorders in this population is high, and diagnosing these disorders is difficult. While there is validity to these concerns, we do not believe they justify universal psychiatric verification of competence in patients requesting assisted suicide.

Psychiatric disorders are common in the terminally ill. Delirium has been noted in 25 to 40 percent of hospitalized cancer patients; in the final stages, up to 85 percent of cancer patients may suffer from delirium.[17] Depression has also been diagnosed in approximately 5 to 58 percent of hospitalized cancer patients, with up to 77 percent of advanced cancer patients having severe depressive symptoms.[18] High rates of psychiatric disorders and interest in physician-assisted suicide have been noted in patients with HIV infection and AIDS.[19] Although the rates of psychiatric disorder climb as medical severity increases, accuracy of diagnosis by primary care physicians diminishes.[20] Not only is depression often missed, but delirium is often misdiagnosed as depression.[21] Psychiatrists may thus offer expertise in diagnosing a mental disorder that primary care physicians lack.

Psychiatric disorders are the commonest cause of impaired capacity to make medical decisions. Yet even the most serious mental disorders may not critically disrupt decisionmaking capacity. It is now widely accepted, for example, that some psychotic patients can provide valid consent to participate in research from which they personally derive no benefit. Meeting criteria for commitment to involuntary treatment no longer implies incompetence to refuse antipsychoticmedication.[22] Clinical and legal consensus now demands that a mental disorder be demonstrated to seriously disrupt the relevant decisionmaking capacity before a patient is declared incompetent and forfeits the right to make those specific decisions him- or herself. Making a psychiatric diagnosis may assist in directing the clinician's attention to where decisionmaking might be impaired, but does not itself prove that decisionmaking capacity has been compromised.

Psychiatrists have raised concerns that depression may cause medically ill persons to choose to hasten their deaths, but the available data indicate variable effects of depression on treatment preference. In one study using hypothetical illness scenarios, elderly depressed patients did choose aggressive medical treatment less often than nondepressed patients in the good prognosis scenarios. However, among these mildly to moderately depressed patients, current depression severity was not as strongly linked to treatment preference as were their estimates of their quality of life in these hypothetical situations.[23] Except in a minority who were severely depressed, successful treatment of depression did not significantly alter treatment preferences.[24] Another study of twenty-two depressed elderly patients revealed that moderate to severe major depression was associated with a high rate of treatment refusal in good prognosis hypothetical scenarios, which showed reversal with depression treatment.[25] A study of 2,536 elderly patients found that scoring in the depressed range on a depression scale predicted a desire for more, rather than less life-saving treatment.[26] Therefore, depression may or may not alter decisions about end-of-life treatment by elderly patients. We have argued elsewhere that depression diagnosis and clinical assessment of the capacity to make medical decisions are distinct tasks.[27]

Studies that examine the psychiatric correlates of terminally ill persons' desire for hastened death are few. For example, James Henderson Brown and colleagues queried patients on an inpatient hospital palliative care service regarding their desire for hastened death.[28] Patients were eligible to participate in the study if they had a terminal illness and either pain or severe disfigurement and severe disability, but were not too sick to consent. Of 331 potential participants, only forty-four were eligible using these inclusion criteria. Ten of forty-four (24 percent) patients desired to die, and all were found to have a "clinical depression." The authors concluded that the desire for death in terminally ill persons does not occur in the absence of psychopathology. However, the criteria for participation, which excluded 287 hospice patients, may have limited the generalizability of their findings. Harvey Max Chochinov and colleagues interviewed cancer patients on a hospice inpatient service and found that 8.5 percent acknowledged a desire for death that was serious and pervasive. Although these patients had higher depression scores than patients who did not persistently desire death, 41 percent did not meet criteria for major depressive disorder.[29] Studies led by William Breitbart[30] and Ezekiel Emanuel[31] also demonstrate that terminally ill persons who express an interest in physician-assisted suicide have higher depression scores, but these researchers did not measure the percentage who met criteria for major depression. Nor did major depression indicate those who would and those who would not be interested in assisted suicide in a future state of severe pain among forty-eight patients with painful metastatic cancer.[32] In total, these studies suggest that though depression is common among persons desiring assisted suicide, it clearly does not account for all of the variance in decision-making.

Moreover, many psychiatrists do not regularly work with seriously ill and dying patients in hospital, nursing home, and hospice settings. In a survey of over 700 Oregon psychiatrists and psychologists, only three respondents reported working with hospice patients in the past year. Only 6 percent of psychiatrists were very confident that they could, within the context of a single evaluation, assess whether a psychiatric disorder was impairing the judgment of a patient desiring assisted suicide.[33]

Psychiatrists' treatment options for the terminally ill are limited by the limited time available for the treatment to be effective and by the severity of the patient's medical illness. Data suggest that psychiatric treatment may or may not affect treatment preferences. Some patients asking for assisted suicide will be willing to try psychiatric treatment and some will not. Even for patients who actively participate in treatment, it will be difficult to determine when enough treatment has been administered—psychiatrists' values as well as their clinical expertise will inevitably determine when the point of "enough" treatment has been reached. For example, how many trials of antidepressant medication are needed before the psychiatrist concludes that the depression is intractable or that the patient is not really depressed?

These observations point to a useful and important role for trained and experienced psychiatrists in the assessment and treatment of seriously ill patients who wish to hasten their deaths. They also argue for more research and better training for psychiatrists in this critical area. They do not, however, make a convincing case for mandatory involvement and a gatekeeping role for the psychiatrist in all cases. . . .

Counterarguments

There are two remaining arguments for psychiatry's role in determining competence to participate in physician-assisted suicide to which we would like to respond. First, some might argue that the problems in assessing competence for suicide are no different from other situations in which competence is addressed. Why do we specifically object to competence evaluation for those requesting physician-assisted suicide? What makes it different from the psychiatrist's role in evaluating competence to stand trial, to make a will, or even more relevant here, to refuse life-sustaining medical treatment? Do not the same problems of subjectivity and potential for bias exist?

There are a couple of critical differences. The evaluation of competence to stand trial, make a will, or refuse medical treatment is not mandatory for every person who is about to undertake these acts. In each of these cases, patient competence is assumed. The psychiatrist is called in only when competence is challenged or questioned by one of the persons naturally involved in the process, such as a lawyer, judge, or relative. We know of no other clinical situation in which psychiatric evaluation for competence is universally required; the presumption for persons standing trial or making medical decisions (even patients who refuse life-sustaining treatment) is that they are competent. Mandating a mental health evaluation for all patients requesting assisted suicide implies a presumption of incompetence. It makes the request for assisted suicide, although legal, adequate grounds for challenging the competence of the person making the request.

In addition, these other decisions or acts for which competence may be called into question are not in themselves morally controversial. No one argues that standing trial or making a will is morally wrong. Quite the contrary, both are viewed as necessary social functions. Thus, it is highly unlikely that a psychiatrist's opinion about competence will be influenced by his view that standing trial or making a will is harmful per se. Refusal of life-sustaining treatment may be considered to be a harm by a minority of our citizens. However, the legal system clearly recognizes this right and the vast majority of health professionals (including psychiatrists) and citizens accept it as a moral right as well. To argue that because psychiatrists are called in to evaluate competence in some cases of treatment refusal, they should be called in on all requests for physician-assisted suicide is illogical. The view that death through assisted suicide is a greater harm to patients than death through treatment refusal reflects social ambivalence about suicide rather than clearly distinct clinical situations. Since the same psychosocial factors—for example, depression, delirium, and anxiety—that affect requests for physician-assisted suicide also affect treatment refusal, a more consistent argument for those advocating the gatekeeper role would be that psychiatrists should be the gatekeepers for all refusals of life-saving treatment as well.

A second counterargument to our position asserts that psychiatrists, despite their shortcomings, are the professionals best qualified to evaluate decision-making capacity and no more biased than other physicians. We do not deny that involvement of psychiatrists in the evaluation and treatment of persons who request physician-assisted suicide can be extremely helpful. The psychiatrist can assist the patient in exploring the often multiple meanings of the request to die. Susan Block and Andrew Billings write, "Most patients, in saying that they want to die are asking for assistance in living—for help in dealing with depression, anxiety about the future, grief, lack of control, dependence, and spiritual despair."[34] The efficacy of psychiatric treatment in the medically ill elderly has been repeatedly demonstrated in recent years.[35] Suffering may be diminished with both psychotherapy and psychotropic medications. The psychiatrist may intervene to improve the patient's relationships with physician and family. Indeed, there are many cases in which psychiatric involvement is absolutely essential.

However, institutionalizing or bureaucratizing such involvement could be problematic. This would imply a greater expertise than is warranted and would shift responsibility from the traditional seat of shared decisionmaking—the patient, the family, and the physician or health care team—to an outside expert who may not have a primary commitment to patient welfare. A required evaluation of competence puts the patient in a "one down" position in which his or her sanity is judged by an outside expert. This intrinsically adversarial position is likely to prevent the development of a therapeutic alliance necessary for the psychiatrist to function in the traditional role as healer. Forcing evaluations in cases where they are neither wanted nor necessary could trivialize the process or turn it into an activity that serves neither patients, society, nor our profession. By making psychiatric involvement optional, a complicated social decision can be kept woven as deeply as possible into the social fabric, allowing society to appreciate rather than avoid its own ambivalence about death, dying, and suicide.

Healers, Not Gatekeepers

We believe that psychiatrists' primary involvement with patients requesting assisted suicide should be in the role of healer rather than gatekeeper. Psychiatric evaluation of the dying patient should always be done for the benefit of the patient. If psychiatric diagnosis is done primarily for social control rather than individual welfare, psychiatrists function as priests or police rather than as physicians. The primary duty of psychiatrists to the dying is not to man the gate to assisted dying, but to nurture autonomous choice and diminish the anguish of the dying process.

We encourage our medical colleagues to involve psychiatrists in the evaluation and care of the dying. Psychotropic medication, supportive therapy, and family intervention can ease suffering and promote autonomous choice. Psychiatric consultation to assess and promote autonomous decisionmaking should be an option initiated by patient, family, or primary physician, not mandated by law. Psychiatrists, on the other hand, must improve their expertise in caring for dying patients and make themselves more available to patients and medical colleagues. An emphasis must be placed on improving the research basis for carrying out psychiatric assessments of dying patients who desire physician-assisted suicide. Legal mandates that require psychiatric certification of competence prior to all cases of euthanasia or physician-assisted suicide hold risks for both the psychiatric profession and the patients it should serve. This practice could distort the role of the psychiatrist as a physician whose first responsibility is the welfare of her patient. It runs the risk of overselling the independence and impartiality of the clinical procedure by which decisionmaking capacity is assessed. It shifts the accountability for value judgments from the traditional context of patient-family-physician.

There is a price to be paid for not making psychiatric consultation mandatory. Some treatable psychiatric disorders will be missed in those opting for assisted suicide. But the benefit for these individuals must be balanced against the serious problems, the arbitrary evaluations and social obfuscation, that would accompany universal mandatory psychiatric consultation. And it may be more difficult politically to endorse or legalize physician-assisted suicide without the psychiatric safeguard. But the societal debate about assisted suicide will be more honest and revealing.

In our culture's current state of ambivalence and confusion about suicide, the moral and medical models run hopelessly together. Using a technical clinical determination of competence to judge the moral acceptability of suicide obscures important value judgments we are making about when life is worth living and when it is not. To foster the most honest debate possible about assisted suicide and to promote truly patient-centered end-of-life care, we should avoid making psychiatrists gatekeepers for assisted suicide.

References

1. Christopher J. Ryan and Miranda Kaye, "Euthanasia in Australia: the Northern Territory Rights of the Terminally Ill Act," *NEJM* 334 (1996): 326–28.

2. W. F. Baile, J. R. Dimaggio, D. V. Schapira, and J. S. Janofsky, "The Request for Assistance in Dying: The Need for Psychiatric Consultation," *Cancer* 72 (1993): 2786–91; Guy I. Benrubi, "Euthanasia: The Need for Procedural Safeguards," *NEJM* 326 (1992): 197–98.

3. Ballot Measure 16. In Oregon voters' pamphlet. Portland, Ore.: Multnomah County Elections Division, 1994.

4. Charles H. Baron, Clyde Bergstresser, Dan W. Brock, Gabrielle F. Cole et al., "A Model State Act to Authorize and Regulate Physician-Assisted Suicide," *Harvard Journal on Legislation* 33 (1996): 1–34.

5. Talcott Parsons, "Definitions of Health and Disease in Light of American Values and Social Structures." In *Patients, Physicians, and Illness,* ed. E. Gartly Jaco (New York: Free Press, 1979), pp. 120–44.

6. Fred Rosner, "Suicide in Biblical, Talmudic, and Rabbinic Writings," *Tradition: A Journal of Orthodox Thought* 11 (1970): 25–40.

7. Presbyterian Senior Services, The Presbytery of New York, "Pastoral Letter on Euthanasia and Suicide," 9 March 1976, p. 3.

8. Gabrielle A. Carlson, Charles L. Rich, Patricia Grayson, and Richard C. Fowler, "Secular Trends in Psychiatric Diagnoses of Suicide Victims," *Journal of Affective Disorders* 21 (1991): 127–32.

9. Robert L. Frierson, "Suicide Attempts by the Old and the Very Old," *Archives of Internal Medicine* 151 (1991): 141–44; Thomas B. Mackenzie and Michael K. Popkin, "Medical Illness and Suicide." In *Suicide Over the Life Cycle: Risk Factors, Assessment, and Treatment of Suicidal Patients,* ed. Susan J. Blumenthal and David J. Kupfer (Washington D.C.: American Psychiatric Press, 1990), pp. 205–32.

10. Robert J. Blendon, Ulrike S. Szalay, Richard A. Knox, "Should Physicians Aid Their Patients in Dying? The Public Perspective," *JAMA* 269 (1993): 590–91.

11. Darien S. Fenn and Linda Ganzini, personal communication.

12. Stuart J. Youngner, "Competency to Refuse Life-Sustaining Treatment." In *End-of-Life Decisions: A Psychosocial Perspective,* ed. Maurice D. Steinberg and Stuart J. Youngner (Washington, D.C.: *American Psychiatric Press,* 1998).

13. Loren H. Roth, Alan Meisel, and Charles W. Lidz, "Tests of Competency to Consent to Treatment," *American Journal of Psychiatry* 134 (1977): 279–84; Allen E. Buchanan and Dan W. Brock, *Deciding for Others* (Cambridge: Cambridge University Press, 1989), p. 77.

14. Youngner, "Competency to Refuse Life-Sustaining Treatment."

15. Linda Ganzini, Darien S. Fenn, Melinda A. Lee et al., "Attitudes of Oregon Psychiatrists Toward Physician Assisted Suicide," *American Journal of Psychiatry* 153 (1996): 1469–75.

16. Fenn and Ganzini, personal communication.

17. Mary Jane Massie, Jimmie Holland, and Ellen Glass, "Delirium in Terminal Cancer Patients," *American Journal of Psychiatry* 140 (1983): 1048–50.

18. Judith B. Bukberg, Doris T. Penman, and Jimmie C. Holland, "Depression in Hospitalized Cancer Patients," *Psychosomatic Medicine* 46 (1984): 199–212.

19. William Breitbart, Barry D. Rosenfeld, and Steven D. Passik, "Interest in Physician-Assisted Suicide among Ambulatory HIV-Infected Patients," *American Journal of Psychiatry* 153 (1996): 238–42.

20. H. C. Schulberg, M. Saul, and M. N. McClelland, "Assessing Depression in Primary Medical and Psychiatric Practices," *Archives of General Psychiatry* 42 (1985): 1164–70.

21. Kathleen R. Farrell and Linda Ganzini, "Misdiagnosing Delirium as Depression in Medically Ill Elderly Patients," *Archives of Internal Medicine* 155 (1995): 2459–64.

22. *Rogers v. Okin,* 478 F Supp 1342 (D Mass, 1979).

23. Melinda A. Lee and Linda Ganzini, "Depression in the Elderly: Effect on Patient Attitudes toward Life-Sustaining Therapy," *Journal of the American Geriatric Society* 40 (1992): 983–88.

24. Linda Ganzini, Melinda A. Lee, Ronald T. Heintz et al., "The Effect of Depression Treatment on Elderly Patients' Preferences for Life-Sustaining Medical Therapy," *American Journal of Psychiatry* 151 (1994): 1631–36.

25. S. C. Hooper, K. J. Vaughan, C. C. Tennant, and J. M. Perz, "Major Depression and Refusal of Life-Sustaining Treatment in the Elderly," *Medical Journal of Australia* 165 (1996): 416–19.

26. Joanne M. Garrett, Russell P. Harris, Jean K. Norburn et al., "Life-Sustaining Treatments During Terminal Illness: Who Wants What?" *Journal of General Internal Medicine* 9 (1993): 361–68.

27. Mark D. Sullivan and Stuart J. Youngner, "Depression, Competence, and the Right to Refuse Life-Saving Medical Treatment," *American Journal of Psychiatry* 151 (1994): 971–78.

28. James Henderson Brown, Paul Henteleff, Samia Barakat, and Cheryl June Rowe, "Is It Normal for Terminally Ill Patients to Desire Death?" *American Journal of Psychiatry* 143 (1986): 208–11.

29. Harvey Max Chochinov, Keith G. Wilson, Murray Enns et al., "Desire for Death in the Terminally Ill," *American Journal of Psychiatry* 152 (1995): 1185–91.

30. Mark D. Sullivan, Suzanne A. Rapp, Dermot Fitzgibbon, and C. Richard Chapman, "Pain and the Choice to Hasten Death Among Patients with Painful Metastatic Cancer," *Journal of Palliative Care,* in press.

31. Ezekiel J. Emanuel, "Empirical Studies on Euthanasia and Assisted Suicide," *Journal of Clinical Ethics* 6 (1995): 158–60.

32. Sullivan et al., "Pain and the Choice to Hasten Death."

33. Ganzini et al., "Attitudes of Oregon Psychiatrists."

34. Susan D. Block and J. Andrew Billings, "Patient Requests for Euthanasia and Assisted Suicide: The Role of the Psychiatrist," *Psychosomatics* 36 (1995): 445–57.

35. J. Stephen McDaniel, Dominque L. Musselman, Maryfrances R. Porter et al., "Depression in Patients with Cancer: Diagnosis, Biology, and Treatment," *Archives of General Psychiatry* 52 (1995): 89–99.

CHALLENGE QUESTIONS

Should Mental Health Professionals Serve as Gatekeepers for Physician-Assisted Suicide?

1. Farberman makes some strong arguments with regard to the importance of involving mental health professionals in cases of physician-assisted suicide. What criteria should be specified in order to determine the competence of the mental health professional to play this role?
2. Sullivan, Ganzini, and Youngner do not believe that there is a convincing case for mandatory involvement of mental health professionals in cases of physician-assisted suicide in general. For what kinds of specific cases could a strong argument be made for requiring such involvement?
3. In 1997 the U.S. Supreme Court ruled that terminally ill people do not have a constitutional right to doctor-assisted suicide, but it also declared that states have the option of enacting assistance-in-dying statutes. What arguments can be made for and against the constitutionality of the right to physician-assisted suicide?
4. What kinds of emotional burdens might be experienced by mental health professionals who become involved in the assessment of terminally ill patients?

Suggested Readings

Block, S. D., & Billings, J. A. (1998). Evaluating patient requests for euthanasia and assisted suicide in terminal illness: The role of the psychiatrist. In M. D. Steinberg & S. J. Youngner (Eds.), *End-of-life decisions: A psychosocial perspective* (pp. 205–233). Washington, DC: American Psychiatric Press, Inc.

Ganzini, L., Fenn, D. S., Lee, M. A., Heintz, R. T., & Bloom, J. D. (1996). Attitudes of Oregon psychiatrists toward physician-assisted suicide. *American Journal of Psychiatry, 153,* 1469–1475.

Groenewoud, J. H. et al. (2004). Psychiatric consultation with regard to requests for euthanasia or physician-assisted suicide. *General Hospital Psychiatry, 26*(4), 323–330.

Peruzzi, N., Canapary, A., & Bongar, B. (1996). Physician-assisted suicide: The role of mental health professionals. *Ethics & Behavior, 6*(4), 353–366.

ISSUE 19

Must Mentally Ill Murderers Have a Rational Understanding of Why They Are Being Sentenced to Death?

YES: American Psychological Association, American Psychiatric Association, and National Alliance on Mental Illness, from "Brief for *Amici Curiae* American Psychological Association, American Psychiatric Association, and National Alliance on Mental Illness in Support of Petitioner," *Scott Louis Panetti v. Nathaniel Quarterman,* U.S. Supreme Court, No. 06-6407 (2007)

NO: Greg Abbott et al., from "On Writ of Certiorari to the United States Court of Appeals for the Fifth Circuit: Brief for the Respondent," *Scott Louis Panetti v. Nathaniel Quaterman, Director, Texas Department of Criminal Justic, Correctional Institutions Division, U.S. Supreme Court, No. 06-6407* (2007)

ISSUE SUMMARY

YES: The *amici curiae* brief argues that mentally ill convicts should not be executed if their disability significantly impairs their capacity to understand the nature and purpose of their punishment, or to appreciate why the punishment is being imposed on them.

NO: The State of Texas asserts that punishment for murder does not depend on the rational understanding, but rather on the convict's moral culpability at the time the crime was committed.

$\mathbf{T}$he complexity of the issue of executing the mentally ill received special scrutiny as a result of the case of Scott Panetti which was heard by the U.S. Supreme Court in 2007. In 1992 Panetti murdered his mother-in-law and father-in-law while his wife and his daughter watched. Panetti, who had a lengthy history of mental illness and psychiatric hospitalizations was sentenced to death. In 2003 Panetti petitioned the Texas state court to determine his competency for execution, but this court ruled him competent. When Panetti brought his case to a higher level, the federal district court found fault with the earlier ruling and summoned three psychologists and a psychiatrist, all of whom concurred that Panetti suffered from mental illness. The court ruled that Panetti was competent to be executed. Panetti's case then went to the Fifth Circuit, and the argument was put forth that a previous U.S.

Supreme Court ruling (*Ford v. Wainwright*) required that Panetti not only be aware of the fact that he would be executed, but also that he have a rational understanding of *why*. Panetti asserted that he was being executed because he preached the gospel, not because of his murders.

The American Psychological Association, the American Psychiatric Association, and the National Alliance on Mental Illness submitted a brief, stating that individuals with psychotic conditions such as that of Panetti may experience delusions and a disrupted understanding of reality; also, they may be unable to connect events or understand cause and effect (i.e., the connection between murder and punishment).

Nathaniel Quarterman, director of the Texas Department of Criminal Justice, asserted that the court should reject the proposition that a murderer must possess a rational understanding of the reasons for execution, to render death an acceptable punishment under the Eighth Amendment of the Constitution (cruel and unusual punishment). Quarterman argued that capital punishment in such cases should not rest on whether or not a convict has rational understanding, but rather on the convict's moral culpability at the time the crime was committed by this person.

POINTS (APA, APA, NAMI)

- Mentally ill convicts are not competent to be executed if they have a disability that significantly impairs their capacity to understand the nature and purpose of their punishment.

- Some psychiotic individuals cannot grasp the essential truth: that their impending execution is retribution for their crimes.

- The Eighth Amendment forbids the execution of individuals who are unaware of the punishment they are about to suffer *and why they are to suffer it.*

- Some psychiotic individuals like Panetti may possess the ability to comprehend facts about the subject of their delusions, but they are often unable to appreciate the personal significance of those facts or to reason about them in a logical way.

- The Fifth Circuit's approach permits the execution of severely delusional individuals even though they believe they are to be executed *for something other than their crimes*, notwithstanding the State's assertions to the contrary.

COUNTERPOINTS (Quarterman)

- Mentally ill convicts are incompetent to be executed only if, because of their illness, they lack the *capacity* to recognize that the punishment (1) is the result of having been convicted of murder, and (2) will cause death.

- Retribution as a permissible theory of punishment depends not on the rational understanding that a convict may or may not have, but rather on the convict's moral culpability at the time of the crime.

- The Court should reject the proposition that a capital convict must possess a "rational understanding" of the reasons for execution to render death an acceptable punishment under the Eighth Amendment.

- The conceded objective of the *amici* APA is not simply avoiding the inhumanity of executing a person who is truly insane, but rather removing from death row as large a class of capital convicts as reasonably possible and thus exempting vast numbers of convicted murderers from execution.

- Requiring a "deep" or "meaningful" appreciation of the State's reasons for imposing the death penalty would create an even greater risk that the Court's test could be circumvented through malingering or abuse.

YES ⬅

American Psychological Association, American Psychiatric Association, and National Alliance on Mental Health

On Writ of Certiorari to the United States Court of Appeals for the Fifth Circuit

The American Psychological Association is a voluntary, nonprofit, scientific and professional organization with more than 155,000 members and affiliates, and is the major association of psychologists in the nation.

The American Psychiatric Association, with more than 36,000 members, is the nation's leading organization of physicians who specialize in psychiatry.

The National Alliance on Mental Illness was founded in 1979 and is the nation's largest grassroots organization dedicated to improving the quality of life of persons living with serious mental illness and their families.

Members of *amici* are regularly called before courts to participate in competency hearings. *Amici* therefore have both pertinent expertise and a strong interest in the establishment of legal competency standards consistent with the best scientific knowledge about individuals suffering from mental illness.

In 2003, the American Bar Association established a Task Force on Mental Disability and the Death Penalty, which included mental health professionals who are members and representatives of *amici*. The Task Force was convened in light of this Court's decision in *Atkins* to address unresolved issues concerning application of the death penalty to persons suffering from impaired mental conditions. In 2005, the Task Force presented a series of recommendations.

[T]he Task Force identified several situations in which the death penalty should not be applied to individuals with mental illness. One category encompasses individuals who, though having been determined competent to stand trial and sentenced to death, suffer from a severe mental disorder or disability that renders them incompetent to understand the nature and purpose of the death penalty. This category would include, for example, individuals whose mental illness worsens in material respects after imposition of valid sentences.[1] Based on the Task Force Report *amici* and the American Bar Association recommended, in substantially similar form, that the death penalty should not be applied to such persons.[2]

From *Scott Louis Panetti v. Nathaniel Quaterman*, Director, Texas Department of Criminal Justice, Correctional Institutions Division, U.S. Supreme Court, No. 06-6407, 2007.

Introduction and Summary of Argument

The Fifth Circuit, in this case and in *Barnard v. Collins*, 13 F.3d 871 (5th Cir. 1994), has adopted a very narrow construction of this Court's decision in *Ford*, a construction that permits the execution of individuals whose severe mental illness precludes them from understanding that the State is putting them to death as retribution for their crimes. The Fifth Circuit recognized that Scott Panetti suffers from schizoaffective disorder, a severe form of psychosis, and that as a direct result he "suffer[s] from paranoid delusions that his [sentence of] execution was the result of a conspiracy against him and not his crimes." *Panetti* v. *Dretke*, 448 F.3d 815, 819 (5th Cir. 2006). The court of appeals nevertheless deemed Panetti competent to be executed under *Ford*.

Amici respectfully submit that the Fifth Circuit's approach is inconsistent with the reasoning of the controlling opinions in *Ford*. Scientific knowledge about schizophrenia and schizoaffective disorder supports the conclusion that persons in Panetti's condition cannot rationally understand the reasons for their execution. Convinced of the reality of their delusions, they simply cannot grasp the essential truth: that their impending execution is retribution for their crimes. Where the prisoner cannot appreciate the reason, his execution cannot further the retributive purpose of the death penalty any more than if the prisoner, as in *Ford*, suffers delusions that he can never be executed at all. As explained further in this brief, for these reasons *amici* American Psychological Association, American Psychiatric Association and the National Alliance on Mental Illness each has resolved that a prisoner is not competent to be executed if he "has a mental disorder or disability that significantly impairs his or her capacity to understand the nature and purpose of the punishment, or to appreciate the reason for its imposition in the prisoner's own case." *See, e.g.*, American Psychological Association Council of Representatives, APA Policy Manual: N. Public Interest (2001) (incorporating policy adopted by the Council of Representatives in February 2006), *available at. . . . Amici*'s approach, which is consistent with *Ford*, requires reversal of the Fifth Circuit here.

In Part I of this brief, *amici* explain that individuals who, like Panetti, suffer from severe psychotic disorders such as schizophrenia or schizoaffective disorder, frequently suffer from bizarre delusions that disrupt their understanding of reality. These delusional beliefs are genuine and often unshakeable, withstanding all attempts to introduce logic or contrary evidence. When they attach to the State's reasons for carrying out the mentally ill prisoner's execution, such delusions can deny the prisoner all rational understanding about "why" he is to be executed. In such a circumstance, proceeding with the execution would not further the purposes of the death penalty. In Part II, *amici* explain that mental health experts can assist the courts in identifying prisoners with mental illness who suffer delusions that preclude them from understanding the actual reasons for their execution. Mental health professionals routinely evaluate patients for the presence of delusional beliefs and generate reliable conclusions as to how those delusions impact the patients' ability to rationally understand information.

Argument

I. The Fifth Circuit's Interpretation of *Ford* v. *Wainwright* Fails to Protect a Class of Severely Mentally Ill Prisoners, in Contravention of the Purposes That Animated *Ford*

A. *In* Panetti *and* Barnard, *the Fifth Circuit Has Interpreted and Applied* Ford *Very Narrowly*

In 1986, this Court held that the Eighth Amendment forbids the execution of individuals suffering from mental illness that renders them incompetent. *Ford* v. *Wainwright*, 477 U.S. 399 (1986). The Court relied on common law to support its interpretation of the Eighth Amendment and identified several reasons why the execution of the insane is unacceptable in a civilized society. *Id.* at 409-410.[3] As one justification, the Court "seriously question[ed] the retributive value of executing a person who has no comprehension of why he has been singled out and stripped of his fundamental right to life." *Id.* at 409. Yet, while suggesting that the Constitution prevents the execution of a prisoner who lacks "comprehension of why he has been singled out" for death, the Court did not provide a substantive test for defining insanity in this context. Justice Powell attempted to do so, in a separate concurring opinion largely devoted to explaining his disagreements with the procedural protections set forth by the four-justice plurality. Justice Powell noted that "today, as at common law, one of the death penalty's critical justifications, its retributive force, depends on the defendant's awareness of the penalty's existence and purpose." *Id.* at 421 (Powell, J., concurring). Accordingly, he concluded that "the Eighth Amendment forbids the execution . . . of those who are unaware of the punishment they are about to suffer *and why they are to suffer it.*" *Id.* at 422 (emphasis added). Justice Powell recognized that the Constitution requires, as a minimum before a prisoner may be deemed competent to be executed, that the prisoner be aware of both the fact that he will be put to death and the reason for that: society's retribution for his criminal acts.

In the case at bar, the Fifth Circuit . . . has ruled that the Constitution permits the execution of a severely delusional man who has no awareness of the true reason for his execution. In upholding Panetti's death sentence, the court of appeals expressly ruled that the Constitution does not bar the execution of an individual "suffer[ing] from paranoid delusions that his execution was the result of a conspiracy against him *and not his crimes.*" *Panetti* v. *Dretke*, 448 F.3d 815, 819 (5th Cir. 2006) (emphasis added). Panetti understands that he has been found guilty of murder and faces execution, but holds the unequivocal and delusional belief that the State is using his crimes as a pretext, and that its real motivation is "to prevent him from preaching the Gospel." *Id.* at 816 (citing *Panetti* v. *Dretke*, 401 F. Supp. 2d 702, 709 (W.D. Tex. 2004)). Relying on *Barnard*, the court of appeals found Panetti's recognition of the State's *articulated* reason for his execution adequate to satisfy the standard set forth in Justice Powell's *Ford* concurrence, despite the court's recognition that Panetti's delusional thinking denies him awareness that the stated rationale is genuine. *Panetti*, 448 F.3d at 819 (noting that "Justice Powell did not state that a prisoner must 'rationally understand' the reason for his execution, only that he must be 'aware' of it").

B. Panetti Is Readily Identifiable As Suffering From Delusions That Commonly Accompany Schizophrenia and Schizoaffective Disorder

Scott Panetti is not an anomaly who by some odd quirk can correctly comprehend the fact of his execution and the State's explanation for it yet who breaks with reality when he ascribes the State's true motivation to a fantastical conspiracy or bizarre purpose. Rather, he is readily recognizable as belonging to the class of mentally ill persons who suffer from severe psychotic disorders that impede their cognitive functioning in some respects while leaving other aspects relatively unimpaired.[4] Such people may possess the ability to comprehend and understand facts about the subject of their delusions, but they are often unable to appreciate the personal significance of those facts or to reason about them in a logical way.

1. Individuals who suffer from delusions firmly hold false, illogical beliefs that cannot be corrected with reason and that interfere with their ability to interpret ordinary experiences.   In the scientific literature, individuals such as Panetti are commonly described as suffering from delusions: false beliefs that cannot be corrected by reasoning and that usually involve a misinterpretation of perceptions or experiences. Such delusions are often characterized by flaws in logical thinking that prevent those who suffer from them from making the right connections between ideas and from testing their beliefs about the world in ways that would enable them to determine the veracity of those beliefs.

Delusional thinking forms part of various psychotic disorders. A delusion has been defined as:

> A false belief based on incorrect inference about external reality that is firmly sustained despite what almost everyone else believes and despite what constitutes incontrovertible and obvious proof or evidence to the contrary. The belief is not, one ordinarily accepted by other members of the person's culture or subculture (e.g., it is not an article of religious faith). When a false belief involves a value judgment, it is regarded as a delusion only when the judgment is so extreme as to defy credibility.

American Psychiatric Association, *Diagnostic and Statistical Manual of Mental Disorders* 821 (4th ed. text rev. 2000) (hereinafter DSM-IV-TR).

Delusional thinking is a hallmark symptom of schizophrenia[5] and of related psychotic disorders, such as schizoaffective disorder.[6] It may also occur as a symptom of mood disorders such as depressive disorders or bipolar disorders.[7] It is particularly pronounced in what is known as the Paranoid Type of Schizophrenia. DSM-IV-TR 313-314. The essential feature of this type of schizophrenia is "the presence of prominent delusions or auditory hallucinations in the content of a relative preservation of cognitive functioning and affect." *Id.* at 313. Typically, persons with this condition suffer from delusions that are categorized as *persecutory* and/or *grandiose*. *Id.* A persecutory delusion, generally speaking, is a delusion whose theme involves a conspiracy or other form of malicious obstruction to thwart the individual's goals. *Id.* at 325. A grandiose delusion is one whose central theme involves the patient possessing a great yet unrecognized talent, sometimes accompanied by the belief that the patient has a special relationship with a prominent person or bears a special message from a deity. *Id.* The two types of delusions are often intertwined: persons experiencing persecutory delusions may reason that, as one textbook puts it, "they must be very important if so much effort is spent on their persecution." Robert Cancro & Heinz E. Lehmann, *Schizophrenia: Clinical Features*, in *Kaplan & Sadock's Comprehensive Textbook of Psychiatry* 1187 (7th ed. 2000).[8]

Psychotic disorders such as schizophrenia distort the mind in certain ways while leaving other functions generally intact. As noted above, an individual with paranoid schizophrenia may possess "a relative preservation of cognitive functioning." DSM-IV-TR 313. Yet such a person, plagued by a delusional psychotic disorder, may have no ability to apply his cognitive functions to test the veracity of the conclusions that he draws; while the *process* of a person's thinking appears normal, the *content* of the thoughts defies accepted reality. For example, a person who is under the delusion that he is the basketball player Michael Jordan may be unable to "test reality" in a way that would disprove his belief. Michael Jordan is tall, athletically gifted, widely recognized, and wealthy. Even after it is pointed out to the delusional person that he possesses none of these characteristics "and even if the person *agrees* that he does not" he may persist in his belief that he is in fact Michael Jordan.

Such persons may understand much of the world around them and have real intelligence. Yet their delusional thought process may consistently lead them to wildly incorrect results. As one psychiatry textbook explains:

> Disturbances of thinking and conceptualization are one of the most characteristic features of schizophrenia. The feature common to all manifestations of schizophreni[c] thought disorder is that patients think and reason . . . according to their own intricate private rules of logic. Schizophrenic patients may be highly intelligent, certainly not confused, and they may be painstaking in their abstractions and deductions. But their thought processes are strange and do not lead to conclusions based on reality or universal logic.

Cancro & Lehmann, *supra*, at 1189. Thus, a person suffering from schizophrenia or schizoaffective disorder may know that he has committed a crime; that the death penalty is imposed on persons who commit such crimes; and that the State has asserted he will be put to death because he committed that crime; and yet be absolutely and unwaveringly certain that his execution is not in fact a response to his crime but is instead an effort to prevent him from preaching the Gospel.

2. Panetti suffers from grandiose, persecutory delusions that disrupt his understanding of the purpose of his execution.   Based upon the record and findings in this case, Panetti clearly falls into this framework. He is not incoherent: the district court found that "at least some of the time, Panetti is capable of communicating, and apparently understanding, in a coherent fashion." *Panetti*, 401 F. Supp. 2d at 708. As one of the State's experts concluded, Panetti possessed a "capacity to understand the Bible, to understand history, movies." *Id.* Indeed, he represented himself at trial, cross-examined witnesses, and applied for subpoenas.

Yet, in the decade preceding his crime, Panetti was hospitalized with diagnoses that included schizophrenia, schizoaffective disorder, and bipolar disorder—all serious mental disorders that, in his case, were accompanied by psychotic symptoms such as auditory hallucinations and delusions of persecution and grandiosity. Pet. 3. While defending himself at trial, he exhibited a wide array of delusional behaviors. His cross-examination tended to be rambling and illogical, and he attempted to subpoena John F. Kennedy, Pope John Paul II, and Jesus Christ. Although Panetti knows that the State claims it intends to execute him for the murders that he committed, he believes in the words of one of the experts who examined him that "God had nullified it, God had forgiven him, God had wiped the slate clean." *Panetti*, 401 F. Supp. 2d at 707. And the district court credited testimony from one of the State's experts who concluded that:

> Panetti does not even understand that the State of Texas is a lawfully constituted authority, but rather, he believes the State is in league with the forces of evil that have conspired against him. [That expert's] testimony is consistent with that of Dr. Conroy, Dr. Rosin, and Dr. Silverman, each of whom testified Panetti believes the real reason he is to be executed is for preaching the Gospel.

Id. at 712; *see also id.* at 707 (Panetti suffers from "grandiosity and a delusional belief system in which he believes himself to be persecuted for his religious activities and beliefs"). As reflected in the findings and the testimony below, therefore, Panetti is able to draw some logical connections but suffers from textbook persecutory and grandiose delusions centered around religion that render him deeply disturbed and deny him any genuine understanding of the reason for his execution.

Although the record does not reflect the methods employed by the doctors who examined Panetti, it is likely that his delusional belief withstood all attempts to "test reality" by confronting him with contrary evidence. A person who is captive to such a delusion would likely be unconvinced by evidence that, for example (1) the State does not, in fact, seek to execute people for preaching the Gospel, and (2) the State has certainly not sought to execute others whose preaching is heard by many more than Panetti's.[9]

C. Contrary to the Rationale of Ford, by Permitting the Execution of Prisoners Who Suffer from Psychotic Delusions, the Fifth Circuit's Approach Permits Executions That Do Not Further the Death Penalty's Retributive Purpose

Insisting that the death penalty must serve its core retributive purpose in every case, Justice Powell wrote in *Ford* that "the Eighth Amendment forbids the execution . . . of those who are unaware of the punishment they are about to suffer and why they are to suffer it." 477 U.S. at 422. In *Panetti,* the Fifth Circuit held that "'awareness,' as that term is used in *Ford*, is not necessarily synonymous with 'rational understanding.'" *Panetti,* 448 F.3d at 821. Accordingly, the court of appeals allowed the execution of an individual who believes that the State's expressed reason for his execution is merely a pretext for the true reason: to stop him from preaching Gospel. The Fifth Circuit's approach fails to recognize the force of the delusions that characterize psychotic disorders such as Panetti's, and thus, contrary to *Ford*, permits executions where the retributive purpose of the death penalty is not served.

As a simple linguistic matter, "awareness of why" a person is to suffer the death penalty might arguably be construed to include mere "awareness of *what the State has claimed as a reason."* But that circumscription of Justice Powell's test otherwise makes little sense. There are individuals, like Panetti, who know what the State says but believe just as surely that the State's claim is not true. The Fifth Circuit's approach permits the execution of such severely delusional individuals even though they believe they are to be executed for *something other than their crimes*, notwithstanding the State's assertions to the contrary.

The Fifth Circuit's standard makes some forms of severe delusion about one's impending execution matter, while others do not. For example, an individual capable of repeating back the State's stated reasons for the execution may not be executed if he believes that his execution is impossible (as in *Ford*), but may be executed if he considers it possible or certain but entirely misapprehends why the death penalty is actually being applied to him. Yet both individuals suffer from debilitating delusional thinking about their forthcoming execution and therefore the retributive purpose of the death penalty is not served in either circumstance. Indeed, Justice Powell plainly recognized that the prisoner's awareness of the "why" was as important to the legitimacy of the execution as his awareness of the "whether." Nor does it appear that the retributive purpose is served more fully when the State executes a person whose delusions cause him entirely to disbelieve the State's asserted rationale than when it executes one who cannot comprehend that rationale in the first place.

Indeed, of the various grounds articulated by the *Ford* majority, none supports privileging one sort of fundamental delusion about an impending execution over another. Whether the ground is that "the execution of an insane person simply offends humanity," 477 U.S. at 407, or that such an execution "provides no example to others," *id.*, or that "it is uncharitable to dispatch an offender into another world, when he is not of a capacity to fit himself for it," *id.*, or that "madness is its own punishment," *id.*, or that executing an insane person serves no retributive purpose, *id.*; *see also id.* at 422 (Powell, J., concurring), there is no reason to spare one individual beset by a delusion regarding whether death awaits or the State's purported reasons for imposing the penalty, yet to execute another individual plagued by a different yet equally irrational delusion regarding the same subject.

D. All Three *Amici* Have Adopted a Common Position on This Issue

For these reasons, with respect to competency to be executed, *amici* and the American Bar Association have respectively adopted substantively identical versions of a recommendation proposed by the Task Force on Mental Disability and the Death Penalty:

> If, after challenges to the validity of the conviction and death sentence have been exhausted and execution has been scheduled, a court finds that a prisoner has a mental disorder or disability that significantly impairs his or her capacity to understand the nature and purpose of the punishment, or to appreciate the reason for its imposition in the prisoner's own case, the sentence of death should be reduced to a lesser punishment.[10]

This recommendation, *amici* submit, draws the proper line between individuals who are competent to be executed and those who are not. The recommendation recognizes that it is impossible to draw a meaningful line among the myriad delusions that may fog an individual's understanding of his pending execution, or the reasons for it.

Specifically, under the recommendation, awareness of the "why" of an execution necessarily includes understanding the reason the death penalty is being applied in one's own case. The Report of the Task Force, which explains the reasoning that underlies each recommendation, stated that an offender who has been sentenced to die

> must "appreciate" its personal application in the offender's own case—that is, why it is being imposed *on the offender*. This formulation is analogous to the distinction often drawn between a "factual understanding" and a "rational understanding" of the reason for the execution. If, as is generally assumed, the primary purpose of the competence-to-be-executed require-ment is to vindicate the retributive aim of punishment, then offenders should have more than a shallow understanding of why they are being executed.

Recommendation and Report on the Death Penalty and Persons with Mental Disabilities, 30 Mental & Physical Disability L. Rep. 668, 675 (2006). In short, it does not fulfill the retributive purpose of the death penalty to execute an individual, like Panetti, who has no rational understanding as to why the pun-ishment is being imposed on him. For that reason, the Fifth Circuit's ruling should be reversed.[11]

II. Mental Health Professionals Can Reliably Identify the Nature and Extent of an Individual's Rational Understanding of an Impending Execution and Routinely Make Similar Assessments in Other Judicial Contexts

In the case at bar, the experts for the State and for the defense largely con-curred in the most important aspects of their assessments. *Panetti* v. *Dretke*, 401 F. Supp. 2d 702, 707–708, 712 (W.D. Tex. 2004) (all experts testified that Panetti possesses cognitive functionality with respect to certain topics and communications, yet suffers delusions, including the belief that he will be executed for preaching the Gospel). Disagreements were limited to the degree, and not existence, of Panetti's delusions pertaining to the reason for his impending execution, *Panetti v. Dretke*, 448 F.3d 815, 817 (5th Cir. 2006), and thus the parties' dispute has focused on the impact of Panetti's functional deficiencies on the ultimate question of "competence to be executed," which is a legal, not a scientific or medical, question.

Expert agreement in this area can be attributed to two factors: first, the underlying scientific and clinical concepts, the nature of psychotic delusions, and the concept of "rational understanding" are well established; second, when the diagnosis is made through an evaluation of the prisoner's currently presenting condition, no extrapolation is needed to assess the prisoner's condition at a remote time in the past.[12] Indeed, the expert consensus on Panetti's diagnosis is consistent with studies showing that mental health professionals using structured interviews and assessing present-oriented functional capacities typically have very high levels of agreement. *See, e.g.*, Gary B. Melton, *et al.*, *Psychological Evaluations for the Courts: A Handbook for Mental Health Professionals and Lawyers* 138 (2d ed. 1997). Thus, mental health experts can provide testimony that can meaningfully inform judicial decisions about competency to be executed with established procedures that have a record of producing reliable, consistent results.

Conclusion

Amici submit that the Fifth Circuit's competence for execution standard permits the execution of individuals who lack any meaningful understanding of the nature and purpose of their punishment, contrary to this Court's decision in *Ford*. *Amici* urge this Court to reverse the judgment of the Fifth Circuit.

Notes

1. Both parties have consented to the filing of this brief. No counsel for a party authored any part of this brief. No person or entity other than *amici* and their counsel made any monetary contribution to the preparation or submission of this brief.

2. In addition to the recommendation discussed in text, the Task Force presented, and *amici* and the ABA adopted, recommendations relating to persons with mental retardation and equivalent impairments of intellectual and adaptive functioning, persons who were mentally ill at the time of the offense, and persons not competent to seek or assist counsel in post-conviction proceedings. *See Recommendation and Report on the Death Penalty and Persons with Mental Disabilities*, 30 Mental & Physical Disability L. Rep. 668, 668 (2006).

3. *Amici* gratefully acknowledge the assistance of Richard J. Bonnie, J.D., Joel A. Dvoskin, Ph.D., Kirk S. Heilbrun, Ph.D., and Diane T. Marsh, Ph.D., in the preparation of this brief.

4. The term "appreciate" approximates the term "rationally understand." *See* Norman G. Poythress, *et al.*, *Adjudicative Competence: The MacArthur Studies* 112 (2002); *see also Martin v. Dugger*, 686 F. Supp. 1523, 1569–1573 (S.D. Fla. 1988).

5. Justice Powell concurred in parts one and two of Justice Marshall's opinion, 477 U.S. at 418, creating a majority for the holding that "the Eighth Amendment prohibits a State from carrying out a sentence of death upon a prisoner who is insane." *Id.* at 409.

6. *Amici* of course have not examined Panetti in person; rather, *amici* rely upon the facts as set forth in the record and on Panetti's prior mental health evaluations.

7. Schizophrenia is typically defined as encompassing two or more of the following five symptoms: (1) delusions; (2) hallucinations; (3) disorganized speech; (4) grossly disorganized or catatonic behavior; and (5) negative symptoms, *i.e.,* affective flattening (diminished emotional expressiveness), alogia (poverty of speech), or avolition (inability to initiate and persist in goal-oriented activities). DSM-IV-TR 299-301, 312.

8. Schizoaffective disorder essentially consists of schizophrenic symptoms coupled with, at some point, either a major depressive episode, a manic episode, or a mixed episode (*i.e.,* an episode in which the individual alternates between major depressive and manic symptoms). DSM-IV-TR 319-323.

9. *See generally* DSM-IV-TR 345-428; *see also id.* at 327 (discussing Mood Disorders With Psychotic Features).

10. It is important to distinguish delusional beliefs from beliefs that are merely wrong. An individual who believes that her husband is cheating on her may be mistaken, but her view may not be delusional, depending upon the facts that she adduces to support her belief. But, the individual who, in one reported case, based such a belief solely on the presence of a red car outside of her apartment, is clearly delusional. *See* Adolfo Pazzagli, *Delusion, Narrative, and Affects,* 34 J. of the Am. Acad. of Psychoanalysis & Dynamic Psychiatry 367, 370 (2006).

11. The record in *Barnard* is much more sparse than in *Panetti;* accordingly, it is difficult to assess the true nature of Barnard's delusions. Because the state court found that Barnard tended to blame his conviction on "a conspiracy of Asians, Jews, Blacks, homosexuals, and the Mafia," 13 F.3d at 876, it is likely that his beliefs would have withstood efforts to test reality by presenting him with evidence that (1) those five groups do not, in fact, work in concert, (2) there is no reason why those groups would have any motive to do him harm, and, (3) most fundamentally, those groups do not control the judicial system, and thus did not bring about his conviction.

12. American Psychological Association Council of Representatives, APA Policy Manual: N. Public Interest (2001) (incorporating policy adopted by the Council of Representatives in February 2006), *available at . . . Mentally Ill Prisoners on Death Row: Position Statement,* American Psychiatric Association (2005), *available at . . .* The National Alliance on Mental Illness adopted an earlier version of this language. *Public Policy Platform of the National Alliance on Mental Illness* 50 (8th ed. 2006), *available at . . .* The ABA adopted a later version of this proposal with a different final clause. *Recommendation and Report on the Death Penalty and Persons with Mental Disabilities,* 30 Mental & Physical Disability L. Rep. 668, 668 (2006).

13. *Amici* and the ABA also resolved that an individual who is found incompetent to face the death penalty should have his sentence permanently commuted to a non-capital punishment. If the death penalty is not commuted but instead is merely suspended in the event the individual's condition were to improve, then the process would force an individual with mental illness to choose between living with psychotic suffering and accepting treatment that might result in his execution. This issue is not implicated here.

14. These characteristics should go far to dispel any concerns this Court may have about the role of mental-disease evidence in this context. *Cf. Clark* v. *Arizona,* 126 S. Ct. 2709, 2734-2736 (2006).

NO

On Writ of Certiorari to the United States Court of Appeals for the Fifth Circuit: Brief for Respondent

Statement of the Case

A. The Crime

Scott Louis Panetti has led a troubled and violent life. Between 1981 and 1992, Panetti was hospitalized on multiple occasions and variously diagnosed with substance abuse and dependence, personality disorders, depression, chronic undifferentiated schizophrenia, and schizoaffective disorder. JA 339-41;1 Federal Petition for Writ of Habeas Corpus, No. 1:99-CV-00260 (W.D. Tex. Sept. 7, 1999) (hereinafter "Federal Petition") (Ex. 14). Although his doctors initially treated him only with therapy, they later placed him on medication, which proved effective in controlling his mental illness. *Id.*, at 462-63 (noting in 1986 that, while taking medication, Panetti "shows no evidence of thought disorder" and "was not paranoid in his attitude"), 466 (observing in 1990 that, after Panetti was stabilized on his medication, he displayed no evidence of "any delusions or any psychotic thinking, or any suicidal or homicidal ideations").

Panetti married his second wife, Sonja, in 1988, and they had a daughter the following year. 31.RR.61. In August 1992, Sonja separated from Panetti because of his drinking and physical threats. 31.RR.62. She took their daughter, then three years old, to live with her parents, Amanda and Joe Alvarado. 31.RR.60-61. Panetti later called to threaten Sonja and his in-laws, saying he would kill both her and the Alvarados or burn down their house. 31.RR.64. On September 2, 1992, in response to these threats, Sonja obtained a protective order against Panetti. 31.RR.65-66; 41.RR (SX 91).

Six days later, Panetti awoke before dawn, 33.RR.695, shaved his head, 31.RR.95-96, and dressed himself in camouflage, 33.RR.679. Arming himself with a rifle, a sawed-off shotgun, 33.RR.696, and several knives, 33.RR.706-07, Panetti drove to the Alvarados' house, 33.RR.696. When he arrived, Panetti broke his shotgun trying to shatter a sliding glass door near Sonja's bed. 31.RR.69; 33.RR.717. He chased Sonja out of the house and confronted her in the front yard, 33.RR.704, hitting her face with the butt of his rifle, 31.RR.73.

From *Scott Louis Panetti v. Nathaniel Quaterman*, Director, Texas Department of Criminal Justice, Correctional Institutions Division, U.S. Supreme Court, No. 06-6407, 2007.

Although Sonja managed to retreat into the house and lock the front door, Panetti shot the lock off and cornered Joe and Amanda Alvarado in the kitchen. 31.RR.42-43; 33.RR.705. He asked Sonja, who was standing in the adjoining hallway, who she would like to see die first. 31.RR.84. Using his rifle, Panetti then shot and killed Joe Alvarado. 31.RR.84. Sonja begged Panetti not to kill her mother, 31.RR.91, but Panetti pressed the rifle against Amanda Alvarado's chest and pulled the trigger, 32.RR.417-18, killing her and spraying Sonja and their daughter with blood, 31.RR.91. Then his rifle jammed. 31.RR.92.

Panetti grabbed Sonja and their daughter and walked them out to his Jeep. 31.RR.92-93. He drove them back to his bunkhouse, 31.RR.94, where he had them wash off the blood, 31.RR.96. When Sonja asked if she could go check on her parents, he responded: "I just shot your parents. No more mommy, no more daddy; get that through your head." 31.RR.96-97. He then forced Sonja to read the protective order aloud. 31.RR.97-98. Sonja asked Panetti if he planned to shoot her and her daughter. 31.RR.98. He replied that he had not yet decided. 31.RR.98.

At dawn, Panetti allowed both Sonja and their daughter to leave the bunkhouse, telling Sonja that he planned to stay there and "shoot two or three policemen" before taking his own life. 31.RR.101. Panetti surrendered to police that afternoon. 31.RR.241. Later the same day, Panetti confessed to the murders, recounting the details of the crime to police. 33.RR.692-737. When asked if he thought that his mental condition excused his behavior, Panetti replied, "it doesn't excuse me from any of that. You know, I made my bed and I'm going to lie in it. . . . I f***ed up. I feel a lot of remorse." 33.RR.734-35; see also JA 208.

Dr. Michael Lennhoff, a psychiatrist, interviewed Panetti several times at the local jail. Panetti stated that he had followed his drug regimen over the preceding year, but he later confessed that he had not taken his medication for one week before the murders. Federal Petition Ex. 14, at 431, 436. Although Dr. Lennhoff noted that Panetti exhibited genuine mental illness, he also concluded that "Panetti may have wanted to impress me with how mentally disturbed he is, perhaps in an exaggerated way." *Id.*, at 434. After a later meeting, Dr. Lennhoff felt that Panetti was "still trying to impress me as not having committed a deliberate crime." *Id.*, at 436.

B. Panetti's Exhaustively Affirmed Conviction and Sentence and the Rejection of His Alleged Incompetence to Stand Trial and to Waive Counsel

Panetti was charged with capital murder. 1.CR.8. The trial court appointed Dr. E. Lee Simes, a psychiatrist, to evaluate Panetti's competence for trial. JA 9. Dr. Simes noted that, despite Panetti's delusional thinking, "his overall story was quite consistent and insightful." JA 13. In particular, Dr. Simes observed that Panetti understood why he was facing capital-murder charges, the significance of those charges, and the significance of the punishment he might receive. JA 13. Panetti also displayed ability to process questions and information and to assist in his defense. JA 13. Dr. Simes concluded that Panetti was competent to stand trial. JA 13.

In April 1994, Panetti moved for a competence hearing. 2.CR.236-41. In the first trial-competence hearing, the jury deadlocked at four for incompetent, three for competent, and five undecided. 3.CR.295-96; 10.RR.379.2 At the second trial-competence hearing, the jury found Panetti competent to stand trial. 13.RR.206-07.

Eight months later, Panetti sent the trial judge a letter explaining that he had stopped taking all medication and, as a result, was "restored to sanity"; he had dismissed his attorneys; he felt competent to represent himself; he did not intend to "act like a lawyer" in his trial; and he would be able to prove that he was insane at the time of the murders. 3.CR.360. Panetti's attorneys then moved to withdraw as his counsel. 3.CR.363-64.

The trial court called a pretrial hearing to inquire further into Panetti's expressed desire to represent himself. 15.RR.5. The judge told Panetti that he personally did not want Panetti to represent himself, 15.RR.10, and asked Panetti's attorneys to confer privately with Panetti about waiving counsel, 15.RR.11. After this consultation, Panetti's attorneys reported that they did not think Panetti should represent himself, but that was his "clear intent." 15.RR.12-13. Panetti confirmed that he wanted to represent himself because he had the right to do so under Texas law and the United States Constitution, and that he was "fully aware" of the penalty for the charges against him. 15.RR.18. Panetti then executed a voluntary waiver of counsel. 3.CR.369. The district attorney informed the court that, because the State was "concerned about protecting the Defendant's rights," he did not want Panetti's attorneys to withdraw. 15.RR.24. When the court reexamined Panetti about his decision, Panetti replied, "I understand everything that's been going on today, sir. I do, however, feel a little bit insulted that I have been asked the same question so many times, Your Honor." 15.RR.25-28. The court held that Panetti had voluntarily and intelligently exercised his right to represent himself and then appointed standby counsel for Panetti. 15.RR.29-30.

At trial, Panetti entered a plea of not guilty by reason of insanity. 31.RR.24. In his rambling opening statement, Panetti informed the jury that he had been diagnosed with paranoid schizophrenia and manic depression in 1986, and that he believed only an insane person could prove the insanity defense. 31.RR.28-29. As Panetti explains in his brief, he exhibited bizarre and incoherent behavior throughout his trial. Panetti Br. 11-15. He did call as witnesses two psychiatrists who had previously treated him, 38.RR.1567-1616, and endeavored to establish through one that, when he did not take his medication, his mental illness could prevent him from distinguishing right and wrong, 38.RR.1574-75. The jury nonetheless found Panetti guilty of capital murder and sentenced him to death. 7.CR.1041-44; 38.RR.1685; 39.RR.102. The Texas Court of Criminal Appeals (CCA) affirmed Panetti's conviction and sentence, *Panetti* v. *Texas*, No. 72,230 (Tex. Crim. App. Dec. 3, 1997) (unpublished), and the Court denied certiorari, 525 U.S. 848 (1998) (Mem.). Panetti then filed a state habeas petition raising fourteen claims, including whether he was competent to stand trial and competent to waive counsel. State Petition for Writ of Habeas Corpus, No. 3310-A, at 3-4 (Tex. Crim. App. June 19, 1997). The CCA denied relief." (pp. 1-5)

"In sum, one jury and four courts rejected Panetti's trial-incompetence claim; one court found him competent to waive counsel and four courts rejected his collateral challenge to that determination; and another jury and two courts rejected his insanity defense. No judge or jury has ever found him incompetent.

C. Panetti's Efforts to Prove Incompetence to Be Executed in State and Federal Court

Once an execution date was set, Panetti filed a motion in the state trial court under Texas Code of Criminal Procedure Article 46.05 asserting incompetence to be executed. JA 355. After concluding that Panetti had failed to make a substantial showing of incompetence, the state court denied his Article 46.05 motion, JA 355, and the CCA dismissed his appeal, *Ex parte Panetti*, No. 74,868 (Tex. Crim. App. Jan. 28, 2004) (*per curiam*) (unpublished).

Panetti then filed a habeas petition in federal district court, asserting that *Ford* v. *Wainwright*, 477 U.S. 399 (1986), prohibited his execution. JA 355-56. The district court granted a stay of execution and allowed Panetti an opportunity to present his renewed allegations to the state trial court. JA 357.

In response to Panetti's second Article 46.05 motion, the state court appointed two neutral experts, Dr. George Parker and Dr. Mary Anderson, to assess Panetti's competence to be executed. JA 59. After conducting a joint interview of Panetti, Drs. Parker and Anderson filed a report documenting their observations and conclusions. JA 70-76. This report reflects Panetti's hostility to Drs. Parker's and Anderson's questions, his tendency toward religious conversation, his attempted manipulation of the interview process, and his general refusal to cooperate with the court-appointed experts. JA 70-73, 75.

Because of Panetti's refusal to cooperate, Drs. Parker and Anderson also relied on several sources of collateral data—including prison records; letters that Panetti had recently written to friends and family; court documents, including documents relating to other competence determinations; discussions with prison staff; and another expert evaluation of Panetti—to help form their relevant opinions. JA 73-75. Based on these data and their personal observations, Drs. Parker and Anderson concluded that Panetti (1) "knows that he is to be executed, and that his execution will result in his death" and (2) "has the ability to understand the reason he is to be executed." JA 75.

In response, Panetti filed a detailed submission criticizing Drs. Parker and Anderson's methodology and contrasting their conclusions with those in a psychiatric evaluation that Panetti had previously presented to the court. JA 79-98. After considering that submission, the state court again denied relief under Article 46.05. JA 99.

Panetti then sought habeas relief in the federal district court, JA 375, which concluded that the state court's determination of Panetti's competence to be executed was not entitled to AEDPA deference because Panetti allegedly failed to receive constitutionally sufficient process, JA 359-61. After granting Panetti's motions for appointment of counsel, discovery, and funds for expert and investigative assistance, JA 358, the district court held an evidentiary hearing on competence, JA 362. At the hearing, Panetti presented expert testimony[.]" (pp. 5–7)

"All of the expert witnesses agreed that Panetti suffers from some degree of mental illness." Although some of the experts labeled this illness schizophrenia or schizoaffective disorder, *e.g.*, JA 144-45, 205, they were collectively unable to agree on a single diagnosis, see JA 239, 313.[1]

The experts did agree, however, that Panetti has the capacity to—and does, in fact—understand that he will be executed. JA 147-48, 207, 236, 243, 245.[2]

Further expert testimony established Panetti's specific understanding that he committed the murders. Indeed, Dr. Rosin testified that Panetti recounted details of his activity on the day of the murders and expressed sorrow for having committed the crime. JA 208; see also JA 148-49 (Dr. Conroy's testimony that Panetti believed that God had forgiven him for killing the Alvarados and had "wiped the slate clean"). Dr. Silverman testified to uncertainty about whether Panetti knows that he killed the Alvarados, but only because Panetti steadfastly refused to answer his questions on this topic. JA 221.

Several experts also concluded that Panetti's delusions created a false sense of the true reason for his execution. *E.g.*, JA 149, 156, 202, 209 (testimony from Drs. Conroy and Rosin that Panetti believes his execution was ordered to prevent him from preaching the Gospel). Importantly, however, these same experts testified that Panetti understands that the State's stated reason for his execution is punishment for capital murder. JA 157, 214.

Dr. Parker testified that portions of Panetti's responses to the experts execution-competence examinations could be attributed to malingering, see JA 241-43; see also, *e.g.*, JA 174, 177, 181 (noting additional reports of Panetti's suspected malingering in the past), and Drs. Parker and Anderson each specifically testified that Panetti has the capacity to understand the reason for his execution, JA 245, 247, 303-04. Both Dr. Parker and Dr. Anderson emphasized that Panetti was deliberately manipulative and uncooperative during his interview with them. JA 239-40, 244-46, 271, 300, 303, 312-14; accord JA 75. They based their ultimate conclusions on Panetti's overall cognitive functionality, as demonstrated through letters he wrote to friends and family, his logical responses to interview questions, and his ability to understand such things as history and movies. JA 242-43, 302-04.

Dr. Parker's suspicions of malingering were corroborated by evidence of psychiatric evaluations conducted in the two years following Panetti's capital trial. For example, Dr. Michael Gilhousen noted that loosening of Panetti's thought processes "appeared to be intentional on his part to create the impression of mental illness." JA 167, II-30. After another interview, Dr. Gilhousen described Panetti's behavior as "obviously manipulative and theatrical." JA 171-72, II-20. Another doctor expressed the belief that Panetti's switching among different voices was "contrived . . . to impress us or lead us to believe that he did have alter personalities." JA 170, II-41.

After hearing all the evidence, the federal district court made three factual findings. First, based on the expert's agreement, the court concluded that Panetti is aware that he will be executed. JA 372.

Second, the district court found that Panetti is aware that he committed both murders. JA 372. The court based this conclusion on Dr. Conroy's and Dr. Rosin's testimony that Panetti knows that he murdered the Alvarados. JA 372. Although the court recognized that Dr. Silverman's testimony cast doubt on this conclusion, the court discounted that testimony, noting that it was based on Panetti's limited responses during his interview with Dr. Silverman. JA 372.

Third, the district court found that Panetti understands the State's stated reason for execution. JA 372. The court based this finding on the testimony of Drs. Conroy and Rosin, and discounted Dr. Silverman's contrary testimony for the same reason. JA 372-73.

Additionally, the district court recounted Dr. Parker's and Dr. Anderson's assessments that "some portion of Panetti's behavior could be attributed to malingering," and it expressly concluded that, although all of the experts had agreed Panetti had "some degree" of mental illness, their testimony collectively "casts doubt on the extent of Panetti's mental illness and symptoms." JA 363.

Finally, the district court noted Dr. Cunningham's testimony that "suggests" that Panetti's delusions prevent him from understanding that Texas is a lawfully constituted authority and lead him to believe that the State "is in league with the forces of evil that have conspired against him," and it observed that this testimony was consistent with the testimony of Panetti's other experts. JA 373. The court made no finding, however, whether these delusions were genuine or the partial product of malingering, because the court deemed it irrelevant to the question of whether Panetti "knows the reason for his execution" within the meaning of the court of appeals's execution-competence test. JA 373.

Based on these factual findings, the district court concluded that Panetti is competent to be executed. JA 373. Although the court denied Panetti's habeas petition, it stayed his execution pending appeal, JA 373, and granted a certificate of appealability, *Panetti* v. *Dretke*, No. 04-CA- 042 (W.D. Tex. Nov. 4, 2004). The court of appeals affirmed the district court's denial of habeas relief, *Panetti* v. *Dretke*, 448 F.3d 815 (CA5 2006); JA 374-84, and the Court granted certiorari, JA 387.

Summary of the Argument

In devoting fully half of his brief to his statement of the case, Panetti endeavors to focus the Court's attention on his lengthy mental-health history, explaining that "incompetency runs like a fissure through every proceeding in this case." Panetti Br. 6. But that fissure has been mostly sealed once and for all by the conclusive determinations of state and federal courts repeatedly rejecting Panetti's direct and collateral challenges to adverse rulings on his insanity defense, his competence to stand trial, and his competence to waive counsel. For that reason, Panetti correctly concedes that, as a matter of law, he is now presumed competent to be executed. *Ibid.*

The state court, the district court, and the court of appeals have all concluded that Panetti has failed to overcome that presumption. The district court found as a factual matter that Panetti knows that he murdered the Alvarados, that he will be executed, and that the State's stated reason for executing him is that he committed two murders. Panetti has not challenged those factual findings on appeal." (pp. 7–11)

"Both Panetti's and his *amici's* proposed standards, which require that a convict rationally understand" the reasons for his execution, are fundamentally flawed. Given the inherent subjectivity and manipulability of such a standard, capital murderers could as a routine matter claim a lack of "rational understanding" through malingering or refusing to cooperate with experts." (p. 12) . . . "Finally, the retributive and deterrent interests served by the death penalty–focused primarily as they are on society at large rather than the capital murderer–do not demand the "rational understanding" that Panetti urges.

The Court should instead adopt a clear and objective test for execution competence. Specifically, the Court should hold that a mentally ill capital convict is incompetent to be executed only if, because of his illness, he lacks the *capacity* to recognize that his punishment (1) is the result of his being convicted of capital murder and (2) will cause his death. This standard controls for the malingering or uncooperative convict, is appropriately tailored to the execution stage of capital proceedings, and serves the twin goals of retribution and deterrence that justify capital punishment. Applying this standard, the Court should hold that Panetti is competent to be executed." (pp. 12–13)

Argument

II. Even If AEDPA Deference Does Not Apply, Panetti's Execution Does Not Violate the Eighth Amendment

Only if the Court concludes that the AEDPA does not bar habeas review should it reach Panettis claim that the court of appeals employed the wrong legal standard for execution competence. Although *Ford* held that the Eighth Amendment proscribes execution of the "insane," 477 U.S., at 409-10, the Court did not define "insanity" or otherwise delineate the constitutional threshold of competence to be executed, *id.*, at 418 (Powell, J., concurring in the judgment), a question which remains unresolved.

Before turning to the merits of that claim, two issues bear emphasis. **First,** there is no dispute that, under *Ford,* executing the insane violates the Eighth Amendment. Executing the insane was forbidden at common law, and it is forbidden today." (p. 19) . . . "And **second,** there is no dispute that, like many capital defendants, Panetti suffers from some degree of mental illness." (p. 19)

"The only legal question before the Court on the merits of this case is what is the definition of "insanity" —that is, what must a court find to conclude that a capital murderer is constitutionally incompetent to be executed." (p. 19)

"Although execution of the "insane" was deemed cruel and unusual in 1971, *Ford,* 477 U.S., at 406-08, the common law did not then draw fine distinctions in mental ability, and thus did not delineate any precise competence standard. Consequently, the standards of the common law are, at best, inconclusive. Likewise, a survey of modern state legislation offers indefinite guidance, as it yields no consensus at all on the mental faculty a capital murderer must possess at the time of his execution. Finally, in the exercise of its independent judgment, the Court should reject the proposition that a capital convict must possess a "rational understanding" of the reasons for his execution to render death an acceptable punishment under the Eighth Amendment. Such a standard is not tailored to the particular interests at stake in the post-sentencing phase of capital proceedings, invites malingering and abuse, and is not necessary to advance the retributive and deterrent justifications for the death penalty.

For all of these reasons, the Court should reject Panetti's and his *amici's* proposed execution-competence standards." (pp. 20–21)

C. The Court Should Hold That the Appropriate Constitutional Standard for Competence to Be Executed is Whether a Defendant Has the Capacity to Recognize That His Punishment is the Result of His Being Convicted of Capital Murder and Will Cause His Death. (p. 33)

"Both Panetti's and his *amici's* proposed execution-competence standards are deeply flawed. The State urges the Court to reject those proposals and instead adopt a clearer and more objective test. Specifically, the Court should hold that a mentally ill capital convict is incompetent to be executed only if, because of his illness, he lacks the *capacity* to recognize that his punishment (1) is the result of his being convicted of capital murder and (2) will cause his death.

The State's proposed standard—derived from *Ford* and the Court's Eighth Amendment jurisprudence—prevents the execution of the truly incompetent, while at the same time (1) incorporating essential safeguards against malingering and noncooperation with psychological examiners, (2) being specifically tailored to the postsentencing phase of capital proceedings, and (3) effectively advancing the modern penological interests behind the death penalty.

> 1. Because of the inherent uncertainties and subjectivity of psychiatric testing, and the risks of malingering and abuse, any standard for competence to be executed should be rigorous and clear." (pp. 33–34)

"The Court has often noted the difficulties that attend even the most skilled psychiatric diagnoses. "[P]sychiatrists disagree widely and frequently on what constitutes mental illness [and] on the appropriate diagnosis to be attached to given behavior and symptoms." *Ake* v. *Oklahoma*, 470 U.S. 68, 81 (1985). For that reason, "a particularly acute need for guarding against error inheres in a determination that 'in the present state of the mental sciences is at best a hazardous guess however conscientious.'" *Ford*, 477 U.S., at 412 (plurality op.) (quoting *Solesbee* v. *Balkcom*, 339 U.S. 9, 23 (1950) (Frankfurter, J., dissenting)). As Justice Powell explained,

> "Unlike issues of historical fact, the question of petitioner's sanity calls for a basically subjective judgment. And unlike a determination of whether the death penalty is appropriate in a particular case, the competency determination depends substantially on expert analysis in a discipline fraught

with 'subtleties and nuances.'" *Id.*, at 426 (Powell, J., concurring in the judgment) (quoting *Addington* v. *Texas*, 441 U.S. 418, 430 (1979)) (citations omitted).

Just last Term, the Court observed that the medical definitions of mental illness "are subject to flux and disagreement," and that such diagnoses "may mask vigorous debate within the profession about the very contours of the mental disease itself." *Clark* v. *Arizona*, 126 S.Ct. 2709, 2722, 2734 (2006). "[T]he consequence of this professional ferment," the Court noted, "is a general caution in treating psychological classifications as predicates for excusing otherwise criminal conduct." *Id.*, at 2734.

Not only are psychiatric diagnoses subjective and frequently conflicting, they are by their nature subject to change. *Atkins* and *Roper* were predicated on constant variables: if a defendant is fifteen or seventeen or twenty at the time of the crime, that age at that instant is fixed and unchanging; likewise, if an individual is of normal intelligence throughout his or her life, that person cannot be expected later to become mentally retarded. In contrast, if a person is sane yesterday and today, that does not mean he or she will be sane tomorrow. As Justice O'Connor cautioned in *Ford*, that mutability carries with it serious risks of malingering:

> "[T]he *potential for false claims and deliberate delay* in this context is *obviously enormous*. This potential is exacerbated by a unique feature of the prisoner's protected interest in suspending the execution of a death sentence during incompetency. By definition, this interest can *never* be conclusively and finally determined: Regardless of the number of prior adjudications of the issue, until the very moment of execution the prisoner can claim that he has become insane sometime after the previous determination to the contrary." 477 U.S., at 429 (O'Connor, J., concurring in part and dissenting in part) (citations omitted) (first two emphases added).[3]

Finally, unlike with age or retardation, capital murderers facing execution may have some ability to voluntarily choose to render themselves incompetent to be executed simply by ceasing to take their medication. Indeed, in the case at bar, the evidence indicates that Panetti's medication had been largely successful in controlling his mental illness, Federal Petition Ex. 14, at 462-63, but that he willingly chose to stop taking it, *id.*, at 431, 436; 3.CR.360.

2. Panetti's proposed "rational understanding" standard has no basis in the Court's precedent and would invite abuse." (pp. 34–36)

a. A "rational understanding" inquiry would engraft Fifth and Sixth Amendment concerns on an Eighth Amendment test.

Although Panetti uses the phrase loosely, "rational understanding" is a specific term of art; it describes the core of several pre-sentencing competence tests. "Rational understanding" was introduced in *Dusky*, in which the Court defined the test for competence to stand trial as whether the defendant has "sufficient present ability to consult with his lawyer with a reasonable degree of rational understanding" and has "a rational as well as factual understanding of the proceedings against him." 362 U.S., at 402 (quotation marks omitted); see also *Godinez* v. *Moran*, 509 U.S. 389, 398 (1993) (concluding that the "rational understanding" test should also be used to measure a defendant's competence to plead guilty and to waive the right to counsel)." (p. 37)

"[A] "rational understanding" is necessary to ensure that defendants do not foolishly or mistakenly relinquish valuable constitutional rights. A defendant faced with such choices must be able to "understand the nature and object of the proceedings against him, to consult with counsel, and to assist in preparing his defense." *Drope*, 420 U.S., at 171.

But a capital convict, unlike a capital defendant, has substantially fewer rights, and there are no significant strategic choices left for him to make. See *Herrera* v. *Collins*, 506 U.S. 390, 399 (1993) (explaining that the presumption of innocence disappears after conviction and listing numerous constitutional rights that defendants enjoy but that convicts do not); *Barefoot* v. *Estelle*, 463 U.S. 880, 887-88 (1983) (discussing the "secondary and limited" nature of federal habeas proceedings); see also *Ford*, 477 U.S., at 421 (Powell, J., concurring in the judgment) (noting that, because the Court's decisions already recognize . . . that a defendant must be competent to stand trial, . . . the notion that a defendant must be able to assist in his defense is largely provided for"). Assuming that a convict is competent to be executed, only the remote possibilities of clemency or commutation—processes that call for no significant strategic decisions by a convict—can prevent the sentence from being carried out.

b. Panetti's conception of "rational understanding" is far too expansive.

Panetti's argument is, in fact, even more aggressive than one for inclusion of only a pure "rational understanding" component. Although he invokes that phrase throughout his brief, the substantive requirement that Panetti asks the Court to incorporate is actually a version of the heightened "knowing and voluntary" requirement that the Court has held applicable, over and above the "rational understanding" competence component, with respect to a defendant's decision to plead guilty or to waive his right to counsel. *Godinez*, 509 U.S., at 400-01 & n.12; *Faretta* v. *California*, 422 U.S. 806, 835 (1975).

As *Godinez* explained, "knowing and voluntary" is not part of any competence test; it is an additional safeguard designed to ensure not merely that a defendant has the *capacity* to understand trial proceedings, but rather that he *"actually does* understand the significance and consequences of a particular decision and whether the decision is uncoerced." 509 U.S., at 401, n.12 (emphasis added)." (pp. 38-39)

"[R]equiring a "deep" or "meaningful" appreciation of the State's reasons for imposing the death penalty would create an even greater risk that the Court's test could be circumvented through malingering or abuse. See *supra* Part II.C.1." (p. 39)

"When viewed in light of the overall death-row population, Panetti's proposal is especially problematic. As a matter of common understanding, most individuals who commit heinous murders are, almost by definition, not entirely sane. Although estimates vary, some sources indicate that as many as 70 percent of death-row inmates suffer from some form of schizophrenia or psychosis. Nancy S. Horton, Restoration of Competency for Execution: Furiosus Solo Furore Punitur, 44 Sw. L.J. 1191, 1204 (1990) (citing Amnesty International, United States of America: the Death Penalty 108-09 (1987)); see JA 142 (expert testimony that most of the convicts in federal Bureau of Prisons hospitals are schizophrenic). Many, if not most, schizophrenics exhibit the type of delusional thinking that Panetti has been observed to exhibit. See Douglas Mossman, *Atkins* v. *Virginia: A Psychiatric Can of Worms,* 33 N.M. L. Rev. 255, 280 (2003); APA Br. 8 (noting that "[d]elusional thinking is a hallmark symptom of schizophrenia" (citing DSM-IV-TR 299-301, 312)).[4] Accordingly, Panetti's "rational understanding" requirement would be applied to a population that is, in significant part, delusional—and thus necessarily *irrational.* See APA Br. 9, n.11." (p. 40)

"[T]he introduction of Panetti's ill-defined—and inherently indefinite— "rational understanding" component would render the execution-competence standard substantially overinclusive. See Mossman, *supra*, at 289 ("Given the high rate of serious mental illness among homicide defendants, granting psychiatric exemptions could leave very few individuals eligible for the death penalty.").

Nor is this potential for exempting vast numbers of convicted murderers from execution an unintended consequence of Panetti's and his *amici's* proposed test. Indeed, *amicus* APA is nothing if not candid, explaining that both its own position and the ABA's is that "an individual who is found incompetent to face the death penalty" should not have his sentence "merely suspended," but should "have his sentence *permanently commuted* to a noncapital punishment." APA Br. 17, n.15 (emphasis added). Thus, the conceded objective of these *amici* (and the predictable consequence of their proposed test) is not simply avoiding the inhumanity of executing a person who is truly insane, but rather removing from death row as large a class of capital convicts as reasonably possible.[5]" (pp. 40-41)

4. Application of the State's proposed test will advance the modern penological interests behind the death penalty.

The Court has recently confirmed that retribution and deterrence are capital punishment's two predominant social purposes. *Roper*, 543 U.S., at 571 (citing *Gregg* v. *Georgia*, 428 U.S. 153, 183 (1976) (joint opinion of Stewart, Powell, and Stevens, JJ.)); accord *Atkins*, 536 U.S., at 318-19. As shown below, application of the State's proposed test will advance each of those interests.[6]

a. The State's test will further the retributive purpose of punishment.

Retribution aims either "to express the community's moral outrage or . . . to right the balance for the wrong to the victim." *Roper*, 543 U.S., at 571; see *Atkins*, 536 U.S., at 319 (explaining that retribution is "the interest in seeing that the offender gets his 'just deserts'"). The Court has repeatedly emphasized the societal focus of retribution. See, *e.g., Thompson* v. *Oklahoma,* 487 U.S. 815, 836 (1988); see also *Schriro* v. *Summerlin,* 542 U.S. 348, 360 (2004) (Breyer, J., dissenting); *Gregg,* 428 U.S., at 183-84 (joint opinion of Stewart, Powell, and Stevens, JJ.). Panetti misunderstands the societal nature of retribution, erroneously equating it with vengeance. Panetti Br. 46 & n.33." (p. 43)

i. The retributive justification for punishment necessarily precedes any execution-competence analysis.

The viability of retribution as a permissible theory of punishment depends not on the "rational understanding" that a convict may or may not have, see *supra* Part II.C.2; cf. Panetti Br. 46, but rather on the convict's moral culpability at the time he committed his crime, *Enmund* v. *Florida,* 458 U.S. 782, 800-01 (1982) (reflecting that "personal responsibility and moral guilt" define a criminal's level of culpability and concluding that execution of one convict for murders that he did not personally commit failed to serve the retributive goal of punishment)." (p. 44)

[I]n the present context the question of culpability will already have been conclusively—and affirmatively—resolved. The issue is not whether the Constitution permits society to *impose* the death penalty on a criminal who was, for some reason, less culpable at the time of his crime, cf. *Roper,* 543 U.S., at 556, 578; *Atkins,* 536 U.S., at 306-08, 321, but rather whether an unquestionably valid death sentence may be *carried out* against a criminal who has subsequently become mentally ill, see *Ford,* 477 U.S., at 425 (Powell, J., concurring in the judgment). This is so because any convict to whom the execution-competence test is applied will necessarily have been adjudicated both sane at the time of his offense and competent to stand trial, removing any doubts about culpability that might in some cases arise from mental illness.

ii. There are substantial problems with the wholly personal view of retribution that Panetti advances." (pp. 44–45)

"Relying heavily on nonjudicial sources, Panetti asserts that retribution requires a condemned prisoner to have a subjective appreciation of the moral impropriety of his criminal conduct and to "suffer the anguish" of knowing the reason for his fate. Panetti Br. 45;" (p. 45)

"Putting aside its lack of support in case law, there are significant problems with Panetti's mind-of-the-criminal approach. First, tailoring the execution-competence test to the innermost thoughts of capital convicts would present substantial practical problems. It is difficult to imagine how anyone other than the convict himself could accurately assess whether he truly appreciates the magnitude of his moral wrong—at least with respect to a convict who is willing to lie about such things. And under Panetti's proposed test, it would be remarkably easy for a convict to feign his way out of a death sentence.

Second, allowing the execution-competence test to be shaped primarily by a personal, subjective view of the retributive rationale would prevent the execution of convicts who genuinely lack moral qualms about their crimes. It cannot be that amoral capital convicts should be excused from death sentences based on amorality alone. Yet Panetti's proposed standard would yield that result." (p. 46)

D. Under Both the State's Proposed Test and the Test That the Court of Appeals Applied, Panetti Is Competent to Be Executed." (p. 48)

Under the State's proposed test, Panetti could properly be held incompetent to be executed only if, because of mental illness, he lacked the capacity to recognize that his punishment (1) is the result of his being convicted of capital murder and (2) will cause his death. To the extent this test varies from that applied by the court of appeals, any such variances are immaterial to the result because, as shown below, the record establishes that Panetti is competent to be executed under either standard.

First of all, it is undisputed that Panetti has the capacity to recognize that the punishment he faces is death. Indeed, the experts all agreed and the district court expressly found that, as a factual matter, "Panetti is aware he is to be executed," JA 363, 372; accord JA 373. Panetti did not oppose this conclusion in the district court, see JA 367, 372, did not challenge it in the court of appeals, and does not challenge it here. Therefore, Panetti is unquestionably "[]aware of the punishment [he is] about to suffer," JA 379 (quoting *Ford*, 477 U.S., at 422 (Powell, J., concurring in the judgment))" (p. 48-49)

The only question that remains is whether Panetti has the capacity to recognize that his punishment is the result of his being convicted of capital murder, or, under the court of appeals's analysis, whether he is aware of why he is to be executed, JA 379. The record establishes that Panetti passes each of these prongs as well.

Dr. Parker and Dr. Anderson each testified that Panetti has the capacity to understand that he is being executed for the murders of which he was convicted. JA 245, 247 (testimony of Dr. Parker), 303-04 (testimony of Dr. Anderson); accord JA 75 (joint report of Drs. Parker and Anderson), and the district court explicitly concluded that "[t]here is evidence in the record to support a finding that Panetti is *capable* of understanding the reason for his execution," JA 367. Again, Panetti does not challenge this conclusion. And under the State's proposed test, it is irrelevant that these witnesses "were unable to reach a formal conclusion that [Panetti] did, in fact, understand" the reason for his execution. JA 364. For the reasons already noted, it is the *capacity* to understand—rather than actual demonstration of understanding—that defines the minimal level of competence needed to satisfy this prong of the State's proposed test. See *supra* Part II.C.3.

And with respect to the court of appeals's test, the district court accurately noted that two of Panetti's own execution-competence experts testified that, "despite his delusions, Panetti understands [that] the State's stated reason for seeking his execution is for his murders." JA 366; see also JA 157 (testimony of Dr. Conroy); JA 214 (testimony of Dr. Rosin). Thus, not only did the district court explicitly find that "Panetti is aware he committed the murders that serve as the basis for his execution," JA 372, but the court further found that "Panetti understands the State's stated reason for executing him is that he committed two murders," JA 372.

The district court also correctly concluded that the alternative sense of "understand" embodied in Panetti's proposal did not match the court of appeals's standard. JA 369" (p. 49-50)

In sum, the record establishes that Panetti: (1) has the capacity to recognize that his punishment will cause his death (and does in fact does recognize this); and (2) has the capacity to recognize that his punishment is the result of his being convicted of capital murder (or, within the meaning of the court of appeals's test, is aware of why he is to be executed). Taken together, these facts conclusively establish Panetti's competence to be executed under both the court of appeals's test and the State's proposed test.

Conclusion

The judgment of the court of appeals should be affirmed." (p. 50)

Notes

1. Citations to the transcript of Panetti's capital-murder trial are noted as "RR" ("Reporters Record"). Citations to the States exhibits admitted into evidence during those proceedings are noted as "SX" ("State Exhibit"). Citations to the pleadings, orders, and motions filed in the trial court are noted as "CR" ("Clerk's Record"). Citations to the federal district court's hearing on execution competence are noted as "FH" ("Federal Hearing"). Citations to the joint appendix filed in this Court are noted as "JA."

2. Panetti incorrectly reports the final vote as nine-to-three in favor of incompetence. Panetti Br. 8, n.6. That vote occurred earlier in the deliberations. 3.CR.290.

3. Dr. Conroy noted that "the major portion of our population in our inpatient units in federal Bureau of Prisons hospitals are diagnosed with some form of schizophrenia," JA 142, and Dr. Silverman opined that most schizophrenics are competent to be executed, JA 227.

4. Lay testimony corroborated this point. Major Miller testified that Panetti cooperated with him in going over the State's pre-execution forms, JA 281, II-42-53, and demonstrated his understanding of the forms' questions about disposition of assets, choice of last meal, and the like. JA 287-88. Additional lay testimony reflected Panetti's demonstrated ability to communicate coherently—and politely—with prison staff. *E.g.*, 1 FH 193-96 (testimony of Terri Hill); 1 FH 200 (testimony of Victoria Williams)."

5. In so noting, Justice O'Connor echoed the concerns of Hale, who, some three centuries earlier, likewise urged courts to guard against the potential for "great fraud" concerning those claiming incompetence. 1 Hale, *supra*, at 35; Legal Historians Br. 15, n.8."

6. Indeed, one death-row study of a limited population noted that half of the profiled inmates exhibited delusional tendencies, which included persecutory delusions (*e.g.*, inmate's belief that he was target of a Jewish conspiracy). Barbara A. Ward, Competency for Execution: Problems in Law and Psychiatry, 14 Fla. St. U. L. Rev. 35, 39-40 & n.26 (1986) (citing Bluestone & McGahee, Reaction to Extreme Stress: Impending Death by Execution, 119 Am. J. Psychiatry

393, 393 (1962)). Other inmates in the study coped with their predicament through obsessive rumination, "thinking furiously about other things, such as appeals, religion, or philosophy." *Ibid.*

7. It will also further the penological interest in incapacitation. See *Atkins*, 536 U.S., at 350 (Scalia, J., dissenting) (quoting *Gregg*, 428 U.S., at 183, n.28) (joint opinion of Stewart, Powell, and Stevens, JJ.)); *Spaziano* v. *Florida*, 468 U.S. 447, 461-62 (1984).